The Birth of Christianity

WORKS BY THE SAME AUTHOR

La notion johannique de l'Esprit et ses antécédents historiques
Paris, Fischbacher, 1902

L'Apôtre Paul et Jésus Christ
Paris, Fischbacher, 1904 (out of print)

Wilhelm Herrmann et le problème religieux actuel
Paris, Fischbacher, 1905

L'Evangile de Marc dans ses rapports avec ceux de Matthieu et de Luc
(Bibliotheque de l'Ecole des Hautes Etudes, Sciences, religieuses, t. XII)
Paris, Leroux, 1909

L'Eucharistic des origines à Justin Martyr
Paris, Fischbacher, 1910

Les sources du recit johannique de la passion
Paris, Fischbacher, 1910

Le texte et les éditions du Nouveau Testament grec
Paris, Editions Ernest Leroux, 1920

Introduction au Nouveau Testament, t. I à IV, 2
Paris, Editions Leroux, 1922-26

Jésus de Nazareth, Mythe ou histoire ?
Paris, Payot, 1925 (out of print)
(English Translation), London, Fisher-Unwin, 1926

Au seuil de l'Evangile, Jean-Baptiste
Paris, Payot, 1928

Critique et histoire. A propos de la Vie de Jésus (Cahiers de la 'Revue d'histoire
et de philosophie religieuses', no. 16)
Paris, Alcan, 1928

Jésus et le messianisme politique. Examen de la théorie de M. Robert Eisler
(Extrait de la Revue historique)
Paris, Alcan, 1931

Jésus et les origines du christianisme ; I, La vie de Jésus
Paris, Payot, 1932 (out of print). (German translation, Zurich,
Rascher et Cie., 1934 and English translation, London,
Allen and Unwin, 1933)

La foi à la résurrection de Jésus dans le christianisme primitif ; Étude d'histoire
et de psychologie religieuses (Bibliothèque de l'Ecole des Hautes Etudes,
Sciences religieuses, t, XLVII
Paris, Librairie Ernest Leroux, 1933 (out of print)

Jésus et les origines du christianisme ; III, L'Église primitive
Payot, 1947

Le Nouveau Testament, traduction nouvelle d'après les meilleurs textes avec
introductions et notes publie sous la direction de Maurice Goguel
et Henri Monnier
Paris, Payot, 1929

The Birth of Christianity

by

MAURICE GOGUEL

Docteur es Lettres, Docteur en Théologie
D.D. (St. Andrews, Glasgow, Lausanne, Uppsala)
Doyen honoraire de la Faculté libre de Théologie
Protéstante (Paris)
Directeur d'Études à l'Ecole des Hautes Etudes
Chargé de cours à la Faculté des Lettres de Paris
Professeur hon. caus. du Collège réformé
de Debreczen

TRANSLATED FROM THE FRENCH
BY H. C. SNAPE, M.A.

New York

THE MACMILLAN COMPANY

1954

This volume (which is a translation of *La Naissance du Christianisme*, Payot, Paris, 1946) is the second of a trilogy entitled *Jésus et les Origines du Christianisme,* of which the first part, *The Life of Jesus,* was published by The Macmillan Company in 1944.

PREFACE

ANYONE who had just seen Jesus die on the cross might well have thought that there was nothing left of him and his work except the memory of a splendid dream, which hard reality had destroyed. Pilate would have been very much surprised if he had been told that his name would go down into history because he had pronounced sentence on a wretched little Jew, who had been brought before him as an agitator and on the suspicion of being a danger to the rule of Rome.

Yet in reality nothing was finished: something was going to begin which would march through the centuries and open up a new age in the history of mankind. A few souls had been so deeply impressed by the person and teaching of Jesus that, although the drama of Calvary was able temporarily to obscure that impression, it could not destroy it. Soon the disciples recovered their confidence in their master and their faith in his divine mission. Their hopes revived and they became convinced that Jesus had overcome death, and that henceforth he would sit on the right hand of God as the Lord in heaven. In this way a new faith was born. At first it found expression in a variety of forms which were gradually absorbed and assimilated into one system of doctrine. In its essential elements this process may be considered to have been completed by the end of the second century in the primitive catholicism of SS. Irenaeus and Tertullian. It is the birth of this faith which I propose to analyse.[1]

There are so many works concerning the birth and early history of Christianity that a catalogue of them would easily fill a book itself. In addition to the volumes needed for evaluating, summarising, and discussing them, several more

---

[1] In my book, *L'Église primitive*, Paris, 1948, I have shown how the constitution of the church expressed the new faith in the field of social relationships and what were the principal aspects of its life.

v

would be needed to compare them and extricate from them the differing orientations, which guide their researches, and to identify those which seem to hold out possibilities of advance. In the footnotes will be found references to the standard works to which students of primitive Christianity refer. The references and discussions have been reduced to a minimum. I have thought it necessary to proceed in this way not only to prevent a work which is already long enough, becoming inordinately lengthy, but also to allow the main features of a process, which is already sufficiently complex, to be clearly delineated. In the present state of historical science it is perhaps more important to elucidate the structure than to discuss every detail. If anyone thinks that I have arbitrarily simplified my task, I would refer him to a series of detailed articles which I have published in the course of many years in the *Revue de l'histoire des religions* and in the *Revue d'histoire et de philosophie religieuses*.[1] I intended all these articles to be only preparatory to the synthesis which I hoped some day to attempt. Anyone who casts a glance over them will, I hope, be convinced that my work is built up on ample research into details which— not always without regret—I have refrained from quoting in order not to weary the reader.

I have made it my duty to be very sparing in analysing and discussing the many hypotheses and theories which have been put forward on numerous historical points concerning Christian origins. I have taken count only of those which provide an opportunity of defining or justifying some particular element in my own conception.

There is one last point which can be conveniently explained here. The history of the formation of the church, which I have here tried to sketch out, forms the first chapter of a general history of Christianity. Nevertheless it treats of one specific fact—if the phrase may be allowed—the formation of a religious society and all that bears on such a fact, not only in the realm of thought but also on the social

[1] It will be seen in the introduction why I formulate the problem of Christian origins in this way.

level, in the fields of both emotional life and moral action. Here is a very different phenomenon from the development of such a society and its adaptation to the various conditions in which it can be called upon to live.

The problem of the birth of the church[1] can be considered as part of a much vaster problem than that of the history of Christianity; it belongs to the general history of religions. I have no idea of doubting the legitimacy and even the necessity of applying to the study of Christianity and, especially to its origins, the methods of religious history, and particularly the comparative method. By comparing Christian facts with the phenomena observed in the bosom of other religions we can elucidate certain aspects of primitive Christianity and comprehend their significance better. Yet I consider that, while we are concerned both to establish facts and grasp their character as well as to explain them, in the present state of historical science we must be very wary of supposing that Christianity is to a large extent made up of elements borrowed from other religions. A religion must be understood as an independent entity which generates its own dynamic. It may be subjected to the influence of other religions or it may borrow to some extent from them; but what it receives or borrows in this way only takes root and is absorbed if it harmonises with some latent quality which thereby gains expression. Those elements, which come from a strange source, in the course of their development generally assume a different significance from that which they possessed in their native environment. As a rule what one religion borrows from another is only material; less often is it the interpretation belonging to the material; very rarely is it the complete complex of ideas, feelings, emotions, and experiences which the material expresses.

M. G.

[1] They will be found enumerated as far as 1941 in the *Bibliographie Gogueliana* inserted by Professor Fridrichsen of Uppsala in part X of his *Conjectanea neotestamentica.*

AUTHOR'S NOTE

THE books of the New Testament and the works of early Christian literature are for convenience mentioned under the names of the authors to whom they are traditionally attributed; this, however, does not imply that they are accepted.

The manuscripts and versions of the New Testament are mentioned by the usual sigla, i.e. those used in E. Nestle's edition of the Greek New Testament (¹Stuttgart, 1941). This table is now universally adopted. The quotations from Irenaeus follow the traditional division of the text as it is reproduced in the Stieren edition (Leipzig, 1853). That given in the Harvey edition (Cambridge, 1857) differs in some respects.

TRANSLATOR'S NOTE

THIS book forms the second volume of a trilogy entitled *Jésus et les origines du christianisme*. The first volume appeared in an English translation in 1933, under the title, *The Life of Jesus*. The third volume was published in 1947 and is entitled *L'Église primitive* but has not been translated.

The author has introduced a few changes and additions in the text and notes of the English edition but substantially this work is a full and un-abridged translation of *La Naissance du christianisme* which first appeared in 1946. The references to *La Vie de Jésus* are to the second edition published in Paris in 1950 under the title *Jésus*.

The quotations from the Bible have been rendered from the Authorised Version except where it fails to give the meaning which it is desired to bring out. In these cases the new translation from the Vulgate has been used.

In most of the passages quoted from Josephus and the Patristic Writers the translations in the Loeb Classical Library have been used.

I desire to record my thanks to Professor S. G. F. Brandon of Manchester University for his permission to make use of the bibliography of modern works appended to his work, *The Fall of Jerusalem and the Christian Church* and the additions to it suggested by him in composing the similar bibliography appended to this work at the author's request.

H. C. SNAPE

Whalley Vicarage
January, 1952

BIBLIOGRAPHICAL NOTES

I. Periodicals

A.G.=*Abhandlungen der königlichen Gesellschaft der Wissenschaften zu Goettingen, Philosophisch-historische Klasse.*

ARCH. F. RELIG.=*Archiv fur Religionswissenschaft.*

BEITR.=*Beitrage zur Religionswissenschaft.*

FORSCH.=*Forschungen zur Geschichte des neutestamentlichen Kanons und der altkirchlichen Litteratur.*

HARV.TH. R.=*The Harvard Theological Review.*

N.G.=*Nachrichten der königlichen Gesellschaft der Wissenschaften zu Goettingen, Philosophisch-historische Klasse.*

R.B.=*Revue biblique.*

R.E.J.=*Revue des études juives.*

R.H.R.=*Revue de l'histoire des religions.*

R.H.L.R.=*Revue d'histoire et de littérature religieuses.*

R.H.P.R.=*Revue d'histoire et de philosophie religieuses.*

S.B.A.=*Sitzungsberichte der Berliner Akadamie der Wissenschaften, Philosophisch-historische Klasse.*

S.H.A.=*Sitzungsberichte der Heidelberger Akadamie der Wissenschaften. Philosophisch-historische Klasse.*

Z.F.TH.U.K.=*Zeitschrift für Theologie und Kirche.*

Z.F.WISS.TH.=*Zeitschrift fir wissenschaftliche Theologie.*

Z.N.T.W.=*Zeitschrift für die neutestamentliche Wissenschaft.*

II. Dictionaries, Encyclopaedias, etc.

BAUER, WÖRTERB.=W a l t e r Bauer, *Griechisch-deutsches Wörterbuch zu den Schriften des Neuen Testaments und der übrigen urchristlichen Litteratur*, Giessen, 1928.

D.A.C.L.=*Dictionnaire d'archéologie chrétienne et de liturgie*, publie par Dom F. Cabrol et Dom H. Leclercq, Paris, 1907 ss.

E.B.=*Encyclopaedia biblica*, published by Cheyne, London, 1899-1903.

HENNECKE, NEUT.APOKR. = *Neutestamentliche Apokryphen in Verbindung mit Fachgelerten* in deutscher Uebersetzung herausgegeben[2], Tubingen, 1924.

KITTEL=G. Kittel, *Theologisches Wörterbuch zum Neuen Testament in Verbindung mit* Bauerfeind, Baumgarten, Behm, Beyer, etc., *herausgegeben*, Stutgart, 1933 ss.

R.E.=*Realencyclopädie fur protestantische Theologie und Kirche, begründet von Hertzog, in dritter Auflage herausegegeben*, von Hauck, Leipzig, 1896 ss.

R.G.G. (the second edition is quoted except where otherwise shown). = *Die Religion in Geschichte und Gegenwart herausgegeben von* F. M. Schiele, Tubingen, 1909 ss. *Zweite Auflage herausgegeben von* H. Gunkel *und* L. Zscharnack, Tubingen, 1926 ss.

VOCABULARY = Moulton *and* Milligan, *The Vocabulary of the Greek New Testament, illustrated from papyri and other non-literary sources,* London, New York, Toronto, 1914 ss.

BEGIN.=*The Beginnings of Christianity,* edited by F. J. Foakes-Jackson *and* Kirsopp Lake, *Part* I, *Vol.* I-V, New York, London, 1920-33.

III. Works frequently quoted

BALDENSPERGER, PROL. VIERT. EV.=W. Baldensperger, *Der Prolog des vierten Evangeliums,* Freiburg in Breisgau, Leipzig, Tubingen, 1898.

BAUER. RECHTGL. U. KETZ.= *Rechtglaübigheit und Ketzerei im alltesten Christentum,* Tubingen, 1934.

BAUER, WORTGOTTESDIENST= *Der Wortgottesdienst der aeltesten Kirche,* Tubingen, 1930.

BOUCHE-LECLERCQ.=*L'intolérance religieuse et la politique,* Paris, second edition, 1911.

BOUSSET-GRESSMANN,REL.D. JUD.=W. Bousset, *Die Religion des Judentums im späthellenistischen Zeitalter in dritter verbesserter Auflage herausgegeben von* H. Gressmann, Tubingen, 1926.

BULTMANN, GESCH.=*Geschichte der synoptischen Tradition[2],* Goettingen, 1931.

DEISSMANN, L. V. O.=*L i c h t vom Osten[2-3],* Tubingen, 1909.

DIBELIUS, GEISTERS.=*Die Geisterwelt im Glauben des Paulus.* Goettingen, 1909.

DUCHESNE, MGR. L., ORIGINES= *Origines du culte chretien,* Paris, 1903.

DUCHESNE, H. A.=*Histoire ancienne de l'Église,* Paris, 1906 ss.

ERBES. TODESTAGE=*Die Todestage der Apostel Paulus und Petrus und ihre römische Denkmaler,* Leipzig, 1899.

GOGUEL MAURICE, EV.DE MC. =*L'Évangile de Marc dans ses rapportes avec ceux de Matthieu et de Luc,* Paris, 1909.

L'EUCHARISTIE=*L'Eucharistie des origines à Justin Martyr,* Paris, 1910.

INTROD.=*Introduction au Nouveau Testament,* I-V, 2, Paris, 1922 ss.

J. DE N.=*Jésus de Nazareth, mythe ou histoire?* Paris, 1925.

J.-B.=*Au seuil de l'Évangile. Jean-Baptiste,* Paris, 1928.

TROIS ÉTUDES=*Trois études sur la pensée religieuse du christianisme primitif,* Paris, 1931.

V.D.J.=*La Vie de Jésus.* Completely recast in a second edition under the title, *Jésus,* Paris, 1950. The references from this book come from the English translation (*The Life of Jesus,* translated by Olive Wyon, London, 1933). The references to the second

French edition have been added.

LA FOI À LA RÉS.=*La foi à la résurrection de Jesus dans le christianisme primitif*, Paris, 1933.

E.P.=*L'Église primitive*, Paris, 1947.

GUIGNEBERT, PRIM DE PI.=*La primauté de Pierre, la venue de Pierre à Rome*, Paris, 1909. *Le Christ*, Paris, 1943.

HARNACK, L. D. ZW. AP.=*Die Lehre der zwolf Apostel nebst Untersuchungen zur aeltesten Geschichte der Kirchenverfassung und des Kirchenrechts*, Leipzig, 1884.

DOGSCH., I.=*Lehrbuch der Dogmengeschichte*, I^4, Tubingen, 1909.

MISSION, *Die Mission und Ausbreitung des Christentums in den ersten drei Jahrhunderten*[3], Leipzig, 1915.

G. A. L.=*Geschichte der altchristlichen Litteratur bis Eusebius*, Leipzig, 1893 ss.

ENSTEH. U. ENTWICK.=*Enstehung und Entwickelung der Kirchenverfassung und des Kirchenrechts in den ersten drei Jahrhunderten*, Leipzig, 1910.

EINF.=*Einführung in die alte Kirchengeschichte, Das Schreiben der römischen Kirche an die korinthische in der Zeit des Domitians (I Clemensbrief)*, Leipzig, 1929.

HEILER, URK. U. OSTK;ALTK. AUTON.=*Die katholische Kirche des Ostens und Westens, I, Urkirche und Ostkirche, II, 1, Altkirchliche Autonomie und*

päpstlicher Zentralismus, Marburg, 1937-41.

HOLL, GES. AUFS.=*Gesammelte Aufsatze zur Kirchengeschichte, ii, Das Osten*, Tubingen, 1928.

KNOPF, NACHAP. Z.=*Das nachapostolische Zeitalter*, Tubingen, 1906.

LEIPOLDT, GOTTESDIENST.=*Der Gottesdienst der aeltesten Kirche*, Leipzig, 1937.

LIETZMANN, H. = *Histoire de l'Église anciene*, traduction de A. Jundt, Paris, 1936 ss.

LIGHTFOOT.=Lightfoot, *The Apostolic Fathers*, London, 1869-85[2], 1889-90. The first part is quoted from the second edition, the second from the first.

LOISY, Q. EV. = *Le quatrième Évangile*, Paris, 1903, [2]1921. Unless otherwise stated I quote from the second edition.

ACTES=*Les Actes des Apôtres*, Paris, 1920.

MYSTERES=*Les mystères paiens et le mystère chretien*[2], Paris, 1920.

NAISS. DU CHRIST.= *La naissance du christianisme*, Paris, 1933.

MEYER, URSPR. U. ANF.=*Urprung und Anfange des Christentums*, Stuttgart, Berlin, 1921-25.

REITZENSTEIN, HELL. MYSTERREL.=*Die hellenisteschen Mysterienreligionen*, Leipzig, Berlin, 1910, 1920, [3]1927. I quote from the second edition.

REVILLE, ORIG. DE L'ÉPISCOP. =*Les origines de l'épiscopat, I* (which is all that appeared), Paris, 1894.

Q.E.=*Le Quatrième Évangile*, Paris, 1901.

ORIG. DE L'EUCH.=*Les origines de l'eucharistie*, Paris, 1908.

SCHURER, GESCH.=*Geschichte des jüdischen Volkes im Zeitalter Jesu Christi*,[3] Leipzig, 1898-1901.

SOHM.=*Kirchenrecht, I, Die geschichtlichen Grundlagen*, Leipzig, 1892.

STRACK-BILLERBECK.=*Kommentar zum Neuen Testament aus Talmud und Midrash*, Marburg, 1922-28.

WEINEL, BIBL. TH.=*Biblische Theologie des Neuen Testaments. Die Religion Jesu und des Urchristentums*[3], Tubingen, 1921.

JOHANNES WEISS, URCHRIST.=*Das Urchristentum*, Goettingen, 1917.

ZAHN, G. K.=*Geschichte des Kanons des Neuen Testaments*, Leipzig, 1888, 1892.

CONTENTS

	PAGE	
PREFACE		v
AUTHOR'S NOTE		ix
TRANSLATOR'S NOTE		x
BIBLIOGRAPHICAL NOTES		xi
INDEX		557

INTRODUCTION

1. *The problem of the birth of Christianity*   1
2. *The chronological setting of primitive Christianity*   21

PART ONE

The Creation of a New Object of Religious Devotion

CHAP.

I. THE BIRTH OF THE BELIEF IN THE RESURRECTION OF JESUS

1. *The burial of Jesus*   30
2. *The third day and the empty tomb*   33
3. *The resurrection*   37
4. *The appearances*   41
5. *The ascension*   60
6. *The tradition and its formation*   61

II. THE BIRTH OF THE FAITH IN THE RESURRECTION

1. *The character of the faith in the resurrection*   66
2. *The origins of the idea of resurrection*   72
3. *The psychological character of the resurrection appearances*   74
4. *The function and character of religious visions*   75
5. *The psychological mechanism of the appearance to Paul*   81

PART TWO

The Failure of Christianity to Develop in the Framework of Judaism

I. THE CHURCH AT JERUSALEM UP TO A.D. 44

1. *The Church at Jerusalem according to the compiler of Acts*   89
2. *Was the Christianity of the Jerusalem Church pneumatick in character?*   95
3. *The theology of the Church at Jerusalem*   98
4. *The life of the Church at Jerusalem according to Acts*   103

CHAP.

II. THE CHURCH IN JERUSALEM AFTER A.D. 44.
THE FATE OF JUDAEO-CHRISTIANITY

1. *What happened about 44*   PAGE 106
2. *James and dynastic Christianity*   110
3. *The mother of Jesus*   118
4. *The domestic history of the Church at Jerusalem after 44*   121
5. *The death of James*   124
6. *The exodus of the Church in 70*   132
7. *The traditions concerning the* desposunoi   133
8. *The Church at Jerusalem after 70*   136
9. *Ebionitism*   139
10. *Jewish Christians and heresies*   145
11. *The significance of Jewish Christianity*   147

III. APOSTOLIC CHRISTIANITY AFTER A.D. 44

1. *Peter at Antioch. The incident between him and Paul*   149
2. *Did Peter evangelise Asia-Minor?*   152
3. *Peter and Babylon. Does Babylon refer to Rome?*   154
4. *Missions from Jerusalem and the Church of Rome*   158

PART THREE

The Development of Christianity within the Framework of Hellenism. The Beginnings of Christian Doctrine

I. STEPHEN AND THE HELLENISTS OF JERUSALEM

1. *Who the Hellenists are*   167
2. *The story of Stephen*   169
3. *Stephen's Speech*   172
4. *The Origins of Hellenic Christianity*   174

II. THE CHURCH AT ANTIOCH

1. *The Hellenists and their mission*   177
2. *The foundation of the Church at Antioch*   181
3. *The name 'Christians' given to the faithful at Antioch*   184
4. *The Church at Antioch after 44*   186
Appendix—Barnabas   189

III. THE APOSTLE PAUL AND PAULINISM

1. *Paul's significance and the character of his thought*   194
2. *The life of the apostle Paul*   205
3. *Paul's missionary method*   221
4. *Paul's theology*   223
5. *Paul's controversies*   250

PART FOUR

The Stabilisation of Christianity and the Formation of its Doctrine

I. TOWARDS STABILISATION

1. *Why Christianity only gradually became conscious of itself as an independent entity*   257

CONTENTS

CHAP.

2. *Primitive diversity and the work of unification*   PAGE 258
3. *Pneumatism and eschatological belief, obstacles to stabilisation*   261
4. *The evolution of pneumatism*   263
5. *The evolution of eschatological belief*   271
6. *The parallelism between the evolution of pneumatism and that of eschatology*   280
7. *The evolution of the idea of authority*   286

II. THE CONFLICT BETWEEN JEWISH AND GENTILE CHRISTIANITY

1. *Paul and the Church at Jerusalem until 43-44*   292
2. *The conference at Jerusalem*   295
3. *The incident at Antioch*   303
4. *The campaign led by Jewish Christians in churches founded by Paul*   305
5. *The epistle to the Romans and the Jewish Christian question*   316
6. *Paul's isolation both at Jerusalem and Rome*   318
7. *The triumph of universalism after* A.D. 70   319
8. *The surviving forms of Jewish Christianity*   321

III. DEUTEROPAULINISM

1. *What is to be understood by the term deuteropaulinism*   323
2. *The Pastoral Epistles*   324
3. *The Epistle to the Ephesians*   328
4. *The synoptic Gospels*   330
5. *The book of the Acts*   337
6. *The first Epistle of Peter*   339

IV. THE EPISTLE TO THE HEBREWS   342

V. THE JOHANNINE THEOLOGY

1. *The Fourth Gospel*   347
2. *The first Epistle of John*   366
3. *The Johannine Apocalypse*   369

VI. CHRISTIANITY AS AN ETHICAL RELIGION IN THE EPISTLE OF JAMES AND THE DIDACHE

1. *The Epistle of James*   373
2. *The Didache*   377

VII. THE PRE-CATHOLICISM OF CLEMENT OF ROME   383

VIII. HERESIES

1. *Heresy and the Church's aspirations after unity. Definition of heresy. The grounds of its appearance*   393
2. *Did the apostle Paul regard the Judaising Christians as heretics?*   396
3. *The gnosticism of Colossae*   401
4. *The gnosticism which is attacked in the Epistle to the Ephesians*   404
5. *The heresies attacked in the Pastoral Epistles*   405

CHAP.

6. *The heresies attacked in the first Epistle of John* PAGE 407
7. *The fight against heresy in the Book to the Seven Churches* 409
8. *Ignatius of Antioch and heresies* 413
9. *The Didache and heresies* 418
10. *The polemic against heresy in the Epistles of Jude and II Peter* 418
11. *Conclusion* 430

IX. TOWARDS EARLY CATHOLICISM 433

PART FIVE

The Reactions Provoked by the Preaching of the Gospel

I. THE PROBLEM

1. *The feelings of the primitive Church towards Judaism* 439
2. *The feelings of the Church towards the empire and the Gentile world* 440
3. *The attitude of Judaism towards the Church* 446
4. *The position of Christianity in the empire. Public opinion* 448
5. *The reactions of the Church* 449

II. THE REACTIONS OF PALESTINIAN JUDAISM TO THE PREACHING OF THE GOSPEL

1. *The feelings of Judaism towards Christianity until 70 and its methods of action* 451
2. *The description given by the compiler of Acts of the attitude of the Jewish authorities towards the church at Jerusalem. A criticism of his description* 454

III. THE REACTIONS OF THE JEWS IN THE DIASPORA AND THE FIRST INTERVENTIONS OF ROME PROMPTED BY THEM

1. *The Christians at first confused with the Jews and enjoying the tolerance accorded to Judaism as a religio licita* 468
2. *The efforts of the Jews to counter Christian propaganda, especially Paul's missionary work* 469
3. *Paul's trial* 489

IV. CHRISTIANITY AND THE ROMAN EMPIRE

1. *The change in the situation in 64 and its causes* 502
2. *The question of the* Edictum Neronianum *and the procedure applied against the Christians* 506
3. *The massacre of Christians at Rome in 64* 510
4. *From Nero to Domitian* 523
5. *The persecution of Domitian* 528
6. *The persecution under Trajan* 537

V. HOW CHRISTIANITY REACTED TO PERSECUTION 545

APPENDIX — BIBLIOGRAPHY OF MODERN WORKS IN ENGLISH 555

Introduction

I.—THE PROBLEM OF THE BIRTH OF CHRISTIANITY

ALBERT SCHWEITZER writes: 'The great and still undischarged task which confronts those engaged in the historical study of primitive Christianity is to explain how the teaching of Jesus developed into the early Greek theology, in the form in which it appears in the works of Ignatius, Justin, Tertullian, and Irenaeus. How could the doctrinal system of Paul arise on the basis of the life and work of Jesus and the beliefs of the primitive community: and how did the early Greek theology arise out of Paulinism? Strauss and Renan recognised the obligation and each endeavoured in a series of works to trace the path leading from Jesus to the history of dogma. Since their time no one who has dealt with the life of Jesus has attempted to follow this course.'[1] This judgement is rather shallow in nature, as the real problem is not only to discover how Christian theology and dogma were formed but also, what is especially important, to discover how the church developed its constitution. For Christianity cannot be reduced to a theology. In addition Schweitzer's appreciation of the paths criticism has followed is somewhat sweeping. But it has to be recognised that research has produced much more both in volume and importance on points of detail than in the way of general outlines and attempts at explanation of the whole.[2] It is very tempting

---

[1] Albert Schweitzer: *Geschichte der paulinischen Forschung*, Tubingen, 1911, p. v. Eng. trans. *Paul and his interpreters*, Black, p. v.

[2] Confining oneself to the works of the twentieth century the following exceptions must be mentioned: Adolph Julicher, *Die Religion Jesu und die Anfange des Christentums bis zum Nicaenum* (325); Adolph Harnack, 'Kirche und Staat bis zur Grundung der Staatskirche', *Die Kultur der Gegenwart, Teil. I, Abt. IV*, Berlin, Leipzig, 1906, pp. 41-160; Johannes Weiss, *Das Christentum*, Gottingen, 1917. The work is incomplete. Only the volume devoted to the apostolic period appeared. The author died before he could edit the volume which was going to deal with the religious state of the ancient world at the time of Jesus. The order in which the volumes were intended to succeed each other show that the complete work was undoubtedly not going to be a general explanation of the origins of Christianity. See by the same author 'Das Problem der Enstehung des Christentums', *Arch. f. Redwiss.*, 1913, XVI, pp. 423-515; Meyer, *Ursp. u. Anf.* Cf. *Ursprung und Geschichte der*

to suppose that the history of Christian origins cannot be treated in any other way but the reasons for this are complex and it is worthwhile pointing out the chief of them.

The history of Christian origins and the New Testament criticism on which it depends are sciences which have only by a slow and difficult process detached themselves from their theological origins; for a long time—and even now on occasion—they had to defend their right to an autonomous existence and, even since they gained that right, they have not always succeeded in ridding themselves completely of the habit of envisaging their problems with a certain theological prejudice. On this account the history of the birth of Christianity has often turned out to be nothing more than the history of the formation of Christian doctrine. But although doctrine is that manifestation of a religion which is most easily grasped, yet it is neither the only one nor always the most important. For this reason also it is nearly always assumed as *a priori* certain that Christianity in its development moved from unity to diversity; in reality, although Christianity has varied in form according to changing environment and different circumstances, at the beginning it appeared under a variety of forms, which a superficial examination fails to disclose. In its earliest history some forces can be detected making for diversity as well as others making for unification and concentration.

Research on Christian origins has not yet arrived at results comparable to those attained in other fields of the history of religions, because (1) theological prejudices have often played hard and fast with research and have had to be set aside,[1] (2) the documents at one's disposal are insufficient[2] and perhaps especially because (3) the problem has been as a rule conceived too narrowly.

Mormonen mit Exkursen uber die Anfange des Islams und des Christentums, Halle, 1912. (Extremely suggestive in many parts, the work of Edouard Meyer is a series of detailed studies sometimes lacking logical order rather than a general exposition.) Loisy, *Naiss. du christ.* Charles Guignebert (*Jésus*, Paris, 1933; *Le monde juif vers le temps de Jésus*, Paris, 1935) made preliminary studies for a complete history of Christian origins which was to be followed by two volumes called *Le Christ et L'église.* Only part of the first volume could be published. It appeared in 1943 together with a lecture on the mystery of Paul given by Guignebert in 1933. The extensive work published under the editorship of F. Foakes-Jackson and Kirsopp Lake (with the assistance of a large number of scholars) under the title *The beginnings of Christianity*, New York, London, is a collection of studies of which only those referring to the book of the Acts have appeared (five volumes, 1920-33).

[1] This applies just as much to those who want to use history in defence of Christianity as to those who want to use it as an instrument of attack.

[2] In these circumstances there is a strong temptation to supply the gaps in our sources of information by hypothesis. A historian as judicious as F. Kattenbusch

The phenomenon, which we are concerned to analyse and explain is not only the formation of a doctrine which found expression in the old Greek dogma but also the establishment of a new religious society, the church, in the life of which doctrine plays a very important but by no means the only part. The terms Christianity and the Church are often used as if they were synonymous. But the first has a wider connotation than the second. Christianity is the whole religious movement which claims Jesus and his activity as its source and origin both in its individual and collective forms; the church is a society, which, without forgetting that its *raison d'être* and purpose lie in a realm beyond, has had to adapt itself to an existence in this present world for its realisation. It is also a society which was several times divided and in the life of which can be discerned at play two forces, one tending to unification, the other to diversification. Both Christianity and the church are wholly centred on the belief in the risen and glorified Jesus. Everything concerning the ministry of Jesus, his teaching and ministry as well as the group of disciples collected round him do not belong to the church's history but to its 'prehistory'. Typically enough there is no word for this: it is an indication of a confusion of ideas and explains why it is so difficult to form a unifying conception of the origins of Christianity.

This confusion comes from the idea to be found as a confessional prejudice in both Catholicism and Protestantism, that Jesus founded the church. The church is a result of his activity but he neither founded it directly himself nor entrusted its foundation to a solitary individual, such as Peter, nor can a group of men such as the twelve apostles be supposed to have been given the mission and power to do it. Jesus did not foresee the church. He proclaimed his return in glory to establish the Kingdom of God and he believed that his return was so near that he gave no instructions to his disciples concerning the interval, which had to elapse until he returned. To quote Loisy's epigrammatic phrase, 'He proclaimed the Kingdom of God and the church was the outcome'.[1]

But Loisy's assertion raises a problem of the first importance which he does not seem to have envisaged. Was the church a

('Die Vorzugstellung des Petrus und die Urgemeinde zu Jerusalem', *Festgabe fur*, Karl Muller, Tubingen, 1922, p. 323) puts forward a theory to justify this procedure. 'We are often tempted', he writes, 'to know more than the texts tells us. We must take a provisional risk. Hypotheses in reconstruction cannot be dispensed with altogether. But we must be very careful in using them.'

[1] Loisy, *L'Évangile et l'Église*, Paris, 1929, p. 153. See also Guignebert, *Le Christ*, p. 3.

substitute for the Kingdom of God or was it felt, at any rate in the beginning, that it was only a stage preparatory to the Kingdom of God? The Pauline conception of the church as the means of edification—taking the word in its full sense and not with the flat insipid meaning which was given to it subsequently—shows that this is the question which has to be answered.

It is often said that history is the resurrection of the past. This is not true. The course of events cannot be reversed. Nothing in the future can be done to recreate the present. So far as history may be thought of as a resurrection of the past it can only be so on entirely partial lines. The possibilities of its being so are directly dependent on the documents at one's disposal. Furthermore, out of all the facts which constituted the real at a given moment, only a small part find a place in the relevant documents and they are not necessarily the most important or the ones of the greatest consequence.[1] At the most history may be a simplified representation of the past but there is even then no guarantee that the facts as a result of such simplification may not to some extent be presented in false perspective. But, dangerous as simplification may be, on other counts it has one advantage. It allows us to see the relationship between the facts which necessarily escapes observation when we are in the presence of the entire complexity of the real. Such a simplified history of primitive Christianity is only possible to a very limited extent. So far as it could be sketched out roughly it would resemble those old maps of Africa, on which beyond the districts touching the coast a few roads and regions were merely marked out and shown without their relative positions being given but with vast tracts of land left white or hachured and marked 'region unknown'. Pierre Termier [2] in his description of the way in which geologists, 'those historians of the earth', study the architecture of the globe, notices that as their observations are restricted to the continents and islands seven-tenths of the earth's surface escapes their investigations. The historians of primitive Christianity are in a similar plight. They are unable to plot the exact position of what they know or to estimate its value because so much has become inaccessible by the oceans of oblivion.

[1] The earliest history of Christianity offers a typical example of this kind. The cultus is one of the most direct manifestations of religion. What we know of the cultus of the first generation of Christians amounts to very little and gives us no general picture.

[2] P. Termier, *Souvenirs d'un geologue*[2], Paris, s.d., p. 358.

The fragmentary nature of the documents at their disposal demands an exceedingly sensitive interpretation. Where the texts are so few, it is possible to make a most minute examination. This is an advantage provided that you always resist the temptation to desire to extract from them more than is there. One particular difficulty emerges from the character of the texts. The term literature may be reserved for those works where the author has some regard for style and expresses what he wishes to say in a way which men of culture can understand. By this definition the writings of primitive Christianity cannot be classified as literature, since they were intended only for a limited group and were not completely intelligible to others. The earliest Christian writers wrote only for the members of the church and therefore did not express all their knowledge, sentiments, and beliefs, because they could assume that their readers already shared them.

Religious literature offers peculiar difficulties in the way of interpretation. A feeling and regard for historical accuracy is missing. Everything in this kind of literature which has the charm of a historical tale is twisted into expressing and justifying the faith, facts and their interpretation being indissolubly bound up together. The memories, which a religious society can preserve of its origin and past, play in its life a double part. On the one hand they express what it is and what it wants to be; at the same time they justify its existence by giving its origins a transcendent character. A religious society makes its memories into a myth which serves to explain the society's formation and justifies its existence.[1]

Christianity is not the religion preached or taught by Jesus. It has for its content the drama of redemption accomplished by his death and resurrection. It depends therefore upon a sacred history culminating in the fact of the resurrection. It is not concerned with the life of a holy man or a hero who serves as an example for those who follow him [2] but with a series of historical facts, which are interpreted as revealing redemptive acts of God. The material may be provided by historical memories and traditions but its elaboration involves a certain disregard for minute historical accuracy. Sacred history in some ways resembles a myth; it differs from a myth as far as both those who weave the story and those who hear it cherish it

[1] Hellenic Christianity developed more rapidly than Palestinian Christianity without doubt because its memories of the ministry of Jesus were more remote.
[2] Although the gospel story was viewed from this angle also in the primitive church.

5

as significant because they are convinced that it is concerned with what is real.

The earliest Christian documents would not make the problem of Christian origins unusually difficult, if they did not happen also to be unilateral in character, owing to the fact that they are a canonical collection.

Tacitus [1] mentions massacres of Christians after the fire at Rome in 64. Josephus[2] mentions John Baptist and the death of James the Just, the brother of Jesus, in 62. Suetonius and Dion Cassius[3] tell of the persecution of Domitian.[4] Pliny informs us of the action taken against the Christians in Bithynia.[5] Apart from these references there is nothing in the history of Christianity in the first century and the beginning of the second known outside Christian sources. Latin writers, in particular Epiphanes and St. Jerome, make some allusions to small groups of Jewish Christians who survived for some time after 70 on the edge of the great church. They also refer to gospels used by these people of which they have preserved a few fragments. The passages in the *Memoirs of Hegesippus* quoted by Eusebius throw an interesting light on the character of Palestinian Christianity, principally as it existed in the period from 70 to the revolt of Barkochba. But, apart from this, our information is confined to Christianity in Asia Minor and Jerusalem. Of the latter we are informed of the earliest phase in its history and of its relations with the former.

In spite of this there is reason to think that Christianity both in the first and second centuries was much more diverse than the sources disclose.[6] Is it credible that Christianity made no advance except in the direction of Asia Minor, Greece, and Italy? It must have spread in several directions at the same time. The catalogue of nations found in Acts ii. 9-11 suggests a vast missionary enterprise which must have been under way when the book of Acts was being edited, i.e. between 80 and 90. We do not know anything about the

---

[1] Tacitus, *Ann.* xv. 44; Suetonius (*Nero*, 16) also mentions the massacres of Christians but does not connect them with the fire at Rome.

[2] Josephus, *A.j.* xviii. 5, 2; xx. 9, 1.

[3] Suetonius, *Domitian*, x. 12, 15; Dion Cassius, lxvii. 14.

[4] Important as they are in certain respects, the texts of Tacitus, Suetonius, and Pliny the Younger, in which Christ is named, do not tell us anything we do not know from other sources. Concerning these texts see my books *J. de N.*, pp. 25 ff.; *V. de J.*, Eng. trans., London, 1933, pp. 75 ff.

[5] Pliny, *Ep.* x. 96.

[6] On this point see my article, 'Unité et diversité du christianisme primitif', *R.h.p.r.*, 1939, XIX, pp. 1-54.

6

origin of Christianity in Egypt,[1] since the traditions which attribute the evangelisation of Egypt to Mark and make him the first bishop of Alexandria are legendary in character.[2]

Intercourse, however, between Syria, especially Antioch and Egypt was easy and frequent and the Jewish colony in Egypt was so important that it must have been, so it seems, one of the first objectives of Christian evangelism. There is another reason why Christianity must have been taken to Egypt at a very early date. Paul writes to the Romans in 58 that he is thinking of undertaking a missionary journey to Spain (Romans xv. 23-4) since he finds that Christ has been preached everywhere in the eastern half of the Mediterranean. He would surely have thought of Egypt rather than Spain, if it had still been virgin country. Of course we cannot exclude the possibility that where there is no mention of a church in existence, evangelism had proved a failure or had left no lasting results. It is also possible that through some accident all the documents referring to a particular church have been destroyed. But such attempts to solve the problem are too simple to give any satisfaction and are tantamount to being unable to offer any satisfactory explanation. Walter Bauer[3] investigated the history of Christianity in Egypt and came to the conclusion that the earliest ecclesiastical authors,

---

[1] Duchesne, *Histoire ancienne de l'Eglise*, Paris, 1906-10, I, p. 331; Harnack, *Mission*[3], II, pp. 706 ff.; Walter Bauer, *Rechtglaubigkeit und Ketzerei im aeltesten Christentum*, Tubingen, 1934, pp. 49 ff. Harnack (*Mission*, II, p. 91, n. 1) believes that he can find proof of the existence of Christianity in Alexandria at a very early date in Acts xviii. 25, where the manuscript D. d. gig. say that Apollos was instructed in the word of the Lord 'in his own country'. But it is rash to see in this anything more than the conjecture of the recursor of D. Some people think that they can find an allusion to Christianity in a letter of Claudius to the people of Alexandria in 41. H. Idris Bell, *Jews and Christians, illustrated from Greek papyri in the British Museum*, London, 1924, pp. 1-37. Cf. Salamon Reinach, 'La première allusion au Christianisme dans l'histoire', *R.h.r.*, 1924, LXXXIX, pp. 108 ff. This opinion cannot be retained. Cf. Guignebert, *Le Christ*, p. 17. Out of the copious literature written about the letter of Claudius I will only quote W. Seston's article 'L'Empereur Claude et les Chretiens', *R.h.p.r.*, 1931, XI, pp. 275 ff., where will be found a reference to the earlier literature on the subject. See also the bibliography given by Dom. Leclercq, 'Judaisme', *D.A.C.L.*, VIII, col. 162. Of the literature later than Seston's article mention must be made of H. Janne, 'Une passage controverse de la lettre de Claude aux Alexandrins', *Revue archeologique*, ser. 5, 1932, XXXV, pp. 268-82. *La lettre de Claude aux Alexandrins et le Christianisme*, *Mélanges* Franz Cumont, Brussels, 1936, I, pp. 273-95 and Marcel Simon, 'A propos de la lettre de Claude aux Alexandrins', *Bulletin de la Faculté des lettres de Strasbourg*, 1943, XXI, pp. 175-183. Seston and Simon think that the letter from Claudius refers to Judaism, Janne refers it to Christianity.

[2] Concerning these traditions see my book *Ev. de Mc.*, Paris, 1909, pp. 13 ff.

[3] Bauer, *Rechtgl. u. Ketz.*, pp. 49 ff.

although they must have had some information of the origin of Christianity in Egypt said nothing about it, because by the standards of early Catholicism the earliest form of Christianity in Egypt was a heresy. In confirmation of this hypothesis, he points out, that in other places as well, Christianity in its earliest form did not conform to what later came to be regarded as orthodox.

Observations such as these regarding the history of the earliest Christian missions show us that what was remembered of the earliest days of Christianity passed through a kind of censorship so that there is only left for us what conformed to the doctrine of the church when it had become fixed in one single form. We can then understand the significance of the fact that with very few exceptions to hand[1] the documents which we have as our sources for the early history of Christianity have a canonical character.[2]

The canon of the New Testament[3] began to be established in the second half of the second century in the course of the church's struggle to preserve its traditions, teaching, and hopes against the

[1] The list of documents which are not canonical and have been preserved is short. Apart from a few passages in the *Memoirs of Hegesippus* mentioned by Eusebius which were not written before the second half of the second century, there are only a few fragments from apocryphal gospels (Jewish Christian Gospels of the Hebrews, the Ebionites, the Nazarenes or the twelve apostles; the Gospel of Peter; the Gospel of the Egyptians) and a fragment from the Apocalypse of Peter. These texts were conveniently collected together by Preuschen (*Antilegomena. Die Reste der ausserkanonischen Evangelien und Urchristlichen Uberlieferungen*, Giessen, 1901). See also the larger collection which extends over a considerably longer period published in German under the direction of E. Hennecke (*Neutestamentliche Apokryphen*[2], Tubingen, 1924). The fragments of the apocryphal gospels and the Apocalypse of Peter cannot be dated before the second century. They belong to types of Christianity recognisably different from that of the great church but they cannot be distinguished and placed with any precision.

[2] I am using the term 'canonical' in a wider sense than that in which it is commonly used, intending it to cover the works of the apostolic fathers (Clement of Rome, the Didache, Ignatius, Polycarp, Barnabas, and Hermas). At one time they were included in the New Testament but were not kept in it because it became clear that the authors of the books did not belong to the apostolic period.

[3] On the history of the canon of the New Testament there exists abundant literature. The most important work of a very conservative character is that of Zahn, *G.K.*, unfinished. Cf. Grundgiss, *Der Geschichte des Neutestamentlichen Kanons*[2], Leipzig, 1904, and the series *Forschungen zur Geschichte des Neutestamentlichen Kanons und der altkirchlichen Litteratur*, published under his editorship from 1881 onwards which contains most of his works. Zahn's ideas were vigorously contested by Harnack, *Das Neue Testament um 200*, Frieburg im Breisgau, 1889, as well as *Die Enstehung des Neuen Testaments und die Wichtigsten Folgen der Neuen Schopfung*, Leipzig, 1914. See also Loisy, *Histoire du Canon du Nouveau Testament*, Paris, 1891; Leipoldt, *Geschichte des Neutestamentlichen Kanons*, Leipzig, 1907-8; Jacquier, *La Nouveau testament dans l'Eglise chrétienne*, Paris, 1911, I; Lagrange, *Histoire ancienne du Canon du Nouveau Testament*, Paris, 1933.

threats of Marcionism and Gnosticism. The canon defined what the church regarded as the authentic standard of its doctrine. By fixing the canon, the church set limits on her own development without consciously intending to make any innovation or arrive at any authoritative decision. She was inspired with the kind of conception of the apostolate and apostolicity which prevailed on the eve of the second generation.

The New Testament was intended to be the *corpus* of apostolic writings which had been preserved by the church; there is nothing to suggest that those who began to close the collection had any other idea in mind except to select books which were supposed to have come from the apostles.[1] But they worked with an artificial idea of the apostolate. Also they could not pick out from the books preserved by the church those which were really old and might have been written by men of the first generation of Christians. In reality, books which possessed a certain inherent authority were considered apostolic much more because their teaching harmonised with that of the church than because they did not bear the stamp of a late period. Books were admitted into the New Testament according to an estimate of their value.[2] That can be inferred from the arbitrary combinations of inconsistent traditions to which recourse had to be made in order to establish *a posteriori* the apostolic character of certain books, notably the Johannine writings and so justify their inclusion in the canon. The New Testament therefore is documentary evidence for the Greco-Roman Christianity of the second half of the second century no less than for that of the first century.[3]

The formation of the New Testament assured the preservation of precious texts but created conditions exceptionally unfavourable for the preservation of other documents, the loss of which historians can only deplore. The canon acted as a veritable censor, with the result

[1] Except always the Gospels of Mark and Luke which were known not to have been written by apostles but possessed such authority that it was impossible to exclude them. Mark and Luke were accepted as apostolic on the ground that the one had Peter's authority the other Paul's. Cf. Irenaeus, *Adv. haer.* iii. 1, 1.

[2] This did not apply when the time came to close the canon finally. This was only done slowly and with much hesitation and delay. When it eventually took place the liturgical practice of the majority of the churches in their readings at public worship was the deciding factor.

[3] Heiler (*Urkirche und Ostkirche*, Marburg, 1937, p. 94) makes the same inference when he writes: 'the New Testament is the document of the catholic church', but he is making a theological not a historical judgement when he adds, 'the New Testament is not only the document of the pure gospel of Jesus Christ; it is also the document of the one catholic apostolic church, which confesses the Nicene creed'.

that they were thrown in the waste paper basket and disappeared. It stands between us and the realities of the first century like a filter or screen which prevents us from seeing in the sequence of events ending in early catholicism anything which fails to harmonise with it. We cannot therefore construct a true and factual history of primitive Christianity, as things are, not just because the preservation of the texts has depended on chance but much more on account of the character of the texts themselves.

While, however, when we consider the facts of the canon, we are compelled to give up the idea of composing a complete history of primitive Christianity, at the same time we can see another way of attacking the problem. That is to investigate the constitution of the early catholic church for which the New Testament is the earliest and most authentic documentary source of information and to pick out of it those elements which we know, with some certainty, belong to Christianity in the first century.

What calls for study is the appearance in history of the early catholic church, i.e. the formation, stabilisation, and organisation of a Christian religious society. The establishment of a society of this kind is the normal result of the advent of a new religious experience.[1] This is not a chance phenomenon but for its appearance depends on certain conditions and laws. It develops with an appearance of inevitability resulting from the process of natural selection, which eliminates those forms without survival value for a religious society, substituting those which we have. A further process of selection operates upon these so as to leave those forms which have the strongest survival value and possess most vitality. This process is determined by the laws of religious sociology and proves a guide for the historian and gives direction to his researches.

The historical method is always the same in principle but varies in application. Military history is not treated exactly as political history. The procedure in studying the history of law is not precisely the same as in studying the history of philosophy or of science or literature. When we come to the history of religions or of one particular religion, we must not abandon the rigorous standard of

[1] In using the term 'religious experience' for want of a better one, I am well aware of the objections raised against its use and do not underestimate their force. (See for instance Hubert and Mauss, *Mélanges d'histoire des religions*, Paris, 1909, pp. xli f.; Loisy, *Les mystères paiens et le mystère chretien*[2], Paris, 1930, p. 345. We mean by the term 'religious experience' only the subjective feeling of being acted upon by a power beyond oneself without any implication that the experience when it arises spontaneously proves to be a source of knowledge.

historical criticism in order to square the result of research with the postulate of this or that theology; neither must we mark out in advance a sphere prohibited to the historian; history is absolutely free from any positive or negative theology and must remain so. The business of the historian is only to establish the facts and set them out in order by their mutual connection. It is not his job to evaluate them and to disengage their deep significance and their spiritual meaning or even to discover if they correspond to a transcendent reality. What is peculiar in religious history comes from the fact that it is concerned with a twofold object, religion being both individual and collective. Primarily it is a complex of feelings, emotions, intuitions, ideas, and representations; in other words, it is a peculiar and specific form of interior life which has direct influence on the intellectual and practical bearings of the subject. If we take into consideration only its exterior manifestations such as doctrine, institutions, and rites, we shall never understand what religion is.[1] While the religious life is the most personal thing in the world, if it is not to evaporate completely, it must find its expression in the social life of a religious society organised in such a way that it can endure.

Social religion emerges from personal religion: the converse is also true. All personal religion comes to birth in the setting of a social religion, even when it assumes a new form. It is purely a question of theory and impossible to verify by observation whether personal or social religion appears first. The religious experience of Jesus occurred in the setting of Judaism to which it owes its form and many of its constituent elements. But it is not the inevitable result of Judaism. In the first century there were hundreds of thousands of Jews in exactly the same position as Jesus and subject to the same influences but there was only one Jesus.[2]

In comparing personal religion with social religion there is a striking analogy with the comparative characteristics of the two kinds of religion distinguished by Bergson[3] as (1) the open or dynamic

[1] Concerning the fact that religious history is in the last resort a study of human experiences and feelings and therefore demands sympathy and understanding of men, see the reflections of H. Usener, 'Mythologie', *Arch f. Rev.* 1904, VII, p. 29. Because in the final analysis the history of religion deals with personalities and every human personality is a mystery, we cannot in this sphere expect to arrive at completely exhaustive results. Snouck-Hurgronje (in Bertholet, *Lehrbuch der Religionsgeschichte*[3], Tubingen, 1925, I, p. 671) writes concerning Mahomet: 'The lives of men who make history in the final analysis evades the historian's criticism.'

[2] Similar observations can be made concerning all religions the origin of which can be known.

[3] Bergson, *Les deux sources de la morale et de la religion*, Paris, 1932.

religion and (2) the closed or static religion, (1) being the spontaneous outburst of spiritual energy, (2) being a certain way of living, thinking, feeling, and acting imposed by the environment. In reality, however, there is no religion purely dynamic or purely static; all that happens is that one characteristic or the other predominates in a religion. The two forms of religion are closely bound up together in so far as a dynamic religion becomes stable and organised, suffers degradation, and gives birth to a static religion. The converse also happens so far as a static religion is the setting from which a dynamic religion can emerge. Religious experience is a form of interior life which in some ways approaches approximately to an emotional phenomenon, in others to an intellectual phenomenon. As it finds an appropriate intellectual symbol to express its emotional impulses, it associates together two apparently contradictory convictions. The first belongs to the pessimistic turn of mind, the conviction of a person that his true destiny is not fulfilled and that neither by his own efforts nor by the natural turn of events will it ever be. There exists no religion for those who are content and satisfied and, while religion is not merely the expression of deep human anxiety, it begins with that. The man who remains anxious is resigned, in despair, or in revolt, according to his temperament; he is not religious. To be religious there must be associated with the pessimistic element an optimistic element, the conviction that the destiny which a man is unable to fulfil if left to himself can be realised by a transcendent power, who is kindly disposed towards him or can be made and kept kindly disposed to him on certain moral or ritual conditions. The destiny of man, the transcendent power, the conditions which must be fulfilled to make this power kindly disposed may be thought of in countless ways. This is what creates the great diversity in religions. That does not matter but without convictions of this kind a living religion cannot exist.[1]

If this religious experience remained purely a matter of feeling without finding any intellectual expression, it would be reduced to a series of isolated moments, which would consequently be unstable and fleeting. In the realm of thought the results of the labour of abstraction are fixed by words which save the trouble of continually repeating the work of abstraction. In the same way the religious feeling

---

[1] It is true that there are certain kinds of religion which do not appear to possess the idea of a transcendent power. Such is the Religion of Humanity developed by Loisy at the end of his life. But it may be asked whether religions of this kind are anything more than the residue of religions.

is fixed and becomes capable of being developed and communicated by finding expression in ideas which are rudimentary and isolated to begin with but later are developed and organised into systems. There is a natural temptation to confuse the projection of religion into the intellectual sphere in this way with religion itself but we must not do this, because, although it is the expression of a religion, as an expression it is only a symbol. That is why Auguste Sabatier[1] says that religious knowledge has a symbolic character. We must go further than that and say that there is no knowledge but only religious symbols.[2]

In every religion there exists an expanding force which compels it to become a conquering power and to assume a social form. Although the conquest of men's minds by a summary or systematically developed doctrine is the plainest form of expansion, there is also active, what is perhaps essential, the mysterious phenomenon of spiritual contagion, the action of soul upon soul, of person on person.[3]

A religion has not really come to a head and found itself until it has given birth to a religious community. But when religion ceases to be personal and becomes social, it changes its character, because the relationship between religious experience and doctrine is reversed. Religious experience instead of preceding doctrine follows it. Intellectual assent to a statement of belief tends to become a substitute for faith; in every case assent precedes experience which becomes dependent on it. Doctrine tends to become an object in itself and a truth in no way dependent on the experience which created it. In this way religion is degraded into a rationalistic system of ideas. Rites and practises also become detached from the religious experience. Religions usually degenerate in the end into a rationalistic theology, a formal morality, and a ritualistic cult. When in this way rites and practises are detached from religious experience, they can only survive as a form of restraint which the religious society exercises on its members. Then the outsider defines religion as 'a bag

---

[1] A. Sabatier, *Esquisse d'une philosophie de la religion d'après la psychologie et l'histoire*, Paris, 1897, pp. 353 ff. (Eng. trans. *Outlines of a philosophy of religion*, London, 1897, pp. 322 ff.).

[2] For the idea that religious representations are only images see the remarks of H. Usener, *Arch. f. Relav.*, 1904, VII, p. 31.

[3] This is what the apostle Paul felt when he explained the success of his preaching of the Gospel by saying that his preaching at Corinth was not with enticing words of human wisdom but in demonstration of the Spirit and of power (1 Cor. ii. 4).

of superstitions which thwart the free development of our faculties'.[1] Sometimes a religion which is nothing more has ceased to live. To take religion in this state of existence and define it as religion is almost the same as taking a decomposing corpse and defining it as life and a living being.

When a religion is living, those who belong to it feel themselves united together by a bond of a peculiar kind. However important to the community may be the bond of experience, convictions and hopes, doctrine and discipline, rites and practices, the specifically religious bond is something different. It does not act directly but indirectly and is made up of the personal loyalty and attachment which each member of the group feels for the transcendent power who is its peculiar religious object. Through him they are united to one another. The Christians of the first generation felt themselves brothers, but brothers 'in Christ', which means that their brotherhood did not depend on some humanitarian conception but on the transcendent action of Christ.

The peculiar religious object which gave birth to the church was the risen and glorified Christ but the faith in the religious object was still only the mental and spiritual necessary condition for the birth of a new religion. If the creative principle of a religious society is transcendent and belongs to something beyond, it is all the same on the level of human and social realities that the religious community comes into existence. Its stable existence for any length of time depends on its submission to the laws governing the stability and life of all human societies. A religious community of which the Christian church is one example is a social phenomenon; if it fails to satisfy the laws governing the life of societies it is doomed to disappear.[2] It must also comply to certain peculiar conditions; otherwise it will change its character and cease to be a religious society. If we analyse the most essential of these conditions we can see to what points the historian of the birth of the church must pay attention.

No society can live for any length of time unless it defines its boundaries in respect of other groups, especially those with which it comes in contact and works. That is why the church possessed a rite of separation and admission. This was the function of baptism.[3] For

---

[1] Salamon Reinach, *Orpheus, histoire génerale des religions*[2], Paris, 1909, p. 4.

[2] Thus Troeltsch (*Die Soziallerhen der christlichen Kirchen und Gruppen*, Tubingen, 1912, p. 5) speaks of 'the sociological consequences of the phenomena of religion'.

[3] This was the primitive significance of baptism. It remained even after other meanings came to be added. See *E.P.*, pp. 295 ff.

this reason also there must be kept alive within the group a conscious-ness of the religious object which gave birth to it. If the group's consciousness of this becomes feeble or disappears, it ceases to have any reason for existing and disintegrates or lets itself be absorbed by one of the religious groups with which it happens to come into con-tact. If its consciousness of the religious object is to be preserved and live, it must from the first be expressed in doctrine. In the past perhaps too much emphasis has been laid on doctrine as the expres-sion of religious speculation and not enough on its sociological function.

For Christianity the development of its doctrine into a system of ideas expressing its religious object so as to ensure its independ-ence with respect to other groups was particularly urgent. For, al-though it had a lively sense of its novelty, yet it kept itself, ideally at any rate, solidly bound up with Judaism from which it had emerged and of which it felt itself to be the fulfilment. Christianity only succeeded after surmounting many difficulties and struggles in formulating its belief in its own independence in such a way that it could feel itself the embodiment of the ideal of Judaism and at the same time independent of Judaism as it empirically existed.

In the realm of doctrine the problem for Christianity to solve in order to find its equilibrium was determined by the fact that, while it had its own peculiar religious object, i.e. the Christ, it did not in any way repudiate the traditional religious object of Judaism, i.e. God. Its conception of Christ and of God had therefore to be reconciled in such a way that they remained united without being confused.

Not only must theologians think out and formulate doctrine but all the members of the group must be fairly clear in their minds what the doctrine is. That is why a teaching office is needed in a religious society. One of the functions of ritual in particular is to keep alive not merely the concept of the particular religious object, but also, what is much more important, a feeling of love for it. The principles and aims of a religious society may belong to the realm of ideas but its life is cast on the level of human realities. On this account a minimum of organisation at least is needed. Circumstances may allow it to become established in the general social setting of its life which it will tend to absorb, or it may be compelled to set its face against its environment and to fight it.

Early Christianity was in the latter plight up to the time of

Constantine.[1] In these conditions it had to create weapons of attack and defence for its own safety. It had also to defend itself against rival religions which were fighting it or trying to find a foothold in its bosom. A religious society has only a precarious existence if it allows its principles and teaching to be contradicted and disregarded by the doctrinal assertions or practical behaviour of its members. It has therefore to exercise disciplinary action on its members with a view to preventing deviations of this kind, to restrain those who would deviate too far and to expel from its bosom those who definitely show themselves to be disobedient to all warnings.

A religious society can only assert itself and maintain its existence after creating the instruments necessary for the discharge of its functions. We have just recounted the most essential of these. A history of the birth of the church will have to demonstrate how the Christian society—or rather how certain forms and groups within this society—gradually adapted itself to the conditions belonging to the stable existence of a religious society, while other groups and forms are shown to have been unable to comply with those conditions and so disappeared, sometimes leaving a confused memory at other times without leaving a trace of their existence.

The history of early Christianity is dominated by the fact that it not only developed on Jewish soil where it was born, but it also underwent a parallel development in the environment to which it was very soon transplanted. At that time it still possessed very great plasticity without any fixed form either in the sphere of doctrine or of organisation. It was not yet a religion but only the germ of one. Greek Christianity was not a religion adapted to a new environment but a religion which grew on Greek or Hellenistic soil from a religious principle indigenous to Palestine and came to maturity in Asia Minor in a form destined to last.[2]

When about 1900 the methods of comparative religion began to be applied to the history of Christian origins, it was thought that many of the problems would be solved by the phrase, 'Christianity is a synchretistic religion'.[3] Generalisations do not enable us to answer

[1] Except for the first generation when Christianity in Jerusalem in its legalistic form was treated by the Jewish authorities with considerable tolerance and the Roman authorities were unaware of the existence of Hellenistic Christianity or confused it with Judaism which enjoyed the privilege of a *religio licita*.

[2] Guignebert, *Le Christ*, pp. 129 f.

[3] This phrase was developed with brilliance by H. Gunkel, *Zum religionsgeschichtlichen Verstandniss des Neuen Testaments*, Gottingen, 1903. See also R. Reitzenstein, *Die hellenistischen Mysterienreligionen*, Leipzig, Berlin, 1910[3], 1927.

the question, whether Greek religious elements have become incorporated in the make-up of Christianity or if some ideological material of Greek origin is to be found there. What is the meaning of this fact, supposing it to be established? An element of one religion is only absorbed by another if the element finds a soil favourable for its development, i.e. if there exists a correspondence in spirit between the foreign element and some principle already present in the receptive religion.[1] In order to decide whether certain elements in a religion have been borrowed from another it is not enough to compare rites, ideas, statements of doctrine, or institutions. It must be seen what is expressed and covered by these things, whether the experiences and feelings, which are the essence of religion, are the same in each case; in other words, we must find out if Greek religious elements have really penetrated into the heart of Christianity or whether Christianity has merely borrowed from Greece certain means of expression.[2]

As Christianity came to be developed on Greek soil, certain terms and ideas which did not mean the same thing for the Jew and the Greek were transposed. Both Semites and Greeks maintained that human personality is made up of two elements, one material, the other spiritual. But the Jew thought that if these two elements are separated, the human personality is destroyed; the body returns to the dust of which it is made, likewise the spiritual element i.e. the breath of life returns to God. For the Greek, on the other hand, the association of the two elements is unnatural and can only be provisional. The soul is bound to a body in which it is shut up as in a prison or tomb; it will only fully expand when it is set free. 1 Cor. xv where Paul argues against certain Corinthians, who deny the resurrection as if it was a denial of any life beyond the grave, shows how certain expressions could bear different meanings for Jews and Greeks. There was here a source of misunderstanding which might have the greatest consequences.

Both Jews and Greeks were dualists in outlook but their dualism differed in each case. The dualism of the Jew was temporal; he opposed the present world to the world to come. The dualism of the Greek was ontological; he expressed himself by spatial images and

---

[1] This is a justifiable comment of Reitzenstein, 'Religionsgeschichte und Eschatologie', *Z.N.T.W.*, 1912, XIII, p. 23.

[2] Guignebert (*Le Christ*, p. 336) appears to me to give the true meaning to the facts when he shows Paulinism to be not a Greek expression of Christianity but 'a Christian adaptation of the spirit behind the Hellenistic mystery religions'.

opposed the world above to the world below which is a symbolical expression for the opposition between flesh or matter and spirit. The transposition of Christianity from the environment of Judaism to that of Hellenism had profound and lasting consequences. The God of Hellenism is a static God who dwells in realms above; man must struggle to rise to God by purifying himself from material elements in order to be able to participate in life divine. The God of Judaism is essentially transcendent but He is above all a god who acts and is constantly intervening in the world's history. He is dynamic. Ever since the creation which was the first victory gained by him over the powers of chaos, He has been in conflict with Satan and this conflict will go on until every hostile power has been annihilated.

In consequence, Greek Christianity in its formation has found it a hard task to think out and express in Greek terms an action of a God who was conceived of in the setting of Jewish thought and to translate into static language a dynamic conception of religion. In those conditions it is not surprising that it has been difficult for Christians to attain perfect balance while on certain points it has not done so even yet.[1]

How much of the early history of Christianity do we need to study for an understanding of the birth of the church? To divide history into periods where there has been continuous development is a device to which recourse must be made if the historian is to arrange his work satisfactorily. Christianity in the course of its history passed through a succession of phases perceptibly differing from one another in aspect and direction, due sometimes to internal developments and at other times changing external circumstances. We have to consider the period during which the church with its essential elements assumed the shape which it possessed at the end of the second century. By then its general structure, although not immutably fixed, was at any rate so formed that, while it afterwards grew still more definite, was yet capable of adaptation to changing circumstances but did not undergo any radical transformation. I shall not, however, attempt within the limits of an outline to write the history of Christianity up to the end of the second century. It will be sufficient to

[1] To give only one example, Christian theology has never discovered a satisfactory solution of the problem of theodicy, i.e. a reconciliation of divine omnipotence with the existence of evil. Perhaps the reason is that it tried to find, by the help of a static conception concerning the being of God, a solution of a problem created by the essentially dynamic conception of a great struggle between God and Satan.

notice the facts concerning the formation of the vital organs of the church.

It took the church more than a century and a half to possess these organs discharging their proper functions. From 70 to 78 Christianity was fully conscious of its complete independence from Jewish communities but it possessed the nucleus of a *corpus* of sacred writings complementary to the Old Testament only a century later. The period running from the death of Jesus to the end of the second century can be quite plainly divided into two about the year 70. At that time Christianity passed through a crisis in both growth and adaptation. Also the first generation of Christians was disappearing and except by the oral tradition the church ceased to be tied to the witnesses of the facts which had created the faith and to those who had proclaimed the earliest forms of doctrine. Tradition then became a preponderant factor, all the more easily because the phenomena of pneumatism abated and tended to disappear, as though the outburst had exhausted those who were possessed. At the same time the expectation of Christ's return and the arrival of a new world assumed a theoretical character and ceased to be a dynamic conviction possessing men's souls. Without forgetting that its consummation lay in its last days, i.e. in the distant future the church settled on earth and took root. This is the end of the period of creative activity and the beginning of that of stabilisation and organisation.[1]

About the same time the church was compelled to adapt itself to somewhat new conditions. Up to 70 those forms of Christianity which were not infected with anti-legalism and anti-ritualism enjoyed a large measure of tolerance from the Jewish community to which they were organically linked. After the fall of Jerusalem Judaism fell back on itself and became identified with Pharisaism. It then turned fundamentally hostile to every form of Christianity. This forced the new religion to become conscious of itself as an independent entity. Even those forms of Christianity which had previously shown themselves unable to understand the position of the apostle Paul were affected. The Judaic opposition to Paulinism lost all meaning if it did not completely vanish. All that was left of Jewish Christianity in Palestine after 70 was reduced to such a precarious kind of existence that Christians emigrated to the Greek world especially to Asia Minor. On account of these happenings the

---

[1] This must be taken *cum grano salis*. Stabilisation and organisation began with the birth of the faith but in the second generation they were the dominant factors at work.

centre of gravity for the church shifted from East to West. Jerusalem and Antioch had originally been the two foci of the church. After 70 the former retained only a theoretical importance; the centre of Christianity was in the Greek world. Gradually and not without resistance from the East the centre of Christianity shifted again and became finally fixed at Rome.

It would be an exaggeration to say that Christianity up to 64 lived at peace with the Roman Empire; for the most part it was unnoticed or rather it was confused with Judaism and enjoyed the privileged position given to the latter. Even, however, before 64, incidents arose, sometimes spontaneously, sometimes through public opinion being inflamed by Jews, but usually only the active preachers of the gospel were disturbed. But this state of affairs came to an end in 64 when after the fire of Rome Christians were accounted responsible for the catastrophe and a large number of them were massacred. The church could no more entertain the illusion that it could find any tolerable *modus vivendi* with the empire. Somewhat against its own wishes it was forced to adapt itself to a new situation where it could not have any legal status.

65 marks the beginning for the church of a new crisis of adaptation and growth in directions which determined its definite characteristics. This does not mean, however, that they were acquired all at once.

We can recognise another transition, real although perhaps not quite so clear, at the end of the first century. In Clement of Rome can be found a distinct formulation of certain essential elements of the catholic conception of the church produced only as an ideal theory but nevertheless as a definite programme.

The pre-catholicism of Clement of Rome can be distinguished from the early catholicism prevalent at the close of the second century by the following features. (1) In early catholicism there was a mystical element which came from Johannine theology in contrast with the emphasis on morals in Clement. (2) Pre-catholicism was still a local form of Christianity peculiar to Rome and it is impossible to know how far it was accepted beyond Rome. But early catholicism is a general form of Christianity catholic in the true sense of the word. At the end of the second century episcopal power and, in a general way, the authority of the clergy had ceased to be a programme as at the end of the first; they had become a reality. Lastly, early catholicism became much more of a system than pre-catholicism ever was; it was equipped also with weapons of organised defence, the essential ones being the rule of faith, episcopal power, and the canon of the New Testament which was the most essential of all. All these came into existence or received precise definition in the course of the second century so that the church could withstand the assaults of heresy.

2.—THE CHRONOLOGICAL SETTING OF PRIMITIVE CHRISTIANITY[1]

Only a few facts of Christian history can be dated by their synchronisation with general history.

The first of these facts in chronological order is the persecution ordered by Herod Agrippa I against leaders of the church in Jerusalem when James, son of Zebedee and also without doubt John his brother, were killed and Peter was forced to leave Jerusalem. The story of this persecution in Acts (xii. 1-19) is immediately followed by that of the king's death, which happened in such impressive circumstances that the compiler of Acts felt that it was God's punishment for ordering the church to be persecuted. The one event must have then followed very quickly on the other. The story to be found in Josephus,[2] although it omits the more legendary charm of that in Acts, confirms it on the essential point by saying that Agrippa reigned for three years; that makes the date of his death 44.[3] Herod appeared in the theatre at Caesarea at some games which he was giving in honour of the emperor. His silver robe was so magnificent that flatterers began to acclaim him as a god. Shortly after the king saw an owl above him and was seized with such violent pain in his stomach that he had to be carried away.[4] He died five days later. According to Dion Cassius[5] the games at Caesarea seem to have been held at the same time as those which took place in the spring in Rome in honour of Claudius' return from Britain. This confirms the story in Acts which tells us that Peter was put in prison at the time of the feast of Unleavened Bread (xii. 3). The persecution therefore took place about Easter 44.

The next fact capable of being dated although with less accuracy

[1] For a discussion of what is only given here in summary form concerning the facts refer to my 'Essai sur la chronologie paulinienne', *R.h.r.*, 1912, LXV, pp. 285 ff. and my *Introd.* IV, 1, pp. 81 ff.   [2] Josephus, *A.j.* xix. 8, 2.

[3] On the accession of Claudius (41) which Agrippa furthered, he received Judaea and Samaria (Josephus, *A.j.* xix. 5, 1; *G.j.* ii. 51, 5; Dion Cassius, lx. 8).

[4] The sudden violence of the disease suggests a crushing attack of appendicitis.

[5] Dion Cassius, lx. 23.

is Paul's stay at Corinth during which he appeared before the proconsul Gallio (Acts xviii. 12-17). The date of Gallio's proconsulate is
fixed by an inscription of Delphi[1] which is unfortunately mutilated
but still indicates that Gallio was proconsul of Achaea in the spring
of 52. Was he then at the beginning or at the end of his period of
office? Governors of provinces entered office in spring[2] and retained
their powers until their successors arrived.[3] In 25 Tiberius decided
that the new magistrates must have left Rome before 1st June.[4] In
42 Claudius advanced this date to 1st April and the following year
he fixed it on 13th April.[5] Gallio's assumption of office can then be
fixed for the beginning of May. The fact that his name is mentioned
in connection with the grant or confirmation by Claudius of privileges to the Delphians makes it probable that he participated in the
negotiations which preceded the imperial decision so that we can
rightly conclude that Gallio was proconsul of Achaea from May 51
to May 52.[6] Did Paul's appearance before Gallio really take place
at the end of his eighteen months' stay at Corinth, as the position
of the story in Acts seems to show?[7] The Acts, after telling of Paul's
break with the synagogue at Corinth, his establishment in the house
of Titus Justus, and the conversion of Crispus with many Corinthians (xviii. 5-8), relates a vision in the course of which the Lord
says to Paul, 'Be not afraid, but speak, and hold not thy peace. For
I am with thee and no man shall set on thee to hurt thee: for I have
much people in this city.' After this vision, Paul settles at Corinth
to preach the word of God for a year and a half (xviii. 9-11). Next to
this story of the vision is placed without any transition or link the
story of Paul's appearance before Gallio (xviii. 12-17), and it is then
said that after this Paul stayed some days longer in Corinth before
embarking for Syria (xviii. 18).

The arrangement of this story shows some anomalies. The incident of Paul's appearance before Gallio is inserted between the

[1] This inscription was published for the first time by Borguet, *De rebus
delphicis imperatoriae aetatis capita duo*, Montepassulano, 1905, p. 63.
[2] Mommsen (*Le droit public romain*, trans. F. Girard, Paris, 1893, p. 294),
gives the date 1st July. It appears to have only a hypothetical value.
[3] Bouché-Leclercq, *Manuel des institutions romaines*, Paris, 1886, p. 203, n. 2.
[4] Dion Cassius, lvii. 14.   [5] Dion Cassius, lvii. 11-17.
[6] This is also the conclusion of Ed. Meyer, *Urspr. u. Anf.* III, p. 37. It is not,
however, completely out of the range of possibility that these dates may be put a
year later.
[7] On this question see my article 'Le vision de Paul à Corinthe et sa comparu-
tion devant Gallion', *R.h.p.r.*, 1932, XII, pp. 321-33. (My previous conclusions
need amendment after this article.) See further, pp. 479 ff.

comment of verse 11 on the duration of Paul's stay at Corinth, which normally would have appeared at the story's end, and the mention of his departure without being connected with it. Also it is plain that a lacuna exists before the story of the vision as nothing is said of the possible risks which the apostle was running and made him think of leaving the town. The story would be much more coherent if verses 9-11 came after verse 17. The accusation of the Jews would have appeared such a threat to Paul that he would have thought of leaving the place. The rearrangement may have been determined by a desire to play down the gravity of the incident. If this is the case then the appearance before Gallio took place not, as is customarily supposed, at the end of Paul's stay at Corinth but considerably earlier, at the time of his break with the synagogue.

Several authors[1] think that the Jews made their complaint when Gallio had just assumed office; they would have hoped to obtain the object of their desires with greater ease from a magistrate who was still badly informed about the situation. Nothing in the text supports this hypothesis.[2] Paul had to leave Corinth in the autumn.[3] The break with the synagogue, the appearance before Gallio, and the vision appeared to have taken place at least a year before his departure, if allowance is made for the important effect of Paul's preaching to the pagan population of Corinth. If the appearance before Gallio took place at the earliest in the spring of 51, which was the date of Gallio's arrival at Corinth, then the autumn of 52 is the earliest date which can be assigned for Paul's departure from Corinth. If account is taken of all the happenings between his departure from Corinth and his arrest at Jerusalem which took place at the latest in the spring of 58, Paul's departure from Corinth cannot be placed as late as the autumn of 53. His eighteen months' stay in Achaea therefore probably lasted from the spring of 51 to the autumn of 52.

A third synchronisation is to be found in the biography of the apostle Paul. His arrest at Jerusalem took place two years before the

[1] Deissmann, *Paulus*, Tubingen, 1911, p. 161; Harnack, 'Chronologische Berechnung des *Tage von Damaskus*', S.B.A., 1912, p. 674.

[2] Preuschen (*Apostelgeschichte*, Tubingen, 1912, p. 113) observes that if the author of Acts had wanted to say what is attributed to him, he would not have said 'Gallio being proconsul'.

[3] When he passed by Ephesus after his departure from Corinth Paul refused to stop there but promised to return (xviii. 19-21) most probably because he wanted to embark for Syria before navigation suffered its annual interruption.

recall of the procurator Felix and his replacement by Porcius Festus (Acts xxiv. 27).[1] The Chronica of Eusebius[2] places the recall of Felix in the eighteenth year of Claudius and the tenth of Agrippa II, i.e. 54. But since according to Eusebius[3] Festus was sent by Nero, there is certainly an error in the Chronicle.[4] But some writers[5] put the recall of Felix at the very beginning of Nero's reign in 55 or 56. In support of this date Harnack observes that according to Josephus[6] when the Jews accused Felix before Nero he only owed his safety to his brother Pallas who fell into disgrace sometime before 13th February 55.[7] Harnack confesses that in giving this last date Tacitus made a mistake of a year and in this way is made to agree with the Chronicle. But Schurer[8] has correctly observed that it is impossible to fit into the four months separating the accession of Nero (13th Oct. 54) from the downfall of Pallas (sometime before 13th Feb. 55) all that part of the period of Felix's government which according to Josephus included his recall, his return to Rome, the complaint of the Jews against him and the intervention of Pallas on his behalf, all taking place in Nero's reign.[9] With Schurer[10] it must be supposed

---

[1] Some authors (V. Weber, *Kritische der Exegese des neunten Kapitels des Romerbriefs*, Wurzburg, 1889, p. 89; Wellhausen, 'Noten zur Apostelgeschichte', *N.G.*, 1907, pp. 8 f.) return to an interpretation which was given in the seventeenth century by Fr. Petau and refer the two years mentioned by the Acts to the duration of Felix's term of office. This opinion, it appears, cannot be retained.

[2] Eusebius, *Werke* (the Berlin academy edition), V; *Die Chronik aus dem Armenischen ubersetzt herausgegeben von J. Karst*, Leipzig, 1911, p. 215. The revision of St. Jerome (Eusebius, *Werke*, vii. 1; *Die Chronik des Hieronymus bearbeitet von R. Helm*, Leipzig, 1911, p. 182), gives the second year of Nero (A.D. 55).

[3] Eusebius, *H.E.*, ii. 22, 1.

[4] Schurer ('Zur Chronologie des Lebens Pauli', *Z. f. Wiss. Th.*, 1898, p. 21 f. and *Gesch.*[3] I, p. 578) shows that for the period which concerns us Eusebius had at his disposal only dates given by Josephus and that those which do not come from this source are pure conjectures. Erbes (*Todestage*, p. 27) supposes that in the sources used by Eusebius the facts were dated by the years of the reign of Agrippa II which were reckoned according to two systems between which existed a difference of five years. Cf. Schurer, *Gesch.* I. p. 589, n. 7.

[5] Weber, *Krit. Gesch.*, p. 182 f.; Harnack, *G.s.L.*, II. 1, p. 233; Wellhausen, 'Noten zur Apostelgeschichte', *N.G.*, 1907, pp. 8 f.; Schwarz, 'Zur Chronologie des Paulus', *N.G.*, 1907, pp. 285 f.   [6] Josephus, *A.j.* xx. 8, 9.

[7] Britannicus' fourteenth birthday (Tacitus *Ann.* xiii. 14-15). According to Suetonius (Claudius 27) Britannicus was born twenty days after the accession of Claudius, i.e. 13th February 41.   [8] Schurer, *Z. f. wiss. Th.*, 1898, pp. 35 f.

[9] According to Acts xxi. 38 the Roman tribune who arrested Paul mistook him for an Egyptian Jew who had just caused a Messianic insurrection which had been completely put down. According to Josephus (*A.j.* xx. 8; *G.j.* ii. 13, 1-5) the riot caused by the Egyptian took place a little after Nero had begun his reign. Unfortunately the chronology furnished by Acts is far from reliable.

[10] Schurer, *Gesch. I.* I, p. 578; *Z. f. wiss. Th.*, 1898, pp. 35 f.

that Pallas even after his downfall exercised some influence[1] or we must even agree with Erbes and Schwertz[2] that the Jews only imagined that Pallas intervened in favour of Felix in order to explain why their complaint which they thought well founded was checked.

The date cannot be placed later than 62 because in that summer Albinus, the next governor but one to Felix, arrived in Palestine and Festus must have held office at least two years, if we take into account the events recorded by Josephus[3] as happening when he was governor. The year 60 is then the latest date for Felix's recall[4] but it might have been one or even two years earlier. I shall retain the year 60, because according to Josephus Festus' term of office appears to have been brief and the interval between Paul's departure from Corinth and his arrest at Jerusalem must have been at least five years.[5]

The setting determined by these three dates must constitute the basis for any attempt to construct the chronology for a biography of the apostle Paul by making use of the short but exact narrative of his relations with the church at Jerusalem in the epistle to the Galatians (i. 15; ii. 10).[6] Three years[7] after his conversion he came to Jerusalem where he remained only fifteen days during which he saw none of the apostles save Cephas and James (i. 19). Then after fourteen years[8] in the course of a second visit he had conversations with 'the pillars of the church', James, Cephas, and John. These conversations which are generally given the somewhat formal title of 'the conference at Jerusalem' must have taken place at the latest

---

[1] Meyer, *Urspr. u. Anf.* III, p. 53, remarks that according to Tacitus (*Ann.* xiii. 23) Pallas succeeded in 55 in getting a prosecution which was brought against him set aside and that up to the end of his life he remained in possession of his large fortune. This shows that his disgrace did not involve for him complete loss of respectability.

[2] Erbes, *Todestage*, p. 17; Schwartz, Zur Chronologie, p. 286.

[3] Josephus, *A.j.* xx. 8, 9-11.   [4] Schurer, *Gesch.* I, p. 579.

[5] Nothing can be made of Acts xxiv. 10, where Paul appearing before Felix says to him that he has governed the people 'for many years'. This may be only a conventional phrase.

[6] In this narrative Paul corrects the tendacious account of his relations with the church at Jerusalem which had been given to the Galatians. He has therefore to weigh all his statements carefully in order not to give his opponents any ground for attacking him.

[7] This must mean 'in the course of the third year'. It may have been less than three years. It is less probable that he means somewhat more than three years as Paul would have been inclined to give the impression of as long an interval as possible between his conversion and his first visit to Jerusalem.

[8] With the great majority of scholars I understand 'at the end of 14 years' although grammatically the phrase can mean 'in the course of the following fourteen years'.

either at the beginning of 44 or the end of 43. Concessions, which were made to Paul's ideas about the freedom of Gentiles from the demands of the Jewish law, may have been sufficient to incense public opinion against the leaders of the church at Jerusalem which was only satisfied by the persecution undertaken by Agrippa.

By working backwards from the date of the conference it is possible to calculate the date of Paul's conversion. Some scholars[1] think that the fourteen years means 'fourteen years after the first visit' and that at first sight seems the natural meaning. But Paul's conversion would then have to be dated 26 or 27 and this is plainly impossible. We must therefore adopt the suggestion of other scholars[2] and suppose that the fourteen years begins from the event which dominates the whole story, i.e. the conversion; we should then place this towards the end of 29 about eighteen months after the death of Jesus.[3]

[1] e.g. Harnack, *G.a.L.* II. 1, p. 237; 'Chronologische Berechn.', *S.B.A.*, 1912, p. 676, n. 1; Zahn, *Einleitung in das Neue Testament*², Leipzig, 1900, II., p. 630.

[2] Ramsay, *The pauline chronology, in Pauline and other studies in early Christian history*, London, 1906; Schwartz, 'Zur Chronologie', *N.G.*, 1909, p. 274.

[3] Concerning the chronological relationship between the death of Jesus and Paul's conversion see *V. de J.*, pp. 166 ff. and *Life of Jesus*, pp. 228 ff.

PART ONE

The Creation of a New Object of Religious Devotion

CHAPTER I

The Birth of the Belief in the Resurrection of Jesus[1]

THE creative source of Christianity was the faith in the risen and glorified Jesus. How did this faith arise? How did there come into being a consciousness of a new object of religious devotion, i.e. Jesus, who had triumphed over death and had become the Christ on the right hand of God?

The death of Jesus on the cross seemed to make definite shipwreck of all the expectations which he had planted in the hearts of his disciples. Soon, however, these hopes were destined to be re-created, enriched with greater assurance than ever before, and founded on the certitude that the master had won a definite victory over death. The church expressed and defended this faith in a cycle of stories which stretch from the death of Jesus to his ascension. The relationship between the faith and the stories is not quite so simple as has been traditionally thought. The stories not only provide the foundation for the faith; they express it and at the same time defend it.

The facts are not unimportant. But even if they could be stated and defined with greater accuracy than is possible, they would not in themselves explain the creation of the faith. If nothing had happened except that the disciples had been the victims of an illusion and had persuaded themselves that their master had returned to life, the appearance of a new religion founded on faith in the resurrection would be capable of explanation. If some document were discovered and established beyond all possibility of dispute that the body of Jesus slowly decomposed in the grave where it had been laid, Christianity with all the gifts of spiritual life which it has given to mankind would not be destroyed. On the other hand, if it were possible to prove that

---

[1] I have devoted a special work to this question (*La foi à la rés.*, Paris, 1933). I shall give here in summary form only the conclusions at which I arrived, referring to this previous work of mine for their justification and for a discussion of questions of detail.

on the morning of the third day the body of Jesus was no longer in the tomb and every possibility of fraud had been excluded, it would not follow that those who were forced to admit this fact would on that account become Christians. A fact means nothing without some interpretation put upon it.

The purpose of studying the stories of the resurrection must be to extract the factual elements on which the faith depended, to outline the character of this faith, and to describe the psychological process which created it.

When Jesus had to allow the possibility of his death to intrude upon his visions of the future, he did not think of it as a check to his work but considered that God would cause him to return on the clouds of heaven as the glorious Messiah. He did not foresee a renewal and continuation of his work on the level of this world's economy but its extension in the realised kingdom of God.

I.—THE BURIAL OF JESUS

Two traditions concerning the burial of Jesus must be distinguished. One refers to what can be called the ritual burial. It would have taken place not to perform a last act of respect to the crucified but solely to avoid transgressing the commandment of Deuteronomy (xxi. 23) which forbids one allowing the sun to rest on the corpse of a criminal.[1] Those who, according to this tradition, buried Jesus were only concerned that his body should not remain exposed and so had no other reason for marking with accuracy the place where they laid it. The other tradition refers to what may be called the honourable burial. It was done in an honourable way in a tomb which could be found again. This tradition alone is portrayed in the stories but there survive distinct traces of the other tradition. In the gospel of Peter (3-5) Herod declares that, if Joseph of Arimathea had not asked for the body of Jesus, the Jews would have buried him to prevent the violation of the precepts of Deuteronomy. The incident of the *crucifragium* in the Fourth Gospel (xix. 31-37) has the same significance. The Jews obtain permission from Pilate to break the

---

[1] Josephus (*G.j.* iv. 5, 5) attests that no one failed to take away the bodies of criminals before sunset. Normally the bodies of crucified persons remained exposed, but the Romans had no difficulty in making a concession on this point to Jewish scruples, since, unless it was the body of a slave, it was customary to give it back to the next of kin. The Jews were accustomed to lay these bodies in a special tomb; they could not be placed in the tombs of their fathers even if only bones survived (*Sanh.* 5 f.; cf. Strack-Billerbeck, I, p. 1049).

legs of the crucified to hasten their death because they wanted to be able to bury the bodies of the criminals before sunset. These two extracts only prove that the Jews would have buried the body of Jesus, even if no one had undertaken to do it himself. We have, however, more direct evidence of a ritual burial in the book of Acts which makes Paul say 'For they that dwell at Jerusalem and their rulers . . . desired Pilate that he should be slain and when they had fulfilled all that was written of him they took him down from the tree and laid him in a sepulchre' (xiii. 27-29). The tradition referring to the ritual burial must have been very much alive to have left traces in a book by a writer, who in his gospel had related the burial of Jesus by Joseph of Arimathea.

The theme of an honourable burial is found in the canonical gospels and in the gospel of Peter[1] but with significant variations. First of all there are variations concerning the personality of the man who took charge of the burial. Joseph of Arimathea is named in all the texts but only Mark and Luke say that he was a member of the Sanhedrin. Luke gives a further detail, it is true, by saying that he was not associated with the designs and acts of his colleagues. They both say that he 'was waiting for the kingdom of God', which means that he was a religious Jew. Matthew calls him a disciple and John[2] reconciles the two traditions by saying that he was a disciple of Jesus but a secret one, because he feared the Jews.[3]

Concerning the tomb there are also variations.[4] Matthew, Luke, and John give the detail that it had never been used before, which Mark seems to ignore. John says that it was 'in a garden in the place where Jesus was crucified'.[5] Peter's gospel has left a trace

---

[1] Mark xv. 42-46; Matt. xxvii. 57-60; Luke xxiii. 50-54; John xix. 38-42; Ev. Pi. 3-5, 23-24.

[2] The traditions followed by the Synoptics is by John combined with another tradition which makes Nicodemus share the lead with Joseph.

[3] The gospel of Peter is vague on this point. It calls Joseph 'the friend of Pilate and the Lord'.

[4] They do not agree about the type of tomb. All the stories assume it to be one of which several examples have been found in the neighbourhood of Jerusalem. This type of tomb is made up of one or more funeral chambers hollowed out in a wall of rock and approached by a fairly low corridor. In front of the entrance was carved a groove along which, presumably with the help of levers, a stone disc was rolled to block up the entrance. Concerning this type of tomb see Vincent et Abel, *Jerusalem, Recherches de topographie et d'histoire,* Paris, 1912 ff., II, p. 96. (I am confining myself to this reference as it would be fastidious and futile to enumerate all the works in which this type of tomb is described with illustrations attached.)

[5] The phrase refers to the passover ritual which prescribed that the paschal lamb must be eaten in the place where it was prepared.

of this when it speaks of the sepulchre being called 'garden of Joseph' (24).

Mark says that Joseph bought a shroud and wrapped the body of Jesus in it before putting it in the tomb. Neither Matthew nor Luke mention the purchase of the shroud but Matthew gives the information that it was new. In John things happen less simply. Nicodemus brings a hundred pounds of a mixture of myrrh and aloes with which he buries the body of Jesus wrapping it up with bandages. None of the stories give any indication that the burial of Jesus might have been incomplete and only provisional.

The story of the anointing at Bethany whether in the form in which we find it in Mark (xiv. 3-9) and Matthew (xxvi. 6-13) or as we find it in John (xii. 1-8) has some connection with those traditions about the burial which tell of the intervention of a woman. It is difficult to find in them any element of solid evidence as the anointing of corpses was apparently not a Palestinian custom.

Although there is nothing in the story of the burial itself to suggest the idea that the burial was only provisional,[1] Mark (xvi. 1) and Luke (xxiii. 56; xxiv. 1) say that the women came to the sepulchre on the morning of the third day in order to anoint the body with spices which they had brought.[2]

The two traditions about the burial cannot be independent. One is the transformation of the other. It is impossible to understand how the tradition of an honourable burial would have become nothing more than a story of a ritual burial without any certain information concerning the position of the tomb. But an evolution of the traditions in the reverse direction is natural, guaranteeing the identity of the tomb and eliminating the harsh suggestion that the body of Jesus was completely deserted by his own friends. At first it is timidly suggested that Jesus was buried by friends through the intervention of someone who was otherwise unknown in the gospel story and in the early church. Only gradually, as the tradition develops, this person comes to be thought of as a disciple. In these circumstances it cannot be doubted that the tradition concerning merely a ritual burial must be regarded as the earlier. From its transformation came the idea of an honourable burial. The earlier tradition in default of all positive evidence sprung from the fact that the narrators

[1] Bousset, *Kyrios Christos*[2], Goettingen, 1921, p. 64; Schwartz, 'Osterbetrachtungen', *Z.N.T.W.*, 1906, VII, p. 30.

[2] Matthew does not say the same thing, but that is because his story of the guard put at the tomb prevented this detail from being put in.

presumed that the Jews treated the body of Jesus in exactly the same way as they usually treated the bodies of criminals. In addition to this there is no particular reason to doubt that this is what happened.

2.—THE THIRD DAY AND THE EMPTY TOMB

The earliest statements of the faith, that of 1 Corinthians xv. 4, speaks of Christ being risen on the third day. If we have here an early element of the tradition, it does not follow that it is a primitive element. The expression 'the third day' is found three times in Matthew (xvi. 21; xvii. 23; xx. 19) and twice in Luke (ix. 22; xviii. 33) in the triple declaration concerning the sufferings, death, and resurrection of the Son of Man, but Mark (viii. 31; ix. 31; x. 34) three times has the phrase 'After three days'; Matthew is also aware of this expression as he alludes to it in xxvii. 63, to recall the prophecy of the resurrection. It has been maintained that the two expressions 'the third day' and 'after three days' are equivalent to each other. Actually they are sometimes in the Septuagint but not always as, e.g. in Hosea vi. 2 where 'the third day' is the equivalent of 'after two days' and not 'after three'.[1]

Matthew also has this logion, 'For as Jonah was three days and three nights in the whale's belly; so shall the Son of Man be three days and three nights in the heart of the earth' (xii. 41). No interpretation however subtle can harmonise this statement with the idea that Jesus was buried on Friday night and rose again on Sunday morning. The tradition therefore originally was not as precise as it had already become in 1 Corinthians xv. 4. It is possible that the two phrases 'the third day' and 'after three days' were at first used without any distinction between them to mean 'after a short interval'. The discovery of the empty tomb in all the stories takes place on the morning of the third day and according to Matthew, Luke, and John the first appearance of the risen Christ took place on the same day but this differs from the tradition followed by Mark and the gospel of Peter which state that the first appearance took place in Galilee.[2]

The necessity of reconciling the appearances with the empty tomb is one of the reasons why the appearances have been moved from Galilee. The story of the discovery of the empty tomb is the

[1] e.g. Gen. xlii. 17-18; Esther iv. 15 ff.
[2] The necessity of reconciling the appearances with the empty tomb is one of the reasons why the appearances have been moved from Galilee to Judaea.

same in form with only insignificant variations in the three synoptic gospels (Mark xvi. 1-8; Matt. xxviii. 1-10; Luke xxiv. 1-11). On the third day at dawn the women met at the sepulchre with spices which they had prepared.[1] They find the stone rolled away and the tomb empty. An angel[2] tells them that the body of Jesus is not there, that he is risen and has gone before them into Galilee. They must tell Peter and the other disciples to go there. 'There', he adds, 'you will see him'.[3] In Mark the women say nothing to the disciples because they are afraid.[4] In Matthew and Luke they deliver the message which had been entrusted to them. Matthew does not say how it is received. Luke says that the disciples do not believe them and consider that they are telling idle tales.[5]

In John's gospel the story of the discovery of the empty tomb is closely associated with two others, (1) the coming of Peter and the nameless disciple to the sepulchre, and (2) the appearance to Mary Magdalen (xx. 1-18). We shall return to these later.[6]

The gospel of Peter has a story in a more developed form. It gives the impression of being a literary amplification which has been quite cleverly constructed from the synoptic story and is completed by the incident of the guard at the sepulchre which it gives with more detail than is to be found in Matthew and contains one surprising element. The way in which the story of the guard at the sepulchre is told makes it difficult to understand how the women were able to enter the tomb. But the story contains one very important original feature. This is the story: 'Mary Magdalen, a disciple of the Lord, because she was frightened of the Jews, who were inflamed with anger, was unable to perform at the tomb of the Lord what women are accustomed to do to the dead whom they have loved. At dawn

---

[1] The incident of placing a guard at the sepulchre compelled Matthew to make the desire to see the tomb the only motive for the women's visit. Concerning the other particulars of his story see further on p. 39.

[2] Luke mentions two angels.

[3] In spite of this announcement Jesus appeared in Galilee to the disciples only and not to the women. In Luke's story where the appearances are placed in Judaea, mention is made of what he said when he was yet in Galilee.

[4] Concerning the way in which the ending of Mark can be explained see *La foi à la rés.*, pp. 176 ff. and my more recent study 'Deux notes d'exégèse: II. Résurrection et apostolat', *R.h.r.*, 1941, CXXIII, pp. 43-56.

[5] Quite a large number of manuscripts (A.B.W. vg. sy^sin. cur. etc.) it is true, add (what is verse 12 of the Received Text): 'Peter arose and ran unto the sepulchre and stooping down he beheld the linen clothes laid by themselves and departed wondering in himself at that which was come to pass'. These words are missing in D and in the early Latin version. They contradict verse 11 and arise from a harmonisation with John xx. 3-10.   [6] See pp. 53 ff.

on the morning of the Lord's day she took her friends with her and came to the sepulchre where the Lord was laid. They were frightened that the Jews would see them. They said to themselves, "If only at least we had been able to weep and lament on the day when he was crucified. Now we would like to do it at his tomb. Who will roll away the stone put at the entrance to the tomb so that we can go in, sit down beside his body, and do what ought to be done? (Now the stone was big.) We are frightened of being seen. If we cannot go in, we will put what we have brought in front of the entrance in memory of him. We will weep and lament until we return home." When they arrived they found the sepulchre open. They went near, bent down and saw a handsome young man dressed in a dazzling dress who said to them, "Why have you come? Who are you looking for? Is it not the crucified? He is risen and he is gone away. If you do not believe, bend down and see the place where he was. He is no more. He is risen; he is gone to the place whence he came." Then the frightened women fled' (50-57).

While this story is on many points an amplified version of what is found in the canonical stories, there is, however, one particular feature which it is difficult to think can be the invention of the compiler. This is the idea that Jesus returned from the tomb straight to the place whence he came, i.e. to heaven. While all the other stories of the discovery of the empty tomb in our possession contain an announcement of an appearance[1] the story in the gospel of Peter does not contain one and even seems to exclude any idea of one by affirming the return of Jesus to heaven. It may well be that there is here a feature originating from an archaic story which is not found in the synoptics.

Some connection exists between the idea that Jesus rose on the morning of the first day of the week and the observance of the Christian Sunday with which the communities founded by Paul seem to have been already acquainted (1 Cor. xvi. 2; Acts xx. 7) and for the existence of which at the end of the first century and in the course of the second there is clear evidence.[2] Apparently the most convincing reason why the resurrection was judged to be on the third day must be found in a belief which was widely prevalent in different quarters of the world that the soul of a dead man remained near the body which it had animated until the morning of the third day

---

[1] Or rather (Matt., John) are associated with a story of an appearance.

[2] *Apc.* 1, 10; *Didache* xiv. 1; Ignatius, *Magn.* ix. 1; Barnabas xv. 9; Justin *Apol. I*, 67, 3, 8.

when it left it altogether.[1] In this way the body of Jesus would be thought of as coming to life again at the very moment when normally death definitely supervened.

In the gospel stories as well as in the gospel of Peter the discovery of the empty tomb with a comment from one or several angels is offered as sufficient proof of the resurrection which is resisted by the disciples, at any rate when they first learn of it. They are convinced only by the appearances. This may well be the result of a literary elaboration which correlated together what were originally two expressions of belief in the resurrection and subsequently became two independent ways of justifying it.

Only in Matthew's gospel (xxvii. 62-66), i.e. half a century after the birth of the faith in the resurrection, are there to be found any traces of a dispute between Jews and Christians about the empty tomb as a matter of empirical evidence. Yet from the very moment when it was first made, the affirmation of the resurrection of Jesus was in dispute. If it originated from the discovery of the empty tomb, how are we to explain why no enquiry was made to contradict the evidence? Certainly no enquiry was made, because if it had been and had proved that the body of Jesus was in the tomb in a recognisable form, how could Christians have maintained their claim that the tomb was empty? At the very least the form in which the belief in the resurrection was expressed would have had to be adapted to the established facts. If no one thought of making an enquiry about the empty tomb, it can only have been because discussion was raised at such time and place as made enquiry impossible. Either those who affirmed that the tomb was empty lived so far away from Jerusalem or such a long time after the burial of Jesus that their statement could not be verified or else no verification was ever possible because the tomb of Jesus could not be identified. This last seems to be the hypothesis which must be retained. At first the affirmation that the tomb was empty was made *a priori*. It was a corollary deduced from the affirmation that Christ was alive in heaven. Once we assume what was the Semitic belief about man, it follows that if Jesus was alive in heaven, his body could not possibly have been left to decompose in the tomb. There was then no necessity to go and look in the tomb in order to declare that it was no longer there. The affirmation of the empty tomb then took on concrete form, the *fonction fabulatrice* came into play; it was imagined and then told how women came

---

[1] In my book *La foi à la rés.*, pp. 167 ff. will be found a list of various texts providing evidence for this.

to the sepulchre on the morning of the third day and found it open and empty.[1] This change became possible as soon as ritual burial became burial made out of respect allowing the position of the tomb to be identified and providing a motive for the visit of the women.

A link had to be forged between the stories of the burial of Jesus and the discovery of the empty tomb. The evangelists were forced to create one. This they did with discretion but also with a rather clumsy repetition which shows that the conflation to which they resort is artificial in character. With discretion they omit any reference to the story of the burial itself in order to leave a part for the women who two days later would find the tomb empty.[2] They confined themselves to saying that the women kept at a distance and looked on. With insistence Mark (xv. 47; xvi. 1) and Matthew (xxvii. 61; xxviii. 1)[3] twice name the women as witnesses who identified the tomb and agreed that it was empty. With a certain clumsiness they fail to create a real connection between the story of the burial and that of the discovery of the empty tomb.

3.—THE RESURRECTION

To leave no doubt that the resurrection was an assured fact, primitive Christianity said that the tomb of Jesus was found empty and that his disciples were shown that it was so. But no attempt was made to describe the fact of the resurrection itself by picturing Jesus coming out of the tomb. There was the feeling that here was a sacred mystery which any attempt at direct description could only profane. Therefore, it was thought, all effort must be confined to ascertaining and establishing its consequences.

On this account we have to go further afield to find stories of Jesus leaving the tomb. We find no reason for supposing that they depend on the earliest traditions. They are simply figments of the imagination. There was a story of this kind in the gospel of the Hebrews but the fragment preserved by St. Jerome[4] mentions only the shroud which Jesus gives back to the servant of the high-priest

---

[1] It is futile to discuss the attempts which have been made to give a natural explanation of the empty tomb (apparent death or the removal of the body). See on this, *La foi à la rés.*, pp. 203-210.

[2] Perhaps, however, there can be found some trace of a tradition which would have effected this in the story of the anointing. See *La foi à la rés.*, pp. 127 f.

[3] In addition with divergences between the two notes of Mark.

[4] Jerome, *De viris inl.* 2.

37

as he leaves the tomb. This reference is made in such terms as preclude any attempt being made to reconstruct what went before.

The gospel of Peter (35-49) contains elements which go beyond what is told in the earlier narratives. But the actual resurrection is not really related. The core of the story is hardly given space at all. Only what happened immediately before and immediately after is reported. It tells us that, immediately before, two angels entered the tomb and, immediately after, they went out with the Jesus whom they held. During the night previous to the Lord's day there is a great noise; the heavens open; two angels come down and go towards the tomb. The stone rolls away of its own accord and they enter. The soldiers see this and go to wake up the centurion and the Jewish authorities. The second part of the story which is the more important yields more evidence than the first. Three men come out of the tomb. Two of them carry the other one while the cross comes behind them. The heads of the two bearers touch the sky while that of the one carried reaches above it. The angels, the story says, have come to find Christ and they have to carry him because before he died his 'power' had left him and he would only find it again in heaven.[1] A voice from heaven asks, 'Have you preached to the dead?' and the cross replies, 'Yes'. While the witnesses of this scene are plunged in thought, the heavens open again and another angel comes down and enters the tomb.[2] In this story there is not found the idea so strongly insisted upon by the gospel stories of the appearances, that he who is risen is recognised as the man whom the disciples have known in the days of his flesh. The identity of Jesus is established in other ways, i.e. by the evidence of angels and the man on the cross. Here we are in the presence of a story which is the product of theological elaboration and must be classed as myth.[3]

Popular tradition tells the public to which it is addressed what it wants to know. The story of the resurrection of

[1] There is an element here which is not exactly docetism but comes from a somewhat peculiar christology which tends to docetism.

[2] This angel appears to have been introduced to prepare the way for the visit of Mary Magdalene and her companions who will find him seated in the tomb.

[3] I mention just as a reminder the glossia to be found in a manuscript of the early Latin version (k, codex Bobbiensis of the fourth or fifth century) in Mark xvi. 4, where it says, 'The women ask who will roll away the stone for them', it reads in this manuscript 'As soon as darkness came over the whole earth during the day about the third hour, angels came down from heaven and, coming out of the tomb (the manuscript has *surgent*: all the editors correct it to *surgentes*) they ascend up to the splendour of the living God: doubtless it is the Christ whose glory fills the sky with light and so the day ends.'

Lazarus (John xi. 39-44) shows that the public were not unable to imagine Jesus leaving the tomb. Yet there was no story of this although it would have been of great value both as propaganda and as apologetic. People had the feeling that they were here in the presence of a very sacred mystery which would only be profaned by any claim to give any very accurate description of it.

There is, however, in Matthew's gospel a story with a thread which might have been expected to end with a description of the resurrection. The tomb is guarded; when the women appear on the scene, there is a great earthquake, an angel comes down from heaven, rolls away the stone and sits on top of it (xxviii. 1-3). But this is not done to allow Jesus to leave the tomb but to enable the women to prove that the tomb is empty. While the soldiers guarding the tomb are so struck with fear that they become like dead men (xxviii. 4) the women are not affected in this way, at any rate not to the same degree, as the angel is able to speak to them after re-assuring them (xxviii. 5). Matthew does not tell of anything happening between the angel coming down and speaking to the women because at that moment nothing did happen beyond the tomb being opened which made it possible to prove that the body of Jesus was no longer there. This is exactly the same point of view which is expressed in Mark's gospel where the one fact proved is that the body has gone out of the tomb. It has not come out like a living person who had been shut up. It has gone direct to heaven.[1]

At some point of time the disappearance of the body of Jesus was not in itself a sufficient proof of the resurrection, a direct manifestation of Jesus restored to life established as a fact was called for and cited in support. This was all the more natural when in actual fact such manifestations did constitute the psychological origins of the faith in the resurrection.

The idea of direct translation to heaven which Jewish tradition asserted to have happened to certain men such as Enoch, Moses, and Elijah, did not imply that of resurrection in the sense of the re-animation of a corpse which had been laid in a tomb, since these men had neither corpse nor tomb.

In all the forms of early Christian thought which we can discern, we find that the religious significance belonging to the resurrection does not lie in the fact that the body of Jesus came to life again on

---

[1] Bickermann 'Das leere Grab', *Z.N.T.W.*, 1924, XXIII, pp. 281-292, shows that the idea of a body laid in a tomb being taken up into heaven is to be found in several Christian legends and had its origin in Hellenism.

earth for a short time, but that it was taken to live in heaven. What gives salvation is Christ's glorification, not his resurrection understood in the sense of the reanimation of his body. If this reanimation became an object of faith, it was because it was regarded as the symbol, proof, and verification of the glorification of Christ.[1]

This is what constitutes for primitive faith the difference between the resurrection of Jesus and those of others which are narrated in the gospels and elsewhere but which no one thought of calling in question,[2] e.g. that of Jairus' daughter (Mark v. 42-43 and parallel passages), the young man of Nain (Luke vii. 11-17), or Lazarus (John xi. 1-44). These resurrections were not thought of as definite victories gained over death. Those who were restored seem to be pictured as having died prematurely and remained mortal.[3] Jesus on the contrary definitely conquered death. 'Christ having risen from the dead dieth no more', writes Paul, 'death hath no more dominion over him' (Rom. vi. 9).

The absence of a story of Jesus coming out of the tomb is not due to accident or design, but to the fact that the earliest conception of the resurrection did not admit of such a happening.

The empty tomb as the objective evidence that Jesus did not remain a prisoner to death is not the only form in which the resurrection was expressed, perhaps not even the earliest. After narrating that the veil of the temple was rent in twain, when Jesus expired, Matthew says, 'The earth did quake, and the rocks rent, and the graves were opened, and many bodies of the saints which slept, arose, and came out of the graves after the resurrection[4] and went into the holy city, and appeared unto many' (Matt. xxvii. 50-53).

The saints certainly did not rise again because an earthquake opened their graves. It was quite a different kind of action with a theological significance. Matthew has preserved here a fragment of a very early tradition which he has scarcely tried to harmonise with

[1] A trace of the idea that Christ went direct to heaven survives also in a variant of the Syriac version of Sinai which in Matt. xxvii. 50 in place of 'yielded up the ghost' has 'and his spirit rose up', i.e. 'he went up to heaven'.

[2] Fr. de Grandmaison (*Jesus Christ, sa personne, son message, ses preuves*, Paris, 1922, II, pp. 464-9) has collected some Greek stories of resurrections, Strack-Billerbeck (I, p. 560; II, p. 545) some Jewish stories. Both show that the idea of resurrection would not have appeared an impossibility in the first century.

[3] A passage from Quadratus, the apologist, preserved by Eusebius (*H.e.* IV. 3) says that some of the dead persons whom Jesus restored to life—he seemed to think that there were more of them that the gospel stories tell of—lived up to Hadrian's time but died afterwards.

[4] Certainly after the resurrection of Jesus. Matthew is here adding to his source.

his story. We can understand what this happening means and how it was thought possible[1] if we bear in mind that the resurrection of Jesus forms the first fruits of the general resurrection. We can see the resurrection of the saints to be both a result of the victory gained by Jesus over death, not on the morning of the third day but at the very moment when he expired and an anticipation of the general resurrection. Such an idea could well ignore any thought of the third day and the empty tomb.

An idea analogous to it is expressed in the saying of Jesus to the repentant thief, 'Today thou shalt be with me in paradise' (Luke xxiii. 43). Here also the victory of Jesus takes the form of a transition to heaven, it is not said how the victory will be shown on earth.[2]

4.—THE APPEARANCES

Whatever theological value primitive Christianity attributed to the empty tomb, it is certain that the faith in the resurrection emerged from the appearances.

The earliest text to speak of the appearances of the risen Christ is 1 Corinthians xv. 3-11. It does not give an account of them but merely alludes to them as facts already known to the reader.[3] Paul only refers to them as evidence in favour of his argument for the resurrection which had been denied by certain Corinthians.[4] Those who have experienced appearances of the risen Christ are mentioned in the following order: Cephas,[5] the Twelve,[6] more than five hundred brethren, James,[7] all the apostles and last of all, Paul

---

[1] 1 Cor. xv. 20-3; Rom. viii. 29; Col. i. 18; Rev. i. 5.

[2] Bousset, *Kur. Chr.*[2], p. 63.

[3] Certain writers (Schmiedel, 'Resurrection und Ascension narratives', *E.B.* IV, col. 4058; Bousset, *Kyrios Christos*[2], Gottingen, 1921, p. 65) believe it possible to infer from the summary character of Paul's reference that at the time when he was writing no detailed stories of appearances were yet in existence. The remark appended to the reference to the appearance to more than five hundred brethren, 'of whom the greater part survive to this day' seems to me to exclude this possibility as it means that anyone could question them, if he wanted. What Paul says of the appearance of Christ to him seems also to exclude this.

[4] This denial did not in their estimation, as Paul understood, mean denial of any life beyond the grave but a spiritualist conception which only expected the survival of the soul.   [5] i.e. almost certainly Peter.

[6] Some texts (D.F.G. 464 lat., etc.) thinking of Judas have 'the Eleven' in place, of 'the Twelve'.

[7] This certainly means James, the brother of the Lord (cf. Gal. i. 19; ii. 1 ff.). Nevertheless, Kattenbusch ('Die Vorzugstellung des Petrus und der Charakter der Urgemeinde', *Festg. f. K. Muller*, Tubingen, p. 329, n. 1) puts forward the hypothesis that it can mean the apostle James whose martyrdom is related in Acts xii 2.

himself 'as one born out of due time'.[1] This text while its authenticity cannot be questioned by any valid argument is not altogether homogeneous. First of all we can see in it a formula which Paul says he had received and is an expression of the common faith of the whole church. It is the earliest expression of faith. Its rhythmic form makes it easily recognisable.

'Christ died for our sin, according to the Scriptures.
And he was buried
He rose again the third day, according to the Scriptures.
And he was seen by Cephas, then by the Twelve.' [2]

To this Paul adds the appearance to more than five hundred brethren with the remark that the majority of them are still alive. This was certainly mentioned with the purpose of hinting that it was possible for anyone to meet them and question them. Because of the commentary accompanying it, this mention of the appearance to more than five hundred cannot have belonged to the kerygmatic formula. Next comes a phrase which is strikingly parallel to the second part of the kerygmatic formula:

'He was seen by James, then by all the apostles.'

It is a formula parallel to that which circulated among those who claimed to follow Peter and appears to have been modelled on it by James' partisans. In conclusion, Paul speaks of the appearance which he himself experienced and describes it in terms which cannot have belonged to a kerygmatic formula. In this way Paul completes and confirms the kerygmatic formula by mentioning other appearances of which he was aware and also his own, the last of all.[3]

Kattenbusch thinks that he would have been held to have experienced by himself an appearance of Christ because respect was due to him as the first apostle to be a martyr.

[1] The term 'abortion' by which for want of a better word ἐκτρώμα is translated is given to the foetus which has been torn away by violence done to the womb of a woman and is dead (cf. Num. xii. 12, Septuagint) and papyrus texts quoted by Moulton and Milligan. *Vocabulary*, art ἐκτρώμα. Without doubt it was a nickname given to the apostle on account of his wan and mean appearance, it he adopted to signify that the beginning of his Christian life was a miracle from God. See A. Fridrichsen, 'Paulus abortivus. Zu I Kor. XV. 8', *Symbolae philologicae O. A. Dainelson octogennario dictatae*, Uppsala, 1932, pp. 78-85.

[2] It is hardly necessary to point out the direct connection between this formula and the declaration of the disciples in Luke xxiv. 34: 'The Lord is risen indeed and has appeared unto Simon'.

[3] This signifies that Paul did not know of any appearances later than his own, not that later ones were impossible. Nothing in Pauline christology suggests or authorises the idea that a limitation was placed upon the period when appearances might take place.

A precise and satisfying connection between the appearances recorded by Paul and those known to us from other sources cannot be established. Luke's gospel contains an allusion to a tradition which recorded that Peter experienced the first appearance but does not recount it.[1] Matthew, Luke, and John, and the book of the Acts, know of appearances to the Twelve but it is just as impossible to harmonise their stories as to discover if Paul is alluding to one of them either in verse 5 or verse 7. The appearance to more than five hundred brethren remains the most obscure in Paul's catalogue. It is surprising that tradition preserved no direct recollection of such an important fact.[2]

St. Jerome[3] recounts the story of an appearance to James as given in the gospel to the Hebrews. After handing his shroud to the servant of the high-priest the Lord goes to the house of James, his brother. James, after drinking the Lord's chalice, swore not to eat before he saw Jesus risen from the dead. On his arrival at James' house the Lord had a table and bread brought to him. He broke the bread and gave it to James, saying, 'My brother, eat your bread, since the Son of Man is risen from the dead'. Even if to suppose that James was present at the last supper did not create difficulties to begin with, it would be impossible to admit a story as historical which against the evidence of all early traditions presumes that there was a single person among the followers of Jesus who waited for his resurrection with conviction. We are in the presence of a story, which originated among those who believed in a Christian caliphate *ad majorem Jacobi gloriam*, and is founded on the single reference in the epistle to the Corinthians.

The last of the appearances mentioned by Paul is his own; it took place in the autumn of 29, about eighteen months after the death of Jesus.[4] Paul makes no reference to a detailed story but the allusions

[1] The special message for Peter with which the women are charged in Mark xvi. 7 suggests perhaps that Mark was acquainted with the same tradition. As I shall suggest further on, it is at first somewhat surprising that the appearance to Peter is not recounted but it is explained by the fact that in the interests of apologetic collective appearances are preferred. In some sense it may be said the *Tu es Petrus* makes up for this diminution in Peter's part.

[2] Von Dobschutz (*Ostern und Pfingsten*, Leipzig, 1903) tried to show that a remembrance of this large collective appearance has been transposed and preserved in the story of Pentecost. It does not seem as if this opinion can be retained although it secured the adhesion of Harnack among others ('Die Verklarungsgeschichte Jesu, der Bericht des Paulus und die beiden Christus visionen des Petrus', *S.B.A.*, 1922, p. 65) and Lietzmann (*Histoire de l'Eglise ancienne*, French trans. A. Jundt, Paris, 1936 ff., I. p. 60).   [3] Jerome, *De viris inl.* 2.

[4] See pp. 25 f. and *V. de J.*, pp. 166 ff. and *Life of Jesus*, pp. 229 ff.

in the epistles (1 Cor. ix. 1; xv. 8; Gal. i. 16; Phil. iii. 7-8) show that the circumstances of this appearance and of the conversion which resulted from it were known in the churches. The place which Paul gave to it in his preaching explains why some of his enemies accused him of preaching himself (2 Cor. iv. 5).

The story in Acts which by a device in compilation is repeated three times (ix. 1-19; xxii. 1-16; xxvi. 12-18)[1] only provides hints about some exterior circumstances. It places the event on the road to Damascus whither Paul is on his way to persecute the church. He is suddenly surrounded by a great light, falls to the ground and hears the voice of the Lord asking him why he is persecuting him and giving him orders to go to Damascus where he will learn what he must do. In Damascus he is baptised by Ananias who lays hands upon him and he receives the Holy Spirit. The incident of Ananias which is missing in chapter xxvi is somewhat suspect in the form in which we have it, as it is completely contradicted by Paul's categorical affirmation in the epistle to the Galatians that his conversion owes nothing to any man.[2] The author of the Acts sees in the vision on the road to Damascus something quite different from the appearances of the risen Christ mentioned in chapter i. He speaks of a voice and a light, he does not say that Paul saw Jesus risen. He flagrantly contradicts the evidence of the apostle (1 Cor. ix. 11; xv. 8). It is the result of the theory held by the compiler of Acts that all the appearances were confined to a period of forty days[3] and were reserved for the apostles alone who had been chosen by Jesus (i. 3; x. 41; xiii. 31). There are clear indications to show that in the source from which the story was taken it had quite a different character. In ix. 5 (cf. xxii. 8; xxvi. 15) Paul, after hearing the voice says, 'Who art thou, Lord?'. It is said that his companions saw no one (μηδένα ix. 7). Ananias says to him, 'The Lord Jesus whom you saw on the road' (ix. 17). A little further on, Barnabas, introducing Paul to the Twelve, tells them how, 'on the road he saw the Lord and spoke to him'

---

[1] Concerning the use of repetition in ancient literature as a means of emphasising the importance of a story, see Von Dobschutz, 'Die Berichte uber die Bekehrung des Paulus', *Z.N.T.W.*, 1930, XXIX, pp. 144-7. Contrary to the opinion of some critics the latest of whom is E. Hirsch ('Die drei Berichte der Apostelgeschichte uber die Bekehrung des Paulus', *Z.N.T.W.*, 1929, XXVIII, pp. 305-12) there are not three stories but three slightly divergent forms of the same story.

[2] Nevertheless the incident must not have been purely and simply an invention as Paul was certainly baptised (Rom. vi. 3; 1 Cor. xii. 13) and that could only have happened at the beginning of his life as a Christian.

[3] Concerning this theory see further on pp. 60 ff.

(ix. 27).[1] These expressions show that, even if the compiler did not intend to tell of an appearance, the source followed by him recounted one. Although it is impossible to attempt to reconstruct this source, it can be seen that it differs from other stories of appearances by giving to Christ the attributes of a celestial being and by stating that those who accompanied Paul were aware that something was happening but did not share the vision.

By saying that Christ was seen by him, last of all, Paul distinguishes the appearance of Christ to him from 'visions and revelations of the Lord' (2 Cor. xii. 1). In some of these visions, e.g. that at Troas (Acts xvi. 9-10) Paul did not see the Christ but only received instructions from him, yet in others he saw the Lord himself. Such plainly is the case of his vision in the Temple at Jerusalem when he went there after his conversion and the Lord appeared to him and ordered him to go and preach the gospel to the Gentiles (Acts xxii. 17-21).[2]

Paul is not the only one who made a distinction between ecstatic visions and appearances of Christ. It is never said that Christ appeared to Stephen or to the seer of the Apocalypse. Yet the former, when he was dying, saw 'the glory of God and Jesus sitting on the right hand of God' (Acts vii. 55-56). The latter beheld Christ in heaven (Rev. i. 9-20). One difference between appearances of Christ and visions is what may be called functional; appearances of Christ created a faith in the resurrection, while ecstatic visions, even though they enriched those who received them, did not fundamentally modify their religious attitude. Another difference appears to be that in the appearances of Christ he was seen on the earth while in the ecstatic vision he was seen in heaven. The most important difference, however, seems to be this; those who enjoyed ecstatic visions felt at the time when they experienced them that they were in an abnormal subjective state of mind, while the percipients of

---

[1] In the same way in chapter xxii. Ananias says to Paul, 'The God of our fathers hath chosen thee . . . that thou shouldst see that Just One and shouldest hear the voice of his mouth. For thou shalt be his witness unto all men of what thou hast seen and heard (xxii. 14, 15). In chapter xxvi the voice from heaven says to Paul, 'I am Jesus whom thou persecutest, to make thee a minister and a witness both of these things which thou hast seen and of those things in which I will appear unto thee' (xxvi. 15).

[2] If there was no evidence apart from that in Acts it would be somewhat open to suspicion. But in 2 Cor. xii. 2-4 Paul speaks of a particularly important vision which he had fourteen years later, i.e. about 43-44. This may well be the vision mentioned in Acts xxii. 17-21, although in Acts the vision seems to take place on Paul's first visit to Jerusalem.

appearances seem to have thought that anyone else who had been in the same place at the same time would have also seen Christ. But one point seems to be of the greatest importance; those to whom Christ appeared regarded the phenomenon as something new and were surprised and troubled by it. On the other hand, those who enjoyed the ecstatic visions which in some cases, notably Paul's, followed an appearance, regarded them as phenomena which they had expected, waited for, and recognised. In some measure their hopes and expectations brought on the visions.

The tradition which survived as it is found expressed in the book of the Acts is, that for a period the length of which is variously described, there was a succession of appearances of Christ, that after this Christ made a final return to heaven and so appearances ceased to be possible. This is not the earliest tradition and it is easy to see how it came about. With the growth of christology it became more and more difficult to think of Christ living the life of glory in heaven and at the same time continually appearing to his disciples on earth. Men's conceptions of the appearances of Christ grew more material-istic because they tended to describe them with greater minuteness, and at the same time details were introduced progressively into the stories to meet the objections raised by those who opposed the idea of the resurrection.

When we consider the part played by the faith in the resurrection in Paul's religious life and thought as a result of Christ's appearance to him, we see that most essential to his faith was not the feeling that Jesus had returned to the environment of his life on earth pre-ceding his passion but a belief in his glorification, i.e. in his transition to life in heaven where death has no more dominion over him (Rom. vi. 9). This idea receives little emphasis in the gospel stories, be-cause, as it seems, influenced by the necessities of apologetic, they have undergone a marked materialisation.

The first story in Matthew, that of the appearance to the women (xxviii. 9-10)[1] is discreet but contains one detail—the women fell down before Jesus and held him by the feet—which implies the resurrection to be material. The second story, that of the appearance to the disciples on a mountain in Galilee (xxviii. 16-20) is told with

[1] This story comes just after that of the discovery of the empty tomb. Although it seems as if Jesus appeared to the women by the side of the tomb and the story finished with the order being given to them to inform the disciples and tell them to meet in Galilee, yet the incident is only narrated just after verse 8 which says that the women told the disciples what they had seen.

46

considerable discretion. No details of the circumstances are given. All that is said is that the Eleven on seeing Jesus worshipped him but some doubted.[1] The two elements to be distinguished in this story are (1) an appearance of Christ, (2) a theological doctrine concerning the mission formed by the instructions given to the disciples by Jesus. The story of the appearance is told with remarkable moderation in a somewhat primitive fashion and is quite bereft of any apologetic tendencies. The element of doubt to be met with here is found elsewhere, e.g. in Luke and John, but there it has quite a different character. Its purpose is apologetic. It seems to show that the disciples did not come to believe in the resurrection with ease, that at first they disbelieved and only finally yielded in the face of incontrovertible evidence. But there is nothing resembling this in Matthew. He does not say how the doubts of some were relieved or even if they were relieved at all. The promise of perpetual aid with which Matthew's story ends can only mean spiritual aid and seems to exclude completely any further appearance of Christ. It is impossible to see in what way one or more appearances could be intercalated between the one experienced by the women and the one experienced by the disciples. On this account Matthew's story resists any attempt to harmonise it with the other traditions.

The stories of the appearances in Luke are not connected with that of the empty tomb by any link as organic as that found in Matthew. The only allusion in the stories of the appearances to the empty tomb is to be found in the Emmaus story in xxiv. 22-24.[2]

The first appearance recorded in Luke is that on the road to Emmaus (xxiv. 13-35). On the evening of the third day two disciples are on their way to the village of Emmaus.[3] On the way they are talking together of what has just happened, when Jesus meets them without being recognised for 'their eyes were heavy'. They speak to the mysterious stranger of their hopes which are now dashed. Three days have passed. 'It is true', they add, 'that some women of their company made them astonished by telling them that they were at the sepulchre, found it empty and saw angels, who told them that

---

[1] There is no need to discuss the desperate attempts which many interpreters have made to eliminate this doubt on the part of the disciples. See *La foi à la rés.*, p. 278, n. 3, pp. 279 f.

[2] These verses appear to be an editor's addition to his source.

[3] The majority of the manuscripts place Emmaus 60 stadia, i.e. about 6 miles from Jerusalem. Some (ℵ. K. Θ. min.) say 160 stadia, i.e. about 3¾ miles. For possible reasons for this variation and proposed identifications see *La foi à la rés.*, p. 282, n. 1.

their master was risen. Some disciples had confirmed the truth of what the women had reported but had not seen the Lord.[1] Jesus then rebukes the two disciples for their incredulity and lack of intelligence and goes on to explain to them the Scriptures which taught that the Messiah must suffer before entering into his glory. On their arrival at Emmaus the disciples persuade their travelling companion to stay with them as the day is far spent. At supper he takes bread, blesses it, and distributes it to them. Then their eyes are opened and they recognise him, but immediately he becomes invisible. The two men then hasten to return to Jerusalem where they find the Eleven and their companions gathered together who tell them, 'The Lord is risen indeed and has appeared to Simon'. They then tell them what has happened to them.

This story is a little masterpiece of dramatic narrative; as the story proceeds, the interest grows. It is written in a lively style with animation. It cannot be the work of Luke as he would not have introduced Cleopas, a figure mentioned elsewhere, and he would have linked the story with that of the empty tomb in a neater manner. The conclusion of the incident is hardly satisfactory. The effect to be expected by the arrival of the two travellers is spoilt as the other disciples already know that Jesus is risen. The original ending of the incident has been touched up to make allowance for the tradition which placed the first appearance in Jerusalem and also made Peter a recipient of an appearance. The author of the unauthentic ending of Mark (xvi. 12-13) knew of the incident in its original form where the two disciples tell of their incredulity only in Jerusalem. If this ending and the phrase about the appearance to Simon is suppressed, a satisfactory link is forged between the Emmaus incident and the following one which tells of another appearance. The disciples at first are sceptical and think that they are in the presence of a ghost. How could an appearance be regarded in this way by people who a moment before had just been confirmed by the evidence of the men of Emmaus? If, on the other hand, the story which these people had just heard left them sceptical, then the meaning of the second appearance which triumphs over their doubts is easily explained.

In this second story—or rather in the second part of the story (xxiv. 36-43)—Jesus is suddenly found in the midst of the disciples assembled together. They think that they see a ghost. He tries to convince them by showing them his feet and hands, making them

[1] This allusion to the empty tomb and a visit of the disciples seems to be an addition to the source.

touch them. Without explicitly saying so the story presumes that these accumulated proofs finally convince them.

A scene of instruction follows that of recognition. It is composed of three closely connected elements. First of all Jesus declares that he has accomplished what Moses and the prophets have written of him and he opens their understanding that they might understand. Next he recalls the prophecy of Scripture on the necessity of his sufferings and death and announces that repentance for remission of sins in his name must be preached to all nations. The commission to do this is given to the disciples by these words, 'Ye are witnesses of these things'. Finally Jesus promises his disciples to send them the Holy Spirit and tells them not to leave Jerusalem before receiving him.

This second story emphasises the material nature of the body of the risen Jesus but this is possibly a result of an apologetic elaboration to show that the disciples did not find it easy to believe in the resurrection and to kill the possibility of their having been in the presence of a ghost. The way in which Jesus is suddenly present among them implies quite a different conception of the state of the risen Christ from that resulting from the reanimation of his corpse.

It is a delicate problem to say exactly what conception Luke's gospel has of the state of the risen Jesus. The mysterious manner in which Jesus comes up to the disciples on the road, the fact that at first they do not recognise him, the manner in which he becomes invisible after breaking bread, cannot be thought of as ordinary arrivals and departures. This is because the risen Jesus is never depicted as having resumed the life which he shared with his disciples. The absence of trays which would emphasise the material nature of the body of Jesus in the Emmaus incident forbids us to see in it simply an allegory of the mysterious presence of Christ in the eucharist. It must be interpreted as a sign of a relatively 'primitive tradition'.

Except for the appearance to Mary Magdalene[1] the Fourth Gospel in its earliest form, i.e. before the addition of chapter xxi. contains two descriptions of appearances. The first is simply placed next to the incident of Mary Magdalene. On the evening of the first day of the week, the disciples are reunited and the doors shut for fear of the Jews, when Jesus suddenly appears in the midst of them and greets them. He shows them his hands and his side and they rejoice together. Then he says to them a second time, 'Peace be with you' and he breathes on them to give them the Holy Spirit and

<hr>

[1] See pp. 53 ff.

bestow on them the power to forgive or retain sins (xx. 19-23). There is no mention of how Jesus left the disciples or of what impression his appearance made on them. The sudden appearance of Jesus and the fact that the doors were shut imply the idea of an immaterial body: the manifestation of the wounds implies the identity of this body with the one which died on the cross. Here is a contradiction which the strangeness of the double greeting increases. The manifestation of the wounds must therefore be considered as an addition for reasons which are plain. The second greeting can then be regarded as a literary device for resuming the thread of the narrative.

Thomas, it is said, was not present when Jesus showed himself to the disciples. When he is told of what has passed he remains sceptical and refuses to believe, 'except he should put his fingers into the print of the nails of Jesus' hands and his hand into the scar of the wound in his side' (xx. 24-25). Thomas' absence is not mentioned at the beginning where it is said that the disciples were gathered together but only at the end as a kind of appendix. From this it can be inferred that the detail was added afterwards so that a second story which laid more emphasis on the material nature of the resurrection could follow. And so eight days afterwards Jesus appears again in the same circumstances, this time Thomas being present; he asks Thomas to touch his wounds and says to him 'Be not faithless but believing', and Thomas says to him, 'My Lord and my God'. Jesus goes on, 'Because thou hast seen, thou hast believed. Blessed are they that have not seen and yet have believed' (xx. 26-29). Although this story is moulded on the one preceding, it is not just a variation told to emphasise the same point. It has a point of its own because it is told for the people who find it hard to believe in the resurrection and demand material proofs. The thought behind the story is that proofs exist which, however, only a man of little faith can need.

A final appearance is recorded in chapter xxi which constitutes an appendix to the gospel. The scene is laid on the edge of Lake Gennezareth without any explanation as to how the disciples returned to Galilee. Seven of them, Peter, Thomas, Nathaniel, the sons of Zebedee and two others go fishing but labour all night without catching anything. In the morning Jesus unrecognised by them stood on the shore and asked them if they had anything to eat. They assured him, No. He told them to cast the net on the right side of the ship. They did so and were not able to draw it up for the number of the fishes. The beloved disciple then said to Peter, 'It is the Lord'. Immediately Peter who was naked put on his coat and threw himself into the water. The other disciples came to the shore and drew in the net. On the land they saw a fire lit, a fish on it and bread. Jesus ordered them to bring the fish which they had caught. Peter then came out of the water and drew in the net which was full of 153 fishes great and small.[1] Jesus invited the fishermen to eat. Then they knew they were in the Lord's presence but no one dared to ask him, 'Who are you?' Jesus took a loaf and a fish and distributed them (xxi. 1-14).

The meal was followed by a conversation between the Lord and Peter. After being assured by putting the question three times that his disciple loved him he entrusted him with the mission of feeding his flock and then predicted his coming martyrdom. At the end of this section Peter asks a question about the fate reserved for the beloved disciple to which the Lord gives a vague reply; the story explains how this reply had been misunderstood so that a legend was accepted that the beloved disciple was not destined to die (xxi. 15-23).

The incoherences in this story of an appearance are obvious. The purpose of the miracle of fishing appears to be to provide food for the disciples and yet no explanation is given of how the bread and fish were provided which they actually found being cooked to give them a meal. When Peter throws himself into the sea after he recognises the Lord who is pointed out to him by the beloved disciple, he seems to do so in order to come up to him more quickly, as the gesture of putting on his coat out of respect seems to show, although it is somewhat unnatural in the circumstances. Yet as soon as he comes on shore he does not run to Jesus but helps his companions who had remained in the ship to draw in the net. We are bound to suppose that the story is a combination of two sources. One told of a lucky catch of fish which Jesus had ordered and was followed by a meal. In the other Jesus made himself known to his disciples by the breaking of the bread with them. This story has some distant analogies with the Emmaus incident. As for the first story it bears a striking resemblance to the incident of the miraculous draught of fishes recorded by Luke (v. 1-11). It is difficult to discover the relationship between the two stories since we know one of them only

[1] The symbolic meaning of this number is unknown to us. It is only necessary to notice that 153 is the triangular number of 17, as in Rev. xiii. 18 666 is the triangular number of 36. This cannot be fortuitous.

when it has become combined with the other and has thus lost its original form. But it seems fairly certain that Luke possesses the story in its earlier form; at any rate Luke's version is nearer to the original than that given by the writer of John xxi and also the story did not originally belong to the cycle of resurrection stories.

This conclusion is supported by the fact that the appearance on the edge of the lake is said to be the third (xxi. 14) while in reality it is the fourth. Two other manifestations of Jesus are numbered in the Fourth Gospel: the miracle at Cana (ii. 11) and the healing of the nobleman's son at Capernaum (iv. 54). The miraculous draught of fishes was originally the third incident of the Galilean ministry of Jesus. As a story of a resurrection appearance it was first altered by being combined with another and then has been reduced to its present form to serve as an introduction to Peter's conversation with Jesus.[1] I shall return to this in my second volume.

The next point to consider is the way in which the two themes (1) the empty tomb and (2) the resurrection appearances have been linked together in the tradition.

Several types of connection can be distinguished. One consists of simple juxtaposition. The most typical example of this comes from the gospel of Peter where the angel interprets the empty tomb as evidence of Jesus' ascension to heaven. This constitutes a consummation following which a resurrection appearance would be altogether out of place. There is a story of an appearance[2] taking place afterwards (58 ff.) but it has no logical or formal connection with the story of the empty tomb. It is quite a separate story with a new beginning.

It must have originally been the same story as that found in Mark, if we agree that the prophecy which Jesus makes in xiv. 28, 'But after that I am risen, I will go before you into Galilee' is a later addition[3] which in its turn has caused xvi. 7 to be inserted announcing a resurrection appearance in Galilee.[4] The words break the organic link between verses 27 and 29 in a very awkward fashion.

[1] See *Egl. Prim.*, pp. 191 ff.
[2] It would be more accurate to say that there is in the fragment in our possession a story suggesting an appearance.
[3] And is missing in a papyrus of Fayoum, *Patr. or.* IV. 2, pp. 95 ff, no. 14.
[4] If this verse is omitted the ending of Mark becomes more balanced. The women by keeping silence on what they had seen and on what the angel had told them are no longer disobeying orders given to them. Consequently we cease to be surprised that we are not told how, in spite of the women's disobedience, the disciples were informed of what the angel had wanted to be brought to their knowledge.

In Luke's gospel[1] there is an example of this type of story where the empty tomb and appearances of Christ are simply placed next to each other.

In Mark's gospel, as we have it, and in Matthew's a connection is made. In the story of the empty tomb an announcement of an appearance is made in the order given by the angel to the disciples to go into Galilee where they will see the Lord. But it looks like an artificial addition because in Mark's story the predicted appearance is never recounted and in Matthew's the appearance does not correspond to what has been foretold. The appearance in Galilee takes place on a mountain which had been appointed by Jesus as a meeting-place (xxviii. 16), although there is no mention of this mountain either in xxvi. 32 or in the angel's instructions.[2]

Matthew, on the other hand, found it necessary to establish a closer connection between the empty tomb and the resurrection appearances by introducing an appearance of the risen Christ to the women near by the empty tomb,[3] but, as we have seen,[4] the story of the empty tomb and that of the appearance to the women are placed side by side without any logical connection between them.

The closest connection between the two themes of the empty tomb and the appearances is found in John's narrative (xx. 1-18) where Mary Magdalene's discovery of the empty tomb culminates in an appearance which originally must have been thought of as a unique appearance preceding Jesus' ascension to heaven. The story is a brilliant composition but is made up out of disparate elements which can be easily distinguished from each other because they are only placed together side by side.

Mary Magdalene comes by herself to the sepulchre for no possible purpose except just to see it, since the body of Jesus was anointed with myrrh and aloes and wrapped up in bandages before it was

---

[1] Verse 12 of chapter xxiv is not reckoned to belong to the authentic text. It is missing in D. it., Marcion.

[2] Perhaps it is right to suppose that behind Matthew's story lies a tradition which knew nothing of the empty tomb and told of an appearance on a mountain in Galilee which Jesus had appointed beforehand as a meeting-place for his disciples. The age and character of this tradition cannot be accurately given. In the light of this conjecture it is legitimate to ask if the prominent place occupied by the discovery of the empty tomb in all the stories concerning the resurrection may not be partly explained as a reaction against the tradition which made Galilee alone the birthplace of the faith in the resurrection.

[3] This introduction also satisfies a desire to harmonise the earliest tradition locating the appearances in Galilee with the later tradition placing them in Judaea.

[4] See pp. 32 ff.

buried. She finds that the stone has been removed and without going near and looking inside the tomb runs to Simon Peter and the disciple whom Jesus loved and says to them 'They have taken away the Lord out of the sepulchre and we know not where they have laid him'. Although all she has seen is that the stone has been rolled away she says, 'They have taken away the Lord'. Although no other woman is ever mentioned in the story, she says, 'We do not know'. Mary Magdalene's encounter with the disciples comes therefore from one source while the story of her visit to the sepulchre comes from another.

Peter and the anonymous disciple run together. The latter arrives first. He bends down to look in and sees the linen clothes on the ground. Simon Peter comes up behind, goes in, and sees the linen clothes lying and the napkin which was about his head by itself.[1] The other disciple then goes in. He sees and believes. After they have made these enquiries they return and ask no further questions about them before the appearance of Christ, on the evening of the same day, to them and others.

We are not told that Mary Magdalene came back to the sepulchre after meeting Peter and the beloved disciple. Yet after they have gone she is depicted as back at the tomb weeping. It is exactly the same situation which existed before she went to meet the disciples. The fragment concerning Peter and the anonymous disciple has been so clumsily inserted into the Mary Magdalene story that it cannot be attributed to the evangelist. It comes from a tradition the origin of which can easily be conjectured. It arose from a desire to make apostles as well as a woman witnesses of the empty tomb.

Verse 11 which says that Mary Magdalene wept beside the tomb originally belonged to the beginning of the story. Kneeling down she saw two angels seated in the place where the body had been laid. They ask her why she weeps and she replies that they have taken away the body of her Lord: she does not know where they have put it. Then Mary Magdalene turns round and sees Jesus standing up but does not recognise him. Why Mary turned round so as to see Jesus is not explained; she is wholly occupied in conversation with the angels. As she must be waiting for their reply it is not natural for her to turn her back on them. What has been said of them serves

---

[1] There exists here a point of argument against the theory that the corpse had been stolen. The body of Jesus would not have been stripped before it was taken away, cf. Baldensperger, *Urchristliche Apologetik Die aelteste Auferstehungskontroverse*, Strasburg, 1909, p. 23.

no purpose because we hear no more of them. It is clear that the ending of the incident about the angels has been suppressed to make room for an appearance of Jesus. An analysis of what follows will enable us to conjecture what the original end of the incident concerning the angels must have been.

Jesus says to Mary Magdalene, what the angels had said to her, 'Woman, why weepest thou?' adding, 'Whom seekest thou?' Mary Magdalene who thinks that she is talking to the gardener says to him, 'Sir, if you have taken him away, tell me where you have laid him and I will take him away'. Jesus then says to her, 'Mary' and she turning round [1] replies to him in Hebrew 'Rabboni' (which means 'Master'). After she has recognised Jesus, it is clear, although the text does not say so, that Mary intends to throw herself at Jesus' feet or to grasp him in her arms, but he stops her doing this and forbids her to touch him because he has not yet gone to his Father.[2] He then orders her to tell the disciples that he is going to his Father and their Father, to his God and their God. Mary Magdalene delivers this message. We are not told how it was received and so we may suppose that they are convinced by what Mary Magdalene told them.

As I have already pointed out, the incident concerning Jesus has been substituted for the end of the incident concerning the angels. We can, however, guess what the end must have been. It is certain that it was an announcement of the resurrection. It is safe to suppose that its wording must have been analogous to the announcement which Jesus himself makes. The angels must have told Mary Magdalene that Jesus had been restored to his Father and his God.

---

[1] It is difficult to explain Mary's gesture which at that moment is repeated. It is equally unsatisfactory to take the word metaphorically in a psychological sense and refer it to a change in mental disposition. Perhaps the text has been altered.

[2] The motive behind this prediction is not clear. Van den Bergh van Eysingh, 'Le Christ chargé d'Esprit', *Premiers écrits du christianisme*, Paris, Amsterdam, 1930, pp. 139 ff., thinks that with a human being Jesus would have lost a mysterious power needed by him for his ascent to heaven, but this idea is altogether at variance with Johannine christology. The idea that contact with the risen Christ would be dangerous for human beings is equally out of the question, if we take into account the stress laid in the resurrection stories, especially those in the Fourth Gospel (xx. 26-9) on the disciples touching Jesus after his resurrection. Perhaps it may be supposed that in his descent into hell Jesus had contracted some taint of which he would not be rid until he was restored to heaven. We must confess that we offer this explanation only in default of a better one. May a better explanation be that we have here a recollection of the story in its earliest form which contained no mention of an appearance.

Schwartz [1] considered that this was the end of John's gospel before it was revised into the form in which we now have it. Schwartz's theory can appeal to purely literary considerations in its favour but it seems certain that the writer who conceived the scene in which angels announce the return of Jesus to God never imagined that an appearance of Jesus could have followed it. It is just as likely that the story has been changed so as to make room for an appearance at the end.[2]

Among the stories to be found in the gospel tradition those concerning the resurrection show the greatest diversity in form and it may therefore be assumed that they have changed the most in the course of development. We have seen in John xxi how a story of a miraculous draught of fishes which originally belonged to the Galilean ministry of Jesus became a story of a resurrection appearance. Conversely it can be proved that a story of a resurrection appearance became an incident in Jesus' ministry: it is the story of the transfiguration (Mark ix. 2-8 and the corresponding passages).[3] The transfiguration provides assent from heaven to Peter's confession with which it is closely connected. The three intimate disciples, Peter, James, and John witness it. The essential elements in the story are the appearance of Jesus clothed in glory, the witness of the two heavenly beings[4] who appear on his right and left hand, and lastly the heavenly voice which declares, 'This is my beloved Son, hear ye him'.

The precise chronological sequence 'six days after'[5] with which the story begins deserves attention. As we can find nothing similar to it except in the stories of the passion and the resurrection, we have here the first sign of transposition.[6]

---

[1] Schwartz, *Aporien in vierten Evangelium*, I. N.G., 1907, p. 348.

[2] A story exists which connects together the empty tomb and an appearance much more closely than in the Fourth Gospel. It is to be found in the *Epistola Apostolorum* (9-10) but this is a late document (written between 160 and 170) and contains not a free development of the tradition but a literary combination of the gospel stories.

[3] See my article 'Esquisse d'une interpretation du recit de la transfiguration', *R.h.r.*, 1920, LXXXI, pp. 145-57 (here will be found a catalogue of the previous literature on the subject); Bultmann, *Geschichte der synoptischen Tradition*[2] Goettingen, 1931, pp. 73 f.; Harnack, *S.B.A.*, 1922, pp. 73 ff.; ed. Meyer, *Urspr. u. Gesch. der Mormonen*, pp. 280 ff.; *Urspr. u. Auf.* III, pp. 152 ff., attack this interpretation.

[4] Identified as Moses and Elijah but originally they may have been angels.

[5] Luke says 'about eight days'. The number eight must have been due to an error in transcription and 'about' must have been added after the error had crept in to smooth out the contradiction with Mark.

[6] Certain incoherences in the story such as that belonging to the three tents which Peter proposes to put up are also proofs of editing.

The declaration of the voice from heaven which is the culminating point of the story closely resembles that made at Jesus' baptism (Mark i. 11, etc.). The author of the story of the transfiguration cannot have believed that the truth which had been revealed only to the three intimate disciples and which they had to keep secret had been publicly proclaimed in the presence of John the Baptist and the crowd.

We cannot help but see a resemblance between the brightness of Jesus' countenance on the mount of transfiguration and the glory of the person of Christ which 2 Cor. iii. 7 ff. declares to be infinitely greater than that which shone on Moses' face as he came down from Sinai. The resemblance is closer still. Paul considers that the resurrection confers on Christ the heavenly attribute of glory and makes him 'the Lord' (Phil. ii. 9-11). Jesus is 'declared to be the son of God with power by (or after) the resurrection of the dead' (Rom. i. 4).[1] What the heavenly voice proclaims on the mountain is that Jesus is the son of God and nothing else. The story of the transfiguration appears to have referred originally to a resurrection appearance where Jesus revealed himself on a mountain (as in Matthew) to the three intimate disciples with the attributes of heavenly glory and in the company of Moses and Elijah or angels.

No story of a resurrection appearance could bear the character of a messianic proclamation, once Jesus was thought of as having been the Messiah from the time his ministry began, as the stories of the baptism show or as having revealed himself as the Messiah to his disciples. The story was therefore transposed and became an incident in Jesus' ministry. This transposition must have taken place before the stories of the baptism had assumed the form in which we have them.[2]

The stories of the resurrection appearances—even the earliest— cannot be harmonised without their being deprived of all their concrete elements and reduced to a bare outline containing nothing but a story of a vision. It would also be necessary to prove that no evangelist intended to relate all the resurrection appearances or even

---

[1] For Paul Jesus is the pre-existent son of God. The resurrection reveals this attribute which until then was unnoticed by the heavenly powers. But behind Paul's formula a more primitive conception can be discovered which maintained that the resurrection made Jesus the son of God.

[2] This interpretation is confirmed by the fact that in the apocalypse of Peter (especially in the Ethiopian recension) there exists a scene resembling that of the transfiguration intimately connected with a resurrection appearance and a story of the ascension.

all those of which he was aware. Alternatively it would be necessary to reduce the stories to a unity by transforming them on the lines of some very complicated system so as to prove that some were derived from others.[1] Anyone will be convinced that no harmonisation is possible if he considers such a problem as the various persons who are supposed to have experienced the first resurrection appearance or the place where it is supposed to have taken place.[2]

No fact was more important for the primitive faith than the resurrection of Jesus; yet, on no fact is the tradition so diverse and incapable of being reduced to a unity. The stories as we have them compel us to admit that they were diverse and incapable of being reduced to a uniform pattern from a very early time. From a single elementary theme there seems to have spontaneously grown and multiplied a host of stories. Some of these stories are simply literary creations with no concrete happenings behind them, such as the appearance to Joseph of Arimathea in the gospel of Nicodemus, to take an example which cannot be called in question but this explanation does not cover all the stories. It is a matter of certainty that in the period following the death of Jesus the disciples were convinced that they saw him alive. Paul's evidence leaves no doubt on this point. He may have been the victim of an illusion but the sincerity of his statements is beyond question. It must be admitted too, that the multiplicity of the stories is explained by a multiplicity of visions.

Of the ten appearances related in the gospels, two only are to individuals;[3] of the six recorded by Paul, three are to individuals. We have here therefore a marked diminution in the number of appearances to individuals in proportion to those experienced collectively. The reason for this is doubtless that on the principle *testis unus, testis nullus* an appearance to an individual seemed less probable than an appearance collectively experienced. In this way the tradition developed into a systematic argument which might win over the indifferent and confound opponents.

The needs of apologetic added to a spontaneous tendency for the tradition to assume a more material and concrete form introduced contradictions into the stories. How could a being, who appeared

---

[1] As Voelter has done, *Die Enstehung des Glaubens an die Auferstehung Jesu*, Strasburg, 1910.

[2] Schmiedel, *E.B.* IV, cols. 4041-4, 4051-2, gives an impressive chart of the contradictions in the stories.

[3] One of these (the appearance to Simon) is only alluded to and another (the appearance to Mary Magdalene) has been inserted as an afterthought into a story which only mentioned one person to begin with.

and disappeared suddenly and entered a room the doors of which were shut, eat and possess a body which could be touched and possessed wounds which were not even healed up? The growing materialisation of the appearances affected the place where they were thought to have happened. By insisting more and more on the idea that the corpse came to life again, men were bound to tend to place the appearances near the tomb where the corpse had been laid. Mark and Matthew[1] have a tradition of an appearance in Galilee, Luke and John[2] of an appearance in Judaea. In the forms in which we have them Matthew and John combine both traditions. One is plainly a transposition of the other and the Galilean tradition can be said for certain to be the earlier. It is impossible to suppose that it could be formed on the basis of a Judaean tradition while the converse development is easy to explain. It comes from a tendency to connect the appearance with the discovery of the empty tomb and from the importance of Jerusalem in primitive Christian thought. There the church came into existence and there it felt for a long time was its seat and centre.[3] Appearances in Galilee on the other hand were quickly forgotten because so far as we know Christianity did not develop in Galilee in its earliest days to any appreciable extent.[4] Furthermore, there were two reasons why the disciples should have been impelled to return to Jerusalem when they had become convinced of their master's resurrection. First, if, as the gospel of Peter says (59),[5] the disciples left Jerusalem in tears and grief, it was natural that their faith being restored to them on a new level of life they should have been inspired to return to the place from which they had set out in despair. They must also have felt impelled to carry the news of Jesus' resurrection to his disciples in Jerusalem. Secondly, there was also the idea that Jesus would return to Jerusalem because he died there.[6]

[1] Before the appearance to the women was put in.
[2] In the gospel before chapter xxi was added.
[3] For a long time the church in Jerusalem was thought to be the true church of which the other churches were no more than colonies.
[4] The silence of Acts about Galilee is typical. It is not named in the missionary programme of i. 8 and only receives any mention at all in a purely editorial passage (ix. 31). If there were any attempts to evangelise in Galilee they must have failed probably because of the way in which Jesus' ministry in Galilee came to an end. See *V. de J.*, pp. 342 ff. and *Life of Jesus*, pp. 359 ff.
[5] This statement is very likely to be true and very probably comes from an early tradition.
[6] K. Hall, *Der Kirchenbegriff des Paulus im seinen Verhaltnis zu dem der Urgemeinde, Gesammelte Aufsitze zur Kirchengeschichte*, Tubingen, 1928, II, p. 55; Lietzmann, *H.* I, p. 61.

The resurrection appearances appear to have been fairly frequent at first but must have soon become rare. A time came when appearances ceased and this gave rise to the idea that the possibility of their happening was confined to a limited period.[1] As the resurrection appearances ceased to be phenomena of actual experience they became merely the data for systematic proof.

As the tradition developed into a fixed form and the resurrection appearances became limited to a closed period, some of the appearances were eliminated as can be seen in the way in which the appearance to Paul is narrated in the book of Acts.[2]

The diversity in the gospel stories cannot be explained except on the assumption that diverse stories were selected from what was formerly a richer tradition still. The preponderance of appearances which were a collective experience has been already noted;[3] it is also very typical. We lack the landmarks which would help us to know how the selection was made from the tradition as it evolved and developed.

5.—THE ASCENSION

The ascension is a late element in the tradition. In the earliest period men appeared to have hesitated in mind between the idea of an indefinite period of appearances and one of a single appearance. All the gospel stories offer a combination of these two ideas. The hesitation is particularly noticeable when Luke's gospel is compared with the book of the Acts.[4] If we ignore the appearance to Simon to which only an allusion is made, the two appearances on the road to Emmaus and to the disciples gathered together in Jerusalem form one story only; they are, if I may say so, one resurrection appearance experienced on two occasions. After Jesus has promised his disciples that they will be endowed with the power of the Holy Spirit, he leads them out as far as Bethany and, while he is blessing them, he is separated from them and is taken up into heaven.[5] The book of the Acts tells us that Jesus showed himself

---

[1] On the other hand this idea must have come into existence when the resurrection appearances were envisaged to possess such material characteristics that it became difficult to combine the glorified life of Christ with his corporeal manifestation on earth.   [2] See pp. 43 ff.   [3] See pp. 62 ff.

[4] Both books are attributed to the same author but the beginning of Acts has been revised. cf. *Introd.* III, pp. 155 ff.

[5] The words 'and he was taken up into heaven' are missing in ℵ D and several manuscripts of the early Latin versions and *syr^sin*. They must be considered authentic; a desire to eliminate the contradiction between Luke's ending and the beginning of Acts explains the suppression.

alive to his disciples for forty days and provided them with many proofs of his resurrection, gave them instructions, and promised them the gift of the Holy Spirit who would give them power to become his witnesses to the ends of the earth (i. 3-8). When he had completed these instructions he was taken up and a cloud received him out of their sight. While they watched him ascending up to heaven two angels explained to them that he would return in the same way (i. 9-12). Compared with the narrative in the gospel that of Acts extends the period of the appearances perceptibly; it also states more definitely that after this period there will be no further appearances. The fact that this idea prevailed over the earliest tradition shows that it must have arisen in response to a profound need.[1]

6.—THE TRADITION AND ITS FORMATION

The faith in the resurrection originates from the appearances. All the other elements in the tradition are the fruit either of reflection or of an elaboration of the stories for purposes of apologetic or, as is most often the case, of both these factors. We may accept with reserve Pascal's saying, 'I only believe those stories for the truth of which the witnesses are prepared to give their lives'. For in every case we have to rely on the good faith of such witnesses. But there is more truth in the statement, 'They saw Jesus because they believed and were convinced that he was living', than in that which lies behind the tradition, 'They believed in the resurrection of Jesus because they saw him living after his death'. The resurrection of Jesus is in reality the resurrection of that faith in him which the disciples had had during his ministry.

Those who experienced the first appearances—and in particular Peter who seems to have had the first one of all, the one which set in motion all the others—had the feeling that they owed to them a faith of which they had no previous knowledge. Others, on the contrary, in particular the apostle Paul, knew of this faith previously but were hostile to it. The two cases differ psychologically and must be considered separately.

[1] It is easy to discern the reasons why the period of the appearances was limited to forty days. Forty is a sacred number. There is a clear correspondence between the forty days of the temptation (Mark i. 13 and corr.) which was the period of preparation for Jesus' ministry on earth and the forty days which preceded the ascension and was the period of preparation for his ministry in heaven. Concerning other traditions which have given other lengths to the period of the appearances (eighteen months, eleven or twelve years) see *La foi à la rés.*, pp. 354 f.

From the stories in the New Testament it is possible to realise that the vision of the risen Christ depended on something more than physical causes. This is a matter of inference rather than evidence. Jesus never appeared to those who were indifferent or hostile but only to men who were his disciples or were destined to become so. The book of the Acts goes so far as to restrict the visions to the Twelve (x. 40-42; xiii. 31); Celsus in the second century was ironical about this, saying that if Jesus had really risen again, he would not have shown himself 'to a silly weak woman' but to those who had proceeded against him, to the man who had condemned him, and finally to everyone.[1] The first affirmation of the resurrection of Jesus probably only referred to his entrance into heaven. The idea that Jesus would triumph in spite of his death appears under this form in the promise accompanying the distribution of the cup at the last supper (Mark xiv. 23 ff. and corresponding passages) and in the reply to the repentant thief (Luke xxiii. 43). It is quite possible that the words of Jesus to Thomas, 'Happy are those who have not seen and have believed' (John xx. 29; cf. xx. 8) contain a note of regret for a form of faith which depended less upon statements of fact.

We find perhaps an echo of a primitive conception, which in support of the reality of the resurrection appealed only to spiritual convictions in Acts ii. 25-36, where Peter appeals not to the empty tomb or to the appearances as evidence for the resurrection but only to Psalm 16.[2] In the same way what is said about the resurrection in reference to the healing of the impotent man seems to have referred only to evidence which is entirely spiritual (Acts iii. 15; iv. 10).

If the faith in the resurrection had originated from the conviction of having seen the Lord living after his death, it does not follow that the proclamation of this fact in its earliest form would have referred to appearances of the risen Christ. It may have been that the first disciples felt a kind of shame which prevented them from recounting certain moments in their spiritual life which they judged too sacred to speak of openly. But this feeling must have been quickly neutralised by the demands of apologetic and by the need which

---

[1] Origen, *C. Celsum*, II, 55.
[2] What is said in this passage about the tomb of David seems so naturally to suggest an allusion to the empty tomb that critics with such diverse views as Loisy (*Les Actes des Apôtres*, Paris, 1920, pp. 290 f.) and Jacquier (*Les Actes des Apôtres*, Paris, 1926, p. 72) think, the former that this illusion was suppressed by a clumsy editor, the latter that it was implied. Both these interpretations are equally arbitrary.

they experienced not to restrict themselves to affirmations but to provide proofs and also to reply to the objections of opponents.

The proof which depended on both the empty tomb and the appearances must have developed in two phases. First of all, the resurrection appearances were referred to by themselves as I Corinthians xv shows, which only refers to the burial of Jesus as a proof of his death. Preachers may have also had to begin by making only vague and guarded references to the appearances as the source of their faith. They may also have mentioned the empty tomb, not as a proof of the resurrection but as a result of it. Later—and without doubt in an environment far away from Jerusalem where the circumstances attendant upon the burial of Jesus had been forgotten or were not known—the statement about the empty tomb changed its character and became a concrete story which was used as a proof.

In other places—and doubtless first in Jerusalem where a memory of the actual circumstances in which Jesus was buried must have lasted for a long time—the empty tomb could not be used as a proof of the resurrection so that the scruples which were felt about speaking of the resurrection appearances were overcome. As the empty tomb or the appearances or both of them came to be used as proofs of the resurrection the stories became more concrete in character and details were introduced which were intended to answer objections which were raised.

By this means also, men were impelled to form ideas concerning the mode of the resurrection and specially concerning the process by which it was realised. The earliest conception to be found on this point is what may be called the idea of passive resurrection such as is offered by the apostle Paul and the book of the Acts. It explains the resurrection as due to an act of the power of God. In the Fourth Gospel (x. 17-18) is found the idea of active resurrection, conceived of as the act of Christ himself who takes back a life of which he had been able momentarily to deprive himself but could not really lose altogether. The development of christology is to be found as the reason for this change. The eternal Logos of God cannot die: only the flesh in which the logos has come to dwell can be tainted.

As the tradition developed, themes which at first were independent of each other became grouped together and organised. The three fundamental moments of the burial, the empty tomb, and the resurrection appearances tended to form one continuous history. Next, as the conception of the appearances became more material, they were confined to a period of limited time. To these three moments was then added a fourth, that of the ascension which is thought of as the beginning of Christ's heavenly life, the first act of which will be to give the Holy Spirit to his own.

As long as the conception of a passive resurrection was dominant, nothing more was needed than simply placing the burial beside the discovery of the empty tomb. The time passed by Jesus in the tomb was thought of as a pause or noticeable break between the terrestrial activity of Christ and his celestial activity which the creative or rather recreative act of God was to make possible. But this held good no longer when the conception of active resurrection was established. If Christ did not die completely—how could it be said that he died completely if he preserved the power of taking back the life which he had freely laid down?—it is difficult to think of him as totally inactive between his death and resurrection.

The Fourth Gospel affirms that the activity of the Son is as incessant as that of the Father (v. 17). The problem then is, 'What did the divine Logos do while the flesh with which the Logos was united lay in the tomb?' The anxiety to solve this problem did not apparently meet with the same scruples which resisted the inclination to picture the resurrection itself. The solution was found by introducing the theme of the descent into hades which appeared at first in the form of the preaching to the dead.

The idea of the mission to the dead arose originally from a natural anxiety. If salvation was only possible through faith in Christ how could the patriarchs and saints of the old dispensation be saved? On the other hand, it was impossible to entertain the idea that the greater part of humanity were condemned to eternal death because they had never had the opportunity to hear the word of Christ which could save them. This gave rise to the thought that one day, either in this world or in the other, all men will hear the word. In John v. 25 it is said without giving an exact date that 'the dead shall hear the voice of the Son of Man and they that hear shall live'. The first epistle of Peter also refers to the preaching to the dead without any mention of the day (iii. 18 f.; iv. 6). At a later date it is stated that Jesus went down to Hades to preach salvation there between his death and resurrection (ev. Petr. 41).

Later on from a combination of the idea that Christ descended into Hades and the old myth of a fight between the powers above and those below emerged the story of the harrowing of hell by Jesus who came and snatched the dead from the clutches of Thanatos, Hades, and Satan. But this does not belong to the early period of the church's history. By the insertion of the theme of the descent into Hades the tradition concerning the resurrection was formed and completed into a continuous story beginning with the burial and ending with the Ascension and Pentecost.

But the affirmation of the resurrection in its completed form became something very different from what it was originally. Originally the expression of an experience it assumed the character of a factual history which can be proved true and must be believed if one is to be saved. This revolutionary change in the primitive character of the tradition is due to what can be considered to be a law of religious development. When the period of creativity comes to an end and one of consolidation follows, the fundamental theme of a new religion and the principal object of its worship become detached from the experience which they symbolise, acquire an objective character, and form the subject of a sacred history and a thesis for systematic apologetic. What Bergson calls the myth-making function intervenes at this stage. The stories created by it, even when they do not correspond with reality or only do so remotely, are still charged with spiritual significance, because, while they may not be entirely products of the imagination, imagination kindles them into life and faith gives them power.

After the original fervour has subsided and the spiritual excitement has died down, the stories produced by it change their character; while to begin with, although they were inaccurate on material points, they formed a true expression of the spiritual realities of a faith, they now become statements of facts in relation to one another which serve both as an expression and perhaps still more as a proof of belief and doctrine.[1]

[1] It is possible that the tradition concerning the resurrection may have been on some accessory points influenced by the old myth of the god who dies and rises again. It is possible that there was not a great difference between the way in which a Christian of the fourth or fifth century thought of the resurrection of Jesus and that in which a worshipper of Attis, Osiris, and Adonis thought of the history of the hero of his cult. But we are concerned with the feelings of Christians of the first generation. While an Adonis, Attis, or Osiris were lost in such a fabulous past that they had become unreal, Christians had the feeling that the drama of the life, death, and resurrection of the Lord had been enacted so recently that they felt they possessed a solid tradition. It must be added that if the faith in the resurrection had been a transposition of a myth, it would have been from the beginning the object regularly celebrated in a ritual, whereas we only find traces of such a cult at a comparatively late date.

CHAPTER II

The Birth of the Faith in the Resurrection

I.—THE CHARACTER OF THE FAITH IN THE RESURRECTION

FROM our analysis of the stories of the cycle of the resurrection we have seen how a tradition developed under the pressure of two demands, (1) to express a faith and (2) to defend it. But how did this faith come into being? The problem belongs not so much to history as to psychology. We can take what facts we like as the beginning of the development of the tradition and in spite of the manifest contradictions existing among them and the impossibility of harmonising them without doing violence to them we may yet suppose that all those facts reported in the New Testament are historically true. But by themselves they cannot explain a faith which looks far beyond them. The facts only express the faith by the interpretation put upon them. First of all then the essence of this faith must be defined as well as its function in the life and thought of primitive Christianity.[1]

It was neither impossible or even difficult for men of the first century to entertain the idea of a dead man coming back to life,[2] but Christians never considered the resurrection of Jesus to belong to the same species as those recounted in many traditions, the great mass of which the public never thought of doubting as having really happened. They were not final victories gained over death. Most of those who had been restored to life were supposed to have perished

---

[1] For further details concerning this chapter as for the preceding one I refer to my book *La foi à la rés.* See also my article 'Le caractère de la foi à la résurrection dans le christianisme primitif', *R.h.p.r.* XI, 1931, pp. 329-52.

[2] The gospels contain several stories of resurrections (Mark v. 22-43; Luke vii. 7-17; John xi. 1-44). Acts has two stories (ix. 36-42; xx. 7-12). A fragment of the apologist Quadratus (preserved by Eusebius, *H.e.* iv. 3, 2) who wrote at the beginning of Hadrian's reign attributed to Jesus more resurrections than are reported by the gospels.

prematurely; it was thought that while their resurrection had restored to them their normal span of life, it had not changed their nature which remained mortal as before. But Christ by his resurrection had finally conquered death. 'Christ being risen from the dead dieth no more, death hath no more dominion over him' (Rom. vi. 9), and the second epistle to Timothy speaks of Christ 'who hath abolished death and hath brought life and immortality to light' (i. 10). The ideas of the Lord's resurrection and his parousia are closely connected. Because Christ has triumphed over death he will return on the clouds of heaven to preside over the universal resurrection and establish the kingdom of God. Thus the resurrection of Christ comprises the idea of his glorification, his entry into the heavenly life of the world to come, and his triumph over death as well as the idea of a return to life.

Whatever forms we may suppose primitive Christian thought to have taken, we are bound to come to one conclusion. The importance of the resurrection does not lie in the fact that it destroyed the ignominy of the degrading punishment of the cross but that it made Jesus a heavenly being, and revealed him as one, able to redeem those who believe on him and to assure them of their salvation. 'God hath made that same Jesus whom ye have crucified, both Lord and Christ', we read in Peter's first sermon preserved in Acts (ii. 36) which constitutes the evidence for the earliest Christian thought[1] and on account of that when the times of refreshing shall come and the restitution of all things which God hath spoken by the mouth of the prophets, Jesus shall be sent as Messiah to blot out the sins of those who shall be converted and to admit them into the heavenly kingdom which shall then be set up (Acts iii. 19 ff.).

Christian thought in this primitive form disclosed by Peter's sermons already possesses two poles. On the one hand it is the cult of the Lord Jesus, i.e. of a being who after a life on earth and his death on a cross is now living and triumphant in heaven. On the other hand it is Jesus who died and at the same time lives and will return. The belief in the resurrection, i.e. in the triumph over death and the elevation to life in heaven unites these two conceptions of Jesus which otherwise would contradict each other.

In the apostle Paul's thought[2] there is a close connection between

---

[1] In Acts ii. 33 is found the equivalent phrase 'being by the right hand of God exalted'. It is repeated in v. 31.

[2] For a complete summary of Pauline thought see further on pp. 223 ff.

Christ's resurrection[1] and the one expected on the last day.[2] From this comes the title given to Christ, first-begotten among the dead, πρωτότοκος ἐκ τῶν νεκρῶν (Col. i. 18; cf. Rom. viii. 29; Rev. i. 5).[3] It signifies not only that Christ's resurrection is the first of all those which will happen but also that it makes the other resurrections possible.

The resurrection is the ground of the justification of believers. On the one hand, faith, and on the other, the sacraments of baptism and the eucharist unite the believer closely to Christ and associate him with the drama of His death and resurrection. The believer by dying with Christ expiates his sins and is freed from the power of the Law, the flesh, sin, death, and demons. 'He rises with Christ and so enters into a new life, the life of the Spirit and is become a new creature'. Although he continues to live in this present world, he belongs to the new celestial world which is that of the Spirit, the world over which the Lord reigns, the Lord who is said to be the Spirit (2 Cor. iii. 17) and which draws from Him the very principle of its existence and its life (cf. Rom. vi. 3-5).

If Paul had considered that the resurrection was only the reversal of the undeserved fate to which Jesus had submitted and nothing more than his rehabilitation, then it could not have brought in its train such far-reaching consequences; it would not have created a new order of things. It might have saved Jesus, perhaps; it would not have saved mankind. Paulinism could not exist without the exaltation of Christ to life in heaven. On the other hand it could dispense with the appearances as their only function is to reveal a transcendent reality.

Christ's resurrection is the ground of redemption as well as justification. Paul has two quite distinct conceptions of how redemption will be realised. They are quite independent of each other; no attempt is made even to harmonise them.[4] According to one conception[5] redemption will be completed at Christ's parousia when he will destroy all hostile powers, last of all, the power Θάνατος, who

---

[1] It is clearly revealed in chapter xv of the first epistle to the Corinthians.

[2] In the case of the elect, who are still alive on earth at the time of the parousia, they will be transferred into beings resembling those who rise again, i.e. they will be endowed with a body which will no longer be terrestrial, psychic, and earthy, but heavenly, spiritual and glorified.

[3] We must consider the title given to Christ in 1 Cor. xv. 20 'first fruits of them that slept' to be the equivalent of the phrase 'first begotten among the dead'.

[4] Concerning these two conceptions see pp. 197 ff.

[5] Stated in 1 Thess. iv. 13-18; 1 Cor. xv. 20-28, 50-57.

brings death to men, and is certainly to be identified with Satan (cf. Heb. ii. 14) although Paul does not expressly do so. Then in Christ the elect will be made alive (1 Cor. xv. 22).[1] Unless the resurrection of Christ is thought to be his exaltation to life in heaven, the parousia with the general resurrection and salvation are not possible.

The other conception[2] casts off the eschatological clothes in which Paul's theology took shape. The believer's destiny ceases to be bound up with the world's. It is no longer thought that the faithful are in a temporary state of sleep and prostration which they will throw off at the parousia. Each one accomplishes his redemption at the time of his death, when the inner man, which grows and is consummated as the outer man perishes, comes into full flower (2 Cor. iv. 16-18). 'To depart', 'not to abide in the flesh', i.e. to die is to be with Christ which is far better for the believer (Phil. i. 21-23).

Paul gives no description of this process either in the second epistle to the Corinthians or in the epistle to the Philippians nor does he offer any theory in explanation of this transition of the faithful to life in heaven. He only envisages it from the point of view of the experience of the believer. Nevertheless he expresses himself in terms which clearly show that it results from an action of the risen Christ. 'Now he that hath wrought us for the selfsame thing is God, who also hath given unto us the earnest of the Spirit', says Paul (2 Cor. v. 5). Further the gift of the Spirit cannot be separated in Paul's thought from the action of Christ and springs from the communion with Christ enjoyed by the believer.

Finally Christ's celestial life plays an essential part in the process of redemption so far as it is a transformation of human nature from a state of *psyche* to one of *pneuma*. By identifying himself with sinful and condemned humanity Christ re-established the link which had united men to their creator once before. Christ died because he identified himself in this way but God has raised him up. Because of this by his action in heaven he is able to exalt those who believe in him to the life of the Spirit.

The theological interpretation of the resurrection outlined in Peter's sermons and developed by Paul expresses a faith which the whole early church shared. From the synoptic gospels and the book of the Acts we can grasp its essentials.

[1] The categorical manner in which Paul expresses himself shows that all men will rise again but those who are not of the elect will meet with a judgement which will send them to destruction.

[2] As is found in 2 Cor. iv. 16-v. 10; Phil. i. 21-26.

The gospel tradition shows us that believers not only looked for light on what Jesus did and taught; they not only found in his words rules of life or the expression of truths which could enrich their devotion. They considered Jesus to be something more than the prophet of the Gospel or the preacher of the doctrine of salvation. He was himself the direct object of their faith. They did not look on him as a historical personage but as a living being. They felt his presence and action. They knew that he was present when two or three were gathered together in his name (Matt. xviii. 20), when they baptised, celebrated 'the Lord's supper', or used his name to exorcise a demon or heal someone sick.

The gospel tradition carries traces of a collective, anonymous, and impersonal effort, which in place of the real sequence of events in the life of Jesus substituted the idea of the realisation of a divine plan. If Jesus was not listened to or followed and came into collision with the authorities of his people, who did not rest until they had him put to death, it was because God had decided in advance that it must be so. The centre of gravity in the life and work of Jesus was sought not in what he had done and taught but in the drama of his death and resurrection, Everything was envisaged in the light projected on the gospel history by the resurrection. It was naturally supposed that Jesus had proclaimed it in advance.[1] The drama of Calvary could only be regarded as the prelude of the victory realised by the resurrection. The factual material of the gospel tradition in this way became subject to a revision which gave the central place to the resurrection.

The stories of the cycle of the resurrection, considered without submitting them to criticism but only for the purpose of trying to disengage from them the ideas and feelings they express, confirm this conclusion.

---

[1] According to the Synoptics Jesus predicted his sufferings, death and resurrection plainly three times (Mark viii. 31; ix. 31-33; x. 32-34 and par.), but the evangelists are careful to indicate very clearly that this information was beyond the understanding of the disciples. According to Luke (xxiv. 13 ff.) the risen Jesus appeared to the two disciples on the road to Emmaus and explained the Scriptures to them which show that the Messiah must suffer before entering into his glory. A little later he appears to the disciples reunited in Jerusalem and explains to them that it was necessary 'that all should be accomplished which was written of him in the law of Moses, the prophets, and the psalms'. Then he opens their understanding that they might understand the Scriptures. Finally he recalls to them that according to the Scriptures it behoved Christ to suffer and to rise from the dead the third day and that repentance should be preached in his name among all nations (xxiv. 44-47).

Christians saw a miracle in the tomb of Jesus when it was found open and empty. The Jesus who afterwards showed himself to his disciples is beyond question the same man who had been buried. His body is real although in some stories it is said to be freed from the contingencies to which ordinary bodies are subject. It appears and disappears suddenly without anybody being able to understand how or why. It can come into a room the doors of which are shut.

Very much less interest is shown in the resurrection itself as a fact, and in the conditions under which it happened than in the ensuing consequences.' Early tradition does not tell us how Jesus left the tomb. When the extraordinary plasticity of the stories of the cycle of the resurrection is taken into account as well as the ease with which they were shaped, transformed, and organised, the silence on this point is very striking. It is explained chiefly by the feeling there was, that the resurrection of Jesus contained a mystery and by the fact that all attention was given to its manifestations and results. Above all things it was desired to explain how the disciples who had been scattered when their master was arrested regained their courage and found a faith which was more assured than before and had become aggressive and victorious.

The book of the Acts lays a still greater insistence on this idea. The pouring out of the Spirit as a result of the resurrection, which the apostles must await at Jerusalem, will make them able to be witnesses of Jesus to the ends of the world. In the subsequent narrative the resurrection occupies a central position in the preaching of the Gospel. The apostles are the witnesses of it.[1]

In the Fourth Gospel as in the Synoptics the resurrection had been predicted in advance by the Scriptures, but the disciples only knew of it after the event (xx. 9). Only then too did they understand the prediction made by Jesus (ii. 21-22). But in the farewell discourses Johannine thought assumes a form perceptibly different from that of the Synoptics. One of the essential themes developed in them is the promise that the disciples will see Jesus again after the imminent separation. But, besides the promise that they will see him again and so change their grief into joy (xiv. 3, 18-19, 23; xvi. 17, 20, 22), there is also the promise to send the Paraclete, i.e. the Spirit (xiv. 16, 25; xv. 26; xvi. 7, 13-15).[2] The ideas of parousia and

---

[1] Among the documents revealing the place held in religious thought and life at the end of the first century by the belief in the resurrection must be mentioned the canticles in the Apocalypse and the fragment of a hymn preserved in 1 Tim. iii. 16.   [2] Concerning the Johannine notion of the Spirit see pp. 358 ff.

pneumatick inspiration are transposed and spiritualised so as to become the idea of the glorified Christ acting upon his own. The Johannine notion of the Paraclete is thus brought into close relationship with the resurrection as a necessary condition of the action of the glorified Christ and a guarantee of the parousia.

John has quite a different conception of the resurrection from Paul but its function in his soteriology is similar. Paul's conception of the resurrection is passive. God raises up Christ by an act of his power. John has an active conception: Christ raises himself, because he has the power to lay down his life and take it up again (x. 17-18). Although his death is represented as a momentary triumph of the Prince of the world, i.e. of the devil (xiv. 30) this idea comes entirely from the tradition since this death is the glorification of the Son of Man (xii. 23). Like a grain of corn which must die to bear much fruit, so the Johannine Christ declares that a man must lose his life in this world to have life eternal. A man must then follow him in his death in order to be 'honoured by the Father' (xii. 24-26). There is no difficulty in seeing here the influence of Pauline ideas.

The Johannine Christ declares that when he is lifted up[1] he will draw all men unto him (xii. 32). This shows the importance of Christ's return to heaven for salvation. Nevertheless the resurrection does not play the same part in John's theology as in Paul's. With John there can be no question of being associated with Christ's death as a condition of being associated with his resurrection, since John considers Christ's death not even to be his temporary annihilation but to be itself his return to heaven, Christ's death only comes into his soteriology because participation in the life divine which the Logos has revealed to men can only begin when Christ has returned to heaven.

2.—THE ORIGINS OF THE IDEA OF RESURRECTION

Attempts have been made to find the origin of the idea of resurrection in the myths of gods who die and come to life again, which occupied an important place in the religions of the ancient world. On secondary points they may have influenced the form assumed by the Christian belief in the resurrection. But no direct derivation can

[1] This term, in accordance with a procedure dear to John, must be regarded as ambiguous. It is an allusion both to the nature of Christ's death and also to his return to heaven.

be discerned. The religion of the worshippers of Attis, Adonis, or Osiris did not possess—or at any rate in only a very feeble degree—that element of love and affection which played such an important part in the Christian faith in its earliest stages and is inseparable from a previous attachment to a living person.[1]

The first germ of the idea of resurrection must be found in the thoughts of Jesus' disciples before their master's death. The faith which possessed their hearts after the crisis of the passion was not new but was transfigured and transposed. The gospels belittle the faith which the disciples had during Jesus' ministry and minimise their loyalty for their master. They were, no doubt, inspired to do this by their own judgement on their past. They made themselves out to have had a certain attachment to their master—they could hardly have done otherwise—but to have been completely blinded to the meaning of the teaching which he had tried to give them on the necessity of his death and resurrection. According to Luke (xxii. 24) when Jesus had just distributed the bread and the cup at the last supper, they disputed among themselves as to who was the greatest among them. They fell asleep at Gethsemane; at the time of the arrest after a timid show of resistance they scattered. They did not appear either at the trial of Jesus or at the time of his crucifixion. They were not there to bury him. Tradition even relates that Peter denied his master in the presence of the high-priest's servants. Even if, as I have tried to show,[2] the episode is not historical, it is none the less significant.

The motive behind this theme which was so amply developed in the tradition was not a spirit of defiance or hostility towards the disciples. It shows that primitive Christianity was so acutely conscious of the novelty of the faith in the celestial Kyrios that it became blind to the fundamental unity which existed between the faith of the disciples before and after the resurrection, who themselves gained the idea that their faith in the heavenly Christ had suddenly flashed into life the day after the passion.

In reality there was more continuity in the thought of the disciples than they themselves perceived. If they had never really submitted to the ascendancy of Jesus and had not attached themselves to him, they would never have continued to follow him,

---

[1] See p. 65, n. 1.
[2] See my study 'Did Peter deny his Lord? A conjecture', *Harv. theol. rev.* 1932, XXV., pp. 1-27; *Life of Jesus*, pp. 485 ff.

when the illusion of possible success had faded and they knew that if they remained faithful they must reckon their lives to be in jeopardy.

Jesus perceived the prospect of his death from the beginning of the crisis in Galilee grow more definite and certain right up to the final drama but it never shook his conviction that he would be manifested in glory as the Messiah. It only made him change his ideas of how his manifestation as Messiah would come about. He thought it would be by a return on the clouds of heaven. After his death he would be exalted to heaven. From thence he would return to preside at the resurrection of the dead and establish the Kingdom of God. When we thus take into account what appears to have been the underlying character of Jesus' thought it is plain that the two ideas of victory over death and participation in celestial life were not absolutely novel. In any case they have their roots in his conviction that in spite of every setback the Kingdom of God will be realised. The belief in the resurrection of Jesus was not therefore ideologically an absolute novelty in primitive Christianity. After a momentary eclipse it was the restoration of the faith which his disciples had shown in him previously.

3.—THE PSYCHOLOGICAL CHARACTER OF THE RESURRECTION APPEARANCES

From an analysis of the tradition we can recognise at least in outline the conditions under which the belief in the resurrection appeared and grew. At the end of a period, the length of which cannot be determined, the disciples, after being disheartened by Jesus' death, regained their courage. What their master had told them about the meaning of his sufferings and death came back to mind and prepared the way for the resurrection of their faith. The realisation of the Kingdom of God ceased to be for them a dream which never could come true. They began to think of Jesus not as dead but as living. This gave rise to the idea that God allowed Jesus to return in order that he might realise his task as Messiah. Jesus first rose again in the heart of his disciples who had loved and believed in him. Renan[1] spoke of 'the divine power of love' and 'the passion of a hallucinated woman which gave to the world a risen God'. Rather than speak of a miracle of love it would have been better to speak of a miracle of faith which prevented those who had for a few months

---

[1] Renan, *V. de J.*, Paris, 1863, p. 434.

lived with tremendous expectations believing that they had been snatched away from them.

Natura non facit saltus. This principle applies to the psychological and moral domain as well. The belief in the resurrection had grown up in the heart of the disciples, before they could be conscious of it, proclaim and preach it.

Their conviction that Jesus was alive in heaven and that they had seen him when he had judged good to show himself gave birth to the idea that the tomb was empty. This at first was simply a corollary of the belief in the resurrection. But gradually it became an independent idea, and as what Bergson has called 'the myth-making function of religion'[1] came into play, stories sprung up telling how women came to the tomb on the morning of the third day and found it empty.

The resurrection appearances which did nothing more than definitely establish belief in the resurrection and rendered men conscious of their belief can from the psychological point of view be divided into two classes. The initial appearance is in one class by itself, Peter's, in all probability.[2] It belongs to a man whose faith and confidence in Jesus had been eclipsed and who was in no way conscious that the Lord was risen. The appearance of Christ to him created both the idea and the belief simultaneously. The other class consists of the remaining subsequent appearances which happened to men who were acquainted with the idea of Jesus' resurrection but had not given him their full loyalty, although they had not rejected and opposed him.

Only of the appearance to Paul have we any knowledge. It is true that we do not know much but we know sufficient to give us a good idea of what happened.

4.—THE FUNCTION AND CHARACTER OF RELIGIOUS VISIONS

Although the appearances of the risen Christ have certain peculiar characteristics, they are not isolated phenomena in religious history. Without entering into a general study of facts of this kind it will be useful to consider as specimens two cases of visions where the psychological mechanism can be easily discerned and light is

---

[1] Bergson, *Les deun Sources*, pp. 207 ff.; Eng. trans., pp. 165 ff.

[2] Perhaps there was at first more than one vision since, although it appears most unlikely, it cannot be absolutely ruled out that men who did not know of other appearances may have experienced them quite independently of each other.

thrown upon the factors determining the appearance to Paul and his conversion.[1] They are the visions which caused the conversions of the Jew, Ratisbonne, and the Hindu, Sundar Singh.[2] Marie-Alphonse was converted to Roman Catholicism on 20th January 1842 at Rome after a vision while contemplating the Virgin Mary. Up till then he was strongly attached to the religion of his fathers and had never forgiven one of his brothers for his conversion to Christianity fifteen years earlier. One of his Roman Catholic friends, Baron de Bussière, kept on pressing him to do the same, but to his persistent demands he replied that born a Jew he would die a Jew. Yet he confessed that he used to visit the church of the Aracoeli where he experienced a mysterious emotion, an emotion which he said was purely religious without being in any way Christian. His friend had given him a medal of the Virgin which had been blessed and which he had promised he would always wear. He had also been given by him a copy of St. Bernard's prayer, '*Memorasse, o piassima virgo*'. He read and re-read it until he knew it by heart and was surprised to find himself repeating it mechanically. On the 20th January 1842 he went with Baron de Bussière to the church St. Andrea della Frati where his friend left him for a moment to make some arrangements at the sacristry for a friend's funeral. Ten minutes later Baron de Bussière rejoined Ratisbonne and found him on his knees in the chapel of St. Michel with his face bathed in tears and in such a state of emotion that he could not give any explanation of what had happened. When he had regained a little calm he explained that he had suddenly been thrown into indescribable mental confusion. The building seemed to disappear from sight. All the light was concentrated on one chapel alone, and there in the centre of the radiating light standing up on the altar was the Virgin Mary, tall and shining, with her face full of majesty and sweetness with the same likeness as shown on the medal. Ratisbonne related later that failing to sleep most of the previous night he seemed to see all the time a tall cross of a somewhat peculiar shape and could not get rid of this vision which obsessed him. A few hours later his eyes fell

---

[1] For an interpretation of Paul's vision and his conversion by means of these visions see my book *La foi à la rés.*, pp. 403 ff. The explanation propounded by me has been criticised by Guignebert, 'La conversion de Paul', *Rev. hist.* 1938, CLXXXII, pp. 7-23 (the article is reproduced in *Le Christ*, pp. 245 ff.).

[2] To these two cases can be added according to evidence which, however, raises some doubts, the case of Edmond Scherer who received a vision of Christ on Christmas Day 1832, which did not change incredulity into faith but indifference into enthusiasm. See *La foi à la rés.*, pp. 405 ff.

on the reverse side of the medal, which he did not remember to have looked at before; there he found the cross, the image of which had haunted him the whole night.

Few visions are as transparent as this one. Even at the time when Ratisbonne said that he was resolved to die a Jew, he was unconsciously a divided soul. On the one side were those things of which he was conscious, the weight of his traditions, pride of race, and the prejudiced attitude to which his condemnation of his brother's conversion had tied him. On the other side below the surface of his consciousness were the forces pushing him towards Catholicism revealed in the emotions which he experienced in the church of Aracoeli, in the impression created by St. Bernard's prayer, in the obsession caused by the face of the Virgin on the medal, and in the impression unconsciously made upon him by the cross on the reverse side of the medal. The former repressed the latter. All this shows that we have here a man with a divided soul where the forces driving him towards conversion are in conflict with those striving to maintain the *status quo.* At first the latter preponderate but the adverse tendencies become all the stronger by being repressed in the unconsciousness. A time comes when they have gathered sufficient power to overcome those which had been repressing them. The old equilibrium is shown to be destroyed by a vision which expresses and justifies simultaneously the new position now realised.

Another vision which must be similarly interpreted is that which made Sundar Singh, who was then fifteen years old, a convinced Christian on 17th December 1904. He belonged to a family who were ardent and practising Sikhs,[1] and up till that time he was violently hostile to Christianity with which he was acquainted through having attended an American mission school. Several times he had burnt or torn up copies of the Bible and had thrown stones and dirt at the missionaries, as evildoers who had come to corrupt everything. He thought of writing a book against Christianity. At the same time—and this was doubtless why his opposition to Christianity took such a violent form—the Bible possessed a secret attraction for him so that he could not stop himself from reading it. It promised peace and rest in mind to those who are tired and heavy-laden (Matt. xi. 28 f.) which was exactly what he was looking for, but he was indignant that a foreign religion could promise him peace, while Hinduism, which he was determined was the finest religion in the

[1] A Hindoo Mahommedan sect.

world, was unable to give it him. He read that God so loved the world that he had given his only-begotten son that all who believe on Him should not perish but have everlasting life (John iii. 16) and he was angry that Christ who could not save himself claimed to save others. On 16th December 1904 this internal conflict ended in an explosion of rage in the course of which he solemnly burnt the Bible which promised peace and only destroyed his own.

The next morning, in the last stage of despair and thinking that as there was no peace in this world he might perhaps find it in the next, he resolved to kill himself by throwing himself under a train which passed near his house at 5 a.m. At 3 a.m., in accordance with Sikh custom, he took a cold ritual bath. Afterwards he emphasised this detail, which made it difficult to think that he was half asleep when what followed took place. After his bath he began to pray, 'O God, if there is a God, show me the true path. I want to be a sadhou (i.e. a saint). If I cannot I am going to kill myself.' About 4.30 a.m. a great light filled the room where he was praying. He thought at first that a fire had started but found out that it was nothing. Turning again to prayer he saw in a luminous mist the visage of a man completely bathed in love. Thinking that it was Bhudda or some other Indian god he was preparing to prostrate himself before the apparition and worship, when he heard these words in Hindustani: 'Why do you persecute me? Reflect that I gave my life for you on the cross.' At first he did not understand: then on the form before him he saw the scars of the Jesus of Nazareth whom he had so violently detested. On his face he read nothing but gentleness and love. Instantly he was changed. 'The Christ', he afterwards said, 'penetrated me like a stream from God; joy and peace filled my soul.' When Sundar Singh got up Christ had disappeared but the wonderful peace remained without ever leaving him. What happened on 17th December 1904 was for him a miracle in the exact sense of the word, a direct and personal intervention of Christ. Sixteen years later he said this:

'I did not imagine what I saw. Until then I hated Jesus and did not pray to him. If it had been the Bhudda I would have said that it was the result of my imagination through my being accustomed to call upon him. No, it was not a dream; you do not dream when you have just had a cold bath. It was a reality, the living Christ.' Sundar Singh had other visions in the course of his life after conversion. He never, however, equated them with the vision at his conversion when he saw Christ with his bodily eyes, while on other occasions he only contemplated him in ecstasy.[1]

[1] Streeter and Appasamy, *The Sadhu*, London, 1921, pp. 5 f.

Three factors go to determine the most satisfactory interpretation to be given to this vision, (1) the restless state of a man who does not find an interior peace of mind for which he longs, (2) an acquaintance with Christianity, which makes him the victim of an internal conflict of motives, being on the one hand attracted to Christianity because it promises him peace and at the same time opposed to it by an instinctive loyalty to his native traditions and a racial pride, which refuses to recognise the value of what is not purely Hindu, (3) an acquaintance with the story of Paul and his conversion. The conflict between the opposing forces lasted a long time. The moment of crisis was marked by an intense internal agitation, by acts of violence, and ideas of suicide. Suddenly calm came: peace followed anguish and the crisis ended by conversion to Christianity.

A conversion which does not originate from a state of indifference but from one of declared hostility is bound to be sudden.[1] The agitated emotional condition of a person whose whole mental life has been thrown into doubt and confusion is eminently favourable for the emergence of visions, which from a psychological point of view are only external projections in a concrete form of the motives of conversion. The person is unable to find the reasons for what has happened to him and is therefore compelled to give himself some explanation. The greater the obstacles to a change of mind seem to him, the more necessary it is for the motives leading to change to be thought of as irresistible.

In the Sadhu's case conversion implied the recognition of the truth of traditional Christian statements about Christ which depended upon the affirmation of his resurrection. It was natural therefore that it should have taken the form of an appearance of the living Christ. Besides this the fact that he knew of the story of Paul's conversion went a long way to determine beforehand, if one may say so, the form that his conversion was eventually to take. Because Christianity satisfied the Sadhu's deepest religious aspirations he felt it was true; because it was true, he was certain that Christ was really living. But the true sequence was reversed in the way in which things appeared to him to have happened. The result of his experience, i.e. the certitude that Christ was really living, he saw as its cause.

---

[1] What is meant by this is that its appearance not its formation is sudden. Every conversion is the end of a psychological process which naturally may be long or short in duration. In certain cases this process works out on the level of consciousness, in others in the region of the subliminal.

Sundar Singh made a clear distinction between his initial vision and the ensuing ecstasies which came to him, because anyone, who lives through a conversion in retrospect, cannot confuse the revelations of a heavenly being in whom he believes, which are granted to him in the subsequent course of his life, with the action by which this being, previously unknown or repulsed by him, won his heart and gained possession of him. The coincidence between Sadhu and Paul, who also made a clear distinction between the vision on the road to Damascus and subsequent 'visions and revelations from the Lord' is too striking to be fortuitous: it is the result of what is common to both conversions.[1]

'The visionary', wrote Edward B. Tylor, 'turns in a vicious circle: what he believes he therefore sees and what he sees he therefore believes.'[2] This summary conclusion does not go to the bottom of things. The faith which brings forth visions and the faith which conversely is created or strengthened by visions are two different phenomena. The former springs from the depths of the unconscious where it has come into activity for reasons which can only partly be discerned. The faith which the vision creates or strengthens is conscious and is expressed in an intellectual formula. Rather than a vicious circle it should be called an ascending line along which faith passes from the region of the unconscious to that of the conscious.

In those conversions which we call slow or progressive this passage is made insensibly. The subject himself cannot notice it. Many people while they would agree that their religious position has changed would be unable to say when precisely their conversion had occurred. But, when a faith is born in the depths of the subliminal self and clashes with opposing forces strong enough to keep it temporarily in check, its passage to the level of consciousness is only made when it has already acquired a certain intensity. Then it is not a progressive ascension but an explosion which breaks all resistance and the resulting disturbance is eminently favourable to the presence of visions.

Those visions which often play an important part in the appearance of new religions present striking analogies with those phenomena

---

[1] A complete study of religious visions would have to include two further facts: (1) the contagious nature of visions, and (2) collective visions, e.g. the visions of Notre Dame de Salette which came to the young shepherd girl, Melanie Calvat, aged fourteen and a half, and her little companion, Maximin, beginning on 19th September 1846, and those which occurred in 1931, at Ezquioga, in the Basque country, a strong Catholic district, where the anti-clerical movement let loose by the revolution in Spain was creating disturbance and anxiety.

[2] Edward B. Tylor, *Primitive Culture*⁴, London, 1903, II, p. 45.

the pathological character of which is indisputable, being the result of a real mental break-down. Yet, as Bergson has shown,[1] the two phenomena must not be confused. Both of them are the outcome of a psychological disturbance and a weakening of the functions of synthesis and control. But this disturbed condition can be due to very different causes. It may be due to a disease in the personality caused by some mental defect or some nervous lesion. Then it is constitutional and lasting.[2] But it may be caused by some intense sentiment, emotion, or spiritual energy in some other form. Then it is only provisional and functional; normal mental balance is more or less quickly restored. It became disturbed because certain psychological elements were enfeebled while others were intensified. It is like the balance of scales which may be disturbed because something has been added to one of the pans or something has been taken away.

The activity of visionaries who are mentally ill or defective must be disordered or can only be on a reduced scale. But on the other hand, those who enjoy visions through being spiritually elated in some way or other may be creative in the realm of thought or action. From their vision they find their personality enriched and strengthened. Applying this criterion to the resurrection appearances we find that they do not belong to that class of visions which are pathological, unless we intend to class as pathological everything in mental and spiritual activity which stretches beyond the level of what is habitual and normal.

5.—THE PSYCHOLOGICAL MECHANISM OF THE APPEARANCE TO PAUL

In the light of the preceding observations we can now consider what happened in the vision of the risen Christ which turned Paul the persecutor into an apostle.[3]

After the belief in the resurrection had come into existence and Paul had come into contact with Christianity[4] he considered the

---

[1] Bergson, *Les deux sources*, pp. 243 ff., Eng. Trans., pp. 195 ff.

[2] It may also be the result of a temporary prehypnotic state such as might be due to the action of certain poisons, e.g. opium, cocaine, hashish, etc.

[3] For certain questions concerning Paul's conversion which I am here obliged to pass over quickly, see *Introd.* IV. 1, pp. 195 ff.

[4] Contrary to the opinion of quite a number of critics we shall see (pp. 462 ff.) that the reasons for questioning that Paul came into contact with the new faith at Jerusalem are insufficient.

disciples of Jesus to be blasphemers, because they claimed that an individual, who quite clearly was under God's curse, as it is written in Deuteronomy, 'Cursed is everyone that hangeth on a tree' (xxi. 23 quoted in Gal. iii. 13), was a messenger from God. Paul persecuted the church because there was a danger that the blasphemy of which it had made itself guilty would bring down the divine wrath on those who tolerated it as well as on those who uttered it. He must then have been aware of the essence of Christianity. He knew that they declared that Jesus after his death had gained a striking revenge, and that several people, nay, even many of the disciples, had seen him alive again, so that they were now able to wait for his glorious return on the clouds of heaven. Paul must also have known something of the teaching of Jesus and possibly some of the sayings of Jesus which he was reported to have said, such as that part of the Sermon on the Mount concerning obedience to the Law of God (Matt. v. 17 ff.), had penetrated deeply into his consciousness. But the principle of Deuteronomy, which made him judge Jesus accursed, held such absolute sway with him that even that strain in the Gospel, which was capable of satisfying his deepest aspirations, could not influence his conscious thoughts.

Paul attributed his conversion to an act of God, which with irresistible power revealed his Son to him, nay, it might be said thrust him upon him (Gal. i. 1-12, 16). This revelation took the form of an appearance of Christ (1 Cor. xv. 8; cf. ix. 1). By showing himself to Paul Christ took possession of him (Phil. iii. 12; cf. 1 Cor. ix. 17); as a result his whole life and thought were changed completely and his scale of values was reversed.

It is easy to follow the course of Paul's thought from the time when his consciousness was suddenly seized with the complete assurance that Jesus was living. God had not only done something extraordinary for Jesus crucified by restoring him to life; he had also anticipated for Jesus the resurrection on the last day and had given him from now on life in heaven, i.e. life in the world to come. Therefore, Paul argued, the disciples were right in saying that Jesus was Messiah of God. The two propositions, 'Jesus is Lord', and 'Jesus is accursed', Paul considered to be equally true. He harmonised them or rather made them dependent on each other by the idea that Christ, to make salvation possible, accepted a complete identification with the whole of humanity and so could take upon himself in his own flesh all the sins of mankind and expiate them by submitting himself to punishment.

The relationship which Paul envisaged between his vision of the risen Christ and his conviction that Jesus was living must be reversed. His vision did not create but revealed a conviction which already existed. The whole problem of the appearance to Paul and his conversion centres round the formation of this conviction.

Some people[1] suggest that an external factor such as a mirage, an attack of fever, a hallucination caused by fatigue, heat, hunger, or some ocular affection caused his vision. These explanations are radically insufficient, although it may be admitted that Paul's temperament predisposed him to ecstatic phenomena. But even if it could be established beyond the realm of conjecture that some external circumstance let loose the crisis on the road to Damascus, it would not explain it. It would be the match which set fire to the powder not the cause of the explosion.

If anything explains the appearance of Christ to Paul and his conversion it can only be his interior life.

Many Protestant interpreters[2] ignore the diversity of forms in which conversion can be clothed and are more or less consciously dominated by the idea that Luther's conversion affords the most suitable guide for interpreting others. With Luther's conversion in mind they suppose that Paul for weeks or months preceding the vision had been passing through a crisis which must be recognised as due to two causes. (1) Paul was attracted by the Church's teaching and impressed by Stephen's attitude before his death. That was the goad against which he tried to kick by persecuting the faithful (Acts xxvi. 14). (2) He needed a rule which was absolute and found the righteousness of the law insufficient because he yearned after such righteousness as would be proof against failure to obey even one solitary commandment of the law. Neither of these ideas can hold water. For one thing when Paul is speaking of his activity as a persecutor, he certainly regrets and condemns it but he never expresses the least remorse but rather boasts of it. This shows that he fully believed that he had acted in accordance with his convictions. As for the idea that his conversion was the outcome of a moral

---

[1] e.g. Renan, *Les Apôtres*, Paris, 1866, p. 179.
[2] e.g. Weizsaecker, *Das apostolische Zeitalter*[2], Freiburg in Brisgau, 1892, p. 72; Weiner, *Paulus*, Tubingen, 1904, pp. 54 ff. and *Bibl. Th.*,[3], p. 416; Deissmann, *Paulus*, Tubingen, 1911, p. 83. It has been disputed by Wrede, *Paulus*, Halle, 1905, pp. 8 f.; Loisy, 'La conversion de saint Paul et la naissance du christianisme', *R.h.l.r.*, N.S., 1914, V, p. 309; 'La carrière de l'apotre Paul', *R.h.l.r.*, N.S., 1920, VI, pp. 451 ff.; Bousset, *Kyrios Christos*[2], p. 106; Heitmuller, 'Die Bekehrung des Paulus', *Z.f.Th.u.K.*, 1917, XVII, pp. 145-7.

struggle,[1] the principal evidence for it comes from the epistle to the Romans (vii. 7 ff.), which is the classic expression of the anguish of a soul which yearns for an ideal it has not yet realised. Further on[2] we shall see that the moral struggle through which there is no doubt Paul passed at the beginning of his Christian life was not the cause but a result of his conversion. But in any case the passage in the epistle to the Philippians (iii. 6), where Paul maintains that he was beyond reproach before his conversion as far as righteousness of the law was concerned,[3] compels us to dismiss from our minds the idea that his conversion was the outcome of a moral struggle. When Paul had become a Christian and because he had become one, his opinion concerning man's capacity to keep the Law of God was quite different from what he thought previously.

Besides, if Paul had considered his conversion to be as Luther did, the recognition or discovery of a truth for which he had been painfully groping, he would in referring to it have expressed feelings of deliverance. Instead he always says that it is a constraint to which he has submitted and that it has thrown him out of the track which previously he had been convinced was the path to salvation (Phil. iii. 12).[4]

At first sight we do not perceive what link there can be between Paul's new estimate of man's capacity to obey the Law of God and his mystical experience on the road to Damascus. All becomes clear, if we remember that Jesus had already submitted the conception of obedience to the Law, i.e. to the will of God to a comparable transformation, when he substituted for the negative prohibitions of the commandments given to them of old time his 'But I say unto you' and his commandment, 'Be ye perfect as your Father in heaven is perfect' (Matt. v. 22 ff.) and placed the ethic of intention against that of the act.[5] Such a revolution in thought cannot have happened twice independently with only a few years between. A change in Paul's attitude following his conversion was determined by the new

[1] Besides Weizsaecker, Weinel and Deissmann, mentioned in the preceding footnote, the idea of a moral crisis is adhered to by Sabatier, *L'apôtre Paul*[3], Paris, 1896, pp. 37 ff.; Fulliquet, *La pensée religieuse du Nouveau Testament*, Paris, 1893, p. 292; Julicher, *Einleitung in das Neue Testament*[7], Tubingen, 1931, pp. 34 f.

[2] See pp. 213 f.

[3] On this text see my study $KATA\ THN\ \Delta IKAIO\Sigma YNHN\ THN\ EN\ NOM\Omega\ \Gamma ENOMENO\Sigma\ AMEM\Pi TO\Sigma$ (Phil. iii. 6); 'Remarques sur un aspect de la conversion de Paul', *Journal of Biblical Literature*, 1934, LIII, pp. 257-67.

[4] The meaning of the term ἔκτρωμα in 1 Cor. xv. 8, must be underlined. See p. 42, n. 1.

[5] See my *V. de J.*, pp. 537 ff. and *Life of Jesus*, pp. 553 ff.

ethical conception proclaimed by Jesus. This reveals one factor in Paul's conversion: his acquaintance with the sayings and teaching of Jesus exercised an unconscious influence against which his whole religious position cried out. But immediately on his conversion it became predominant and played a part in his thought's development, the importance of which has often been ignored.

While Paul's conversion was not preceded by any crisis of which he was aware, there had gone on in preparation for it intense activity in his subliminal self. There the affirmations of Christians concerning their master's resurrection and their expectation of his return on the one hand and on the other the new ethical ideal preached by Jesus had been secretly working upwards gathering strength while on the level of consciousness they were repressed by the statement of the law concerning a curse belonging to the cross and by loyalty to the traditional forms of Judaism. As in the case of Ratisbonne and that of Sundar Singh, a moment came when the activity in the unconscious gained such strength that in the end it triumphed over every obstacle and found a positive conclusion. It then burst forth in the field of consciousness and became objectified in a vision which the apostle judged to be the direct presence of Christ himself. Trying to account for what had happened to him he considered that Christ had personally intervened in his life and had caused his conversion.

The first appearances were different in character, because they happened to men who had been attached to Jesus but had never thought of his returning to life. Nevertheless, as far as one can judge in the absence of any direct documentary evidence, the vision's mechanism appears to have been the same. Before there was any belief that he would appear posthumously there existed the conviction that Christ was alive in heaven. This explains the visions. As for the belief that Christ was alive in heaven, it was only the reappearance of convictions which had developed while as disciples they had lived with their master. The dark hours of the passion had repressed them without completely robbing their hearts of them. When they had returned to Galilee and had recovered themselves, their old convictions came alive again. But they could not subsist in their previous form. As long as Jesus was alive they could expect that he would manifest himself as the Messiah in glory.

After his death faith in him could only last or be reborn if he had triumphed over death and so could be regarded as a living person. Faith in the heavenly Christ not only extended the hopes which the disciples had placed in Jesus; it exalted and adapted them to the changed circumstances which seemed at first to have brought them grievous disappointment. This explains the presence of a conviction which did not develop slowly and calmly but showed itself with such intensity that it assumed the explosive form of a vision. For this reason, as soon as this faith began to spread, a veritable epidemic of visions occurred of which there is no doubt the stories preserved to us give only a dim picture. It is certain that very quickly afterwards they became rare and stopped altogether. Paul felt that he enjoyed the last of them. Things were then stabilised; the belief in the resurrection assumed a different character. It ceased to express a mystical experience and took on the aspect of an affirmation of fact which was to be turned into a dogma.

PART TWO

The Failure of Christianity to Develop in the Framework of Judaism

CHAPTER I

The Church at Jerusalem
up to A.D. 44

SOON after Jesus' death, at the end of a few days or at most a few weeks, the belief in his resurrection and glorification was firmly held by his disciples. Thus a new religion was set up but if it was to last various conditions had to be fulfilled which did not exist at first. First, the new faith had to become aggressive, and to do that had to extend beyond the narrow confines of the little group among whom it had originated. Secondly, it had to define its position, especially in respect of the Jewish faith, which those who considered Jesus to be the Messiah sitting on the right hand of God had no idea of repudiating.

I.—THE CHURCH AT JERUSALEM ACCORDING TO THE COMPILER OF ACTS

The process by which both these conditions were realised began at Jerusalem. The book of Acts is our only source of information concerning the very early history of Christianity at Jerusalem. Although the compiler of this book only wrote as late as between 80 and 90 he had excellent sources of information. In particular he made use of a written source[1] containing missionary sermons which in the opening chapters he put into the mouth of Peter.[2] Besides this he had nothing else concerning the very early history of the church at Jerusalem except various traditions of a somewhat legendary character and some more prosaic notes describing the life of the first Christians. But he does not seem always to have understood

---

[1] If it had been an oral source it would have conformed to the postpauline thought which was current in the period when Acts was compiled. But this is not the case.

[2] It is impossible to decide if they were his actual speeches. The question is without interest. The important thing is that they express a very primitive form of thought.

them very clearly as, e.g. concerning the community of goods, which held sway among the disciples. What is more serious, he naïvely projected into his description of the early church in Jerusalem a representation of it as it existed in his own time as well as personal memories of his own concerning Greek Christianity in the Pauline communities. To extract from his story reliable information concerning the first Christians a very close criticism is therefore needed.

We must begin by recollecting the professed purpose of this history. It proposed to show how by the action of the Spirit the gospel was carried from Jerusalem to the ends of the earth. But this design was only partly realised, partly because his sources proved insufficient and partly because he never became their real master.[1] Chapter ii provides the key to the whole story, where it is narrated how, on the day of Pentecost, the promise of the Holy Spirit made by Jesus to his disciples was fulfilled, and how the disciples by the action of this Spirit were given power to be witnesses to their master. The day of Pentecost was the real birthday of the Church, because on that day it became a missionary body. At the first effort by the preaching of Peter 3,000 persons were converted. The Twelve did not have a monopoly of the Spirit, but possessed the privilege of being able to confer it by the imposition of hands.[2] The compiler of Acts considered that the apostles retained all power because they were both guardians of the Spirit and by their witness maintained the tradition which had brought the church into being. While some stories[3] appear to suggest that the assembly of the faithful possessed a right of decision, the power of initiative belonged to the Twelve whose mouthpiece was Peter.[4]

The work of conquest begun on the day of Pentecost is followed by the healing of an impotent man performed by Peter and John. The impression produced by this miracle and the explanation given

[1] Perhaps also because he intended to write a third volume, a project which he was unable to realise.

[2] Concerning this see the characteristic story of the Samaritans converted and baptised by Philip, one of the Seven, but they did not receive the Holy Spirit until Peter and John came from Jerusalem and laid their hands upon them (viii. 14-25).

[3] The story of the election of Matthias as an apostle in place of Judas (i. 15-26) and that of the institution of the ministry of the Seven (vi. 1-6) (see *E.P.*, pp. 86 ff.).

[4] Besides apostles in two passages (xi. 30 and xv. 2 and *passim* in this chapter also) mention is made of elders or presbyters. They are also named in xxi. 18 besides James. Their function cannot be defined and it must be supposed that here is a projection into the past of the function played by the college of presbyters in the churches at the end of the first century.

by Peter mark a new step forward: 5,000 persons were added to the church on this occasion. But at the same time difficulties began. The sensation caused by the healing awoke the attention of the authorities.[1] Peter and John were arrested and the next day were brought before the Sanhedrin. Not till then was it known that they had been with Jesus.[2] Their boldness made an impression on the tribunal, which only forbade them to speak in the name of Jesus before releasing them. Peter replied to this that one must obey God rather than men and that they could only speak of what they had seen and heard. In spite of this outburst they were freed and rejoined their companions with whom they prayed to God for courage to withstand the threats against them. While they prayed, the place where they were shook; they were all filled with the holy Spirit and preached the word of God with boldness (iii. 1-4, 31).

The life of the church went on without hindrance for a period the length of which the story in Acts does not allow us to determine. Suddenly, without any explanation, the high priest Annas[3] caused the apostles to be arrested and put in prison. They were brought before the Sanhedrin,[4] who on the advice of one of their members, Gamaliel, did not take extreme measures against them but only caused them to be whipped and again forbade them to speak in the name of Jesus. They took no notice of this prohibition (v. 17-42).

The hostility of the Jewish authorities, even if it was as active as the compiler of Acts makes it out to have been, did not hinder the

[1] It is surprising that the attention of the authorities had not been attracted to them by the events of Pentecost. It is a proof that in the earliest tradition the healing of the impotent man was the first appearance of the new faith outside the circle among whom it originated. This is confirmed by the pouring out of the Spirit at the end of the incident which is an earlier doublet of the story of Pentecost.

[2] This feature is also hard to reconcile with the story of Pentecost.

[3] All the manuscripts have Ἀναστὰς δὲ ὁ ἀρχιερεὺς (The high priest getting up) and the versions give this reading also, with the exception of one manuscript alone, *b.* of the old Latin version, Samuel Berger, *Un ancien texte latin des Actes des Apôtres retrouvé dans un manuscrit provenant de Perpignan, Notices et extraits des manuscrits,* t. XXXV, Ire partie) Paris, 1895, p. 194, which has 'Annas the high priest'. This is no doubt the primitive text, as Blass admits (in his edition of Acts *secundum formam quae videtur Romanam,* Leipzig, 1896). The high priest then in office was Caiaphas. Annas, his father-in-law and predecessor, had been deposed in 15. The same mistake is made in Acts iv. 6. In Luke iii. 2 Annas and Caiaphas are given as being high priests at the same time which is quite impossible.

[4] At this point (v. 21-26) is placed an incident of a miraculous deliverance. In the morning the apostles were no longer in prison but at liberty preaching in the temple. The Sanhedrin had them brought before them without violence because of their popularity. This is an embellishment on the tradition, made by the compiler of Acts who, it must be supposed, makes the Jewish authorities hostile to Christianity but not the people.

expansion of the church but its very growth created a difficulty and to overcome it measures had to be devised. For the first time mention is made of the existence of two groups within the church, the Hebrews and the Hellenists. The compiler appears to have thought that they only differed in the language which they used; the former group had never left Palestine and so spoke Hebrew or Aramaic, while the latter spoke Greek because either they or their parents belonged to the dispersion.

Friction occurred between the two groups: the Hellenists complained that their widows fared worse than the others in the distributions which were made daily to those members of the church who were in need. Peter proposed, to satisfy them, that, as the apostles had too much to do to be able to give their attention to charitable distributions, seven men should be appointed for this purpose. This suggestion was accepted: seven men, all bearing Greek names, were nominated and the apostles laid their hands on them (vi. 1-6). The compiler read into this incident the institution of the diaconate as it existed towards the end of the first century, but all we know of the seven shows that they were the leaders and preachers of the Hellenist group, while the Twelve were of the Hebrew group. This is particularly plain from what is told of one of them, Stephen, whose preaching provoked violent opposition from the Hellenistic Jews. Stephen was accused of blasphemy and stoned after a more or less regular trial. His death was followed by a persecution which the author of Acts says extended over the whole church so that everyone was forced to scatter except the apostles, who remained at Jerusalem (vi. 7-8, 3). In actual fact only the Hellenists[1] were subject to persecution; they were compelled to leave the city and become evangelists.

Two detailed stories follow telling of the activity of one of them, Philip (viii. 4-40) and of the conversion of Saul of Tarsus, who had been one of the most active agents of persecution (ix. 1-30). The author then comes back to the church in Jerusalem and states that it enjoyed peace and walked in the fear of the Lord (ix. 31). Following this comes a series of stories about Peter's mission. Two miracles are attributed to him, the healing of an impotent man at Lydda (ix. 32-35), and the resurrection to life of a woman, Tabitha-Dorcas, at Joppa (ix. 36-43).[2] Then comes the story of Cornelius (x. 1-11, 18).

[1] Guigenbert, Le Christ, p. 128.
[2] These stories offer striking analogies, the first with the healing of the impotent man at the gate of the temple, the second with the resurrection of Jairus' daughter by Jesus.

A centurion of Caesarea, who 'feared God', i.e. a man who was drawn towards Judaism, received through a vision an order to summon to his house Peter who was at Joppa. Peter also received an order in the same way to comply with this invitation. In spite of his Jewish scruples he went to the Gentile's house and preached the Gospel to those he found there assembled. As the holy Spirit fell on them while he was speaking, his remaining scruples were destroyed and he commanded them to be baptised. On his return to Jerusalem Peter became an object of criticism to certain members of the church belonging to the 'party of the circumcision',[1] because he had entered the house of a Gentile. He defended himself by recounting what had happened and the whole assembly gave glory to God for granting to Gentiles repentance unto life. The author of Acts attached capital importance to this story.[2] He considered that it explained and justified the preaching of the gospel to the Gentiles and that it attributed to the leader of the Twelve an initiative heavy with consequences although, as we shall see,[3] when others followed his example they met with lively opposition from part of the church in Jerusalem and some of its leaders.[4] The story is important because it throws light on one of the essential characteristics belonging to the conception which ruled the mind of the compiler of Acts, namely, the idea all the power of initiative in matters of importance to the church's life belonged to the church at Jerusalem, especially to the group of the Twelve who governed it.[5]

The story of the persecution ordered by Herod Agrippa I in the spring of 44[6] is the last fact of immediate concern to the church at Jerusalem to be reported in the Book of Acts.[7] It is placed in the

---

[1] Further on I shall try to determine the sense and meaning of this expression.

[2] This is shown by the fact that all the elements of the story are repeated twice by a clever arrangement.　　　　　　　[3] See pp. 177 ff.

[4] One reason sufficient in itself for doubting the historicity of this incident is that the personality of the centurion seems to have been moulded on that of the centurion at Capernaum (Matt. viii. 5 f.; Luke vii. 2 ff.); Meyer (*Urprung u. Auf.* III, pp. 141 f. Cf. Grundmann, 'Die Apostel zwischen Jerusalem und Antiochien', *Z.N.T.W.*, 1940, XXXIX, p. 129) remarks that the note in X. 1 saying that the centurion Cornelius belonged to the Italian cohort cannot be historical, as this cohort could not between 41 and 44 have been stationed at Caesarea which at that time belonged to the kingdom of Agrippa I.

[5] Another example of this can be found in the story of the foundation of the church at Antioch (xi. 19-26). This story is post-dated and transposed by making Barnabas, who appears to have been one of this church's founders, a delegate from the church at Jerusalem to that at Antioch when Jerusalem had learnt of its foundation.　　　　　[6] See pp. 465 ff. concerning this persecution.

[7] There is of course also the story of the conference at Jerusalem in chapter xv but it is post-dated and also refers not so much to the church at Jerusalem as to

middle of a story of a journey made by Barnabas and Saul to Jerusalem to bring assistance following a prediction of famine which prophets from Jerusalem who had come to Antioch made there (xi. 27-30 and xii. 24-25). After a bare mention of the martyrdom of the apostle James, son of Zebedee, most of the narrative is devoted to Peter's imprisonment and his miraculous deliverance. After he came out of prison he went to the house of Mary, mother of John Mark, where he found the brethren assembled praying for his deliverance. Then he left Jerusalem; he seems never to have returned (xii. 1-23). Before departing Peter ordered those whom he found at Mary's house to tell of his deliverance to 'James and the brethren'. As James is singled out by name he must have been from this time onwards a particularly important person in the church. This is very surprising as he is not previously mentioned.[1] In what follows James appears as the principal person and real leader of the church at Jerusalem. Not only the story of Acts but also the epistle to the Galatians show that he played an important part at the conference of 43-44.

We must now examine the material used by the author of Acts to express his own idea of the history of the church at Jerusalem. The first stages of the church's development are marked by the story of Pentecost and that of the healing of the impotent man. Originally they were parallel and not successive to each other. Their character shows that the church had no clear remembrance of the way in which the new faith emerged out of the group among whom it originated. We must therefore presume that it must have happened by easy imperceptible stages without attracting attention. This hypothesis is strongly supported by an allusion in the incident of the healing of the impotent man to an enquiry by the Jewish authorities, after they discovered that those who had been with Jesus were devoting themselves to missionary activity. In spite of this their activity must not have seemed very dangerous since, except for the brief squall raised by Herod Agrippa's persecution, they were left undisturbed.

Did the missionary activity of the Twelve extend beyond Jerusalem? It is impossible to say. The evangelisation of Samaria was the work of a Hellenist and what is told of Peter's missionary activity lacks consistency. One thing only can be retained as certain:

its relations with the Gentile Christian churches. I shall come back to this story later on. See pp. 298 ff.

[1] For further details see *E.P.*, pp. 86 ff.

Peter was remembered as a missionary.[1] But we have no means of determining whether his missionary activity preceded or followed his departure from Jerusalem.[2]

2.—WAS THE CHRISTIANITY OF THE JERUSALEM CHURCH PNEUMATICK IN CHARACTER?

While the incident of the healing of the impotent man may be a piece of genuine history, the same cannot be said of the story of Pentecost. We have only to recall its main outline. While the Twelve[3] were reunited in one place which is not specified but may be the upper room, a mighty wind was heard. Tongues of fire alighted on the head of each of them; they were filled with the holy Spirit and began to speak in foreign tongues to the great surprise of those Jews who had come to keep the feast from all parts of the diaspora. But some maintained that the apostles were the worse for drink (ii. 1-13). It is plain that the author wished to tell of an outburst of glossolalia[4] but had never met with this phenomenon in his own experience. It was not then current in his own time. The compiler only knew that it had played a big part in the church's past history but the traditions in his possession referring to it belonged to Greek Christianity. He failed to take into account the differences between this form of Christianity and that at Jerusalem and so introduced phenomena belonging to the former into his picture of the life of the church at Jerusalem. He was also compelled to form his own idea of what glossolalia were from the word itself. He understood it to be the power to express oneself in an idiom acquired by some extraordinary

[1] The Pauline epistles also show this. See 1 Cor. ix. 5.

[2] Guignebert, *Le Christ*, p. 124, thinks that if Peter ever preached outside Jerusalem, it could only have been after the dispersion of 44.

[3] The text does not say precisely 'the Twelve'. The subject of the first sentence is 'all' but the next sentence shows that in all probability it means the apostles.

[4] Glossolalia is the language of ecstasy which is often inarticulate and sometimes appears at times of exaltation and religious excitement. Concerning glossolalia in general see Flournoy, *Des Indes à la planète, Mars. Étude sur un cas de somnambulisme avec glossolalie*[3], Paris, Geneva, 1900; Lombard, *Essai d'une classification des phénomènes de glossolalie. Archives de psychologie, VII*, 1907. *De la glossolalie chez les premiers chrétiens et des phénomènes similaires*, Lausanne, Paris, 1910; Mosiman, *Das Zungenreden geschichtlich und psychologisch untersucht*. Tubingen, 1911; H. Rust, *Das Zungenreden. Eine Studie zur kritischen Religionspsychologie*, 1924. Besides the story of Pentecost there is also a question of glossolalia in two further passages of Acts (viii. 17 and xi. 44-46) which both fit in with the compiler's theory and belong to incidents of more than doubtful historicity. There is perhaps also an allusion to glossolalia in viii. 17.

means. We are therefore in the presence of a story which has been quite artificially constructed. It is not even possible to infer from it that the church at Jerusalem was acquainted with the phenomena of glossolalia.

It is a matter of prime importance to know if Palestinian Christianity was acquainted with glossolalia and pneumatism in general. These facts played such a considerable part in Greek Christianity, especially in Paul's. Their appearance gave believers the feeling that they were being invaded and possessed by a power, which was not their own but belonged to the holy Spirit, directing their words and acts.[1]

What is to be said of the appearances of the risen Christ, which belong to the beginning of Christianity at Jerusalem and must certainly be classified as phenomena of pneumatism, since they are a symptom of the excitement belonging to a new faith? Do they by themselves give Palestinian Christianity a pneumatick character?[2] We noted in the last chapter[3] that the first Christians, in particular Paul, made a very sharp distinction between the appearances of the risen Christ and ecstatic visions by attributing to the former an objectivity not to be found in the latter. While it is true that in the case of the apostle Paul, which is the only one we can follow in detail, an initial appearance gave rise to the phenomena of pneumatism, as is shown by the interpretation Paul put upon them, we have no right to generalise from this one case. For between Pauline Christianity and that at Jerusalem there was this one essential difference. Paul regarded the new faith as cut off from the cultural framework of Judaism, while Christians in Jerusalem felt it to be enshrined in the old framework so that they were not nearly so conscious of the novelty of the Gospel. Furthermore this feeling grew weaker as ensuing conversions made Jewish influences and Judaisers stronger. We are therefore led to the conclusion that while the resurrection appearances constituted phenomena pneumatick in character which gave birth to Christianity in Jerusalem, they lasted only for a limited period and do not prove that this characteristic

---

[1] Concerning this question see my article 'La conception jérusalémite de l'Église et les phénoménes de pneumatisme', in *Mélanges Franz Cumont*, Brussels, 1936, pp. 209-23; K. Kundsin, *Das Urchristentum im Lichte der Evangelienforschung*, Giessen, 1929, p. 31, had remarked already that pneumatism was a feature of Greek Christianity.

[2] Light was thrown on the organic relationship between the appearances of Christ and pneumatism particularly by Wellhausen, 'Kritische Analyse der Apostelgeschichte', *A.G.*, 1914, p. 6.   [3] See p. 43.

persisted. Only by examining the stories in Acts which refer to or appear to refer to pneumatick phenomena can we hope to arrive at more precise conclusions.

We cannot help but be struck by the artificial nature of the theory put forward by the author of Acts concerning the relationship between the Spirit and apostleship. It is exactly the reverse of the oldest which is that held by St. Paul. It can only be briefly described here.[1] The compiler of Acts considers the pouring forth of the Spirit to be a result of apostleship. Paul considers it to precede apostleship. Apostleship for him is a charisma which God has established in the church (1 Cor. xii. 28). Compared with Paul's conception that of the book of the Acts shows a perceptible narrowing down. In the latter possession of the Spirit is a privilege for a small number, while for Paul it is a general possession since, 'if any man has not the Spirit of Christ he is none of his' (Rom. viii. 9). It is clear that the book of the Acts does not attach such importance to the Spirit and apostleship as Paul does; to explain this we must suppose that it was written at a time when the phenomena of pneumatism were dying out, if they had not died out already, and when the idea of a charisma is no longer understood in its primitive sense.

The second story of the outpouring of the Spirit on the apostles (iv. 23-31), although it is more primitive than the one in chapter ii, shows a curious deviation in the conception of the charismatic gift of evangelism. The Spirit no longer speaks by the apostles or lends a persuasive power to what they say but, what is very different, only inspires them with courage to speak in the face of threats.

As for miracles of healing, if we put on one side the stories referring to Peter which seem to be purely literary inventions, apart from some general remarks of an editorial nature there is only one concrete story, that of the healing of the impotent man at the gate of the temple (iii. 1 ff.). The explanations given by Peter concerning this cure show that reference is not being made to a 'gift of healing' as is mentioned in 1 Cor. xii. 9 or to à 'virtue' which Jesus possessed and felt went out of him when the woman with an issue of blood touched the hem of his garment according to Mark v. 30, but only to an invocation which brought into play the power of Christ. It is not so much a miracle of healing as a healing through prayer.[2]

---

[1] For more details I refer the reader to *E.P.*, pp. 86 ff.

[2] We must consider the compiler responsible for the grossly materialistic conception which we meet in v. 15-16 where it is said that the sick were healed when

We notice the same sort of thing concerning visions. They abound in the second half of Acts which tells of Paul, while they are rare in the first half.[1] Only those belonging to the legendary story of Peter at the house of Cornelius can be mentioned.

The election of Matthias in place of Judas by supernatural intervention through drawing lots cannot be used to support the idea that pneumatism played any part in the history of the church at Jerusalem. It is only the revival of an old superstition. Nobody is inspired in any way since it is left entirely to God to show who must be chosen.

No inference can be drawn from the story of Ananias and Sapphira, the historicity of which is very doubtful (v. 1-11). We must recognise here the feeling of the church that it had such little power to ensure its own purity that it had to leave to God the task of excluding from its bosom those who had compromised it too deeply.[2]

3.—THE THEOLOGY OF THE CHURCH AT JERUSALEM

Why did pneumatism play such a small part in the life of Christianity at Jerusalem that for most purposes it hardly existed there at all, while in Greek Christianity its part was considerable? One reason lies in the fact that pneumatism found a more favourable soil for its development in the Greek environment than in the Judaism of the first century, which considered the age of prophecy to be closed not to be reopened until the times of the Messiah.[3] In

they were covered by Peter's shadow. That this is due to the compiler is confirmed by the fact that he recounts a detail of the same kind in reference to Paul, when he says that cures were made by means of handkerchiefs which he had used and had been impregnated with his sweat.

[1] We must naturally put on one side those belonging to persons of the Hellenistic group (Stephen, Philip, and Ananias of Damascus).

[2] The non-pneumatick character of Christianity at Jerusalem receives some support from a fact noted by Meyer (*Urspr. u. Anf.* II, p. 442, n. 5) that the Synoptics tell of no miracle performed by Jesus at Jerusalem, except for the cursing of the fig-tree (Mark xi. 12-14, 20-25; Matt. xxi. 18-20) and also from a fact noted by Lonmeyer, *Galilaea und Jerusalem*, Gottingen, 1936, p. 76, cf. p. 98, that Jamus is never represented as inspired.

[3] Ps. lxxiv. 9; Isa. lxiii. 11; Joel ii. 28 f.; Zech. xiii. 2-6; 1 Maccabees iv. 44 ff.; ix. 27; xiv. 41. Cf. J. Bonsirven, *Le Judaisme Palestinien au temps de Jésus-Christ*, Paris, 1935, I, p. 256. Guignebert (*Le monde juif vers le temps de Jésus*, p. 84, n. 2) maintains that prophecy was not completely extinct but by basing his argument on the calling of John Baptist in Luke iii. 2, he makes his contention unacceptable since it depends on a Christian document. Bousset-Gressman, *Rel. d. Jud.*, pp. 394 ff., supports the same hypothesis by more consistent arguments, in particular, by referring to a clear mention of ecstatic phenomena in the Jewish apocalypses. But allowance must be made for the fact that these descriptions are only literary imitations in character and constitute nothing more than a surviving literary form.

the Greek environment on the contrary enthusiasm in the etymological sense of the word was still alive. Popular preachers and philosophers felt that they were the mouthpieces of the gods and on that score claimed attention.[1] While Christianity in Jerusalem felt that it was a new religion, it was both theoretically bound up with Judaism and also in material contact with it. On the other hand, Paul, who moulded Greek Christianity so clearly with his own imprint, and was much more conscious of the absolute novelty of the Gospel could only find an explanation for his own radical conversion in the compelling intervention of Christ in his own life, not just at the very beginning of his career as a Christian but extending over his whole Christian life.

There are also definite theological reasons to explain why pneumatism has such a small place in the life of Palestinian Christianity. We can see them clearly if we consider the kind of theology to be found in the sermons of Peter.

In the first of these sermons, the one woven into the context of the story of Pentecost,[2] Jesus is described as a man approved of God as his envoy by the miracles wrought by his hands. Two points must be emphasised: the term 'man' which is applied to Christ and the idea that Jesus was in his miracles only an instrument used by God. Peter goes on to recall how the Jews caused his death by Gentile hands.[3] But his death was the realisation of a purpose predetermined in the will and foreknowledge of God (ii. 22-23). This idea is merely suggested without being put into precise form. Nothing is said of this divine plan or of the part which Jesus was to play in it. No reference is made to Old Testament prophecies. The idea is put forward in a very rudimentary form without any of the later developments. An affirmation of the resurrection follows without any reference to the empty tomb or to the resurrection appearances.[4] It rests on nothing but an exegetical argument and the testimony of the apostles to what can only be a spiritual experience and refers only to the act by which God has raised up Jesus (ii. 24-32). Raised now

---

[1] Reitzenstein, *Hellen. Mysterrel.*, pp. 12 ff., 19, 48 f., 99 ff.

[2] There is no need in this sermon to take into account the references to the outpouring of the Spirit. They are additions of the editor for the sake of making a link between the sermon and the story which forms its context.

[3] The conception of the respective part of the Jews and the Romans in the passion to be found here is subordinate to that existing in the gospels (see *V. de J.*, p. 392 and *Life of Jesus*, p. 464) but here it is only a detail added by the compiler. In the main it is certain that the Jews were not ignorant of the death of Jesus.

[4] See p. 62.

to the right hand of God, he has received the Spirit who had been promised and has poured him over his own disciples.[1] The house of Israel must now know that God had made this Jesus whom it had crucified Lord and Christ (ii. 33-36). The idea that Jesus only became Messiah through his exaltation to heaven is very primitive. After this declaration Peter draws the practical consequences in reply to his audience's request as to what they ought to do: 'Repent and be baptised everyone of you in the name of Jesus Christ for the remission of sins and ye shall receive the gift of the Holy Ghost'.[2] This exhortation is supported by the declaration that the Spirit is promised to the Jews and their children and to all that are afar off as many as the Lord shall call.[3] Peter exhorts them to save themselves from this untoward generation (ii. 38-40), i.e. to separate themselves from them to escape being shut out from the Kingdom of God, which is the fate hanging over them. As it is a generation and not a world which is untoward, it must follow that the sin of which they must repent has been committed by the Jewish nation through putting Jesus to death.

The second sermon which comes after the healing of the impotent man follows the same line of thought. Jesus is described in it as $\pi a\hat{\imath}s$ $\theta\epsilon o\hat{\upsilon}$. This expression has a double meaning as it can mean either 'servant' or 'child of God'. We must understand it in the first sense and so see one of the processes through which the idea of the divine sonship of Jesus is introduced and formed. The term 'servant of God' is equivalent to the term 'a man approved by God' which was used in the first sermon. This servant, Jesus, has been rejected by the Jews.[4] They have put him to death, although he was 'the prince of life', i.e. it was his function to give men the true life or to lead them to it. God has raised him up. Peter and his companions are witnesses of this (iii. 15).[5] The Jews and their leaders in putting Jesus to death acted in ignorance but by this means God has realised what he had promised by the mouth of all the prophets. Then comes, as in the first sermon, an exhortation to repentance which will assure

---

[1] This appears to be an addition of the compiler.

[2] Here also can be recognised an addition of the compiler.

[3] 'Those who are afar off' may be Jews of the diaspora or Gentiles. The former may be the meaning in the original and the latter that given to it by the compiler.

[4] The theme referring to Pilate wishing to release Jesus and the Barabbas incident is slightly developed here. But as it is derived from an elaborated form in the gospel tradition it must be accounted the work of the compiler.

[5] As in chapter ii we have no allusion here to the empty tomb or to the appearance.

forgiveness of sins. The fruits of repentance are described somewhat differently from chapter ii. Not only will the Jews be restored to their alliance with God from whom they have been separated by the wrong which they have done to Jesus but repentance will also bring positive results by allowing the times of refreshing to come from the Lord and the sending of the predestined Messiah, Jesus, who must remain in the heavens until the restitution of all things spoken of by the prophets[1] (iii. 19-21). To support this statement Peter quotes a series of passages from the Old Testament, which speak of the coming of a prophet who shall deliver the people. He refers them to the second coming of Jesus, which alone will have a messianic character. God has raised up and sent his servant for the Jews[2] to bless them and turn them from their wicked works.

This passage appears to be referring to the first coming of Jesus, as the repentance of the Jews is conceived as the condition of Jesus coming as Messiah. The thought of the sermon is not perfectly coherent. According to verse 17 the Jews put Jesus to death through ignorance and Peter appears to excuse them on that account. We cannot suppose that the compiler has touched this passage up, as, if he had done so, he would have made the thought more coherent. It seems better to explain this contradiction by the gropings of thought which is trying to express itself.

The only remark to be noted of the words put into the mouth of Peter when he is questioned by the authorities is that there is none other name except that of Jesus by which men can be saved (iv. 12).

In the speech before the Sanhedrin the same theme keeps cropping up: God has raised up Jesus, whom the Jews had put to death and has raised and exalted him to be prince and Saviour, to give Israel repentance and forgiveness of sins, i.e. to persuade them to repent so that forgiveness will be assured them. Because the resurrection shows the gravity of the wrong they have done Jesus, in itself it constitutes an appeal to repentance, and furthermore, the

---

[1] To understand how the restoration of all things, i.e. the arrival of the new age can depend on the conversion of the Jews, we must remember that the end of redemption is not only the salvation of men but also the glory of God by the establishment of his reign, which can only take effect when a messianic people is established through the repentance of the Jews or, failing that, through the conversion of the Gentiles.

[2] The text has the words 'to the Jews first' but, as nothing in what follows envisages the extension of salvation to the Gentiles, it must be supposed that the words 'at first' have been added by a compiler who was a universalist to a source which was not so.

fact that Jesus has become the Saviour guarantees the efficacy of repentance. Of this the apostles are witnesses[1] (v. 30-32).[2]

The theology of these sermons is still very simple and its form floating; yet its attitude is quite distinct. They show a functional christology which explains the person and work of Jesus by what he did not by what he was. It has two poles, one in the past in the ministry of Jesus as prophet and healer, the other in the future in the work which he will accomplish on his return as Messiah and redeemer. In the meanwhile he sits at the right hand of God but he is apparently inactive and there is nothing to show that he intervenes either in the individual's life or that of the community of those who believe in him and expect him. There is no reference in these sermons to anything comparable to the activity which according to Paul the Christ-Spirit exercises in the life of believers and of the church. Verse 33 of chapter ii, which is of an editorial character,[3] speaks of the Spirit which Christ has received and has poured over his own disciples as something which remains external to him and has no direct relationship with him.

When the fact that Christianity at Jerusalem was not pneumatick in character is placed in this theological framework the reason for it is plain and we can see it in its true character. It was a form of Christianity where the Christ played no active part.

The framework of the theology of Peter's sermons is completely Jewish and eschatological.[4] It centres round an expectation of salvation but does not possess the assurance of a salvation which has been already realised. It is true that the hope of salvation differs from that to be found in Judaism; it does not rest only on the promises of God and the words of the prophets but also on the ministry of Jesus and especially on his exaltation as Messiah at the right hand of God. Yet it always remains a hope. Men continue to wait for the coming of the Messiah who will grant forgiveness of sins[5] and will realise

[1] To the witness of the apostles is added that of the Spirit which God gives to those who obey Him. This has no organic connection with what goes before and is due to the compiler.

[2] We are not using Peter's sermon at the house of Cornelius as it does not come from the same source as the first chapters.

[3] This is one of the elements by which the sermon is adapted to the story of the outpouring of the Spirit, which is the sermon's setting. It makes an awkward division between verses 32 and 34.

[4] It does not appear to have envisaged the idea of the salvation of the Gentiles.

[5] This sin is thought to be especially that which the Jews committed by putting Jesus to death. Consciousness of sin is far from having in Peter's sermons and the book of Acts the tragic character which Paul gives to it.

the Kingdom of God. But this Messiah is known; he has lived on earth. This is a novelty for Judaism and one must be careful not to underestimate the importance of this. The expectation of his coming could assume a more concrete form and increase in tenseness through being charged with a personal loyalty. The Jewish people have committed a crime against the man who is to be the Messiah and they must repent of it to obtain forgiveness for it. The preaching of the gospel begins then to assume the character of an appeal to repentance in quite a different sense from what it had been with John Baptist and with Jesus, a fact which contributes to giving the conceptions of sin and forgiveness a central position in Christian thought.

In order to understand completely the part played by the theology in Peter's sermons in the formation of Christian doctrine we have to do more than consider it by itself. We must take account of what is essentially there without yet being formally expressed. There are present certain ideas logically leading to developments which did in fact take place later on. Such, for example, is the idea that the sufferings, death, and resurrection of Jesus were arranged by God in advance. In chapter ii. 23 f. a quotation from Psalm xvi is used as the only argument for this as the author sees in it a prediction of the resurrection. Starting from the idea that God willed the death of Jesus, one was bound to ask how it was possible to know that God willed it and why he did so. An answer to the first question came from the use of prophetic exegesis and this proved one of the factors in the development of the gospel tradition.[1] An answer to the second question was given by developing the idea of God's plan of redemption using the death of Jesus as a necessary means for the accomplishment of human salvation.

While Peter's sermons yield only a functional christology, yet we can also see in them the germ of an ontological one. The idea that after the resurrection Jesus became Messiah, the prince of life, was bound to lead to the idea that his whole nature had been transformed by the resurrection.

4.—THE LIFE OF THE CHURCH AT JERUSALEM ACCORDING TO ACTS

The book of the Acts gives some information about the life of the first Christian community in notes of a fairly general character (ii. 43-47; iv. 32-35; v. 12-16) which form, however, precious sources

---

[1] On prophetic exegesis see *J. de N.*, pp. 125 ff. and *Life of Jesus*, pp. 175 ff.

of evidence. They show us a group united in a brotherhood whose religious life had two centres, the temple where they participated in the worship of Judaism[1] and 'the house'[2] where they celebrated together the breaking of the bread, i.e. a eucharist which looked entirely to the reunion in the future with the Lord in the consummated Kingdom of God without any idea of a present blessing associated with the idea of union with Christ through the celebration of the meal.

It has been suggested that although only the word 'house' is used for the meetings of Christians, in reality they formed a synagogue (called the synagogue of the Galileans or of the Nazarenes), one of the many synagogues at Jerusalem which the Jews formed according to their particular affinities without any thought of separation.[3] But Acts xii. 12 show us that the Christians met together in the houses belonging to those of them who could accommodate them.

The author emphasises the spirit of fellowship which reigned among the members of the church and says that they had everything in common, that they sold their possessions and distributed the proceeds among them according to everyone's need (ii. 45). The same information is given with more precision in iv. 34, but the facts show this to be only an ideal picture. If the community of goods was a rule imposed on members of the church, how has the action of Barnabas been remembered who sold some land in his possession to give the price to the church? (i. 36-37).[4] Apart from the detachment shown by Christians perhaps sustained by their belief

---

[1] Acts mentions specifically participation by Christians in Jewish prayers but says nothing of their attitude towards the temple sacrifices. It does not appear to have been negative like that of the Essenes. This is true whatever may be our opinion of the historicity of the detail mentioned in Acts xxi. 23 f., where it is said that James requested Paul on his last visit to Jerusalem to associate himself with four brethren who had vowed a vow and to purify himself in front of the sacrifice. Johannes Weiss, *Urchrist.*, p. 39, remarks that if the Christians had abstained from sacrifices entirely they would not have preserved the saying of Jesus, 'When you offer sacrifice . . .' (Matt. v. 23-24).

[2] In place of the singular κατ οἶκον the Western text has the plural κατ οἶκους which appears to suggest that there were too many Christians to meet in one house. The Western recensors have taken κατ οἶκον too literally and did not understand the author's intention which was simply to distinguish between the particular assemblies of Christians and those of the Jews.

[3] e.g. the synagogues of the Libertines which I shall speak about later on, p. 170, n. 2.

[4] In the Ananias-Sapphira incident (v. 8-11) Peter expressly declares that they could preserve their goods. The case of Mary can also be recalled. She kept the ownership of her house (xiii. 12).

in the imminent end of the world and the development of a service of assistance which appears to have grown considerably [1] the only fact to be inferred from this legend is that the little Galilean colony which formed the initial nucleus of the church lived in common and had only one purse.[2]

[1] What form this service took cannot be defined in detail. In the same passage, which appears on other accounts to reflect a later organisation, daily distributions (in money or in kind?) and common meals are mentioned in succession.

[2] It was perhaps originally formed out of the sale of what they possessed in Galilee, e.g. Peter had a boat and what with difficulty they had been able to keep when they came to settle in Jerusalem. Guignebert admits this, *Le Christ*, pp. 104 f.

CHAPTER II

The Church in Jerusalem after A.D. 44
The Fate of Judaeo-Christianity

THE years 43-44 were both for the church in Jerusalem and in a more general way for the development of Christianity a period of crisis. Simultaneously, or almost simultaneously, three things happened. At first sight they appear to have taken place independently of each other but further examination shows a close bond between them. Undoubtedly they mutually reacted upon each other and are closely linked together, even though they did not spring from the same root.

We are faced with a double difficulty both when we come to study and bring to light these events and when we try to explain and interpret them and analyse their consequences. First of all, the direct information at our disposal, which at any rate does not amount to much, only allows us at the most to see these events as isolated happenings without telling us anything of their causes, their possible relationship to each other, or the repercussions which they caused either at Jerusalem or beyond.

Secondly the events at Jerusalem to be considered here had causes and effects which were both local and general.[1]

I.—WHAT HAPPENED ABOUT A.D. 44

Here are the three things which happened at Jerusalem in the years 43-44 given in their chronological order.

1. The church at Jerusalem discovered quite suddenly, it seems, that the position of the community founded at Antioch twelve years

[1] This could have been avoided by adopting another plan and following more exactly the chronological order of events but, after weighing everything up, it appeared that, although there might be some inconveniences, it would be better without dividing the study of Christianity at Jerusalem or in Greece up into pieces, to treat all the reactions resulting from the preaching of the Gospel together.

earlier was very different from its own, although it had not been ignorant of its existence without, however, ever having until then had occasion to enter into relations with it.[1] From its first beginnings Gentiles had been admitted into it without any demand being made upon them to be circumcised or to comply with the observance of the Jewish law. Christians of Jewish origin seem to have shown no anxiety or scruple at living in close religious communion with men who, despite their conversion to the gospel, remained none the less from the point of view of Jewish ritual impure Gentiles. A journey made to Antioch by some Christians from Judaea[2] disclosed an outlook in this church quite different from that which characterised the church at Jerusalem. The Jews attempted to impress upon the Gentile converts at Antioch that they could not be saved unless they had themselves circumcised according to the Mosaic custom. They met with lively opposition from Barnabas and Paul, especially the latter. As agreement was found to be impossible it was decided that delegates of the Christians at Antioch should go up to Jerusalem to discuss the question there. At Jerusalem a rupture was avoided but not without difficulty and, although the two contradictory positions could not be really reconciled and an agreement arrived at, yet it was agreed in principle that the leaders of the church at Jerusalem should recognise the validity of Paul's apostleship and preaching and extend 'hands of fellowship' to Barnabas and Paul. They were thus given complete freedom to preach the gospel to the Gentiles, without anything being fixed or determined concerning what the relations should be between Jewish and Gentile Christians when circumstances brought them together. Furthermore, it was only a personal agreement made between 'the pillars of the church' themselves.

The mass of the faithful do not appear to have followed them but to have persisted in their intransigent attitude.

2. At the beginning of 44 just before the Passover the church received a sharp attack. The Jews publicly expressed their opposition to the Christians which Herod Agrippa appeased by having James

---

[1] Although, because the divergences between the church at Jerusalem and that at Antioch were for a long time ignored, conflict was avoided, it made it all the more bitter when it eventually flared up. The divergent positions had had time to harden and grow definite.

[2] The passage Acts xv. 1, which informs us of this does not tell us if it was by chance these Jewish Christians came to Antioch or if they had been sent by the leaders of the church at Jerusalem or by some of them who had learnt or suspected that the church at Antioch did not take up the attitude towards the Gentile converts which appeared at Jerusalem to be normal. I shall return to this question later.

and, doubtless his brother John too, put to death and imprisoning Peter. He escaped early in the morning of the day when he was to be brought to trial. His escape is told as a miraculous deliverance; it must have been surrounded in mystery to protect from discovery those who had facilitated it.

Agrippa's persecution was violent but brief; it did not touch the masses of the faithful but only certain of the leaders of the church, those who belonged to the party which had met Paul with concessions, which the church in Jerusalem, to judge by his subsequent attitude, does not appear to have approved of. Did persecution cease because the deaths of James and John together with Peter's departure were sufficient to satisfy public opinion or was it because Herod's sudden death, followed by the re-establishment of the rule of procurators, brought back a situation where it was more difficult for the Jews to express in action their hostility towards the Christians? Apparently the first explanation is to be preferred, as the story in Acts shows quite clearly that Herod left Jerusalem for Caesarea, which appears to show that he had lost interest in the Christians. We may then presume that the emotions which had stirred Jewish public opinion were allayed after the conference, both because they received satisfaction and also because it was seen that, taking all things into account, the church at Jerusalem remained loyal to Judaism and made no concession to Paul's position.

Although the evidence for the conference is quite independent of that for the persecution and the compiler of Acts placed the conference at Jerusalem out of its chronological order so that the two events are not mentioned in sequence, it is not rash for us to think that they were intimately bound up together and that Jewish public opinion was stirred up against the Christians by the concessions made to Paul.

3. The third event which happened in 44 quite clearly was a result of the persecution as it is concerned with Peter's departure from Jerusalem. But it is possible that it was caused by a situation existing both before the persecution and the conference. For Peter does not seem to have returned to Jerusalem when the storm had passed, and none of the apostles are ever mentioned any more in the history of the church at Jerusalem after 44,[1] while the direction

---

[1] This does not mean that the party was not represented at Jerusalem afterwards. We shall see that representatives of the apostolic tradition emigrated from Palestine to Asia after 70.

of this church passed into the hands of James. The change therefore was not only a change of personnel caused by circumstances but also a change of government favoured by circumstances which must have been prepared for beforehand.

Harnack[1] notes that according to a tradition which appears to have been widespread,[2] the apostles, in obedience to the Lord's orders, remained twelve years in Jerusalem before scattering over the world to preach the gospel and suggested that there could be found in this a confused memory of the fact that the apostles left Jerusalem in 44. But we must rather see in this tradition an effort to harmonise two elements in the conception of apostleship to be met with in the book of the Acts, (1) the idea that the apostles directed the life of all the Christian communities from Jerusalem, and (2) the idea that the essential function of the apostles was to scatter all over the world and preach the gospel.[3] Besides this the interval from the death of Jesus to 44 is sixteen not twelve years and, even if the number twelve is supposed to be given as an approximation and for reasons of symbolism, the difference is too great for it to be a true recollection of the period during which the church at Jerusalem was under the direction of the Twelve.

Harnack [4] thinks that the direction of the church passed into the hands of James as a result of a change in its composition. Strongly Hellenistic at first, he supposes that it became Jewish through the occurrence of a large number of Jewish conversions; in this way he explains that the Seven and the Twelve successively disappeared and that finally the direction of the church came into the hands of James. There may be an element of truth in this idea but in the form in which it is presented by Harnack it cannot be retained. First of all, as we shall see later on,[5] if the Hellenists and the Seven had to leave Jerusalem at an early date, it was not owing to an internal conflict within the church, but to the violent hostility to which Jews treated them after the death of Stephen.[6] Furthermore,

---

[1] Harnack, *Mission*, II, p. 96; cf. I, p. 45.

[2] *Kerygma Petrou*, a fragment mentioned by Clement of Alexandria, *Strom.*, VI, 5-43. Apollonius, mentioned by Eusebius, *H.e.* V. 18, 4; *Acta Petri cum Simone* 3. Cf. Von Dobschutz, *Das Kerygma Petri*, Leipzig, 1893, pp. 52 ff.; Harnack, *S.B.A.*, 1912, p. 678.

[3] The importance of this idea was reinforced by the fact that from some particular date the churches which could do so strove to attribute to themselves an apostolic origin.   [4] Harnack, *Mission*, II, p. 96, n. 2.   [5] See pp. 461 ff.

[6] It may be asked, it is true, if the complaints concerning the way in which the Hellenist widows were treated in the distribution of alms, did not mask a conflict of another kind. This, however, does not appear likely; the purpose of the story is

although there are reasons for thinking that Peter did not adopt such a rigorist attitude as James on the question of Gentile converts conforming to the ritual obligations of the law and was ready in some measure to accommodate himself to circumstances, he stayed nearer to James than Paul on this question, especially in the period previous to 44 when he had not yet entered into relations with the church at Antioch.

Nevertheless there may have been some rivalry between Peter and James which ended in the disappearance of Peter and the Twelve leaving the primacy to James with the *desposunoi* [1] as his successors and doubtless as assistants as well. Their disappearance took place before 44, i.e. before the time when the question of the position of Gentiles in the church cropped up at Jerusalem. [2]

After the departure of the apostles two opposing developments took place. James and his group grew more exacting in their demands upon the Gentiles to observe the law. Peter, on the other hand, after coming to Antioch and submitting to the influence of Greek Christianity became perceptibly more liberal in his outlook towards Gentile converts. [3] A divergence may have grown up between Peter and James, even opposition, but we have no evidence for its existence in the period preceding 44.

2.—JAMES AND DYNASTIC CHRISTIANITY

Further back [4] I have remarked on the strangeness of the fact that James is only mentioned for the first time in the Acts in chapter xii. 17, in reference to Peter's departure from Jerusalem in 44,

clearly to explain the coexistence of the Twelve and the Seven, which the author has understood on the lines of the orders existing in his own time, i.e. of deacons subordinated to presbyters or episcopoi. It was therefore natural for him to treat the Seven as deacons and to come to regard the incident concerning the distribution of alms as the occasion which brought their ministry into being.

[1] This term means 'those who are connected with the Lord'. To our knowledge it was used for the first time by Julius, the African, in his 'Letter to Aristides', Eusebius, *H.e.* i. 7, 14, as a title for the members of Jesus' family.

[2] It is true that in xi. 2 it is said that, when Peter returned to Jerusalem from his visit to Cornelius, 'they of the circumcision' reproached him for entering the house of a Gentile. There could not have been at Jerusalem a party of the circumcision before 44, because it was not known that Gentiles had been admitted into the church at Antioch without obligation. In addition to this the Cornelius incident has no historical value.

[3] We do not know how long he remained at Antioch or when he left it, but it appears certain that for the whole of the latter part of his life he lived in Greek Christian churches.   [4] See p. 94, n. 1.

although he had been an important and influential person for some time past, since on Peter's departure from Jerusalem the direction of the church falls to him. We have also established the fact[1] that a group was formed at an early date, which claimed for James the distinction given to Peter by the original tradition, of having experienced the first appearance of the risen Christ, and created the phrase 'he was seen of James, then of all the apostles'. To appreciate the significance of these facts we must consider as a whole the tradition preserved by the church concerning James. There are two distinct elements in the tradition which are quite unconnected. On the one hand, there is a very clear remembrance of the fact that while Jesus was alive his brothers did not believe in his mission. Mark (iii. 21) relates how on one occasion, when the crowd were pressing so closely round Jesus to hear him that he could not even take a meal, his own people (i.e. the members of his family), tried to get hold of him by saying that he was beside himself, i.e. he was mad.[2] A little later on after the Pharisees had accused Jesus of being possessed by a devil the following incident is narrated. Someone comes to tell Jesus that his mother, his brothers, and sisters are present calling for him but he, knowing that they were doing this to prevent him from doing his work, replies, 'Who is my mother or my brethren?' And he looked round about on them which sat about him and said, 'Behold my mother and my brethren! For whosoever shall do the will of God the same is my brother, and my sister, and mother' (iii. 31-35). Besides this passage the Fourth Gospel expressly says that the brethren of Jesus did not believe in him (vii. 5).

On the other hand, a remembrance of the part played by James in the early church has been preserved. We have not only to mention the evidence of the book of Acts but we must recall the evidence of the apostle Paul, which is perceptibly earlier. In 1 Cor. xv. 7, he recalls the tradition according to which James experienced an appearance of the risen Christ. It must have been widely prevalent at the time he was writing, as he shows no doubt on the subject. In the Epistle to the Galatians (i. 19) he says that on his first visit to Jerusalem he saw no one but Peter and James, the brother of the Lord, but no other apostle.[3] Three years then, after the death of

[1] See p. 42.
[2] The whole import is clearly shown by this incident being placed next to the story of the Pharisees accusing Jesus of being possessed (iii. 22-30).
[3] Much discussion has taken place, which in many respects has proved fairly futile, whether the passage means that Paul saw no other apostle except James apart from Cephas, or whether he saw no other apostle except Cephas but that

Jesus, James was already a person of importance in the church. Paul's version of the conference at Jerusalem which he gives a little further on (ii. 1 f.) shows the importance of the part played by James in it. He figures at the side of Cephas and John—and even before them—among the pillars of the church at Jerusalem; lastly, 1 Cor. ix. 5 shows without specially naming James how much consideration the early church gave to the brethren of the Lord.

Tradition makes James the first bishop of the church at Jerusalem. According to Clement of Alexandria,[1] 'on the day after the ascension Peter, James (the son of Zebedee) and John, although they had been given more honour by the Lord than any of the others, did not lay claim to the distinction of being the first bishop of Jerusalem but James the Just was chosen'.[2] Tradition, however, does not preserve any memory of the circumstances in which James returned to the faith which he had at first rejected.[3] This suggests a comparison with the case of Paul. Acts shows him first as persecutor and then as believer, but these two phases of his life are connected together by the story of his conversion. No story of the conversion of James has survived. This can only be explained by supposing that the group who were attached to the Twelve recalled to mind and brought up against James and his party the incredulity of the brothers of Jesus during his ministry.

The early church at Jerusalem lived in the expectation of the return of the Lord, waiting for the day when he would return to

he saw James. For the latest discussion of this question see H. Koch, 'Zur Jacobus frage, Gal. i. 19', *Z.N.T.W.*, XXXIII, 1934, pp. 294-309. Koch is in favour of the latter meaning. Both are grammatically possible. If we assume the broad meaning which Paul always gives to the term 'apostles' there is nothing in any case in Gal. i. 13 to justify the arbitrary combinations which have been used to try and identify the brother of Jesus with James, the son of Alphaeus, who figures in the list of the Twelve.

[1] In a fragment of the *Hypotyposes*, quoted by Eusebius, *H.e.* ii. 1, 2; Jerome, *De viris inl.* II, supports the same tradition.

[2] In what follows he goes so far as to say that Jesus himself made James bishop of Jerusalem, Epiphanius, *Haer.* lxxviii. 7; Chrysostom, *In ep. ad Cor. hom.* xxxviii. 4, Eusebius already knew of this tradition (*H.e.* vii. 19). He reports that there was shown at Paneas, which was formerly Caesarea Philippi—'still or previously' Harnack says (*Mission*, II, p. 96, n. 1)—the seat of James 'who received from the Lord and the apostles the bishoprick of the church at Jerusalem'. The book of the Acts must have been unknown where the tradition grew up about James being the first bishop of Jerusalem.

[3] The story of the gospel of the Hebrews concerning the appearance of Jesus to James was not made up to provide this explanation since it suggests that James recognised much more explicitly than anybody else the Lord to be the historic Jesus.

reign over his own. As the disciples had to have direction while they were waiting for this, it was supposed that those most qualified to act on behalf of the Lord provisionally as his deputies or vicars were those who were most closely connected with him while he was living on earth. At first sight it is natural to suppose that the Twelve made up his spiritual family. But when the brothers of the Lord rallied to him, the idea occurred to some that those who were members of the natural family of Jesus because they were connected to him by ties of blood ought to take his place provisionally.

This introduced an element into Christianity, in one of its forms at least, which has been justly compared by Edouard Meyer to the part which the Kaliphate played in the beginnings of Islam. 'It is extremely significant', he writes, 'that in the earliest days of Christianity, as in Islam and in Mormonism, as soon as the prophet had died, a dynastic element appeared and tried to assert itself.' The brothers of Jesus are held to have a share in the same divine power as the master and themselves assert this claim.[1] We can justifiably say that a dynastic Christianity supplanted apostolic Christianity at Jerusalem in 44. This fact throws light on the meaning of the polemical point implied in the references made by Mark and John to the attitude of the brothers of Jesus towards him during his ministry.

This polemical point is not the only one to be noted in the gospel tradition. There is a point, strongly emphasised, in the *Tu es Petrus* (Matt. xvi. 17-19) and in the *Pasce oves* (John xxi. 15-17)[2] which is an adaptation of the former to a somewhat different conception of the church: Jesus here entrusts his mission and the power of legislation and government in the church to Peter and not to James.[3] Similarly the power of remitting or retaining sins is given by him to the Twelve and not to his brothers (Matt. xviii. 18; John xx. 22-23). He announces to them that in his kingdom they will sit on thrones to judge the twelve tribes of Israel (Matt. xix. 28; Luke xxii. 28-30).[4] Lastly, to them and not to the *desposunoi* is given first the promise

---

[1] Meyer, *Urspr. u. Anf.* III., p. 224. Before Meyer, Johannes Weiss (*Urchrist.*, pp. 558 ff.) had already emphasised the importance of this fact.

[2] Concerning the meaning of these two texts see *E.P.*, pp. 184 ff.

[3] Foakes, Jackson, and Lake, *Beginn.* I, p. 330, suppose that the *Tu es Petrus* was thought of at Antioch as a defence for Peter against James.

[4] Concerning this logion see my article 'La demande des premières places dans le Royaume messianique et le logion sur les trônes', *R.h.r.* 1941, CXXIII, pp. 32 ff.

and later the gift of the Holy Spirit (Luke xxiv. 49; Acts i. 8; ii. 1 ff.; John xx. 22).[1]

Lastly, the Fourth Gospel contains the incident of Jesus entrusting his mother to the beloved disciple (xix. 26-27) which we cannot help but consider to be an antidynastic point; it is written in terms which would lead the chance reader to think that the death of Jesus would leave his mother alone and deserted, without any other sons to look after her. It is possible that this incident originated in the confusion created by the fact that there was in the church at Jerusalem a woman with the name of Mary who had a son John with the surname Mark (Acts xii. 12).

None the less, it remains true that the author of this incident did not know or did not wish to recall the presence of the brothers of Jesus in the church and dissociated his mother from them.

The antidynastic points to be found in the book of the Acts and in the gospels are all the more striking since dynastic Christianity seems to have been an entirely Palestinian affair and there is no sign that it played any part in Greek Christianity. The antidynastic polemic never existed in the Greek environment in which the gospels were written. What we find in them must be considered the survival of a polemic which had been much more active in an earlier period.[2]

[1] On the contrary I do not think that the interpretation of Johannes Weiss (*Urchrist.*, p. 559) can be adopted which also finds an antidynastic point in the demand of James and John for the first places in the messianic kingdom (Mark x. 35-40; Matt. xx. 20-23). For the reasons which compel me to reject this interpretation see the *Note d'exégèse* mentioned in the preceding footnote, pp. 37 ff.

[2] The polemic between the partisans of dynastic Christianity and those of apostolic Christianity has a curious echo in the second century. Hegesippus in his story of the death of James (in Eusebius, *H.e.* ii. 23, 6) says that he only was allowed to enter into the sanctuary (i.e. into the holy of holies where only the high priest entered once a year) and that he wore vestments of linen following the custom of the priests, not of wool. He thus makes him out to have been a high priest. The same tradition is to be found in Epiphanius (*Haer.* xxix. 4; lxxviii. 13) who refers to Eusebius, Clement of Alexandria, and others and describes James as a high priest with greater precision by saying that he wore the *petalos*, the gold plate which adorned the tiara of the high priest (Exod. xxviii. 36 f.; xxix. 6; xxxix. 30-31; Lev. viii. 9). Jerome (*De viris inl.* 2) and Andrew of Crete (*Vita Jacobi*, ed. Papadopoulos Kerameus, x. 21) support the same tradition. For the attempt made by Eisler to defend the historicity of this tradition, *ΙΗΣΟΥΣ ΒΑΣΙΛΕΥΣ ΟΥ ΒΑΣΙΛΕΥΣΑΣ* Heidelburg, 1929, II, pp. 580 ff., on the subject of Eisler's system, see my observations 'Jésus et le messianisme politique. Examen de la théorie de M. Robert Eisler' (*Rev. hist.* 1929, CLII, pp. 217-67). In this tradition can be seen only a legend, the purpose of which is to glorify James. There is a very similar tradition about John which can have no greater value. The evidence for it comes in a letter of Polycartes of Ephesus to Victor of Rome (Eusebius, *H.e.* iii. 31, 3). It is there said of him that he was 'high priest, having worn the *petalos*, martyr

When we come to analyse the traditions concerning Palestinian Christianity in the period from 70 to the revolt of Barkochba, we shall find that the rights conceded to the *desposunoi* were derived at that time, not only from their common parentage with the Lord, but also from the fact, that like him they claimed to be descended from David. From this it can be legitimately inferred that the hopes for the future entertained by dynastic Christianity at this period had acquired or resumed an outlook distinctly nationalistic. Did they possess this already before 70? To attempt to answer this question we must examine the form which belief in the Davidic descent of Jesus assumed. It appeared very early on; the Apostle Paul affirms it in the most distinct manner in Romans i. 3. From the infancy narratives right up to the solemn entry of Jesus into Jerusalem the evangelists declare it in such an explicit manner that it is unnecessary to quote the texts. It seems quite clear that it depended on a dogmatic assumption rather than historical evidence. Men were not induced to believe Jesus was Messiah because they knew he was descended from David. It was rather the reverse. They thought he was descended from David because they considered him to be Messiah. It is also very doubtful if many Jewish families possessed any exact knowledge of their ancestry at the beginning of the first century of our era.[1]

The gospel tradition, however, contains a pericope, which shows a somewhat critical attitude towards the Davidic descent. It is Mark xii. 35-37 and corresponding passages.[2] Jesus has just been subjected

and doctor'. This tradition can only be explained as a replica of that concerning James being a high priest. Nevertheless it affords evidence of the persistence of opposition between the partisans of the apostles and partisans of the *desposunoi*.

[1] This difficulty was perceived in antiquity by Julius the African who, in his 'Letter to Aristides' (an important part of which is quoted by Eusebius, *H.e.* i. 7), explains that the genealogies of the families of pure Hebraic race were preserved right up to the time of Herod the Great but Herod caused them to be destroyed so that he could not be reproached for not being of the Jewish race. A few persons, however, says Julius the African, remembered their genealogies and even preserved copies of them. They lived in the towns of Nazareth and Kochaba and scoured the rest of the country to find their genealogy in the *Book of the Days* (13-14). This story shows a singular contradiction. Julius the African says, on the one hand, that genealogies were preserved up to the time of Herod and that the Lord's parents had to re-establish theirs by making enquiries throughout the whole country. At the same time he says that they made use of a *book of days* which if it existed at all must have been at a given place. This enquiry would certainly have been made before the orders of Herod as he would have first ordered the *Book of the Days* to have been destroyed. Again an enquiry made at that time by people who claim to have knowledge of their genealogy defies explanation. The whole statement is quite inconsistent and does not contain a shred of truth.

[2] I am considering it here only in the form in which Mark gives it. The texts of Matthew and Luke only differ by insignificant variations.

to a whole series of insidious questions by the Jews in an attempt to place him in an embarrassing position and extract from him some compromising answer. He turns round, takes the offensive, and asks questions of his interlocutors. Quoting from a passage in Psalm cx. 1 which was currently interpreted in a Messianic sense, he asks them how could David in speaking of Messiah call him 'Lord', if he is his son. The question assumes that the title Lord implies Messiah's superiority over David while the title son implies subordination to him. The Jews cannot reply to this question. We are not concerned to know how far in a more or less mutilated form this story preserves the words of Jesus. What we want to know is in what sense the evangelists have understood the question and whether they thought any reply possible or called for. Some commentators[1] judge this passage to be a criticism of the idea of the Davidic descent of Messiah. In any case it cannot be supposed that this was the meaning which the evangelists gave to this story since when they wrote the Davidic descent of Jesus was a well established dogma.

Before we try to see what meaning can be given to Jesus' question we must consider two passages in the Fourth Gospel. It is said in vii. 40 f. that when the people in the crowd heard Jesus teaching in Jerusalem, they said, 'He is the Christ' to which others made the objection, 'Shall Christ come out of Galilee? Hath not the scripture said, That Christ cometh of the seed of David and out of the town of Bethlehem where David was?' A little later, when Nicodemus observes to the Pharisees who were much enraged against Jesus that the Law does not allow anyone to be condemned without being heard, they reply to him, 'Art thou also of Galilee? Search and look; for out of Galilee ariseth no prophet' (vii. 52). Something similar is found in i. 45 ff. when Philip says to Nathanael, 'We have found him, of whom Moses in the law, and the prophets, did write, Jesus of Nazareth, the son of Joseph'. Nathanael replies disdainfully, 'Can there any good thing come out of Nazareth?' As soon as Nathanael allowed himself to be led to Jesus who told him that he had seen him at a distance under a fig-tree—this scene is not described and it is futile to try and picture it—he cries out, 'Rabbi, thou art the Son of God; thou art the King of Israel'. The meaning of this is quite clear. The evangelist is alluding to an

---

[1] Among others, H. J. Holtzmann, *Hand-commentur zum Neuen Testament*, Tubingen, Leipzig, 1901, I, I³, p. 166; Loisy, *Les Évangiles synoptiques, Ceffond*, 1908, II, p. 362; Bultmann, *Gesch.*, pp. 145 ff.

objection which the Jews must have been making at the time against those who affirmed the Messiahship of Jesus. He meets it with what is for him the one thing decisive, the evidence of faith. This explains why in chapter vii the objection is stated without any reply.

We can easily understand a mystic like the fourth evangelist taking up this attitude but it is more difficult to attribute it to the synoptic evangelists who appear to have been spirits of another kind from John's. When they treat this question of the Davidic descent of the Messiah they give no reply to it because they consider that the reply is obvious and can presume that their readers know the answer. We can see what the reply would be in the passage in the Epistle to the Romans concerning it. In it the person of Jesus is defined from two complementary points of view and it is plain that either of them treated in isolation would fail to provide a satisfactory definition. From the point of view of the flesh Christ is the son of David but this is a condition of Messiahship not its efficient cause. From the point of view of the Spirit or through the Spirit he is son of God. If then Jesus was only son of David he would not be Messiah, i.e. 'Lord' over David and superior to him. This is the meaning of the declaration put into the mouth of Jesus. We can see here a point directed against the *desposunoi* who, because they said that they were sons of David, believed that they had the right to a special place in the church and to direct it. The fact that this fragment found its way into the tradition received by Mark and is reproduced by him without perhaps properly understanding it appears to prove that even before 70 ideas of the Davidic descent of the Messiah were mentioned and discussed, it being maintained that it held good for Jesus but that it could not justify any pretensions the *desposunoi* might put forward. It is thus permissible for us to think that even before 70 future expectations had assumed a nationalistic character in dynastic Christianity.

Finally, a passage in the book of Acts (i. 6-8) makes a polemical point against the nationalistic bias in the expectations for the future entertained by the *desposunoi*. They may have inherited this or themselves created it. After Jesus has announced to his disciples that in a few days they will receive the baptism of the holy Spirit, they ask him if at this time he will restore the Kingdom to Israel. Jesus meets this question with a kind of demur by declaring to them that it is not for them to know the times and seasons which God has put in his own power, i.e. He has not only not revealed them but He has not yet fixed them.[1] He repeats, as if it were the only thing that mattered to the disciples, the promise of the holy Spirit. Apocalyptic preoccupations are thus opposed by the argument that concerning the time when the events of the end will happen they are in any case unpredictable. Is there anything more in this passage? The question put by the disciples shows that they considered that the baptism of the Spirit would coincide with the national restoration which they were expecting. Jesus' reply denies this coincidence, at least so far as the realisation of their hopes is concerned. The pouring out of the Spirit is quite near, but when the restoration of the nation will take place cannot be known. It would be going too far to see in Jesus' reply a rejection of the idea of a national restoration; it is not even implied. There is nothing more than a censure passed on excessive importance being attached to this idea. From this it can be inferred that dynastic Christianity had given its hopes and expectations a nationalistic colour. We are all the more justified in interpreting this passage in this way because, while the idea of a national restoration does not appear again in Acts, the compiler in mentioning views of the future makes Peter speak of 'times of refreshing and the re-establishment of all things' (iii. 20-21) and Paul of 'the hope of the resurrection of the dead' (xxiii. 6).

3.—THE MOTHER OF JESUS

Is there any relationship between the dynastic movement of the first generation of Christians and the tendency, which began to show itself a little later—only after 70, since it is not yet formed in Mark's gospel—to attribute to the mother of Jesus an important place in Christian piety? To reply to this question we will pass in review what the tradition says about Mary.

Mark's gospel only mentions her in addition to her sons and daughters in their attempt to seize Jesus and prevent him from following his work (Mark iii. 20-21, 31-35). At the time when Mark was writing it cannot be supposed that Mary played any part in the life of the church. In the gospel of the infancy told by Matthew, Mary plays quite a passive part. She is an instrument used by God and nothing more. It is very different in the story told by Luke where Mary is no longer eclipsed. In the scene of the annunciation, after she has been told of God's designs, she acquiesces in them with

[1] For the reasons why this moment is conceived as not having been fixed by God, see p. 101, n. 1.

a humility and confidence which the narrator wishes to put forward as a pattern.[1]

After the adoration of the shepherds it is said that 'Mary kept all these things and pondered them in her heart' (ii. 19).[2] We must also recall the words addressed to her by the old man, Simeon (ii. 34-35). He says that 'a sword shall pierce her heart' which seems to associate her closely with the drama of the passion. The man who conceived and wrote this gospel could not have thought that Mary remained a stranger to the Christian faith and had no place in the church. It is surprising that after this Luke does not name Mary again and only speaks of her when he recalls a speech of Jesus disavowing her by declaring that he regarded only those who do the will of God as his mother and brethren (viii. 19-21).[3] The infancy gospel is a fragment borrowed from an earlier tradition. Its Palestinian origin is

[1] I am not taking into consideration here the *Magnificat* because there is doubt concerning its attribution. While the great majority of the manuscripts introduce it with the words, 'And Mary said', the reading, 'and Elizabeth said', is found in three manuscripts of the Latin version (a.b.l*). St. Jerome attests that this reading was found in some manuscripts of his time which is confirmed by the evidence of Nicetas. It is given by some of the manuscripts of the Latin version of Irenaeus. In one of the two passages quoted by Irenaeus (iv. 7, 1) the Armenian version which seems to have been made from the Syriac and not from the Latin there are the words, 'And Elizabeth said'. The other passage where Irenaeus quotes the *Magnificat* (iii. 10, 1) is not known in the Armenian version. It looks as if Irenaeus must have attributed the *Magnificat* to Elizabeth. See E. Ter Minassiante, 'Hat Irenaeus Lc., 1, 46, Μαρία oder Ελιζάβετ gelesen?' *Z.N.T.W.*, 1906, VII, pp. 191 ff. In verse 56 after the *Magnificat* we read 'and Mary stayed with her' (Elizabeth), although if she had just spoken we should have expected 'and she stayed with Elizabeth'. Since it is difficult to suppose that Elizabeth would be substituted for Mary, the reading 'Elizabeth' apparently must be retained, unless we adopt the ingenious hypothesis of Loisy (*Ev. Syn.* I, p. 303) that the oldest text had no proper name at all. In that case, both because Elizabeth is the last subject expressed in what precedes the *Magnificat* and because of the concluding words, the *Magnificat* would have to be attributed to Elizabeth. Among the critics who have pronounced to this effect can be named: Voelter, *Die Apokalypse des Zacharias im Evangelium des Lukas, Theol. Tidschr.*, 1896, XXX, pp. 244 f.; Loisy (under the pseudonym of Jacobe), 'L'origine du Magnificat', *R.h.l.r.*, 1897, II, pp. 424-32 and *Ev. syn.*, I, pp. 304 f.; Harnack, 'Das Magnificat der Elizabeth', *S.B.A.*, 1900, pp. 538 ff. The traditional attribution has been maintained by Catholic commentators and by others, e.g. F. Spitta, 'Das Magnificat, ein Psalm der Maria und nicht der Elizabeth', *Theol. Abhandl. f.*, H.-J. Holtzmann, Tubingen, 1902, pp. 61-94. The later attribution of the poem to Mary is a symptom of the growing importance attributed to her.

[2] The same remark is made after the episode of Jesus as a boy of twelve years old in the temple.

[3] Mention must also be made of xi. 28, where after a certain woman of the company had cried out, 'Happy is the womb that bare thee and the paps which thou hast sucked', Jesus reproves her and says, 'Yea, rather, blessed are they which hear the word of God and keep it'.

plain, not only from its style and numerous reminiscences and quotations from the Old Testament to be discerned in it, but also from the fact that salvation is conceived in it as reserved for Israel. The rest of Luke's gospel gives us the tradition in the form in which it was to be found in centres of Greek Christianity (Antioch perhaps) in the last third of the first century. Christianity in this form seems either to have had less interest in the mother of Jesus than Palestinian Christianity or else the interest developed more slowly, which is confirmed by the fact that in the Pauline epistles no allusion to her person is found.[1]

Mary is never mentioned in Acts except for a reference to her in i. 14, which we suspect is due to a late addition. This permits us to doubt if she ever came to Jerusalem.

We find no mention of the mother of Jesus in the sphere of Greek Christianity until we come down to the Fourth Gospel.[2] What can be noticed in it concerning her shows quite a complex position which reveals divergent preoccupations and gives the impression of not being completely stabilised. John does not speak of the mother of Jesus in vii. 5, where he mentions the incredulousness of the brothers of Jesus. In the story of the miracle of Cana (ii. 1-11) Mary is beside Jesus: she believes in his mission and does not doubt his power to perform miracles, but the way in which Jesus receives her suggestion and denies her any right to give him advice shows the author's preoccupation to affirm Jesus' complete independence of her. We can justifiably ask ourselves if we must not see here a protest against a particular conception of Mary's part. In addition to this, the fourth evangelist differing from the synoptics places Mary among the women stationed not in the presence of the cross at a distance but directly at its foot and he relates how Jesus before he died entrusted her to the beloved disciple (xix. 25-27). This scene presumes that up to then Mary had lived with her son and that his death was going to leave her deserted. It is hardly possible to harmonise this conception with the description of the ministry of Jesus given by both the synoptics and the fourth evangelist but it is none the less characteristic of it.

[1] The fact that in Gal. iv. 4 Paul says that Christ was born of a woman cannot be counted an allusion to Mary. This phrase, which is stating the natural conditions of human birth, shows that Paul did not take into account the personality of the mother of Jesus.

[2] The interest which the Fourth Gospel takes in the person of Mary, although limited in other respects, is all the more striking considering that the theory of the incarnation of the Logos tends to liberate the person of Jesus from its human ties.

Very important differences therefore exist between the tradition concerning the mother of Jesus and that concerning his brethren. Both of them, as was quite natural, sprung up on Palestinian soil but greater interest was shown in the brethren than in the mother and made itself much more strongly felt. The latter interest extended also much more rapidly to Greek Christianity at the cost, however, of being integrated into it in a less durable form.

They do not possess the same nature. The interest in the brethren was first and foremost of a practical nature conditioned by the part which they played in the church and by the rights and authority which they claimed to possess. The interest in Mary was never practical: at first it was purely theoretical and later became devotional as well. We have no reliable evidence that Mary was ever a member of the church and played any part in it. Attention was called to her by the appearance and development of the idea of the supernatural birth. At first she is represented as a purely passive instrument; then gradually, as Luke shows us, she became more like an active than a passive instrument because she of her own volition acquiesced in God's designs. Latei on, when the idea of Mary's perpetual virginity sprung from that of the supernatural birth, she came be be considered, not only the instrument of the incarnation but a collaborator in effecting it. But scarcely can even the beginning of this development be traced in the period with which we are concerned.[1] In reality therefore there is no connection between the tradition concerning the brethren of the Lord, which reflects historical facts, and that concerning Mary, which belongs to the realm of theology. We must therefore conclude that Christianity at Jerusalem was not interested in her.

4.—THE DOMESTIC HISTORY OF THE CHURCH AT JERUSALEM AFTER 44

We know very little of the domestic history of the church at Jerusalem during the period when it was under the government of James, which lasted from 44 to the eve of the Jewish War. While this may partly be due to the fact that the period was not marked by any striking events, there is certainly also another reason. The book

---

[1] Apart from certain surviving cults of feminine divinities the development of the cult of Mary was helped forward by a devotional need of popular piety for an object nearer and more accessible than God and Christ and for a being with the attribute of feminine and maternal tenderness who might be worshipped.

which would explain why the Jewish authorities considered it a of the Acts which is our only source for this period was written at a time when Jewish Christianity, which is properly called Ebionitism, of which dynastic Christianity was a continuation, had ceased to count in the life of the church. There is no doubt that traditions and memories were preserved of what happened at Jerusalem between 44 and 70 but, as there was hardly any contact between Jerusalem and Greek Christianity, the Christian community where the book of the Acts was written did not know of them. The little that this book has to tell us concerning the life of the church at Jerusalem in the period which we are considering, refers to its dealings with the apostle Paul. The author is very discreet in what he says on this point, because he thought it inopportune to recall with precision memories of past conflicts which had lost their point and did not fit in with the idealised picture of the early days in the life of the church which he wished to draw.

As for the organisation of the church at Jerusalem after 44, such information as we have, together with the tradition which makes James the first bishop of Jerusalem, provides the impression that James possessed such personal power that, even if he had not had the formal title, he was the first representative of monarchical episcopacy as it came to be established and accepted in the whole church in the first half of the second century. In addition to him presbyters are mentioned (Acts xv. 2 and several times in this chapter, and xxi. 18) but in such a way that we can form no idea of their attributes and functions. The author may be only projecting into the past the part played by the council of elders in the Hellenistic communities at the end of the first century but there is a certain fascination in the idea that the elders at Jerusalem were the other members of the family of Jesus. Since James exercised power because he was a brother of the Lord it is difficult to think that the other *desposunoi* had no particular position of authority. It can therefore be presumed that a kind of council gathered round James which, however, his strong personality prevented from being anything but a decorative and honorary body.

Concerning the material position of the church we have no direct information. From the fact that it could live in peace it may be inferred that it must not have been numerically very important,[1]

---

[1] It goes without saying that neither Acts ii. 31 not Acts iv. 4, must be taken literally which mention respectively the conversion of 3,000 and 5,000 persons at once, nor Acts xxi. 20 which speaks of thousands of Jews who believed.

negligible force. From the fact that Paul organised a collection for the benefit of the church at Jerusalem at the request of its leaders and came to bring the proceeds in 58, it may be concluded that the church at Jerusalem was in financial and economic straits.[1]

Only one text makes us think that the churches of Judaea suffered at the hands of the Jews after 44. Writing in 51 to the Thessalonians and speaking of the tribulations through which their church had passed, Paul draws a parallel between them and what the churches of Judaea had had to bear at the hands of the Jews (1 Thess. ii. 14). Some questions arise concerning this text which makes it less positive than at first sight it seems. What precise evidence did Paul possess concerning what was happening in Judaea, while he was in Macedonia and then in Greece? Paul is speaking of tribulations which the Thessalonians had suffered in the past; he is primarily thinking therefore of what had taken place when their church was founded. It may well be that he is thinking similarly of Judaea and has in mind the persecution which had compelled the Hellenists to leave Jerusalem, i.e. an event which at the time when he was writing had happened twenty years previously.

A more positive reason for doubting if the peace of the church was disturbed between 44 and 70 is the fact that, when Paul came for the last time to Jerusalem, the flood of Jewish hatred which was released against him at that time did not rebound in any way on the Christians at Jerusalem.

Concerning the internal disposition and attitude of the church towards Gentile converts, there is no doubt that from 44 to 58 the church not only maintained its hostility but increased it. To convince oneself of this it is only necessary to compare the much warmer reception which Paul encountered at Jerusalem in 43-44 with that which he found in 58, when James thought it necessary to take precautionary measures before he came into touch with the faithful.[2] The attitude of the church at Jerusalem developed in this way partly through the influence of James but also probably because conversions of Jews which were thus facilitated made the church all the more firmly fixed in this outlook.[3]

---

[1] Although the collection was something more than an offering of material assistance. See *E.P.*, pp. 262 ff.

[2] I shall return to this point in greater detail. See pp. 318 f.

[3] Confirmation of the anti-Pauline attitude of the church at Jerusalem is furnished by the fact that it is to her and her leaders to whom the opponents of Paul in Galatia and Greece refer. It is not certain if they were their agents but they certainly reflected their ideas. See pp. 309 ff.

Although the church at Jerusalem between 44 and 58 became more anti-Pauline, this does not mean, however, that its legalism was so rigorous that it wished to impose the whole of the Jewish law on Gentile converts. As we shall see later on,[1] the story in Acts xv combines two things: a tradition concerning the conference at Jerusalem and another tradition concerning a decision taken by the church at Jerusalem at a date, which cannot be accurately given but which is certainly later than the conference, when definite rules were drawn up on the relationship between Christians of Jewish origin and Gentile converts. These rules were purely negative and what was demanded from the Gentiles was to abstain from what was particularly abominable in the eyes of Jews, the eating of things sacrificed to idols, from things strangled, and from blood, i.e. from eating flesh of animals which had not been ritually slaughtered, and lastly from marriages within the degree prohibited by the Jewish law.[2] Such a decision showed a *modus vivendi* rather than any real concessions. Jews would have been able to agree to this. It shows, therefore, a very trifling deviation from Judaism.

5.—THE DEATH OF JAMES

It is not as paradoxical as it might seem at first to see the only bloody deed which is recorded in the history of the church at Jerusalem between 44 and 70, i.e. the execution of James the Just in 62, to be the result of a reconciliation between the church and Judaism. Josephus actually explains his death as due to the jealousy of the high priest, which presumes that James' influence extended beyond the bounds of the Christian community. On the death of James we have two independent sources of evidence, which are difficult to reconcile with each other. The earliest is that of Josephus[3] in Book xx. 9, 1 of *Jewish Antiquities*. This is what is told there.[4]

' The younger Annas, who, as we said, had received the High Priesthood,[5] was bold in temperament and remarkably bold in daring. He

[1] See p. 303.

[2] For my justification of this interpretation of what has been called 'the decree of Jerusalem' see p. 307. The text of it is not the same in the Eastern recension as in the Western recension of the book of the Acts.

[3] Meyer (*Urspr. u. Anf.* III, p. 74) thinks that Josephus was a witness of James' death.

[4] Translator's note. I am reproducing the English translation of the passage from Eusebius, *H.e.* ii. 23, 21-24, by Kirksopp Lake in Loeb Translations, Eusebius, London, 1926.

[5] In 62 after the death of Festus and before the arrival of his successor Albinus.

followed the sect of the Sadducees, who are cruel in their judgements beyond all the Jews, as we have already explained.[1] Thus his character led Annas to think that he had a suitable opportunity through the fact that Festus was dead and Albinus still on the way. He summoned a council of the Sanhedrin, brought before it the brother of Jesus, the so-called Christ[2] whose name was James, and some others, on the accusation of breaking the law and delivered them to be stoned. But all who were reputed the most reasonable of the citizens and strict observers of the law were angered at this and sent secretly to the King,[3] begging him to write to Annas to give up doing such things, for they said that he had not acted rightly from the beginning. And some of them also went to meet Albinus as he journeyed from Alexandria, and explained that it was illegal for Annas to assemble the council without his permission. Albinus was influenced by what was said and wrote angrily to Annas threatening him with penalties, and for this reason King Agrippa deprived him of the High Priesthood when he had held it for three months and appointed Jesus, the son of Dammarus.'

The authenticity of this text has been much discussed. Eusebius[4] knew it in the form in which we have it; but Origen three times[5] speaks of the destruction of Jerusalem as a punishment inflicted on the Jewish people for the murder of James and each time quotes Josephus as his authority. Several critics, however, consider that he only had before him a text which had been edited by a Christian. Schurer[6] thinks little reliance can be placed on the text. Zahn[7] declares it to be unauthentic. But as Origen does not say from what book he borrows his story, it may well be that he is quoting from memory and that, as Edouard Meyer[8] suggests, he is combining the story of James' death with the stories of John Baptist's death and the defeat inflicted by Aretas on Herod Antipas, which Jewish

[1] In *A. j.* xiii. 10, 6, Josephus says that the Pharisees were more indulgent than the Sadducees in applying the law. In xviii. 1, 4, he says that, when the Sadducees arrive at the magistrates' courts, in spite of themselves they are obliged to conform to the practice of the Pharisees, because otherwise the people would not support them.

[2] This is consonant with the passage xviii. 3. 3, which is certainly unauthentic in the form in which we have it and must have replaced an authentic passage. *V. de J.*, pp. 58 ff. and *Life of Jesus*, pp. 78 ff.

[3] Herod Agrippa II, to whom belonged in theory the power of nominating and deposing the high priests, but who in fact acted only in accordance with the wishes of the procurator. [4] Eusebius, *H.e.* ii. 23, 21-24.

[5] Origen, *C. Celsum*, i. 47; ii. 13; *Comm. in Matt.*, x. 17.

[6] Schurer, *Gesch.* I, p. 581.

[7] Zahn, *Bruder und Vetter Jesu, Forsch.*, 1900, VI, pp. 301 ff. Zahn shows himself very severe on Josephus' evidence because of the confidence with which that of Hegesippus inspires him. [8] Meyer, *Urspr. u. Anf.* III, p. 73, n. 2 (to p. 74).

opinion judged to be a divine punishment for the murder of the prophet[1] and also with the story of the assassination of Jonathan, which God punished by stirring up the Romans against the Jews.[2] Juster sees[3] in the story of James' death nothing but a Christian fiction. He compares Josephus' story with John xviii. 31, where the Jews remind Pilate that they do not possess the right to put anyone to death, and notices that Albinus, when he came to take possession of his office, could not help but know the limits of the Sanhedrin's powers. He thinks, therefore, that the text of Josephus in speaking of a Sanhedrin without full power is expressing a Christian fiction. But if the Sanhedrin retained in principle under the rule of the procurators all its rights, why does Josephus never mention its intervention except in the trial of James? Besides it would have been contrary to all the principles of Roman policy and the most elementary prudence not to control and limit the Sanhedrin's powers.[4] If the story of James' death in the *Jewish Antiquities* had come from a Christian pen, would it have contradicted the story told by Hegesippus, which seems to have been very popular in Christian circles?[5] There is no reason to question its authenticity.[6]

It seems difficult to suppose that Roman rule in Judaea fell completely into abeyance during the absence of a procurator. It may well be that the complaint lodged against Annas was that he had not waited for the arrival of Festus' successor and had been satisfied to have the assent of some subordinate official. This would afford a better explanation as to why Albinus exacted only a moderate penalty from Annas.

The statement that the enemies of the high priest went for an audience to Albinus is open to suspicion, both because it serves as a double to the story of an audience with Agrippa when he is requested to ask the high priest to be more moderate, and also because it is impossible that Albinus could not have had the most precise knowledge of the extent of his powers. If Annas had committed a flagrant illegality he would have met with something more than bare censure. Every-

---

[1] *A.j.* xviii. 5, 2.   [2] *A.j.* xx. 8, 5.

[3] Juster, *Les Juifs dans l'Empire romain*, Paris, 1914, II, pp. 149 ff.

[4] Buchsel, 'Die Blutgerichtbarkeit des Synhedrins', *Z.N.T.W.*, 1931, XXX, pp. 202 ff. Cf. *V. de J.*, pp. 406 ff. and *Life of Jesus*, pp. 451 ff. Leitzmann's reply to Buchsel ('Bemerkungen zum Prozess Jesu', *Z.N.T.W.*, 1932, XXXI, pp. 78-84). Cf. 'Der Prozess Jesu', *S.B.A.*, 1931, XIV, pp. 9 f. (partly in proof). I do not consider this decisive. See my observations on this subject, 'A propos du procès de Jésus', *Z.N.T.W.*, 1932, XXXI, pp. 299-301.   [5] Zahn, *Forsch.*, VI, pp. 254 ff.

[6] Its authenticity is admitted by Salomon Reinach in *Oeuvres de Flavius Josephe*, IV, p. 283, n. 3.

thing is much clearer if we allow the sentence referring to a visit by the Jews to Albinus to be the clumsy gloss of an editor, who believed that the high priest had abused his power and thought that he could not have remained in office without the consent of the procurator.

When then Josephus' story is reduced to its essential elements, it tells, as Lietzmann says,[1] of a blow struck by force against James by the high priest, which was made possible by the absence of a procurator and was condemned by public opinion, which shows that the high priest must have acted from personal motives rather than anything else.

We do not know what accusations were brought against James and those accused with him. Josephus was not badly informed, neither did he not wish to speak of the affair because it concerned Christianity; if this had been so, he simply would have passed over the whole affair in silence. Probably he only considered the incident worth reporting because it resulted in the deposition of the high priest. The accusation that he had violated the law was evidently only a pretext, as the protest of the stricter legalists proves. How too could James have been accused of violating the law, when a tradition which was so widely scattered that it cannot be dismissed as pure fiction held him to be a rigorous legalist? If the real motive behind the trial was an attack on the Christian faith,[2] then it must be supposed that public opinion was still favourable to the Christians in 62 and would not allow, if it could help it, Christians to be disturbed. But it appears more probable that Ananias and James were rivals in influence. The high priest whose preoccupations were political rather than religious would have been jealous of the popularity enjoyed by James. This is confirmed by the fact that those who perished with him do not appear to have been Christians; otherwise the church at Jerusalem which was not rich in martyrs would have preserved their memory.

The second story of James' death in our possession, that of Hegesippus,[3] is called by Edouard Meyer[4] 'fantastic legend devoid

---

[1] Leitzmann, *Z.N.T.W.*, 1932, XXXI, p. 80.

[2] As Leitzmann thinks among others (*H.*, I, p. 189) who considers that he finds justification for his opinion in the fact that James was stoned which was the punishment for blasphemers.

[3] Preserved by Eusebius, *H.e.* ii. 23. Concerning Hegesippus see Zahn, *Forsch.* VI, pp. 250 ff.; A. Puech, *Histoire de la Littérature grecque chrétienne*, Paris, 1928, II, pp. 265-269. Hegesippus came originally from Palestine and must have been very nearly a contemporary of Irenaeus. He came to Rome round about 164 and wrote his *Memoirs* between 174 and 189.

[4] Meyer, *Urspr. u. Anf.* III, p. 73, n. 2; Schwartz ('zur Eusebius Kirchengeschichte, I. Das Martyrium des Jakobus des Gerechten', *Z.N.T.W.*, 1903, IV, pp. 48-61) had already criticised him with the same severity.

of any historical value'. Zahn on the other hand[1] considers it of so much value that he sacrifices the evidence of Josephus for it. Lastly, Eisler[2] has attempted the impossible by trying to harmonise two stories which, beyond the fact that they both record the death of James, have nothing in common.

This is how Eusebius. tells the story of the martyrdom of James. The Jews made him appear before the people and summoned him to deny his faith in the Christ. Far from giving way James proudly confessed it. The Jews then taking advantage of the fact that Festus had just died could act on their own initiative without the consent of a procurator and so put James to death (ii. 23, 2). After giving this summary, in which he combines details borrowed from Josephus with others which come from Hegesippus, Eusebius recalls that he had previously (ii. 1, 4-5) quoted a passage from the seventh book of the *Hypotyposes* of Clement of Alexandria according to which 'James the Just was hurled from the pinnacle of the temple and beaten with a fuller's stick until he died'. He then quotes an important passage from the fifth book of the *Memoirs* of Hegesippus concerning the death of James. This is the text given: [3]

The charge of the Church passed to James the brother of the Lord, together with the Apostles. He was called the 'Just' by all men from the Lord's time to ours, since many are called James, but he was holy from his mother's womb. He drank no wine or strong drink, nor did he eat flesh; no razor went upon his head; he did not anoint himself with oil, and he did not go to the baths. *He alone was allowed to enter the sanctuary*, for he did not wear wool but linen, and he used to enter alone into the temple, and be found kneeling and praying for forgiveness for the people, so that his knees grew hard like a camel's *because of his worship of God, kneeling and asking forgiveness for the people*. So from his excessive righteousness he was called the Just and Oblias, that is in Greek Rampart of the people *and righteousness, as the prophets declare concerning him*. Thus some of the seven sects among the people, who were described before by me (in the *Commentaries*), *inquired of him what was the gate of Jesus, and he said that he was the Saviour. Owing to this some believed that Jesus was the Christ. The sects mentioned above* did not believe either in resurrection or in one who shall come to reward each according to his deeds, but as many believed did so because of James. Now, since *even* many *of the rulers* believed, there was a tumult *of the Jews and the Scribes and Pharisees*

[1] Zahn, *Forsch.*, VI, pp. 232 ff.; Dom. Leclercq, 'Jacques le Mineur', *D.A.C.L. VII*, col. 2110, implies the same criticism when he judges the story of Hegesippus to be 'without doubt historical'.　　[2] Eisler, *ΙΗΣΟΥΣ*, II, pp. 580 ff.
[3] ii. 23, 4-18, English trans. Loeb. Those passages which Schwartz, *Z.N.T.W.*, 1903, IV, pp. 48-61, finds to be interpolations are printed in italics.

saying that the whole people was in danger of looking for Jesus as the Christ. So they assembled and said to James, '*We beseech you to restrain the people since they are straying after Jesus as though he were the Messiah. We beseech you to persuade concerning Jesus all who come for the day of the Passover*, for all to obey you. For we and the whole people testify to you that you are righteous and do not respect persons. *So do you persuade the crowd not to err concerning Jesus, for the whole people and we obey you.* Therefore stand on the battlement of the temple that you may be clearly visible on high, and that your words may be audible to all the people, for because of the Passover all the tribes, with the Gentiles also, have come together.' So the Scribes and Pharisees *mentioned before* made James stand on the battlement of the temple, and they cried out to him and said, 'Oh, just one, to whom we all owe obedience, since the people are straying after Jesus who was crucified, tell us what is the gate of Jesus?' And he answered with a loud voice, 'Why do you ask me concerning the Son of Man? He is sitting in heaven on the right hand of the great power, and he will come on the clouds of heaven.' And many were convinced and confessed at the testimony of James, and said, 'Hosanna to the Son of David', Then again the same *Scribes and Pharisees* said to one another, 'We did wrong to provide Jesus with such testimony, but let us go up and throw him down that they may be afraid and not believe him'. And they cried out saying, 'Oh, oh, even the just one erred.' And they fulfilled the Scripture written in Isaiah, 'Let us take the just man for he is unprofitable to us. Yet they shall eat the fruit of their works.' So they went up and threw down the Just, and *they said to one another, 'Let us stone James the Just', and they began to stone him* since the fall had not killed him, *but he turned and knelt saying, 'I beseech thee, O Lord, God and Father, forgive them, for they know not what they do'. And while they were thus stoning him one of the priests of the sons of Rechab, the son of Rechabim, to whom Jeremiah the prophet bore witness, cried out saying, 'Stop! What are you doing? The Just is praying for you.'* And a certain man among them, one of the laundrymen, took the club with which he used to beat out the clothes, and hit the Just on the head, and so he suffered martyrdom. *And they buried him on the spot by the temple, and his grave stone still remains by the temple. He became a true witness both to Jews and Greeks that Jesus is the Christ,* and at once Vespasian began to besiege them.

At the end of his story Eusebius insists that intelligent people thought that James' death was the cause of the city's siege which immediately followed[1] and then he adds that Josephus also tells of the death of James in Book XX of the *Jewish Antiquities* and quotes

---

[1] II, 23, 19. He supports his opinion by a quotation from Josephus but gives no indication as to its origin and seems to have borrowed it from Origen.

his story. Eusebius, who had emphasised Clement's agreement with Hegesippus[1] says nothing about the plain contradictions between Josephus and Hegesippus, although they could not have escaped his notice. At the least he could not have been completely convinced of the accuracy of one of the stories quoted by him.

Schwartz[2] reveals a series of incoherences, repetitions, and contradictions in the narrative of Hegesippus from which he infers that Eusebius had used an interpolated edition of Hegesippus' *Memoirs*.[3] But the story has to be treated with the greatest reserve even after these additions have been excised. What is said of James as high priest is quite impossible. An execution in the temple and a tomb on the very spot where it was performed are so utterly improbable that neither the subtle ingenuity of Zahn[4] or of Eisler[5] can attenuate it. Even the substance of the story is open to suspicion. How could the enemies of James, being well aware of his ascendancy over the people and his attachment to the Christian faith, hope that he would speak in the tenor desired by them and from a tribune which to say the least of it was peculiar?[6] James' declaration about the Son of Man on the right hand of the Great Power recalls too closely the words of Jesus before the Sanhedrin for it to be considered as anything except of literary origin.[7] We are here in the presence of an edifying legend, where the author has had no regard for verisimilitude or for chronology.[8]

[1] This agreement proves nothing, as Clement has merely given a summary of Hegesippus' story.

[2] See further back p. 127, n. 2.   Joh. Weiss *Urchrist.*, 554, n. 1 (on p. 555 also) notes the lack of coherence in Hegesippus' story which he explains by supposing that he made use of an older tale and embroidered it.

[3] Ad Schlatter, *Der Chronograph aus dem zehnten Jahre Antonins*, Leipzig, 1894, pp. 76 ff., attempted to extract a coherent story by making a distinction between elements from a reliable source and clumsy emendations made by Hegesippus. His system is ingenious but arbitrary. Martin Dibelius, *Der Jakobusbrief*, Meyer, XV[7], Gottingen, 1921, p. 13, no. 3, also recognises that there must have been some disorder in Hegesippus' text.

[4] Zahn (*Forsch.* CI, pp. 233 f.) suggests that they made James climb up on to one of the porticoes which surrounded the temple court and threw him out of the temple from the side facing the torrent of the Cedron.

[5] Eisler (*IHΣOYΣ*, II, p. 538) thinks that the text is speaking not of a tomb but a commemorative plaque.

[6] Schwartz, *Z.N.T.W.*, IV, 1903, p. 57, remarks that the pinnacle of the temple is a common feature of both the story of Hegesippus and the story of Jesus' temptation.

[7] James' prayer for his executioners calls for the same remark as it is an echo of that of Stephen (Acts vii. 60).

[8] Dibelius (*Jakbr.*, p. 14) sees in the story of Hegesippus the earliest typical example of a Christian legend of martyrdom. G. Kittel ('Die Stellung des Jakobus

The two stories of Josephus and Hegesippus contradict each other on all essential points. First the date, Josephus gives 62, Hegesippus immediately before the siege.[1] According to Josephus there was a trial; Hegesippus mentions nothing like a trial.[2] According to Josephus James was put to death with others; Hegesippus says that he died alone.

We have to choose between the two stories. Apart from the absurdities in the story of Hegesippus that of Josephus has the advantage of being connected with a historical fact, the deposition of Annas, and also it is given a precise chronological date, the interval between Festus's death and Albinus' arrival. Josephus' story cannot be accounted for as a Christian fiction, neither can it be explained as a literary creation.[3] On the other hand, it is easy to show that Hegesippus' story forms a legend. The religious imagination loves to paint the death of a venerated personage in heroic colours. It makes a martyr of James, although he was not brought to his death on account of his faith, and those who died with him were not Christians.[4]

From the fact that James appears to have been a dangerous rival to Annas it may be concluded that the church occupied a position of importance at Jerusalem in 62. Since it was only James who was seized by the high priest, James' personal influence not the church's must have alarmed him.

The story which Eusebius tells[5] following Hegesippus of James being replaced by Simeon, son of Cleopas and the Lord's cousin,[6] as bishop of Jerusalem, needs to be treated with great caution. Eusebius introduces it by the formula, 'It is related', which shows that he himself will not guarantee the veracity of what he is going to tell. After James' death and the capture of Jerusalem which followed

---

zum Judentum und Heidenchristentum', Z.N.T.W., 1931, XXX, p. 145) also denies it any historical value.

[1] Zahn (Forsch. VI, pp. 234-235) says 66 but this date does not agree with the story of Hegesippus.

[2] Eisler (IHΣOYΣ, II, p. 586) tries to harmonise the two versions by the idea that the Sanhedrin, being prevented by the Rome authorities from acting in broad daylight, held a secret session and then in order to execute the sentence feigned a popular outbreak to which the Roman authorities could more easily close their eyes than to a regular execution.

[3] The authenticity of the text of Josephus is admitted by Dibelius, Jahrb., p. 13, and by G. Kittel, Z.N.T.W., 1931, XXX, p. 146.

[4] There is no doubt that because James' companions in punishment were not Christians the church's tradition has passed them by in silence or forgotten about them.   [5] Eusebius, H.e. iii. 11, 1.

[6] He says, 'cousin of the Lord, of whom it is related'.

it, the apostles[1] met together with his kinsfolk according to the flesh
of whom the majority were still living to nominate a successor to
James. Simeon was chosen because of his kinship to the Lord.[2]
This tradition was constructed to establish a regular succession of
bishops of Jerusalem. It could only have happened at a time when
James had died and the legend of the siege of Jerusalem being a
punishment for his being put to death had had time to mature.

6.—THE EXODUS OF THE CHURCH IN 70

We have no direct source of information concerning the church's
attitude in the troubled period which preceded the siege of Jerusalem,[3] although there was an open struggle between the peace
party which had at its head men like Gorion, the son of Joseph the
Pharisee, Simon son of Gamaliel, the former high priests, Annas
and Jesus, and the party of resistance to the death led by John of
Gischala. By terror and assassination the Zealots came to dominate
the city. Annas and Jesus were assassinated; another leader of
their party, Zacharias, the son of Baruch, was brought to trial and
just after he had been acquitted was stabbed by his accusers.[4] The
anachronistic allusion of the gospel tradition to this murder, describing it as the last crime of the Jews after which God would bring
on this generation all the innocent blood which had been spilt since
that of Abel the Just (Matt. xxiii. 35; Luke xi. 51),[5] shows that the
Christians at Jerusalem were not on the side of the Zealots. Schurer[6]
makes the murder of Zacharias the date of the exodus of the Christian
community who in obedience to a revelation left Jerusalem to take
refuge at Pella.[7] Eusebius says that it took place 'before the war'.

---

[1] It is unnecessary to emphasise the extreme unlikelihood of the presence of
the apostles in Jerusalem after 70 or even in 62.

[2] Elsewhere (*H.e.* iv. 22, 4) Eusebius quotes a sentence from Hegesippus which
says that 'after the martyrdom of James the Just, Simeon, son of Cleopas, the Lord's
uncle, was made second bishop of Jerusalem, being preferred over all the others
because he was the Lord's cousin'.

[3] See Schurer, *Gesch.* I, pp. 617 ff.; Lietzmann, *H.* I, pp. 189 ff.

[4] Josephus, *G.j.* iv. 5, 4.

[5] Loisy, *Ev. Sym.* II, p. 386; Wellhausen, *Einleitung in die drei ersten Evangelien*[2],
Berlin, 1911, pp. 118-123; *Das Evangelium Matthaei*, Berlin, 1904, pp. 119-121; *Das
Evangelium Lucae*, Berlin, 1904, p. 62; Meyer, *Urspr. u. Anf.* I, pp. 234 ff.; Reitzen-
stein, 'Das mandaische Buch des Herrn des Grosse', *S.H.A.*, 1919, XII, pp. 41 ff.;
Bultmann, *Gesch.*, p. 120. Bultmann, however, thinks that the text might be before
70.   [6] Schurer, *Gesch.* I, p. 619.

[7] Eusebius. *H.e.* iii. 5, 3. On the possibility of identifying this prophecy with
the synoptic apocalypse see *V. de J.*, pp. 406 ff. and *Life of Jesus*, p. 428. Cf. Epi-

The revolt broke out in 66 when the rupture with the Romans came to a head, but the exodus could only have taken place in the spring of 68 when Vespasian prepared to lay siege to Jerusalem[1] or in that of 70 when the city was effectively besieged by Titus. The latter interpretation recommends itself from the fact that the chapter in which Eusebius relates the exodus of the Christian community begins by mentioning the arrival of Vespasian which took place on 1st July 69.

The exodus of the Christians does not prove that they had detached themselves from the national aspirations of the Jews and that they were indifferent to the fate of Jerusalem;[2] it only proves that they neither shared the sentiments and hopes of the Zealots nor yielded to the tyranny with which they were threatening Jerusalem.[3]

7.—THE TRADITIONS CONCERNING THE DESPOSUNOI

Although the traditions collected by Eusebius in the *Notebooks* of Hegesippus concerning the *desposunoi* must be used with extreme caution on matters of detail, they help us to gain a good idea of the character of Palestinian Christianity after 70 and to some extent of it previous to that. They show that its views of the future were nationalistic in character and reveal the preponderating role played by the *desposunoi* in it due as much to their kinship with Jesus as to their Davidic descent.

phanius, *Haer.* xxix. 7; *De mensuris et ponderibus*, 15. Hoennicke (*Das Judenchristentum im ersten und zweiten Jahrhunderten*, Berlin, 1908, p. 104) thinks that here Eusebius depends on Hegesippus or Julius the African. This is improbable because he does not quote these two authors as he usually does. Eusebius does not speak only of the departure of the Christians of Jerusalem but of the Christians of Judaea. Such a general exodus seems to have been hardly probable. Cf. Knopf, *Nachap. Z.*, p. 11. Schwartz (ed. of the *Histoire ecclésiastique* in the Berlin collection of the Fathers, Leipzig, 1903-9, III, pp. ccxxvi f.) throws doubt upon the historicity of the flight to Pella for reasons which do not appear to be decisive.

[1] Upon hearing of Nero's death he resolved to keep all his forces to support his chances of becoming emperor.

[2] It would not be quite the same to admit with Meyer (*Urspr. u. Anf.* III, p. 584) and Lietzmann (*H.* I, p. 189), that James' murder helped the Christians to resolve to leave Jerusalem. It can hardly be supposed with any plausibility that the two facts harmonise both on account of the interval of time between them and also because the man who put James to death was the high priest Annas who subsequently was one of the leaders of the peace party.

[3] Harnack (*Mission*, II, p. 97) remarks that the exodus of the community was only possible because it must not have been very numerous.

According to Eusebius[1] from the time of Vespasian onwards the Roman authorities had been searching for the descendants of David to put them to death. In another place[2] Eusebius says that Domitian gave orders for all those who claimed to be of the race of David to be put to death. He mentions in this connection the two grandchildren of Jude, the Lord's brother.[3] The story which he tells about them comes from two sources: (1) an early tradition according to which they were denounced by heretics, and (2) the story of Hegesippus which contains the rest of the story. After the accused had been brought before the Emperor[4] they confessed that they were of the lineage of David. They possessed a small farm worth 9,000 denarii which they cultivated themselves, as their hard hands showed and on which they paid tax. They also declared that Christ's kingdom would not be terrestrial but altogether heavenly. Domitian recognised them to be simple and inoffensive people and had them set free.[5] A combination of two traditions can be perceived in this story, one concerning measures which were taken against men who would eventually have been able to embody the national aspirations of the Jews and another concerning a persecution which heretics had initiated against the church. To connect these two elements together somehow or other Eusebius says that after Domitian perceived that Jude's grandchildren were inoffensive persons and released them he gave orders for the persecution to cease. All this lacks consistency. The story may well have originated in nothing else but the tradition that Vespasian took measures against David's descendants and the reflection that the *desposunoi* must have been victims of them. We can only guess the reasons why this story was placed in the reign of Domitian and not Vespasian. The only fact which can be retained, therefore, is the importance of the part played in the church by the *desposunoi*. This is confirmed by another

[1] Eusebius, *H.e.* iii. 12, following Hegesippus. It is not said here that the *desposunoi* were searched and disturbed at that time. Meyer (*Urspr. u. Anf.* I, p. 73, n. 2) concludes that the idea of the Davidic descent of the family of Jesus did not yet exist. According to him it only appeared between Vespasian and Domitian with Matthew's and Luke's gospels. It is, however, plainly mentioned in Rom. i. 3 in such a form that it seems likely to have been the same in both Hellenistic and Palestinian Christianity. It may well be that Hegesippus has become confused and attributes measures to Domitian which elsewhere he puts down to Vespasian or perhaps that the leaders of the Jerusalem community escaped under Vespasian because they were still at Pella.　　　　[2] Eusebius, *H.e.* iii. 19, 20.
[3] According to a fragment of Hegesippus (De Boor, *Neue Fragmente des Papias, Hegesippus und Pierius in bisher unbekannten Excerpten aus der Kirchengeschichte des Philippus Sidetes*, Leipzig, 1888, p. 169), they were called Zoker and Jacob.
[4] Eusebius, *H.e.* iii. 20, 6.　　　　[5] Eusebius, *H.e.* iii. 32, 6.

passage from Hegesippus,[1] according to which the grandsons of
Jude, after their liberation, directed the churches until the time
of Trajan, both because they were martyrs and because they
belonged to the Lord's family. In another place,[2] quoting the text
of Hegesippus word for word, Eusebius employs the expression,
'they directed the whole church'. Tradition here makes a transposition and amplification. Because the grandsons of Jude at the
most directed small Palestine communities it made them the leaders
of the whole church.

Government by Jude's grandsons is said to have lasted until
Trajan's time, although according to Hegesippus himself Simeon's
episcopate, the immediate successor of James, lasted the same
length of time. There were then several divergent traditions or,
as is more probable, men who only shared in the church's government within the framework of a plurinominal episcopacy were
thought of as monarchical bishops. Eusebius,[3] following Hegesippus,
gives the following account of the martyrdom of Simeon, who at
the time was 120 years old. Denounced by heretics, both because
he was a Christian and also because he was a descendant of David,
he was tortured for several days. Atticus, a man of consular rank,
with other witnesses of his sufferings were astonished at his resistance. At the end he was crucified.[4] Simeon's great age is not
the only difficulty contained in this story. The conjunction of two
motives for the accusation, Christianity and Davidic descent, must
also be added. The tortures suffered by the old man before he
died are better explained on the hypothesis that he was accused
of Christianity than on the supposition that he was being suppressed as an eventual claimant to a throne. The political motive
may well have been an additional cause because of the importance attached to the relationship of the leaders of the church to
Jesus and David.

There may be some connection between the idea that heretics
denounced the bishop Simeon and Jude's grandchildren and the
story told by Hegesippus[5] concerning a certain Thebutis. Disappointed at not being chosen bishop on James' death, he began to
corrupt the church which up to then had remained pure, i.e. pure

---

[1] Eusebius, *H.e.* iii. 20, 6.   [2] Eusebius, *H.e.* iii. 20, 6.
[3] Eusebius, *H.e.* iii. 32, 1-6.
[4] Eusebius adds, always following Hegesippus, that subsequently Simeon's
accusers were in their turn put to death also because they were descendants of
David.   [5] Eusebius, *H.e.* iv. 22, 4-6.

from heresy, by spreading abroad the errors of the seven Jewish heresies.[1] The genealogy of heresies mentioned by Hegesippus in reference to this is pure phantasmagoria; from his story one thing can be retained, i.e. the preference given to the *desposunoi* in the election of those called to direct the churches stirred up opposition, which, however, it is certain did not altogether arise from disappointed ambitions. We have no means of proving if the rivals of the *desposunoi* went to such extremes as to denounce them to the Roman authorities. In any case it is best to be reserved on this point, since ecclesiastical tradition always likes to paint heretics in the blackest colours and does not hesitate to attribute to them deeds which call for the greatest censure. It may be that rivalry between the *desposunoi* and their enemies only served to attract the attention of the Roman authorities. The fact that the heretics who had denounced Simeon were themselves put to death favours this hypothesis.

8.—THE CHURCH AT JERUSALEM AFTER 70

Eusebius[2] gives a list of the bishops of Jerusalem which is divided into two parts. The first part contains fifteen names from James to Judas in Hadrian's time. After 134, when Hadrian forbade all Jews to live in Aelia Capitolina, which had been built on the site of the ruins of Jerusalem,[3] the composition of the church changed and it had uncircumcised bishops, whose names form the second part of the list. The first was Marcus.

Eusebius lists fifteen bishops up to 134. This is a large number, especially if we take into consideration that the second, Simeon, died in Trajan's reign. There would then have been thirteen bishops in succession to him within a period of twenty years, which allows for each bishop an average episcopate of eighteen months. This is very short. Zahn[4] thinks that the names of bishops of neighbouring

---

[1] Zeiller (in Lebreton and Zeiller, *L'Église primitive* [Fliche and Martin, *Histoire de l'Église*, I, Paris, 1935], p. 394) sees in Thebutis an extreme Judaiser. This is pure conjecture.

[2] Eusebius, *H.e.* iv. 5. This list is found with some variants in Epiphanius, *Haer.* lxvi, 21 f.

[3] According to Epiphanius (*Haer.* xxix. 7) most of the Christians of Jewish race who were compelled to leave Jerusalem emigrated to Transjordania, while some of them went into the other regions of Syria.

[4] Zahn, *Forsch.* VI, p. 300. Johannes Weiss (*Urchrist.*, pp. 561 f.) gives the same explanation.

churches have slipped into the list.[1] Harnack[2] suggests that monarchical episcopacy did not exist at Jerusalem before 134 and reckons the list of bishops to be a list of presbyters. It may be that names of *desposunoi* have also slipped in.

From the time when the Christian community took refuge at Pella, the mist which covers the history of Palestinian Christianity grows still thicker. It will be found that for two or three centuries or a little longer Jewish Christianity remained only as the sect of Ebionitism[3] and vegetated, surviving by itself before disappearing, 'obscurely and miserably', as Mgr. Duchesne says.[4] Edouard Meyer for his part says, 'The church of Jerusalem on leaving Jerusalem for Pella ceased to have any significance and played no further part'.[5] Ebionitism ceased to be a factor in the development of Christianity and for this reason fell into an oblivion, which would have been still more profound, if the fragments which survived to the fourth century had not tickled the curiosity of writers like St. Jerome and Epiphanius who have recorded a few details about it.

Most of today's scholars[6] suppose that, when peace was re-established, the Christians who had fled to Pella—or at any rate part of them—returned and settled in the ruins of the city. Mgr. Duchesne, however, thinks that in the sixty years which elapsed from the capture of Jerusalem to the revolt of Barkochba there was nothing at Jerusalem except the camp of the tenth legion *Fretensis*.[7]

Josephus says[8]:

Caesar ordered the whole city and the temple to be razed to the ground, leaving only the loftiest of the towers, Phasael, Hippicus, and Mariamne, and the portion of the wall enclosing the city on the west: the latter as an

---

[1] Mgr. Duchesne (*H.a.* I, pp. 120 f.) who does not allow that the Christians returned to Jerusalem after 70 thinks that it gives the names of bishops of Pella and other colonies of the Jerusalem church. Yet he thinks (p. 119)—what would be more difficult to contradict, cf. Schurer, *Gesch.* I, pp. 685 f.—that at the time of the revolt of Barkochba the Jews occupied the ruins of the holy city for a period.

[2] Harnack, *G.a.L.* II. 1, pp. 221 and *Mission*, II, p. 96. This is also Schlatter's opinion (*Die Kirche Jerusalems vom Jahre* 70-120), Gutersloh, 1898, p. 30. Schwartz (ed. of the *Histoire ecclesiastique*, III, p. ccxxvi) and Meyer (*Urspr. u. Anf.* III, p. 585, n. 1) consider the list to be without value.

[3] Harnack (*Dgsch.*, I[4], p. 330) asks if the term 'Jewish Christianity' should be kept for Ebionitism after 70. But Ebionitism is not a late appearance. It is the survival of a type of Christianity which existed well before 70.

[4] Duchesne, *H.a.* I, p. 127.   [5] Meyer, *Urspr. u. Anf.* III, p. 585.

[6] Harnack, *Mission*, II, p. 97; Knopf, *Nachap. Z.*, p. 12; Hoennicke, *Judenchristentum*, pp. 105 ff. and especially Schlatter, *Die Tage Trajans und Hadrians*, Gutersloh, 1897; *Die Kirche Jerusalems von* 70-130, Gutersloh, 1898.

[7] Duchesne, *H.a.* I, p. 118.

[8] Josephus, *G.j.* vii. 1, 1. [I am quoting from Loeb Eng. trans.]

encampment for the garrison that was to remain,[1] and the towers to indicate to posterity the nature of the city and of the strong defences which had yet yielded to Roman prowess. All the rest of the wall encompassing the city was so completely levelled to the ground as to leave future visitors to the spot no ground for believing that it had ever been inhabited.

This passage from Josephus is not as decisive evidence as Mgr. Duchesne thinks; he mentions the order to destroy the city but only tells of the destruction of the ramparts. The statement that it was no longer possible to guess that Jerusalem had ever been an inhabited place need not be taken literally. The three towers remaining with part of the rampart sufficed to show that it had been a large city. The very importance of the Roman garrison left at Jerusalem must have required a large number of people dwelling round the Roman camp. Something remained or was reconstructed which was occupied by the insurgents in the course of the revolt of Barkochba[2] and had to be recaptured by the Romans.[3] Eusebius seems to be nearer the truth than Josephus when he speaks of half the city being destroyed by Titus and the remainder by Hadrian.[4] He states[5] that right up to the time when the city was besieged by Hadrian there was at Jerusalem a very large Christian church. Epiphanius reports[6] that when Hadrian entered Jerusalem, there was among the city's ruins a synagogue and on Mount Zion a little church. These pieces of evidence cannot be put on one side, although the description of the church as 'very large' must be treated with reserve, unless it must be understood in a moral and not a material sense, as must also Epiphanius' identification of the church of Zion with the upper room where the apostles were reunited after the ascension.[7]

There is evidence for the presence of Jewish Christians in various districts bordering on Palestine.[8] It may be that they came

[1] Josephus, G.j. vii. 1, 2, says that attached to the tenth legion were some squadrons of cavalry and cohorts of infantry.

[2] Schurer, Gesch. I, pp. 685 ff.   [3] Schurer, Gesch. I, p. 691.

[4] Eusebius, Dem. evang. vi. 18, 10. See also other texts which have been reunited together by Schurer, Gesch. I, p. 692, n. 126.   [5] Eusebius, Dem. evang. iii. 5, 10.

[6] Epiphanius, De mensuris et ponderibus, xiv. 1. Cf. Haer. xxix. 7.

[7] For the traditions referring to this church see Dom Leclerq, 'Cenacle', D.A.C.L., II, cols. 3032-3037.

[8] Epiphanius (Haer. xxix. 7. Cf. xviii. 1; xxx. 2, 18; xi. 1) names the Basanitides and the Batanaea as places where Jewish Christians were to be found in his time, whom he supposes to be descended from the refugees at Pella but the fact that Ebionites lived in those regions in the fourth century does not prove that they had been there since the end of the first.

to them for the same or similar reasons as those which compelled the Christians of Jerusalem to take refuge at Pella or perhaps they gradually left the country which belonged to the Jews or on account of the hostility which they met in it.

Apart from Symmachos, the translator of the Old Testament, the Ebionites do not seem to have produced any writer. According to Eusebius,[1] Origen held from a certain Juliana who had inherited them from Symmachos some notes written by him on the Scriptures and *Notebooks* in which he had discussed Matthew's gospel, doubtless to prove that the gospel belonging to his own sect was superior.

As for Hegesippus, in spite of his Palestinian origin and the peculiar interest taken by him in the church at Jerusalem, he belongs to the great church. Otherwise, Eusebius[2] would not have said that he had collected in the five books of his *Notebooks* 'the pure tradition of the apostolic preaching'. He tells us nothing about the peculiar ideas of the Ebionites.

9.—EBIONITISM

Their ideas then are only accessible through the writers of the great church who only had a superficial knowledge of them and were not really interested in their theology. The first one to mention them is Justin Martyr.[3] He distinguishes two groups among them. He refuses to describe as Christians those of them who claimed to impose the Jewish law on all believers and considers that they were excluded from salvation. On the other hand, those who did not deny concessions to believers who do not observe the law were saved. Justin also knows that some of them see in Christ simply a man, the offspring of men, ἄνθρωπον ἐξ ἀνθρώπων γενόμενον (48, 4), i.e. they deny the pre-existence and supernatural birth, believing that Jesus has become Messiah by election and choice (ἄνθρωπον γεγονέναι αὐτὸν καὶ κατ' ἐκλογὴν κεχρίσται καὶ Χριστὸν γεγονέναι) (49, 1), which Tryphon observes agrees with the Jewish conception of the Messiah.[4]

---

[1] Eusebius, *H.e.* vi. 17.   [2] Eusebius, *H.e.* iii. 8, 1.   [3] Justin, *Dial.* xlvii-xlix.

[4] In speaking of those who attribute to Christ a wholly human origin in chapter xlviii, Justin describes them as being of our *genos*. Some early commentators, like Neander, because they did not wish to think that Justin permitted heretics to be Christians corrected 'our' to 'your'. This correction would be permissible if the word genos could be understood to mean 'race'. The result would be that as Justin in *Dial.* lxxxii speaks of 'false doctors among us' it must be supposed that he does not consider heretics to be outside the church.

Irenaeus adds to this information[1] that those who profess this christology are called Ebionites. Like Justin he says that they deny the virgin birth and affirm the necessity of observing the law. He claims that they only use Matthew's gospel[2] and reject Paul's epistles. Origen[3] gives almost the same information; he considers that the Ebionites differ very little from Jews.[4] He remarks, however, that some of them believe in the supernatural birth.[5] Eusebius[6] distinguishes two groups, who were both equally attached to the law, but one of them denied the supernatural birth while the other affirmed it but rejected completely the idea of pre-existence, which, says Eusebius, makes them as impious as the other group. Both consider Paul an apostate and reject his epistles.[7] Eusebius adds that they use the gospel of the Hebrews only and think little of the other gospels and that they observe the Sabbath and also keep Sunday like other Christians in memory of the Saviour's resurrection.[8]

With Epiphanius and St. Jerome[9] we come to the time when information becomes more circumstantial but more confused as well as more difficult to interpret. They do not refer to anything more than fragments of groups of Jewish Christians who had survived up to the fourth century. According to Epiphanius they were quite strongly influenced by sects of Jewish heretics.

What matters most is to grasp the relationship between Ebionitism and the Christianity of the first generation. The reality of this

---

[1] Irenaeus, *Adv. Haer.* i, 26, 2; iii. 11, 7; 21, 1; iv. 33; v. 1, 3.

[2] In reality a gospel akin to Matthew's.

[3] Origen, *C. Celsum*, ii. 1; v. 61, 65; *De principiis*, iv. 22; *Hom. in Genesim*, iii. 5; *in Jerem.* xvii. 12; *in Matt.* 16, 12; 17, 12.

[4] Ἰουδαῖοι καὶ οἱ ὀλίγῳ διαφέροντες αὐτῶν Ἐβιωναῖοι Comm. *in Mt.*, xi, 12 (Ed. Benz-Klostergmann, Leipzig, 1935, p. 52).

[5] Origen, *C. Celsum*, v. 61.   [6] Eusebius, *H.e.* iii. 27.

[7] Among the Ebionites appeared the story reported by Epiphanius (*Haer.* xxx. 16, 25) according to whom Paul's enemies hawked about a story that he was a Greek by birth and had himself circumcised out of love for the high-priest's daughter but because she repelled him he harried the Jewish people with his hatred.

[8] We do not think that the pseudo-clementine writings and their *grundschrift* must be classified with the sources concerning early Ebionitism in spite of the hypothesis developed on this subject, particularly by O. Cullman, *Le problème littéraire et historique du romain pseudo-clémentin*, Paris, 1930 (see my observations on his book in *Revue de philologie*, LXIX, 1933, pp. 105-109). Schwartz, 'Unzeitgemasse Beobachtungen zu den Clementinen', *Z.N.T.W.*, 1932, XXXI, pp. 151-199) seems to me to have presented with force the reasons there are for considering the Pseudo-clementine writings to be a romance without any historical value direct or indirect.

[9] Epiphanius, *Haer.* xviii. 1; xxix. 7; xxx. 2-18, 20, 34; xl. 1; Jerome, *Ep. ad August.*, 112, 13. Jerome's evidence is important for what it says about the Jewish Christian gospels concerning which there is a certain confusion elsewhere. See on this subject my book *J.-B.*, Paris, 1928, pp. 163 ff.

relationship is first of all established by the name or names belonging to the group. In the second and third centuries the name is Ebionites[1] to which in the fourth century was added that of Nazarenes. The word *ebionim* (the poor) is a biblical Hebrew word and not Aramaic; it expresses a religious ideal and does not refer to indigent people but to those who feel detached from the world.[2] The community at Jerusalem called itself by this name[3] and the Jewish Christians kept it because it meant for them a link between themselves and the primitive church, although it is quite certain that the Greek Christians never possessed it. The very fact that this name was not given to Christians outside Jerusalem shows as James Weiss says that it was 'a relic of a very early period'.[4] Nothing shows better the distance separating the Ebionites from the great church than this simple fact. What they considered to be a name of which they could be proud became in the eyes of the Greek Fathers a mark of heresy and in those of Eusebius a sign of intellectual poverty.

The term Nazarene used by Epiphanius to designate a particular group of Jewish Christians has quite a different origin.[5] The heresy of the Nazarenes (Acts xxiv. 5) seems to have been the earliest designation given to Christianity by the Jews. The Greek church was led by the way in which its christology developed to prefer to retain the name 'Christians', which was first used by strangers to the faith (Acts xi. 26). Christians from all quarters appropriated a name which originally was used as a term of abuse. Those who treated of heresy forgot the origin and meaning of the terms, Ebionites and Nazarenes, and indulged in venturesome etymology. The terms formed a link between Palestinian primitive Christianity

[1] Certain Fathers (Hippolytus, *Philosophoumena*, vii. 34; x. 22; Tertullian, *De praescr. haer.*, 33; *De carne Christi*, ii; Epiphanius, *Haer.* xxx. 1) supposed the word Ebionites to be derived from the founder of the sect, Ebion, who had published his ideas among the refugees at Pella. Almost alone among recent critics, Hilgenfeld, *Judentum und Judenchristentum*, Leipzig, 1886, p. 101) still believes in the existence of Ebion. For a discussion of this question see Hoennicke, *Judenchristentum*, pp. 229 f. Eusebius (*H.e.* iii. 27) explains the name Ebionites as due to the poverty of the thought of these heretics. 'Their name', he says, 'well suits the poverty of their thought.'

[2] Cf. *Ps. Sal*, 5, 2; 10, 7; 16, 2. Cf. Wellhausen, *Ev. Mt.*, p. 14. Johannes Weiss, *Urchrist.*, p. 569. A. Causse, *Les pauvres d'Israel*, Strasbourg, Paris, 1922.

[3] Gal. ii. 10; Rom. xv. 26. Perhaps also Minucius Felix, *Octavius*, 36; Holl, *Ges. Aufs.* II, p. 60; Schwartz, *Z.N.T.W.*, 1932, XXXI, p. 190.

[4] Johannes Weiss, *Urchrist.*, p. 569. Weiss notes with reason that the fact that the fathers give divergent explanations of the name, Ebionites, proves the archaic character of this designation.

[5] See *J. de N.*, pp. 64 ff., concerning the relationship which Epiphanius falsely established between the Christian Nazarenes and a Jewish sect of Nazarenes.

and the sects of Jewish Christians. This is shown by the heresies themselves of which the Fathers accuse the Ebionites. The Ebionite christology which denies the supernatural birth is a survival from an early stage in the development of christology belonging to the time when the earliest version of the story of the baptism took shape.[1] It is not so much that the Ebionites differed from the great church as that the thought of the great church underwent development if not transformation.[2]

Something must be said of the attitude of the Ebionites towards the law. They did not innovate[3] but remained fixed in the attitude taken up at the first by the church at Jerusalem against Paul and the men of Antioch. The Fathers have been just as inaccurate in saying that the Ebionites rejected Paul's epistles. The truth is, that on this also, they remained fixed in the attitude common to all before these epistles existed or before they had yet been collected together into a *corpus*.

They lived out of touch with the great church and even in opposition to it being unable to accept the idea that the law had been superseded. They kept on using a gospel which they had composed themselves or had adapted for themselves, and had no knowledge of the gospel canon of the Greek church.

The Ebionites were not innovators but traditionalists who refused to subscribe to the hellenisation of Christianity; their group was a fragment of primitive Christianity in an air-tight case, protected completely from the influence of Greek Christianity.[4] This does not mean that it underwent no change at all. Left behind on the edge of Palestine, in regions where Jewish sects of a heretical and more or less synchretistic nature flourished, it submitted to

[1] See my book, *J.-B.*, pp. 139 ff. [2] Johannes Weiss, *Urchrist.*, p. 570.
[3] This is not quite true if we agree with various writers: Schlatter, *Dir Kirche Jerusalems vom Jahre* 70-130, pp. 11 f.; Knopf, *Nachap. Z.*, pp. 16 ff., that the Ebionites returned to rabbinic discussion. According to various Talmudic texts (the texts and translation of these are to be found in Strack, *Jesus die Haeretiker und die Christen nach den aeltisten judischen Angaben*, Leipzig, 1910, pp. 4 ff., 23 ff.* R. Eliezer was accused of heresy and trying to find an explanation for this accusation remembers that, when he was discussing a question of the law (Is it right to use money from prostitution for building latrines for the high priest?), he had made the mistake of expressing pleasure at a maxim which Jacob of Cephas Sekhanja, a Christian, said came from Jesus and of giving it his approval. Schurer (*Gesch.* II, p. 372) thinks this story a legend. It would be only wise to accept it with reserve. If it is historically true it would be of interest, especially on the point of view felt by Jews towards Christians. To give it the meaning attributed to it by Schlatter and Knopf we should have to prove that Jacob of Cephas Sekhanja did not quote the maxim solely in order to embarrass Eliezer.
[4] Johannes Weiss, *Urchrist*, pp. 595 ff.; Meyer, *Urspr. u. Anf.* III, p. 595; Schwartz, *Z.N.T.W.*, 1932, XXXI, pp. 191 ff.

their influence all the more easily because its doctrine was rudimentary and lacked form and structure.

In the surviving fragments of the gospels of the Jewish Christians
when they are compared with the canonical gospels and in particular
with Matthew's, we usually find a few variants which have no
significance[1] or disclose an attachment to James, the Lord's brother.[2]
The gospel of the Hebrews, however, contains a version of the story
of the baptism, which has some interesting peculiarities.[3] When
Jesus comes out of the water, the whole fount of the Holy Spirit
(*fons omnis spiritus sancti*) comes down and rests upon him, saying
to him, 'My Son, I have been waiting for your coming in all the
prophets in order that I might dwell in you. You are my first-
begotten Son[4] who reigns for ever.' The conception contained here
has been influenced by gnosticism; there is no trace of sonship or
adoption. The Holy Spirit is a Power who seeks to incarnate himself
and succeeds in doing so in Jesus.[5]

In the gospel of the Ebionites[6] John Baptist instead of eating
locusts (ἀκρίδες) and wild honey (Mark i. 3, 4)[7] eats 'wild honey,
which tastes like a fritter in oil'. The assonance of the words ἀκρίδες
and ἐγκρίς shows that the author wishes to touch up the traditional
text by altering it as little as possible to adapt it to an ascetic vege-
tarianism.[8] Elchasaism[9] is interesting as showing the importance

[1] Such an example is the fragment of the gospel of the Hebrews preserved by
St. Jerome (*in Mt.* xii. 13) where the man with the withered hand, whose healing
is told by Matthew (xii. 9-13) accosts Jesus and says to him, 'I was a mason, I
gained my livelihood with my hands, I pray you, Jesus, make me whole, in order
that I may not be put to the shame of begging for my bread'.

[2] e.g. the story of the appearance of the risen Jesus to James. See p. 43.

[3] We know of it through Jerome, (*in Jes.* 11, 2).

[4] The term *filius primogenitus* must not be interpreted to imply a supernatural
birth. The word spirit (*ruah*) is feminine in the Semitic languages. Cf. the fragment
of the gospel of the Hebrews preserved by Origen (*in Joh.*, t. ii. 12), 'My mother,
the holy Spirit, took me by one of my hairs and transported me to the great mountain, Tabor'.   [5] Johannes Weiss, *Urchrist.*, p. 575.

[6] The text is preserved by Epiphanius, *Haer.* xxx. 13.

[7] A detail missing in Luke and in Tatian's *Diatessaron*, ii, possibly for similar
reasons to those which have determined the transposition to be noticed in the
gospel of the Nazarenes.

[8] How wide this tendency was in primitive Christianity is shown by Grégoire,
Les sauterelles de saint Jean-Baptiste, Byzantion, 1929-30, V, pp. 109-128.

[9] The principal sources of information for Elchasai and elchasaism are: Hippolytus, *Philosophoumena*, ix. 13-17; x. 29 and Epiphanius, *Haer.* xix, xxx, liii. The
prophet's activity began a little before 101; his book was drawn up in 116. It was
brought to Rome about 200 by Alcibiades of Apamaea who tried to propagate the
sect and was opposed by Hippolytus. Concerning elchasaism see H. Waitz, in
Hennecke, *Neut. Apokr.*, pp. 422 ff.; Lietzmann, *H.* I, pp. 197 ff.

which people who had become Ebionites attached to gnostic speculations. Elchasai lived in Transjordania. He claimed to have had a vision in which Christ appeared to him looking like a giant with the Spirit by his side having the figure of a woman. He considers Christ to be the Great King, the son of the Great God, and to have had a series of successive incarnations. Elchasai observed the Jewish law but rejected animal sacrifices. He taught that as the world was shortly coming to an end God was offering to sinners a last chance of salvation by means of a second baptism together with the invocation of the seven elements.[1] In addition to this he taught cosmological speculations from which he deduced a distinction between lucky and unlucky days.

Ebionitism and Elchasaism have certain elements in common but a synchretistic gnosticism had influenced the latter more strongly than the former.[2] According to Epiphanius and St. Jerome all that the Ebionites did in the way of writing was to reproduce and combine what they received from previous writers. There is no doubt that Jewish Christianity was dead and finished soon after the fourth century without having brought any appreciable influence to bear on the development of Christianity after the fall of Jerusalem. Some of its adherents were compelled in the end to join neighbouring catholic communities while the rest were left to be absorbed in synchretistic sects.

Ebionitism is a religion which missed its way because it never succeeded in making the principle which gave birth to it independent and strong. Why did it fail to do so? Because, unlike Paulinism, it never possessed the conviction that the Christ was present and active. It considered Jesus to be the teacher who was to return to save and reign in the new world which he was to establish. As soon as the conviction that the world was soon coming to an end disappeared, it[3] could only consider him a master of wisdom, while even in this respect his importance was perceptibly dwarfed by the absolute authority which the Jewish law continued to exercise. In these circumstances Christianity ran the risk of being nothing more than a theme for cosmological speculation, as is shown by Elchasai

[1] The sky, water, the holy spirits, the angels of prayer, oil, salt and earth.
[2] According to Lietzmann (*H*. I, p. 197) elchasaism had no influence on Jewish Christianity and is only interesting as a symptom of the influence of gnosticism in Syria. According to Meyer, on the other hand (*Urspr. u. Anf.* III, p. 599) it had a direct influence on Ebionitism.
[3] The Fathers make no reference to the eschatology of the Ebionites. The fact may not be without significance, although the limited amount of evidence at our disposal does not allow us to draw any precise conclusions.

and in a lesser degree in the story of the baptism in the gospel to the Hebrews. Ebionite christology remained rudimentary for other reasons beside the fact that it failed to enjoy benefits which the doctrine of the logos conferred on Greek Christian thought. For the Ebionites could have found in their own environment material likely to stimulate speculation. Greek christology set out to explain the fact of redemption. For that reason, in spite of the speculative form it had to assume, it always preserved a sense of religious values which proved a rampart of defence for Greek Christianity against those forces which might have transferred it into a philosophy. Ebionite christology, because it had no real religious character and content, developed perforce into mere speculation and instead of making Ebionitism permanent facilitated its absorption into synchretism.

10.—JEWISH CHRISTIANS AND HERESIES

Further on[1] we shall see that there seems to have been quite an important emigration of Christians from Palestine to Asia. It is certain that this must explain why Paul was so little remembered and his influence so weak in this province in the second century. These emigrants appear to have belonged to the party following the apostles. Edouard Meyer,[2] however, thinks that he can find a polemic directed against powerful threats from Jewish Christianity in the pastoral epistles and in Ignatius.

A passage in the epistle to Titus (i. 10-16) speaks of speculations and Jewish practices.[3] After having said that the bishop must be capable of teaching sound doctrine and refuting heretics, the epistle goes on as follows:

For there are many unruly and vain talkers and deceivers, specially they of the circumcision: whose mouths must be stopped, who subvert whole houses, teaching things which they ought not, for filthy lucre's sake. . . . Wherefore rebuke them sharply, that they be sound in the faith; not giving heed to Jewish fables, and commandments of men, that turn from the truth. Unto the pure all things are pure: but unto them that are defiled and unbelieving is nothing pure: but even their mind and their conscience are defiled.

The passage refers to some speculative theory[4] which involved fasting and abstinence. But while the author says that these doctrines

---

[1] See p. 259, n. 2.   [2] Meyer, *Urspr. u. Anf.* III, p. 587.
[3] The same tendencies perhaps are at work in Titus, iii. 9; 1 Tim. i. 4; vi. 3 f.
[4] No doubt concerning genealogies of angels and aeons (because of Titus, iii. 9 and 1 Tim., i. 4).

prevailed among those of the circumcision, they must not have been purely Jewish. The prohibitions hinted at cannot have been those of the law since they are described as commandments of men.

Ignatius opposes heretics with vehemence and describes the thought and practices of some of them as ' Judaism': but we do not know exactly what the word connotes. Ignatius' mind is neither accurate or robust. With him protestations of loyalty to sane doctrine and invective against heresy take the place of argument. Ignatius came in contact with various groups of heretics; it is just as impossible to enumerate and define them as to determine to what in each of them his polemics refer. We can only discover with a measure of approximation traces of Jewish heresy.

In the epistle to the Magnesians after vituperating against heterodoxies and futile myths Ignatius describes heresy as a way of life according to Judaism, but he makes no allusion to anything concrete except the observance of the sabbath and not Sunday (9. 1). When Ignatius describes the heresies of Judaisers as myths, does he mean the kind of speculations referred to in 1 Tim. i. 4 and Titus iii. 9 or is he only using a term of abuse to which we must not give too precise a meaning? He indulges in a polemic concerning the observance of the sabbath in which he describes those who do so as persons who deny the resurrection. Is there anything more in this beyond the fact that Sunday is essentially a commemoration of the resurrection? We cannot decide.

In chapter vi of the epistle to the Philadelphians readers are put on their guard against preachers of Judaism but there is no reference to circumcision or to observing the law, although Ignatius declares that it would be better to hear Christianity preached by a circumcised person than judaised by an uncircumcised person. He may be concerned here with a Judeaohellenic gnosis such as that described in the epistle to the Colossians.

The same epistle contains a passage, the text of which is uncertain and the meaning obscure but it seems according to the most probable interpretation to be concerned with judaising heretics. Ignatius exhorts his readers to do nothing in a spirit of contentiousness but to act as if they had learnt of Christ (κατὰ Χριστομ θίαν). Some people say, 'If I do not find it (as for certain what is taught in the church) in the documents I do not believe it belongs to the faith of the Gospel'. The documents here in question must be the books of the Old Testament.[1] To those who demand in this way scriptural proofs, Ignatius first of all replies, 'It is written', i.e. proofs exist, but when his interlocutors doubt him and say that that is just the question, Ignatius breaks off the discussion and declares that for him, 'the irrefutable proofs are Jesus Christ, his cross and resurrection' (8. 2). He is engaged with Christians who were attached to Judaism and more than ordinarily struck by certain contradictions between the Old Testament and the Gospel. Perhaps too the passage may reflect the impression which certain Jewish objections had made on some members of the church.

The heresies fought by Ignatius and labelled as Judaism seem to have sprung up under the influence of Jews rather than Jewish Christians.[2]

If Jewish dynastic Christianity appeared in Asia it met with resistance as is proved by the way in which the legend of James being high priest is countered by that of John being high priest.[3] The fact is that the foundations of Greek Christianity were so strong from the beginning that they could never be called in question. The most that Jewish Christian influence could do was to inspire certain communities, notably that from which the Book to the Seven churches emerged, with a lively hatred for the Nicolaitanes,[4] who had in fact developed a tradition which they had received from Paul and claimed that they had freed themselves from the last relics of Jewish ritualism.

II.—THE SIGNIFICANCE OF JEWISH CHRISTIANITY

In the synthesis formed by primitive catholicism only one element can be imagined to have had its origin in dynastic Christianity. This is monarchical episcopacy: James, i.e. the James described by the tradition, seems to have been its first representative.[5] But

[1] For the reasons which lead us to prefer this interpretation to interpreting it as referring to the record of the trial of Jesus. See my book, *J. de N.*, p. 94.

[2] Schwartz (*Z.N.T.W.*, 1932, XXXI, p. 191) thinks that there were Jewish Christian influences at work in Asia but that they were quickly absorbed.

[3] See p. 132, n. 4.

[4] See my study, 'Les Nicolaites', *R.h.r.* 1937, CXV, pp. 1-36. There are reasons for thinking that the group to which the author of the Book to the Seven churches referred may have only represented a minority but its influence was extensive compared with its numbers. This fact may have been one of the reasons why the memory of Paul declined in Asia.

[5] There is a certain affinity between the idea of apostolic succession and of the dynasty of the *desposunoi*.

there is no exact reason for supposing that a direct connection existed between them and such resemblances as exist can be explained by the fact that similar causes were at work in both cases.[1]

Dynastic Christianity contributed nothing to primitive catholicism because, when Christianity shifted its centre of gravity to the Greek world, it discarded all the forms which linked its fate to that of Judaism. Doubtless the process would have been less rapid and not so complete if the events of 66-70 and the national catastrophe which struck Judaism had not intervened. Christianity did not see in these events a misfortune brought about by unfavourable political circumstances but judged them to be God's punishment for a nation which had refused to recognise the Messiah and had had him put to death.[2] The tradition preserves Jesus' harsh words about Jerusalem, and his prediction of its destruction;[3] it reduces his ministry at Jerusalem to a brief series of conflicts, and, above all, attributes sole responsibility to the Jews for the death of Jesus. All this amounts to a condemnation of the Jewish people which assured for Christianity definite autonomy and made Jewish Christianity an obsolete religion.

Jewish Christians turned from the offensive to a defensive position in A.D. 70. When they ceased trying to impose their way of looking at things on Greek Christians they lost one of the forces which had galvanised them into life.[4] As Judaism crystallised and became identified with Pharisaism keeping itself hostile to every form of Christianity, Judaising Christians were placed in a delicate and precarious position.[5]

The turn taken by events was unfavourable to Jewish Christianity. But it disappeared because it contained within itself the seeds of its own decay. It was not viable and failed to grasp the new object of devotion, i.e. the heavenly Christ, in such a way as to ensure its autonomy beside the God of Judaism. When Jewish Christianity ceased to think that Messiah was going to come or at any rate relegated his coming to a nebulous future, it could only think of Christ as the revealer of wisdom from on high or as an object of cosmological speculation. In other circumstances Jewish Christianity might perhaps have been the means of a revival of Judaism; the hostility displayed by Judaism after 70 made this impossible. It could not become a new religion because it was powerless to divest its main principle of its Jewish clothes.

---

[1] See *E.P.*, pp. 86 ff.
[2] Meyer, *Urspr. u. Anf.* III, p. 584.
[3] There is no reason to doubt the authenticity of these words.
[4] Hoennicke, *Judenchristentum*, p. 241.   [5] *Ibid.*, p. 243.

CHAPTER III

Apostolic Christianity After A.D. 44

I.—PETER AT ANTIOCH. THE INCIDENT BETWEEN
HIM AND PAUL

THE situation arrived at in 44 when Peter had to leave Jerusalem
was never subject to question afterwards. Neither he nor any of the
Twelve appeared ever to have returned to Jerusalem. It may be
because the situation gradually created there and firmly established
by Peter's departure made it impossible for him to try and resume
the direction of the church. Or perhaps he may have recoiled at
the idea of a struggle, the issue of which would be doubtful and
which in any case would be prejudicial to the church's interests.
Or again perhaps he may have found himself at Antioch, where
he seems to have stayed quite a long time, absorbed in activities
which gave his life a new orientation. Peter had the reputation of
being a missionary right from the time of the conference at Jerusalem; he was conceived to have been entrusted before anyone
else with the mission of preaching the gospel to the Jews (Gal. ii.
7, 8). The events of 44 may conceivably have had the effect of releasing him—somewhat against his will, it is true—from the direction
of the church at Jerusalem, and of allowing him to give himself up
completely to missionary work in districts where Jews lived and to
extend his travels still further. This last supposition receives perhaps
some confirmation from the tradition which states that the apostles
on the Lord's orders first of all remained twelve years in Jerusalem
before they scattered themselves across the world to preach the
gospel everywhere.[1] This, however, has no absolute value, as it may
well have sprung up to put an interpretation favourable to Peter
on what was in reality a check in his career.

We noted in the preceding chapter[2] the traces left in the gospel
tradition of an attack on the *desposunoi*, which could only have
arisen and grown in a group attached to the Twelve. This attack,

[1] See pp. 108 f.   [2] See pp. 112 f.

149

however, only characterises one aspect of the relationship between the group of the apostles and the dynastic group. In spite of the friction generated between them they are only variants of the same type of Christianity. What separated them was less important than what united them. We can see this in their attitude towards Paulinism, in face of which, except for some fleeting differences, they realised a true common front.

We have two accounts of the conference of 43-44, which are very unequal in value, one from the epistle to the Galatians (ii. 1-10) and the other from the book of the Acts (iv. 1-29). They do not suggest even a shade of difference between the attitude of James on the one hand and that of Peter and John on the other. Later on, while Peter was living at Antioch, he found it possible, on grounds of expediency rather than principle and under the influence of his new environment, to agree to important concessions such as eating with believers of Gentile origin, who had remained uncircumcised. This no doubt meant celebrating the Lord's Supper with them. But we are not to suppose that his attitude had in any way fundamentally changed from that taken up at the first by the church at Jerusalem, when some of James' party went to Antioch and Peter not wishing to wound their susceptibilities cut off his relations with the Gentiles.[1] When afterwards efforts were made to judaise the churches founded by Paul with ensuing crises in Galatia and Corinth, Paul's enemies appear to have claimed Peter and the other apostles as well as James and the authorities of the church of Jerusalem to have been behind them. How far were they authorised to do this? Had they really been sent by them? Paul does not seem to be quite clear on this point; he is always certain that those who were working against him in Galatia and Greece knew that their motives were akin in spirit to the attitude of Peter and James which Paul thoroughly understood. Peter and James may not have taken the initiative in going and attacking Paul on his own ground and they may even have judged their partisans' zeal to have been inopportune but they were all united in opposition to Paul's negative attitude towards the law.

The check received by Peter in 44 opened up for him a new sphere of activity. It enabled him to have a much more lasting and profound influence on the general development of Christianity than if he had remained in Jerusalem, where he would have had no

[1] Possibly he intended to take them back after the partisans of James had departed.

contact with Greek communities and would have been isolated within the framework of Judaism.

Concerning Peter's activity after he left Jerusalem we are limited in direct and certain information to the account of Galatians ii ff. which tells of his stay at Antioch.[1] This seems to have been quite long in duration and to have been extended owing to his influence there. It is shown by the fact that Barnabas and the Christians of Jewish origin at Antioch followed his example and also by the fact that tradition makes out that he founded the church there and became its first bishop.[2]

At the time of the occurrence which set Peter and Paul at loggerheads with each other the situation at Antioch had changed since the first visit of the Judaeans on the eve of the conference. Paul's dominating preoccupation then was to safeguard his missionary work by opposing the demand that converted Gentiles should be compelled to accept circumcision. He appears to have had no fears that the Christians at Antioch had allowed themselves to be influenced by his enemies. He was thus not so much advocating his personal views as defending the position of the church at Antioch. He was fighting to safeguard 'the liberty which we enjoy in Christ' to quote his own expression (Gal. ii. 4). But when the incident took place which it is certain happened on his return from his first long missionary journey the situation had completely changed. Paul was now filled with dread to see the Gentile Christians of Antioch impressed by the changed attitude of Peter and Barnabas and accepting Jewish practices in the belief that without them they would remain only half-Christian and deprived of real assurance of salvation. Only Peter's influence and his missionary activity could have made possible this change in the situation at Antioch. The epistle to the Galatians (ii. 7-8) shows that Peter's missionary activities had been to the Jews only. Peter's converts had not formed a Judaising community of their own apart from the original church at Antioch but had somewhat modified its

[1] The text of the epistle to the Galatians does not say that Peter came to Antioch as soon as he had left Jerusalem.

[2] The *Chronicon* of Eusebius (year from Abraham 2055 in the Armenian translation, ed. Karst, p. 214; 2058 in the Latin version of Jerome, ed. Helm, p. 179), attributes to Peter the foundation of the church at Antioch, but it names Evodius as the first bishop (year from Abraham 2058 in the Armenian translation, ed. Karst, p. 215; 2060 in the Latin version of Jerome, ed. Helm, p. 179). In the *Ecclesiastical History* (iii. 36, 2) Eusebius speaks of Ignatius as the second after Peter to succeed to the bishopric of Antioch. Origen (*Hom. VI in Lucam Delarue*, III, p. 938) says the same thing. Jerome (*ad. Gal.*, ii. 11 and *De viris inl.* 1) makes him the first bishop of Antioch.

spirit and shifted its centre of gravity. The new converts who had come from Judaism participated in the common life of the church and in all probability had no precise idea of the conditions which the Jewish law laid upon the Gentiles. The situation at Antioch seems thus to have become somewhat confused and this explains the logical contradiction in Peter's conduct when the partisans of James arrived.

It may be that Peter left Antioch to escape the troubled atmosphere which the incident unavoidably created. We cannot know for certain, since, as we shall see,[1] the church appears to have ranged itself on his and Barnabas' side and not on Paul's. It seems more probable that we cannot determine when Peter left Antioch[2] because, in accordance with the principle which inspired the missionaries of the first generation, he wanted always to go in advance. The way in which Paul speaks of the apostles, the brothers of the Lord and Peter as missionaries shows that Peter had a roving commission (1 Cor. ix. 5).

We do not know where Peter went when he left Antioch. The traditions that he contributed to the foundation of churches at Corinth and Rome are, as we shall see,[3] quite inconsistent and meet with decisive objections. This does not prove that he did not go to Corinth and Rome after churches had already been established there. But he does not seem to have exercised any profound influence which has left any distinct trace in either of them. Later on both these churches, especially Rome, claimed Peter for their founder for reasons, however, which had nothing to do with any memory of his activity among them.

2.—DID PETER EVANGELISE ASIA-MINOR?

Some authors believe that they can find in the first epistle preserved as that of Peter[4] an indication of districts where he worked as a missionary. The epistle is addressed to Christians in a vast area which includes Pontus, Galatia, Cappadocia, Asia, and Bithynia.

[1] See p. 305.

[2] It is impossible to make much of the dates given for Peter's departure from Antioch in the Chronicon of Eusebius (the third year of Caligula's reign (39) in the Armenian trans., ed. Karst, p. 214; the second year of Claudius' reign (43) in the Latin version of Jerome [ed. Helm, p. 179]).   [3] See pp. 308 ff.

[4] The second epistle cannot be used in the same way. It was written later in the second half of the second century and is a literary fiction completely dependent on the first.

It takes the form of an exhortation to believers who have to suffer for their faith.[1] It encourages them to patience and faith by invoking the example of Christ who had had to suffer and die before he partook of glory. Bernhard Weiss[2] believed that it was addressed to communities founded by Peter in the course of a journey previous to Paul's missions in Asia. This theory meets with a series of difficulties which seem to be decisive. The narrative in Acts and the epistles of Paul which are addressed to churches in Asia give a very clear impression that no other missionary had preceded Paul in Asia. The Jewish communities in the diaspora were closed groups but there were around them groups of proselytes who constituted as it were a bridge between the Jews and the Gentile world, so that it seems impossible for the preaching of the gospel to have been strictly confined to them without extending to the Gentiles. The ideas contained in the first epistle of Peter far from showing an archaic form of Christian thought are post-pauline. It contains phrases derived from Paul but vulgarised and cheapened and to a large extent deprived of their mystical content. There is also to be found in it the conception of Christ preaching to the dead, which belongs to quite an advanced stage in Christian thought. On the other hand, the problem of the Jewish law has disappeared from the horizon; the victory of universalism has been so complete that it is taken for granted and needs no defence. From its character the first epistle of Peter can hardly be dated before 80 and must therefore have been written after the apostle's disappearance. For even if the tradition which says that he died in the course of the massacres which followed the fire at Rome is far from certain, we can at any rate retain the year 64 as the latest date which can be given for his death.

It is plain that Peter may have come to Asia in the period following Paul's activity there. The very fact that an epistle attributed to him is addressed to Christians of this area may be evidence that he was remembered to have been active there. This inference is plausible but by no means conclusive. The attribution of the epistle to Peter is late and quite conceivably could have happened well after its first revision. The epistle may well have been put under the apostle's patronage owing to the authority attached to his name from the beginning of the second century onwards.

[1] For the situation and time to which it refers see p. 339, n. 1.
[2] Bernhard Weiss, *Lehrbuch der Einleitung in das Neue Testament*[3], Berlin, 1897, pp. 407 ff. Most of those who defend its authenticity reject Weiss's theory. See for example the criticism of Zahn, *Einl.*[2], II, p. 3.

3.—PETER AND BABYLON. DOES BABYLON REFER TO ROME?

We have one other more reliable piece of evidence for a tradition concerning Peter. Unfortunately its meaning is ambiguous. At the end of the epistle we read, 'The church that[1] is at Babylon, elected together with you, saluteth you; and so doth Marcus, my son' (v. 13). What are we to understand by the term, Babylon? Three meanings are possible: Babylon in Mesopotamia, Babylon a small town which was situated in the delta of the Nile beside a camp which became old Cairo, and lastly, Babylon as a symbolic name which in theory may have stood for Jerusalem but much more probably stood for Rome as in the Apocalypse. The first interpretation was supported formerly by Jacques Cappel and Bengel,[2] more recently by Weiss, Kuhl, and Knopf.[3] The fact that we know nothing of the evangelisation of Babylonia[4] in early days does not constitute a valid objection to this, when we remember the very fragmentary character of our knowledge of the earliest developments of Christianity. It is sometimes objected that Babylon was in the first century in ruins and a desert.[5] But this objection is not in any way decisive. According to Josephus[6] Jews to the number of 50,000 left the city in the middle of the century for Seleucia. Josephus' evidence, even if the numbers mentioned are subject to a heavy reduction, shows that Pausanias and Pliny the Elder must not be taken literally when they speak of the city being a complete

---

[1] This is the commonly accepted interpretation. There is only one other possible, i.e. by adopting the reading of 'the church co-elect', but this reading is too isolated. Mill (*Novum Testamentum*, Oxford, 1707, p. 718) and Bengel (*Gnomon Novi Testamenti*, Tubingen, 1742, p. 1026, in the eighteenth century, and in our day (Guignebert, *Prim. de Pi.*, Paris, 1909, p. 169) are induced by the phrase in the context 'Mark my son' to think that it refers to Peter's wife whom according to 1 Cor. ix. 5, he took about with him in his travels. But Mark was from Jerusalem and not Galilee and can only have been Peter's spiritual son. The suggestion therefore, tolerably bold as it is, falls to the ground.

[2] Jacques Cappel in *Critici Sacri*, Amsterdam, 1618 ff., VIII, 1, p. 172. Bengel, *Gnomon Novi Testamenti*, p. 1026.

[3] Bernhard Weiss, *Lehrb. d. Einl. i. d. N. T.³*, p. 416; Kubel, *Die Briefe Petri und Judae* (Meyer XII⁶) Go., 1897, pp. 60, 287 f.; Knopf, *Die Briefe Petri und Judae* (Meyer XII⁷), pp. 200 f.

[4] The late traditions which make Peter a missionary to Babylonia (the earliest appears in Photius, *Bibl.*, 273) can only be accounted for by presuming that they were suggested by the text of the epistle. Concerning them see Zahn, *Einl. i. d. N.T.*, Leipzig, 1900, II, pp. 20 ff.

[5] Pausanias (viii. 33, 3) says that at Babylon only the walls remained. Pliny the Elder (*Hist. nat.* vi. 26, 32) says that the city returned to solitude.

[6] Josephus, *A.j.* xviii. 9, 8-9.

ruin.[1] As apart from this the Jewish emigration cannot be considered to have been complete, the hypothesis that a mission was sent at an early period to Babylon cannot be ruled out as impossible. It meets, however, with one difficulty, which is that if a Christian church existed at Babylon, it is difficult to conceive how Babylon could have come to be a symbolical expression for Rome.

The second interpretation, which supposes that Babylon stands for a military camp in the Nile delta north of Memphis in the occupation of one of the legions stationed in Egypt[2] was suggested in the eighteenth century by Jean Le Clerc[3] and has been defended by Salomon Reinach.[4] I have already given my reasons for thinking[5] that Egypt was evangelised at an early date. But the traditions supported by Eusebius[6] and the monarchian prologue to Mark[7] which attribute the earliest evangelisation of Egypt to Peter and make Mark the first bishop of Alexandria are too late and inconsistent to be taken into serious consideration. It is also difficult to attach any weight to the argument in favour of Babylon in Egypt which depends on the existence of the word ἀρχιποίμην (literally, head shepherd: sovereign pastor) in the epistle of Peter (v. 4). Deissmann[8] discovered this word on the label attached to the mummy of a certain Ptenis who is described as 'youngest of the *archipoimenes*': it has also been found in a papyrus of 338[9] where a certain Kametis is mentioned as *archipoimen* at the head of a list of shepherds. But the word is also found in two documents which are not Egyptian but Syrian, in the Old Testament of Symmachos (4 Kings iii. 4) and in the *Testament of the Twelve Patriarchs* (Judah viii. 1).

Salomon Reinach's argument in favour of the Egyptian theory rests on the close connection which he maintains existed between the three pseudopetrine documents, the second epistle, the gospel of Peter, and the apocalypse of Peter. The two last appear to be of

---

[1] Josephus (*A.j.* ii. 15, 1; xv. 2, 21) himself says this. Cf. Philon, *Leg. ad. Cajum*, 282. According to Strabo (xvi. 1, 5) most of Babylon was destroyed and Diodorus (iii. 9, 9) says that only a small part of the city was inhabited.

[2] Strabo, xvii. 1, 30; Josephus, *A.j.* ii. 15, 1.

[3] Jean le Clerc, *Le nouveau Testament du Notre Seigneur Jesus, Christ traduit sur l'original gree avec des remarques*, Amsterdam, 1703, on I.P. 5, 13.

[4] Salamon Reinach, *Rev. archeol.*, 1908.

[5] See pp. 6 ff.   [6] Eusebius, *H.e.* ii. 16, 24.

[7] *Nam Alexandriae episcopus fuit.* (Leitzmann, *Das Muratorische Fragmen und die monarchianischen Prologe zu den Evangelien, Kleine Texte*, I[2], Bonn, 1908, p. 16).

[8] Deissmann, *Licht vom Osten*[2], Tubingen, 1909, p. 67 (with reproduction).

[9] *Pap. Leipzig*, 97, xi. 4.

Egyptian origin. Reinach thinks that the first epistle also should be added to these three. The connection between the apocalypse and the second epistle was shown by the fact that both mentioned[1] the transfiguration. But it appears now since the Ethiopian text was discovered to be much less close than was supposed when we only had the Greek text. For the former makes it plain that what was supposed to be the story of the transfiguration should be placed after the resurrection and is really an account of a resurrection appearance. The connection therefore between the second epistle and the apocalypse is much less close than Reinach imagined. Furthermore, the resemblance between the two epistles of Peter is quite external and excludes the possibility of any common origin. The second epistle refers to the first in order that it may be taken for an epistle of Peter (iii. 1) but the attribution is as exaggerated in the one as reserved in the other. The two documents, it may be said, are not products of the same workshop. Reinach's theory therefore rests on an insecure base. It must also be added that the theory itself is the product of pure guesswork and meets with grave difficulties. It presumes that there was in Egypt rivalry between the two churches of Alexandria and Babylon. Babylon, in order not to be outdone by its rival which claimed to have been founded by Mark, imagines that it may claim Peter as its founder. Two observations will suffice. The tradition which makes Mark the founder of the church at Alexandria lacks any support before the fourth century. It is impossible to agree to a reckless extrapolation. He judges the tradition to have been in existence as far back as the period preceding the revision of the first epistle of Peter, although it could only belong to the time of the last revision. The second observation is this. If Reinach's hypothesis is correct, it is a matter of considerable surprise to find the author of the epistle proceeding in such a discreet manner to claim Peter for Babylon in Egypt.

The preceding observations do not allow us to rule out altogether the Egyptian hypothesis : it is still possible but there is not the least indication of a positive nature in its favour.

Since neither of the two literal interpretations of the term Babylon have proved convincing, we must consider the interpretation which makes Babylon a symbolic designation for Jerusalem or Rome.

In Revelations xi. 8 it says that the bodies of the two assassinated

---

[1] On this Ethiopian text see my article 'A propos du texte nouveau de l'Apocalypse de Pierre', *R.h.r.*, 1924, LXXXIX, pp. 191-209.

prophets remain exposed for three days 'in the street of the great city, which spiritually[1] is called Sodom and Egypt, where also our Lord was crucified'. It is perfectly clear that Jerusalem is meant, but it is difficult to determine the origin of the fragment which the author of the Apocalypse has inserted in his work. It is certainly previous to 70 and must come from some Greek Christian community, which was annoyed with Jerusalem for the way in which Paul had been treated, or from a community which in the intestine quarrels preceding the siege of 70 was hostile to the Zealots, who through assassination created a reign of terror in the city. But this does not matter much, as, whatever interpretation is kept, it establishes the custom of naming a city with which one has a grievance by the name of a city or district known for its impiety.

In the eighteenth century Louis Cappel and Fr. Harduin maintained that the Babylon of the first epistle of Peter was Jerusalem.[2] Their theory had no great success. It met with two decisive objections. Except for the fact that two men from Jerusalem are mentioned by name in the letter, Silvanus,[3] through whom as an intermediary it was written (v. 12)[1] and Mark (v. 13) there is nothing in the letter implicit or explicit to show or indicate a conflict which would explain that severe judgement on Jerusalem was meant in such terms as the majority of readers could not have failed to understand. The second objection is that the epistle certainly belongs to a date after 70, which would be a time when Jerusalem had ceased to play any part at all.

The Roman interpretation given in antiquity by Eusebius and Jerome[5] is supported by the designation of Rome as Babylon in the Apocalypse (xiv. 8; xviii. 2 ff.).[6] It meets, however, with one real

[1] This means: from the point of view of the Spirit's, i.e. God's judgement on the city.

[2] According to Drach, *La sainte Bible avec commentaires Epîtres catholiques*, 1872, p. 67, mentioned by Jean Menier, *La première Epître de l'apôtre Pierre*, Mâcon, 1900, p. 329.

[3] Always it being supposed that he is identical with Silas, Paul's companion, which is not absolutely proved correct. It is also not absolutely certain that Silas was of Jerusalem as Acts says.

[4] Or we may agree with the attractive suggestion put out by Bornemann, 'Der erste Petrusbrief, eine Taufrede des Silvanus', *Z.N.T.W.*, 1919-20, XIX, pp. 143-165, that a speech of Sylvanus has been used.

[5] Eusebius, *H.e.* ii. 15, 2; Jerome, *De viris inl.* 8.

[6] This designation had been in existence for some time in certain Jewish texts (4 Esdras iii. 1 f.; xxviii. 31; Or. Sib. v. 159 ff.). Because of their date (second and third centuries) we cannot make anything out of certain remarks of rabbi who call the Alexandrine doctors with whom they differed Babylonians.

difficulty through the contradiction between this designation and the conciliatory attitude of the epistle towards the Empire.[1] But this difficulty is not insurmountable, because there are serious reasons, which lead us to think that the epistle only assumed the form in which we know it at a late date and that the opening greeting with the epistolary conclusion, which by themselves turn it into a letter of Peter, were only added last of all without doubt at a time when the relations between the church and the Empire were not what they had been when the body of the epistle was put together.

We may then retain the hypothesis that Babylon means Rome as at least the most likely to be correct, although we cannot be definitely certain of it. We cannot, however, draw any certain inference from it concerning the activity and presence of Peter at Rome. For the attribution of the letter to the apostle may well date from a time when the Roman tradition concerning Peter had already begun to develop. We know that it has been the subject of considerable discussion and still is. Later on we shall see[2] that it rests on a distinctly fragile foundation and appears to have been inspired by ecclesiastical preoccupations rather than historical memories.

The result of our enquiries into the evidence for Peter's missionary activity is fairly meagre and does not correspond to the importance which Paul shows was attached to it.

Peter was certainly not the only missionary who carried Christianity from Jerusalem to the Jewish communities of the diaspora and to the Greek world but of the others we know still less than we do of him.

4.—MISSIONS FROM JERUSALEM AND THE CHURCH OF ROME

On one point, however, their work can be proved to have produced an important result. It concerns the foundation of the church at Rome. Its origin goes back to a very early date[3] for this reason. Almost everyone agrees that the text of Suetonius[4] which speaks

---

[1] See in particular the loyal exhortation of ii. 13 f. which expresses the idea that if the conduct of Christians is beyond reproach the magistrates will protect them against their enemies.   [2] *E.P.*, pp. 184 ff.

[3] We do not think any useful purpose is served by discussing the tentative paradox of Leon Hermann (*De Golgotha au Palatin*, Brussels, 1934) who wants to go back as far as 29 for the arrival of Christianity in Rome. See the criticism of his thesis and method made by Guignebert, *R.h.r.*, 1935, CXI, pp. 290-295.

[4] Suetonius, *Claudius*, 25. 4. For the interpretation of this text, see *J. de N.*, pp. 48 f. and *Life of Jesus*, pp. 97 f.

of Claudius expelling the Jews of the city because they were disturbed *impulsore Christo* refers to an agitation caused in Roman Jewry by the preaching of the Gospel. The date of this expulsion must be the year 49.[1] The Ambrosiastre provides evidence that the church of Rome was not founded by an apostle.[2] This is striking evidence in face of the tendency to attribute an apostolic origin to the great churches. The tradition which makes Peter the founder of the church of Rome depends on the evidence of Irenaeus[3] who does not define in what circumstances Peter came to Rome, secondly on the evidence of Eusebius[4] according to whom he came to Rome to fight Simon the Magician. The legend, however, concerning Simon at Rome originated in a blunder of Justin who mistook a statue of the Sabine god, *Semo Sancus*[5] for one of Simon the Magician. As for the idea that 'another place' to which Peter went on leaving Jerusalem (Acts xii. 17) is Rome, apart from the fact that it would be difficult to reconcile it with his arrival at Antioch, to retain it as Belser[6] does we must be convinced *a priori* that the church of Rome was founded by Peter. It is also equally impossible to suppose in the absence of any allusion to it in the epistle to the Romans that the church was founded by emissaries from Paul.[7] The theory that pilgrims who had heard Peter at Jerusalem on the day of Pentecost brought the gospel to Rome savours far too much of fantasy and guesswork.[8]

The gospel must have been brought to Rome between 40 and

[1] The birth of the church of Rome in the bosom of the Jewish colony there is supported by the fact that Aquila and Priscilla who were among the Jews expelled from Rome were already Christians when Paul met them at Corinth (Acts xviii. 1-2).

[2] Preface of the commentary on the Epistle to the Romans: *Nulla insignia virtutum videntes nec aliquem apostolorum susceperunt fidem Christi.*

[3] Irenaeus, *Adv. Haer.* iii. 3, 2.

[4] Eusebius, *H.e.* ii. 14, 6.   [5] Justin, *Apol.* i. 26, 2.

[6] Belser, *Einleitung in das Neue Testament*[2], Freiburg in Breisgau, 1905, p. 489. This is not the opinion of all the Roman Catholic critics. Duchesne (*H.a.* I, p. 55) believes the tradition that the church at Rome was founded by Peter 'lacks sufficient foundation to win the assent of history'.

[7] Wieseler, *Zur Geschichte der neutestamentlichen Schriften und der Urchristentums*, Leipzig, 1880, p. 62.

[8] Reuss, *Epîtres pauliniennes*, Paris, 1878, II, p. 7. Zahn (*Der Brief des Paulus an die Römer*, Leipzig, 1910, pp. 8 ff.) although he does not go so far, believes the church of Rome to have originated at an early date. We are pressing much too hard the texts in Rom. xiii. 11 if we think that they prove that the church at Rome came into existence at the same time as Paul's conversion and support this opinion by the mention of Andronicus and Junias who are said to be apostles before Paul (Rom. xvi. 7) without any indication, however, that they took part in the foundation of the church of Rome.

50 by missionaries who came from Jerusalem.[1] As the young church survived the expulsion of the Jews it must have rapidly extended beyond the borders of the synagogue.

There is no doubt that Paul learnt of the existence of a church at Rome and was put in touch with some of its members[2] by Aquila and Priscilla, whom he met on his arrival at Corinth. When he was looking for new ground for his activities after the crises in Corinth and Galatia he saw where he could do best to prepare for the evangelisation of Spain and to assure himself of a good reception wrote his epistle to the Romans.

Whether the majority of the members of the church at Rome at that time were of Jewish or Gentile origin has been much discussed. The epistle itself does not help us to answer the question for certain one way or the other. It only tells us what Paul thought about it. It is quite possible that his judgement was formed by Aquila and Priscilla, who had been strongly influenced by him, and that he believed it approximated much more closely to his views than it did in reality. A reading of the epistle leaves us with no clear impression on this point as is shown by the diversity of the interpretations which have been put forward.[3] The framework of

[1] This is supported by a passage from St. Augustine (*Ep.* 102. 8) which invokes the evidence of Porphyry and says that the *lex Judaeorum* penetrated to Italy after the death of Gaius Caesar (41) or in his reign (*post Caesarum Gaium aut certe ipso imperante*). Since Judaism had arrived in Rome well before this time the information can only refer to the *lex Judaica nova*, i.e. the Gospel.

[2] Since the time of Keggermann (*De duplici epistolae ad Romanos appendice*, 1767) and especially since the time of David Schule (*St. u. Kr.*, II, 1829, pp. 609 ff.) many critics, because they were surprised that Paul gives personal greetings to so many members of a church he had not visited, considered Rom. xvi. 1-16 to be a fragment of an epistle to the Ephesians or to be an epistle itself to the Ephesians. This hypothesis had a certain vogue but can hardly be maintained any longer. It raises grave difficulties and also it can be easily understood that in order not to appear a stranger in Rome Paul took care to mention by name all the members of the church whom he could possibly know directly or indirectly.

[3] Ancient exegesis considered it self-evident that the majority of the Christians at Rome were of Gentile origin. This opinion was questioned at an early date by Koppe (*Novum Testamentum perpetua annotatione illustratum*, Gottingen, 1824, IV[3], p. 13) and was forcibly attacked by Baur (*Ueber Zweck und Veranlassung des Romerbriefs*, Tubingen, Zurich, 1836, 3, pp. 114 ff. Cf. *Paulus*[2], Leipzig, 1866-1869, I, pp. 343 f., 368 f., 405). The idea that the epistle was addressed to Jewish Christians prevailed until 1881, when a reaction was provoked by a study from Grafe (*Ueber Veranlassung und Zweck des Romerbriefs*, Freiburg in Breisgau, Tubingen, 1881). Opinion is still fairly well divided. Compromising theories have also been put forward. H. Schultz (*Die Adresse des letzten Capitels des Briefs an die Romer*, *Jahrb. f. deutsche Theol.*, 1876, XXI, pp. 105-130) and Heinrici (*Die Forschung uber die paulinischen Briefe*, Giessen, 1886, p. 25) suggested that the Christians of Rome were of Gentile origin but passed for Jews. For more details see *Introd.*, IV, 2, pp. 274 ff.

the epistle (i. 10-15; iv. 14-16; xvi) hints at readers of Gentile origin. The question of the collection is raised in such a way that it can only be understood as addressed to Gentiles and of the many individuals who are greeted in chapter xvi only three are shown to be Jews.[1] The majority of them, therefore, must have been non-Jewish. Many passages in the body of the epistle must be interpreted in the same way. Thus in iii. 3 Paul speaks of Jewish incredulity in quite an objective manner. He calls the Jews, 'My brethren, my kinsmen according to the flesh'. He does not say, 'We also, are Israelites', but, 'I also, I am an Israelite'. Every exhortation to remain humble and not to become proud at having taken the place of the Jews in the economy of salvation can only be supposed to be addressed to Gentiles.[2] Paul indeed tells his readers that Abraham and Isaac are their ancestors (iv. 1, 12; ix. 10) but he also tells the Galatians that they are the seed of Abraham, although they are unquestionably of Gentile origin, and he speaks of 'our fathers' when he is writing to the Corinthians, who are similarly Gentiles, about the Israelites in the desert (1 Cor. x. 1). Other indications of Jewish origin which Zahn thought he recognised do not stand up to examination.[3] As we read the epistle we grow more inclined therefore to favour the idea that the church at Rome was for the most part Gentile Christian in character or at least Paul thought it so and we are supported in this opinion by Mark's gospel, which was probably written at Rome[4] and presumes that its readers have no knowledge of Jewish customs.[5]

[1] Andronicus, Junias and Herodion (xvi. 7-11); Aquila and Priscilla (xvi. 3); Mary (xvi. 6); Rufus and his mother (xvi. 13), were also certainly Jews.

[2] In iii. 9 Paul is speaking of the privilege and advantage accruing to the Jew from circumcision and asks, 'are we better than they', but this cannot be understood in the opposite sense. Paul is thinking of himself not his readers as linked with Judaism.

[3] e.g. vii. 4-6, where Paul tells his readers that before their conversion they were under the yoke of the law (Zahn, *Br. a.d. Rom.*, p. 332). But in Gal. iii. 22, Paul says that the scripture hath concluded all under sin, all, i.e., both Jews and Gentiles together. Zahn (p. 574) also sees in the instruction concerning the weak brethren (xiv. 1-15, 13) a sign of the Jewish Christian character of the Roman community, as otherwise he considers that the contrast between Paul's tolerance shown in Rom. xiv. 5, and his intransigent attitude expressed in Gal. iv. 10 f. cannot be explained. Zahn considers that at Rome Paul was dealing with persons who continued to practise the Jewish law and not as in Galatia with Gentiles who had adopted it. But there is no proof at all that the scruples of the weak brethren arose out of observance of the Jewish law; they appear rather to have had a neopythagorean origin especially since there is nothing to show that the weak brethren at Rome had imposed a rule upon themselves as a condition of salvation.

[4] Bacon, *Is Mark a Roman Gospel?* Cambridge, Massachusetts, 1919. Cf. *Introd.*, I, p. 367.

[5] e.g. the explanations given of purification (vii. 2-4) and of corban (vii. 11-13).

The Epistle to the Romans is, however, addressed to readers who are familiar with the Old Testament and in whose regard Paul does not wish to be thought of as contemptuous of the law and hostile to the people of Israel. The Christians of Rome therefore must have been subjected to some judaising influences, although they do not seem to have been effected by propaganda of a particularly judaising nature. Paul's only fear was that their attitude towards the law was not strong enough to prevent their falling before any future onslaught of Judaisers. He never reveals his apprehensions very explicitly but they can be seen from the following sentence which appears to be a postscript in his own hand to the letter which had been dictated to Tertius, 'Now I beseech you brethren, mark them which cause divisions and offences contrary to the doctrine which ye have learned; and avoid them. For they that are such serve not our Lord Jesus Christ, but their own belly' (xvi. 17-18).

Such may have been the state of things or possibly the situation may have been transformed by the action of Judaisers between the time when Paul was writing to the Romans and that of his arrival at Rome as a prisoner. One thing, however, is certain. They did not give him a very warm welcome. It is true that Acts recounts that warned of his coming the brethren came as far as Appii forum and the three taverns to meet him[1] and that their welcome gave him courage (xxviii. 15). But this note somewhat unexpectedly is placed not before but after Paul's arrival in Rome has been mentioned (xxviii. 14). It is therefore an addition made by the compiler of Acts to his sources because he did not wish to leave the impression that the Christians at Rome received Paul as a prisoner with indifference. In his last chapter, however, he declares that Paul received the Jews at Rome with whom he desired to have conversations and all those who came to him but he does not say that he also received a visit from the members of the church. This attitude of reserve which the church at Rome took up towards Paul when he was a prisoner shows that it was biased against him and ranged itself on the side of his enemies. Confirmation of this fact comes from certain passages in the pastoral epistles[2] which appear to refer to

[1] i.e. about thirty-eight and twenty-eight miles respectively from Rome on the Appian way. Guignebert (*Le Christ*, p. 318) notes that it is hardly natural that two places separated by only ten miles should be given as the *rendezvous* of the delegation from Rome and the apostle.

[2] Concerning the use made in the pastoral epistles of fragments of letters written by Paul while he was a prisoner in Rome, see *Introd.*, IV, 2, p. 500.

the imprisonment and the trial of Paul at Rome. We cannot be certain that 2 Timothy iv. 16 f. refers to these things, being a passage in which Paul complains that at his first appearance in court no one stood by him but all forsook him. We cannot decide for certain whether this text refers to the imprisonment at Caesarea or at Rome. 2 Timothy i. 15-18 does not raise the same doubt as Rome is mentioned by name. 'All they that be in Asia be turned away from me.[1] The Lord give mercy to the house of Onesiphorus.[2] For oft he refreshed me. He was not ashamed of my chain; but when he was in Rome, he sought me out very diligently and found me. The Lord grant unto him that he may find mercy of the Lord in that day.'

This text shows us that some time a change took place in Paul's condition; most probably it refers to Paul's transfer to a prison the result of which was that he lost touch with the church, so that, when Onesiphorus comes from Asia to Rome to help the apostle, the church cannot tell him where he could find him. In spite of this, Onesiphorus succeeded in discovering him. What a stranger could do the church could have done too if it had been anxious about the apostle's departure.

Paul was then certainly deceived in thinking that the church at Rome had absorbed his conception of the gospel. It stood not with him but with his enemies. This provides us with a very weighty reason for thinking. that it was founded by a mission from Jerusalem.

We have no direct knowledge of the history of the church at Rome for a period of some thirty years following Paul's death and the fire at Rome which had resulted in the massacre of Christians. Slowly it had to be reconstituted without perhaps being able to resume completely all the traditional threads which had been snapped by the terrible bloody losses which had been inflicted on it. The church, however, arising from the old one which seemed to have been destroyed was not an entirely new creation.

In the last decade of the first century, although at the time it had again to suffer from the persecution of Domitian, there was at Rome an important and flourishing church which enjoyed

[1] There is no doubt that Paul is referring to some of his collaborators and friends who had come to help him but had been discouraged by the delay in the trial and other reasons and so returned to Rome.

[2] The reason why Paul speaks of the house of Onesiphorus and not of Onesiphorus himself is undoubtedly because in the interval Onesiphorus had died.

consideration from the other churches. This is shown by the epistle of Clement of Rome to the Corinthians which was written about 96.[1]

As we shall see later on,[2] this document reflects Christianity of an ethical nature such as can be found in Christianity at Jerusalem in its later stages. At the same time it is also tinged in a somewhat superficial and verbal way with Paulinism.

[1] Concerning the circumstances in which this epistle was written see *E.P.*, pp. 137 ff.
[2] See pp. 383 ff.

PART THREE

The Development of Christianity within the Framework of Hellenism

The Beginnings of Christian Doctrine

CHAPTER I

Stephen and the Hellenists of Jerusalem

FROM what the book of Acts tells us about Stephen the Seven and their group, we can see that in addition to the Christians attached to Judaism, who impressed the church at Jerusalem with the character it retained right up to the time of the revolt of Barkochba, there was also at Jerusalem at a very early date, since it was already in existence at the time of Paul's conversion, another Christian group known as the Hellenists. Both their outlook and their way of life seems to have been quite distinct from that of the group known as the Hebrew which was in the majority. Our information about the Hellenists comes from the story in Acts concerning Stephen, especially from the sermon for which the story is the setting.

I.—WHO THE HELLENISTS ARE

There has been much discussion on the term Hellenist which the author of Acts uses without any explanation.[1] It is generally supposed to mean Jews who spoke Greek because either they or their fathers belonged to the diaspora.[2] We meet with the word for the first time in Acts but it was not used subsequently with this meaning. The Post-Nicean Fathers and Julian the Apostate use it as a synonym for Gentiles. As it is derived from a verb in $\iota \zeta \omega$ it implies a particular tendency.[3] The term Hebrews which in the Acts is used as an antithesis to Hellenists is seldom used to denote Jews who speak Hebrew, except once or twice by Philo, who generally uses it to describe the Israelites in the time of the Patriarchs.[4] We meet with the term 'Synagogue of the Hebrews' in inscriptions

---

[1] See H.-J. Cadbury, ' The Hellenists', *Begin.* V, pp. 59-74.
[2] This is the meaning adopted by Bauer (*Worterb.*) and F. Zorell (*Lexicon graecum Novi Testamenti*[2], Paris, 1931 s.v.).   [3] Cf. Ἰουδαΐζειν in Gal. ii. 14.
[4] Philo, *De confus. ling.*, 129. *De congr. erud. grat.*, 43 s.

THE BIRTH OF CHRISTIANITY

at Rome,[1] Corinth,[2] and Philadelphia in Lydia.[3] We cannot be certain that it means synagogues which had been founded by people who continued to use Hebrew, as funerary inscriptions from the Jewish catacombs at Rome[4] use the same term Hebrew but are sometimes written in Greek or Latin script. While we have no direct evidence it seems most reasonable to suppose that the only difference between Hellenists and Hebrews was one of language.[5] The author of Acts certainly considered the Hellenists to be Jews because he mentions them before he tells of the first conversion of a Gentile, i.e. Cornelius and in the list of the names of the Seven he discloses the fact that one of them was a proselyte (vi. 5).

The two facts (1) that they differed in language, (2) that the Hellenists were driven away from Jerusalem at a very early date explains why no conflict appears to have arisen between the two groups, although their outlook in thought was very different. They must have at least gone each their own way without being unknown to each other.

It is true that this is not the picture given to us by the story in Acts; but we cannot altogether trust it on this point. Without creating any link between the preceding story, that of the appearance of the Twelve before the Sanhedrin (v. 17-42),[6] it goes on to say that at that time, as the number of the disciples grew, the Hellenists murmured against the Hebrews because their widows were neglected in the daily ministration.[7] As Peter considered this complaint well founded, he summoned an assembly of the faithful to whom he declared that the apostles could not neglect the most important of their duties, the ministry of the word, i.e. preaching

[1] C.I.G., 9909; Schurer (Gesch. III, p. 46) thinks that it refers to a synagogue which was made up of Jews who continued to speak Hebrew.

[2] Deissmann, L.v.O., p. 9, n. 2. Deissmann reproduces the inscription.

[3] Keil und von Premerstein, Bericht uber eine dritte Reise in Lydien, Denkschriften der Akademie der Wissenschaften in Wien, 1914, LVII, pp. 32 ss., n. 42.

[4] For these inscriptions published by Nic. Muller, N. Bees and Kaibel, see Cadbury, p. 65, n. 5.

[5] Cadbury's interpretation (p. 69) which makes the Hellenists to be Gentile converts to Judaism finds no possible confirmation in Acts xi. 20, which refers to Gentiles. B.D.², etc. have Ἑλληνιστάς, while Ἕλληνας is only to be found in א^c. A.D.*, and a few minuscules. The reading Ἑλληνιστας seems to come from a correction of ευαγγελιστας in א*. This reading does not make sense and must have originated in a fusion of the words Ἑλληνιστας and ἐυαγγελισομεον which follow each other.

[6] This story is completely devoid of any historical value. See pp. 455 ff.

[7] It may be as has sometimes been supposed (see e.g. Guignebert, Le Christ, p. 78), that the compiler of Acts substituted the grievance concerning the distribution of alms for a more serious motive of another kind.

and prayer for serving tables[1] and that it would therefore be best to entrust the work of assistance to seven approved men, full of the Holy Ghost and wisdom. After this proposal had been agreed to, seven men were chosen and presented to the apostles who after praying laid their hands on them. This was the symbolic gesture both in Judaism and in primitive Christianity for giving authority to anyone to perform a function[2] (vi. 1-6).

We have already noted[3] that in this story the author of Acts had in mind the organised ministry existing in his own day which subordinated deacons to presbyters and bishops. By it he wanted to explain two conflicting traditions, (1) that a group of twelve men, (2) that a group of seven exercised in the church the most primitive of the functions which they considered to be identical with those existing in the church at the end of the first century. But the list of the Seven contains only Greek names. It would have been a singular proceeding in order to ensure an equitable distribution of the alms among the members of two groups, which if not rivals were at any rate distinct, to have entrusted the duty to men who were exclusively chosen from only one of them. We know something about two of the Seven if not three and what we know does not conform to the idea that they distributed alms. Stephen was a preacher and teacher; Philip was an evangelist. Nicholas also appears to have been a teacher if we are right in supposing that the group of heretics called the Nicolaitanes who are attacked at the beginning of Revelation are connected with him.[4]

The story therefore in Acts vi. 1-6 has no direct historical value. It provides evidence, however, for the existence at Jerusalem of a Christian group who had as preachers and leaders the Seven and not the Twelve, and who being formed of people who spoke Greek would in other ways which cannot be defined be subject to the influence of Hellenism.

2.—THE STORY OF STEPHEN

The compiler of Acts considers the story of the institution of the ministry of the Seven to be the prelude to the story of Stephen. The only link, however, to be found between the two stories is the name Stephen which figures in the list of the Seven. Actually they

[1] This seems to show that the author seems to think of the service of alms as a meal offered by the church to the poor.
[2] See *E.P.*, pp. 401 ff.   [3] See pp. 91 f.   [4] See pp. 409 ff.

are separated by a short editorial note (vi. 7) which mentions an increase in the number of the disciples and the conversion of many priests. We can distinguish two elements in the section vi. 8-viii. 7 devoted to Stephen, which must first be considered separately: a story and a speech.

Stephen, full of grace and power, accomplishing signs and wonders, provokes hostility from certain members of the synagogue of the Libertines, Cyranians, Cilicians, and Asians,[1] who not being able to resist the Spirit by which he spoke, stir up false witnesses who accuse him of having blasphemed against Moses and God. He is brought before the Sanhedrin and the false witnesses give their accusation definite form by saying that Stephen declared that Jesus of Nazareth would destroy this place[2] and would change the customs given by Moses (vi. 9-15).

In answer to the interrogation of the high priest Stephen makes a speech in which he vigorously accuses the people of Israel of idolatry. By his speech Stephen stirs up his audience into fury in the face of which, full of the Holy Spirit, he declares that he sees the heavens opened and the Son of Man[3] seated on the right hand

[1] Although the text is not exactly clear, it seems to refer to one synagogue and not several. It is surprising that one section of the members of this synagogue are called after their legal status: the Libertines (there is no doubt that they were descended from the Jews whom Pompey had brought to Rome as slaves, many of whom had been subsequently freed. Cf. Schurer, *Gesch.* II, p. 431). The other sections are called after their place of origin or domicile. Preuschen (*Apostelgeschichte*, p. 37) following the Armenian catena proposed to correct Λιβερτίνων to Λιδύων (people from Lydia). Blass (*Philology of the Gospel*, London, 1898, pp. 69 f.) proposed Λιβυστίνων. These corrections are unnecessary, R. Weill ('La Cité de David, Compte rendu des fouilles exécutées à Jérusalem sur le site de la ville primitive (campagne 1913-14'), *R.e.j.*, 1920, LXXI, pp. 30-34. Cf. Clermont-Ganneau, *Découverte à Jérusalem d'une synagogue de l'époque hérodienne*, *Syria*, 1920, I, pp. 190-197; Fr. Vincent, *Découverte de la synagogue des Affranchis à Jérusalem*, R.B., 1921, XXX, pp. 247-297) while making excavations at the extremity of the hill of Ophel discovered a Greek inscription in which it is said that 'Theodotus, son of Ouettenios (Vettenius), priest and archisynagogus, son and grandson of archisynagogi, built this synagogue for the reading of the law and teaching the commandments, as well as the hostelry, the rooms, and the baths to serve as an inn for those who come from afar', and that 'this synagogue was founded by his fathers and forbears with Simonides'. The inscription must belong to the first century before the fall of Jerusalem. The fact that Theodotus' father has a Latin name shows that he must have been a slave in Rome and had been freed. The synagogue to which Theodotus added arrangements for lodging pilgrims must have been in existence in the early years of the first century. It is not unreasonable to identify it with the one mentioned in Acts.

[2] i.e. Jerusalem and the Temple.

[3] This is the only passage in the book of Acts which contains the term, Son of Man.

of God (vii. 54-56). He is then dragged outside the city and stoned, after the witnesses[1] had laid their clothes at the foot of a young man named Saul. As he dies, Stephen cries out, 'Lord Jesus, receive my spirit', and then, 'Lord, lay not this sin to their charge' (vii. 57-60).[2] Mention is then made of Saul's approval of his death and of a great persecution against the church which compelled all the faithful to scatter except the apostles[3] (viii. 1). The burial of Stephen is then mentioned (viii. 2). The story finishes with a note about the persecution of the church led by Saul (viii. 3).

The end of the story is not altogether coherent. The three notes about Saul (vii. 58; viii. 1, 3) make a triplet and are not smoothly integrated into the text; they certainly originated with the compiler. Stephen's burial is mentioned in such a peculiar place as to make one think that it is a note which has been clumsily put in afterwards as an afterthought. Furthermore, it is not clear from the story if Stephen was executed after a proper trial or was massacred as the victim of a popular movement. The compiler has combined two traditions which differ in detail but agree on essentials. This does not at bottom affect the value of the story in Acts.

It is far otherwise concerning the false witnesses. Here the story is doubly suspect. First of all Stephen, instead of protesting against the ideas which have been falsely attributed to him, maintains in his speech that the Israelite cult was an idolatrous form of worship. From this there should have been drawn the logical conclusion that it ought to be abolished and the place where it was celebrated destroyed. There also exists a disturbing parallelism[4] between the false witnesses, who accused Jesus before the Sanhedrin of having proclaimed that in three days he would destroy the temple and build it again, meaning by that, that he would change the whole form of Jewish worship,[5] and those who bring an accusation against Stephen so closely resembling that brought against Jesus that it cannot be independent of it. Both these considerations show that we are in the presence of an idea which

---

[1] According to *Sanh.* vi. 4 it was their duty to throw the first stones.

[2] In the same way that Stephen's vision calls to mind the declaration of Jesus before the Sanhedrin (Mark xiv. 62 and par. passages) the words attributed to him recall to mind those which Luke puts into the mouth of the dying Jesus (xxiii. 34, 46) but can only be accepted as authentic with reserve. See *Life of Jesus*, p. 536.   [3] Concerning this persecution see pp. 460 ff.

[4] This parallelism is shown to be still more striking by the one drawn by the author between Stephen's death and Jesus'.

[5] Concerning the authenticity and meaning of this saying see *V. de J.*, pp. 491 f. and *Life of Jesus*, pp. 507 f.

Christians belonging to the time and environment when the tradition had become set considered so outrageous that they could not admit that it was Jesus' or Stephen's and thought that it could only be attributed to false witnesses.

3.—STEPHEN'S SPEECH

An analysis of Stephen's speech and an examination of its context affords direct confirmation of this opinion. The first part consists of a somewhat ample presentation of the religious history of Israel. Its tone is quite peaceable without any polemics (vii. 2-41).[1] Until it mentions the making and worship of the golden calf, the speech conforms to traditional Jewish thought. After that it falls away and takes on a tone which no Jew could help but think was blasphemous. It declares that from the time Israel worshipped the golden calf God turned away from them and gave them up to worship the host of heaven. This idea which is the basis of the whole of Stephen's thought, is supported by a saying of Amos who said that the Israelites did not worship God in the wilderness but idols, Moloch and Remphan (vii. 42-43).[2] The building of the temple at Jerusalem is regarded as putting the crown on Israel's revolt against God and making it beyond redemption (vii. 48-50).

The second and concluding part of the speech is short compared with the length of the beginning. It is also so obscure that it seems to have been mutilated.[3] Only fragments of the original conclusion remain. Stephen reproaches his audience for remaining as rebellious to the Holy Spirit as their fathers had been. The latter persecuted the prophets who predicted the coming of the Just One; they have put this Just One to death, they have received the law by the disposition of angels and have not kept it (vii. 51-53).

Although there is little connection between these affirmations certain ideas can be deduced from them. We see, for example, that

[1] Stephen's historical summary differs on a few counts from the stories in the Old Testament. These are noted in the commentaries. The same divergences are found in Philo.

[2] vii. 44-47 unexpectedly follows the traditional line of thought closely but so flatly contradicts what has gone before and what follows that it must be considered the compiler's addition to soften the boldness of Stephen's thought.

[3] The compiler has tried to explain the want of balance between the two sections of the speech by the suggestion that the fury of the audience compelled Stephen to condense what he wanted to say. In reality the speech is not cut short or interrupted; it is mutilated.

even after the revolt of his people God did not leave them as he sent the prophets to them and above all as he sent them the Just One. We do not see what part Stephen considered the Just One to play; we recognise only that the hostility shown towards him is not excused as it is in one of Peter's speeches (iii. 17) through ignorance on part of the Jews, which in short was excusable, but is the crowning point of the opposition which they have always shown to God's interventions. What survives of the speech of Stephen is completely negative in character. It forms an indictment against the Jewish people not an exposition of Stephen's faith. We can, however, form some idea of his positive thought by extending the lines of thought of which there are in his speech plain indications. Two conclusions to this speech can be thought of. One would be a call to repentance that the Jews should at last be converted and that the Just One would forgive and save them. But if Stephen thought on these lines, they would have been the same as Peter's and we can see no reason why the tradition was unable to agree to this and eliminated the positive part of the speech. Must we therefore suppose that Stephen's thoughts ran in a different direction? He may have thought that God has definitely turned away from Israel and that henceforth he will turn to the Gentiles to establish his kingdom. This interpretation finds confirmation in the fact that it was the Hellenists who took the initiative at Antioch in preaching the gospel to the Gentiles.[1]

The additions and mutilations made by the compiler to Stephen's speech prove that he did not compose it. The idea that Judaism became such a decadent religion that Christianity was a completely new religion belongs to the antipodes of his thought.

If we grant that the story of Stephen is connected to the persecuting activity of Saul of Tarsus in an artificial way, theoretically it is not inconceivable that the compiler of Acts by inserting the story where we find it has committed an anachronism and that Stephen's thought in reality belongs to a much later stage in the development of Christian thought. But the fact that Jerusalem is the scene of Stephen's activity does not allow us to keep this conjecture. The judaising character of the church at Jerusalem was quickly accentuated; ideas such as those of Stephen could have only manifested themselves without creating a violent reaction

---

[1] The initiative may have been taken by different people independently. Guignebert, *Le Christ*, p. 126, appears to us to go too far with his hypothesis that the Hellenists were the first to propagate the new faith.

within the fold of the church before the Christians in Jerusalem had adopted a definite attitude. We have no trace in the story in Acts of any such reaction.

We cannot see in Stephen's speech a projection into the past of Pauline ideas or of the issues raised by Paulinism. Paul only considered the worship of the Jews to have perished because the redemptive work of the Christ had been accomplished. Until then it was the legitimate form of worship desired by God.

Furthermore, Stephen's speech does not contain a late interpolation made under the influence of ideas similar to those of Marcion. For Stephen considered that the religion of Israel had come to an end, not because it did not originate in a revelation of God but because Israel revolted against him and persisted in its revolt in spite of the calls of the prophets who were sent to it.

4.—THE ORIGINS OF HELLENIC CHRISTIANITY

The question of the origins of Stephen's thought cannot be separated from that of the origins of Greek Christianity. Certain scholars who have had very little following such as Heitmuller,[1] Schutz,[2] W. Bauer,[3] and Lohmeyer[4] especially, start with the fact that Galilee was only judaised at a late date and therefore in only a superficial way.[5] On this they have sketched out or developed a theory that in this province a religion new in form came into existence from Jesus himself when he was alive which was much more distinct from Judaism and its law than the religion which must have developed later at Jerusalem. This form of Christianity, they argue, spread into the neighbouring Hellenic areas even as far as Damascus where it made a conquest of the man who was later to be the apostle Paul. This theory meets with a series of objections of which it is sufficient to point out the principal. First of all we are in the presence of a construction which is quite theoretical and rests on no positive fact. It is a hypothesis which has been put forward to explain facts which can be given a simpler and more natural explanation. What is more serious is that we have no trace

[1] W. Heitmuller, 'Zum Problem Paulus und Jesus', *Z.N.T.W.*, 1922, XIII, pp. 320-337.   [2] R. Schutz, *Apostel und Junger*, Giessen, 1921.
[3] Bauer, 'Jesus der Galilaer', *Festgabe fur Ad. Julicher*, Tubingen, 1927, pp. 16-34.   [4] Lohmeyer, *Galilaea und Jerusalem*, Gottingen, 1936.
[5] This opinion meets with a serious objection in the fact that Galilee during the Jewish war and before was one of the most active centres of opposition to Rome and of political messianism resting on a religious basis.

of the early existence of any form of Christianity in Galilee.[1] This hypothesis creates a paradox for which we can find no plausible explanation. The paradox rests on the fact that while from a form of Christianity which sprung from the activity of Jesus in Galilee there developed a theory which placed the emphasis on the accomplishment of redemption through the death and resurrection of Jesus, the church at Jerusalem, where the drama of the passion was enacted, attached much less importance to it and considered what the Christ would accomplish on his return to be the essential redemptive act.

We must look rather to the thought of Jesus in what appears to have been its final form if we are to discover the origin of Stephen's ideas. They appear to have been organically connected with it. As is shown by the ecstatic vision which Stephen received before his death in which he saw the heavens open and the Son of Man sitting on the right hand of God his thoughts were tending in the same direction as those of Jesus when he declared before the Sanhedrin that the Son of Man would sit on the right hand of God and come on the clouds of heaven.[2] Like Jesus too, Stephen thought that the Son of Man when he showed himself in glory would change the whole form of Israel's worship. This was what Jesus meant when he spoke of destroying and rebuilding the temple. The Jewish form of worship with its legalistic setup from which it could not be separated created a gulf between Jews and Gentiles and placed the latter beyond the reach of the covenant with God. Its destruction would have enabled the Gentiles equally with the Jews to have partaken of salvation. It is therefore fairly certain that the Hellenists who came to Antioch were the first or among the first to preach the gospel to the Gentiles.[3]

It is not surprising that Stephen's ideas caused the Jews to react so violently that the Hellenists could not remain in Jerusalem.[4]

---

[1] Galilee is only mentioned once in the book of Acts in a passage (ix. 31) which was certainly added by the compiler.

[2] Concerning this declaration see *Life of Jesus*, pp. 507 f. and *V. de J.*, pp. 493 f.

[3] It does not then seem legitimate to suppose with Guignebert, *Le Christ*, p. 179, that the election of the Seven marked a schism in the church at Jerusalem. It is more natural to suppose that the Seven without ever having been formally elected were the centre and leading element in the Hellenist group corresponding to the Twelve in the Hebrew group.

[4] This of course does not exclude the possibility that some remained. It seems perfectly reasonable to count as a Hellenist Mnason mentioned in Acts xxi. 16 (cf. p. 489, n. 1). This, however, does not mean that the Hellenists as a group did not count for anything in Jerusalem after Stephen's death.

We do not know how far the church itself was associated with this reaction. One thing is certain: it was in no way influenced by the Hellenists.

Considered in the framework of Christianity at Jerusalem the Hellenist movement was nothing more than a passing incident leaving no traces behind it. It was remembered because the action of the Hellenists was so important in the extension of Christianity beyond Jerusalem. As we shall see in the next chapter, members of their group were the evangelists who had to leave Jerusalem, came to Antioch and preached to Gentiles. In this way they founded a church which became one of the most powerful centres for the spread of the gospel in the first generation and was for a long time one of the mother-churches of Christendom. Force of circumstances rather than any concerted plan of action drove the missionaries at Antioch to preach the gospel to Gentiles. But they would not have profited by the circumstances which arose and would not have refused to ask those who were converted to comply with the Jewish ritual, if they had not had quite a different perception of the relationship between the gospel and Judaism from that of the Hebrew Christians in Jerusalem. It would be more accurate to say that the Hellenists saw a problem to which other Christians were blind.

Stephen's solution does not seem to have exercised much influence in Christian thought. His radicalism alarmed them: they refused to accept it. The expressions used by Stephen to describe his conception of the relationship between the new religion and the old, tradition transferred from him to false witnesses. There is no form of Christian thought known to us which recalls his ideas. We do not meet with anything in primitive Christianity which we can suppose to have come from them. What, however, is most important in the history of thought and is really creative of new orientations is not always to find the solution to a problem but to formulate a problem which up to then has not been thought of. This is what Stephen did. After him others were able to find solutions to the problem of the relationship between the new religion and the old, which met with more success than his, perhaps showed greater balance, smoothed the paths of transition and at the same time made it easier for Christianity to retain the heritage of Israel's religion. It nevertheless remains true that Stephen by formulating the problem laid the foundations of Christianity's independence.

CHAPTER II

The Church at Antioch

I.—THE HELLENISTS AND THEIR MISSION

DRIVEN from Jerusalem by persecution the Hellenists came into touch with new surroundings. These provided them with the opportunity for successful activity of a more intense nature than was possible for them when they formed a small group within the Jewish community at Jerusalem.[1] The Hellenists were certainly much more inclined to evangelism than the Hebrews could ever have been; this was due to the fact that they had the feeling that Judaism had come to a dead end, that to obtain salvation man must pursue the path which had been opened up by the Just One, which was not the same as that of the Jewish ritual.

The narrative in Acts clearly shows a connection between the dispersion of the Hellenists and their mission. 'They that were scattered abroad', it says, 'went everywhere preaching the word' (viii. 4). This undoubtedly was the first mission to pass beyond the districts of Judaea in the immediate neighbourhood of Jerusalem. It began at a very early date since it took place before Paul's conversion. Our information about this Hellenistic mission is only very fragmentary. We have for instance no knowledge of the circumstances in which the church at Damascus was founded although the story of Paul's conversion (Acts. ix. 2, 10 ff.) proves that it was then existing. It is, however, natural to suppose that it came into existence through a Hellenist mission.[2] In the same way we have no details concerning the activities of those, who according to Acts xi. 19 went to Phoenicia and Cyprus,[3] neither concerning the mission

---

[1] We noticed that the same fact can be observed of Peter whose missionary activities became much more intense after he left Jerusalem.

[2] The idea advanced by Lohmeyer (*Galilea und Jerusalem*, Goettingen, 1936) that it may have been one of the fruits of Galilean Christianity and had no connection with Jerusalem Christianity is an ingenious conjecture perhaps but there is no adequate evidence to support it.

[3] It may be, at least so far as concerns Cyprus, that this silence must be explained by the fact that these missions gained no results. The story of Paul and

177

which founded the church of Caesarea, although it may be supposed
from Acts viii. 40 and xxi. 8 f. that its foundation should be attributed to Philip. This may be due to other causes besides the fact
that the compiler of Acts had only imperfect and incomplete information about these missions. It may well be that he mentions
them in only a summary fashion because the fact that a missionary
group came into existence without any initiative from the Twelve
and outside their control did not conform to his own conception.
This hypothesis is supported by the fact that the story—or rather
the simple mention of the event—of the mission which founded
the church at Antioch has clearly been transposed and postdated.
A very striking doublet exists between viii. 4 which introduces the
story of Philip's mission in Samaria and his evangelising work
between Azot and Caesarea after the persecution following Stephen's
death and xi. 19 which the compiler of Acts places after quite a
number of stories[1] and so dates perceptibly later.[2] He mentions the
arrival of Hellenists at Antioch who had been scattered by persecution and turning also to the Gentiles founded a church which soon
assumed a position of very great importance.

viii. 44 *They that were scattered abroad went everywhere preaching the word.*

xi. 19 *They which were scattered abroad* upon the persecution that arose about Stephen *travelled* as far as Phenice and Cyprus and Antioch, *preaching the word* to none but unto the Jews only.

οἱ μὲν οὖν διασπαρέντες
διῆλθον εὐαγγελιζόμενοι
τὸν λόγον

οἱ μὲν δυν διασπαρέντες ἀπὸ
τῆς θλίψεως τῆς γενομένης
ἐπὶ Στεφάνῳ διῆλθον ἕως
Φοινίκης καὶ Κύπρου καὶ
Ἀντιοχείας μηδενὶ λαλοῦντες
τὸν λόγον εἰ μὴ μόνον
Ἰουδαίοις

Barnabas' journey across Cyprus (Acts xiii. 4-12) contains no mention of their finding groups of Christians there.

[1] Stories of Philip's missions (viii. 4-40). The conversion of Paul of Tarsus (ix. 1-30). Stories of Peter's missions (Peter at Lydda and Joppa. The conversion of the centurion Cornelius) (ix. 32-xi. 18).

[2] This is also supported by the fact that the first notice of the dispersion is placed before Paul's conversion, i.e. according to our chronology at a date later than the summer of 29. On the other hand the author of Acts seems to place the second notice telling of the foundation of the church at Antioch about 40 or 41.

The same note serves as an introduction to both sections. The author certainly borrowed the note from a source which must have told of the activity of those who had been scattered and founded the church at Antioch rather than of Philip's; the structure of the first sentence is more suitable for the introduction to the story of a group's activity than an individual's.

Why didn't the author of Acts relate the foundation of the church at Antioch in the same context as he found it mentioned in his source? It cannot be because he was wedded to the idea of narrating at once the story of the evangelisation of Samaria to which for some reason or another he attached great importance. There was nothing to prevent him from placing the activity of Philip in Samaria side by side with that of the anonymous missionaries at Antioch.

The position of the story can only be explained as due to a transposition made of set purpose, expressly intended to convey the impression that the church at Antioch was founded after the centurion Cornelius had been converted. In this way the impression is given that the apostle Peter and the Twelve took the initiative in preaching the gospel to the Gentiles. Furthermore, by making out that the church at Antioch was only founded just before the conference at Jerusalem, he considerably lowered the prestige of this church which had refused to give way to the demands of Christians who had come from Judaea. On the other hand, by the same stroke the authority of the church at Jerusalem is heightened and it is made to seem less improbable for a question which had risen at Antioch to have been submitted to the judgement of the church at Jerusalem. In reality we know that nothing of the sort took place at the conference but that the men of Antioch and those of Jerusalem conferred together as between equals.

The story of the evangelisation of Samaria by Philip (viii. 4-25) is fairly full but except for two details which must be accepted with considerable reserve contains nothing out of the ordinary. The story is evidence for the fact that Samaria was evangelised and attributes this to Philip but tells us nothing concrete about it.

One of the episodes which must be considered concerns the incident of Peter and John's visit to Samaria, when they went as

According to Acts (xi. 26) Paul passed a year at Antioch before he came to Jerusalem for the conference. His arrival at Antioch would then have taken place towards the end of 42. According to the narrative Barnabas must not have been at Antioch for a long time before this.

delegates from the church at Jerusalem after it had learnt of the conversions made by Philip. The two apostles make what is a veritable confirmation circuit, as the Samaritans whom Philip had converted and baptised receive the holy Spirit when the two apostles lay their hands on them.[1] Here is to be found an addition made by the compiler to his source. His intention is perfectly clear; he wishes to make out that the evangelisation of Samaria was under the control of the church at Jerusalem in order that his narrative may conform to his artificial *ex post facto* conception of the apostolate and inspiration running through the whole book of Acts.[2]

Among the Samaritan converts was a certain Simon who had formerly practised magic. He gave out that he was 'some great one' and all the Samaritans from the least to the greatest said that he was 'the great power of God' (viii. 9 f.). It would be foolish to suppose that we can portray Simon's appearance and describe his ideas from what the later heresiologues tells us of him and his followers. He was doubtless one of the prophets mentioned by Origen,[3] who thought themselves the vehicles and organs of a divine revelation. Simon subsequently was reckoned the typical heretic, the great enemy whom Peter came to fight and destroy at Rome. An early form of this tradition more simple in character has influenced the story in Acts. Simon is treading an evil way. He asks Peter to give him in exchange for money the power of conferring the holy Spirit by the laying on of hands and draws upon himself a very stern admonition. He is not, however, obdurate beyond redemption since Peter calls upon him to repent. This call does not fall on deaf ears as he asks the apostle to pray that the threats hanging over him of which the apostle has spoken may not be realised. This must have been the tradition at a time when it was still hoped that the followers of Simon would rally to the church.

Following the story of evangelisation of Samaria comes the anecdote of Philip's conversion of the Ethiopian eunuch (viii. 26-40).

[1] If needed, the fact that the author of Acts believes that the privilege of conferring the Holy Spirit by the imposition of hands was confined to the apostles is plainly supported by Simon's demand made to Peter that he should give him the same power in return for money (viii. 18 f.).

[2] See *E.P.*, pp. 86 ff.

[3] Origen, *Celsum*, vii. 8 f. According to Origen *Celsum*, vi. 11 the Samaritan Dositheus gave himself out to be the Messiah promised by Moses. According to Hippolytus (*Philosophoumena* vi. 40) Marcus declared that he possessed 'the supreme power which comes from invisible and unnamed places'. Cf. also the story of Apsesthos and his parrots told by Hippolytus (*Philosophoumena* vi. 8) concerning this idea of the prophet or the son of God, see Wetter, *Der Sohn Gottes*, Gottingen, 1916.

In this the miraculous plays a big part. It is also noticeable that we are here in quite an advanced stage of theological thought as Isaiah liii is used to explain the death of Jesus.[1] All that can be gathered from this episode is that Philip left behind the reputation of a great missionary and that his activity must have ranged in the district of Ashdod and Caesarea where we find him residing at the time when Paul stayed in Caesarea on his way for the last time to Jerusalem (xxi. 8 f.).

2.—THE FOUNDATION OF THE CHURCH AT ANTIOCH

The book of Acts tells of the foundation of the church at Antioch in remarkably sober terms. The compiler of Acts, after mentioning the Hellenists who were scattered abroad upon the persecution that arose about Stephen and then came to Phenice, Cyprus, and Antioch, says as follows:

And some of them were men of Cyprus and Cyrene, which, when they were come to Antioch, spake unto the Grecians, preaching the Lord Jesus. And the hand of the Lord was with them: and a great number believed, and turned unto the Lord (xi. 20-21).

No proper name is given; the affair is related with simplicity and sobriety. The author of this note has reported a fact without apparently possessing any clear comprehension of its significance and consequences. The text gives us no indications as to the circumstances in which the initiative to preach to the Gentiles was taken, whether it was the result of a preconcerted plan of action, which was formed from preconceived theories, or whether favouring circumstances happened to arise, which drove the Hellenists at Antioch to take the decisive step of opening the gates of the church to the Gentiles. If we ought to stick to the latter hypothesis, then it must remain true that, if the Hellenists were wise enough to be able to profit by circumstances as they arose, they were not prevented by any feeling that those who did not observe the law could not receive grace and salvation.

The significance of the establishment of Christianity at Antioch, the third city in the Roman empire, and the most important in the East,[2] must be emphasised. For the first time Christianity gained a foothold in one of the capital cities of the ancient world and established a church in a place which through its connections with every

---

[1] Apart from this passage the only other explicit quotation from Isaiah liii is in 1 Peter ii. 22-25.   [2] Harnack, *Mission*, II, p. 124.

part of the world was destined to become a focus from which the new faith spread in every direction.

The story in Acts does not tell us directly that the church at Antioch was in any perceptible way different in character from that at Jerusalem. This silence is intentional; fortunately we can fill the gap. At Antioch those who were Gentiles were not compelled to keep the law; there is no doubt that those who had been converted from Judaism continued to observe Jewish customs to some extent at any rate; they must not, however, have been very rigorous legalists as they agree in their religious life to have close relationships with believers who had remained uncircumcised and to share meals with them (most probably the Lord's supper) (Gal. ii. 12). The book of the Acts supports the epistle to the Galatians on this point by saying (xv. 1) that the Christians of Gentile origin at Antioch were both surprised and disturbed when Judaeans came to Antioch and told them that they could not be saved unless they were circumcised in accordance with the Mosaic custom. This was plainly a rule which they had never heard mentioned before.

After the church at Jerusalem had learnt of the foundation of the church at Antioch it sent Barnabas there (xi. 22). Between this despatching of Barnabas to Antioch and that of Peter and John to Samaria exists a remarkable parallelism. In both cases the purpose is the same, to forge a link—at least after the first blow had been struck—between a church which had been founded by Hellenists and the mother church in Jerusalem which was represented by the Twelve. But the action taken was not the same, Peter and John's mission to Samaria is plainly a gloss in the story and entirely the product of the author's imagination. He supposed the occasion demanded it. But on the other hand we know for certain that Barnabas came to Antioch. To prove it we have only to recall that both the Acts and the epistle to the Galatians state that Barnabas with Paul represented the church of Antioch at the conference at Jerusalem, that afterwards he was first of all with Paul and then with Mark a missionary sent out by the church at Antioch, and that, as his presence at the time of the incident at Antioch proves, he appears to have stayed at Antioch in the intervals between his missionary journeys.[1] If added to this it is remembered that Acts xi. 20 states that men from Cyprus and Cyrene took the initiative in preaching the gospel to the Gentiles at Antioch and that Barnabas did in fact come from Cyprus (Acts iv. 36), there appears no doubt that we

---

[1] His name heads the list of prophets and teachers at Antioch in Acts xiii. 1.

have every reason to think that Barnabas must be reckoned to be one of the founders of the church at Antioch.[1] He must have gone there immediately after the death of Stephen.[2]

The epistle of the Galatians states (i. 21) that Paul stayed in Syria and Cilicia in the interval between his two missionary journeys, i.e. the eleven years preceding the conference at Jerusalem. The apostle does not mention Antioch by name as connected with the conference and only refers to it as the place where Peter and he met and faced each other.[3] But there is no doubt that it was from Antioch Paul set out to Jerusalem and that it was on behalf of the church there that he fought at the conference. Acts xi. 25-26 states that it was Barnabas who went to Tarsus to look for Paul and brought him to Antioch about a year before the Jews came to Antioch on their mission which resulted in the conference. What is this information worth? Acts ix. 27-28, states that, when Paul came to Jerusalem after his conversion,[4] the disciples with whom he tried to come into contact withdrew, because they did not know that he had become a Christian, until Barnabas brought him to the apostles. The story in Acts at this point lacks certainty and coherence: it does not explain how Barnabas could know of Saul's conversion, while the other Christians in Jerusalem were still unaware of it.[5] The way in which the compiler of Acts recounts this affair enables us without hesitation to maintain that Barnabas and Paul were in such close contact with each other that we can understand that the former considered that the presence of the latter would be useful at Antioch.

[1] Guignebert, *Le Christ*, p. 191.

[2] A similar fact is to be noted concerning Silas whom Acts xv. 22 mentions was sent to Antioch with Judas Barsabas to report the decisions of the conference at Jerusalem. Acts xv. 33 says that Judas Barsabas and Silas after accomplishing their mission left the brethren in peace and returned to those who had sent them, while a little further on (xv. 40) it says that Paul left Barnabas and chose Silas to help him. The editors of the Western text noted the contradiction and tried to iron it out by the addition of what is verse 34 in the received text. This, however, only emphasises the incoherence. After having said that Judas and Silas returned to those who had sent them there is added, 'Notwithstanding it pleased Silas to abide there still and Judas departed by himself'.

[3] Perhaps Paul avoided mentioning Antioch by name because at the time when he was writing the letter to the Galatians his relations with this church were not what they had been.

[4] The Acts makes out that Paul came to Jerusalem shortly after his conversion. The epistle to the Galatians (i. 18) proves that he came considerably later 'after three years'.

[5] At the time when Paul made his first visit to Jerusalem, it would have been difficult for his conversion three years before to be unknown.

3.—THE NAME 'CHRISTIANS' GIVEN TO THE FAITHFUL AT ANTIOCH

The compiler of Acts also mentions one detail concerning the church at Antioch which I have refrained from considering before now to prevent my analysis from being overweighted with what should be known of the argument it has caused.

'And the disciples were called Christians first at Antioch' (xi. 26).[1] Against Bauer who maintained that the word Χριστιανός could only have come into existence in the West R. A. Lipsius[2] pointed out that, although similar formations are not impossible in Latin,[3] the use of words ending in ανος, -ηνος, -ιανος for names of partisan groups is common in Asia.[4]

The text of Acts clearly shows that the name 'Christians' was given to members of the church by outsiders. It was certainly devised[5]

---

[1] The forms Χρητὸς and Χρηστιανός are met with in various texts: pap. mag. Egyptian (Wesseley, *Abh. d. Wiener Akad. d. Wiss*, 1888, II, p. 75) amulet (Kaibel *Inser. gr. Siciliae et Italiae*, Berlin, 1890, no. 2413); epitaphs from Syracuse (Kaibel, no. 78. 154. 196), from Asia Minor (*C.I.G.* II, 2883, *d.* 3857 *g.p.* 3865 1) from Syria (Le Bas-Waddington, *Voyage archéologique en Syrie*, Paris, 1870, III, p. 582, no. 2558). The original text of *Sinaiticus* had Χρηστιανούς instead of Χριστιανούς. It is the same in Acts xxvi. 28 and 1 Peter iv. 16, i.e. in the two other passages in the New Testament containing the words 'Christian' or 'Christianity'. We must remember also the phrase from Suetonius, *impulsore Chresto*. In the earliest inscriptions from Phrygia containing the term 'Christian' can be found the forms Χριστιανόι, Χρειστιανόι, Χρηστειανόι, Χρηστιανόι (inscriptions mentioned by Harnack, *Mission*, II, p. 191, Ramsay, *Cities and Bishoprics of Phrygia*, Oxford, 1895, pp. 558 ff. and Anderson, *Paganism and Christianity in New-Phrygia*, in Ramsay, *History and Art of the Eastern provinces of the Roman Empire*, 1906, pp. 214 ff.). The earliest material evidence for the use of the term 'Christian' appears to be a *graffito* from Pompeii, deciphered in 1862, which has since disappeared. It contains the letters . . . HRISTIAN . . . . The inscription is too mutilated to be capable of interpretation. Concerning this *graffito* and the literature devoted to it see V. Schultze, *Christeninschrift in Pompeii*, *Z.f. Kirchengesch.*, 1881, IV, pp. 125-130; D. Leclercq, 'Pompei', *D.A.C.L.*, XIV, col. 1403-1404.

[2] R. A. Lipsius, *Uber den Ursprung und aeltesten Gebrauch des Christennamens*, *Gratulationsprogramm der theol. Facultat Jena fur Hase*, 1873. Cf. De Labriolle, *Christianus*, *Bulletin Du Cange*, 1929-30, V, pp. 69-88.

[3] Gerke, *Der Christenname ein Scheltname*, *Festschrift zur Jahrhundertfeier der Universitat Breslau*, 1911, pp. 360 ff., maintains the Roman origin of the term.

[4] F. Blass, Χρηστιανόι Χριστιανόι, *Hermes*, 1895, XXX, pp. 465 ff. See also Lecoultre, *De l'etymologie du mot 'chretien'*, *Rev. de theol. et de philos.*, 1907, XI, pp. 188-196.

[5] It cannot have been devised by Jews who would have taken care not to give a name to their enemies which would have given them a claim to consider themselves the true servants of the Messiah.

by Gentiles.[1] It may well have first been used ironically and contemptuously;[2] this would explain why for a long time it was not used by believers themselves.[3] Later, when persecutions began and the *nomen* became a criminal offence, Christians no longer repudiated it, as, if they had done so, they would have been disavowing their faith and denying their Lord. It then became a title of honour. The fact that we do not meet with the term 'Christians' in the writings of the first generation, and only rarely in those of the second and that it only became anything like current in the time of the Apologists does not constitute a valid objection to the information given in Acts xi. 26.[4] In favour of the term originating at Antioch, Harnack[5] uses an argument which is not without value, even though we must not consider it decisive. This is that Ignatius is the only one of the apostolic Fathers to use the terms Christian and Christianity. We can therefore agree with the majority of the commentators of Acts[6] that the term Christian was coined by Gentiles at Antioch to describe the new converts shortly after the foundation of the church there.

Nevertheless this fact is significant. The fact that the term Christian was at first only used of Gentile Christians[7] supports the hypothesis that the church at Antioch was Hellenic in character. It also affords evidence for its importance inasmuch as outsiders found it necessary to have an appropriate term by which they could

[1] The Gentile origin also explains why we have the two variants Χρηστιανόι and Χριστιανόι. The name Χριστὸς meant nothing to a Gentile, while we meet with the name Χρηστὸς although not very frequently (*C.I.G.*, 194, 427, 1337, 1723, 2027, etc.). Cf. Blass, *Hermes*, 1895, XXX, pp. 465 ff. Dom Le Clercq, 'Chretiens', *D.A.C.L.* III, col. 1468.

[2] Preuschen (*Apgesch.*, p. 74) has suggested that those who claimed Christ (the Anointed) as their leader were ironically called 'the anointed ones'. Theophilus of Antioch (*Ad. Autol.* i. 12) knew that the name 'Christian' originally was used ironically.

[3] There are thus three contexts in the New Testament containing the word.

[4] The evidence from Tacitus (*Ann.* xv. 44) must be added which shows that the term 'Christians' was in current use in Rome in 64. This evidence cannot be rendered invalid by supposing that Tacitus is using an anachronism and has projected into the past a term which had only become current in his own time.

[5] Harnack, *Mission*, I, p. 398. Harnack also relies on the tradition which makes Luke a native of Antioch. But the tradition is not strong enough to be used in this way.

[6] It is sufficient to mention Loisy (*Actes*, pp. 468-470) who cannot be suspected of accepting the evidence of Acts without question.

[7] Harnack (*Mission*, I, p. 397, n. 3) quotes from a text which has not yet been edited and mentions 'Christians and Jews who confess Christ'. The author of this text evidently does not consider the latter to be understood under the term 'Christians'.

call its members. It proves also that the church was quite distinct from the synagogue and even from the proselytes attached to it.[1]

4.—THE CHURCH AT ANTIOCH AFTER 44

I have not here concerned myself with the events which disturbed the church at Antioch in 43-44 nor with the repercussions following upon it from the quarrel between the apostle Paul and the Judaising Christians. I shall return to them in another chapter. We will only note at the moment that it may well have had its origin in a difference in attitude between the church at Antioch and the apostle. Perhaps the Gentile Christians at Antioch would not have found it so difficult to accept circumcision if Barnabas and Paul especially had not exerted themselves with such vehemence against the demands of the Judaeans. Nevertheless, at the conference at Jerusalem, Paul felt that he was defending the cause of the church at Antioch as much as his own personal position. It is quite possible that he entertained some illusions on this subject and that the Christians at Antioch were much less keen than their apostle to hold fast to 'the liberty which we have in Christ' and attached less importance to the question at issue than he did. The difference between Paul and the Christians which was slight at first seems to have grown wider afterwards. It was not yet present in 43-44. The fact that Paul at the conference gained recognition for his apostleship and his gospel gave him a free hand to continue his missionary work among the Gentiles. The church at Antioch must have considered this result to be an encouragement for projects which it had undoubtedly already formed.

We have no need to think that it was due to chance that immediately after the conference the church at Antioch inaugurated a series of great missionary enterprises. A note of a very modest nature (xiii. 1-3) tells us of the origin of the mission from Antioch, and we have no reason to question its value.[2] It mentions six prophets and teachers:[3] Barnabas, Simeon surnamed Niger, Lucius of Cyrene,

[1] If Christians were only a group within the fold of Judaism, people outside would not have distinguished them from Jews or at any rate would not have been sufficiently interested in them to have given them a proper name.

[2] If it was written by the author of Acts himself Paul would not have been mentioned the last after six men who left behind them a much fainter impression in the history of primitive Christianity.

[3] Harnack (*Mission*, I, p. 323, n. 2) considers that the six persons mentioned were both prophets and teachers combined. Loisy (*Actes*, p. 501) thinks that the

Manaen, who had been brought up with Herod the Tetrarch,[1] and Saul. While they rendered worship to the Lord and fasted, the holy Spirit commanded them to set apart Barnabas and Saul for the work for which he had destined them. And when they had fasted and prayed, they laid their hands on them and sent them away.[2] The revelation here mentioned, it is certain, only served to put into definite action a project which had already been envisaged and entrusted to Barnabas and Saul.[3] Missionary enterprise is here thought of as inspired and directed by the Spirit. On the level of human activity and thought they do not act on their own personal responsibility but as delegates of a church. In the realm of fact it clearly means that the church at Antioch organised the journey and paid the expenses incurred. After the story of the journey, to which I shall return later on,[4] the envoys gave an account of what they had done before an assembly of the church at Antioch and showed 'all that God had done through them and how he had opened a door of faith unto the Gentiles' (xiv. 27). While this journey certainly does not stand out as the first time that the gospel was preached to the Gentiles, nevertheless it was the first large enterprise of a systematic character undertaken for this purpose. Its date can be fixed with certainty as the spring of 44. We cannot say how long it took or fix even approximately the date when Barnabas and Paul returned to Antioch, on which appears to depend the date when a serious quarrel arose between Peter and Paul.

In short, while Paul was kept far away by his missionary activity, Peter was turned out of Jerusalem, came and settled in Antioch.

terms 'teachers' and 'prophets' applied to two different classes of people and noticing that the conjunction between Lucius and Manaen is τε not καὶ classifies Barnabas, Simeon, Niger and Lucius of Cyrene as prophets, Manaen and Saul as teachers. Ramsay (*Paulus in der Apostelgeschichte, deutsche Uebesetzung von H. Groschke*, Gutersloh, 1898, pp. 54 f.) had already made this distinction before Loisy. If it is true that Paul makes a distinction in 1 Cor. xii. 28 between the ministry of a prophet and that of a teacher, it is not rigid. The same man can combine in his own person several gifts of the spirit. Such was the case for example in Paul, who was an apostle, a prophet and a teacher as well as possessed with the gift of tongues without mentioning any other gifts which he might have possessed. Loisy thinks that except for the name Saul which was added sometime later the list composed the founders of the church at Antioch. This hypothesis should be retained although it can never be proved that it is right.

[1] Or, perhaps, foster-brother.

[2] The origin of this note may well be found in the story of Paul's missions which appears to have been the principal source used for the second half of the Acts.

[3] The sequel shows that John Mark (xiii. 5b) was their companion from the start, although he only played a subordinate part. [4] See pp. 218 f.

There by degrees he became so influential that, when Paul and he had quite a keen dispute with each other, the church did not take Paul's side.[1]

We have very little information about the subsequent history of the church at Antioch. As the church at Jerusalem showed a marked decline after 70 the influence of the church at Antioch must have considerably increased. It preserved its Hellenic character as is shown by the fact that most of the names in the list of bishops of Antioch are Greek in form. It must, however, have been subject to Jewish influences. They may have met with some success as is shown by the fact that among the heresies which Ignatius attacked there is one for which he uses the term 'Judaism'.[2]

For want of any direct evidence some scraps of information can be gained from certain traditions. While they must be accepted on points of detail with much reserve they at least provide support for the belief that the church at Antioch preserved its importance. Acts (xi. 27-30) relates that the prophet Agabus about 43 came from Judaea to Antioch and predicted a big famine. Upon hearing this the church determined to send Barnabas and Paul to Jerusalem with money to help the church there. As we shall see further on[3] the episode cannot be retained as historical. It may have arisen from a confused memory of the fact that, at the conference at Jerusalem which was held at that time, Paul had asked the Gentile churches to come to the financial aid of the church at Jerusalem which was in a bad way materially. If we accept this interpretation we are not bound to drop Harnack's.[4] He considers the story in Acts to be a kind of symbolical expression of the assistance rendered by the rich church of Antioch to neighbouring churches when they found themselves in need.

In the second decade of the second century the letters of Ignatius show us a man who for all his protestations of humility is proud to be bishop of Antioch and believes himself qualified by his position to instruct the other churches. His authority is certainly that of a confessor but he also speaks as bishop of Antioch. He calls this church 'the church of Syria' which after the torment of persecution had recovered 'its ancient grandeur' (Sm. xi. 2). When he asks the churches to whom he has occasion to write or to send a message to send delegates to Antioch we cannot be sure that it is only because the church needs support when it has no bishop. It may be also

[1] See pp. 303 f.   [2] See pp. 414 ff.
[3] See p. 294, n. 1.   [4] Harnack, *Mission*, II, p. 125.

because being the metropolitan church of Christendom and the most important church in the East respect from its neighbours was due to it.[1]

It goes without saying that no positive direct value can be attached to the affirmation of St. John Chrysostom that no church could rival that of Antioch for the number of relics it possessed[2] any more than to the tradition which says that it was Ignatius who, instructed by angels, introduced the chanting of the responses into the forms of worship.[3] These traditions, however, may be considered as proofs of the prestige which the church at Antioch claimed for itself and of the glory shed upon it by its past.

APPENDIX—BARNABAS

Barnabas played a very important part in the church at Antioch. He may even have been one of its founders. He appears to have reflected Paul's outlook rather than Peter's.

The first time we find him mentioned is in the note of Acts iv. 32-37 which describes the community of goods then characterising the church's life. We read: 'And Joses, who by the apostles was surnamed Barnabas[4] (which is being interpreted, The son of consolation) (or of exhortation)[5] a Levite of the country of Cyprus[6] having land, sold it, and laid it at the apostles' feet' (iv. 36-37).

The etymology of the name Barnabas as given in this note has been the subject of much discussion.[7] Many attempts which have

---

[1] Harnack, *Mission*, II, p. 126.

[2] St. John Chrysostom, *Hom. in coemet. appel.*, 1.　　　[3] Socrates, *H.e.* vi. 8.

[4] This is the translation given by most of the commentators; it is the most probable. We may, however, translate it as Lake and Cadbury (*Begin.* IV, p. 49) note 'Joseph surnamed Barnabas who was of the number of the apostles'.

[5] The *paraclesis* is a religious discourse made up of exhortation, encouragement, consolation, and even reproach. The meaning given to the name Barnabas shows that he was a man who was peculiarly versed in this kind of instruction.

[6] It is unnatural for the two terms 'Levite' and 'Cypriote' to be associated with each other. The word γένος would have to be watered down considerably, much more than is legitimate, if it is to mean not that Barnabas was a Cypriot by race but that he was descended from Jews who had come to Cyprus to live there. It is certainly much better frankly to recognise the contradiction and to suppose that the compiler of Acts made Barnabas a Levite because he wanted to obliterate the memory of the fact that he was not a pure Jew by race.

[7] On this subject in addition to the commentaries, see Klostermann, *Probleme am Aposteltext*, Gotha, 1883, pp. 8 f. Schmiedel 'Barnabas', *E.B.* I col. 484 ff.; Dalman *Die Worte Jesu* I, L., 1898, p. 32; *Grammatik. d. jud. palast. Aramaischen*, Leipzig, 1894, p. 142, n. 1; Deissmann, *Bibelstudien*, Marburg an der Lahn, 1895, pp. 175 ff.; *Neue Bibelstudien*, Marburg an der Lahn, 1897, pp. 15 ff.; 'Barnabas', *Z.N.T.W.*, VII, 1906, pp. 91-92.

been made to explain it have not ended in any really satisfying result. It is plainly a popular derivation and therefore not more than a guess, a product of imagination to give an honourable and edifying meaning to a name which creeted some surprise when it belonged to an evangelist. It was pagan and contained the name of the Babylonian god Nebo to whom it signified that its bearer was attached. Barnabas is to be equated with the form Barnebous (son or worshipper of Nebo) which appears on two inscriptions.[1] As an explanation of the fantastic derivation given in Acts iv. 36 it has been suggested[2] that, as this derivation was more applicable to the name Manaen rather than the name Barnabas, it originally belonged to the name Manaen in the list of prophets and teachers at the beginning of chapter xiii and that through a mistake it was applied to the name Barnabas instead of Manaen and then was transferred from chapter xiii to chapter iv. This hypothesis is too complicated to be at all probable.

From iv. 36-37 we learn that Barnabas was a member of the church at Jerusalem at an early stage and that as a preacher he had notable powers of persuasion. We learn also that tradition tried to camouflage his name which contained that of a pagan god and made him out to be a Levite in order to compensate for his Cypriot origin. On this account it may well be that he was of Gentile origin, perhaps not exactly a proselyte as Nicholas is said to have been in vi. 5 but the son or grandson of a proselyte unless we are to suppose on account of his kinship to John Mark of Jerusalem (Col. iv. 10) that he was of mixed descent, having on one side ancestors belonging to the tribe of Levi, and on the other ancestors who were Cypriotes.[3]

[1] An Aramean inscription from Palmyra of 114 of our era (De Vogue, *Syrie centrale*, *Inser. semit.*, Paris, 1868, p. 53). A Greek inscription from the third or fourth century of our era from Nicopolis in the north of Syria (K. Humann *und* O. Puchstein, *Reisen in Kleinosien und Nordsyrien*, *Textband*, Berlin, 1890, p. 398. (Cf. Deissmann, *Bibelst.*, p. 177; *N. Bibelst.*, p. 16, n. 1.) The transformation of the vowel *e* (in Nebo) into *a* does not cause difficulty as it is current in the transposition into Greek of the name Nebo and compounds in which it occurs. In Isa. xlvi. 1 where the LXX (in the manuscript B) Aquila and Theodotion have Νεβυου Symmachus has Ναβω. Nebucadnezzar is rendered by Nabouchodonosor in the LXX; this form is also found in Berosus, Josephus, and Strabo. See also the transposition of Nebouzaradan into Nabouzardan (manuscript A in 2 Kings xxv. 8). The form Nabu adopted by the people of Syria and Palmyra is a contraction of the full form Nabun. Syrians and Palmyrans transcribe n b w, from which comes the biblical Nebo, used both as the name of a god (Isa. xlvi. 1) and of a mountain (Deut. xxxii. 49) and of a town (Numb. xxxii. 3, 38). (I owe this information to my colleague André Parrot.) [2] Lake-Cadbury, *Begin.* IV, p. 49.
[3] He would then have been similar in descent to Timothy, born of a Jewish mother and a Gentile father (Acts. xvi. 1).

While we have no right to say that Barnabas belonged to the Hellenist party in Jerusalem, it is not improbable that he was more tolerant than most Christians at Jerusalem in his attitude towards Jewish ritual law because he was of Gentile or semi-Gentile descent. In the book of Acts he seems to hold a position of his own as he is described as the mediator between Paul and the Twelve after the former's conversion. I shall not give the reasons here which lead us to think that Barnabas was one of the founders of the church at Antioch and not just a delegate who was sent afterwards to create a link between it and the church at Jerusalem.[1] In any case, immediately on arrival at Antioch Barnabas felt himself to be a member of the church there and behaved as if he were one. His authority there seems to have been much greater than Paul's. This perhaps was due, not only to the fact which Acts reveals that he was well known there before Paul but also and perhaps more so to the fact that Barnabas was a more supple character and less self-assertive than Paul, so that he did not create that friction which Paul seldom completely avoided in his dealings with the churches he had founded.

It would be an exaggeration to say that Barnabas held prior place before Paul in the church at Antioch. Nevertheless, in the first part of Acts Barnabas is always mentioned before Paul (xi. 30; xii. 25; xiii. 1, 7 and also xiv. 14; xv. 12, 25), while Paul takes first place from the time the missionaries reach Antioch in Pisidia (xiii. 43, 46, 50; xv. 2, 22, 35). This cannot be a tendacious touching up of the narrative; if the compiler had wished to show Paul's superiority over Barnabas he would have proceeded more systematically. We must therefore suppose that the situation gradually changed in the course of the voyage. It must be presumed that Paul gained the upper hand because he was bolder in initiative and capable of much more intense activity so that in the end Barnabas' gentler nature was overpowered by Paul's strong personality.

The incident mentioned in Galatians ii. 11 ff. supports the idea that on the question of the ritual law Barnabas' position was not the same as Paul's, although according to v. 43-44 they formed a common front against the claims of the judaisers. The difference between the two men was perhaps less one of doctrine than of temperament. On the question of ritualism Barnabas did not hold such rigid and fixed ideas as possessed the mind of Paul; he was much more influenced by the practical needs of the situation and so avoided the opposition and strife which Paul stirred up.

[1] See p. 182.

Paul and Barnabas separated when they were planning a second missionary journey. It is difficult to believe that the only reason for their separation was, as the story in Acts (xv. 36-40) tells us, due to a divergence of view concerning the suitability of taking John Mark with them. On the previous journey he had accompanied Barnabas and Paul no further than Cyprus, when he left them to return to Jerusalem. The separation of Barnabas and Paul may well have resulted from the incident at Antioch, while the reference to John Mark may have been introduced in place of the real cause of the separation to make it appear less serious. The significance of the separation must not be exaggerated. Later on in the epistle to the Galatians Paul mentions Barnabas as a man who on one occasion had been carried away by an evil example but had fought by his side for the defence of the gospel and Christian liberty. In the first epistle to the Corinthians he shows him to be a missionary who had co-operated with him whole-heartedly and had followed the same methods. He mentions him in terms which show that both he and Barnabas belonged to a group of missionaries which was a different one from that to which the other apostles, the brothers of the Lord and Cephas belonged. Like Paul Barnabas worked with his hands to gain his livelihood (1 Cor. ix. 6).

Acts xv. 36-39 states that after being separated from Paul Barnabas with John Mark left for a missionary journey to Cyprus. We have no reason to doubt the truth of this; no value, however, can be attached to late documents[1] which give an account of his missionary activity and martyrdom in Cyprus. They are legends intended to lend glory to the church in Cyprus and give it the right to affirm its independence from the church in Antioch.[2]

In the same way the traditions which put Barnabas among the sixty-six disciples[3] as well as of what is said of him in the *Acta Petri* (ch. 4) or in the pseudo-clementine literature (*Hom.* i. 9-16; *Rec.* i. 60, 61) cannot be retained.

A theological treatise which, in the form of a letter contains an allegorical interpretation of the Jewish sacrificial cult and appears to have been written about 130, is preserved under the title of the epistle of Barnabas. Tertullian[4] also attributes to Barnabas the

---

[1] Περίοδοι καὶ μαρτύριον τοῦ ἁγίου Βαρνάβα τοῦ ἀποστόλου (end of the fourth century or the beginning of the fifth). *Acta Barnabae auctore Marco* (the same period). *Enkomion Barnabae* by the Cypriot monk Alexander (sixth century).

[2] Harnack, 'Barnabas', *R.E.* II, p. 412.

[3] On this subject see Hennecke, *Neut. Apokr.*, p. 125.

[4] Tertullian, *De pudicitia*, 20.

epistle to the Hebrews but the way in which he does it shows that he was not making a personal guess but following a tradition of which we have no other knowledge. There can be no question of attributing either of these two compositions to Barnabas. The epistle to the Hebrews is not a composition of the first Christian generation neither is what is called the epistle of Barnabas for much more cogent reasons. The attribution of them to Barnabas is only of interest as showing what the primitive early church remembered of his career.[1]

[1] There also existed at a fairly early period a gospel of Barnabas of which nothing survives (except according to Resch two quotations which have little significance. That they belong to it can only be purely a matter of conjecture. See above Hennecke, *Neut. Apok.*, p. 64, n. 2). Concerning the gospel of Barnabas see Harnack, *G.a.L.*, I, p. 18; Zahn, *G.K.*, II, p. 292.

CHAPTER III

The Apostle Paul and Paulinism[1]

I.—PAUL'S SIGNIFICANCE AND THE CHARACTER OF HIS THOUGHT

WHEN the Hellenist missionaries at Antioch turned to the Gentiles and did not ask them to submit to the demands of the Jewish ritual law, they instinctively felt that their faith could not remain strictly confined within the framework of Judaism. Subsequently Barnabas and the church at Antioch showed some hesitation in their attitude towards those who maintained that Christians were obliged to keep the ritual commands of the Jewish law. Although they instinctively felt that the gospel was independent from Judaism they had not clearly grasped the fact and given it formal expression.

Nevertheless the set-up of the Hellenic church at Antioch marked an important stage in the establishment of Christianity as a religion independent of Judaism, but this advance still needed to be consolidated. The relations between Christianity and Judaism had to be clearly thought out to secure the former's independence. This was the task of the apostle Paul or, one should rather say, one aspect of his task. He cut the gospel free from the chains with which Judaism was in danger of strangling it. At the same time his missionary journeys caused its vigorous expansion while the incomparable power of his preaching gave it forms of expression which have lasted for centuries and even now form the classic expression of the Christian faith.

For this reason the figure of Paul towers above the whole of the first generation of Christians, although he was not the first nor the only missionary of his time and he certainly was not the most influential.[2] Both in the very heart of the church and even in the

---

[1] The literature about Paul and Paulinism is extremely abundant. The most essential references will be found in my book, *Introd.* IV, 1-2. Albert Schweitzer's book (*Paul and his Interpreters*) is especially important for the theological interpretation of Paulinism.

[2] 1 Cor. ix. 4-6, shows, however, that Paul felt that he and Barnabas of the

communities founded by him he met with misunderstanding and hostility. He died in isolation, in the midst of general indifference from believers, but scarcely ten years after his disappearance, the cause for which he had struggled and which appeared to die with him, that of Christian universalism freed from all ritualism, had gained complete victory. Less than a generation after his death, what could be recovered from his letters was collected into a *corpus* [1] and remained the principal source of Christian theology.

Paul defined the relationship of Christianity with Judaism and in this way gave it a structure which was never subsequently modified in spite of Marcion's attempts to do so, and so far as can be seen could never be called in question without shaking the very foundations of Christianity. He proved Christianity to be the fulfilment of the promise made to Abraham and thus forged a definite link between Christianity and the religion of the patriarchs, Moses, and the prophets along the lines hinted at by Jesus, while his theory that Christ had brought to an end the reign of the law brought to birth the universal religion which was potentially present in the gospel.

It may be said that Paul's doctrine of salvation provided an explanation of Christian experience and laid the foundations of christology in a form which the Hellenic spirit could assimilate.

We know that some historians have claimed that Paul was the second founder of Christianity and have thought his labours to have been as important as those of the first if not more so.[2] Yet this is to misunderstand his work. In the development of a religion we have to distinguish between devotion to a new religious object on the one hand, which is a real creative act, and on the other hand, the way in which this experience is expressed together with the organisation of a religious society without which it cannot be preserved in a settled condition. There is no doubt that without Paul Christianity would never have become established in the form in which we find it. Perhaps it might have evaporated away but with Paul and without

missionaries of the first generation formed the group which made the greatest sacrifices for their work.

[1] The *corpus paulinum* seems to have been formed at the beginning of the last decade of the first century between the composition of the book of Acts and that of the epistle of Clement of Rome to the Corinthians. This must have taken place in Greece. On this question see Zahn, *G.K.*, I, pp. 811-839; Harnack, *Die Briefsammlung des Apostels Paulus und die anderen vorkonstantinischen christlicher Briefsammlungen*, Leipzig, 1926; Lietzmann, 'Einfuhrung in die Textgeschichte der Paulusbriefe', *An die Romer*[2], Tubingen, 1933, pp. 1 ff.

[2] It is to be noticed that Guignebert following many others maintains this thesis in his last book *Le Christ*.

Jesus it would never have been born. The work of Jesus cannot be compared with that of Paul; they do not belong to the same species and were not undertaken with the same purpose.

There is nothing more untrue than the idea that Paulinism is an abstract theological system. None of the ideas expressed by Paul or of the doctrines formulated by him mean anything if they are divorced from the religious experiences which suggested them and of which they are the expression. Paul was anything but a theorist. His interior life, his activity as a missionary and leader of the churches formed an indissoluble whole, and a whole which was constantly in motion. His ever active thoughts were centred on the idea of a movement. His theology was not of a God as a being but of a God who wills and acts. It is perfectly true that at the basis of Paul's thought lies a complete theology which he had inherited from Judaism concerning God, the creation, man, his destiny, and his position in the world and before God. But Paul does not demonstrate it as his theology; it forms the assumptions of Paulinism not Paulinism itself.

It is a commonplace to mention the systematic character of Paul's thought and to describe the apostle as the first and greatest Christian thinker and the creator of the church's theology. The epistles contain the elements of a vast apocalypse, which begins with the revolt of Satan against God and even with the creation of the world while its end is the glory of God. Satan caused men to fall into sin by forcing them to give him and the demons the worship and adoration which was due only to God. In this way he associated them with the revolt by which he desired to make himself equal with God.[1]

The entering of sin into man and the world provoked God's anger, which would have brought the corrupt world with the rebel spirits and sinful men to an end, if God, moved by pity and for the sake of his glory, had not undertaken a work of redemption which is superimposed on his work of creation. Both man and the universe are to be redeemed or perhaps we should say man is to be redeemed in a cosmic setting.[2]

[1] Rom. i. 18-23. Paul does not expressly mention Satan's revolt against God but it was an idea current in Jewish thought. It is implied in the christological argument developed in Phil. ii. 6-11, where it is said that Christ did not seek to make himself equal with God. The negative form of the sentences at the beginning show that this picture of Christ is like one side of a diptych. On the other side there is a corresponding picture of a celestial being, Satan, who wished to be equal with God, i.e. to gain for himself the worship due to God.

[2] See my article 'Le rôle de l'elément cosmologique dans la sotériologie paulinienne', *R.h.p.r.*, 1935, XV, pp. 335-359.

Paul gave to this general framework which he did not create but inherited from Judaism his personal interpretation, which far from being systematic and coherent shows flagrant contradictions. These appear not only on secondary questions but on such essential points as the interpretation of the death of Christ, the conditions of attaining salvation, and the calling of the Gentiles which the abrogation of the Jewish law made possible.

Although I wish to anticipate as little as possible the analysis of Pauline thought which I shall give later on, I must make this point clear because it must be grasped if one is to see Paulinism in correct perspective.

The importance which the apostle attached to the idea of the death of Christ cannot be exaggerated. It is such an essential element in his preaching that the whole faith rests on Jesus-Christ crucified (1 Cor. i. 23; ii. 2) or on the cross of Jesus-Christ (1 Cor. i. 17, 18). We meet, however, with ideas concerning this important point which cannot be harmonised with each other. In 1 Corinthians v. 7, where Paul says 'Christ our passover is sacrificed for us', he seems to conceive the death of Christ to resemble the sacrifice of the paschal lamb, while elsewhere (Gal. iii. 13; Rom. v. 17; viii. 3) he seems to be thinking of another type of levitical sacrifice, of purification, redemption, or expiation. In the epistle to the Colossians (ii. 14-15) Paul declares that by the cross Christ has triumphed over hostile demonic powers and has plundered them. We meet with a similar but not identical idea in 1 Corinthians ii. 8 which says that none of the princes of this world knew of the plan of redemption conceived of by the wisdom of God, for, had they known it, they would not have crucified the Lord of glory.[1] In other passages Paul has recourse to the idea of substitution to explain the efficacy of the death of Christ. In Galatians iii. 13 he says that Christ hath redeemed us from the curse of the law, being made a curse for us.[2] Although this is not really the idea of substitution it closely resembles it. Paul nearly always returns to it, when he is trying to explain how the death of Christ makes the justification of the sinner possible. It is the idea of expiation through the union of the innocent with the

[1] The idea expressed here is that the spiritual powers, who direct the march of events, by crucifying Jesus, i.e. by causing Pilate to put him to death, without knowing it have contributed to God's plan for the salvation of sinners and for their own destruction. We can see here the old folklore-theme of the tricked demon.

[2] The preposition ὑπέρ is ambiguous in the Koine and sometimes means 'in place of' and at other times 'on behalf of'. In Gal. iii. 13, the meaning 'in place of' must be preferred.

guilty. God treated Christ 'who knew no sin' as if he was the sin itself and in his flesh condemned this sin (2 Cor. v. 21) so that, when Christ died, divine justice was satisfied and forgiveness made possible.

These various interpretations of the death of Christ are not all on the same level. The idea of the condemnation of sin in the flesh of Christ has a greater importance than any of the others. Paul does not just state it once in passing but returns to it again and again and upon it bases his whole theory of the sinner's justification. The other ideas, however, are not to be considered null and void. The problem covers them all: why cannot we find in Paul a homogeneous theory of redemption through the death of Christ? We cannot escape it by taking refuge in subtle interpretations for the sake of unifying the divergent ideas which Paul puts out. If we were to find a solution by this method which would have to satisfy us on other counts, we should have to make use of ideas and arguments which cannot by any means be attributed to the apostle. Deissmann[1] suggests that the various formulae concerning the death of Christ to be found in the epistles should be considered as parallel but independent attempts to explain and express experiences which by their very nature escape strict definition. A real unity exists between them but it comes from the religious experience to which they all refer, like the unity between the views of a mountain as seen from the four points of the compass.

If we enquire into what Paul considers to be the conditions for the accomplishment of salvation, we shall meet with analogous statements which, however, are much sharper in form.

The believer who has been justified and united to Christ by faith and the sacraments is no longer in principle a being of flesh but has become a spiritual being. He continues, however, to live in the flesh. Justification thus keeps a theoretic character; it is not salvation. The believer is only saved by hope (Rom. viii. 24). The death and resurrection of Christ guarantee for him a deliverance which, however, has not yet been realised. To the question, 'How will salvation be accomplished?', Paul's theology provides not one answer but two, 1 Thessalonians iv. 13-18 and 1 Corinthians xv. 20-58 say that in order to be able to inherit the kingdom of God the man who is flesh and blood will have to undergo a transformation. Paul says that those who die before the return of the Lord will remain until then in a state of sleep or provisional prostration and

---

[1] Deissmann, *Paulus, Eine kultur- und religionsgeschichtliche Skizze*, Tubingen, 1911, p. 95.

then will rise again with a body which will be no longer terrestrial, carnal, and psychical, but spiritual and heavenly. The others among whom Paul ranges himself will undergo an instantaneous transformation as soon as the Lord appears to make the final assault which will end in the establishment of the reign of God.[1]

In other contexts Paul does not make the parousia to be the means by which salvation is accomplished and so renders it practically useless, at least so far as the elect are concerned. In 2 Corinthians iv. 16-v. 10 he distinguishes two elements in man. One he calls the outward man: it is the human personality so far as it is determined by the fact that it is descended from Adam; it is dominated by the powers of death and destined to destruction. Paul pictures this destruction as progressive, death in the customary sense of the word only signifying the final end. The inward man which grows as the outward man perishes is the new creation which is realised in him who is 'in Christ'. The believer who knows that this new personality has been born and is growing in himself longs for the time when it will be able to escape out of the fetters and limitations which life in the flesh imposes upon it. The same idea is to be found in the first chapter of the epistle to the Philippians which expresses a real yearning for death as the time when the apostle will be fully 'with Christ'. The idea of an intermediate period of sleep between the death of each believer and the parousia of the Lord is quite foreign to the eschatology of both the second epistle to the Corinthians and the epistle to the Philippians. Further on we shall have to enquire why these two eschatologies exist side by side and how it can be explained;[2] for the moment it is sufficient to point them out and to observe that Paul never seems to be at pains to harmonise his views on the individual and collective accomplishment of salvation.

The idea of the calling of the Gentiles to salvation also had capital importance for Paul. Its importance was not only theological but also practical since he never ceased in the whole of his career to struggle in its defence. Paul had far too much respect for the authority of the Old Testament ever to free himself from the idea that there was a fundamental difference between the chosen people and the Gentiles. Besides this he retained a feeling of national pride even though his assurance of salvation which he had entertained before

[1] There is no doubt that Paul did not mention the idea of the transformation of those who will be still alive at the parousia in the first epistle to the Thessalonians, because, when he wrote of this development, he was not concerned with those who had died before the parousia.

[2] See pp. 272 ff.

his conversion had collapsed (Phil. iii. 4-6; 2 Cor. xi. 21-22).[1] The whole argument of Romans ix-xi shows how Paul remained attached to an instinctive and dogmatic belief in Israel's privileges. The phrasing of Romans i. 16 must be understood literally. Salvation was intended first for the Jews and only afterwards for the Gentiles.

Although universalism is a peculiar characteristic of Christianity it was not an absolute novelty. Ad. Lods[2] showed that the idea of a universal church without any distinction of race and rite was the ultimate aim and end of the religion of the prophets but was hindered and thwarted in Judaism by a series of contrary forces. The new faith triumphed over these forces and universalism spontaneously sprang up in the primitive church. It was present as a fact before any theory arose to justify it *a posteriori*. Paul is the only man to our knowledge who felt the need to formulate a theory in support of it. But he offered and sketched out a whole series of explanations which, however, cannot be unified. I shall enumerate them in the order of the documents in which they are described.

Galatians iii. 16 states that the promise made to Abraham, which Paul[3] considered to be the foundation of the religion of Israel was not intended to benefit all the descendants of the patriarch but only one of them. By means of rabbinic exegesis Paul deduces this from the fact that the text of Genesis (xii. 7) speaks of 'his seed' and maintains without taking into account that the word is a collective noun in the singular that the promise refers to Christ alone and through his mediation to all those who believe in him and belong to him, whether they are Jews or Gentiles. 'And so', he concludes, 'the blessing of Abraham is come to the Gentiles' (iii. 14). In this theory the function of the law is quite subordinate and provisional. It came 430 years after the covenant and cannot annul it (Gal. iii. 17). Its function is simply to exercise a provisional discipline like a schoolmaster (iii. 24).[4] Furthermore, it 'concludes all under sin' (iii. 22), i.e. to say it must make all, Jew and Gentile alike, feel convinced that there is no possibility of salvation at all apart from Christ. This, however, is not altogether coherent. Two functions are attributed to

---

[1] To these may be added Rom. ix. 1-5, in which two sentiments are mixed up together: pride of race and Paul's feelings of loyalty to his own people.

[2] Ad. Lods, 'Les antécédents de la notion d'Église en Israël et dans le judaisme', *Origine et nature de l'Église, Conférences à la Faculté libre de théologie protestante de Paris*, Paris, 1939, pp. 9-50.

[3] In this passage at any rate, as he appears elsewhere not to ascribe to the law such a subordinate function.

[4] The word pedagogue means here supervisor not teacher.

the law, (1) a temporary function, which belongs especially to the ritual law. This is to provide a discipline for humanity so long as it is spiritually under age, i.e. until Christ comes; (2) a permanent function which is to create a consciousness of sin. This function persists in the Christian economy as the development of Paul's own Christian life clearly shows.[1] Thinking especially of the ritual function of the law Paul shows in Galatians iii. 11 that it is only valid until the arrival of the inheritor of the promise, i.e. Christ.[2] When the work of Christ is accomplished, the law ceases to be valid. No particular act of God or Christ was necessary to make it null and void just as no particular act is needed to put an end to the powers of guardians over the property of their wards when they attain their majority.

The long argument in Romans ix-xi shows that in principle salvation was intended for the Jews alone; it was only offered to the Gentiles because the Jews did not accept it; in spite of Jewish incredulousness God's plan to establish a Messianic people must be accomplished. Jewish incredulousness therefore made the salvation of the Gentiles possible. As Paul meditates on Israel's destiny, he comes to form the grandiose idea that God has used the incredulousness of the Jews as a means of making the salvation of the Gentiles possible but once this result is obtained the incredulousness of Israel will not last. And so Israel in one way and the Gentiles in another will all be saved.

While, as we have seen, the epistle to the Galatians states that the law became null and void as soon as Christ's work was accomplished, the epistle to the Colossians gives us a different idea (ii. 14-15). The separation between the Jews and the Gentiles was founded on the law. Christ by the cross destroyed the law. He gained a victory over the powers in revolt and destroyed the document which was hostile to the Gentiles, i.e. the law which condemned them to remain outside the covenant with God and cut them off from every hope of salvation. Christ nailed it to the cross and annulled it.[3] Ephesians ii. 14 f. presents the same idea where it is said that Christ by his death destroyed 'the wall of separation' between the Jews and the Gentiles and united humanity.

[1] See *E.P.*, pp. 450 ff.

[2] It looks as if he must mean up till the time when his work is completed. The phrasing here is somewhat vague which is due to the fact that Paul is thinking of Christ's work theologically not historically.

[3] A reference to the custom of cancelling a bill or contract by pricking it with a hole.

Thus the epistle to the Galatians, the epistle to the Romans, as well as the epistles to the Ephesians and the Colossians express the idea that the law has lost its force and that it cannot be resisted any longer or imposed upon the Gentiles; but this idea is expressed and defended by three different theories which cannot be harmonised.

From these observations it must first of all be inferred that Paulinism does not possess the systematic character which is sometimes ascribed to it. But this is not all and is not the most essential point. The most important thing to be inferred from these notes is that in Paulinism, theology compared with religious experience is a secondary element both psychologically and chronologically. Experience creates the expression, while from the second generation onwards the doctrinal statement led to the experience.[1]

To prevent any misunderstanding I must be more precise. While in the case of the apostle Paul a direct connection between experience and doctrine can be established it must not be supposed that his theology is essentially subjective in character and is nothing more than speculation on his own personal experience. On the contrary, he considers it to be the expression of an objective redemptive drama the reality of which does not depend in any way upon the experience of believers or on the benefits they can gain from it. This is the logical conclusion of a number of considerations which can be clearly indicated.

To begin with, Paul writes of his own experience in such a way that it is clear that it is not just his own but that of all believers and the whole church. To give only one example, in Galatians iv. 4 he writes, 'God sent forth his Son . . . made under the law, to redeem them that were under the law, that we might receive the adoption (i.e. that we might become sons of God)', and speaking to the Galatians, he continues, 'and that you might be sons of God (i.e. what proves that you are is that) God hath sent forth the Spirit of his Son into your hearts, crying, Abba, Father'. This passage is quite characteristic with 'we' and 'you' being interchanged.

In the second place, Paul reckons that the Old Testament reveals the doctrine of redemption and adoption to those from whose eyes the veil has been removed which had prevented the Israelites from grasping it.

---

[1] See my article 'Paulinisme et Johannisme, Deux théologies ou deux formes d'expérience religieuse?' *Trois études sur la pensée religieuse du christianisme primitif*, Paris, 1931, pp. 43 ff.

Paulinism has two characteristics which at first sight may seem to contradict each other. In the epistle to the Galatians Paul declares in the most categorical manner that he holds his apostleship and his gospel which in his eyes are inseparable, direct from God and Christ.

Before his conversion he was acquainted with the *kerygma*, i.e. the Christian preaching. He knew that Jesus' disciples preached that God had raised up Christ and had exalted him on to his right hand but he held this preaching to be absurd and blasphemous. He had read in the book of Deuteronomy (xxi. 23) this rule, 'Cursed is he who is hung on the tree'. How could it be conceived that God had accomplished a miracle of resurrection in favour of a man, on whom had rested the weight of God's curse, and furthermore had raised him to his right hand? He could only then use all his resources to fight such blasphemous preaching which, if tolerated, might bring the wrath of God of Israel. He came to believe in the resurrection of Jesus, not because the Twelve affirmed it but because he himself experienced an appearance of Christ, because he was convinced that he had seen Jesus alive after his death, in the same way as previously Cephas, the Twelve, more than five hundred brethren, James, all the apostles, i.e. all those enumerated in 1 Corinthians xv. 4-7 had seen him. 'Have I not seen Jesus our Lord?' he says in 1 Corinthians ix. 1. It is difficult to say precisely what this appearance of Christ was but it is beyond argument that what happened on the road to Damascus he considered to be an act of God by which God revealed to him His son in order that he might preach Him to the Gentiles (Gal. i. 15-16). It must be added that Paul never felt that his conversion was the only moment in his life when God intervened. During the whole course of his life as a Christian and an apostle he felt that both his thoughts and his acts were guided by the Spirit of God.

Thus the governing circumstances which brought Paul to the faith contained all the elements which might have led him—and I am tempted to write which ought to have led him—to think himself to have been endowed with a completely new and fresh revelation. But instead of founding a new religion on the revelations which he had received and continued to receive, he adhered to a religion, which at any rate in principle, had been previously established, although it did not possess any fixed form in the realm of worship, doctrine, organisation, etc. Everything was still fluid and in a state of becoming. Yet he determined to maintain contact with it in spite of all the difficulties and even the dangers to which he was thereby exposing himself.

In 1 Corinthians xv what he first quotes as a proof of the resurrection of Jesus is the tradition which he has received and transmitted, expressed in the rhythmic phrases which form the earliest confession of the church's faith.

> Christ died for our sins, according to the Scriptures
> And he was buried
> He rose again the third day, according to the Scriptures
> And he was seen by Cephas, then by the Twelve.

After giving a list of appearances of which he knew—it does not seem as if it was intended that the list should be exhaustive—he mentions the one which he himself experienced merely by way of an appendix and describes it as the last of all, which only means that he did not know of any later than his own.[1] Paulinism is thus both a personal religion springing from inspiration and a religion inherited from a tradition. It is easy to understand the reason for this. Paul's gospel was summed up in Christ crucified or in the cross of Christ. He did not reckon the drama of the cross to be a metaphysical drama which had been unfolded outside the realm of time and space. It is a drama which had taken place at a particular moment of time and in a particular place on earth. He who was both its victim and its hero may have been more than man, but he was so fully clothed in humanity that he could represent humanity before God together with human sin and, if one may say so, could incarnate this sin in his own person. How otherwise could God have condemned this sin and thereby have expiated and annulled it with its consequences in the flesh of one who did not know sin so making possible salvation from sins? (Rom. viii. 3; 2 Cor. v. 21.) But Paul did not witness the drama of the cross.[2] He only knew of it through the church at Jerusalem and the Twelve, who were its leaders and mouthpiece. Paul was anxious to keep in touch with the Twelve, because they were the bearers and guarantors of the tradition, in spite of all the difficulties which this brought upon him.[3]

---

[1] In the Pauline christology there is nothing to justify the belief that from a particular moment of time no further appearances could occur.

[2] It is often supposed that he was not in Jerusalem during Jesus' ministry and trial there. This may be so. But it is also possible that Jesus' trial and execution made less impression than the gospel stories suggest and many of the inhabitants of Jerusalem may not have known about them.

[3] When Paul came to Jerusalem for the last time after the crises in Galatia and Greece, his purpose was to assure himself that the agreement of 43-44 still held good. He was not sure that he would receive a warm welcome from the church at Jerusalem and he could not help but know that his presence at Jerusalem would offer provocation to the Jews as they considered him a renegade and an

Paulinism is a theology based on a tradition for another reason. When Paul became a Christian he did not feel that he had ceased to be a Jew on that account. On the contrary, he had become more truly and fully what he had not been before, because his conversion revealed to him the true meaning of the Old Testament.

In 2 Corinthians iii. 3, 12 ff. Paul finds a personal meaning of his own in the incident concerning the veil with which Moses covered his face when he came down from Sinai to prevent the Israelites being terrified by the bright light which shone from his face through having contemplated the glory of God.[1] He gives the incident an allegorical interpretation. The Israelites have Moses' veil on their face when they read the Old Testament and it makes them blind to the fact that it witnesses to Christ. For that reason Paul did not consider that by his conversion he had broken with Judaism. On the contrary he thought that it had given him a deeper knowledge of the true meaning of the Old Testament.

2.—THE LIFE OF THE APOSTLE PAUL

Paul's thought was so closely bound up with his personal life and preaching that, if we are to understand it, we must begin by giving a short biographical sketch.

There is no doubt that St. Paul[2] was born in the first decade of

apostate and had been trying to create some incident which would make it possible to get rid of him. Rom. xvi. 17, which was written by Paul to the Romans when he was preparing to leave for Jerusalem, shows that he took into account the dangers which he was going to face.

[1] His interpretation of the story is different from that of the Old Testament because he supposes that Moses had had to wear the veil to prevent the Israelites from being able to say that the brightness had disappeared.

[2] Traditional exegesis (in antiquity, e.g. Origen, *Comm. in ep. ad. Rom. praef.*; Jerome, *In philem.*, 6; Augustine. *Conf.*, VIII, 4, etc., and among modern commentators, e.g. Meyer, *Ursprung. u. Anf.*, III, p. 197) considered that Saul took the name of Paul in memory of the proconsul Sergius Paulus, the first Roman to be converted by him (Acts xiii, 6 ff.). A change of name was legally possible (Mommsen, 'Die Rechtsverhältnisse des Apostels Paulus', *Z.N.T.W.*, 1901, II, p. 84). Dessau. *Der Name des Apostels Paulus Hermes*, 1910, XLV, p. 347, mentions the case of a Cypriot who adopted the name of C. Ummidius Quadratus, one of Sergius Paulus' predecessors. It is not impossible that the compiler of Acts may be explaining the double name of Saul-Paul in this way. But the apostle in accordance with current usage (see the examples given by Deissmann, *Bibelstudien*, pp. 182 ff.) seems to have had two names at the same time which sounded like each other, one Semitic and the other Greek. Also as a Roman citizen Paul must have had a *nomen*, a *praenomen*, and a *cognomen*. Zahn ('Paulus', *R.E.* XV, p. 70) suggests that Saul was his *nomen* and Paul his *cognomen*. G. A. Harrer ('Saul who is also called Paul', *Harv. Th. Rev.*, 1940, XXXIII, pp. 19-34) has suggested another

the Christian era[1] at Tarsus in Cilicia (Acts ix. 11; xxi. 39; xxiii. 3). His Jewish origin was only called in question by his enemies at a late date.[2] His family possessed the double rights of being citizens of both Rome[3] and Tarsus.[4] We do not know how they acquired them. They do not appear to have belonged to the lowest classes of the population.[5] Although they were domiciled abroad they remained strongly attached to their national traditions, as they boasted that they were of pure Hebrew race and belonged to the tribe of Benjamin (Phil. iii. 5).[6] Paul was a Pharisee and was taught by the Rabbi.[7]

interpretation. He makes 'Paul' not a proper name but a surname (*signum* or *supernomen*) which it was customary to give in Macedonian Egypt. This hypothesis is not so convincing as that which considers 'Saul' and 'Paul' to be two of the three official names of the apostle.

[1] Acts vii. 58 makes him out to have been a young man (νεανίας) at the time of Stephen's death about 30. We can hardly suppose from the part which he played in the persecution that he was then less than 25 years old. In the letter to Philemon v. 9, written between 58 and 60 he describes himself as an old man πρεσβύτης). The conjecture of Bentley and others reading πρεσβέντης (ambassador of Christ) is not convincing. Paul, at the age of 55, considering the life he had led, might well have called himself an old man.

[2] Epiphanius (*Haer.* XXX. 16, 25) states that the Ebionites questioned the Jewish origin of Paul by saying that being a Greek by race Paul had himself circumcised in the hope of marrying the high-priest's daughter. Because she rejected him he detested Judaism and attacked it. This is a legend concocted to explain prejudicial views and affords no reason for thinking that there is any historical tradition behind it. Paul's Jewish origin has been called in question by some modern writers (Krenkel, *Beitrage zur Aufhellung des Geschichte und der Briefe des Apostels Paulus*[2], Braunschweig, 1895, pp. 4 f.; Toussaint, *L'Hellénisme de l'apôtre*, Paul, Paris, 1921, p. 190) without adequate reasons. Jerome (*Comm. in Philem.*, 23; *De viris inl.* 5) collected local traditions which stated that Paul's family originated in Gischala in Galilee and came to reside in Tarsus when he was still a small boy. But they have no value and are to be considered a product of local patriotism.

[3] It has sometimes been doubted whether Paul was really a Roman citizen (e.g. Hausrath, *Jesu und die neutestamentlichen Schriftsteller*, Berlin, 1908, II, pp. 197 ff.). It is true that although the law did not allow a Roman citizen to be scourged he submitted to being scourged three times (2 Cor. xi. 25) but the law may have been violated to his loss as it was at Philippi according to Acts xvi. 37. (Cf. Schurer, *Gesch.* III, p. 85, n. 24; Juster, *Les Juifs de l'Emp. rom.*, II, p. 15, n. 8, p. 165, n. 2.) Paul may have renounced his privileges as a Roman citizen in order to maintain his union with his own people. He laid claim to them at Jerusalem because he had finally broken with them and there was no advantage in not making use of them.

[4] On the possibility of holding double rights of citizenship see Schurer, *Gesch.* III, p. 86; Mommsen, *Z.N.T.W.*, 1901, II, p. 82, n. 2.

[5] Wendland, *Die urchristlichen Literaturformen*, Tubingen, 1912, p. 353; Boehlig, *Die Geisteskultur von Tarsus*, Gottingen, 1913, pp. 128 f.

[6] It is for that reason no doubt that his Jewish name was that of the only king who belonged to the tribe of Benjamin.

[7] In Acts xxiii. 6, Paul declares himself to be 'a Pharisee, the son of a Pharisee'. Some authors (Renan, *Les Apôtres*, p. 165; Harnack, *Mission*, II, p. 44; Johannes

We have some information concerning his personal appearance. Some of it[1] must be received with great caution, while the rest consists of Paul's personal allusions to his physical weaknesses. They are too vague for us to be able to give them any precise meaning. This much can be admitted. Paul's appearance had nothing imposing about it (2 Cor. x. 10) and he suffered several attacks of painful illness, which may well have been the symptoms of a chronic complaint.[2] He speaks of it as an angel of Satan which buffeted him, as a thorn which was in his flesh from which he had prayed three times to be freed but the Lord had refused (2 Cor. xii. 7-9). The many and various diseases which it has been suggested were meant by this evil, haemorrhoids, ophthalmia, leprosy, Malta fever, chronic rheumatism, and many more, show that we have not got sufficient information to make a retrospective diagnosis. All we know is that Paul was puny and unhealthy, extremely sensitive, and subject to alternating bouts of enthusiasm and despondency; his influence owes nothing to his physical make-up. His fiery soul had only a feeble body at its disposal.

Weiss, *Urchrist.*, p. 13) take this literally, although it is not certain that the party of the Pharisees were represented in the diaspora. 'Father' was the title given to the Rabbi. (Cf. Matt. xxiii. 9 and the title of the treatise Pirke Aboth = the traditions of the fathers.) Acts xxiii. 6 and Gal. i. 14 in which Paul speaks of the traditions of the fathers probably only mean that he had been taught by the rabbis. This is how Lietzmann, *An die Calater*[3], Tubingen, 1932, p. 7, interprets it.

[1] This applies to the description of the apostle given in the *Acta Pauli et Theclae* (ch. 3). (Tertullian *De baptismo*, 17, states that these Acts were written about 180 by a presbyter from Asia, *amore Pauli.*) Some writers (Renan, *Les Apôtres*, p. 170; Zahn, *G.K.* II, pp. 903 f.; Salomon Reinach, 'Thecla', *Cultes, mythes et religions*, Paris, 1912, IV, pp. 243-249; Meyer, *Urspr. u. Anf.* III, p. 413) think that this description can be retained on the strength of the supposition that as it is not generally flattering an admirer of Paul would not have imagined it. But we cannot judge the description by modern aesthetic standards. It must be remembered that the writer of *Acta Pauli et Theclae* had distinct ascetic tendencies. In addition to this, the arguments advanced by those who reckon the portrait to be only a literary creation seem to us to be more convincing. Such are the opinions of Clemen ('Miszellen zu den Paulusakten', *Z.N.T.W.*, 1904, V, pp. 228 f.; C. Schmidt, *Acta Pauli*[2], Leipzig, 1905, p. xvii, and Vouaux, *Les Actes de Paul et ses lettres apocryphes*, Paris, 1913, pp. 122 f.; R. Eisler (*ΙΗΣΟΥΣ* II, pp. 414 f.) believes that he can find contradictions in the portrait and on this propounds a theory that an authentic description of the apostle has been touched up to make it more flattering. It is much more reasonable to see in these contradictions which are by no means flagrant the result of two opposing tendencies similar to those which were at work in descriptions of Jesus. Sometimes he was described as the most beautiful of the children of men and at other times as the man who had taken on himself all the sufferings of mankind.

[2] Gal. iv. 13. I Thess. iii. 1. I Cor. ii. 3. II Cor. xii. 7-9. See also *Intr.*, IV, I, pp. 129 ff.

At Tarsus[1] he received his early education. This fact is important. Situated at a place where four roads meet, at the entrance to the passes of the Taurus mountains which lead to the interior of Asia Minor Tarsus was a link between two worlds. Subject to the influences of Syria, Macedonia, and Rome alike, the seat of an important Jewish colony, through Tarsus there flowed the religions and philosophies of both the East and the West. In the time of Paul it was the centre of a new syncretistic religion: the mysteries of Mithras had perhaps already penetrated there. According to Strabo's evidence[2] it could count as a rival to Athens and Alexandria.

Paul's early education was Greek both in form and language. Greek is his mother tongue and the way in which he expresses his ideas, reasons, and argues, shows an acquaintance with the logical forms used by the Stoics.[3] There is abundant evidence to show that he used the Septuagint and never quotes from the Hebrew Old Testament.[4] The Greek of his letters is not a translation of Aramaic. Wendland[5] plainly proves that Paul's style is not Attic Greek but refuses to describe it as non-literary and popular in form. Norden[6] goes so far as to consider his works a Greek classic and von Willamowitz-Moellendorf[7] considers that although his style was careless he made masterly use of the rhetorical forms used by the sophists of Asia Minor. Paul's letters show a complete disregard for balance and harmony in composition. Constantly the course of his argument is broken up by incidents and digressions and becomes disjointed with anacoloutha. His thought is often extremely condensed; important elements are taken for granted or scarcely hinted at. It seems as if Paul could not find the words to fit his thoughts quick enough, because he was accustomed to dictate. In spite of these defects Paul's letters show incomparable power and real eloquence. Although his genius was too original and tumultuous to allow him to bend it to classic form, he was a true master of the literary art and the art was Greek not Jewish.[8]

---

[1] Concerning Tarsus and its culture see Boehlig's book, *Die Geistesk. v. Tarsus.*
[2] Strabo, xiv. 10, 13-15.
[3] See Bultmann's book, *Der Stil der paulinischen Predigt ubd die kynisch-stoische Diatribe*, Gottingen, 1910.
[4] Vollmer, *Die alttestamentlichen Citate bei Paulus*, Freiburg in Brisgau, Leipzig, 1895, p. 103.   [5] Wendland, *Urchristl. Literaturf.*, p. 353.
[6] Norden, *Antike Kuntsprosa,*[2] Berlin, Leipzig, 1909, I, pp. 506 ff.
[7] Willamowitz-Moellendorf, *Die Kultur des Gegenwart, Teil.* I.
[8] Paul's vocabulary (cf. Th. Naegeli, *Der Wortschatz des Apostels Paulus*, Gottingen, 1905) is that of the common language of his time, strongly tainted, however, with that of the LXX. While the syntax is generally speaking correct, it is characterised by the frequent use of conjunctions and connecting particles.

We are not on this account compelled to put on one side the statement in Acts xxi. 40 that Paul was acquainted with Aramaic[1] nor that in Acts xxii. 3, that he had been the pupil of Gamaliel in Jerusalem.[2] He did not, however, receive from him his early education. His ways of thinking and feeling are so essentially Jewish that he must have been familiarised with the teachings of Judaism from his childhood onwards in his father's house. He must have come to Jerusalem later merely to finish his education in Rabbinics.

Although Paul was a Jew of the diaspora and imbued with the idea of Israel being the chosen people he had nothing to do with politics. The sincerity of his loyalty to Rome was never questioned. Although he was constantly haunted by the apocalyptic hope what he hoped for was the establishment of the kingdom of God not the restoration of national independence and the political triumph of Israel. Just because he was born and grew up in a Greek environment his conscience was perplexed by the problem of the Gentile world and he acquired a largeness of view which was destined to find an answer in his conception of Christianity as a universal religion.

If it is supposed that Hellenism exercised any influence on Paul it has to be remembered that he never makes a quotation from any of the Greek authors[3] or alludes to the teachings of the Greek philosophers.[4] These facts are negative: they only prove that the apostle never looked for any confirmation of his preaching in Hellenism and that he possessed some of the Jew's contempt for the foreigner.

[1] We cannot, however, consider this to be proved by the use of a few Aramaic words in the epistles (Maran Atha [1 Cor. xvi. 22], Abba [Gal. iv. 6, Rom. viii. 15] as these are words of liturgical significance which have passed into the forms of worship used by the Hellenic churches.

[2] Concerning Gamaliel or Gamaliel the Elder, see Dalman, 'Gamaliel', *R.E.* VI, p. 364; Schurer, *Gesch.* II, pp. 364 f.; Strack-Billerbeck, II, pp. 636 ff. If the statement of Acts means anything more than a desire to make Paul the disciple of an illustrious rabbi, he owed the essential traits of his personality much more to his temperament than to his master. Several opinions of Gamaliel can be quoted which show that he was thought of as a discreet and moderate kind of man. The book of the Acts (v. 34) describes him advocating a policy of tolerance towards the Christians. Although the episode may have no historical value (see pp. 491 ff.) it shows that Gamaliel had a reputation for moderation and discretion.

[3] It is true that in 1 Cor. xv. 33 is to be found an iambic trimeter borrowed from Menander : 'evil communications corrupt good manners', but the sentence may have become a proverb.

[4] I am not taking into account the speech on the Areopagus, which I do not think can be attributed to Paul (cf. *Introd.* III, pp. 267 f.), and in Phil. ii. 6 I retain the reading in the manuscripts, ἁρπαγμόν (robbery) and reject the conjecture ἀπράγμον (a sinecure) suggested independently of each other by Salomon

It is possible that he was not so far removed from Greek polytheism as he imagined. He does not deny the existence of many celestial and divine beings but places upon them a different interpretation. He does not reproach the Gentiles for worshipping beings who do not exist but for worshipping beings who 'by nature are no gods' (Gal. iv. 8), or for worshipping 'devils and not God' (1 Cor. x. 20). He states plainly that there is only one God, the Father, but this statement which seems to affirm an intransigent monotheism is followed by an explanation which unexpectedly weakens its significance: 'for though there be what are called gods, whether in heaven or in earth (as there be gods many and lords many), but to us there is but one God, the Father' (1 Cor. viii. 5-6). Paul did not invent this interpretation of polytheism; the first sign of it appeared in Ecclesiasticus, xvii 17; it became more explicit in Jewish angelology, especially in that to be found in the book of Enoch, but what is peculiar to Paul is the way in which he connects polytheism and sin and also the way in which he interprets polytheism by the Jewish idea of the fall and on this interpretation bases his doctrine of redemption.

The Hellenistic Judaism of Tarsus and a Gentile environment made such an impression on the future apostle that he presented his gospel in a form which enabled it to spread through the Greek world. Apart from the fact that Paul lived successively at Tarsus and Jerusalem[1] we have practically no other information concerning his youth.[2]

Reinach ('L'indolence des dieux', *Rev. des Études grecques*, 1916, pp. 238-244; *Cultes mythes, et religions*, Paris, 1923, pp. 301-306, and by Anton Fridrichsen, 'Quatre conjectures sur le texte du Nouveau Testament', *R.h.p.r.*, 1923, III, pp. 441-442). This conjecture would introduce into the text a polemic against the Epicurean idea of the impassibility of the gods. I do not think the text can be corrected as there is no ambiguity in the manuscripts and the meaning is perfectly clear.

[1] He appears to have served the Sanhedrin as a *schliah* (messenger, apostle). Cf. *E.P.*, pp. 86 ff.

[2] In accordance with the custom of the Rabbi, whose ministry must have been of a voluntary nature (Schurer, *Gesch.* II, p. 318), Paul learnt and practised a trade, that of making tents (a maker of harness there is no doubt rather than a weaver). See *Introd.* IV, 1, pp. 150 ff.). There is also the question whether in accordance with the custom of the Rabbis he did not marry as a young man. It seems impossible to think that he was married when he wrote 1 Cor. vii. 8, but he may have been a widower, as was thought in antiquity Methodius of Olympia (*Symposium* III, 12) in the sixteenth century Luther (see the texts mentioned by Krenkel, *Beltr.*, p. 27) and in recent times especially J. Jeremiah. The question has been debated between him ('War Paulus Witteer?' *Z.N.T.W.*, 1926, XXV, pp. 310-312; 'Nochmals: War Paulus Wittwer?'. *Z.N.T.W.*, 1929, XXVIII, pp. 321-333) and Fascher ('Zur Wittwerschaft des Paulus', *Z.N.T.W.*, 1929,

The question whether he had ever seen Jesus during his ministry[1] is not so important as was once thought. At the very most they may have seen each other in the streets of Jerusalem. He did not hide the fact that he persecuted the Christians but rather boasted of it. It is much more likely then that if he had taken part in the plots against Jesus he would have boasted that he had assisted in the death of the Lord. His conversion would have been all the more remarkable.[2] Most probably Paul never heard the new faith mentioned until the disciples returned from Galilee convinced that their Master had risen again, unless, as some suppose, he only heard the new faith mentioned for the first time at Damascus. He must have been shocked to hear a man proclaimed as the messenger of God and the Messiah on whom according to the principle laid down in Deuteronomy (xxi. 23) had fallen the curse of God, inasmuch as he had been hung on a tree. Even if what he had heard of Jesus and his sayings had secretly influenced him, the conviction that the divine curse was laid upon Jesus would only have allowed him to think that those who proclaimed that God had made him triumphant over death were liars and blasphemers who deserved heavy punishment.[3]

We have already seen[4] that the idea that Paul had any share in the popular movement which caused the death of Stephen must

XXVIII, pp. 62-69). The tradition of the primitive church that Paul was married (Clement of Alexandria, *Strom.* III, 52; Origen, *Comm. in ep. ad. Rom.* I, 1, a recension interpolated into the epistle of Ignatius to the *Philadelphians*, 4) rests on an erroneous interpretation of 1 Cor. ix. 5 and possibly on the more or less conscious desire to establish a parallel between Peter and Paul. As for the idea put forward by Clement of Alexandria (*Strom.* III. 6) and Eusebius (*H.e.* iii. 30) which Renan (*Saint Paul*, Paris, 1869, pp. 148 f.) revived as a hypothesis, that the vocative γνησίε σύζυγε ought to be translated 'dear wife' and not 'dear Synzygos' or 'true comrade' and is none other than Lydia the seller of purple (Acts xvi. 14, 40) it is better left to those who love historical romance. The fact that Paul is described as 'a young man' (Acts vii. 58) the first time he is mentioned makes it improbable that he was then married. When we read 1 Cor. vii it is difficult to imagine that he married after he became a Christian.

[1] Concerning the discussions raised by this question and the solutions suggested see *Introd.* IV, pp. 176 ff.

[2] The text of 2 Cor. v. 16 round which the discussion principally centres is hypothetical in form (if we have known . . .). It does not authorise any positive conclusion.

[3] There is no need to think with Wellhausen, *Israelitische und judische Geschichte²*, Berlin, 1897, p. 386, that Paul, made wise by hatred, thought that as the gospel developed it would be the ruin of Judaism. Pfleiderer (*Das Urchristentum²*, Berlin, 1902, I, p. 63) and Meyer (*Urspr. u. Anf.*, III, p. 34) believe that Paul tried by persecuting the Christians to smother a secret attraction he felt for their faith. What, however, the apostle himself says leaves no doubt concerning the sincerity of his hatred for Christianity. [4] See p. 171.

be considered doubtful or at least precarious. But on the other hand, although certain critics have tried to prove that it is certain that Paul only came into contact with Christianity in the diaspora at Damascus and there came into conflict with it, their arguments are not decisive.

Paul's conversion took place near Damascus in the autumn of 29.[1] As Paul rarely alludes to it in his epistles he must have already given a detailed account of it to those to whom he was writing. For that reason he never gives any details on how it happened. He simply says that the Lord showed himself to him (1 Cor. ix. 1; xv. 8), that God revealed his Son to him (Gal. i. 15) that he was apprehended of Christ (Phil. iii. 12). On the other hand, the book of the Acts gives three versions of the story relating how the conversion happened (ix. 1-19; xxii. 3-16; xxvi. 9-20). But its evidence has little value, because the appearance of Christ described by the source has been reduced to a vision of an indeterminate nature.[2] The only feature which can be retained is the localisation of the event in the neighbourhood of Damascus. Acts states that Paul was left by the vision quite helpless; he only understood what the vision meant after a Christian from Damascus, Ananias, had laid his hands upon him. Paul's solemn declaration in Galatians i. 11-12 that he received his gospel directly by a revelation from Jesus Christ without having been taught by anybody prevents the Ananias episode from being considered historical as it is given in the story of Acts.[3]

When we were considering the birth of the faith in the resurrection[4] we saw what explanation could be given of the psychological process by which a persecutor was turned into an apostle. Paul's conversion was for him a revelation of the son of God (Gal. i. 15); he saw Jesus alive in glory and the experience compelled him not only to revise all his previous judgements about the new faith but completely to reorientate his thought. But the conversion did not cause the apostle to make a complete break with his religious past. He did not reject the fundamental elements of his thought and replace them by others. Formally, at any rate, Paul always used the same notions of God and his Kingdom, of man and sin, of salvation

---

[1] See pp. 25 f.   [2] See pp. 44 f.

[3] If the episode was a complete invention in every way, the person who laid his hands upon Paul would not have been given the name of the deceiver, Ananias. We know (Rom. vi. 3; 1 Cor. xii. 13) that Paul was baptised and it is difficult to see when he could have been except at the beginning of his life as a Christian. It would therefore be possible that Ananias baptised him when he introduced him to the church at Damascus.   [4] See pp. 81 ff.

and redemption. The problem of religion was still couched in the same terms, the problem of salvation. Paul still had the same yearning after righteousness, thinking of it not as an ideal but as the divine proclamation of a sentence, which opened the gates to the kingdom of the new world. But to the question, 'On what conditions will man who is a sinner be able to gain the verdict of acquittal?' after his conversion he gave quite a different reply from what he had said before. 'But what things were gain to me',[1] he writes to the Philippians, 'those I counted loss for (i.e. in comparison with) Christ, yea doubtless, and I count all things but loss for the excellency of the knowledge of Christ Jesus my Lord; for whom I suffered the loss of all things, and do count them but dung that I may win Christ, and be found in him,[2] not having mine own righteousness which is of the law, but that which is through the faith of Christ, the righteousness which is of God by faith' (iii. 7-9).

As a Jew he considered the law to be a kind of contract between God and his people. God said to the Israelite, 'Do this and you will live'.[3] By obedience the Jew created for himself a right to salvation; he realised the conditions which God had imposed as the duty required.[4] Paul felt that he had amply fulfilled these terms and showed that he was beyond reproach as far as legal justice was concerned (Phil. iii. 6). But after his conversion he considered justification by obedience to the law to be possible in theory but beyond realisation in practice. We can see a startling contrast when we compare the proud assurance of the Pharisee as it is expressed in Philippians iii. 6 with the poignant phraseology of Romans vii. 13 ff.[5] which cannot possibly be an abstract argument but is the echo of the

[1] Paul is referring to the claims to righteousness which he could put forward from the Jewish point of view.　[2] On the day of judgement.

[3] This is a conception of the law not as the revelation of an abstract ideal but as a means of grace. What it commands and what it forbids constitute a minimum with which God may be satisfied.

[4] In addition to this the Jew is the object of a peculiar indulgence with which God will judge the members of his own people. The whole of chapter ii of the epistle to the Romans is a denunciation of the idea that God will not judge the sins of the Jew as he judges those of the Gentile. This is what chapter xv of Wisdom expresses. Furthermore, the Jew profited by the sacrificial system which blotted out involuntary disobedience of the law. Cf. G. F. Moore, *Judaism in the First Centuries of the Christian Era*, Cambridge, Mass. I, pp. 257-267. On the whole question see my article: '*ΚΑΤΑ ΤΗΝ ΔΙΚΑΙΟΣΥΝΗΝ ΤΗΝ ΕΝ ΝΟΜΩΙ ΓΕΝΟΜΕΝΟΣ ΑΜΕΜΠΤΟΣ*', *Journal of biblical literature and exegesis*, 1934, LIII, pp. 257-267.

[5] Chapter vii of the epistle to the Romans has been the subject of so many different interpretations that it is quite impossible even to enumerate them. I have limited myself to describing the one which I think should be adopted.

personal experience of an anguished soul who judges the law of God to be holy and good but feels himself bound to a wicked power which prevents him from obeying it. When did Paul have this experience? Not before his conversion as otherwise he would not have written Philippians iii. 6. Neither is it an experience which came to him as he was writing to the Romans. The contrast is too vivid between his description of moral despair and his shout of triumph and deliverance which ends the passage, 'Thanks be to God through Our Lord Jesus Christ'. The situation which Paul is describing has been resolved. The crisis must have taken place after his conversion before the apostle had regained his balance in Christian thought and action.

It may well be that the words of Jesus preserved in Matthew v. 17 f. taught Paul to see that, if the principle of legalism, on which the religion of Israel rests, is worked out to its logical conclusion, it demands not only that some acts must be done and others avoided but also that the whole conduct and life of a man, his motives and inner convictions, should be obedience to the will of God. But this explanation is not sufficient because in Romans vii, Paul not only complains that he cannot do what is good but also that there is some kind of constraint which drives him to do what is wrong. His conversion therefore transformed his whole conception of man's capacity to obey the law and do the will of God.[1]

In one sense it may be said that Paul formed his theology by integrating into what had long been his philosophy the new faith in the risen and glorified Christ to which he became converted by his experience of the risen Christ on the road to Damascus.[2] But it must be added that the original vision, important as it was, was not the only source of his Christian life, faith, and thought. It must not be separated from the visions, ecstasies and revelations which followed

[1] In Paul's estimation the doctrine of justification by keeping the law had been robbed of two supports, (1) the idea that God regarded the chosen people with special favour, and (2) the sacrificial system; (1) was undermined by the forces which impelled Paul towards universalism. As for (2) many Jews were not particularly attached to the sacrificial system, while Paul's uncompromising mind did not permit there to be any other condition, even as an accessory, for salvation except the cross of Christ. It should also be noted that Paul's epistles do not contain any polemic against the idea of justification through sacrifices, from which it can be inferred that this idea must not have held an important place in Paul's thought as a Jew.

[2] This idea is developed with force by Auguste Sabatier, *l'Apôtre Paul, Esquisse d'une histoire et de sa pensée*[3], Paris, 1896, particularly in pp. 52 ff., too much, however, to the neglect of other considerations.

and made up that 'life in Christ' experienced by the apostle, of which his theology was only the expression.[1]

Paul maintained that there was a close connection between his conversion and his calling to be an apostle and evangelist. God had revealed his Son to him because he wished him to preach the gospel to the Gentiles (Gal. i. 16). From the very beginning of his life as a Christian he seems to have been convinced that he was called to preach the gospel; it is not quite so certain that he knew immediately that he was called to preach it to the Gentiles.

After his conversion he was in Arabia (Gal. i. 17).[2] It has been thought[3] that after the shock of his conversion he retired into solitude to put his ideas into order, but action always followed his thoughts so quickly that it appears probable that he must have preached the gospel to the Nabateans.[4] Support for this idea may be derived from the fact that according to the Acts Paul began immediately after his conversion to preach the gospel at Damascus, provoking such hostility thereby from the Jews that he had to escape by night, being let down over the wall of the city in a basket (ix. 23-25). The truth of this episode is confirmed by 2 Corinthians xi. 32-33 which, however, states that Paul's enemies were the Nabateans and the ethnarch, Aretas.[5] This source must be preferred. The hostility of Aretas and the Nabateans would not have just been due to the fact that Paul had been in retreat in their country for the purpose of elaborating a new theological system. He must have been preaching the gospel there and so had stirred up opposition.

Did his audience consist of the numerous Jews in the district or did he preach to the Gentile Nabateans as well? In the epistle to the

[1] G. Wetter (*Die Damaskusvision und das paulinische Evangelium, Fastschrift Julicher,* Tubingen, 1927, pp. 80-92) emphasises the part played by revelations in the whole of Paul's life. But he seems to me to have underestimated the importance of the appearance of Christ on the road to Damascus.

[2] If Josephus' terminology is used, Arabia must mean the Nabatean kingdom to the East and South of Palestine, extending from the district of the Euphrates to the Red Sea. In face of the evidence of the epistle to the Galatians it is difficult to understand how Meyer (*Urspr. u. Anf.,* I, p. 175, n. 3 on page 174) can speak of Paul's stay at Damascus lasting for three years.

[3] This is what such as Zahn, *Der Brief des Paulus an die Galater,* Leipzig, 1905, p. 68; Meyer, *Urspr. u. Anf.,* III, p. 339; Leitzmann, *H.* I, p. 109 think.

[4] As is admitted by Loisy, 'La carrière de l'Apôtre Paul', *R.h.l.r.,* N.S., 1920, VI, p. 445, and Guignebert, *Le Christ,* p. 296.

[5] Damascus was not at that time in the hands of the Nabateans. The ethnarch therefore must not have been the governor of the town but chief of the Nabatean colony. There is no doubt that he had placed agents at the gates of the town to seize Paul or to assassinate him as he was leaving the town.

Galatians there are hints, but nothing more, to suggest that at a given moment a change took place in the purpose and object of Paul's missionary activity. After mentioning a mission to Galatia in opposition to Paul and those who were behind it Paul writes, 'And I, brethren, if I yet preach circumcision, why do I yet suffer persecution?'[1] (v. 11).

To preach circumcision is not exactly the same as to preach to Jews but Paul is never frightened of using somewhat exaggerated expressions and may well have thought that to preach only to the Jews was to remain a prisoner to the law. He may therefore be writing of a time when he did not incur the opposition of the Judaisers because he was not yet addressing himself to the Gentiles. There is a passage in the book of the Acts which supports the idea that Paul's missionary activity underwent a change of direction if it can be retained as authentic.

Paul's speech after his arrest at Jerusalem recounting his conversion finishes with these words, 'And it came to pass that, when I was come again to Jerusalem, even while I prayed in the temple, I was in a trance; and saw him[2] saying unto me, Make haste, and get thee quickly out of Jerusalem: for they will not receive thy testimony concerning me. And I said, Lord, they know that I imprisoned and beat in every synagogue them that believed on thee: And when the blood of thy martyr Stephen was shed, I also was standing by, and consenting unto his death, and kept the raiment of them that slew him. And he said unto me, Depart; for I will send thee far hence unto the Gentiles' (xiii. 17-21).

The compiler of Acts put these words into the mouth of the apostle, because he wanted to explain why Paul's missionary activity had a different aim from that of the Twelve and to stamp the principle of preaching the gospel to the Gentiles with the highest authority he could think of.[3]

If Paul had had a vision like this on his first visit to Jerusalem it would have taken place three years after his conversion, i.e. after

---

[1] The word ἔτι (yet) is missing in D.G. *it*. These manuscripts are not of great value. The word may have been suppressed to prevent the idea being given that Paul's preaching varied. It is not impossible that it came through the same word being repeated which is to be found at the end of the sentence.

[2] Him, i.e. the Lord Christ.

[3] It is very tempting to identify this vision with that alluded to by Paul in 2 Cor. xii which must have been particularly important. But the difficulty about this is that the vision in 2 Cor. xii took place about 44 when Paul was already known as the apostle to the Gentiles.

his activity in Arabia. Then when he says to the Galatians, 'If I yet preach the circumcision! . . .' he must have been thinking of his mission in Arabia as where he was doing this, i.e. while he still considered the gospel to be confined within the bounds of Judaism. This is possibly what he meant; but this explanation is far from being absolutely convincing and meets with difficulties which cannot be easily solved.

Paul's brief visit to Jerusalem after his hurried escape from Damascus was undertaken with certain precautions; it was kept secret as Paul met only Peter and James and saw none of the other apostles (Gal. i. 18-19).[1] From that time he was hated by the Jews and regarded with suspicion by the Christians. This cannot be explained unless he had addressed himself to the Gentiles and so made it clear that he had taken up a position in opposition to the Law.

For the period following up to 43 we only know that Paul was at work in Syria, Cilicia, and above all in Antioch. It is certain that his activity was crowned with success. They heard reports of him in Judaea and glorified God in him (Gal. i. 23-24). With Barnabas he withstood the pressure which Judaisers who came to Antioch tried to bring to bear on converted Gentiles and then came to Jerusalem to defend their cause.

The results of the conference at Jerusalem[2] did not exactly fulfil Paul's wishes but through his tenacity of purpose he gained recognition of his apostleship and his gospel from the 'pillars of the church'—not without difficulty it is true. In this way it became possible for him to embark on extensive missionary undertakings without any fear that his work would be compromised in advance by opposition from within the church.[3]

It will be sufficient to recall in outline[4] his three missionary journeys.[5] The narrative as it is given in the book of Acts varies very much in value according to the sources at the disposal of the

---

[1] See p. 111, n 3.   [2] See pp. 295 ff.

[3] In Gal. ii. 2 Paul says that he came to Jerusalem 'lest by any means he should run or had run in vain'. This shows that he had the feeling that opposition from the Christians in Jerusalem would have made his missionary work impossible or have spoilt the results. The events which followed showed that he was mistaken with regard to the way in which he was received at Jerusalem.

[4] For a criticism of the account of these journeys given by Acts and for details which cannot be given here see my *Introd.* III and IV. I shall return to these journeys when I am dealing with the opposition which Paul incurred.

[5] It is convenient to make use of the terms first, second, and third journeys as they are hallowed by custom but it must not be forgotten that Paul had previously made other journeys in Arabia, Cilicia and Syria.

compiler of the narrative. He seems to have had fairly good sources of information on the details of the journeys in Macedonia and Greece, but for the rest of his narrative he seems only to have had a simple itinerary at his disposal which he embroidered with attractive but often legendary elements and inserted in it speeches which cannot have been Paul's[1] but were either composed by the compiler himself or borrowed from some collection of missionary speeches.

Paul made the first journey with Barnabas, crossed the island of Cyprus, then went into Asia Minor through Perga and preached at Antioch in Pisidia, Iconium, Lystra and Derbe; then the missionaries retraced their steps and came back to Perga where they embarked for Antioch (Acts xiii. 4-14, 28).

Paul chose Silas as his companion for the second journey after he dismissed Barnabas,[2] went through Syria and Cilicia and visited Derbe, Lystra, and Iconium. At Lystra he found a new companion in Timothy who proved to be a very precious friend.[3] The first part of the journey was devoted to visiting churches which had been founded previously. Next Paul went through[4] Phrygia and Galatia.[5] Then after he had made attempts to enter Mysia and Bithynia, the provinces of Asia, which for reasons we are unacquainted with failed, he passed over into Macedonia in accordance with a dream, which together with the obstacles which had compelled him to give up his previous plans he believed showed him what was the will of God. He stayed at Philippi, Thessalonica, and Berea. His preaching in Macedonia met with great success but also

---

[1] The speeches in the synagogue at Antioch in Pisidia (xiii. 16-41), before the Areopagus (xvii. 22-31) and to the elders of the church at Ephesus who came to Miletus (xx. 18-35).   [2] See p. 304.

[3] According to Acts xvi. 1-3 Timothy was the son of a Jewish mother and a Gentile father and Paul had him circumcised 'because of the Jews' before he took him as his companion. In Col. iv. 10-11, however, at the time when Timothy was with him and is mentioned as the joint-author of the epistle Paul that Mark and Jesus-Justus are the only Jews working with him. From this it can be inferred that Timothy was uncircumcised.

[4] The texts of Acts (xvi. 6) says only that Paul went through Phrygia and the region of Galatia but gives no details perhaps in order not to bring to mind the disagreeable happenings which must have happened later in Galatia. The verb διέιχομαι which is used here in Acts means to go through a country and preach the gospel.

[5] We think that it refers to Galatia, the country properly so called, i.e. the old kingdom with the capital Ancyra, what the commentators call Northern Galatia. For the reasons why I prefer this theory to that which would make it refer to the districts in the south of the Roman province of Galatia where the churches founded by Paul were situated see *Introd*. IV, 2, pp. 147 ff.

with lively opposition not only as Acts informs us from the Jews but also from the Gentiles. Paul was compelled to flee from Philippi to Thessalonica, then from Thessalonica to Berea. Finally he had to leave the province, pursued, it seems, by the public authorities, who only allowed him to return in peace at a later date towards the end of his third journey.[1] He made a brief stay at Athens and then came to Corinth, where at first he only wished to stay until he could return to Macedonia. When he saw that he could not return he decided to devote himself to the evangelisation of Corinth and remained there for eighteen months. After this he made a brief halt at Ephesus and returned to Antioch (xv. 40-xviii. 22).

A little time after he set out on a fresh journey which proved to be the last. For the second time he went through Phrygia and Galatia and arrived at Ephesus where he stayed[2] two or three years.[3]

This sojourn in Asia was a particularly critical period in Paul's life. While he was there he had to face grave difficulties which came to a head in Corinth a little before those which cropped up in Galatia.[4] For his stay there the evidence from Acts is poor and not very trustworthy.[5] Accurate information, however, comes to us from the epistle to the Philippians,[6] 1 Corinthians xv. 32 where Paul says that he fought with wild beasts at Ephesus, and 1 Corinthians xvi. 9 where he says that his enemies were numerous, proving that in Ephesus Paul met with great difficulties and very probably was put in prison and threatened with capital punishment.[7] The epistle to the Philippians also shows us that Paul met with trouble even in the very heart of Asiatic Christendom from people who were jealous of him and tried to replace his authority by their own (i. 15-17). At the same time the Jews were straining to draw to their side those whom his preaching had turned from polytheism.[8] It looks as if the compiler of Acts wanted to throw a veil over all this.

[1] See pp. 474 ff.
[2] The stay in Asia was interrupted at least once by a rapid journey to Corinth.
[3] Two years according to Acts xix. 10; three years according to Acts xx. 31. It may well be that the two years refer only to the time spent by Paul teaching in the school of Tyrannus. It is also possible that of the three years Paul stayed in Asia two were spent in Ephesus.
[4] Concerning the crises at Corinth and in Galatia see further on pp. 305 ff.
[5] Thus the detailed story of the riot caused by the silversmith Demetrius appears to refer to an anti-semitic movement which did not concern Paul or the Christians.
[6] For the reasons which make me think that the epistle to the Philippians was written at Ephesus while Paul was in prison there and not as is most generally thought while he was a prisoner at Rome see *Introd.* IV. 1, pp. 369 ff.
[7] See pp. 485 ff.   [8] Those are the persons referred to in Phil. iii. 2 ff.

When Paul left Ephesus in Asia he wanted to pass through Macedonia which so far he had been unable to revisit, then to go to Corinth and try to restore his authority there. In Macedonia he learnt first, that the Corinthians, following a stern letter which he had written to them and the intervention of Titus, had regained their senses and had put a stop to their opposition, and secondly, that the Galatians had been worked upon by Judaising missionaries and were on the point of giving way to their demands and accepting circumcision. It is well known how the crisis in Galatia ended.[1] As far as Greece is concerned the church at Corinth seems to have submitted completely to Paul who met with no trouble there during his stay of three months (Acts xx. 3) at the beginning of 58, at least so far as the church was concerned. For it is unlikely that during these three months the Jews would have showed no signs of a hatred which at the time of his departure drove them to form a plot to assassinate him on the journey which he had planned to Jerusalem.[2]

This journey to Jerusalem had been planned for some years. It went back to the time when in fulfilment of the promise made by him at the conference of 43-44 Paul had organised a collection for the church at Jerusalem in Galatia, Asia, Macedonia and Greece.[3] At first he was undecided whether he would accompany in person the delegates of the churches who were to bring it (1 Cor. xvi. 3-4). After the crises in Galatia and Greece he felt it necessary to put his relationship with the leaders of the church at Jerusalem to the test to get to know exactly what they felt towards him. By undertaking the journey to Jerusalem he got a clear idea of the dangers to which he was going to be exposed at the hands of the Jews in Jerusalem, and he was not fully assured of being favourably received by the Christians there.[4] His fears were justified. The church received him with marked reserve and was unconcerned as to his fate when he found himself in difficulties. As for the Jews, they caused a riot in the course of which he would have been massacred if Roman troops had not intervened in time to seize him.[5]

[1] See pp. 315 ff.
[2] When Paul learnt of this plot he modified his itinerary and instead of embarking direct for Syria made a detour by passing through Macedonia and Asia (Acts xx. 3).
[3] Concerning this collection see my article, 'La collecte en faveur des Saints de Jérusalem', *R.h.p.r.*, 1925, XV, pp. 301-318.
[4] This can be inferred from Rom. xv. 30-31 where Paul makes an insistent demand on the Romans to pray that he may be delivered from them that are rebellious in Judaea, i.e. the Jews and that the collection may be well received by the church.
[5] Concerning the trial which then took place and the end of Paul's life see pp. 488 ff.

When Paul's missionary activity was in this way forcibly interrupted, he had the feeling that his work in the Eastern half of the Mediterranean was ended and he was preparing, after passing through Rome, to find a new field for his activity in Spain.

3.—PAUL'S MISSIONARY METHOD

Paul's missionary method is shown to be a curious mixture of irrational and supernatural impulses expressed in dreams and visions and reasoned plans formed after considered reflection, a curious combination of calculation and improvisation. It seems as if Paul's purpose was not to evangelise whole districts systematically but to create a number of strategic points from where the faith might afterwards spread. For this purpose he chose the large cities[1] which by their situation were places not only where trade routes joined but also where the philosophic and religious streams of the ancient world met. Here there was a floating rootless population, which had lost its political, religious, and social traditions, possessed no stability and was particularly vulnerable to the preaching of the gospel.

This missionary method, which might be described as a method of projection in contrast to a method of progression is followed by what might be called a process of diffusion. It seems to have been the method followed by the majority if not all of the missionaries of the first generation both from Jerusalem and from the Hellenistic Christians (1 Cor. ix. 5).[2] It affected the way in which Christianity developed in important respects. At the end of the first generation the Eastern basin of the Mediterranean from Jerusalem to Rome (Rom. xv. 18)[3] contained a fair number of Christian communities

[1] This is because Paul found it easiest in such cities to gain his livelihood. From one church at least, however, he accepted financial help. That was the church at Philippi (Phil. iv. 15-16; cf. 2 Cor. xi. 9), but he always refused to receive anything from the church at Corinth (1 Cor. ix. 3 ff.; 2 Cor. xi. 9-10; xii. 13-18), doubtless because his disinterestedness was questioned there.

[2] This method seems to have been followed by the moralists, itinerant Greek preachers. See Rengsdorf, 'ἀπόστολος', Kittel, *Theol. Worterb.* I, p. 411.

[3] Perhaps in other directions as well. We do not know much about the Christian mission in the first generation apart from references to Paul's missionary activities. I only wish to note one point concerning Egypt. The legends attributing its evangelisation to Peter and Mark are late and inconsistent. But it may be supposed that Egypt had already been evangelised when Paul wrote the epistle to the Romans. Wishing only to preach where Christ had not yet been named (Rom. xv. 20) he wanted to undertake the evangelisation of Spain. Would he not have preferred Egypt if it had still been virgin ground for evangelisation. There is no reason for thinking that Christianity had spread only in a westward direction.

which existed in isolation from each other. They only had occasional contact with one another and were not bound up together in one central organisation. The contrast between this complete absence of any general organisation and the exceedingly strong feeling among these communities that they were spiritually one, a feeling which showed itself in action, e.g. in the hospitality which Christians received from the churches when they were travelling,[1] constitutes an important fact.

Both in the realm of thought and organisation and in other respects development must not have been the same everywhere. Christianity covered a vast area and as long as it still lacked fixed forms could show diversity without being divided. In the second generation a movement towards unification set in which at the end of the first century came to a head in two forms which might be described as pre-catholic, the Fourth Evangelist in Asia representing one form and Clement of Rome in the West representing the other. A century later we can see appearing with Irenaeus and Tertullian what may be called pre-catholicism.

Although Paul felt that he had a special mission to the Gentiles he was not on that account prevented from preaching also to the Jews. Between the Jews and sympathetic Gentiles who gravitated round the synagogues it was impossible to draw a clear line. Two reasons, one theoretical, the other practical, prevented Paul from refraining from altogether preaching to the Jews. When he offers the gospel as 'the power of God unto salvation to every one that be-lieveth, to the Jew first, and also to the Greek ' (Rom. i. 16) he means that in principle salvation is intended for the Jews and that it is only because they reject it that it is offered to the Gentiles. When-ever Paul arrived at a fresh town, he did not feel that he had any right to address himself to the Gentiles exclusively until at any rate the Jews had rejected his message. The synagogue services with the opportunities which they provided for every worshipper to preach to the community offered to the Christian missionaries a pulpit ready to hand where they could get into touch with both Jews and proselytes and through them with other Gentiles. Ac-cording to the Acts, Paul preached everywhere in the synagogue

From 1 Cor. ix. 5 we know that the missionaries from Jerusalem, those whom Paul calls the other apostles, the brethren of the Lord and Cephas, were also itinerant but we do not know in what countries they were active.

[1] See *E.P.*, pp. 167 ff. This hospitality was also abused. The Didache formulates precise rules to remedy this abuse.

until he was expelled from it. When that happened he set up in another place, at Corinth in the house of Titus Justus, at Ephesus in the school of a certain Tyrannus which he rented. Acts here rather describes Paul's arrangements as if they were the execution of a formal plan. The services of the synagogue could only be a temporary means of preaching the gospel. They were sufficient for the beginning of a mission but were unsuitable for instructing those who had to become more clearly conscious of their faith, and it is difficult to see how baptism and the eucharist could have been celebrated in them. Even when the growing groups of Christians were not expelled from the synagogues they could not remain in them indefinitely; they had to find places for meeting which could be their own.

Paul had helpers in his missionary work; two groups can be distinguished. One was composed of missionaries like Barnabas, Silas, Titus, perhaps Apollos as well, who sometimes were associated with him for a common task but otherwise were engaged in their own work. Others such as John Mark for the first part of the first journey and Timothy especially were more like subordinates and auxiliaries. Paul also gained assistance from people who did not accompany him on his travels but helped him in the communities to which they belonged. Such were Aquila and his wife Priscilla, Sosthenes, Epaphras, Archippus and others.

When Paul thought that his activity had made sufficient impression in a church so that it could be left alone, he withdrew himself from it; he kept in touch with it by correspondence[1] and whenever the opportunity came returned and visited it. As he said, he carried with him constantly the 'care of all the churches' (2 Cor. xi. 28).

4.—PAUL'S THEOLOGY

It is often said that the one source of all Paul's thought was his conversion.[2] To a large extent this is true as long as we do not take it rigorously. It has already been noted that the religious problem remained the same for Paul after his conversion as it was before and that he used the same material for his ideas in both parts of his life. Furthermore, he never confined the action of God and Christ in him to the one moment of his conversion. He was an inspired man,

---

[1] We only possess a small part of this correspondence.

[2] Particularly was this idea developed in a book of Sabatier, *L'apôtre Paul Esquisse d'une histoire de sa pensée*, Paris, 1870³, 1897.

who felt that he was possessed if not continuously at any rate constantly by the Spirit of Christ inspiring his thoughts and dictating his words and actions. This life 'in Christ' or 'in the Lord' or 'in the Spirit' was the never ceasing spring of Paul's life and thoughts pushing him forward with unfailing power.

Paul's theology is based upon the idea of a divine plan of creation in two stages on which a plan of redemption was superimposed, when sin had made it impossible for God to complete His plan of creation and He refused to allow the work which He had undertaken for His glory to end in failure.

Paul maintains in 1 Corinthians xv. 44-49 that there is a psychic body and a spiritual body.[1] Adam, it is said in Genesis ii. 7, was created a living *psyche*.[2] The second Adam, on the other hand, is a life-giving spirit. Paul states that not the spiritual but the psychical comes first (xv. 46).[3] The first man is earthly,[4] while the second man comes from heaven. These are the marks of human nature of which the two Adams are the prototypes. Paul explains that man, so far as in his nature he is descended from Adam, i.e. flesh and blood, cannot inherit the kingdom of God (1 Cor. xv. 50). Flesh here does not mean what it has become since the fall which has made it the seat and cause of sin; but the flesh as God originally created it, innocent as far as sin is concerned, capable of sinning but not inevitably bound to sin. Even if there had been no fall, the creation would not have been completed without the appearance of the second Adam, who had to be the bridge across which it would pass from the carnal level to the spiritual level. He would, however, have accomplished not an act of redemption but an act of creation similar to the first act of creation in which he had also played a part. The statements of the cosmological function of Christ are not as explicit as those in Hebrews i. 2-3 and John i. 3, but it is clearly said in Colossians i. 16 that 'by him all things were created, that are in

---

[1] The first is corruptible (ἐν φθορᾷ), in dishonour (ἐν ἀτιμίᾳ), in weakness (ἐν ἀσθενείᾳ); the second is incorruptible (ἐν αφθαρσίᾳ), in glory (ἐν δόξᾳ), in power (ἐν δυνάμει) (1 Cor. xv. 42-43).

[2] There is here a double antithesis, on the one hand, that of ψυχή and πνεῦμα, on the other hand, that of a life possessed only as a deposit which leaves man mortal compared with the life which Christ possesses so far as he can give life.

[3] This idea is certainly borrowed from an older doctrine. Although Paul only means by it the two stages through which the world and mankind were to pass, it is clear that it does not harmonise with the idea of the pre-existence of Christ and his function as an organ of creation.

[4] This term, which comes from Gen. ii. 7, refers both to the place of man's habitation and the substance of which he is made.

heaven, and that are in earth, visible and invisible, whether they be thrones, or dominions, or principalities, or powers.[1] All things were created by him, and for him: and he is before all things and by him all things consist.' This is not just an improvisation put forward to meet the cosmological gnosis of the Colossians since a similar contention is to be found in 1 Corinthians viii. 6 where Paul writes, 'But to us there is but one God, the Father, of whom are all things, ἐξ ὃυ τὰ πάντα and we in him (made for him) (ἐις αὐτόν) and one Lord Jesus Christ by whom (δί ὃυ) are all things and we by him' (δί αὐτοῦ)'. But until Paul came into collision with the Colossian gnosis the idea of the cosmological function of Christ had remained in the background of his mind because it was not of practical interest.[2]

What was the end of creation? It is easy to see what it is when we consider what there was at the beginning before creation when God alone existed.[3] At the end of all things when the τέλος shall be attained as mentioned in 1 Corinthians xv. 24 God will be all in all (xv. 28). God all in all is something different and something more than God by himself. The realisation of the state defined by this phrase was the end of the plan of creation. As it miscarried as a result of the fall, it is now the end of the plan of redemption which God has imposed upon the former plan without annulling it. It may thus be said that Paul's God is an expanding God. If we wished from a practical rather than a theoretical point of view to define Paul's God we might say that he is the one who has the right and alone the right to worship and obedience.

According to the opening chapters of the epistle to the Romans, the first sin which was the source of all others is idolatry, giving to others the adoration due to God and due to him alone. If it is compared with what we read in the christological hymn[4] in Philippians ii. 3 it is clear that the fall has a cosmic character and that the fall of man is only man's compliance with Satan's revolt against God.

[1] i.e. all the beings of the celestial hierarchy.
[2] I cannot therefore subscribe to the opinion of Guignebert (*Le Christ*, p. 288) who thinks that Paul obtained the idea that Christ has cosmological function from the Colossian gnosis.
[3] From the theological point of view Christ the son of God seems to have been inseparable from Him.
[4] In this hymn the first characteristics given of the attitude of the pre-existent Christ are not positive but negative. This leads us to think we have in the fragment one side of a diptych and that the corresponding side would give the picture of another heavenly being also existing ἐν μορφῇ θεοῦ who wanted to claim equality with God (ἔιναι ἴσα θεῷ), i.e. put himself forward as an object to be worshipped by the created world.

It is true that in virtue of his omnipotence God could have created beings who could do nothing but worship him but, if he had done this, he would as it were, have only been worshipping himself and nothing would have been added to his glory. In short, worship[1] can have no value unless it is free. God therefore created free beings, i.e. beings capable of giving or refusing him their worship and obedience and of offering it to other beings. God therefore undertook a risk in his work. It might miscarry and it did. God—always because of his omnipotence—could have destroyed a world which did not respond to his expectation and stood in his way and have left it to resume his attempt at another time as would have been necessary for the final accomplishment of his purpose. One passage in the epistle to the Romans (iii. 25) seems to suggest that it might appear that God ought to have done this if he had been mindful of his righteousness and holiness.

But God is patient and merciful. Instead of destroying his work he left the plan of creation to develop on its own and imposed upon it a plan of redemption which fits into that of creation, partly because they both have the same purpose, i.e. to create for God a community of worshippers and also because Christ is the organ by which both plans are to be realised. From this it follows that Christ's work is both positive and negative, negative as it destroys sin and its consequences and positive, as it creates the bridge across which man may pass from the realm of the flesh to that of the spirit. This helps to give the impression at first sight that Paul's soteriology shows a certain amount of contradiction in its phraseology. The results of justification are not described as the restoration of human flesh to the pristine purity of Adam's before the fall or to that of Christ's but the man who is justified is said to be dead to the flesh and become a spiritual being. This gives rise to the paradoxical character of Paul's ethic with its curious mixture of indicatives and imperatives summed up perhaps in the sentence, 'Make yourself in fact what you are in principle'.[2]

All this is due to the way in which experience compelled Paul to modify the lay-out of Jewish traditional eschatology. This contained two successive worlds, (1) the old world, i.e. the world of the flesh where since the fall God's rule is limited by that of Satan and demons, and (2) the new world, which was to come and would be

---

[1] On all these questions see my article, 'Le Paulinisme théologie de la liberté', *Rev. de théol. et de phil.*, 1951, pp. 93-104.

[2] Concerning Paul's ethics see *E.P.*, pp. 450 ff.

the reign of God, i.e. a state of things in which neither men nor things would offer any obstacle to God's will. Between the two worlds and separating them from each other was to appear the Messiah who would destroy the powers hostile to God and establish his reign. Paul transformed the bipartite lay-out, or if it be preferred, he substituted a tripartite lay-out in its place. He interpolates between the reign of Satan and the reign of God an interim period when the two worlds coexist together which will last from Christ's resurrection to his parousia. Paul at first thought this period to be short. In 1 Thessalonians iv. 1 and 1 Corinthians xv. 51-52 he expresses himself as if the parousia would take place while he was still living, and he thought that those of the elect who had died before the parousia had gone into a state of sleep or provisional annihilation from which they would emerge at the last day at the call of Christ. In Philippians i. and 2 Corinthians we find a different conception. At the moment of their death the elect will enter into communion with Christ who will be free from the limitations imposed upon him as long as he lived in the present dispensation.

Sabatier[1] tried to explain this dualism as due to a change in Paul's thought brought about or rather occasioned by a mortal danger to which Paul was exposed and to which he refers at the beginning of the second epistle to the Corinthians.[2] At some time or other his situation was such that he despaired of life. The truth contained in this hypothesis is that if we want to understand how Paul's ideas evolved we must see them in the light of his personal experience. But in spite of that the hypothesis cannot be accepted. First of all, in Sabatier's time, it was assumed as self-evident that the epistle to the Philippians was the last of the Pauline epistles to be written but today this is very much doubted and there are many scholars who consider it to be one of the earliest, being preceded only by the epistles to the Thessalonians and the first to the Corinthians. But a more decisive fact is that there are not two phases in Paul's eschatology but two currents which run side by side without commingling. One comes from Judaism and is a collective eschatology. The other which is an eschatology for the individual springs from Paul's experience as a Christian. The two passages expressing individual eschatology contain statements implying collective

---

[1] Sabatier, 'Comment la foi chrétienne de l'apôtre Paul a-t-elle triomphé de la crainte de la mort?' *Revue chrétienne*, 1894, pp. 1 ff.

[2] The allusion is not clear to us but it was to the Corinthians who knew what Paul was speaking about.

eschatology. In the first chapter of the epistle to the Philippians we find Paul desiring death because it will put an end to what in the present dispensation imposes limits on communion with Christ but we also find in the same epistle a most distinct statement of collective eschatology. 'We find our true home in heaven. It is to heaven we look expectantly for the coming of our Lord Jesus Christ to save us; he will form this humbled body of ours anew moulding it into the image of his glorified body, so effective in his power to make all things obey him' (iii. 20-21). In 2 Corinthians v. 10 also we find an argument concerning the growth of the inner man as the outer man decreases ending with a statement implying the conception of collective eschatology as it contains that of the last judgement implying that each individual's destiny will not be decided until the last day. 'For we must all appear before the judgement seat of Christ, that everyone may receive (the wages) the things done in his body, according to that he hath done, whether it be good or bad' (v. 10).

It is easy to see that the two currents to be found in Paul's eschatology do not spring from the same source. The collective eschatology comes from Jewish tradition, while the individual eschatology springs from Paul's peculiar experience of mystic communion with Christ as a Christian. But we must not consider the elements of collective eschatology to be found in Paul to be nothing more than a survival. They express an essential feature in Paul's thought, the knowledge that the end of redemption is not only to save a large but undefined number of individuals but the establishment of the people of God who will give him the worship and obedience due to him. There will come a time when God's work which is being carried out in time will attain its end. That will be the $\tau \acute{\epsilon} \lambda o s$ referred to in 1 Corinthians xv. 34, the resurrection of the elect, the time when the hostile powers have been destroyed and God will be all in all. Paul retained a certain amount of collective eschatology, because this conception which was essential to Paul's thought individual eschatology failed to express, although he could never be satisfied with the thought that death might interrupt the believer's communion with Christ even for a moment.

Paul envisages the problem of redemption in two spheres of reference at the same time, i.e. in terms of righteousness and justice and also in terms of power.[1] Righteousness must not be sacrificed.

[1] The Swedish theologian, G. Aulen, has made this remarkably clear in his book *Christus Victor*. Eng. Trans. S.P.C.K. 1951.

For that reason Christ became at one with human sin or took it upon himself—Paul's thought oscillates between the two conceptions— and expiated it by his death. But man must be freed from the servitude of Satan into which he has fallen. This is to think of redemption in terms of power. This is why Paul thought of the cross of Christ as victorious over Satan (1 Cor. ii. 6 ff.; Col. ii. 15) and it is known what an important place is given in the epistle to the Romans to the conception that the body is freed by faith in Christ from the bondage of Satan and has entered into the service of God.

A dualism therefore exists in Paul's conception of redemption. Right up to the time of St. Anselm, as Aulen has shown, Christian theology wavered between the two conceptions; since St. Anselm the juridical conception has prevailed with the result that to some extent Paulinism has been given a false interpretation.

Sin made it impossible for the divine plan to be carried out. Mankind and creation became infected with a principle of corruption which destined them for destruction. The purpose of the creation could only be accomplished through redemption. Christ is the agent of redemption as he had been of creation. His redemptive action is not a substitute but an addition to what ought to have been the second stage in his creative activity. For the accomplishment of the end of creation in spite of sin several conditions must be fulfilled, some of them negative, others positive. First God's anger against sin and sinners must be appeased without justice being sacrificed; hostile powers must be defeated or destroyed in order that the normal order of the cosmos which had been disturbed by Satan's revolt may be restored; in particular, mankind must be rescued from their power which had brought upon him sin and death. Lastly, human nature itself must be transformed from its carnal to a spiritual condition.

There are thus two lines of thought in Paul's soteriology which are closely bound together but are quite separate strands. Each of them corresponds to one particular aspect of Paul's experience of salvation, but his ideological material in each case has a different origin. The idea of redemption, forgiveness, and deletion of the consequences of sin, is merely a product of theological reflection derived from the conviction of forgiveness and salvation felt by those who had been influenced personally by Jesus. This is a heritage received by Paul from the first Christian community. On the other hand, the conception of a double creation and the transformation of human nature seem to have been foreign to primitive Christian thought.[1] Its origin must be looked for in Hellenised Judaism such as was to be found in Alexandria. The idea of spirit and flesh being in conflict with each other and spirit being unable to expand until it is freed from the bond connecting it to the flesh is a Greek conception.[2] The idea of the body being the tomb or prison of the spirit from which it desired to escape was strange to the Jew, who considered that a spirit could not exist without a body. In Paul's conception of the flesh and the spirit being in conflict can be traced some Greek influence, limited, however, in extent, since Paul remained unable to conceive of the existence of a spirit without a body as is shown by the argument of 1 Corinthians xv. There it is supposed that because the Corinthians deny the resurrection of the body they do not believe in any life hereafter at all.[3]

We find in Philo a conception of the two Adams similar to that of Paul's.[4] Philo draws his inspiration from the two stories of the creation of man in Genesis (i. 27; ii. 7) and lays down that there is one man created in the image of God and possessing his spirit, i.e. the spiritual and heavenly man.[5] Another man was only fashioned by God and animated with his breath.[6] Paul may have known this theory or one like it but he transformed it by reversing the order in which the two men appeared. It is plain that on this point he contradicted a current doctrine which was known to his readers. He makes use of it but gives it a new meaning.[7] Paul identifies Jesus dead, risen, and glorified with the Messiah for whose coming, as a Jew, he had been waiting. This with the way in which Paul thought of salvation determined the attitude of Paul's mind as a Christian. The conditions under which he became a Christian led him to consider Christ and his work from the angle of the cross. It must be

[1] Although it may be implied in the idea of the transformation of the present economy into the future economy, this, however, is only of the future.

[2] See E. Rohde, *Psyche, Seelencult und Unsterblichkeitsglaube der Griechen*[3], Tubingen, Leipzig, 1903, especially II, pp. 121 f.; J. Carcopino, *La Basilique pythagorieienne de la Porte Majeure*, Paris, 1927, pp. 251 ff.

[3] Paul gives expression to the desire of being delivered from the body of sin but his ideal is the ἀπολύτρωσις τοῦ σώματος (Rom. viii. 23), the deliverance of the body by a transformation which would prevent it from being the cause of sin.

[4] See Brehier, *Les idées philosophiques et religieuses de Philon d'Alexandrie*, Paris, 1908, pp. 121 ff.; Bousset-Gressmann, *Rel. d. Jud.*, pp. 353 ff.; Meyer, *Urspr. u. Anf.*, II, pp. 346 t.; Lietzmann, *Kor.* p. 85.

[5] In the *de opificio mundi*, p. 134, p. 32, Philo identifies the first man, i.e. the one whose creation is recounted in Gen. i. 27 with the logos. This may be the origin of Paul's identification of Christ with the heavenly Adam.

[6] Philo, *de leg. alleg.* I, 31, p. 49.

[7] It may also be that we have here an argument against the gnostic idea of the redemption of a spiritual being who had fallen into matter.

recognised that while Paul did not deny the importance of Christ's words and teaching[1] his essential work he considered lay in his death; the gospel was for him the cross of Christ (1 Cor. i. 23-24; ii. 2). The whole of his soteriology consists of nothing but an interpretation of the death of Christ and an explanation of the paradox of the curse of God hanging over his Son. Apart from this, faith in Jesus as the Messiah compelled Paul to divide the task of the Messiah, the idea of which he had inherited from Judaism, into two parts, one of which was left to be accomplished at the return of the Lord.

Although Paul felt that he always preached the same gospel he did not come to perfect knowledge at one stroke; he even had the feeling that perfect knowledge never could come in the present economy (Phil. iii. 13; 1 Cor. xiii. 9-12). While his thought as a Christian became enriched and developed he did not feel that it really underwent change.[2] At a time when the church did not yet possess traditional doctrine or fixed dogma his theology acquired its expression under the influence of practical considerations relative to his preaching and his mission.

To understand Paul's conception of the way of salvation we must gain some idea of his anthropology. It is difficult to grasp, because he never gave his psychology any systematic expression but much more so because of his somewhat loose terminology[3] which he borrowed from popular speech. Its ambiguity shows a certain looseness in his thought which comes from the fact that in Paul's mind the two ideological streams from Palestine and Greece were commingled. His anthropology was fundamentally Hebraic but tinged with Hellenism, especially with regard to the terms and notions used to express it.

Paul generally describes human personality to be made of three elements: a body, a soul ($\psi v\chi\acute{\eta}$), i.e. a vital principle which animates it and a spirit ($\pi v\epsilon\hat{v}\mu a$ or $vo\hat{v}s$) (1 Thess. v. 23).[4] He also uses the term heart ($\kappa a\rho\delta\acute{\iota}a$) to define all the immaterial element in human personality. This term comes from the Old Testament and seems to

[1] On this subject see my *Life of Jesus*, p. 116 ff.

[2] Sabatier (*L'Apôtre Paul*) made an attempt to trace the development of Paul's thought. It is an interesting attempt but must now be reckoned obsolete.

[3] To give only one example Paul uses the word 'heart' for the source of all evil thoughts (Rom. i. 21-24) and also for what in man is receptive of God (Rom. ii. 15; x. 10; 2 Cor. i. 22; Gal. iv. 6).

[4] Concerning this conception see the article by P. Festugiere, 'La trichotomie de 1 Thess. v. 23 et la philosophie grecque', *Recherches de science religieuse*, 1929, XIX, pp. 385-415.

have belonged to popular speech. The heart has both an affective character (Rom. ix. 2; x. 1) and an intellectual character (1 Cor. vii. 37; 1 Cor. iii. 15). It is receptive towards God (Rom. v. 5; 2 Cor. i. 22; Gal. iv. 6, etc.) but it is also the source of evil passions (Rom. i. 24) and is evil (Rom. i. 21).

The term νοῦς comes from the Greek language. In Romans vii. 22 it is the interior self which is in harmony with the law of God, but in other parts of the epistle (i. 28) it is an evil *nous* (ἀδόκιμος) to which God has abandoned idolaters.

Like the heart the *nous* appears to have been a conception religiously and ethically neutral.[1]

Paul also speaks of the conscience (συνείδησις).[2] Sometimes this word is associated with the heart and appears to be synonymous with it; sometimes it refers to what a man feels about himself to his power of judging himself (Rom. ii. 15; ix. 1; xiii. 5; 2 Cor. i. 12, etc.).

The most important point concerns the body σῶμα. Chapter xv of the first epistle to the Corinthians gives a lesson on the resurrection which turns entirely on a misunderstanding. Certain Corinthians were denying the resurrection. Paul thinks that that implied that they denied the existence of any kind of life beyond the grave, while the Corinthians in question as Greeks meant that the life beyond the grave would be the life of the soul which would expand fully, when it was freed from the body in which it was now shut up as in a prison or tomb. As a Jew, Paul cannot think of the life of a soul without a body. The Greeks thought of the body as a material thing while Paul thought of it as a form, the expression of personality. How otherwise could Paul have spoken of a spiritual body? This also is an impossible conception for us whose minds have been formed on Platonic and Cartesian lines.

There is lastly in the Christian a spirit which does not come from himself but is a gift of God, a gift, however, which is appropriated by him who receives it so far as it becomes a constituent element in his personality renewing it and making it into 'a new creature'. Paul's feeling of being possessed by the Spirit and being inspired has something in common with that of a man possessed who feels a power within him not belonging to him which cannot be resisted. The distinguishing mark of the spirit for Paul is that this power

[1] Rom. xii. 2 speaks of a renewal of ourselves which gives us knowledge of the law of God.

[2] This term is only found in the New Testament in Paul's letters or in writings subject to the influence of his thought.

becomes integrated into the personality to which it gives new life and so makes it the true self. At the same time, however, this new creation is not wholly finished, because the terrestrial man cannot be completely transformed into the heavenly man in the present economy.

Paul considers the phenomena of pneumatism to be the manifestation of a supernatural force and uses them as valuable evidence. But this is only the exterior side of his conception. The Spirit not only produces phenomena which attract extraordinary attention but also sets in motion saving activities in the depths of human personality which gradually invade the personality until they emerge from the region of the unconscious to the realm of the conscious. Paul was acquainted with a prayer 'in tongues' where the Spirit prays without the conscious personality being able to be associated with it. The complete prayer is that prayed by the Spirit but shared by the *nous* (1 Cor. xiv. 14-15). Paul allots to the Spirit the widest sphere of action He has ever had in Christian thought. He does not reject the spectacular phenomena of pneumatism but seeks to discipline them (1 Cor. xiv). He considers them to belong to another order of happenings, i.e. of hidden spiritual motions which cannot be given expression (Rom. viii. 26) belonging to the life of the believer and creating joy and peace for him (1 Thess. i. 6; Rom. xiv. 17; xv. 13), his hope of justification (Gal. v. 5; 1 Cor. vi. 11), his assurance of sonship with God (Rom. viii. 15), and the glorious liberty of the children of God (2 Cor. iii. 17; Rom. viii. 21). Lastly, to them belongs the love of God, the crown of the Christian life, which gives him hope and patience in afflictions (Rom. v. 5) and agape (1 Cor. xiii). The action of the Spirit not only brings forth the fruits of the Christian life but through the action of the Spirit the Christian life comes into existence. Faith comes from preaching and the power of preaching comes from the Spirit. By contrast the author of Acts considers the possession of the Spirit to be a luxury for the Christian, a kind of privilege which comes to some Christians on rare occasions but Paul reckons it to be the primordial, constituent essential of the Christian life for, 'if anyone hath not the Spirit of the Lord, he is none of His' (Rom. viii. 9).

To some extent the apostle abides by the Hebraic conception of the *rouah Jahve* which seized the prophets of Israel and made them speak.[1] In Paul's thought the Spirit not only uses men for God's

---

[1] Sabatier, *Mémoire sur la notion hébraique de l'Esprit*, Paris, 1879; Ad. Lods, 'Trois études sur la littérature prophetique', *R.h.p.r.*, 1931, XI, pp. 211 ff.

designs but also transforms them. Paul is much more eager to describe and define the action of the Spirit than to say what the Spirit himself is. The statements of the epistles on this subject are vague and sometimes contradictory. In Romans viii. 9-11 Paul gives one definition after another of the Christian life, saying that the Spirit of God lives in him, that he has the spirit of Christ, that Christ is in him and that the spirit of him who has raised up Jesus from the dead lives in him. All these expressions are equivalent to each other and interchangeable. In other places the Spirit is the conscience God has of himself (1 Cor. ii. 11).[1]

In 2 Corinthians iii. 17 Paul gives this formal definition of the Spirit: 'The Lord[2] is the Spirit' but immediately afterwards he does not speak of the Lord who is the Spirit but of the Spirit of the Lord. He says, however, in Galatians ii. 19, 'Christ lives in me'. Usually he speaks of the believer who has the spirit of Christ[3] rather than of the believer who has Christ in him. This is partly perhaps due to the fact that it is somewhat difficult to grasp the idea of the Christ as being both a person living a transcendent life in heaven and at the same time active in the hearts of believers. Also the expression 'the gift of the Spirit' implying that there are various degrees of the Spirit also implies, what is of some importance, that the action of the Spirit will only yield its full fruit in a life beyond. The Christology developed in Philippians ii. 6-11 describes how Christ after humbling himself to die on the cross received the title of *Kyrios* (Lord) which gave him the right to be worshipped by every being. This shows that Christ only acquired the attribute[4] which made him and the Spirit identical[5] in his existence after death in

---

[1] Gal. iv. 29 says that Isaac was begotten 'according to the Spirit' while Ishmael was begotten according to the flesh. This might imply an action of the spirit in the religion of Israel. But this is an isolated passage. Paul usually thinks of the action of the spirit in connection with the glorification of Christ. In Gal. iv. 29 the phrase 'according to the Spirit' may quite well be only implying the idea of the plan of redemption.

[2] i.e. Christ glorified. The fact that the term Lord applies both to God and to Christ goes some way towards identifying the Spirit of God with the Spirit of Christ.

[3] i.e. possessed by. In Paul's thought the believer possesses the Spirit and is possessed by him.

[4] This is a very different conception from that in the Fourth Gospel which makes the glorification of Christ to be the same as his return to the state in which he was previous to the incarnation (xvii. 5).

[5] All the same in 1 Cor. x. 4 Christ is identified with the spiritual rock which followed the Israelites in the desert. This passage, however, reproduces a Jewish idea (Strack-Billerbeck, III, pp. 406 ff.). The passage 1 Cor. xv. 45 describing the second Adam as a 'life-giving spirit' is much more important but it puts the

glory. It was only possible for the Spirit to act upon believers after Christ was glorified since Galatians iv. 6 states that possession of the Spirit is evidence of justification.

Paul's originality lies in the conception that the action of the Spirit is not only the symptom but also the cause of what has happened and is happening in the life of the believer. The conception of the Spirit is thus placed in the centre of the Christian life. The Spirit makes the believer a new creature and that is the one thing that counts in Paul's estimation (2 Cor. v. 17; Gal. vi. 15).

The expressions 'in Christ' 'in the Lord' and 'in the Spirit'[1] are most characteristic of Paul's vocabulary.[2] Deissmann[3] has shown that they cannot be explained as coming from the Septuagint or as hellenisms. They express the relationship between the believer and Christ and the state of the believer when his life, mystically united to Christ, is no longer his own but belongs to Christ. Paul places the emphasis not so much on the mystical union itself as on its fruits shown as the gifts of the Spirit. He is thinking of a close communion with Christ but such is its nature that the human personality is not destroyed in its realisation. To be 'in Christ' therefore is through the drama of the death and resurrection of Christ to have passed from existence in the flesh the end of which is death to a new order which Christ's resurrection has inaugurated in a celestial realm. This realm is not only subject to Christ but also takes its life from him.

Paul's doctrine of the Spirit is a psychological description and an explanation of the birth and growth of the life of the believer. The Spirit is not a developing power but a transforming force. Flesh and spirit are two opposing powers in conflict with each other (Rom. viii. 7). They do not belong to the same order of creation (1 Cor. xv. 45). But Paul also believes that they are in conflict as a

accent on the action of Christ over the new humanity of which he is the prototype and this action only comes into play after his glorification.

[1] There are also the phrases 'in Christ Jesus' and 'in Jesus Christ' but never 'in Jesus'. The expressions 'in the Lord' and 'in the Spirit' are equivalent to each other through the equation 'The Lord is the Spirit' (2 Cor. iii. 17). The expression 'in God' is only found once (Col. ii. 3) but it is not so much a peculiar concept as an extension of the concept 'in Christ'.

[2] The frequency with which this group of expressions is used shows how much Paul has influenced the various writers of the New Testament. Apart from the Pauline and pseudo-Pauline epistles the expression is found in the Johannine writings five times less frequently than in the *corpus paulinum* and in the Acts and the first epistle of Peter ten times less frequently than in the *corpus paulinum*.

[3] See his monumental study, *Die neuetestamentliche Formel 'in Christo Jesu'*, Marburg an der Lahn, 1892.

result of sin. Romans vii gives a description of a being who is flesh and whose flesh is the seat and cause of sin but at the same time is Spirit or at any rate aspires to become Spirit because there is something in him which approves of the law of God and would like to conform to it. There is here a combination of two different theories, (1) that of a double creation in which flesh and spirit are two stages through which mankind must pass; (2) a doctrine of the fall which makes flesh the seat of sin. This is not an essential dualism but is due to an accident. In other words there are not existing from eternity two conflicting principles but the dualism is the result of a disorder which came into the world. Paul's doctrine of the fall which dominates all his thought is an inheritance from the Jewish tradition. God created the universe through the instrument of Christ. In the universe existed a whole series of celestial beings of a spiritual nature: Thrones, Lords, Powers, Dominions, Archangels, and Angels.[1] Satan, one of the first grade of this hierarchy, wanted to make himself equal with God by claiming adoration for himself and enlisted on his side part of the heavenly hierarchy. The revolt also infected mankind, as men worshipped demons in the shapes of men or animals (Rom. i. 21-23). The revolt therefore is a fact which involves more than men; the drama has a cosmic character; its end will be the annihilation of the powers hostile to God (1 Cor. xv. 24-25). But as Paul's concern is wholly of a practical nature he envisages the drama from the human point of view.

God might have destroyed a rebellious world and Paul seems to think that he ought to have done so and that in not doing so he failed in appearance at least to act with justice. He had in mind a task of redemption by accomplishing which he declares his righteousness as it shows his true character in his long-suffering and patience (Rom. iii. 26). But sin is not free from punishment. 'The wages of sin is death' (Rom. vi. 23), this is an axiom of Pauline thought. Adam's sin has brought in its train a corruption of his nature which extended to his descendants. All have sinned and death has been brought into the world (Rom. v. 12).[2] Man has become the slave of sin, of the flesh which is now the seat of sin, of death and of the demons.

[1] Paul's classification of celestial beings is not precise.
[2] Paul's thought oscillates between three conceptions: (1) Death is a result of man's carnal nature. Adam was mortal, although before the fall he was not inevitably condemned to die. (2) Death is God's punishment. (3) Death is a result of man's falling into the hands of demons especially Thanatos, a personification of death, who is probably identical with Satan. Cf. Heb. ii. 14.

By his work Christ has gained a victory over the demons, re-conciled sinners to God,[1] caused the beneficiaries of God's plan to pass from life in the flesh to life in the spirit, and opened the way for the resumption and realisation of God's initial plan.

When Christ reappears at the end of time he will destroy all the hostile powers but his victory will only be a consequence of the fact that he has become *Kurios*. If the rulers[2] of this world had had previous knowledge of God's plan they would not have crucified Christ and so made way for their own destruction (1 Cor. ii. 8) since Christ by dying on the cross spoiled the powers and principalities and triumphed over them (Col. ii. 15).

Paul not only thinks that Christ has gained a victory over the demons but also that he has freed men from the domination of sin. The law could not free men because flesh prevented it,[3] but God realised salvation by sending his Son in sinful flesh making him one with humanity. Being in the flesh he condemned sin (Rom. viii. 3). Then God raised up Christ, glorified him, and made him Lord and Spirit. Christ's resurrection anticipated the general resurrection on the last day. Thus it inaugurated the new world.[4] But while Christ has been given his place in the celestial realm he has not severed the links which he had forged with humanity so that the δικαίωμα τοῦ νόμου, i.e. the satisfaction granted to the demands of the law and righteousness was not the wholly negative satisfaction of justice through the destruction of the sinner. It had a positive character and if the collective union of Christ with humanity becomes a personal reality for an individual sinner it can bring him into the life of the Spirit. As Christ has been freed by his death from sin, although he

---

[1] This is what Paul calls justification. As Christ has borne the punishment which the sin of humanity deserved, the sinner who has been united to him lives in compliance with the law, and furthermore, shares in the life of glory which God has bestowed on Christ.

[2] i.e. the demonic powers who inspired those who put Jesus to death. For the meaning of 1 Cor. ii. 8 see *J. de N.*, pp. 121 ff.

[3] The function of the law is to make sin abound (Gal. iii. 19; Rom. v. 20; vii. 7). But Rom. vii. 10 has the expression, 'the commandment for life'. On the other hand, in Rom. viii. 3, Paul says that by sending his Son God achieved what could not be done by the law because of sin. The contradiction vanishes if we bear in mind the idea of two plans, (1) of creation and (2) of redemption. The law was intended to be a preparation for the creation of life by the coming of the second Adam in the form of a humanity which was carnal but not sinful. In spite of sin God still gave the law in accordance with his previous decision but, now that human flesh had become the seat of sin, the law could not fulfil the original purpose for which God had intended it.

[4] Schweitzer, *die Mystik des Apostels Paulus*, Tubingen 1930, Eng. trans., *The Mysticism of Paul The Apostle*, London, 1931, has made this point quite clear.

accepted its consequences, in the same way the sinner who is united to Him by faith[1] is also liberated.

Union with Christ brings both liberation from the dominion of sin and also reconciliation with God as well as a transition to the life of the Spirit.

In combining the two ideas of the abolition of sin and the transition to another sphere of life Paul betrays an apparent incoherence in his thought. In theory the Christian is a being who has been substantially changed (Rom. viii. 4-9; Col. ii. 11-12); his life, however, goes on in the same conditions as before. Although justified, the Christian is still capable of sinning. We must look for an explanation of this paradox in the Jewish antecedents of Paul's thought. As a Jew Paul waited for the end of the age when the Messiah would intervene as a redeemer. With the coming of the new world which the Messiah was then to bring in for the elect the old world was to disappear.[2] By his belief in the resurrection of Jesus, Paul was compelled to believe also that with it the new world began its existence. He does not give this belief up but adapts to it the idea of one economy succeeding another by suggesting that during the period separating Christ's parousia from his resurrection which as before he considers must be very brief they coexist together. In this period the flesh is still in existence and while the demons have been conquered and their power broken as far as concerns those who belong to Christ, they have not been destroyed; they still reign in the present world and can influence even those who have been justified if they are not on the watch. For although dead to the flesh they still live in the flesh. While they have ceased to be slaves of sin they are not incapable of sinning and are not completely out of the grip of the demons. This paradox is explained if we bear in mind that Jewish apocalyptic has quite a different meaning for Paul from what it once had, because the death and resurrection of Christ has now accomplished the salvation of the elect, which formerly Paul looked

[1] While Paul certainly considers that there is in faith an intellectual element such as a mental image of God and Christ, primarily he thinks of it as a mystical phenomenon, an act which unites the believer to Christ. Elsewhere Paul states that his union with Christ is realised through participation in the sacraments, baptism and the eucharist. I shall return to the relationship between faith and the sacraments which are the two methods of union with Christ, when I am dealing with the sacraments.

[2] Paul's thought oscillates between the two ideas of the world's destruction and the world's renewal. The latter idea seemed to dominate his mind in the end. See my article, 'Le caractère et le rôle de l'élément cosmologique dans la sotériologie paulinienne', *R.h.p.r.*, 1935, XV, pp. 335 ff.

forward to as something to happen in the future. But some apocalyptic still remains, since all the results of the act of redemption have not yet been worked out.

From this paradox follows the doctrine of sanctification which is of capital importance.[1] Paul states it in a somewhat illogical form. Instead of a statement as we should expect he gives exhortation.[2] Paul does not describe how he who has become a new creature brings forth the fruits of the Spirit; he exhorts him to do it (Gal. v. 13). Exhortations and warnings against the sins into which Christians are liable to slip take up a considerable part of the epistles. Paul was never inclined to antinomism although his disciples and his opponents have sometimes taken his phraseology in this sense;[3] he never thought all the acts of a justified Christian were free from sin or that sanctification could be realised automatically.

Paul's answer to the problem of sin in the life of the believer shows clearly what he thought about sanctification. If he had thought that by justification men were made incapable of sinning, when he discovered that certain Christians had been guilty of grave and even scandalous offences, he would have been bound to think that they had been mistaken in thinking that they were justified and would have considered that their conversion had not taken place but was still to come. But he deals with the affair of incest at Corinth in quite a different way (1 Cor. v. 1 ff.). He does not suggest that salvation once acquired cannot be lost or that the Christian who has

[1] This importance can be almost measured in material terms by the amount of space taken up by moral exhortation (paranesis) in the epistles.

[2] One detail will illustrate this fact. After the argument and exposition of justification by faith Paul says in Rom. v. 1, 'Being then justified by faith, *let us have* peace with God'. The subjunctive, $\dot{\epsilon}\chi\omega\mu\epsilon\nu$, which is hortatory is given by the best manuscripts and by the majority of the manuscripts ($\aleph$ A.B.C.D.G.P. etc.). The reading $\dot{\epsilon}\chi o\mu\epsilon\nu$ (we have) is given by $\aleph$ B.G.P., etc. There is no doubt about the priority of the reading $\dot{\epsilon}\chi\omega\mu\epsilon\nu$. Lietzmann, *Rom.*, p. 58, recognises this but thinks that logic demands the reading $\dot{\epsilon}\chi o\mu\epsilon\nu$. Our logic doubtless does so but not Paul's. He claims that the reading $\dot{\epsilon}\chi\omega\mu\epsilon\nu$ arose from the fact that Tertius, who wrote at Paul's dictation (Rom. xvi. 22), misunderstood what Paul had dictated, as the difference in the pronunciation of the first century between *o* and *w* was hardly noticeable. But the hypothesis is too arbitrary to be accepted. Even if it were accepted it still remains true that the reading for $\dot{\epsilon}\chi\omega\mu\epsilon\nu$ seemed for a long time the natural one. It only caused surprise when Christian thought had so developed that the eschatological character of Pauline thought was quite ignored.

[3] Certain phrases used by Paul may have lent themselves to this misunderstanding. Most of them are due to the fact that owing to the lack of terms sufficiently exact, Paul had to use the same word for the ritual law which had been abolished and for the moral law which is still in force. We have only to read 1 Cor. x. 20-21 to agree that Paul did not succeed in formulating his thought clearly because the word law had this double meaning.

relapsed into sin is of necessity cut off from salvation. The solution adopted by him in this case of incest is clearly improvised and cannot be squared with his soteriological principles. He pronounces that the guilty party be delivered over to Satan for his flesh to be destroyed in order that the spirit may be saved on the day of the Lord. This really means that instead of losing salvation, which would have been the logical result of his sin, he will suffer premature death which will be the punishment inflicted upon him as a result of being handed over to Satan.[1] Paul could be satisfied with such a solution and considered that sin was a kind of anomaly in the life of a believer because he had been compelled to dissociate justification from complete redemption and ascribe them to two separate moments of time. In the Jewish doctrine of the redemption wrought by the Messiah they were closely connected together and took place at the same moment of time, i.e. on the arrival of the new world.

The term itself, justification, suggests the idea of the judgement which God—or rather the Messiah in his name—will pronounce on each individual by which he will be admitted into the kingdom of heaven or cut off from it.[2] While God cannot break his own promise and condemn a man who has observed all the commandments of the law, as he has said, 'Do this and you shall live', he is still free to acquit a man who deserved condemnation. Formally the problem of justification is exactly the same for Paul as a Christian as it was for him when a Jew. But after his conversion he was convinced that nobody could observe the law in its entirety and therefore nobody could be justified by it. No one therefore has any right to salvation but by grace only, God justifies those who belong to Christ. Consequently, the last judgement has lost much of its importance. The individual's destiny is not decided on the last day but on the day when he believes in Christ or refuses to do so. Although Paul takes care solemnly to affirm the reality of the last judgement his thought is much the same as that of John who denies it.

To the formal conception of justification corresponds the material conception of salvation or redemption. Salvation is the state in which

---

[1] In 1 Cor. xiv. 30-32 Paul explains in the same way cases of disease and death which have occurred at Corinth. He considers them to be punishments which God has inflicted upon those who have profaned the Lord's supper to prevent their perishing with the world.

[2] Concerning the nature of the idea of judgement in primitive Christianity see my lecture, ' Le jugement dans le Nouveau Testament', in *Compte-rendu de la séance de rentrée de la Faculté libre de théologie protestante de Paris*, 4 Novembre, 1942, pp. 5-20.

the elect will be when they belong exclusively to the new world. Salvation therefore belongs to the future. 'We are saved by hope', Paul says (Rom. viii. 24).[1] This means something more than we have the hope of salvation. We should have said a salvation which is to be completed in the future rather than a salvation belonging to the future. Paul calls Christians, 'those who are saved' (1 Cor. i. 18; 2 Cor. ii. 15), not those who will be saved. Salvation so far is prevented from being completed because it is negative in character rather than positive. 'We shall be saved by him from wrath', Paul says (Rom. v. 9). This means that when God's wrath bursts on the world, Christians will be preserved from it, because their faith in Christ has justified them, i.e. because God's judgement has already been pronounced on them and they have been acquitted. Romans v. 10 and vi. 5, state that participation in the resurrection of Christ belongs to the future but other passages (Rom. viii. 2; Gal. ii. 18 f.) state that it is already realised. The resurrection is the cause of justification and at the same time the prototype of what will happen to each member of the elect when he definitely enters the new economy. Paul says that we wait impatiently to become sons of God (Rom. viii. 23) but at the same time he writes to the Galatians, 'You are all sons of God through faith in Christ Jesus' (iii. 26) and again, 'The proof that you are sons of God is that God has sent into your hearts the Spirit of his Son who cries, *Abba*, that is Father' (iv. 6-7). In the same way he writes to the Romans that they have received a spirit of adoption who makes them sons of God (viii. 15). The Christian is only really saved and become a spiritual being and a son of God so far as he has received the Spirit. Furthermore, as long as the present economy lasts he can only have a foretaste or earnest (Rom. v. 5; vii. 6; viii. 4 ff., etc.). A man's salvation therefore is real but incomplete as long as he is flesh and blood since flesh and blood cannot inherit the Kingdom of God (1 Cor. xv. 50). This means flesh in its pure state not flesh corrupted by sin.

Paul is thinking of justification as something to come when he speaks of it as possible in theory but in practice unrealisable through the works of the law (Rom. ii. 13; iii. 20, Gal. ii. 16). Of justification by faith he uses both the present and the past (1 Cor. vi. 11; Rom., iii. 24; v. 1-9; viii. 30). He does not say, 'We are justified by hope in the same way that he says that we are saved by hope. This could hardly be explained if the achievement of salvation was an

[1] Cf. Rom. v. 8-10; vi. 5; viii. 11 ff.

inevitable result of justification. The importance which Paul attaches to sanctification and the insistent tone of his moral exhortations show quite clearly that he reckoned the loss of salvation to be more than a theoretical possibility or merely a text for moral teaching. He puts it forward as a possibility for himself as, e.g. in 1 Corinthians ix. 27, in which he affirms that he submits himself to a severe discipline, 'for fear that after preaching to others he himself might be a castaway'. The whole of his conduct in the affair of incest shows that he did not think that salvation was definitely assured to those who had been once justified.[1]

In a number of passages, however, in the epistles, Paul declares with impressive conviction that salvation is assured. Such is Romans viii. 1, 'There is no more condemnation for those who are in Christ Jesus'. Or again there is Romans viii. 31 ff. and all Paul's exhortations show that it rests with man to continue in God's mercy, 'If God be for us, who can be against us? He that spared not his own Son, but delivered him up for us all, how shall he not with him also freely give us all things? . . . Who shall separate us from the love of God? . . . We are more than conquerors through him that loved us.'

These declarations come after an argument leading up to them in which Paul speaks of the Spirit, who comes to strengthen the weakness of believers, and intercedes for them, and he declares that God makes all things work together for good to them that love Him (viii. 26-28). But the love which the believer gives to God is neither the cause nor even the condition of salvation; it is the result of election. Those who have it are those who have been called according to predestination (viii. 29-30). A distinction must be drawn between predestination as a theory and the conviction which an individual may have that he is predestined. According to Romans ix. 19-23 the notion of predestination is an inference derived from the idea of God as sovereign, whose decisions no one can call in question; but predestination is only affirmed here in a hypothetical form. 'If God wished . . .', Paul writes. Paul, however, seems at bottom to be quite positive in his belief in it, since in support of what is put in the form of a hypothesis he quotes from Hosea and Isaiah. But he who is predestined can only find comfort from being so, if he lives in God's mercy without which he will be cut off (Rom. xi. 22).

---

[1] The possibility of losing salvation follows also from instruction about the dangers of idolatry (1 Cor. x. 1 ff.).

Paul not only gains his idea of predestination from his conception of God's power and freedom but also from his conviction that God had intervened in his own life. This gave the idea practical value. He perceived that God had realised his designs for him for which he had been predestined from his mother's womb (Gal. i. 15). He saw the working of divine grace in his life as a Christian and his activity as an apostle. 'By the grace of God I am what I am', he writes (1 Cor. xv. 10). Paul cannot separate the two ideas of predestination and election; he finds here not so much a theological problem as a psychological one. Convinced that he possessed the spirit he could not explain why he alone had been chosen since to say that he was chosen is only to express his assurance that he has been saved. We are here in the presence of something very intimate in the life of the apostle.

In chapters ix to xi of the epistle to the Romans especially, which contain Paul's meditation on the destiny of the people of Israel, Paul is led to develop ideas about predestination which are more like intuitions than clear-cut and balanced doctrine; some of them are incongruous with those expressed elsewhere in a more precise fashion. Paul explains that Israel has been shown to be unbelieving and as a result of her unbelief the Gentiles have been called but the Gentiles must not on that account allow themselves to become proud, since, if they do not live in the mercy of God, i.e. if they do not persevere in faith and sanctification, they in their turn will be pruned away. As for the Jews, if they do not remain stubborn in their unbelief, God is sufficiently powerful to graft them anew on to the tree from which they have been cut off to make room for the Gentiles (xi. 13-24).[1] This is not just the theme of an exhortation intended to impress upon the Gentiles the necessity for perseverance and vigilance, since in the sequel (xi. 25-36) Paul unfolds a mystery, a truth which he claims to be a revelation: Israel's unbelief, he affirms, which has caused her rejection, was willed by God for the purpose of making the election of the Gentiles possible, but, when

---

[1] In Rom. xi. 17 ff. Paul uses the allegory of the ungrafted olive tree to express his thoughts. It is not, however, worked out to perfection. The ungrafted tree symbolises the people of Israel and its branches are cut off in order that branches of wild olive which symbolises the Gentiles may be grafted in their place. This is one anomaly as it contradicts the usual practice and purpose of arboriculture. To this he adds another anomaly by suggesting that later on the branches which have been cut off can be grafted on again to the trunk to which they originally belonged. Paul constructed his allegory like an algebraic formula and in this way it resembles apocalyptic imagery. It is not the image of a poet with a sense of reality as the images used by Jesus were.

the end which God has in view has been attained, i.e. when the Gentile masses have been brought into a state of salvation, Israel in her turn will be converted and so saved. This does not agree with other explicit statements of the apostle that the whole of humanity is not predestined for salvation. Paul speaks here of the fullness of the Gentiles[1] and of 'all Israel'. On this subject, therefore, his thought oscillates; sometimes he thinks that only a portion of mankind, partly Jewish and partly Gentile have been chosen to form a Messianic people; at other times, while it cannot be said that he thought salvation fully universal, since it seems impossible on his soteriological principles for the dead to be saved without having faith,[2] yet we cannot help but ask ourselves, if at times he did not have a vision of salvation being largely universal, and given to the whole of humanity both Jew and Gentile. This would be only, however, to extrapolarise a line of thought to which he never gave accurate expression, since in spite of this his dominating thought was that no-one, not even all those who are justified, are assured of salvation.

Although he felt that he possessed salvation, that he was predestined and elect, he could not rid his mind of all doubts that his salvation was not absolutely assured. He could only solve his doubts by an act of faith in the power and love of God.[3]

Paul also resolutely opposed the convictions of those who thought that as justification had delivered them from the domination of demons and the flesh they no longer were under any obligation to withstand the peril of idolatry and so could give rein to all the instincts of the body which, because it was not destined for salvation, did not matter from either the religious or moral point of view. These were the views which the 'strong' or 'gnostics' at Corinth had inferred from Paul's teaching.[4] Their watchword was, 'all is allowed'. Above all they maintained that the Christian who was

[1] It is true that it may be asked if the term τὸ πλήρωμα τῶν ἐθνεῶν (xi. 25) ought not to be understood as meaning those Gentiles who are destined for salvation; but the parallelism of the expression with 'all Israel' in verse 26 seems to exclude this meaning.

[2] Nothing in Paul can be found to suggest a preaching of the gospel in the abode of the dead. Apart from this it would be difficult to reconcile the idea with Paul's conception that the dead remain in a state of prostration until the resurrection.

[3] See on this point my article, 'Les fondements de l'assurance du salut chez l'apôtre Paul', R.h.p.r., 1937, XVII, pp. 105-144.

[4] I shall return to this question in the second volume when I deal with the moral crisis which took place at Corinth when among other things the antinomism of the 'strong' was in conflict with what Paul considered to be the excessive scruples of another group.

well informed about the demons and Christ's victory over them had no need to be bothered any more about them or to avoid action which could bring him into contact with them again. In the same way they considered that everything concerning the life of the body, whether it were questions of sex or food, was of no importance, because it was doomed to be destroyed. Paul sharply recoiled from these ideas: the demons, he said, still possessed some power and the body was not just an exterior and provisional clothing for the soul but a vital part of human personality which was not destined to be destroyed but to be transformed. 'The body is for the Lord', he writes, 'God hath both raised up the Lord and will also raise us up[1] by his power. . . . Your bodies are the members of Christ' (1 Cor. vi. 14-15).[2]

Paul's soteriology begins from his own experience of salvation; but he was not content just to describe what happens when a sinner is forgiven and begins a new life. He also explains the experience by looking at redemption from an objective point of view. We have already seen in what way he describes the mechanism of justification. We must now analyse his conception of the person of the redeemer who accomplishes justification.

Paul's christology consists partly of an elaboration of the data provided by his own religious experience and partly of a development of ideas belonging to the framework of his thought before he was a Christian. Some of them were Jewish and some Greek. Paul's Christ is not simply a man who has been raised to the dignity of Messiah and Saviour by his resurrection or by the outpouring of the Spirit upon him at his baptism. On the other hand Paul's christology is not as highly metaphysical as that to be found in the epistle to the Hebrews or the Fourth Gospel. It comes between

[1] This resurrection implies a transformation.
[2] The argument is somewhat incoherent. On questions of eating Paul judges the libertine right. He writes as follows, perhaps making one of their formula his own, 'Meats are for the belly (κοιλία) and the belly for meats. But God shall destroy both it and them' (vi. 13). This implies that in the world to come man will not have to eat any more and that his digestive organs will not exist any longer. But when he passes to the problem of sex he argues differently. He uses the term σῶμα. The libertines must have developed the argument that sexual activity resembled eating and was only concerned with organs doomed to be destroyed which the celestial man would not possess. Paul makes a distinction between what will disappear in the transformation accompanying the resurrection called by him κοιλία or to which the κοιλία belongs and what on the other hand will remain glorified called by him the σῶμα. He reckons that sexual activity belongs to the σῶμα since he says that debauchery is a sin committed by a man against his own σῶμα and even goes so far as to say that it is the only sin of this character (vi. 18).

these two extremes of Christian theology but is nearer to the second than the first. His Christ is pre-existent as Messiah and Son of God.[1] Paul's christology is therefore clearly metaphysical; but it preserves also a functional character. While what Christ is explains the work which he accomplished, it is also through this work that he became the *Kurios* and he was not this in his pre-existence.

While Paul categorically affirms Christ's pre-existence, he appears to have very little interest in speculating in what state Christ pre-existed or what function he could then undertake. It was only his interest to fight the Colossian gnosis which made him develop the idea of Christ's function in the creation. He writes: 'He is the image of the invisible God, the first-born of every creature,[2] for by him all things were created, that are in heaven, and that are in earth, visible and invisible, whether they be thrones, or dominions, or principalities, or powers; all things were created by him and for him. . . . And he is the head of the body, the church' (i. 15-18).

These ideas resemble those to be found in the epistle to the Hebrews and the Fourth Gospel. It was not only opposition to the gnosis at Colossae which led Paul to express these ideas; they were already implied in a passage in the first epistle to the Corinthians where Paul is laying down the attitude of Christians with regard to the multiplicity of gods and lords and writes: 'But to us there is but one God, the Father, of whom are all things, and we in him; and one Lord Jesus Christ, by whom are all things, and we by him' (1 Cor. viii. 6).

But from the point of view of the position of the believer and his own salvation this cosmological work of Christ has no importance. And so Paul had no occasion or need to develop and express his ideas about it until he was faced with the gnosis at Colossae and

[1] This is plain from a large number of texts in which Paul declares that God has sent his Son or that he has sent the Messiah (e.g. Gal. iv. 4; Rom. viii. 3). In the digression on Christology in Phil. ii. 6-11 it is said that Christ pre-existed 'in the form of God' but this condition is distinguished from that of equality with God which alone gives the right to adoration. There is, however, in the opening greeting of the epistle to the Romans (i. 4) a phrase which might very well be taken as adoptionist in christology 'determined (or declared) to be the son of God with power according to the spirit of holiness by (or beginning from) the resurrection from the dead'. It may well be an expression surviving from an adoptionist christology but Paul uses it, not in the sense that the resurrection established Jesus as Messiah, but that it manifested him as such.

[2] The parallelism between this phrase with that of Col. i. 18, 'first-born among the dead' proves what the context also shows, that Paul thinks not only that Christ was created before all other beings but also that by him the other beings were created.

compelled to oppose it. Paul's christology was determined by practical needs and not by speculative interests. Paul was much more interested in what Christ had done than in what he was and of what he had done the accomplishment of human salvation interested him most. Paul's epistles—and for that matter his general teaching—do not seek to treat of the Christ as a philosophical problem but to persuade those to whom they are addressed to adopt towards the Christ the attitude which will lead to their salvation.

Paul considers the activity of the pre-existent Christ to be just this, that 'in the form of God' as Messiah and Son of God he allowed himself to become man. Paul makes his pre-existent action an act of obedience. Although he actually did speak of the Son of God who loved him and gave himself for him (Gal. ii. 20) Paul usually describes the work of Christ as an act of obedience and so reserves to God all the initiative and efficacy in the work of redemption.[1]

The term ἐκένωσεν (literally he divested himself; he emptied himself) used by Paul in Philippians II. 7, must not be pressed too far. It certainly does not contain all the subtleties found in it by later dogmatic theology. It only has to be noted that it refers to a real emptying and not merely an apparent one. In the epistle to the Galatians Paul describes Christ as born of a woman and born under the law (iv. 4). By this phrase he means to show that Christ is the same as other men[2] save for sin alone which he has not known (2 Cor. v. 21).[3]

Although Paul is much more interested in the drama of the death and resurrection of Christ than in his ministry and teaching, a careful examination of the epistles shows[4] that allusions to the life of Jesus and recollections of his sayings have more importance in his thought than the few express quotations incline one to think. Paul

[1] The term grace which often occurs in the epistles refers to the grace of God. It is particularly clear in 1 Cor. xv. 10 where after Paul has spoken of the appearance of Christ to him and of his work as an apostle he concludes, 'But by the grace of God I am what I am and his grace which was bestowed on me was not in vain'.

[2] The expression 'born of a woman' comes from the Old Testament and means 'born in the customary way'. It would be a gross mistranslation to think that it referred to a supernatural birth, an idea with which Paul was unacquainted.

[3] Paul never explained how he could reconcile the full humanity of Christ with the fact that he was without sin, although he taught that sin and death are a taint attached to all the descendants of Adam (Rom. v. 12). It can only be supposed that he would have interjected that as the second Adam, Christ stands for the beginning of a new age and not the continuation of the old.

[4] See my book, L'apôtre Paul et Jésus Christ, Paris, 1904, pp. 69-99, which also contains the early bibliography for this question, and my Life of Jesus, pp. 119 f.

makes the attitude of Jesus to be in all circumstances a standard and an example which the faithful must try to imitate. In the same way his sayings have an absolute authority which leaves no room for argument.[1]

Paul's thought is foreign to any kind of docetism. He never thinks of the humanity of Christ as purely appearance. If he had not been human his redemptive work would have only been valuable as an idea. Mankind could not have derived any benefit from it. If we wanted any additional proof that Paul thought Christ was really human, we should find it in the fact that Paul only thinks of the resurrection as passive: Christ is raised by an act of God which is the equivalent of an act of creation. He is not only restored to the state in which he was before he became man by God but he also receives the title of 'Lord' from God which he did not possess in his pre-existence and becomes identified with the Spirit (2 Cor. iii. 17), i.e, he sums up in him all the reality of the celestial world. With the resurrection began a new age in which the Spirit is given to believers. Paul's thought at this point is not perfectly coherent in form. The identity of the Lord and the Spirit and the fact that only after the resurrection Christ received the dignity of Lord imply that he was not Spirit in his pre-existence or at any rate he was not the Spirit. Yet Paul says that the second Adam was made a life-giving spirit (1 Cor. xv. 45) which implies that he is in essence the same as the spirit. The idea of the second Adam and the theory of glorification do not originate from the same ideological current.[2]

According to a passage in the first epistle to the Corinthians (xv. 24-28) where Paul seems to be dependent on Jewish apocalyptic Christ's reign which is implied by his office as *Kurios* is not destined to be eternal. After the parousia, when he will have destroyed all

[1] This is particularly plain from the difference between the verses 10 ff. in 1 Cor. vii, and verses 25 ff. in the same chapter. In the first passage concerning the indissolubility of marriage Paul quotes a commandment of the Lord (the saying in Mark x. 11-12 or one like it) in such a way that it puts an end to all further argument. In the other passage he declares that on the subject of virgins he had no commandment of the Lord. He gives his own opinion and emphasises that it is that of a man inspired and one to whom the Lord has given grace to be faithful and therefore that it is an authorised interpretation of the Lord's thought: in spite of this he argues and uses persuasion in such a way that he shows the difference between the commandment of the Lord and the word of an inspired man.

[2] That Paul borrowed his speculations concerning the two Adams from some older source which he had failed completely to assimilate may be inferred from the following fact. Paul explains the action exercised upon humanity by the two Adams of which they are the prototypes in 1 Cor. xv. 45 ff. by what they are and in Rom. v. 12 by what they do.

hostile powers including last of all Death itself, he will restore the Kingdom to God his Father and God will be all in all. This conception does not agree with Paul's christology; it is only the survival of the Jewish idea of the Messiah's reign being provisional and preparatory for the realisation of the kingdom of God.

There is a close organic relationship between Paul's own experience of salvation and his thought about Christ. But all the ideological material which he uses to express his christology belongs to a period previous to his faith, to his conversion, and even to Christianity itself. The Jewish doctrine of the Messiah provoked less than we might at first sight be inclined to think. What it contributed referred to the final function of Christ and his triumph over the demonic powers.[1] The speculations of hellenised Judaism about the Logos, Wisdom, and the hypostases, were the most important source for Paul's christology. The idea of Christ as *Kurios* led Paul to place him among the celestial beings and above them and to make him the first-born in order to give him the first place in all things (Col. i. 18). In this way Christ was identified with Wisdom and the Logos through whom God created the world. In the same way the idea that Christ by his work completes the creation by transforming it on to a spiritual level implies his pre-existence as the ideal prototype and head of creation as well as his superiority over all created things.[2]

Paul's soteriology has sometimes been described as a mystery of salvation and redemption and it has been suggested that this explains its structure. Paulinism in short, it is said, grew up in the atmosphere of the mystery religions; but true as this may be, we are not entitled to infer from this that it originated out of them. We can define and explain a theology much more by its spiritual content than by its form and ideological material. The Greek mysteries emphasised a transformation of human nature as their aim rather than a man's capacity to realise a certain moral ideal which, however much it may attract him, he cannot attain in his natural state. There is practically nothing in common between Paul's vision of Christ as his saviour together with the feelings with which Christ

---

[1] Again it must be noted that certain elements of Jewish doctrine, particularly so far as it refers to the provisional character of the reign of the Christ were, as has already been seen, clumsily integrated into Paul's thought.

[2] This is without prejudice to the statement in 1 Cor. xv. 46 that not what is spiritual but what is physical comes first, as this appears to refer to the two kinds of humanity and not to their prototypes. We cannot, however, be certain that we do not find here a certain contradiction in Paul's thought.

inspired him and the sentiments of the initiated for the saviour heroes of the mystery cults. Paul's soteriology was not formed by transforming a Greek mystery and putting the Lord Christ in the place of Mithra, Attis, or Osiris. Its structure did not arise in this way. Paul only availed himself of terms and ideas, which the mystery cults had elaborated and vulgarised, for the purpose of expressing his own ideas and experiences and even this he did only to a limited degree.

5.—PAUL'S CONTROVERSIES

When Paul became a Christian he found that he had to adjust his new outlook to the framework of his previous ideas. As a missionary he was compelled by the necessities of preaching to define and explain his phraseology in order to withstand certain errors[1] and to defend his own interpretation of the gospel against others, particularly against that with which the Judaisers opposed him. All these factors influenced the structure of Paul's thought and the phrases which he used. The last mentioned factor in particular gave Pauline thought a dialectical and polemical twist which however, is superficial and not of its essence. Paul attacked certain misconstructions put upon his thought and what he conceived to be certain misinterpretations of the gospel not as the champion of a particular orthodoxy or in defence of some objective truth which a man might fail to grasp at the peril of his salvation; his polemical style is to be explained rather as the fruit of a masterful temperament which could not brook the slightest contradiction.

In Galatia Paul came into collision with the Judaisers who tried to compel converted Gentiles to keep the Jewish law. They could not further their ends without censuring Paul himself and questioning the authority of his preaching. But what he considered to be at stake was not his personal reputation in the churches of Galatia but faith in Christ as the one sufficient ground of salvation. Paul's adversaries do not seem to have attacked his positive teaching. All they maintained was that to be able to enjoy salvation a man must keep the Jewish law. Against this Paul contended that faith in Christ is of such a self-sufficient and uncompromising nature that to attach any further conditions of any kind to the redemptive action of

---

[1] Due perhaps to the action of strange preachers, who had sprung up spontaneously in some of Paul's audiences, or again to the resurgence of pagan habits of mind and ways of life, which conversion had repressed without radically destroying.

Christ is to question its efficacy and efficiency. Paul goes so far as to say that to observe the law is to surrender justification by faith, to be stripped of grace, and to have despaired of Christ and faith in him completely (Gal. v. 1-4). Paul was not fighting here for the victory of a particular theology or the exclusion of some heresy; he was attacking a spiritual attitude which lacked full confidence in the redemptive power of Christ and so endangered the salvation of those adopting it.

The crisis at Corinth[1] was of a different character. It was more confused than the crisis in Galatia which came later because Paul's adversaries followed different tactics. They certainly also intended to judaise the church but they did not disclose their plans immediately; they first tried to ruin Paul's personal authority before they attacked Paul's gospel and for the purpose cleverly exploited the situation at hand. The crisis also was much more complex. It arose not just through the activity of missionaries opposed to Paul coming from without but also from internal causes.

I shall have to return to this crisis later on (a) because it forms a turning point in the struggle between Judaeo-Christianity and Gentile Christianity[2] and (b) because it throws light on the ethical conceptions and moral life of the primitive communities.[3] I am only referring to it here for the light it throws on Paul's thought and for the reactions provoked by his thought among the Greek communities.

At the time of the crisis the church at Corinth had lost something of its first fervour and also found itself deprived of Paul's firm and constant directing hand. At the same time Judaising missionaries were causing confusion. While things were in this condition the old pagan outlook which conversion had repressed without radically destroying took on a new lease of life.

From the very beginning there had been a latent misunderstanding between Paul and the Corinthians due to the fact that they interpreted Greek terms, which Paul used to express Semitic ideas, in their original sense. This was made clear on an important point. This is not only important for the light which it throws on what happened at Corinth but it also shows the direction Christian thought was going to take later on and reveals the importance of this fundamental fact, that Christianity originated on Semitic soil but while it was still in a fluid state and had no fixed form was transplanted on to the soil of Greece and there grew to maturity.

[1] Concerning the circumstances of this crisis see Introd. IV. 2, pp. 87 ff.
[2] See pp. 305 ff.   [3] See *E.P.*, pp. 561 ff.

In 1 Corinthians xv. Paul discusses a theory put forward by the Corinthians—or rather by certain Corinthians—that there was no resurrection of the dead. He assumes that they deny that there is any life after death. But this was not what the Corinthians thought. They thought that there was only a life after death for the soul and not for the body. This in Paul's eyes was quite unthinkable. Two conceptions therefore confront each other, the conception of the immortality of the soul and the conception of resurrection.[1] They are not really combined because they are irreconcilable. They remain placed beside each other in every Christian eschatology and have the character of a mongrel kind of spiritualism.[2]

There thus grew up at Corinth a form of spiritualism which Paul found himself unable to accept and even to understand. Its presence was plainly evident in the antinomism which Paul attacked with force and even with indignation whether it was attributed to him by the people who claimed that they were following him or by his enemies.[3] Although it was quite foreign to the direction of his thought, none the less, it was put forward as a logical inference which could be supported by certain statements of Paul's concerning Christian liberty. Misunderstanding on this point was further aggravated by the ambiguous phraseology used by Paul when he was teaching about the law. He never made any clear and precise distinction between the moral law which still remained valid in substance and the ritual law which Paul judged had not merely been repealed but was declared by Paul with growing emphasis as he became more and more involved in controversy to be an enemy of faith.

This was not just a passing incident. In the whole history of the Christian ethic there are these two elements representing two conceptions between which it oscillates; the Christian life is sometimes thought of as obedience to law, at other times as the free outburst of the new personality created by faith expressing itself in the realm of conscious life. Sometimes it is thought of in both these ways at the same time.

[1] Only conditional immortality and resurrection since it is only concerned with that of those who have been redeemed by Jesus Christ.

[2] This is shown by the various liturgies for the dead actually used in Christian churches. They affirm also the immediate celestial blessedness of the souls of the elect and their resurrection on the last day, i.e. they express two eschatologies which are really an extension of the two aspects of Paul's eschatology.

[3] e.g. see Rom. iii. 8 where Paul treats an antinomist interpretation of his gospel as a calumny.

The crisis at Corinth was a domestic issue between Paul and the Christian community. The crisis at Colossae so far as it can be called a crisis is explained by external factors. It was due to the efforts of persons outside the Christian community who tried to win over Christians to the worship of angels and heavenly powers, a religion which derived its inspiration from a Judaeo-Hellenic cosmological gnosis.[1] We shall see at a later stage[2] Paul's reactions to this tendency by an insistence on the cosmological function and position of Christ. This gave quite a new direction and character to Paul's thought and made quite a perceptible difference to the future understanding of Paul's ideas and their subsequent influence. As a result Christian thought not only developed as a theology but also as a philosophy and cosmology, not only as a doctrine of the relationship between man and God and of redemption wrought by Christ but also as a complete explanation of the universe. Through the influence of Paulinism in this direction Christian thought not only grew into a *fides qua creditur* but also into a *fides quae creditur*.

I have not tried at this point to distinguish and define the part played by Paulinism in the growth and development of Christianity. The remaining part of my book will show that. Both directly and indirectly Paul will be seen to have been an influence at almost every point. His influence was shown under several aspects. Through him the infant religion spread over a wide area and was firmly planted in the Greek world, marked with his own powerful personality which with remarkable originality had grasped the essentials of the new faith and given them shape and form. As he tried to find expression for his thoughts he created formulae, which may not have been in logic perfectly coherent and balanced but nevertheless came to stand as the classical formulae of the faith. They acted as a framework for all the subsequent development of Christian thought and determined the very form itself which faith and religious experience was to assume in the generations to come.

[1] Perhaps those who were disposed to follow the teachers at Colossae made out that although it was only from Christ that salvation could be expected it would be just as well to secure the goodwill of the heavenly powers or at any rate their neutrality for the time being while they still retained some of their power.

[2] See pp. 401 ff.

PART FOUR

The Stabilisation of Christianity and the Formation of its Doctrine

CHAPTER I

Towards Stabilisation

I.—WHY CHRISTIANITY ONLY GRADUALLY BECAME CONSCIOUS OF ITSELF AS AN INDEPENDENT ENTITY

THE first generation of Christians both in Palestine and in Greece showed themselves boiling and seething in a state of intense spiritual fermentation. Their hearts were possessed with tremendous hopes; they were waiting for the realisation of their salvation in a coming new order and they were convinced that the time of deliverance was so near that it had almost already begun. Groups of men, some in Jerusalem and Judaea and what was significant already even in Samaria, others at Antioch and a little later all over Asia Minor, Macedonia, Greece, and even in Rome, as well as in other parts of the world, believed that the ministry, death, and resurrection of Jesus were the decisive events in human history ushering in the final age of man and the world, the last act of the drama to which the fall had been the prelude, when the purpose of God in creation, in spite of Satan's revolt, would be definitely realised in mighty acts.

The small groups of Christians dotted about across the Roman Empire were numerically small and were out of touch with each other without any organised social ties. Individually they were small in numbers, unimportant, and with little social influence. But they all were possessed of such a powerful dynamic that they were destined to gain one victory after another. Considered separately they might appear to be negligible but in a very short space of time the many groups which sprung up over a wide area were consolidated into one body. In this way they disclosed their true character and it was made evident that they were going to change if not the face of the world at any rate the spiritual orientation of humanity.

The message of salvation through Christ was proclaimed and published with such intense fervour that it could only be described as a new religion in view of its latent potentialities. If it was to exist first of all in its own right as a religion in the full sense of the word its doctrines needed to be formulated and systematised and the life of the Christian communities required unification. It is true that there were signs that both these objectives were beginning to be realised but so far what had been done was in its nature improvisation; it was the result of instinctive response and spontaneous suggestion; there was no co-ordination or system. No real continuity could be discovered, as we have already seen when we were dealing with the various theories formulated one after another by Paul in expressing and defending his ideas concerning the abrogation of the law and the election of the Gentiles.[1]

Christianity in its infancy found it hard to become conscious of itself as a religion in its own right. That is why there is such a striking contrast between, on the one hand, the intensity of the new faith on its appearance and the rapidity of its growth and expansion and on the other the slow and almost hesitating way in which it found forms and system for its expression in the realm of doctrine and institutions and organisation for its realisation in its social environment. There is no question that from the very first Christians both in Palestine and in Greece were sharply conscious that in their faith there was something new, but they considered that what was new was more than anything else the fulfilment and expansion of Judaism. Paul was the only one of the first generation who understood that in being the fulfilment of Judaism Christianity passed beyond Judaism and left it behind. But no one really followed his guidance. Because Christians of the first generation failed to grasp this their faith remained a prisoner in the cradle of the Judaism in which it had been born. Christianity was only on the way to becoming a stabilised religion, when the church became conscious of being an independent entity in its own right or rather when circumstances compelled it to become so.[2]

2.—PRIMITIVE DIVERSITY AND THE WORK OF UNIFICATION

In the first generation there existed Christianities rather than Christianity. The faithful belonged to communities far apart from each other which were only able on rare occasions to come into touch with one another but in spite of this felt bound to each other by a powerful spiritual bond. They were convinced that they were servants of the same Lord and the elect of the same Saviour. But while they all felt that they had the same beliefs, the various communities expressed the new faith in different ways, each one in ignorance of

[1] See pp. 198 ff.   [2] See the next chapter.

what the others were doing. They were therefore independent of each other even if they were not more or less opposed to each other. The result was that when Christians from different communities met each other, contact was difficult and sometimes sharp conflicts occurred such as that which sprung up at Antioch in 43-44 and did not subside until the apostle Paul disappeared. We saw[1] that at the beginning of 44 the apostle Peter and almost certainly other representatives of apostolic Christianity with him were compelled to leave Jerusalem and take up their abode in the Greek world and that this prepared the way for the fusion of types of Christianity which up to then had been distinct. With this event the process of fusion began. The same thing happened probably on a much bigger scale after 70 when life became difficult for Christians in Palestine. Many of them emigrated, most probably in different directions, although on this point we are only certain that some went to Asia.[2]

[1] See p. 110.

[2] Our knowledge of the emigration of Christians from Palestine to Asia depends in the first place on the evidence of Papias. Concerning this evidence see *Introd.* II, pp. 141 ff. In the fragment of the preface of his book *Explanations of the sayings of the Lord* preserved by Eusebius (*H.e.* iii. 39, 3-4) Papias mentions two persons, Aristion and John the elder, who certainly lived in Asia because he states that he made a note of their remarks at the very time when they were made. This is clear from the fact that Papias, when he speaks of them, uses the present tense and not the aorist which he uses when he is speaking of the other witnesses to the tradition referred to by him. The period when the conversations of Aristion and John the Elder took place cannot have been previous to the second decade of the second century. As Eusebius rightly comments (39, 5 ff.) Papias makes a very sharp distinction between these two men and another group consisting of Andrew, Peter, Philip, Thomas, James, John, Matthew, direct disciples of Jesus, of whom he only speaks in the past tense, as people who were no longer living at the time when he was making his enquiries and concerning whom he makes no mention which could lead anyone to think that they had had any contact with Asia. But the men of the other group, Aristion and John the Elder are described by Papias in the same terms used by him of the first group, i.e. 'Disciples of the Lord'. τοῦ κυρίου μαθηταί. It cannot be supposed that any direct disciples of Jesus were alive in Asia between 110 and 120. If there were they would have been more than one hundred years old. This is most unlikely and there is no doubt that if it had been so, Papias could not have failed to emphasise the fact as a proof of the direct link between him and the Lord. Many critics have suggested various emendations, e.g. 'disciples of them', 'disciples of John', 'disciples of the Lord'. Ingenious and attractive as these may be they are not called for. The term was used in Palestine of Christians and is not found in any Greek document. There is justification for thinking that the title, μαθηταί τοῦ κυρίου, was brought by Christians from Palestine to Asia where it then came into use. It showed the prestige they enjoyed from the fact that they came from the country of the Lord and which they could legitimately claim as the bearers of a tradition which was always felt to have special value and importance. Beside the evidence of Papias must be placed that of Polycrates of Ephesus in his letter to Victor at Rome (Eusebius, *H.e.* v. 24, 2 ff.). He speaks of the 'great stars', i.e. distinguished persons who fell asleep in

When these emigrations took place, the importance of the church at Jerusalem was practically reduced to nothing, and Christianity shifted its centre of gravity to the Greek world, with the result that the general situation hastened and favoured the fusion of the various groups of Christians and the unification of the different types of Christianity represented by them.[1]

If Christianity was to be stabilised, the organisation of the communities had to become strong and fixed. Furthermore, the church's doctrine had to become generally established and gradually to give its actual organisation as it became consolidated through the effect of circumstances rather than the execution of a preconcerted plan the character of an organisation endowed with divine rights.[2]

If the church was to express its faith it could not remain content with loose improvised formulae which were more or less uncoordinated but these formulae needed to be defined and systematised so that all Christians could accept them as the best expression of their faith. For this purpose they had to become objective in character, not just the means of handing on certain experiences but the symbol of an objective truth, which a man had to confess he believed not just that he might enjoy a religious experience but that he might participate in salvation. If the church was to become a stable society a 'sound doctrine' had to be established and imposed on each individual Christian. This meant that experience and doctrinal forms stood together in a new relationship. At first the experience

---

Asia. First he mentions Philip, as having died at Hierapolis with two of his daughters who remained virgins all their life. He mentions another of Philip's daughters who must have been married and died at Ephesus after having lived in the Holy Spirit. He mentions next John the apostle as having died at Ephesus. The tradition about John is due to a confusion between the apostle and the elder both of whom are mentioned by Papias but in two different sentences but they have been mixed up by Irenaeus. The tradition is quite legendary in character as it says that John was high-priest (see p. 114, n. 2), but it shows the importance which the churches in Asia attached to the fact that they could count among their members Christians of Palestinian origin. As for the tradition concerning Philip, it does not refer to the apostle, as Polycrates says, but to Philip, one of the Seven, mentioned by the book of the Acts, and must be retained as historical. Acts xxi. 8-9 says that he was living at Caesarea with his four daughters who were virgins and prophetesses in 58 when Paul passed through Caesarea on his way to Jerusalem. In addition to this evidence both the Fourth Gospel and the Johannine Apocalypse show that a stream of Palestinian thought and tradition flowed into Asia.

[1] When I was discussing the form of Jewish Christianity which survived after 70 I showed that those types of Christianity which could not be absorbed in the resulting synthesis either disappeared or were left on the fringe of the church (p. 16).

[2] On this aspect of the stabilisation of Christianity see *E.P.*

created the forms. Gradually the process was reversed. The forms created the experience. Faith was no longer an outburst of spiritual enthusiasm which then went on to seek a symbol for its expression. It had to be created by imparting and receiving information.

These conditions were only realised after a long process of development. First efforts were quite fumbling and produced little fruit but we can plainly discern them from the time of the first generation of Christians being made on certain points, particularly by the apostle Paul. They only became intense and coherent in the second generation and came to fruition first of all in the pre-catholicism of Clement of Rome and then in the primitive catholicism of St. Irenaeus and Tertullian.

It will be noticed that the West undertook the major share of the work in the achievement of stabilisation and also that the church of Rome, endowed with a legal mind and an innate capacity for organisation and government typical of the Latin mentality, played the leading part. This becomes clear from the end of the first century with Clement of Rome; Rome continues to do so and her part grows in importance in the second century culminating in the attempt of Victor, bishop of Rome, when the date of keeping Easter was being disputed, to compel those churches of Asia, which claimed to follow their own traditions, to fall into line with the custom of the great majority of the other churches. But these did not for the most part claim the right to impose their own custom on any who followed a different one. The East being more mystical and less logical in outlook did not resist Rome's endeavours at organisation and unification; it complied with the process without actively participating in it. Most of the heresies which delayed the work of stabilisation came for a long time from the East and for that very reason made efforts at unification appear all the more necessary. The case of montanism is typical in this respect.

3.—PNEUMATISM AND ESCHATOLOGICAL BELIEF, OBSTACLES TO STABILISATION

There is no doubt that in the first generation the work of unification and stabilisation only proceeded in a very jerky fashion for one very important reason. In its earliest days the church was dominated by two forces which acted like an obstacle or at any rate as a brake to any progress towards stabilisation and organisation. They were (1) pneumatism and (2) eschatological convictions.

Pneumatism, whether it is individual or collective, is a creative factor in the life of a religious community making for spontaneity and innovation. As long as pneumatism is at work it cannot make terms with any limitations or be confined within the framework of any organisation. Before yielding to its demands a church must be assured that the Spirit revealed is that of God and not a demon. The Spirit blows where it listeth; no one can think of imposing bounds upon its activity. Yet quite early on the danger was felt which the reign of the Spirit might bring to the church.[1] In the instructions given by Paul in 1 Corinthians xii.-xiv. we see Paul concerned to control perhaps not the activity of the Spirit but at any rate the manifestations of the spirit within the framework of the cultus and in subordination to the higher interest of edification.[2] In his introduction (xii. 2-3) Paul gives the reasons for the necessity for proving the origin of inspiration. 'Ye know that ye were Gentiles, carried away unto these dumb idols, as ye were led. Wherefore[3] I give you to understand that no man speaking by the Spirit of God calleth Jesus accursed: and that no man can say that Jesus is the Lord,[4] but by the Holy Ghost.' The criterion therefore by which the authenticity of inspiration can be recognised is the harmony between its message and the faith of the church. But important as the criterion laid down here is its implications must not be misunderstood. It is not intended to restrict the liberty of the spirit but only to prescribe ways in which it might be known if the Spirit causing the prophet to speak came from God or from demons, because Paul believed in both inspiration by demons and inspiration by God. But the rule also implies a measure of limitation. Paul has two ideas in mind: (1) the Spirit can only convey the truth, and (2) the church possesses the truth. In principle Paul only intends to resolve a problem of form, i.e. of the origin of inspiration; but as always happens, form and content cannot be entirely separated. Without intending to

[1] The earliest Christian document in our possession, the first epistle to the Thessalonians, gives the recommendation not to quench the Spirit and not to despise prophesyings (v. 19-20). This is an early reaction against a tendency to mistrust inspiration. If it is remembered that according to 2 Thess. ii. 2, a prediction that the paruosia was coming almost immediately had been made in the name of inspiration, this tendency may well have been the result of a feeling that inspiration sometimes provoked a dangerous agitation in the churches.

[2] As to how Paul's rules of discipline to which manifestations of charisms had to be submitted made it possible for regular and organised forms of worship to appear, see *E.P.*, p. 266.

[3] i.e. in order that you may be able to recognise whether an inspiration comes from God or from demons.

[4] This means to contradict or confess the faith of the church.

do so, Paul lays down a criterion for the content of inspiration, although he only wished to pronounce upon its origin. We must, however, distinguish between the implications of the principle laid down by Paul and what it in fact meant for him. The reasons why inspiration was fated to diminish in importance in the course of the second generation are clear. While we must not suppose that Paul intended to detract from its authority, however much in fact he did so, we have to recognise that he had at least the vague feeling that if the faith was to be stabilised some co-ordination was demanded between teaching given by revelation and the truth possessed by the church.

Like pneumatism all the eschatological beliefs and convictions possessed by the first generation of Christians that they were living on the eve of a great cosmic revolution were of necessity obstacles to any process of stabilisation. What was the good of forming an organisation on the supposition that it was going to endure while all the time it was on the point of disappearing? A movement towards stabilisation could only become effective when eschatological beliefs had lost their force even if they had not disappeared and had become theories which had no effective influence on men's minds and wills. Then the church could be established on earth with the feeling that it was destined to pass its life there, it is true, not for ever, but at any rate for an almost unlimited period of time.

If we are to understand how stabilisation became possible, we must follow the course of pneumatism and eschatology in the first two generations of Christians.

4.—THE EVOLUTION OF PNEUMATISM

I shall begin by simply stating the facts. We shall then find a striking parallelism between the two developments of pnemuatism and eschatology which will help us to explain the facts.

Pneumatism was a characteristic phenomenon of the first generation of Christians especially in the communities belonging to the Greek world. It did not disappear all at once but was only present in the second generation in a much attentuated form and was a thought-form rather than anything else; to a very large extent it became a form which had lost its primitive content. Then towards the end of the first century survivals of real pneumatism existed but they caused some embarrassment which shows that pneumatism was not in complete accord with the current needs of the church.

The synoptic gospels which began to be compiled about 70 use the prophetic form to describe inspiration and only give it quite a small place. It only appears in the promise that help will be given to those who will be persecuted to whom the Spiri͡t will dictate what they are to say when they are questioned about their faith.[1] Luke's gospel, no doubt because it is in some measure Pauline in thought and follows a Pauline tradition, lays much more stress than Matthew and Mark on the promise of the outpouring of the Spirit. There is no doubt that we must agree with Harnack[2] that the original text of Luke in the Lord's prayer gave not 'Thy kingdom come', but 'May thy Holy Spirit come upon us and purify us' (xi. 2).[3] When Jesus is going to leave his own the last words which he says to them are to order them not to leave Jerusalem before they had received the Holy Spirit who had been promised to them (xxiv. 49).

The Synoptic gospels were edited in a Hellenic environment after 70. It can only be supposed therefore that inspiration had ceased to play in this environment the same part it had done twenty years before. It is true that much more stress is laid upon inspiration in the book of Acts which possesses a positive theory on the subject of the Spirit, but as we have seen[4] the theory is artificial, nothing more than a formal survival of Paul's conception, no longer depending on personal experience or on any direct acquaintance with the facts of pneumatism.

The epistle to the Ephesians teaches that the mystery of Christ —he refers to the reconciliation of the Gentiles—has been revealed by God unto His holy apostles and prophets by the Spirit (iii. 5).

[1] Matt. x. 19. Cf. Mark xiii. 11 (= Luke xxi. 12-15); Luke xii. 11-12. A similar idea is shown in the story of the martyrdom of Stephen which describes him as having had at the time of his death an ecstatic vision in which he saw the heavens open and Jesus on the right hand of God (Acts vii. 55-56).

[2] Harnack, 'Die ursprungliche Gestalt des Vaterunsers', an article published as an appendix to 'Ueber einige Worte Jesu die nicht in kanonischen Evangelien stehen', *S.B.A.*, 1904, pp. 195-208.

[3] The readings given by two minuscules, 700 (xi⁶s.) and 162 (xii⁶s.) and supported in addition by Gregory of Nyssa and Maximus the Confessor. Marcion also knew of it and Harnack found reminiscences of it in the *Acts of Thomas* and in the liturgy of Constantinople. The support for this reading is not considerable or large but it is very significant as liturgical use fixed the Lord's prayer so firmly in one form that it is less likely that it was altered at a late date than that a primitive reading persisted here and there which differed from the liturgical form. In the saying about the answer to prayer which is a kind of commentary on the Lord's prayer Matthew (vii. 11) speaks of 'good things' which the Father will give to those who ask Him. But Luke (xi. 13) speaks of the gift of the 'Holy Spirit'. It is true that the text varies somewhat but that is because many manuscripts have been influenced by a harmonising tendency. [4] See pp. 95 ff.

This is Paul's idea of inspiration in a restricted form, since inspiration is confined to a particular category of persons belonging to the past.[1]

The epistle to the Hebrews suggests that it was only in the past that the preaching of the gospel was accompanied by 'signs and wonders, with divers miracles and gifts of the Holy Ghost' (ii. 4). In theory Christians possess the Spirit (vi. 4); to give up the faith and the Christian life is an offence to the Spirit of God (x. 29), but as it is supposed that through the Holy Spirit Christ was himself offered to God as a pure victim (ix. 14) plainly the Spirit is operative in the life of Christians through the redemptive work of Christ which they share.

The first epistle of Peter also shows that the function of the Spirit in the preaching of the gospel was remembered (ii. 12) but the word Spirit is principally used in the epistle in reference to the heavenly life which Christ has entered upon after he has suffered (ii. 18), the life to which Christians are destined, provided that they emerge victorious from the trials of suffering and especially from those of persecution. Every Christian is exhorted to practise the charism which he has received. This, however, refers not to the Spirit but to the manifold grace of God (iv. 10). This makes one think that the idea of inspiration was outside the range of his thought or perhaps inspired him with distrust.

In the pastoral epistles Timothy is exhorted not to neglect the gift that was given him 'by prophecy[2] with the laying on of the hands of the presbytery' (1 Tim. iv. 14) or again to 'stir up the gift of God which is in him by the putting on of Paul's hands' (2 Tim. i. 6). The gift is therefore connected with a ritual gesture by which a group or individual who hold authority and power qualifying them for the discharge of certain functions in the church transmit this power and authority to someone else after they have been assured that the person who is to be given authority possesses the aptitudes necessary for exercising these functions. Previous ideas have been

[1] The idea expressed in ii. 20 that apostles and prophets are the foundation on which the church is built fails to agree with the idea expressed by Paul in 1 Cor. iii. 11. According to the epistle to the Ephesians, Christ is not directly the foundation of the church but the revelation received by the apostles about it. For the implications and causes of this transformation see my article 'Autorité du Christ et autorité de l'Écriture', R.h.p.r., 1938, XVIII, pp. 101-125.

[2] It is difficult to say exactly what the function of prophecy is supposed to be here. It appears to be nothing more than a formal survival of the charismatic conception of the ministry.

remembered and changed but all thought of living pneumatism has disappeared.[1]

The evidence of the post-Pauline literature is remarkable in its homogeneity. Inspiration has ceased to be a spontaneous outburst. Paul's conceptions have not been altogether forgotten or repudiated but what has been remembered of his ideas is not applied to spontaneous happenings but to an organised ministry of the church under its control which is entrusted to certain individuals; one of its functions is to see that the 'sound doctrine' is not subject to any change.[2]

In this conception of the ministry the real pneumatic element had no part. It must therefore be presumed that it had completely disappeared. Clear traces of it can still be found at the end of the first century in the form of prophetism and the itinerant ministry.

Prophetism and ecstatic phenomena have a place in the Johannine apocalypse largely because the church felt itself in danger through persecution and this created a psychological disturbance and caused a current of excitement to run through the church. But they may have been more general in character since the Fourth Gospel[3] gives a big place to the doctrine of inspiration, although it does not seem to take into account any kind of ecstatic phenomena. The doctrine is also to be found in the first epistle of John. The book of the Acts mentions the four daughters of Philip who were prophetesses (xxi. 8-9). This shows that prophets were held in esteem or at any rate were remembered for a long time. The letter of Polycrates to Victor supports this.[4]

---

[1] See *E.P.*, pp. 392 f.

[2] This change in ideas from the Spirit being originally thought of as a creative and liberating force to its conception as a power making for conservation was expressed by Wellhausen, *Israel u. Gesch.*, p. 375, in a plain and even somewhat brutal, but forceful simile, 'The Holy Ghost became the ghost of the church; it fluttered about in the councils of the church like an owl or a bat'. Van Der Leeuw (*Phanomenolgie der Religion*, Tubingen, 1933, p. 626) in considering the function of inspiration not only in Christianity but in the growth of religions in general, says that the vessel which the action of the Spirit creates becomes its coffin.

[3] The position of the church according to the Fourth Gospel does not seem to be tragic except in chapters xv-xvii which may have been added at a later date. See *Introd.* II, pp. 370 ff.

[4] Eusebius, *H.e.* v. 24, 2. It should be noticed that when Polycrates mentions Philip and his daughters as among the first rank of 'the stars of Asia' he does not recall that they were prophetesses. This is a sign of the change in appreciative values which took place in the course of the second century. The survival of prophetism was not peculiar to Asia. Hermas mentions the existence at Rome in the middle of the second century of a type which was clearly that of an ecstatic visionary. It is of course true that this appears to have been rather an isolated case.

The doctrine of the Spirit contained in the Fourth Gospel is an extension of the Pauline doctrine emptied of all exterior manifestation and ecstatic element.

In the period following the compilation of the Fourth Gospel use seems to have been made of some of its rather simple phrases about the Spirit, e.g. the Spirit being the interior fount of inspiration, the revealer of all truth, to defend doctrines which were out of harmony with the church's thought or in the sphere of morals were producing results which contradicted the moral principles of Christianity. On this account the author of the first epistle of John took care to use phrases which show greater caution and slightly differ in meaning. He puts his readers on guard against ascribing the action of the Spirit of Christ to what in reality is inspired by antichrist and teaches that the criterion by which to judge one source of inspiration from another is the confession that Jesus has come in the flesh (iv. 1 ff.). In other words, he lays down the same criterion as Paul had done which is whether what the Spirit teaches is in harmony with the forms used by the church to express its faith.

The Johannine doctrine of the Spirit is not just a survival of pneumatism at a time when it had generally speaking disappeared or was for the most part on the decline. It is the expression under the influence of Pauline forms of thought of the experience and life of a powerful religious personality and the appearance of Christianity with a new dynamic in the bosom of a religion which had grown completely static.

The Johannine doctrine therefore has a personal and even individualistic character and cannot be altogether explained as a stage in the evolution of pneumatism which had been determined by historical causes of a general kind.

The itinerant ministry of apostle, prophet, and teacher which the Didache shows us survived in Syria[1] about the year 100 is quite different in character. The author of the Didache holds inspiration in unqualified respect. To condemn a prophet who speaks under the action of the Spirit is the only sin which cannot be forgiven (xi. 7).[2] But mere inspiration causes him some uneasiness and embarrassment. It might almost be said that while he respects the

[1] Or perhaps in Egypt.
[2] The authority given to the prophet is shown by the fact that when he presided at the eucharist 'he could celebrate the eucharist in any form he wished' (x. 7). This means that he had the right to improvise prayers instead of reciting those given in chapters 9 and 10.

principle of inspiration he mistrusts people who are inspired. One reason for this is that preachers went from church to church and just because their ministry was itinerant they easily escaped all control with the result that there could easily slip into their ranks schemers, false prophets[1] who pretended to be inspired, and men 'making traffic of Christ' (xii. 5). That this danger was already recognised is significant; it shows that the ministry of inspired persons was now somewhat out of place in the life of the churches. To guard against the danger of the churches being exploited by people who had little with which to recommend themselves the author, guided by common sense, suggests a few tests such as finding out whether such people had an axe to grind[2] and whether they practised what they taught.[3]

Even when a man has been recognised as a truly inspired prophet, his activities must be under control. While in principle a prophet must be received as the Lord himself (xi. 4), he must in fact only be received and listened to, if what he taught agreed with what the faithful had already been taught, if he did not teach a doctrine which destroyed what was established, and if his teaching was for the increase of righteousness and knowledge of the Lord (xi. 1-2).[4] Enquiry must also be made if he have 'the behaviour of the Lord' (xi. 8).

Even when it is plain that the itinerant prophet is an approved prophet and that his teaching does not contradict that of the church his preaching cannot be accepted without reserve and conditions. The author does not express his thought on this point in any general or abstract manner but lays down a rule which applies to a concrete case. Unfortunately the text is somewhat obscure.

No prophet who has been tried and is genuine, though he enact a worldly mystery of the church, if he teach not others to do what he does himself, shall be judged by you. For he has his judgement with God, for so also did the prophets of old (xi. 11).

Harnack[5] suggests the most reasonable interpretation of the text

[1] The expression is found at least six times in the Didache. The false prophet is not a man possessed by demonic inspiration and therefore in the service of satanic powers hostile to God, as is the case in the earliest texts; he is a person who pretends to be inspired because he has an axe to grind. See Fascher, *Prophetes, Eine sprach- und religionsgeschichtliche Untersuchung*, Giessen, 1927, p. 188.

[2] xi. 5, 6, 9.   [3] xi. 10.

[4] This is the same as the principle laid down in 1 Cor. xii and in 1 John iv.

[5] Harnack, *Lehre der zwolf Apostel*,[2] Leipzig, 1893, pp. 44 ff. Harnack's interpretation is adopted by many critics, notably by Knopf, *Die Lehre der zwolf Apostel, Die zwei Clemensbriefe*, Tubingen, 1920, p. 32, and with some hesitation by H.

and makes out that to understand what the author means by 'the worldly mystery of the church' we must refer ourselves to Ephesians v. 32-33 where the author writes in reference to marriage, 'This mystery is great'. This phrase refers not to marriage proper but to the relationship of Christ to the church, of which marriage is a kind of symbolic figure. This idea in the second century gave birth to all kinds of speculations[1] which were intended to justify ascetic practices and to make an ideal of absolute chastity. It must be noted that the allusion to 'the prophets of old'[2] refers to those of their activities which have some resemblance to those of inspired persons. People are not to be called upon to imitate their actions which may appear para-doxical and seem offensive to any fine feelings and even to the moral conscience. The nature of the author's advice not to pass judgement needs to be underlined; no defence of their conduct is implied. He is uncertain whether they are not to be condemned but as they are prophets who are under consideration he thinks that it must be left to God alone to pronounce judgement upon them. Finally, it should be noted that the author expresses himself somewhat enig-matically as if he wished only to be understood by people of his own time and so avoid informing others of practices which baffled him and seemed to set a bad example. If this is so it must mean something more than denying prophets the right of imposing or even recommending celibacy. It must refer to the mystical unions of virgins and ascetics living together in chastity which were prac-tised in the early church and are most probably referred to in the instructions of 1 Corinthians vii. 36 ff.[3] The good sense of the author of the Didache revolted at this kind of practice which could only too easily end in scandal and moral catastrophe. But as the men who follow this practice are inspired he did not dare to condemn them. He is careful to leave them to God's care. This shows that,

Hemmer, *Les Péres apostoliques*, Paris, 1926, I-II,[2] p. xcix. Hennecke (*Neutest. Apokr.*, p. 561) hesitates between this interpretation and that which makes out that it refers to ascetic practices which the prophet may be allowed to follow but must not wish to impose upon others.

[1] On this subject see the texts mentioned by Harnack in his commentary on the passage.

[2] Harnack thinks that it refers to prophets of the first generation of Christians. It seems better, however, to adopt the interpretation given by others, e.g. by Knopf, p. 33 and to suppose that it refers to the prophets of the Old Testament, particularly Hosea and his matrimonial troubles. Bryennius, the first editor of the Didache (*ΔΙΔΑΧΗ ΤΩΝ ΔΩΔΕΚΑ ΑΠΟΣΤΟΛΩΝ, ΕΝ ΚΩΝΣΤΑΝΤΙΝΟΠΟΛΕΙ*, 1883, p. 44) gave this interpretation.

[3] On this subject see Achelis, *Virgines subintroductae*, Leipzig, 1902 and Lietz-mann, *Kor.*, pp. 35 ff.

while he does not admit anything wrong about them, his personal opinion is that inspiration cannot be taken as a very sure guide on these things. He tries whatever may be thought about them to prevent his readers from having anything to do with them and lays it down that prophets who have contracted these kind of unions should not ask for them to be imitated.

There is one point more which has to be considered because it illustrates the change from an itinerant and charismatic ministry to a stable and administrative one. The author of the Didache considered that only inspired men are really qualified to direct the Christian communities but it frequently happened that a church did not enjoy a ministry of this kind. In chapters ix and x are provided written prayers to be used when there is no prophet present to preside over the eucharist who could improvise his own prayers; at the same time in chapter xv those churches without teachers and prophets were to appoint someone from the bishops and deacons to discharge their ministry. They are to take care to choose two men for this function who are disinterested, speak the truth, and have been proved. They are to esteem them as highly as if they were actually prophets and teachers. This simple recommendation shows that there was held to be a wide difference between the prophetical ministry and that of bishops and deacons. Furthermore, while prophets and teachers possessed the authority of the Spirit, bishops and deacons gained theirs through election, which implies that their authority lacked any transcendent character and was simply a delegation of the powers of the community.[1]

Peculiar circumstances might arise when a truthful and proved prophet wanted to settle permanently in a community. The author recommends that when this happens he must be provided for (xiii). But if he is an itinerant prophet, he is only to be provided for a day or two days at most which he will pass in the church which he is visiting and that on his departure he is only to take the provisions necessary for a day's journey.

On the evolution of pneumatism the Didache provides evidence of two kinds. First, we have evidence about a particular locality from which we have no right to generalise because it refers to one

[1] There is quite a clear distinction between the two ministries so far as the Didache concerning the prophet who settles down to live in a church instructs the faithful to give the first fruits of all their goods so as to provide for him (xiii). Nothing of this kind is mentioned for the bishops and deacons. It can only be supposed that this was taken for granted as it is laid down in xiii. 4 that where there is no prophet the first fruits are to be given to the poor.

particular group of churches. It proves that inspiration had become decidedly rare and only survived in the form of an itinerant ministry which had become quite exceptional in character. Secondly, we have evidence of a more general kind in the Didache showing a growing dissatisfaction with inspiration and increasing difficulty in accommodating it to the normal life of the communities. This must have been due to general causes and have been found in other communities besides the one to which the Didache refers, with the result that it must have helped to hasten the disappearance of pneumatism or at any rate to its becoming ineffective.

But a movement like pneumatism did not disappear all at once or altogether. Heinrich Weinel[1] maintained that he found traces of it surviving in the Christianity of the second century right up to the time of Irenaeus. His description needs to be revised and it would be found that he has exaggerated considerably; there is some truth in what he says but the evidence shows that hardly anything of pneumatism survived except outbreaks of a sporadic kind.

5.—THE EVOLUTION OF ESCHATOLOGICAL BELIEF

We pass on now to the evolution of eschatology.[2] In outline it closely resembles that which we traced for pneumatism.

The terms eschatology and apocalyptic we often hear used as if they were synonymous. This is a source of confusion. If we hold strictly by etymology every religion which teaches that salvation can only be realised or achieved in a life beyond, would have to be described as eschatological. The term is generally used in a narrower sense and applied to conceptions which link the fate of the individual to that of the world and the attainment of salvation to the establishment of a new cosmic order and in addition are distinguished by the belief that the arrival of this new world is imminent. Apocalyptic adds to these elements the idea that it is possible to know in advance at what time the cosmic drama will be unfolded and the timetable which it will follow.

Christianity came to birth and gained possession of men's souls as a great hope. The first generation of Christians lived feverishly

---

[1] H. Weinel, *Die Wirkungen des Geistes und der Geister im nachapostolischen Zeitalter bis Irenaeus*, Freiburg in Breisgau, Leipzig, Tubingen, 1899.

[2] On this question see my article, 'Eschatologie et apocalyptique dans le christianisme primitif', *R.h.r.*, 1932, CVI, pp. 382-434, 489-524.

waiting for the great day when the Lord would come and establish his kingdom. Their slogan *Maran atha* 'The Lord comes', affirmed their faith: and also their prayer 'Lord, come'.[1] Furthermore, at a very early stage of its history Christianity went back to the Jewish apocalyptic conceptions rejected previously by Jesus.[2]

The belief that Jesus by his resurrection had gained a victory which was a definite assurance of salvation lent strength to the outlook towards the future which the primitive faith derived from its Jewish origins, since Jesus' resurrection was the promise and assurance that he would return to accomplish and complete the work of redemption.[3] The first Christians had the feeling that they were strangers on earth and pilgrims who yearned to enter their own heavenly country (Heb. xi. 13; 1 Pet. ii. 11).

The earliest Christian preaching loved to conjure up by drawing inspiration from such a text as Psalm 110 the time when all the enemies of Christ would be put under his feet (Acts ii. 34-35; 1 Cor. xv. 25 ff.; Heb. x. 13. Cf. ii. 6 ff.; Mark xii. 36 and par.) when the 'restoration of all things' would be accomplished (Acts iii. 19-21). In the epistles to the Thessalonians (1, iv. 14-18; 2, ii. 3-12) and in the first epistle to the Corinthians (xv. 20-28, 51-52), Paul sketches out a complete scheme of apocalyptic on exactly the same lines as those of Jewish thought.[4] But his thought also takes another turn as he looks to the emergence in the individual of a new reality, the

[1] For the meaning of *'maran atha'* see W. Bauer, *Worterb. s.v.* (bibliography) and Strack-Billerbeck, II, pp. 493 ff. Paul uses the phrase in 1 Cor. xvi. 22 without translating it which shows that it had been absorbed from the soil of Palestine where it originated into the liturgy of the Greek churches. It may be that the conviction of the presence of Christ may have been so intense in these churches that the phrase had acquired a new meaning and that instead of a prayer it had become an affirmation of faith. We find it as a kind of confession of faith in the eucharistic formulae of the Didache (x. 6). The equivalent of it is found at the end of the Apocalypse (xxii. 10-20) in a form which combines affirmation and prayer.

[2] See *V. de J.*, pp. 469 ff. and *Life of Jesus*, pp. 569 ff. Apocalyptic seems to have been integrated into Christian thought at a very early date. It had already happened when the first epistle to the Thessalonians was written, the earliest Christian document in our possession. The apocalyptic teaching (iv. 13 ff.) which it contains is not given as a novelty. The reasons which Loisy (*Naiss. du christ.*, p. 17; *Remarques sur la littérature épistolaire du Nouveau Testament*, Paris, 1935, pp. 88 f.) has put forward for considering this instruction to have been added later appear to me unconvincing. See my observations on this subject, 'Les épîtres paulliniennes d'après M. Loisy', *R.h.p.r.*, 1936, XVI, pp. 508 ff.

[3] See my article, 'Parousie et résurrection', *Trois Etudes*, pp. 3-41.

[4] These passages do not show any spontaneous development in Paul's thought as the apostle was compelled to write them in order to correct mistaken ideas entertained by his readers. This shows at any rate that apocalyptic ideas belonged to the periphery and not to the centre of Paul's thought.

interior man created in the believer by the Spirit of Christ which, however, will only come to fruition when each individual passes on to the beyond (2 Cor. iv. 16 ff.; Phil. i. 23 ff.).

There is something more here than a few surviving fragments of an apocalyptic conception which Paul's Christian thought had really left behind; the collective apocalyptic still surviving corresponds to an essential element in Paul's thought, viz. the idea of the consummation of the church which will only be possible at the end of the history of mankind.[1]

Generally speaking, primitive Christianity accepted the world beyond into which Christ had entered by his resurrection in a rather vague way, while Paul, owing to the form his conversion gave to it, believed in its reality with tremendous intensity. Although primitive Christianity believed in the present reality of heaven so that it inclined to think that the present world was definitely disappearing apocalyptic on that account was not eliminated and was not completely integrated anew into Christian thought. A compromise was established; apocalyptic tendencies survived in an attenuated form. For this reason Matthew's gospel[2] gives the Sermon on the Mount as the charter of a new society the relationship of which to the new Kingdom of God is not defined with any exactness. The word 'church' can be found twice in this gospel (xvi. 18; xviii. 17) which points to the existence of a semi-organised Christian society which has ceased to believe that its existence on earth is only of a temporary nature. The demand which the composition of the gospels satisfied was that for a coherent narrative of the life of Jesus and can only have come about when the conviction that the Kingdom of God was going to be set up at a particular time had died out. Mark (xiii. 32) and Matthew (xxiv. 36) added to the synoptic apocalypse a saying of Jesus which declares that the Father alone to the exclusion of the angels and even of the Son knows the time of the parousia.[3] Even if it is to be understood as referring to the exact moment of the parousia and not to the period when it will happen[4]

---

[1] I shall have to return to this point later on to show its importance with reference to Paul's teaching about the church. See *E.P.*, pp. 39 ff.

[2] And already in the Logia which is shown by a comparison between the Sermon on the Mount in Matthew (v-viii) and the Sermon on the Plain in Luke (vi. 20-49) to have contained an outline-programme in a simpler form however.

[3] This saying is such a flat contradiction of the idea of Christ possessing omniscience that it is impossible for it to have been created by the tradition.

[4] In 1 Thess. v. 1-3 after Paul has affirmed the unpredictable character of the parousia by the simile of the thief who comes in the night, he expresses his thoughts more precisely by the simile of a pregnant woman who does not know the exact

it is none the less significant because it is in opposition to the principles of apocalyptic.[1]

In Palestinian Christianity eschatology seems to have dwindled in importance principally for reasons of an external and general kind, but in the case of Paul's eschatology there were other reasons much more closely connected with his religious life. This fact deserves examination and its import and the consequences flowing from it must be noticed. It partly explains why Paulinism was the form into which what became primitive Catholicism synthesised and set, although Paulinism appears to have been hardly understood or followed in the first generation.

Eschatology[2] grew feeble and in the end disappeared in Palestinian Christianity because it was spent and exhausted. Its disappearance was due to negative causes and was a negative fact. With it disappeared the religious dynamic which it had expressed. On that account Palestinian Christianity was left enfeebled and out of balance and, so far as it showed itself unbending to the influence of Greek Christianity, doomed to disappear, because it was not sufficiently distinguishable from Judaism.[3] The same causes, it is true, were at work in Greek Christianity, but there were also other influences at work. Eschatology did not just disappear in a negative fashion but was transformed into something positive. The forces at work in the first generation under the forms of pneumatism and eschatology became thought of as realised and spiritualised. Hence they did not disappear but only assumed a new form.

With Paul it is plain that eschatology did not gradually fade out. Something else happened. While in one sense his eschatology did lose its tenseness[4] it became a realised and spiritualised eschatology.

moment when she will be seized with the pangs of child-birth. She is not ignorant, however, at what period they will come.

[1] Mark (xiii. 33-37) gives this teaching in the parable which comes at the end of the synoptic apocalypse. He compares Christians to servants to whom the master has entrusted his house and who must keep awake so that on his return he will not find them asleep. This theme occupied a large place in Christian exhortation as it can be found in the epistle of James (v. 1-8) which except for this reference does not contain any eschatological ideas at all. We shall see later on (pp. 276 f.) that there is no doubt that the Didache ends by developing an apocalyptic theme merely as a subject for exhortation. By using the theme of the end as a subject for exhortation in this way the church helped to preserve eschatology as a live element in Christian thought.

[2] The same is true of the decline of pneumatism in Palestinian Christianity.

[3] See p. 144.

[4] The instruction given in 2 Thess. ii. 1-12 shows that faced with feverish expectation that the world was coming to an end almost immediately Paul felt it

He did not think of salvation as only to be expected in a future world, whether near or afar off; he thought of it as something already real and grasped by the believer in the experience of being possessed by the Spirit who had made him a new creature, a being of the new heavenly world. An eschatological element still survives in the fact that salvation will only be completed in another economy but it will be the flowering of a reality which is already present and will depend in a much less degree on what will happen at the last day.

After Paul the eschatological element continued to decline and its decline became accentuated. In the epistle to the Ephesians Christ's crucifixion is the moment when he is victorious over the Powers and subdues them (i. 20-22). The dualism of present and future is combined here with another dualism, that of the world below with the world above and from now henceforward the elect have been placed 'in the heavenly world' or 'among the heavenly beings'.[1] The pastoral epistles hardly preserve any eschatology at all except the idea of the beyond and a few formulae concerning an expected manifestation of the Lord in such an attenuated form that they can be considered nothing more than survivals.[2]

An ontological dualism expressed in spatial language of a Greek type serves as the framework for the thought of the epistle to the Hebrews. The judgement and the resurrection figure among the elementary doctrines (vi. 1-2). The author recognises that Christ's reign is not yet complete (ii. 8; x. 13) but the second of the two passages containing this idea is inserted between two categorical affirmations concerning the complete and definitive character of his sacrifice (x. 12, 14) which score a polemical point against those who made salvation depend on what would happen at the last day. The judgement is invoked in x. 27 as a terrifying prospect for the enemies of God but the idea of Christ's return mentioned in ix.

necessary to restrain himself or at any rate to be more careful and reserved in affirming the coming of the parousia as imminent.

[1] It is true, it seems that the formula ἐν τοῖς ἐπουρανίοις which occurs no less than six times in the epistle to the Ephesians has been borrowed from the gnosis which the epistle attacks. The author makes it his own in order to neutralise it but it is uncertain whether it signifies any clear and definite idea at all, or whether it always means the same thing. In any case it is not an idea to which the author had been led by the internal development of his thought.

[2] The term parousia is replaced by that of 'manifestation' (1 Tim. vi. 14; 2 Tim. iv. 1, 8; Titus ii. 13). This term is also used in reference to the ministry of Jesus (2 Tim. i. 10). It looks as if the author wished to avoid suggesting the whole apocalyptic set up which had become associated by tradition with the term parousia.

28 has no soteriological function as it will be 'without sin'. It belongs to a conception analogous to Paul's idea of creation in two stages and of the coming of the second Adam who will raise humanity on to the spiritual plane.

The first epistle of Peter shows a return to eschatology; it is certainly connected with the confusion into which Christians had been thrown by the tribulations they had had to bear for their faith. The expectation of salvation is much more tense in this epistle than in the other writings of this period with the exception of the Johannine apocalypse, but more than anything else it is an aspiration after deliverance from persecution without any resulting thought of an apocalyptic drama.

The Johannine apocalypse is very different in nature as it was written under the impression that the church and the empire were engaged in or about to engage in a struggle to the death, a struggle which on the face of things was unequal but nevertheless the church would emerge from it triumphant because its cause was that of God. The author of the Apocalypse conceives this triumph in the form of the destruction of the present world and its replacement by a new world. John's book might have, it seems, opened wide the gates to the apocalyptic flood and brought the church back to a stage which the deuteropauline writings had largely passed beyond. This is not the case, because although the Johannine apocalypse borrowed its materials from Jewish sources it gave them a completely new interpretation. The Messiah whose triumphant intervention John invokes is a Messiah who has already gained his victory; he is 'the one who was dead and is alive for evermore' (i. 18; ii. 8); he is 'the Lion of the tribe of Judah who has prevailed' (v. 5). That is the tone not of hope but of triumph and assurance as shown in the canticles of the apocalypse. As with Paul the centre of the drama's gravity has been displaced, it is no longer in the future; it is in the past. Victory has definitely been gained.

After many ups and downs for quite a long period during which it sometimes met with strong resistance, the Apocalypse attained its place in the canon. This legitimised in a fashion the periodic outbursts of apocalyptic which have taken place in the history of Christianity and ensured that they happened within the confines of the church and not in opposition to the church from outside and so allowed them to be brought under control more easily.

Ought the conclusion of the Didache to be compared to the Apocalypse? Chronologically they are close to each other. Eschatology is only represented in the body of the book itself by some elements of eucharistic prayers (ix. 4; x. 5-6);[1] it is much more amply represented in the conclusion which is almost like a little apocalypse. It says that it will avail nothing to have lived a long time in the faith if a man is not found irreproachable when the Saviour returns. This moment of time is described as a terrible ordeal. Evil will multiply at the last times, false prophets and destroyers will appear, sheep will become wolves, love will be changed into hatred. Then antichrist will appear, the deceiver of the world who will show himself as the Son of God, he will accomplish signs and prodigies, will dominate the earth and commit such crimes as he has never committed before. Men will be put to the proof of the fire, many will fall and perish, but those who survive in the faith will be saved. Then the signs which herald the drama will appear (the stars falling, trumpets sounding, a resurrection not of all but only of the saints), then the world will see the Lord coming on the clouds of heaven (xvi. 3-7). This picture reveals an outlook so different from that of the author of the Didache in the rest of the book that its composition cannot be attributed to him. He must have borrowed it from some source. It may be asked if he understood what it originally meant. Possibly the last chapter of the Didache contains only a few stereotyped formulae of a somewhat conventional kind which have no positive meaning except so far as they serve as moral exhortation. In fact, one of the possible ends to the development of apocalyptic and eschatology is that they become nothing more than texts for moral exhortation.

Another line of development comes to an end in the Fourth Gospel, the principal intermediate stage being indicated by the thought of Paul. The end is the complete spiritualisation of both apocalyptic and eschatology which is tantamount to their elimination. The conception seems most likely to have been that of somebody who was the centre of a small and select group rather than belonging to the church of its time, although it nevertheless influenced contemporary collective thought.

Under the influence of Judaeo-Alexandrine philosophy the idea of the co-existence of the two worlds to be met with in Paul became, it might be said, stabilised; it no longer refers to the temporary

---

[1] These prayers were not composed by the author of the Didache but borrowed by him. They appear to have originated in a very different environment from that in which he lived. We must therefore be very careful in using them to describe the author's thought.

situation between Christ's resurrection and his parousia. The lower world is that of the flesh and sin; but John gives to sin a completely negative conception.[1] He considers it the natural state of man which lacks the life which is real. In the same way the flesh is character-ised by its powerlessness and not by its corruption. It serves no purpose as it is the Spirit who gives life (vi. 63). The only positive sin which deprives a man of any possibility of life is the refusal to receive the word of Christ (xv. 22). For those on the contrary who receive the word, Christ becomes 'the way' which leads to the world of true life (xiv. 6). The gift of life is spoken of sometimes as present (iii. 36; v. 25; vi. 47) and sometimes as future (iii. 36; xi. 26) but the future mentioned is not so much a survival from primitive eschatology as a result of the fact that the evangelist's ideas are given in speeches supposed to have been made by Jesus during his ministry, although his return to heaven and his glorification are necessary antecedents for his being able to give his own the Spirit, who will assure them the life which is real (vii. 39). John works with two conceptions of life: one is of life as completely physical, earthly and only transitory; the other is of life as spiritual, heavenly and eternal. The two kinds of life cannot be associated with each other and have no connection with each other. As for the heavenly life, the Johannine Christ speaks of it as a blessing which the believer already definitely possesses. but also as a gift which he will possess in the future. It must be understood that a time will come when the spiritual life will be the only one and it will be shown that physical death has no power over it (xi. 25-26). John makes no suggestion as to when or how the believer will pass to eternal life in its purity but it is clear that his eschatology follows the same lines as the indi-vidual eschatology of Paul and that we must interpret this as a change in the framework of Paul's thought and suppose it to happen to each believer at the end of his physical life.

It is also affirmed in the Fourth Gospel that Christ will return, but the idea of his return not only is deprived of any apocalyptic element but is transformed. Christ returns as the Spirit given to believers. He returns not in an external and material form but as a spirit within the interior man. It does not happen at an exact moment in history but is continuous with the whole life of believers.[2] It is therefore closely parallel to the activity which according to Paul

[1] Concerning the Johannine conception of the flesh and sin see pp. 152 f.
[2] Concerning this doctrine see my article, 'La notion johannique de l'Esprit et ses antécédents historiques', Paris, 1902, pp. 109 ff.

creates 'the life in Christ' the only difference being that Paul explicitly affirms a material return as well, which John appears to omit.

The first epistle of John is more precise on this point as on others and even corrects the teaching of the gospel. It conceives the juxtaposition of the two modes of life resulting from the existence of believers in the world to be a kind of conflict. The possession of the life given by the Spirit and salvation have lost something in the way of being actually realised. The question of their consummation and fruition loses its importance and at the same time eschatological preoccupations once more receive consideration.[1]

In the Gospel salvation is realised by the Spirit given to the faithful.[2] By this Spirit he is protected against the enmity of the world (xv. 18-20; xvi. 2; xvii. 11-13).[3] Pneumatism detached from all exterior manifestations of an ecstatic character is spiritualised and at the same time eschatology has become realised to such an extent that for all practical purposes it has disappeared. As for apocalyptic it is completely eliminated; the only question considered is a spiritual return of Christ. Salvation loses all connection with the world's destiny and is put in quite another sphere. The idea of judgement is discarded and that of resurrection has only a symbolic value.[4]

On these points also the epistle, compared with the Gospel, shows a perceptible regression. The life of the elect in the world is no longer thought of as simply a cause of suffering but it is also a cause of sin. The thought of the epistle is thus directed afresh towards the future and the idea of the parousia (ii. 18; iii. 2) without, however, any return to apocalyptic ideas. Nothing shows better how far removed from apocalyptic the thought of the first epistle of John is than the curious charge to be found in this writing in the concept of the antichrist. Antichrist is no more a transcendent personal power opposing Christ. There is no more one antichrist but antichrists who are heretics (ii 18; cf. 2 John 7).[5]

The development of eschatological ideas does not end in their neutralisation through being spiritualised but rather in what might

---

[1] *Not. joh. de l'Esprit*, pp. 149 ff.

[2] This Spirit is given sometimes by God at the request of Christ (xiv. 15-16) or in his name (xiv. 26), sometimes by Christ (xv. 26). He is also Christ returning to his own (xiv. 18; cf. xiv. 2-3). The Spirit is also described as being the Father and the Son coming to live with the faithful (xiv. 23).

[3] Sometimes in place of the gift of the Spirit Christ promises to his own the fulfilment of prayers made in his name (xiv. 13; xvi. 23 ff.).

[4] See pp. 359 f.

[5] It is rather different, however, in iv. 3 f. Heretics here are not antichrists but inspired by the spirit of antichrist who is in the world.

be described as their quiescence in the condition of a chrysalis reducing them in a large measure to being theories, which ceased to influence men's minds directly but nevertheless remained a latent force in the Christian conscience liable to come to life if favourable circumstances occurred. This is not only due to the fact that these ideas were too closely bound up with the conditions in which Christianity came to birth for them to disappear completely but also to the fact that they expressed one of the essential elements of Christian belief, i.e. that salvation is never completely consummated as long as the present economy lasts. John's radicalism did not triumph. The church clung to the idea of the last judgement as one of its essential teachings. But it did not disavow the Johannine doctrine of eternal life realised here and now.

The Johannine Apocalypse and the Fourth Gospel are the terminals of two processes of development which are so different from each other that one is tempted to say that they conflict with each other, one of them affirming that salvation will be realised in a realm beyond by the destruction of the sinful world, the other insisting on a new kind of life which is present here and now. The church has made no choice between these two conceptions as it has not done between that of resurrection and of eternal life; it appropriated the two chains of series of ideas without co-ordinating them into a completely balanced and logical system; they correspond to two elements in Christian experience neither of which can be sacrificed to the other.

6.—THE PARALLELISM BETWEEN THE EVOLUTION OF PNEUMATISM AND THAT OF ESCHATOLOGY

We can thus find a striking parallelism between the evolution of pneumatism and that of the eschatological conviction. Both of them began with phenomena of great intensity; then at the beginning of the second generation they became cooler in intensity and grew rare without, however, completely disappearing, but it was found more and more difficult to give them any appropriate place in the life of the church. At the same time their character perceptibly changed. Pneumatism was not completely disowned but was brought under control and its force canalised. Instead of being a source of spontaneity, creativeness and novelty as it was originally, it became a guarantee of the tradition. Although eschatology was never completely rejected it ceased to be a dynamic idea and became a theory except so far as it expressed the church's conviction that its life would extend beyond that of the present world. It counted for so little that it no longer hindered the church from being established in the world and taking root in it. On the other hand, it possessed for a long time sufficient force to keep the church to some extent detached and disinterested in the life of the world.

Pneumatism and eschatological conviction were not so much destroyed as kept within bounds. Both of them remained in the bosom of the church as latent forces always ready to break out into life as we can see from the sporadic outbursts of pneumatism, eschatology, and even apocalyptic, which have occurred in the history of the church often in association with each other.[1]

The parallelism between the two developments is to be explained by the fact that, broadly speaking, the same causes are at work in both. Two of them leap to the eyes. The first is the fact that the phenomena belonging to both of them, because they express a spiritual ferment and need an atmosphere of excitement for their appearance, the more intense they are, the quicker they both exhaust themselves. The second is that, while they stand for essential factors in the creation of a religion they are ill adapted to a religion's needs when it has acquired a past and become a tradition so as to be well on the way to being expressed in a stable organised society.

If, however, we are satisfied with this explanation we shall only see the exterior aspect of things; we should fail to grasp the more profound causes of the development both of pneumatism and eschatology and to perceive the real reason for the similarity in their development.

The case of the apostle Paul is typical. If there ever was an inspired man he was one. He had visions, revelations, ecstasies; he prophesied and spoke in tongues.[2] No one was convinced with greater intensity than he that he was living at the end of time and belonged already to the world of the future. But he laboured to discipline the manifestations of his charismata (1 Cor. xiv). He interpreted them in such a way as to give the ecstatic elements a secondary importance without completely eliminating them. He

---

[1] These outbursts sometimes have been rather superficial phenomena, resulting from taking scripture literally. But it would be a mistake to take them all as that and nothing more.

[2] It is quite possible that other forms of pneumatism were manifest in his life, notably the gift of healing which was practised by him.

reckoned the essential action of the Spirit to be the creation of a new personality in the believer and in groups of believers the formation of a new society, i.e. the church. He was also compelled to pour cold water on the excitement created among the Thessalonians by waiting for the parousia (2 Thess. ii. 1). While he always remained faithful to collective eschatology, believing that salvation would achieve its consummation at the end of the world, he also developed an individual eschatology believing that the destiny of the believer did not depend on that of the world.

It is not a sufficient explanation to say that there were two Pauls, co-existing at the same time, one an inspired enthusiast, the other an administrator with an acute sense of what was needed in the life of the church to give it balance and enable it to fulfil its educative function. The reverse is rather the truth; the celestial realm and salvation ceased to be objects of hope and became objects of present experience. Paul never lost the feeling of being subject to impulses as an inspired man without being able to understand them or even to associate himself with them. Evidence for this is shown by what he says of extempore ecstatic prayer wherein the Spirit prays in the believer without, however, the believer being able to follow it with his *nous* or conscious personality, which cannot be associated with such activity. He does not belittle the value of such facts as possible proofs of the presence and action of God in the life of the believer and the church but he does not rely on them exclusively.

Eschatological convictions underwent a similar transformation through the idea that since Christ has been glorified the new world has become a reality to which the believer belongs although he continues to live in the old world.

Although Paul was not aware of the change which his ideas underwent, eventually it was quite clear what had happened. In place of the temporal dualism of Jewish tradition could be found an ontological dualism expressed in spatial metaphors (earth and flesh on the one side, heaven and spirit on the other)[1] apparently resembling the dualism of Greece which is ontological and not temporal. Is this a pure accident[2] or is Christianity already being

[1] This opposition is already implied in Paul's temporal dualism since the present world belongs to the flesh and the world to come to the Spirit. This conception is reflected in the theory of the two Adams as it is expressed in 1 Cor. xv. 45 ff. Paul would seem to have held it before his conversion, quite independently therefore of his experience of salvation in his life as a Christian.

[2] A pure accident but one which without doubt facilitated the hellenisation of Christianity.

hellenised? It would be going too far to say that Hellenism exercised no influence at all on Paul. The only influences which counted as far as Paul's thought was concerned were religious. Hellenism provided Paul with certain means of expression for translating his thoughts and his religious experience especially. Its importance must not, however, be overestimated. Within the bounds of anthropological considerations, which must be taken into account on these points, Paul remained quite impervious to the Greek dualism of body and soul as is shown by the discussion in 1 Corinthians xv, where he never thinks of life beyond the grave in any other way except as through the resurrection of the body.

This is a matter of ideology rather than anything else. If we find that neither Paul nor his successors have ever completely substituted an ontological dualism in place of a temporal one, the reason is that the Christian conscience has always kept faithful to a dynamic conception of God which has its roots in the Old Testament and plainly is closely connected with an eschatological conception.

The Christian God, like the Jewish God, is a God who acts, who created the world by a victory over chaos and since the fall has been in conflict with satanic powers, who is labouring for the salvation of the elect and will at the end destroy all his enemies. On the other hand, the God of Hellenism is static in character. He is an ideal which man must strive to attain. Wherever a dynamic conception of God holds good, there is also an eschatological orientation, since if God acts we are bound to be interested in the purpose and ends of his activity. That is why in Christianity eschatology was more than a mere survival. We find Paul's eschatology to be of a realised and spiritualised character; this sprung from religious motives. Paul experienced in his Christian life in place of a mere hope a consciousness of salvation and life in Christ as something still incomplete but nevertheless real.[1]

We can see here that spiritual experience, i.e. therefore pneumatism exercised a direct influence on Paul's eschatology. Can we therefore infer from this that pneumatism and eschatology are psychologically speaking organically connected with each other? Certain facts lead us to question the truth of this. It has particularly to be noted that in contemporary Judaism at the time of the birth of Christianity, while eschatological ideas held a central and dominating position, pneumatism was dead except in some surviving forms.[2]

---

[1] Which remains a hope even when it is guaranteed by the word of God.
[2] These survivals were probably phenomena of mimesis caused by reading and meditating on the stories of the visions of the prophets of Israel.

The current conception was that the age of revelation and prophecy was closed and would only revive in the Messianic times. It may also be added that Jesus himself had very strong eschatological convictions but they were not accompanied by any phenomena of ecstasy or vision.

Although these facts are not without significance, we must not draw hasty conclusions from them which they do not warrant. It seems probable that pneumatism and eschatology are not entirely independent of each other but that a connection exists between pneumatism and a certain type of eschatology. The character of an eschatology is not so much determined by its content alone as by the spiritual forces behind it and the reasons given in support of it. Jewish apocalyptic grounded its hopes on the declarations of God which it was believed could be extracted from inspired scripture by study and meditation, and also on a tradition in the making of which elements taken from foreign religions had played a part, notably Mazdeism. The grounds for hope were thus quite exterior to the hope itself and the object hoped for belonged entirely to the future. Such an eschatology could be described as completely futuristic.

Paul's eschatology and following him the church's eschatology are of a different kind. In Paul's judgement the Kingdom of heaven is a present reality both for Christ-Kurios himself and for those who belong to Christ and are united to him but it is not yet the only reality. The Spirit has bestowed on believers his first-fruits already and given them the assurance that the Kingdom of heaven is present and real so that they have become spiritual beings and are integrated into the kingdom now. Such an eschatology is no more completely futuristic; it is a realised eschatology and it is pneumatic experience which has made it so. Thus it is not by accident that we find in Paul and in John in a slightly different form realised or spiritual eschatology existing side by side with pneumatic experience.[1]

In Christianity in Jerusalem the situation seems to have been different. Here the object of hope remained to be realised through the achievement of Christ when he returns. As we have already seen,[2] while Christ has become Messiah by his resurrection and in virtue of this sits on the right hand of God, he is waiting for the time when he will return and complete the work of redemption; but

---

[1] John's experience should be described as mystical rather than pneumatic. The difference between them which in essence is one of emphasis lies in the fact that Paul's experience was accompanied by ecstatic phenomena which in the case of John were lacking.   [2] See pp. 99 f.

for the present he exercises no positive influence neither on the individual nor on the collective life of believers. For that reason phenomena of pneumatism if not completely absent from Christianity in Jerusalem were in any case very rare and played no part comparable to that which they did in Paul's Christianity. Christian eschatology in Jerusalem, however, was not the same as Jewish eschatology. It differs in at least one important aspect. The Messiah who would bring in the Kingdom was not an ideal and expected person whom the people were waiting for; he was a personality known and beloved; Christians were not waiting for his coming but for his return; they could well recollect his character in a concrete fashion and so regarded him as their pattern whom they must imitate in their whole moral life. While this entailed a certain attenuation in the futuristic character of their eschatology it meant that they could not have immediate experience of Christ's action and consequently of the reality of the kingdom of heaven. This still remained an object of hope and not of experience.[1]

The simultaneous neutralisation and spiritualisation of pneumatism and eschatology were revolutionary processes which changed the outward form of Christian religion. But this profound change did not create any disturbance or cause any crisis,[2] while, thanks to the realisation of eschatology and the spiritualisation of pneumatism at the hands of Paul the religious dynamic which belonged to them

---

[1] Jesus' eschatology differs both from Paul's and that of Christianity in Jerusalem. It may be described as an eschatology reinforced by the conviction, which John Baptist's also possessed, that the age of the Law and the prophets had come to an end (Matt. xi. 13; Luke xvi. 16) and that a new age had begun. The Kingdom of God had come (Mark i. 15). The current translation, 'The Kingdom of God is at hand', is not accurate. It must be translated, 'is come'; the meaning is that a decisive fact has happened, the kingdom is nearer than it was before. In addition to this Jesus was certain that the kingdom was being realised not only because he put his trust in the promises of God but also because his certitude sprang directly from his intimate communion which he felt he had with God continuously in his life. This was equivalent to the pneumatic experience completely devoid, however, of any ecstatic element. In the second half of his ministry, when his prophetic consciousness had become Messianic, there was added the conviction that through his sufferings he would realise the conditions which must be fulfilled if it was to be possible for the Kingdom of God to come (see *V. de J.*, pp. 306 ff. and *Life of Jesus*, pp. 390 ff.). This is equivalent to eschatology becoming realised in a peculiar form.

[2] Certain enemies of Christianity (either from without or heretics) attacked the teaching of the church on the ground that the prophecies referring to the parousia had not been fulfilled (2 Peter iii. 3-10. Cf. 1 Clem. xxiii. 3 f.; 2 Clem. xi. 2-4) but it is sufficient to look at the reply made by the author of 2 Peter when he says that for God a thousand years are as a day to see that the author has no expectations of the parousia at all and is quite untouched by the objection.

did not evaporate but assumed new forms which were better adapted to the needs of a society which was destined to have a long life before it.

The disappearance of pneumatism would have involved the disappearance of Christianity itself if the conviction and conception of authority as well as the spiritual power expressed in pneumatism had not found a new equilibrium.

7.—THE EVOLUTION OF THE IDEA OF AUTHORITY

Jesus, without ever rejecting the authority of the Old Testament, went behind the letter of scripture and found the living authority of God with whom he lived in close communion. The whole Christian conception of authority reflects this double aspect of the position of Jesus. The authority of the Old Testament remained in its entirety[1] as it always had been but to it another was added springing from the prophetic authority which Jesus was convinced he himself possessed. His disciples and those who were converted by them accepted this authority in the same way as those had done who were with him during his ministry but it had become infinitely greater and transcendent in character through faith in the resurrection. In addition the principle of imitating Jesus played an important part. The authority of his sayings gave birth to the idea of Jesus as legislator, an idea which did not altogether correspond to historical fact.[2]

Paul never invokes the sayings of Jesus to establish and defend his interpretation of the drama of redemption except in 1 Corinthians xi. 23 ff. where he is giving directions concerning the Lord's Supper and is trying to correct errors in the manner of celebrating it which had happened at Corinth. He is very much more interested in Jesus as Saviour rather than as teacher or preacher and finds the supreme authority in Jesus not in what he said but in what he had become after his glorification and in what he had achieved through the drama of his death and resurrection. All this has been revealed to him by God through his Son (Gal. i. 16), a revelation which began with the christophany which produced his conversion and had been continued ever afterwards in his life 'in Christ', which was a life

---

[1] In fact the authority of the Old Testament is only formal, being material for allegorical exegesis at first, then through usage the whole theology of the church comes to depend on it.

[2] It is sufficient to recall the part played by the 'commandment of the Lord' in Paul (1 Cor. vii. 10, 25) and by the Sermon on the Mount in Matthew's gospel.

inspired, directed, and maintained by the activity of the Lord, who is the Spirit.

Although the Spirit was the supreme authority in Paul's life as a Christian and consequently in his theology, yet there was another foundation to his faith in addition to an entirely subjective revelation. The existence of a Christian community was no negligible factor in his conversion and influenced the formation of his thought as a Christian. It led him, instead of founding a new religion on the basis of his revelations, to give his loyalty to a religion which was already in existence. Paul accepted the authority of the Spirit as in some degree objective because a close connection existed between this Spirit which he identified both with Christ glorified (2 Cor. iii. 17) and the historic Jesus of Galilee. The authority of the Spirit could not therefore be separated from that of a historic tradition which received a religious and theological interpretation.[1]

Thus we find in every form of primitive Christian thought known to us an objective and a subjective element combined, a historical tradition and a religious interpretation. This gave Christianity the feeling of dependence upon a sacred history, i.e. a history made up of events which faith judged to be acts of God. An objectivity was in this way given to faith which prevented Christianity from deteriorating into subjective revelation while at the same time the disappearance of inspiration was compensated for by an enlargement in the part played by tradition.

The conception of authority prevailing in the last third of the first century which remained the same in character in all subsequent development contains the same elements as existed in the primitive period but organised in a different manner. Some of them are strengthened and accentuated; others have become attenuated or transposed. All have been adapted to meet a new situation. The authority of the tradition, especially of the doctrinal tradition, had become perceptibly stronger. In the Pastoral epistles inspiration has become a principle of conservation. This fact corresponds to the inversion which took place in the course of the second generation between experience and form, when loyalty to the form of words

---

[1] This combination of two aspects of authority is found in a less precise form in the collective conscience of the church. This is particularly to be seen in the synoptic gospels. They contain a historic tradition which in the form and shape in which it is presented expresses a doctrine. The speeches of Peter in the book of the Acts are similar to this, as in them historical evidence as to what Jesus was during his ministry and spiritual witness to his resurrection are closely associated with each other (see p. 62).

became the condition of experience and participation in salvation. The weakening in experience which this inversion expresses corresponds to a decline in the spiritual level of the life of the church, which seems to be in accordance with a law that, what a religious society gains in extension it loses in intensity and fervour. Yet the principal cause of what is here to be found is more general in character. No religion can live without being convinced that it is absolute; it is thus compelled to maintain its unchanging character throughout the ages and in spite of all the changes which time brings. The authority used to justify doctrinal conceptions in this way becomes a conserving and not a creative principle, a source of immobility rather than change.

This transformation was at least foreshadowed as early as the first generation. While Paul in preaching the gospel aimed primarily at what might be called a spiritual contagion and counted only on the action of the Spirit and the power of God for success in his preaching, it is none the less true, that in his missionary activities he made extensive use of certain formulae and very largely devoted himself to teaching a doctrine. The conquest of men's intelligences was not the end in view but through the force of circumstances themselves was one of the means he used. The further we get away from the creative period the more important became this element in preaching.

In the second generation this transformation gave a new character to the forms of doctrine and the system which explicitly or implicitly contained them. Detached from experience they came to express an objective truth and tended to become co-ordinated with other elements of secular knowledge which believers might think they possessed, whatever was their origin; consequently they tended to become all-embracing explanations of God, the world, man, and his position before God and in the world. But this movement did not end in making a philosophical system. As van der Leeuw[1] rightly observes, however rational and objective may be the form in which a religious doctrine is expressed, it can never be entirely the same as a philosophy or system of ideas. It is possible to suppose and conceive that it would cease to be a religious doctrine if it was not also an object of belief and became detached from all subjective spiritual experience. On the religious level it only has value so far as it is a confession of faith, i.e. so far as it determines a certain spiritual attitude and possesses the character of an act of worship, taking the word worship in its widest sense.

[1] Van der Leeuw, *Phenom. d. Red.*, p. 421.

By assuming an objective character, doctrine is both detached from the experience which gave birth to it and the personality who formulated it. It loses its personal character to become the expression of the thought of a society. The result of this process inevitably involves both a declension in thought and a marked decline in the spiritual level. A comparison between Paulinism and Post-Paulinism shows this. In the latter we do not find the same rigour of thought, spiritual power, and mystical intensity, as are to be found in the former. But what is in reality the result of a law of the development of a religion cannot be described as its degeneration or decadence. A religion can only originate from a personal experience[1] but it must be added that, if it is to expand beyond the limits of an individual ephemeral life, its individual character must be effaced and replaced by a collective character. This implies a sacrifice but without it the most original and profoundest experience is destined to remain sterile. 'Except a corn of wheat fall into the ground and die it abideth alone; but if it die it bringeth forth much fruit' (John xii. 24). When the individual experience is effaced it becomes ripe for collective religion.

We must not lose sight of this if we wish to appreciate properly what is especially to be seen in the pastoral epistles. They present the idea of a deposit of doctrine received by the church and to which assent must be given in order to be saved. The belief that an immutable doctrine was necessary was strengthened by the reactions which the first heresies caused. At first they were instinctive but became sharper and more systematic in form, as heresies became more sharply opposed to doctrine propounded by men who arrogated to themselves the right to speak in the name of the church although they probably consisted only of a minority. To fight heresy it became necessary both to define and rationalise doctrine and in particular to ascribe to it an authority and origin which put it outside the pale of discussion.

The position of the pastoral epistles on this point is still somewhat hesitating. They show the conception of a sacred doctrine of which the church is the guardian. Care must be taken in transmitting it that nothing is altered, but no account is given of the circumstances and conditions in which it was entrusted to the church. The fiction attributing the letters to Paul is sufficient as it puts the 'sound doctrine' under apostolic patronage. Afterwards the theory is more sharply defined as the doctrine of apostleship grows according to

[1] Van der Leeuw, *Phenom. d. Red.*, p. 626.

which the Spirit was entrusted to the apostles, giving them a commission to found the church and therefore first of all to preach the
gospel which implied formulating, i.e. establishing the doctrine. The
true doctrine is that of the apostles and the only valid and legitimate
organisation belonging to the church is that given to it by the
apostles.[1] There is a close correlation between the two things: as
is shown by the pastoral epistles and a little later on by the epistles
of Ignatius; the ecclesiastical organisation is called into being to
defend the true doctrine against the innovations of heretics and this
is one of the essential functions of its ministers.

The fact that a certain type of doctrine itself created an authority
which rapidly gained the supremacy reacted on the other forms of
authority known to the first generation. In this phase of development in Christian thought the sayings of Jesus were no more used
just to stimulate efforts towards sanctification and to solve such
practical questions as arose in the life of the church and the individual Christian but to establish and justify doctrines. Signs of this
change are perceptible in the synoptics but they are expressed with
some reserve. While it is said that Jesus instructed his disciples on
the necessity of his sufferings and death, it is also explained that
they were only able to understand what was said to them after his
resurrection when they had received the Holy Spirit. In the Fourth
Gospel what the author considers to be true doctrine makes up the
substance of the speeches put into the mouth of Jesus. Not until we
come to the epistle to the Hebrews (ii. 3) do we find the idea explicitly stated that Jesus preached the doctrine of salvation which
those who heard him had to repeat afterwards.[2] This idea, however,
was not the one which subsequently prevailed, striking as the
justification would have been which it would have given to doctrine.
For that to happen they were too keenly aware of the difference between the teaching of Jesus and the Christian message,
i.e. between the *Evangelium Christi* preached by Jesus and the
Evangelium de Christo, the doctrine of salvation through the death
and resurrection of Jesus, which was the entire content of the
apostolic preaching.

---

[1] See *E.P.*, pp. 86 ff.

[2] It may be asked if we have not an idea like this in 1 Tim. vi. 3 which makes
an attack on 'anybody who teaches otherwise (than the church) and consents not
to wholesome words, even the words of our Lord Jesus Christ, and to the doctrine
which is according to godliness'; but as the following verses emphasise the moral
consequences of heresy the sayings of Jesus seem to be thought of here primarily
as ethical rules.

The various forms of authority which found a place in the stabilised church were reunited into one bundle by the doctrine of the apostolate which was modified to satisfy new conditions. Doctrine became the apostles' teaching and, while at first bishops, who claimed to be guarantors that the doctrine was faithfully transmitted, were not regarded as the successors of the apostles, they were at any rate according to the theory of Clement of Rome considered to be the legitimate successors of the first bishops, who had received their charge from the apostles.[1]

The system was completed and defined in the course of the second century when gnosticism and marcionitism endangered the church. The function of bishops and that of the confession of the faith then became all important. The conception of apostolic authority received clear and concrete form in the idea of a sacred Scripture of the New Covenant. This we can see definitely appearing in the last third of the second century onwards.[2] All these developments were placed under apostolic patronage. The apostles were reckoned to have been the first bishops. The confession of the faith which was the primitive baptismal symbol of the church of Rome in a slightly developed form became the apostolic symbol. The New Testament was conceived to be a collection of apostolic books. This was the end of a process of development which began with nascent Christianity, a movement of enthusiasm dominated by the idea that the world was soon coming to an end and ended in early Catholicism, i.e. in an organised church with established doctrine and institutions.

[1] See *E.P.*, pp. 68 ff.
[2] The canon of the New Testament was set up from this time forward with the four gospels, the book of Acts, Paul's epistles, the first epistle of Peter and the first epistle of John to which the Apocalypse was sometimes added. The exact delimitation of the collection was only slowly made with considerable care.

CHAPTER II

The Conflict between Jewish and Gentile Christianity

I.—PAUL AND THE CHURCH AT JERUSALEM UP TO 43-44

HARNACK could say that nothing in the New Testament bears more clearly the marks of Jewish Christianity than the eleventh chapter of the epistle to the Romans,[1] and yet, during the whole of his career, especially from 44 onwards, Paul was in conflict not only with Judaism but also with Jewish Christianity at Jerusalem which remained faithful to the Jewish law. As we have already seen[2] the circumstances which gave rise to Paul's conversion caused Paul to break with the doctrine that man could become justified by keeping the law, which while he was a Jew by religion he considered to be the guarantee of salvation. Through meditating on the problem of the law, which was thus forced on his attention, he became convinced that it had ceased to be of any value as a means to salvation. In this way he became the exponent of universalism in its widest sense although he was not its only representative. Independently of him, before even he became a Christian, the Hellenists, who were driven away from Jerusalem, founded a church at Antioch, in which Christians of Jewish origin and converted Gentiles who did not observe the law lived side by side without any friction for a period of fifteen years, i.e. until they were disturbed from outside. Paul, however, and other representatives of Gentile Christianity seem to have differed on one point. The latter seem to have acted from instinct and impulse and not to have shown themselves intransigent towards those who wished to maintain Christianity within the framework of Judaism, while Paul gave universalism a dogmatic foundation in the light of which he judged any attempt to compel converted Gentiles to keep the law a betrayal of the gospel. In defending his ideas he gave no consideration to opportunism. He was not concerned to make bridges.

[1] Harnack, *Dgsch.*, I, p. 318 (n. 2 on p. 317).   [2] See pp. 212 ff.

It is not therefore a matter of luck that the documents which have survived to tell of the conflict between Jewish Christianity and Gentile Christianity which began at Antioch at the end of 43 represent it to be almost a personal quarrel between Paul on the one side and Peter and James on the other. Baur and his school,[1] it is true, exaggerated the importance of the conflict; it may be that the majority of the faithful were not interested in it, as they thought, but it is quite certain that in re-acting from the exaggerations of the Tubingen school subsequent scholars have underestimated its significance.

On Paul's relations with the church at Jerusalem up to 44 we have two sources of information: (1) the epistle to the Galatians and (2) the story in the book of Acts. The evidence from the epistle to the Galatians may be described as tendacious in the sense that the purpose of the story given by Paul (i. 15-ii. 10) is to show that he does not hold his apostleship from the church at Jerusalem. Both in his selection of the facts and in the manner of his presentation Paul is telling his story to demonstrate a thesis; but we can be quite sure that the facts narrated are accurate for this reason. Paul had to weigh very carefully his record on every point narrated by him because, if he had made any statement which was not absolutely correct, his adversaries would not have failed to score off him. Paul may not have told everything[2] but what he has told must be retained. The story in Acts was written a long time after the events had happened at a time when the situation had completely changed. The author had at his disposal only material of unequal value and much of it was mediocre in quality. He elaborated and moulded it to fit a conception of the origins of the church which he formed from what he found it to be between 80 and 90. Therefore, when the two sources contradict there is no doubt that preference must be given to the epistle to the Galatians.

In the beginning of this epistle Paul recollects the circumstances

---

[1] Concerning Baur and his system see H. Schmidt-J. Huassleiter, 'Baur' (F-C.), *R.E.* II, pp. 467-483; K. Bauer, 'Baur' (F-C), *R.G.G.* I, cols. 818-828 and especially A. Schweitzer, *Paul and his interpreters*, pp. vi. f., 12 ff. Of Baur's works I will only mention the first sketch which he gave of his system (*Die Christus-partei in der korinthischen Gemeinde Der Gegensatz des paulinischen und petrinischen Christentum. Der Apostel Paulus in Rom. Tub. Zeitschr. f. Theol.*, 1831, 4, pp. 51-136) and the book in which he develops his system, *Paulus, der Apostel Jesu Christi. Ein Beitrag zu einer kritischen Geschichte des Urchristentums*, Stuttgart, 1845, second edition revised by Ed. Zeller, Leipzig, 1866-87.

[2] We shall see further on that Paul passes over some important points with extreme rapidity. There may be some which he passes over in silence.

which led to his conversion and then declares that he did not confer with flesh and blood nor did he go up to Jerusalem to those who were apostles before him but that he went into Arabia and then returned to Damascus (i. 16-17). To confer with flesh and blood would mean to come to Jerusalem and to ask the first apostles to confirm his vocation and complete his instruction as a Christian. Paul mentions first, not what he did but what he did not do after his conversion because he wishes to correct the description which had been given to the Galatians of his relations with the church at Jerusalem.[1]

Only three years later he came to Jerusalem and made contact with Cephas.[2] He saw also James but none other of the apostles[3] and stayed there only fifteen days (Gal. i. 18-20). The particularly solemn manner in which he affirms the truth of his story by calling God to witness shows that he wants to correct the story of his relations

[1] Traces of this tendacious narrative are to be found in the story in Acts which passes over in silence the journey to Arabia and makes Paul come to Jerusalem immediately after his conversion (ix. 26). In my book, *L'apôtre Paul et Jesus-Christ*, pp. 53 f., I have contended that this journey was not historical. Actually three visits to Jerusalem are mentioned in Acts while Galatians says that there were only two. I now think that the visit mentioned in Acts xi. 27-30; xii. 25 must be reckoned to be a doublet of the one mentioned at the beginning of Acts xv. This is post-dated as the letter sent by the apostles and elders to the Gentile Churches after the conference is only addressed to the churches in Antioch, Syria, and Cilicia and ignores those founded by Paul and Barnabas in the course of the missionary journey which is recounted in chapters xiv and xv of Acts. On the other hand the motive given for the journey made by Paul and Barnabas to Jerusalem in Acts xi. 27-30 (to bring relief from the church in Antioch) cannot be accounted as historical. If that had been the reason why Paul and Barnabas visited Jerusalem in 44, would they have been asked 'to remember the poor' (Gal. ii. 10) and even then, if they had done so, would not Paul when he mentioned this request have not said that he had not waited to be asked to think of them? The author of the book of Acts appears to have had two sources at his disposal, a tradition in Antioch which gave a summary account of the despatch of Paul and Barnabas to Jerusalem and an account of the conference which came from Jerusalem. He failed to recognise that these two sources referred to the same journey and on that account he placed one before Paul's first missionary journey and the other after it. This explanation of things seems much closer to the truth than that of Lyder Brun ('Apostelkonzil und Aposteldekret', L. Brun *und* A. Fridrichsen, *Paulus und die Urgemeinde*, Giessen, 1921, p. 2) who suggests that the journey mentioned in Acts xi. 30 was made by Barnabas alone and that the relief sent by the church at Antioch gave to the Christians in Jerusalem the idea of asking Paul to interest the other Gentile churches in the difficult situation in which they were fixed.

[2] The verb ἱστορῆσαι which is used here is found fairly frequently in classical Greek and in the papyri. It means to examine, to become acquainted with, more rarely to make enquiries of. The last meaning cannot be accepted here as παρὰ Κηφᾷ and not Κηφᾶν would then be needed.

[3] Concerning the interpretation of this text see p. 111, n. 3.

with Jerusalem which had been given to the Galatians. Why did Paul make his first visit to Jerusalem in such secrecy? Was it that his sharp *volte-face* would have so annoyed the Jews that it would have been dangerous for him to show himself in Jerusalem? This may be true, but at the same time the fact that he did not disclose his visit to members of the church compels one to suppose that the Christians in Jerusalem even then felt some prejudice against him. Possibly they reproached him for having failed to show respect to the Twelve in not coming to them immediately after his conversion. Perhaps also they did not entirely approve of the way in which he had preached the gospel in Arabia. It may be that Paul came to Jerusalem because he desired to adjust his relations with the mother church so as to be able to devote himself without any qualms to the evangelisation of the Gentiles. We may then suppose that he only gives the visit a brief mention because he failed to get from it all he hoped for.

Concerning the following ten years Paul only says that he stayed in Syria and Cilicia and that the churches in Judaea, to whom he was unknown by face, glorified God because he now preached the faith which previously he had persecuted (i. 20-24). The brevity of this note is explained by the fact that nothing important took place affecting Paul's relations with the church in Jerusalem during this period.

2.—THE CONFERENCE AT JERUSALEM

At the end of 43 or at the beginning of 44 Paul came back to Jerusalem with Barnabas; they brought with them Titus, a Gentile who had been converted and remained uncircumcised. This journey was undertaken in accordance with a revelation. This must mean that a revelation showed Paul that the best way of resolving the question which had just arisen at Antioch was to discuss it with the authorities of the church at Jerusalem. He was concerned about the position of Gentile converts and their obligations with respect to the law. Paul does not say so because his readers were as aware of it as he himself was. The person of Titus was the incarnation of the problem. Would the Christians in Jerusalem regard Titus as a brother although he was uncircumcised or would they demand that he must be circumcised? In that case would Paul give way to them or would he bring on a rupture? The situation was grave; compromise seemed impossible.

Paul realised perfectly well that if he refused to budge, a rupture with Jerusalem would bring grave consequences in its train on his labours. He wanted to prevent his missionary activities from being clogged and sterilised. Also how could he resign himself to the church, i.e. the body of Christ being divided?[1] But against this he was convinced that to agree to circumcision being imposed on the Gentiles was to betray the gospel. For to do so would be to admit that salvation could depend on other causes and conditions besides the cross of Christ.

Our information concerning the position of the Christians in Jerusalem is not so direct. Their loyalty to the Jewish law, it seems, must have prevented them from making any concessions. Yet they did not resign themselves to a rupture but, at the risk of not being followed by the mass of the faithful in Jerusalem and unable to ignore the fact that their gesture would present practical problems the solution of which they could not yet see, they consented to offer to Barnabas and Paul 'hands of fellowship'. What they had done in spite of its leaving an irreducible opposition behind it must have given them the conviction of a deep unity which nothing could break because both parties felt that they had the same Lord and worshipped the same Lord in the same way.

The story of what happened at Jerusalem which is given in the epistle to the Galatians is not easy to follow, both because it is somewhat abrupt owing to the emotional state in which Paul was when he wrote it and also because it passes over certain points very quickly in spite of their importance.

Paul says, 'I communicated unto them that gospel which I preach among the Gentiles but privately ($\kappa\alpha\tau'$ $\imath\delta\iota\alpha\nu$) to them which were of reputation' (ii. 2).[2] The two clauses of the sentence cannot refer to the same act because the particle makes a contrast between them and it would be hardly natural for the same people to be referred to first of all by the vague term 'them' and then immediately afterwards by the more precise term 'those who were of reputation'. The only term which 'them' can refer to in what precedes it is the word 'Jerusalem'. Paul therefore must have begun by communicating his gospel to an assembly of the church at Jerusalem. As he says

[1] See my article, 'Quelques remarques sur l'unite de l'Eglise dans le christianisme primitif', *Bull. de la Fac. libre de theol. protest. de Paris*, May 1936, pp. 1-9.

[2] The expression 'them which were of reputation' ($\delta\iota$ $\delta o\kappa o\hat{\upsilon}\nu\tau\epsilon s$) in classical Greek (cf. Bauer, *Worterb.*, s.v. $\delta o\kappa\epsilon\omega$) frequently means the authorities. Paul does not seem to be applying the term here to the leaders of the church. He is using it somewhat ironically. Like the term 'pillars' it must have been a customary designation. On one occasion Paul adds to the words $\epsilon\hat{\iota}\nu\alpha\iota$ $\tau\iota$ (those who seemed to be somewhat) $\delta\iota$ $\delta o\kappa o\hat{\upsilon}\nu\tau\epsilon s$ (ii. 6); on another occasion he adds $\sigma\tau\nu\lambda o\iota$ $\epsilon\hat{\iota}\nu\alpha\iota$ (who seemed to be pillars) (ii. 9).

nothing of the way in which they received it, it can only be presumed that they did not receive it as he desired and expected. The church at Jerusalem refused to recognise what Paul preached as the gospel. He did not allow himself to be discouraged but more or less on his own authority held private conversations with the leaders of the church at Jerusalem in order to try and turn the check which he had just endured into a success of some kind.

Paul does not retrace the ups and downs of the discussions, doubtless because he did not wish to show what resistance he encountered, but he goes so far as to make an allusion to 'false brethren'[1] to whom he refused to make any concessions even of a provisional nature.[2] In a jerky style which shows how hot the strife must have been, Paul states the results of the conversations. His statement is moderate because he does not want to revive a controversy which he wishes to consider closed and also because if he gave the story in greater detail he would have had to recollect what powerful and tenacious resistance he met which limited the positive results gained by him. Incomplete as they were, however, they were not negligible. Paul made no concession and Titus was not circumcised; nevertheless the pillars of the church, James, Cephas, and John offered hands

[1] Paul says that 'false brethren were unawares brought in to spy out our liberty which we have in Christ Jesus' (ii. 4). This seems to refer to those who raised the question of circumcision in the church at Antioch and returned to Jerusalem to fight Paul there. Apparently they were members of the church at Jerusalem. The expression 'those who were brought in' does not seem then to refer to what they did at Jerusalem since they were not strangers brought in there but Paul was the stranger. Paul uses the expression because he is thinking of those who were brought into the churches in Galatia to stir up trouble in them.

[2] Some scholars think that Paul would have agreed to Titus being circumcised. In Gal. ii. 3 f. he says that Titus was not compelled to be circumcised but he mentions false brethren and says (according to the text of the great majority of manuscripts and versions, which is also the reading adopted by the editors) 'I did not yield to them, even for an hour'. The negative is omitted by D, some Latin versions (d.e.) Tertullian, Victorinus, Ambrosius, and the Peschitto. In spite of the weakness of this evidence certain critics (Renan, Lake, Spitta, Johannes Weiss) prefer this reading. The only gain in this reading is that it destroys an anacolouthon but it is well known that anacoloutha are frequent in Paul's writings. If we adopt this reading it must mean that Paul, in the hope of conciliation, made a concession without Titus being compelled in any way but he did not consider that it constituted a precedent. In support of this interpretation Acts xvi. 3 can be quoted which says that Paul circumcised Timothy. But it has already been seen (p. 218, n. 3) Acts cannot be used as good evidence on this point. It must be added that, if Paul had been perhaps not disloyal to his principles but at any rate so inconsistent as to allow Titus to be circumcised, this fact would have been brought up against him by his opponents in Galatia and Paul would have been compelled to defend himself on the point. The text of the majority of the manuscripts must therefore be retained and we must suppose that Titus was not circumcised.

of fellowship and recognised that he had received a commission to preach the gospel to the Gentiles as Peter had received his commission to preach it to the Jews. The only demand made upon him, which he recognised as reasonable, was to remember the poor, i.e. to impress upon the Gentile Churches their duty to come to the material aid of the church in Jerusalem (ii. 3-10).[1]

Paul came to Jerusalem accompanied by Barnabas who had been named with him as a delegate by the church at Antioch. But in the story in the epistle to the Galatians Barnabas is scarcely named and Paul speaks as if he came alone to defend the case of Gentile Christianity. Is this only because in the crisis in Galatia which led him to refer to the conference only his authority and not Barnabas' was concerned? Or was it because when they were in Jerusalem Barnabas did not defend the cause of Christian liberty with the same energy and firmness as Paul? Or perhaps when Paul was writing to the Galatians Barnabas was not so firm as at first when he was under the influence of Paul? There may be some truth in each of these explanations.

The results of the conference must not be misunderstood. They were in the main negative; a schism which would have been disastrous was avoided. The problem which had arisen was not solved. No arrangements had been made to place the relations between Jewish and Gentile Christians on an organised basis and the concessions made to Paul were only authorised by leading personalities who were not followed by the mass of the faithful as they did not agree with them. What success Paul had in 44 was mainly negative in character and less complete than the account in the epistle to the Galatians would lead us to believe.[2]

The account of the conference given in chapter xv of Acts cannot be easily harmonised with that given in the epistle to the Galatians. It lacks homogeneity. First of all it tells how on Paul's return to Antioch from their first missionary journey people came from Judaea[3] and stirred up trouble among the converted Gentiles by telling them that they could not be saved if they were not circumcised according to the Law of Moses. Paul and Barnabas withstood this demand and, as apparently they could not come to terms, it

---

[1] Concerning Paul's response to this demand see *E.P.*, p. 167 and my article, 'La collecte en faveur des Saints à Jerusalem', *R.h.p.r.*, 1925, V, pp. 301-318.

[2] Guignebert, *Le Christ*, p. 308.

[3] We cannot know from the text whether they were people from Jerusalem who had come to Antioch for private purposes or whether they had been sent by James to exercise pressure on the church.

was decided that Paul and Barnabas and some others[1] should go
up to Jerusalem to confer with the apostles and elders on the issue[2]
(xv. 1-2). Paul and Barnabas gave an account of the results of their
missionary activities without apparently any reference to the problem
which had arisen at Antioch and for solving which they had come
to Jerusalem. After they had been heard some converted Pharisees
got up and maintained that Gentiles must be circumcised and
taught to observe the law of Moses (xv. 6). This feature in an artificial way refers back to what was said in verse 1 about Judaeans
coming to Antioch.[3] No mention is made of any opposition to this
contention on the part of Paul and Barnabas. It is said that the
apostles and elders met together to examine the point at issue. A
great debate took place but we are not given any clear picture of
what course it took or any account of those who took part in it. The
narrative only mentions how Peter and James intervened. Peter
recalls the conversion of Cornelius and gives vent to ideas which
are nothing else but Paul's doctrine of justification by faith (xv. 6-11).
Then Paul and Barnabas, without actually intervening in the debate,
give an account of the signs and wonders which God had done on
their mission (xv. 12). This forms a doublet to verse 4. Next James
declares that they must not trouble the converted Gentiles further
but that in order to avoid giving offence to the Jews they must ask
them to refrain from things sacrificed to idols, from marrying within
the degrees prohibited by the Jewish law,[4] and from eating both
things strangled and blood[5] (xv. 13-21). James' proposition is

[1] We cannot tell if the others were other members of the church at Antioch or
if they were those who had come from Judaea and had been maintaining circumcision to be necessary.

[2] The Eastern text which is to be preferred leaves it open whether they came
to discuss the question with the apostles and elders or to submit it to their decision.
The Western text gives the latter interpretation but it must be considered to be a
secondary reading.

[3] The Western text identifies the Pharisees of Jerusalem with the Judaeans who
came to Antioch but in such a way that it is plainly a gloss.

[4] In defence of the meaning given by me to the word πορνεία see Strack-
Billerbeck, II, pp. 729 ff.; Bentley (cf. Resch, *Das Aposteldekret nach seiner ausserkanonischen Textgestalt*, Leipzig, 1905, p. 20) and later independently of him,
Joseph Halévy (*Notes évangéliques, IV. Le concile de Jérusalem et sa décision, Rev.
sémitique*, 1902, X, pp. 228 ff.) made an ingenious suggestion that πορνεία should
be amended to πορκεία (pork). The meaning would be satisfactory but it is difficult to suppose that the same textual error would happen in three passages (xv.
20, 29; xxi. 25).

[5] For the reasons which compel us to adopt the Eastern text and follow it here
see *Introd.* III, pp. 91 ff. The Western text was revised at a time when the importance of the Jewish ritual for the first generation of Christians had ceased to be

adopted and a letter drawn up to inform them of it. Judas, Barnabas, and Silas are chosen to take the letter and accompany Paul and Barnabas to Antioch.

We have already noted[1] that the idea that Silas was a delegate sent to Antioch is open to suspicion, because after his return to Jerusalem has been mentioned, he is found again at Antioch where Paul takes him as a collaborator. A more serious reason for refusing to place any reliance on the story in Acts is that, when Paul came for the last time to Jerusalem, James informed him, as though he did not know it before, of the decisions which according to Acts xv were taken at Jerusalem, when Paul was present and even gave his assent to them (xxi. 25).

The story in Acts xv combines two traditions, one referring to the conference of 43-44, the other to a decision which the church at Jerusalem made at a much later date to fix a minimum of ritual observance for Gentile converts to agree to keep in order that Christians of Jewish origin might be able to enter into relations with them. When the two traditions were fused that concerning the conference at Jerusalem was bound to have been altered.

What were the positive results of the conference at Jerusalem? Paul says, 'For they who seemed to be somewhat added nothing to me: But contrariwise, when they saw that the gospel of the un-circumcision was committed unto me, as the gospel of the circum-cision was unto Peter (For he that wrought effectually in Peter to the apostleship of the circumcision, the same was mighty in me toward the Gentiles;) and when James, Cephas, and John, who seemed to be pillars, perceived the grace that was given unto me, they gave to me and Barnabas the right hand of fellowship; that we should go unto the heathen and they unto the circumcision'. This text is somewhat harsh in tone, which shows what an emotional state Paul was in, when he wrote it. It raises many questions which cannot always be answered with complete assurance. Are Paul and Cephas mentioned here as individuals or as the representatives of two missionary groups? The fact that of the Jerusalem party Paul mentions only Peter would incline one to the former interpretation,

---

understood; by suppressing things strangled and adding the precept 'not to do to others what one would not wish to be done to oneself' the reviser of D. trans-formed ritual rules into a little moral catechism. The rule, 'Do not . . .' is shown to be an addition by the fact that an imperative is used, although what precedes is in the infinitive. Logically the Western text would presume what is an absurdity, viz. that murder and adultery were regarded as permissible in the Greek churches before the church at Jerusalem intervened.　　　　[1] See p. 183, n. 2.

while the fact that the right hand of fellowship was offered, not only to Paul, but also to Barnabas would incline one to decide in favour of the latter. According to Acts xv Paul and Barnabas both came to Jerusalem to defend the thesis that converted Gentiles should not be compelled to observe the Jewish ritual law. Paul therefore was not alone in pleading his cause any more than Cephas was on the other side. Only we have to take into account the fact that according to Paul's report of the incident at Antioch[1] in Galatians ii. 11 f. Barnabas does not seem to have been as wholehearted as Paul but to have been ready to agree to concessions and accept a compromise. This may be the reason why Paul considered himself to be, if not alone, at any rate the most authentic representative of the mission to the Gentiles and that is why he states that he was the only one to refuse to yield to any demand that the Gentiles should observe even the minimum of the Mosaic law. Perhaps Peter is named as the only representative of the mission to the Jews because he had been the only one of the three pillars of the church to evangelise outside Jerusalem and Judaea.

But the most important and delicate of all the questions raised by the story of the conference at Jerusalem concerns the distinction made between the gospel of the circumcision and that of the uncircumcision.[2] It is often supposed that we are merely concerned here with a division of missionary work and this interpretation may be supported by the fact that, while it is possible to conceive of the idea of a double apostolate, it is much more difficult to attribute to Paul the idea of two gospels, i.e. if we assume from what he states in Galatians i. 6 that there is no other gospel than that which he has preached to the Galatians. But the idea of a division in the missionary work meets with serious difficulties. Jews and Gentiles were not strictly separated from each other. There were Gentiles in Palestine and many synagogues in the diaspora. Although Paul considered that he had been chosen by God to preach the gospel to the Gentiles he was neither on theological nor practical grounds prevented from addressing himself to the Jews as well. That there was no theological reason preventing him may be seen from Romans i. 16 where Paul wishes to define what the gospel is and says

---

[1] Paul does not say exactly when this incident happened. It seems to have occurred after the missionary journey which Paul and Barnabas made together and is recounted in chapters viii and xiv of Acts.

[2] On this question see Fridrichsen's very suggestive article, 'The Apostle and his message', *Inbiundningar till Dokordpromotionerna*, Uppsala, 1947.

that it is the redemptive power of God for the Jew first and then for the Gentile. This shows that Paul not only had no idea that he was prevented from preaching to the Jews but also that he did not feel himself free to preach to the Gentiles until he had been rejected by the Jews. The practical grounds are that, when Paul arrived at a town where he had no connections, he used the service in the synagogue as an opportunity for addressing part of the population, i.e. Jews and proselytes or simply sympathisers with Judaism, who *a priori* must have been the people most accessible to his preaching.

Fridrichsen proposed to make the distinction between the two apostolates not ethnic but geographical. To Peter would have been apportioned the evangelisation of Palestine, to Paul the Jewish world. But Paul's complaint against those who came and disturbed the churches in Galatia was not that they had violated the agreement concluded at Jerusalem but that they had come and insinuated themselves into churches which they had not founded.

Fridrichsen rightly emphasised that the two conceptions of apostolate and gospel are interrelated with each other. The apostle is the man who has received a message and has been given the duty of transmitting it. If there are two apostolates there must be two gospels. In actual fact, the gospel which was preached to the Gentiles contained elements which were not of necessity in the gospel as it was preached to the Jews. When Christian preachers were giving their message to Jews they did not ask them to give up all their old hopes and beliefs but only to acknowledge that their hopes had been realised in the person of Jesus Christ. When Paul refers to the conversion of the Thessalonians he speaks of the way in which they had turned towards God by turning away from dumb idols to serve the living and true God (1 Thess. i. 9). We have here a negative element which had no place in the conversion of a Jew.

But between Paul's and Peter's gospel[1] there is a difference and Fridrichsen is right to insist on this. Paul's christology of the Kurios is not the same as the Jerusalem christology of the Messiah, with the result that there is a gospel of Paul differing from Peter's. Fridrichsen is also right in finding in this christology the real foundation of universalism. Jesus who in his pre-existence was Messiah and Son of God was by being glorified raised to the rank

[1] We are using this name in a somewhat conventional and symbolic way as in fact we do not know what really was Peter's theology.

of Lord of the universe. This was what enraged Jewish particularism and constituted the message which the gospel was able to bring to the Gentiles.

Account has to be taken of these considerations to appreciate the significance of the conference at Jerusalem. It did not resolve the problem which was then raised but, what was a great advance, it prevented a rupture, the consequences of which would have been catastrophic, and it secured a principle which was destined to assure Christianity its full autonomy while at the same time it maintained its spiritual contact with Judaism and appropriated its religious heritage. But much time had yet to pass and Paul had to suffer in many struggles before the cause of universalism and freedom of Christianity from all Jewish ritualism had triumphed in fact, as it had triumphed in principle at Jerusalem in 43-44. It must be added that universalism did not triumph in the second generation merely because Paul's ideas came into favour after he had disappeared, and because his letters, even before they had been collected into a *corpus*, were exercising an influence which they did not possess in his lifetime. Apart from this, another cause of the triumph was the attitude of Judaism after 70 when it became hostile to every form of Christianity, although previously it had in a large measure shown itself tolerant towards those forms of Christianity which continued in the framework of the worship and ritual of Judaism. It then excluded them from the synagogues[1] and thus threw them into the arms of Greek Christianity, or rather compelled them to live in such extremely precarious conditions that they could not survive.

3.—THE INCIDENT AT ANTIOCH[2]

It is proved that, while the conference at Jerusalem made it more or less clear that a rupture could not be tolerated, it did not solve the questions raised. If it were necessary, the incident at Antioch referred to by Paul in Galatians ii. 11 ff. would make this explicit and would make it all the more plainer with what reserve and discretion the accounts in Acts xv must be treated. The time when it happened is not given. Paul only says, 'When Cephas came

---

[1] It is probable that when John ix. 22 says that the Jewish authorities decided to exclude from the synagogue anyone who recognised Jesus as Messiah—to speak of it happening in Jesus' lifetime is an anachronism—it is reflecting a decision which may have been taken after 70 in many synagogues.

[2] See my article, 'Le recit d'Actes XV, l'histoire de Corneille et l'incident d'Antioch', *R.h.p.r.*, 1923, III, pp. 138-143.

to Antioch'. That can only have been after 44 as it would have been hardly natural for Paul to do anything else except follow the chronological order in telling his story.[1] The incident must have taken place when Paul was staying at Antioch between his first two missionary journeys.

As Peter was with a church which was partly composed of people who were originally Gentiles, he had no scruples in eating with them,[2] but as soon as some of James' partisans arrived,[3] he was afraid of offending them or incurring their censure and broke off relations with the Christians of Gentile origin; other Christians of Jewish origin and even Barnabas followed his example. Paul described his conduct without any reserve as hypocrisy and considered it to be an attempt to bring pressure to bear on Christians of Gentile origin. He publicly rebuked Peter for his conduct as hypocritical (Gal. ii. 11 ff.). Paul's condemnation is hardly fair. If he had desired to grasp the reasons for Peter's conduct he would have realised that he could not please one party without offending the other. The only mistake he had made was in taking up an attitude on his arrival at Antioch without sufficiently considering whether he could maintain it under all circumstances. Paul does not say what was the issue of the incident because the results were not favourable to the cause he championed.

In any case the conflict affected the rest of Paul's career with the most dire consequences. It disturbed his relations with the church at Antioch and, what was more serious, with the church at Jerusalem. It left him an isolated individual right up to the time of his death. As a result of the incident at Antioch Paul and Barnabas were separated, and in spite of the explanation given in the story in Acts it seems to have been a rupture permanent in character, which put an end to a collaboration which had lasted many years, first at Antioch, and then at Jerusalem, where the two missionaries had together championed the rights of Christian universalism. According to Acts (xv. 36-41) the separation was caused by a divergence

[1] However, in what appears to be quite an arbitrary fashion, Grundmann ('Die Apostel zwischen Jerusalem und Antiochia', Z.N.T.W., 1940, XXXIX, p. 135) works on a hypothesis suggested by H. Boehmer in unrecorded lectures and conjectures that the incident happened while Peter was on his way to Cornelius' house at Caesarea.

[2] This must mean to partake of the Lord's supper with them.

[3] It is impossible to say whether they were sent by James or whether they came to Antioch for private reasons. We have to remember that precisely the same question arose in the same circumstances with reference to the Judaeans who came to Antioch and raised the question of circumcision for the first time.

of view as to whether it was the best course to take on a new missionary journey as an assistant John Mark who had left Paul and Barnabas after they had traversed Cyprus on their first missionary journey (xiii. 13). It has been suggested that we have here what Guignebert[1] calls 'a white lie' on the part of the compiler of Acts to cover up the real reason for the separation. Such a hypothesis is not to be ruled out if at any rate we suppose that John Mark deserted because he did not entirely approve of the universalist twist which Paul gave to the mission. It is not inconceivable that Barnabas too, although he was overshadowed by Paul, did not entirely approve of his recklessness.

The incident at Antioch caused Paul's relations with the church at Jerusalem to grow more difficult. The Christians at Jerusalem may well have considered that Paul's attitude at Antioch put an end to the agreement which the pillars of the church had made with him in 43-44 and that they were no longer bound to have any regard for him. Paul was left alone to withstand Judaising propaganda which was going on even in the churches which he had founded and, when he came up to Jerusalem for the last time, the church there gave him a very cool if not frankly hostile reception.

4.—THE CAMPAIGN LED BY JEWISH CHRISTIANS IN CHURCHES FOUNDED BY PAUL

There is no doubt that the first efforts made by Judaisers to attack Paul in churches founded by him took place at Ephesus. Later on the campaign extended from there both to Greece and to Galatia. We can see the first traces of it in the epistle to the Philippians.[2] In it the apostle explains that, since it has been recognised that he has been made a prisoner on account of the gospel and not for any crime or breach of the common law, which in fact would have compromised both himself and the cause he served, his imprisonment and trial have promoted rather than impeded the progress of the gospel.

While he was forced to be inactive, others had begun to preach the gospel or had continued to do so with renewed ardour. Among

---

[1] Guignebert, *Le Christ*, p. 308. Guignebert also notes (n. 1) that John Mark may have deserted after they had crossed the island of Cyprus owing to some scruple he felt as a Jewish Christian.

[2] I believe that the epistle was written at Ephesus while Paul was a prisoner here, as I think. See *Introd.* IV, 1, pp. 369 ff.

them he distinguished two groups inspired by different motives. One group out of affection for Paul desired to see that the work which was so dear to him was maintained; the motives of the other group were not sincere; they were inspired by jealousy and a spirit of contention with a desire to cause him pain (i. 12-18). Some of them therefore wanted to profit by the opportunity which offered itself for supplanting Paul's authority by their own. It may be presumed that they were not just inspired by personal ambition but wished to secure the supremacy of a judaising conception of the gospel. But as Paul did not see this he could rejoice that the gospel was being preached with redoubled zeal without stopping to think of the motives behind it.[1] Otherwise his liberation put an end to the attempt before it had had time to develop sufficiently for its real character and purpose to be clearly disclosed.

Our information about all this is so scanty that unfortunately we cannot tell if the people who were behind this movement in Ephesus came from outside or not and whether they were the same people who later on set to work in Greece and Galatia or at any rate belonged to the same group. In any case the conjecture is plausible and what Paul says in 1 Corinthians xvi. 9 of 'many adversaries' whom he met in Ephesus is an argument in its favour, as it might well be that these adversaries were not only enemies from outside.

This, however, was nothing more than a preliminary confused skirmish since Paul was taken by surprise by the more systematic

---

[1] The critics who remain faithful to the traditional supposition that the epistle to the Philippians was written while Paul was a prisoner in Rome naturally see things in a different light. See e.g. O. Cullmann, 'Les causes de la mort de Pierre et Paul d'après le témoignage de Clement Romain', *R.h.p.r.*, 1930, X, pp. 294-300. They think that those who began to preach the gospel through jealousy and love of argument could not have been only Jewish Christians and explain that Paul does not judge them to be agitators from Corinth and Galatia because old age had given him a certain serenity and detachment. Without mentioning the other difficulties which face the conception that the epistle to the Philippians was written in Rome it meets with two objections which seem insurmountable: (1) As Paul arrived in Rome as a prisoner without having ever been there before and his relations with the church seem to have been reduced to a minimum we do not see how his imprisonment could have had any influence whatever on the way in which the gospel was being preached; (2) we cannot explain the contrast between the serenity which Paul shows towards those who preach the gospel in a way which he cannot approve of and the vigour of the curse which he lets forth in Gal. i. 6-9 against anyone who preaches a different gospel from his own as due to a spirit of detachment which he had gained in old age through meditation. The virulence of the polemic of chapter iii against 'the enemies of the cross of Christ' (iii. 18) shows that when Paul was writing the epistle to the Philippians he had lost none of his combative spirit.

campaign undertaken by the Judaisers to detach the churches in Greece and Galatia from him.

Their tactics were not the same in each case. While they worked by gradually worming themselves in secretly in Greece, in Galatia they attacked directly. Perhaps because Paul's enemies, by going to work carefully and slowly in Greece, had given him time to intervene and re-establish the situation they adopted different methods in Galatia. Sufficient analogies exist between the two campaigns for us to be able to see that they were part of a single plan to judaise Paul's churches. While, however, the general purpose of the action is clear, it is difficult to pick out what part the church at Jerusalem played, both as regards its leaders and the apostle Peter. But one thing is certain; between 44 and 58, the date of Paul's last visit, the church at Jerusalem had come to regard him with growing hostility and defiance. The compiler of Acts, who minimises and even hides the friction between Paul and the church at Jerusalem, shows that this was so. He reports that when Paul arrived at Jerusalem, James told him of thousands of converted Jews who held him to be a renegade preaching apostasy and trying to persuade the Jews of the diaspora not to circumcise their children any more and to give up the Mosaic customs (Acts xxi. 21). James also did not dare to bring him into the presence of the church until he had given public proof of his loyalty to Judaism (xxi. 22-26). The compiler of Acts implies that James did not agree with the opinion he was reporting but he does not say that he tried in any way to withstand it and when Paul was in prison neither James or any other member of the church at Jerusalem raised a finger to come and help him or ease his lot.[1]

From the attitude taken up by the church at Jerusalem in 58 it may be presumed that it was not entirely ignorant of the campaigns fought in Greece and Galatia against Paul.

The crisis in Corinth was complex in character and was due to many causes. It came to a head extremely quickly. The eighteen months which Paul spent at Corinth (Acts xviii. 11) were not long enough for the education of the church there to be so far advanced that when he left there was no possibility of any deflection arising. After his departure at first the church continued to develop normally (1 Cor. i. 5-9) without anybody from outside creating any difficulties for its members.[2] For some time Apollos followed up Paul's

---

[1] Concerning the attitude of the church at Jerusalem in 58 see pp. 345 ff.

[2] Christians at Corinth maintained good relations with their heathen fellow-citizens. They submitted the differences arising between them to the law-courts

work by teaching there along Paul's lines but with different gifts. The crisis, which arose quite suddenly, seems to have been due to two different causes. First of all there was a resurgence of the pagan mentality which conversion had repressed rather than destroyed. This accentuated certain latent misunderstandings, which were due to the fact that the Corinthians understood and interpreted in the light of Greek ontological dualism, what Paul had taught in the framework of Semitic temporal dualism. In this way the Corinthians failed to take into account the gulf between their ideas and those of the apostle and separated the destiny of the soul from the body. At the same time, under the influence of the Greek spirit, they came to think of the gospel as a philosophy and to imagine that those who preached it were leaders of rival schools which they supposed was customary and were in existence side by side in opposition to each other. The church at Corinth thus became divided into parties and the fact of having been baptised by this particular person or that played a large part in their formation (1 Cor. i. 13 f.). Disturbance of this kind threatened secretly to undermine Paul's authority and to make the church receptive to other influences than his. To this were added misunderstandings which became more and more aggravated. The Corinthians, although loyal to Paul, complained that they were misunderstood by him. The other reason for the crisis was the fact that circumstances compelled Paul to postpone several times a journey to Corinth which had been promised several times so that bad feeling grew.

The trouble became much more acute when interventions from outside took place. That they took place there is no doubt whatever; but of what their nature was our knowledge is much more vague and interpretations differ considerably. The obscurity is due in the first place to the fact that the epistles contain allusions which were perfectly clear to the Corinthians but are not so to us. But in addition to this, Paul, especially at the beginning of the crisis, does not seem to have known how far the Judaisers, who claimed that they were acting under the authority of Peter, James, and the church at Jerusalem, were in fact sent by the 'pillars of the church' and, if they had been, whether they had not considerably gone beyond the instructions given to them.

Although the formation of a party of Apollos was certainly due to his missionary activity in Corinth it does not necessarily follow

(1 Cor. vi. 1 ff.) and accepted invitations to partake of feasts in pagan homes even when they took place after sacrifices (1 Cor. viii. 10; x. 27).

that Cephas' party was formed in the same circumstances, i.e. that Peter came to Corinth.[1] The majority of commentators reject the idea of this visit,[2] at any rate during the period covered by the letters of Paul which have been preserved to us and the period before that. The way in which Paul describes himself as the sole founder of the church at Corinth (1 Cor. iii. 6; iv. 15) destroys any value in the evidence of Denys of Corinth, who in a letter written about 170 to Soter of Rome[3] expressed himself as follows: 'By this exhortation[4] you have closely united the trees of the Corinthians and Romans which were planted by Peter and Paul, for both planted in our Corinth, both taught us the same doctrine, and both, having taught together in Italy, submitted to martyrdom at the same time'. Denys says nothing to show that what he recounts is already known to the Romans; he invokes no tradition to justify his statement. What he says is only a legend which the Christians of Corinth had created because they wished to be able to invoke the same illustrious patronage as the church in Rome.[5] But we cannot call it so much a legend as an erroneous and tendacious interpretation of certain passages in the first of Paul's epistles to the Corinthians such as i. 12 or ix. 5.

The existence at Corinth of a party of Cephas (1 Cor. i. 12) could only prove that Peter came to Corinth if it was absolutely certain that to be of the party of Cephas must mean that one had

---

[1] Concerning the coming of Peter to Corinth and his part in the campaign against Paul see my article, 'L'apôtre Pierre a-t-il joué un rôle personnel dans les crises de Gréce et de Galatie?' *R.h.p.r.*, 1934, XIV, pp. 461-500, in which is given the history and a bibliography of the question.

[2] See e.g. Renan, *Saint Paul*, pp. 376 ff.; Reuss, *Les ep. paulin.* I, p. 140; Julicher, *Einleitung in das Neue Testament*[2] *neubearbeitet in Verbinding mit*, E. Fascher, Tubingen, 1931, p. 82; Belser, *Einl.i.d.N.T.*, pp. 118 f.; Bauer, *Rechtgl. u. Ketz.*, p. 117. Against this view can be mentioned Bernh. Weiss, *Einl.i.d.N.T.*, p. 196, n. 1; Harnack, *Dgshch.*, I, p. 180, n. 2; *Mission*, I, p. 63, n. 2; Link, *Die Dolmetscher des Petrus*, St. u. Kr., 1896, p. 427; Schwartz, *Charakterkopfe der antiken Literatur*, II[2], Leipzig, 1911, p. 137; Meyer, *Urspr. u. Anf.*, III, p. 441, n. 1; Leitzmann, *Korinther*, 1931, p. 7 (in the first (1923) edition Leitzmann did not express this opinion); 'Die Reisen des Petrus', *S.B.A.*, 1930, pp. 153-156. The critics who are favourable to the idea that Peter came to Galatia give expression to various shades of opinion, e.g. Harnack says that the idea that Peter came to Galatia is not as improbable as is ordinarily supposed, while Edouard Meyer says that he cannot understand how anyone could doubt that he did so.

[3] Quoted by Eusebius (*H.e.* i. 25, 8).

[4] This may refer to the letter of Clement of Rome or to a more recent letter of the church of Rome to the church of Corinth. Both are mentioned in a fragment of Denys given by Eusebius (*H.e.* iv. 23, 11).

[5] Zahn (*G.K.* I, p. 806, n. 4) thinks that Clement of Rome would have already known of this tradition. For the reasons why I cannot retain this interpretation see *R.h.p.r.*, 1934, XIV, pp. 429-491.

been instructed and baptised by him. But, even if those who claimed Paul or Apollos as their leaders invoked the fact that they had been baptised by them, it is quite certain that when the crisis blew up that many more people must have belonged to Paul's party than the handful who had been baptised by him (1 Cor. i. 14). If Cephas' party came into existence perhaps in opposition to Paul and perhaps also in opposition to Apollos that does not prove that it was set up in the same fashion. Because Cephas was chosen as the patron of an opposition party like this it can only be inferred that men in-invoked his authority to fight Paul's.[1]

There is thus no positive proof that Peter came to Corinth but there are very strong reasons for doubting whether he stayed there in the period preceding the editing and collecting of Paul's letters. If he came there without any intention of opposing Paul, how are we to explain that Paul never alludes to his presence and, if he came to try and influence the church, how could Paul have ignored or pretended to ignore such an intrusion?

Traces that persons from outside intervened in the church at Corinth are positive but lack detail and are difficult to explain. In 1 Corinthians iii. 10 Paul speaks with some irritation of those who came to build on the foundation which he had laid at Corinth. He is not thinking of Apollos because he has shown his agreement with him by the metaphor: 'I planted, Apollos watered' (1 Cor. iii. 5).

Chapters x to xiii are part of what is called the severe letter and form a defence of Paul's apostleship and a somewhat lively polemic against those who had tried to belittle him in the eyes of the Corinthians. These people who came to Corinth fortified with letters of commendation are certainly identical with those described

[1] In support of the idea that a party of Cephas may have been established without Peter coming personally I do not rely on there being also a party of Christ because I do not believe that such a party existed. The words in 1 Cor. i. 12, 'I am of Christ', cannot be understood as defining what ought to be the normal attitude of Christians, because they are in exactly the same style as the watchwords of the parties. Two reasons prevent us from supposing that there was at Corinth a party which claimed Christ as its leader in a way of which Paul could not approve. (1) Nothing in the first or second epistle suggests that this self-styled party of Christ could in any way be thought of as like the parties of Apollos or Cephas; (2) the idea that there was a party of Christ meets with the objection that Paul opposes to the division of the church the fact that Christ is not divided and that Paul has not been crucified for the Corinthians any more than Apollos or Cephas and that they have not been baptised in the name of Paul. This compels us to consider the words, 'I am of Christ', to be a clumsy gloss. Concerning this hypothesis and other ideas which have been developed with reference to the party of Christ see *Introd.* IV, 2, pp. 118 ff.

in 1 Corinthians iii. 10 ff. One of the arguments they used against Paul was that, because he refused to be maintained by the churches, he showed himself to be a man who did not dare to lay claim to the privileges of an apostle because he knew that really he was not an apostle (2 Cor. xii. 13). Paul had already replied at length to this argument in chapter ix of the first epistle. If Peter had come to Corinth he would have been one of those described in 2 Corinthians x ff. since in any case Paul had shown that he could not lean on Peter's authority to fight his adversaries; but who could have given Peter these 'letters of commendation' by which the intruders tried to give themselves credit? Did not Peter figure among those to whom Paul ironically alludes as the 'chiefest of the apostles' (2 Cor. xi. 5; xiii. 11)?

The general tone of the correspondence, especially of chapters x to xiii of the second epistle, written in the most acute moments of the crisis, cannot explain why Paul never mentions by name or clearly designates his opponents, if they were well-known persons, although he has no need to be tactful. On the other hand, all is clear, if the agitators at Corinth in their opposition to Paul claimed the support of the apostles in such a vague manner that Paul could not discover what truth there was in it, i.e. if they had really been sent by them and in any case if they had not gone beyond their instructions and even whether they were not acting contrary to the Apostles' intentions and ideas. Paul was opposed by people who took credit to themselves that they were Christ's in a different way from Paul or at any rate claimed that, as a champion of Christ, Paul was inferior to them (2 Cor. x. 7). Paul's reply was that he would not compare himself to those who wanted to commend themselves (x. 12), and he emphasises that his work gave him an authority which the Corinthians could not fail to recognise.

He had previously said in 1 Corinthians ix. 2 'If I be not an apostle to others, yet doubtless I am to you; for the seal of mine apostleship are ye in the Lord'. He had then been attacked before by people who had come from outside and had not accomplished at Corinth a work comparable to his. He returns to this point in 2 Corinthians x. 13-17 and makes great play with the fact that he has not, like his enemies, wormed himself into a church which he has not founded.

Paul has in mind that they had been comparing him to the apostles in Jerusalem when he says that, if anyone thinks he is 'of Christ', he is also (2 Cor. x. 7). He is not questioning the fact that they are Christ's but he is denying them a monopoly. He returns to the theme later on in xi. 16 and taking the rhetorical precaution to say that he speaks as a fool he shows that he has a much better claim to be Christ's on every account than they could ever show. Between these two passages is inserted another of a different character and one frankly aggressive in tone. He will continue to do, he says, as he has done, so as to cut away the ground from those who would gladly boast that they are no different from him and wish that he was no different from them. He means that they wished that his disinterestedness had not been a reproach to their cunning (xi. 12). Paul insinuates that behind the agitators at Corinth are fickle persons with an axe to grind and gives rein to violent invective, calling them false apostles, deceitful workers, who disguise themselves as apostles of Christ as Satan is disguised as an angel of light and he promises them the reward they deserve (xi. 13-15). It is plain that in saying this he does not have in mind the apostles at Jerusalem. He does not attack them personally and, while he may speak of them with some bitterness and irritation, quite plainly it is because those who were at work in Corinth were trying to make use of their name.

We do not know what right the agitators at Corinth had to claim that they were backed by James and Peter. Paul, however, did not think that they had been sent by them and it would be surprising if he had been deceived about this.

In the epistles to the Corinthians Paul is not defending his gospel but his apostleship. Plainly then no direct attempt had been made to judaise the church. Yet at times Paul seems to have guessed that they were trying to undermine his authority in order that later they could attack his gospel. When Paul is giving instruction concerning party-strife and has in mind the party of Cephas he alludes to a form of teaching of which he evidently did not approve as he compares it to a building constructed of materials which have no strength and will not stand up to the test of the fire on the day of judgement (1 Cor. iii. 10-17). But Paul does not say that those who came after him to Corinth have been trying to destroy his work, as he says that they have worked on the foundation laid by him. The last sentence in the paragraph, it is true, suggests something else; 'Know ye not that ye are the temple of God. If any man defile the temple of God, him shall God destroy; for the temple of God is holy, which temple ye are' (iii. 16-17). Paul therefore has a more or less passing suspicion that the activity of the party of Cephas may be more serious than the facts of which he was aware would warrant him in thinking.

Rather more definite evidence of a similar kind is found in the severe letter. 'If he that cometh', writes Paul, 'preacheth another Jesus, whom we have not preached, or another spirit[1] which ye have not received, or another gospel, which ye have not accepted ye might well bear with him' (2 Cor. xi. 4). But after saying that he does not affirm as in Galatians i. 6-8 that he would know no gospel save his own. He is therefore only formulating an extreme hypothesis to show how far the credulity of the Corinthians would go but he does not stop there and immediately returns to defending his apostleship.

Does this mean that the crisis at Corinth was only concerned with a question of personal prestige. This is improbable. It seems much more probable that the agitators wished to bring the church at Corinth over to keeping the law; they thought that they would be much more likely to achieve their object if they did not divulge their purpose at first but began by destroying Paul's authority. Events spoiled their tactics. The crisis took a very grave turn and then suddenly subsided in a manner favourable to Paul.[2] By dissimulating their intentions to begin with his enemies gave him time to intervene before it was too late. Once his authority was reestablished there could be no further question of detaching the Corinthians from the gospel which he had preached to them.

The crisis in Galatia[3] was quite different in character. It broke out very suddenly. Towards the end of his stay in Asia or after his arrival in Macedonia, Paul learnt—we do not know how—that the Galatians had been worked upon by opposing missionaries and were on the point of giving up the gospel which had been preached to them and going over to observing the Jewish law. It is not clear who had troubled them or what their relations were with the authorities of the church at Jerusalem whom they claimed as their leaders. Paul himself does not seem to have been clear on these points. The ill-concealed irritation and bitter, almost scornful irony, with which he treated the pillars of the church who had made him important concessions in 44, show that he considered them responsible for what took place in Galatia.

Paul speaks of 'certain' persons ($\tau \iota \nu \epsilon s$) who were troubling the Galatians (Gal. i. 7) but he does not seem to have thought of them

---

[1] The text has here the word $\lambda \alpha \mu \beta \acute{a} \nu \epsilon \tau \epsilon$ (= you receive) which makes the sentence meaningless. I omit it supposing it to be a clumsy gloss.
[2] See *Introd.* IV, 2, pp. 137 ff.   [3] See *Introd.* IV, 2, pp. 166 ff.

as more or less irresponsible agents simply carrying out someone else's orders. In another context (v. 10) he writes: 'but he that troubleth you shall bear his judgement, whosoever he be', apparently referring to somebody of importance whom the Galatians knew as well as he. The two passages do not harmonise with each other perfectly; we must therefore conclude that they contain only conjectures founded on dark and obscure hints.

If Paul had known that Peter or somebody else of equal importance had been at work in Galatia he would not have failed to mention him by name, as the tone of the first two chapters shows that he felt no need for any tact as far as the pillars of the church were concerned. He makes no direct reference to Peter or James because he knew of nothing which authorised him to think that either of them had been at work in Galatia or were directing from a distance the campaign which had been carried on there.[1] The situation seems to have closely resembled that which we found existed at Corinth. The opposing evangelists did not make direct attacks on Paul's apostleship but maintained that the authority of James, Peter, and the Twelve was greater than Paul's and therefore Paul's teaching must be completed and even corrected by the teaching given at Jerusalem. But we cannot discover whether Peter and James were behind the campaign, whether they approved of it or judged it inopportune. It is not even certain if they were aware of it. The only thing which we can take as certain is that the authorities of the church at Jerusalem shared, in principle at least, the views of the missionaries opposed to Paul.[2]

What was the outcome of the Galatian crisis is not known.

---

[1] We cannot therefore agree with Edouard Meyer's opinion (*Urspr. u. Anf.*, III, p. 434) who thinks that there is no reason to doubt that Peter came to Galatia to resume the conflict which he had led against Paul at Antioch. Leitzmann (*S.B.A.*, 1930, pp. 153-156) adopts Edouard Meyer's thesis but is compelled to justify it instead of confining himself to a bare affirmation.

[2] H. J. Ropes ('The singular problem of the Epistle to the Galatians', *Harvard Theological Studies*, Cambridge, Massachusetts, 1929, XIV) develops an idea adopted from Luetgert (*Gesetz und Geist, Eine Untersuchung zur Vergeschichte des Galaterbriefs*, Gutersloh, 1919), viz. that in the epistle to the Galatians Paul had had to defend the authority of the Old Testament against people who were attacking it. It is true that he insists on its authority but in doing so he would seem to be replying to accusations that he misunderstood it. Hirsch ('Zwei Fragen zum Galaterbrief', *Z.N.T.W.*, 1930, XXIX, pp. 192-197) suggested that the agitators in Galatia were men who had once shared Paul's views but had rallied round the cause of legalism for the sake of avoiding the kind of difficulties which faced Paul but it is difficult to see how they could have thought of such tactics in circumstances like those in Galatia where legalism had been brought in from outside.

Shortly after its occurrence Paul wrote the epistle to the Romans. The theme of the epistle to the Galatians is set out again and developed in a calmer tone which may be taken as evidence that the crisis found a happy solution. But the weight of this argument is diminished by the fact that, as Paul desired to conciliate the Romans whose collaboration he needed for the evangelising work which he intended to undertake in Spain, he must have thought it necessary to avoid lending an aggressive character to the account which he was giving of his doctrine and offering it in a form which showed that it had been called in question by a group of people who possessed unquestioned prestige. In favour of the supposition that the issue was favourable, Paul's visit to Jerusalem immediately after the crisis may be quoted. If the authorities in Jerusalem had been in any way responsible for the rupture which broke out between Paul and the churches in Galatia he would not still have thought it possible and desirable for him to maintain contact with Jerusalem. But this also is not a conclusive reason because Paul fails to state clearly what part the authorities in Jerusalem played in the diffi- culties he had just encountered; just because he was uncertain he needed to know if the agreement on principles which he had gained only with difficulty in 43-44 still held good.

Other reasons which are also in no way conclusive might lead us to think that the Galatians gave way to ritualistic legalism. There is no mention of any representative of the churches in Galatia among those who accompanied Paul to Jerusalem with the collection (Acts xx. 4). But 1 Corinthians xvi. 1-4 shows that the collection had been organised and completed in Galatia before it had been made in Greece where the crisis delayed its execution.[1] It may be possible therefore that the collection was completed in Galatia and brought to Jerusalem before the crisis came to a head. That would explain why Paul restricts himself to a simple allusion to what he had done 'to remember the poor'. We may even ask ourselves if, when the Galatians came to Jerusalem to bring their collection, the attention of the Christians in Jerusalem was not then drawn to their churches and there was suggested to them the idea of making good use of their opportunities to try and gain them over to the conception of the church ruling in Jerusalem.

Whatever may have been the issue the two crises in Greece and Galatia show that the differences of opinion which existed in 43-44 far from being narrowed in the following years were only aggravated

[1] In Macedonia the collection had been delayed by persecution, 2 Cor viii. 1 ff.

Lietzmann[1] thinks that the conference in Jerusalem, the incident at Antioch, and the crises in Corinth and Galatia were stages in a developing process. After the incident at Antioch the Christians in Jerusalem would have considered that the agreement of 43-44 had been broken and would have engaged in open conflict against Paul. A systematic campaign would have been devised and organised by James and directed by Peter. For his case Lietzmann relies principally on the supposition that Peter came to Corinth for which we have seen there is not sufficient evidence. But Lietzmann was certainly right in stressing the importance of the incident at Antioch as it affected the relations between the Jewish and Gentile Christians, not only because it showed that, in spite of the concessions which some of the leaders of the church in Jerusalem made, the rank and file stuck to the idea that observance of the law was necessary for salvation but also because the unyielding attitude adopted by Paul provided those who were dissatisfied with the agreement of 43-44 with an excuse for considering it broken by him, from which they concluded that they were exempt from showing any consideration to Paul at all.

5.—THE EPISTLE TO THE ROMANS AND THE JEWISH CHRISTIAN QUESTION

The epistle to the Romans may be considered to be at least in an indirect form evidence for the relations between Paul and the Jewish Christians. Paul wrote it because he wanted to forestall any influence which those who had attacked him in Greece and Galatia might exert in Rome as they might arrive there before him. But he did not write the epistle for this purpose alone. Neither is the epistle a direct apology for Paul's gospel.[2] Paul of course explained the doctrine of justification by faith because he wanted to counteract erroneous and tendacious interpretations which had been given. But he argues with discretion and has no adversary in mind. He does not seem to have done this merely because he thought it wiser not to disclose to the Romans, what perhaps they did not know, that his gospel had been attacked and opposed. To explain the epistle to the Romans we must also entertain the idea that, after a period of conflicts in which the essentials of his theology had been called in

[1] Leitzmann, 'Die Reisen des Petrus', S.B.A., 1930, pp. 153-156.
[2] In particular it should be noted that Paul in the epistle to the Romans confines himself to affirming his apostleship without feeling any call to defend it.

question, Paul felt the need for drawing up a balance-sheet of his ideas and formulating the most essential affirmations of his gospel on a new basis. The composition of the epistle to the Romans proves that when Paul wrote it he did not consider that the conflict had come to an end but that he had not in any way been disturbed by the opposition which he had incurred.

At a time when he was preparing to begin a new period of activity which was to carry the gospel of salvation to Spain, Paul wanted to clear up his relations with the church at Jerusalem and so sought to resume contact with its leaders. The opportunity to do so was provided by the visit to Jerusalem to be made by the delegates from the churches in Asia, Macedonia, and Greece who were to bring the collection; he determined then to accompany them although at the beginning he had been undecided (1 Cor. xvi. 3-4). He must have judged that it was vital to go up to a meeting at Jerusalem as he was well aware of the dangers to which he was exposing himself, both from the Jews who could not fail to see in his visit to the Holy City a cause for provocation and from the Christians there also as he was by no means assured of receiving a warm welcome from them. The epistle to the Romans gives very clear evidence on this point. 'Now I beseech you, brethren, for the Lord Jesus Christ's sake, and for the love of the Spirit, that ye strive together with me in your prayers to God for me; that I may be delivered from them that do not believe in Judaea; and that my service which I have for Jerusalem may be accepted of the saints' (Rom. xv. 30-32).

In the epistle to the Romans Paul resumes the contentions which he had formulated in the epistle to the Galatians in the heat of the conflict and he does not yield an inch to the Judaisers. But he also shows in this epistle the deepest and, it may be said, the most passionate attachment to his own people. He begins his imposing picture of Israel's destiny which he draws in chapters ix to xi with a moving declaration of his patriotism. Plainly he is replying to the accusations brought against him that he was an apostate and a renegade. Paul then goes on to explain Israel's incredulity by the idea that it is part of a vast divine plan to make the vocation of the Gentiles possible. At the end in due season Israel will be converted. Their conversion will be like life from the dead (xi. 15), i.e. the coming of the new age.

The tone of profound emotion running through this passage shows that we must see in it something more than an extract from a philosophy of history. Paul is here replying to an accusation which had touched him in the very fibres of his being, the accusation that he was the enemy of the people of Israel and had misunderstood the peculiar election which had fallen upon them. Such an accusation does not seem to have been brought against him in Galatia or at Corinth. There is no doubt that it must be regarded as a fact, that of all the accusations brought against him by the Jews, the most damaging to his reputation was in the church at Jerusalem, and this made it all the more urgent for Paul to get in touch again and be on the spot.[1]

6.—PAUL'S ISOLATION BOTH AT JERUSALEM AND AT ROME

As far as the Jewish Christians were concerned there seems to have been no appeasement; on the contrary, defiance if not hostility seems to have only increased towards Paul at Jerusalem between 44 and 58, the date of his last visit there. What happened between the time of his arrival in Jerusalem and the time when we lose all trace of him leaves no doubt as regards this. According to Acts xxi. 20 ff. he was welcomed by the elders and James. But James did not dare to introduce him to the church until he had given public proof of his loyalty to Judaism by agreeing to associate himself with some brethren who had to discharge a vow by submitting themselves to a rite of purification and offering a sacrifice. That Paul was ready to do this is not as unlikely as has been sometimes thought. While he had protested against the claim that the law must be imposed upon Gentile converts Paul had never maintained that Christians of Jewish origin must stop observing it. Acts, however, does not afford us sufficiently sure evidence for us to be able to consider it certain that things happened in this way. Whatever happened Paul was found in the temple when, spontaneously or not, a riot started up and Paul would have been massacred if the tribune who saw what was happening in the temple from the fortress of Antonia had not intervened in time with his soldiers who arrested him. Lengthy legal proceedings followed which were only to end at Rome at the earliest five years later.[2] Acts does not mention that the church at Jerusalem made any request to come to Paul's aid or ease his lot before he was transferred to Caesarea or during the

---

[1] A secondary motive behind it may also have been Paul's desire to restrain the tendencies of certain Gentile Christians who went further than he did and declared that Israel had been definitely robbed of her privileges.

[2] See pp. 488 ff.

two years he stayed as a prisoner there. This silence is significant. The author of Acts was dominated by the idea that perfect harmony always reigned between the apostle Paul and the church at Jerusalem so that he could not have failed to mention any favour the Christians at Jerusalem might have done for Paul. What is no less significant is that at the time when Jewish hatred was unloosed against Paul the peace enjoyed by the church at Jerusalem does not appear to have been disturbed, which shows that the Jews did not consider the Christians to be in agreement with Paul any more than they thought themselves in agreement with him.

Three years passed between the time when Paul wrote to the Romans and when he arrived a prisoner in the city. Possibly the Judaisers used this delay to win over the church at Rome to their cause or perhaps Paul had been deceived in thinking that it was favourable to his conception of the gospel. In any case, the apostle was received at Rome with marked indifference;[1] he lived there in distinct isolation without receiving from the church any assistance or comfort during his imprisonment and trial. The Christians in Rome showed no interest in guaranteeing his defence. It is quite possible that their attitude discouraged the Asiatics who came to Rome, made them disloyal to the apostle and resolved to return to Asia. Perhaps the very fact that the apostle was left a prisoner alone and isolated is the reason why we do not know how his trial ended.

And so after the incident at Antioch which brought to an end a short period during which Paul might have thought that his relations with the Christians in Jerusalem were on such a footing that he had been left complete freedom of action his situation persistently grew worse. He became more and more isolated and misunderstood even in the churches founded by him and everywhere he went he met with fierce opposition which had been fomented from outside. As the years passed his isolation grew and opposition increased. After a long period of imprisonment during which both the church in Rome as well as that in Jerusalem showed no interest in him he died in the end without perhaps the church being even aware of the fact.

7.—THE TRIUMPH OF UNIVERSALISM AFTER A.D. 70

It might well have seemed that the cause of universalism was lost with Paul and that the church by refusing to go with him had condemned itself for the rest of its existence to remain shut up in

[1] See pp. 161 ff.

the framework of Judaism so that it could never be anything more than a Jewish sect. But ten years passed and the situation was completely reversed. Universalism won the day.[1] In all Christian literature written after 70 as it has been left to us, universalism entirely devoid of any ritualism is accepted as a fact and no one thinks that there is any need to justify it. How can such a sudden change be explained? It is most unlikely that the spiritual values expounded by Paul to justify his position would have had more influence when he had disappeared than they had when he was alive, especially at a time when the epistles had not yet been collected into a *corpus* and could therefore be known only to a few people and consequently only exercised a very limited influence. The change came about, not from internal but from external causes; they are not psychological or religious but sociological. As we shall see later on[2] while Judaism showed itself fanatically and violently hostile to the Christianity of Stephen, who wished to reform the cult, and to that of Paul, who wished to free Christianity from the yoke of the law, it showed itself tolerant towards the forms of the new religion practised by those who wished to remain within the framework of the old law. At this time Judaism was not yet uniform but welcomed within its fold groups whose ideas were as diverse and even as contradictory as those of the Pharisees, the Sadducees, the Essenes and many other groups. Discussion between representatives of these different sects could be keen; no one seems to have thought that his rivals were not to be tolerated. As long as Christianity remained faithful to the practice of the law it was only one sect among many others.

The catastrophe of 70 transformed the situation. Judaism fell back upon itself; it became a rigorously closed body of doctrine and hostile to any other doctrinal form. It opposed therefore every form of Christianity, even those which remained loyal to the law. The Christian faith, i.e. to confess Jesus to be the Messiah became a damnable heresy. In this situation the decision had to be made which by a singular anachronism the fourth gospel applies to the time when Jesus was alive, 'The Jews had agreed already that if any man did confess that he was the Christ, he should be put out of the synagogue'. Thus Christianity had the feeling of independence thrust upon it in most cases from without rather than acquiring it for itself. The little groups who showed themselves incapable of accommodation were excluded on that account from the church and

[1] Except in the little groups of Jewish Christians who remained on the edge of the church.   [2] See pp. 444 ff.

wrote off their own future. After 70 it became impossible to belong to both synagogue and church at the same time. One had to make a choice between the two groupings. To enter the synagogue and abide there was to repudiate faith in Christ and to refuse to recognise him as Messiah.

The practice of the Jewish law became then an anomaly in the church and at times gave the impression of being a heresy. The problem of the relationship between Christianity and Judaism took on a different aspect. It was not a question of practice but of ideology: it was the theological problem of the two covenants.

Finally, it may be asked if all the efforts of Paul had not been futile. Since external circumstances gave or imposed on Christianity the feeling of independence, had he fought and suffered to no purpose? A more compliant attitude on his part would have made no difference to the final result. The only part which he seems to have played was to foresee by a stroke of genius the way in which Christianity had to develop in order to realise its possibilities. But this is only to look at the exterior aspect of things. Except for the little groups of Jewish Christians who remained impervious to the activity of Greek Christianity the church was able to adapt itself to the situation in which it found itself after 70 without apparently any crisis arising. That this was so is surely due to the fact that Paulinism had prepared for the church a new structure of thought and a new centre of gravity.[1]

8.—THE SURVIVING FORMS OF JEWISH CHRISTIANITY

A problem which dominated the life of a society for a generation and created opposition and grievous schisms did not disappear without leaving traces behind it. But after 70 we can still see the opposition between Jewish and Gentile Christianity in existence but it is nothing more than a survival. Two points only have to be noted here to which we will return later.

While it is quite certain that certain groups of Christians of Greek origin were completely freed from any ritual practice, others

---

[1] We must not perhaps attribute this work exclusively to Paul. In the first generation of Christians there were other forms of Greek thought besides Paul's, notably that which came to a head in the epistle to the Hebrews. Nevertheless it remains true that none of these forms of thought seem to have exercised an influence as profound and extensive as Paul's. The church then has not been the victim of accident or mistake in always remembering Paul as the champion of Christianity's independence in the first generation.

possibly through atavism believed that certain abstentions ought to be imposed. This might provoke friction between them. Such seems to have been the case in the conflict between the author of the book to the Seven Churches and the Nicolaitani[1] but the Nicolaitanian practices are condemned not because they are violations of the law but because they are tainted with idolatry. The author of the letters is not thinking of imposing on Christians any other burden beyond abstaining from sacrifices to idols and from *porneia*, i.e. from marriages within the degrees prohibited by the Jewish law. He seems rather to react against the tendency of certain persons to go much further in the practice of ritualism (ii. 24-25).[2] Conversely the heresy which Ignatius fought against under the name of 'Judaism' may have been some Jewish Christian doctrine or practice which had survived.[3]

The second point to note refers to the controversy concerning the date of Easter which took place in the second half of the second century.[4] It was a conflict between two liturgical practices, one belonging to Asia which had grown up on the pattern of the celebration of the Jewish passover[5] while the other which had been introduced much later at Rome and most probably under her influence in the other provinces of the church made Easter primarily a commemoration of the resurrection, which from the first generation onwards the institution of Sunday had placed in the centre of Greek Christian worship. But the conflict involved no question of Jewish ritualism and it was not any loyalty to Judaism which made the Quartodecians faithful to their traditional way of keeping the feast of Easter.

---

[1] Concerning the Nicolaitan heresy see pp. 409 ff.

[2] The author of the Didache takes up a similar position with regard to food. 'And concerning food, bear what thou canst', he writes (i.e. observe as far as possible the Jewish rules). 'But keep strictly from that which is offered to idols, for it is the worship of dead gods' (vi. 3). The difference between the two rules suggests that the one concerning foods is inspired only by an anxiety not to offend those who had scruples on this account. They must have been Christians as the Didache wishes the members of the church to make themselves distinct by not having the same fast-days as the Jews and not using the same forms of prayers (viii. 1-2). Also incidentally they are to have their worship on Sunday (xiv. 1). But while the author of the Didache directs them to assemble together on Sunday he does not say that he gives this direction so that they would show themselves distinct from the Jews. [3] See pp. 409 ff. [4] See *E.P.*, pp. 411 ff.

[5] At least as far as the date is concerned, because the observance of the Passover had taken on a new meaning in the Jewish Christian church in the fact that it had become a commemoration of the death of Christ and the accomplishment of redemption through it.

CHAPTER III

Deuteropaulinism

I.—WHAT IS TO BE UNDERSTOOD BY THE TERM DEUTEROPAULINISM

THE name deuteropaulinism is used to cover those forms of Christian thought which were most widespread in the church in the period following 70. The term is convenient and shows clearly the dominating character of a theology which was an extension of Paul's in a vulgarised and bastard form. Although convenient it lends itself to misunderstandings and needs definition to distinguish the various meanings which can be given to it.

The term deuteropaulinism can be understood in a narrow sense and in a wide sense. In the narrow sense it is the theology expressed in the pastoral epistles and the epistle to the Ephesians, which through interpolations became the expression of a Pauline theology adapted to a new situation. The first epistle of Peter is also a document expressing deuteropaulinism in this sense of the word. When we use the word in its wider sense the term deuteropaulinism applies to the more complex forms of thought which analysis reveals to be a combination of a Pauline current with another current derived from apostolic Christianity. To a very large degree the synoptic gospels and the book of Acts so far as they are not works of history belong to this category.

The Johannine theology as it is found both in the two first epistles[1] and the Apocalypse as well as in the gospel might also be included. It is better not to do so, as, although it is unquestionable that these documents show Pauline influences, the theology which they express is so original that it is something more than a theology of epigoni.

For different reasons I shall not classify the epistle of Clement of Rome to the Corinthians as one of the documents showing deuteropaulinism. Pauline formulae exercise very superficial influence on it

[1] There is no need to take into account the third epistle as it contains nothing doctrinal.

and, although its author shares certain prejudices with the compiler of the pastoral epistles, the spirit expressed in it is very different from that of the Eastern Christianity to be found in the other documents I have just mentioned.

2.—THE PASTORAL EPISTLES

The thought expressed in the pastoral epistles hardly belongs to any particular personality but is common to the environment in which the author lived, probably Asia in the last decade of the first century,[1] or perhaps in the first or even the second decade of the second at a time when the memory of Paul[2] still dominated Asiatic Christianity. These epistles are in the form of instructions sent by Paul to his young[3] collaborators, Timothy and Titus, whom he had charged with missions the nature of which is not sharply defined.[4] These instructions reveal that the author is zealous to endow the churches with an organisation which will ensure them the services of a regular ministry and can protect them from new and pernicious ideas of heretics. The author wants to defend the sound doctrine but he does not seem to think that it was necessary to define in what it consists. Doubtless his readers are supposed to know what it is. But the fact that sound doctrine is not expounded is symptomatic. It at least shows that the author's theological thought runs along traditional and conventional lines and is not personal and active.

The churches whose life is reflected in the pastoral epistles are not the same in appearance to what they were in Paul's time. They have become perceptibly larger bodies and have come into touch with

[1] For this date and the general character of the pastoral epistles see *Introd.* IV, 2, pp. 476 ff.

[2] In the course of the second century Paul was hardly remembered at all. Asiatic Christianity had come to claim John instead of Paul as its founder. The reasons for the disappearance of Paul's influence in Asia are not clear; they may have been complex. Asiatic Christianity may have changed somewhat in character following the immigration of Christians from Palestine after 70. Also Paul's authority may have been impaired by the way in which Marcion and the Gnostics tried to make use of the Pauline epistles in support of their own ideas. Later on Irenaeus corrected this when he depended on the Pauline epistles to defend the true doctrine. On this subject see Werner's book, *Der Paulinismus des Irenaeus*, Leipzig, 1889.

[3] Timothy and more especially Titus would not as the epistles appear to suggest have been so young or so inexperienced at the time which we would have to date the epistles if they were authentic.

[4] The instructions given to Timothy sometimes presume that he is exercising in some church the functions of a bishop or an elder and at other times that he has been charged to organise the churches in a complete district.

fresh strata of the population; they contain a sufficient number of rich persons that it is necessary to give them special instructions (1 Tim. vi. 17); they have sufficient resources at their disposal that they can organise a complete system of assistance.[1] An important part of the activities of elders, bishops, and deacons must have been devoted to the labours of administration, since impartiality figures among the qualities required of those aspiring to ecclesiastical functions (1 Tim. iii. 3, 8; Titus i. 7).

People from outside have their eyes fixed on these churches; those at their head have therefore to be men of good reputation (1 Tim. iii. 7). Christians have sometimes to suffer for their faith. The recommendation to be politically loyal (1 Tim. ii. 16; Titus ii. 8; iii. 1) shows that sometimes they were tempted to revolt against the authorities. They are recommended to submit because it is the best way to live a peaceful life. The author is certainly also thinking of those who may be called to witness their faith before tribunals when he speaks of the good confession of Jesus before Pontius Pilate as the model to imitate (2 Tim. vi. 13).[2]

To judge by the exhortations of the author of the Pastorals the moral state of the churches left something to be desired.[3]

The formulae of Paul's thought are to be found in the pastorals but they have lost their edge. They are no longer expressing an experience but establish or presume the existence of a doctrine, which has been entrusted to the church and must be transmitted. Redemption is conceived of as a moral transformation, as the revelation of a new way of life which is opposed to the natural life with its material passions and carnal covetousness (2 Tim. iv. 3). The affirmation that the work of Christ has made this change possible has become hardly anything more than a formal phrase; the author is much more interested in the consequences flowing from the change than in the change itself.

Paul's idea that the holy life was the result of the death of the old man has gone; it is rather thought of as the condition of salvation which will be realised in a life beyond. Devotion which consists both of faithfulness to the teaching and holy living[4] is described as useful (ὠφέλιμος) because it holds out promises both for the present

---

[1] See *E.P.*, pp. 126 ff.

[2] See the splendid suggestive article by G. Baldensperger, 'Il a rendu témoignage devant Ponce-Pilate', Strasburg, Paris, 1922.　　　[3] See *E.P.*, pp. 561 ff.

[4] 1 Tim. vi. 3 ἡ κατ' εὐσέβειαν διδασκαλία (the doctrine which is according to godliness) shows the close connection between godliness and correct credal belief.

life and for the future (1 Tim. iv. 8 ff.). He who loves justice, godliness, faith (or faithfulness), love, patience, and gentleness, and fights the good fight[1] can be assured that he is grasping eternal life to which he is called (1 Tim. vi. 11-12). Christ has been given as a ransom for all (1 Tim. ii. 6). It is the 'mystery of godliness' which a fragment from a christological hymn extols without, however, disclosing any exact soteriology.

> God was manifest in the flesh,
> Justified in the Spirit[2]
> Seen of angels,
> Preached unto the Gentiles,
> Believed on in the world,
> Received up into glory.
> (1 Tim. iii. 16.)

The author quotes it as part of the sound traditional teaching but he fails to explain how these facts determine and condition the new moral life of believers. It is interesting to note that he does not himself create the formulae which he uses to express his faith. There seems to be the same sort of thing in another passage (Titus ii. 11-14) which also seems to be an extract from a confession of faith:

For the grace of God that bringeth salvation hath appeared to all men teaching us that denying ungodliness and worldly lusts, we should live soberly, righteously, and godly, in this present world; looking for that blessed hope, and the glorious appearing of the great God, and our saviour, Jesus Christ; who gave himself for us, that he might redeem us from all iniquity, and purify unto himself a peculiar people, zealous of good works.

Here is the echo of Pauline formulae but the thought behind them is distinctly debased. Divine grace is no longer the power which creates a new personality; its function now is only to teach and to persuade men to change their lives so that they will be saved. Salvation is the result not the cause of the sober, righteous, and devout life to which divine grace leads.

The Pastorals contain no eschatological ideas beyond belief in the life beyond and a few phrases about waiting for the Lord's appearance, which, however, are only survivals.[3]

---

[1] The author does not say against whom this fight is waged which is characteristic of the vagueness of his thoughts and the traditional nature of the phrases used by him.

[2] As we do not know what preceded this fragment from a hymn we cannot determine what is the meaning of the phrase, 'He was justified by the Spirit'.

[3] Concerning the weakening of eschatological belief in the Pastorals see pp. 275 ff.

The author has in mind communities which are firmly established but whose life is not what it ought to be both from the moral and religious point of view. He uses phrases which have by now become traditional in order to remind them of the doctrine. He does not require of them mystical experiences but wants them to accept a system of truths as they have been handed down and to see that they have practical consequences in their lives. Theology has a negative rather than a positive interest for him. He is concerned to repress the sins which would damage their moral life and salvation. The gospel is 'godly edifying which is in faith' (1 Tim. i. 4), i.e. a divine rule of life which comes from God, a kind of law for the believer, which conforms to the 'words of our Lord Jesus Christ' (1 Tim. vi. 3). The faith, which is a transmitted deposit has become an orthodoxy (1 Tim. i. 18; vi. 20; 2 Tim. i. 5; ii. 1, etc.).[1] Ecclesiastical organisation exists to assure its conservation. The Holy Spirit is no more a revealing and creative power but has become a force making for conservation (2 Tim. i. 14). The essential duty of Christians is to persevere, as the truth has been given once and for all and all novelties must be avoided (1 Tim. iv. 16; 2 Tim. ii. 19, 22; iii. 15).

The Pastoral epistles show that their author's theology was quite rudimentary in character and in form completely negative and polemical. His concern is to fight false doctrines and those who propagate them (1 Tim. i, 3 f.; iv. 6 f.; 2 Tim. ii. 15; iv. 2-5; Titus i. 9). Although the heretics whom he attacks do not seem to have belonged to groups organised outside the church, he does not think that they have a place in it. He does not address his remarks to them; he does not advise that efforts should be made to convince and gain them over; he limits himself to putting his readers on guard against them.

There is no doubt that he does not explain how the church has become the guardian of the truth, because it is implied that the authority of the apostle Paul is behind the doctrine. Only incidentally he says that, 'if any man teach otherwise, and consent not to wholesome words, even the words of our Lord Jesus Christ, and to the doctrine which is according to godliness, he is proud' (1 Tim. vi. 3). but, as we have already seen,[2] the words of the Lord seem to have been thought of here not as the source of doctrine but as the standard of moral conduct.

---

[1] Jean Reville, *Les origines de l'épiscopat*, Paris, 1894, I, pp. 283 ff.; Wendland, *Urchr. Literaturformen*, pp. 365 f.   [2] See p. 290, n. 2.

2.—THE EPISTLE TO THE EPHESIANS[1]

The epistle to the Ephesians makes Paul's thought the collective thought of the community and Christ-mysticism Church-mysticism.

This was a reaction against a Judaeo-Hellenic cosmological gnosis which was trying to insinuate itself into the church.[2] On that account, as had already happened in the epistle to the Colossians, developments relative to the cosmological function and place of Christ assumed an important place. This preoccupation influenced other theological elements in the epistle. Most notable of these, is that sin is no longer thought of as merely an ethical and human fact but as a cosmic and almost physical fact. It is thought of as a man's obedience to the lusts of the flesh as a result of the power which the demons have exercised over humanity since the fall; but evil and sin are also explained as due to a separation between the celestial and terrestrial world which the cosmic powers, and in particular, the ruler of the power of the air (ii. 2) maintain as they are in revolt against God. Here can be seen Greek influence at work in the epistle to the Ephesians as its thought lies within the framework of a dualism which is not temporal but ontological. The cosmic order is disturbed and men are confined in the lower world and cannot share in the celestial life. Christ re-establishes the cosmic unity and 'gathers together in one', i.e. reunites in one single body all things, both those on earth and those in heaven, and so reopens for men access to the heavenly world (i. 10).

Concerning the heavenly beings the interpolator's thoughts are somewhat vague.[3] We meet with the idea that Christ's resurrection and glorification have subordinated all the heavenly beings to him and that his triumph has been the realisation of a plan which God in his infinite wisdom had hidden from the spiritual powers and had only revealed to them at the time of its accomplishment. The epistle quotes (iv. 8) a passage from Psalm 68 and speaks of Christ as having made a triumphal ascent and thus defeated the demonic powers. While he may not have completely freed men from the influences drawing them on to sin (ii. 2), he has broken their irresistible

[1] See my article, 'Esquisse d'une solution nouvelle du problème de l'épître aux Ephésiens', *R.h.r.*, 1935, CXI, pp. 254-284; 1936, CXII, pp. 73-99.

[2] Paul had already attacked this gnosis in the epistle to the Colossians but when interpolations were made to the epistle to the Ephesians it seems to have assumed new forms. Concerning this gnosis, see p. 404.

[3] Schlier, *Christus und die Kirche im Epheserbrief*, Tubingen, 1930.

domination and given men the power to fight them (v. 6 ff.). But we do not find any traces of the idea that they have been destroyed. The fact that Christians have to fight them rules out the idea that they accept the sovereignty of Christ. The idea that Christ has triumphed through the cross does not completely harmonise with the idea that their revolt still persists.

The epistle says of the readers of Gentile origin to whom it is addressed that before the coming of Christ they were destined to death because of the sins in which they were living according to the era of this world, i.e. the prince of the power of the air who is in the children of rebellion (ii. 2). This refers to conditions which have now passed away. To the Gentiles who were dead because of their trespasses God has given life with Christ and has set them up with him 'among the heavenly beings' or 'in heavenly places'[1] (ii. 5). The epistle to the Ephesians does not show the same kind of incoherence in its soteriology as we find in Paul's. When the epistle says that God has made us sit together in heavenly places in Christ Jesus (ii. 6), or that he hath blessed us with a spiritual blessing (i. 3), and when it says to the faithful that they are saved (ii. 8), while Paul says that they are only saved by hope (Rom. viii. 24), it fails to make the distinction which the apostle did between justification gained and realised and redemption which is yet to come. Its soteriology is not eschatological and it has made the terms used by Paul in a realistic sense into metaphors expressing the idea of a new mode of life.

It shows a further incoherence. It describes the believer's deliverance from the powers who cause him to sin and the access to a new life as already achieved, but in spite of that, it is still necessary to fight against Principalities, against Powers, against the Rulers of the darkness of this world, in a word against the evil powers who exist among the heavenly beings (vi. 12). The fact that Christ has become the head of the cosmic body is not therefore sufficient to restore order and bring back all the beings of the celestial hierarchy to obedience. But the epistle gives us no hint as to how their hostility will be finally overcome.

The epistle to the Ephesians shows how an established form of Christian thought found a place for a chain of ideas which were foreign to Christianity and were assimilated without any effect on Christian essentials.

The conception of salvation to be found in it has two aspects, one ethical and therefore individual, the other cosmic and therefore

---

[1] For the expression ἐν τοῖς ἐπουρανίοις see p. 275, n. 1.

collective. Beings who were dead because of their sins receive life, negatively through the forgiveness which is granted to them, and positively by Christ, who coming to dwell in their hearts makes them founded and rooted in love (iii. 16-18) and perfect men 'unto the measure of the stature of the fullness of Christ' (iv. 13). On the other hand, the change made by redemption is the position of man in the cosmos. He ceases to belong to a divided universe in which what is on earth has no connection with what is in heaven. He is given a place in a connected and unified organism of which Christ is the head.

As far as Judaism and Paulinism are concerned this combination is not altogether new. In Jewish thought salvation was bound up with the coming of a new world and Paul's soteriology remained faithful to this idea. Paul, however, made this God's second plan and failed to develop it systematically. He introduced the idea of a second Adam and so made it a second creation rather than a restoration of the first creation. But the cosmic transformation for which Paul awaits is also a unification, as the hostile powers will disappear and at the end 'God will be all in all' (1 Cor. xv. 28). But the soteriology of the epistle to the Ephesians differs from Paul's in this respect, that after the cosmos has been transformed by being made one, salvation will follow, but Paul puts the accomplishment of salvation first, with the transformation of the cosmos flowing from it as a result. The epistle to the Ephesians simply puts the ethical and cosmic elements side by side; Paul connects them together into one organised whole. The reason for this is that the mind of the interpolator of the epistle to the Ephesians did not work spontaneously. He made some of the gnostic formulae his own, not because he wanted to solve particular problems which had arisen in his mind or because he had a strong interest in cosmological speculations, but because he wanted to persuade those, whom these speculations were attracting, to worship and adore the Christ.[1]

4.—THE SYNOPTIC GOSPELS

F. C. Baur was the first to realise that the gospels are not merely records of history but that each of them reflects its own Christian theology; while this is true, he drew from it inferences which it did not warrant by reckoning the gospels to be apologies for Jewish or

[1] Concerning the conception of the basis of the faith maintained by the epistle to the Ephesians see pp. 404 f. and its conception of the church see *E.P.* p. 54.

Gentile Christianity or that synthesis of both of them which was realised later in primitive Catholicism. There are only shades of difference in the forms of thought in the first three gospels and they are only of secondary importance. We must not attribute to these differences too much importance, especially as it raises a question of method which must first be examined.[1]

It would be very dangerous to try and describe each of the gospels by the material which has been used in their composition. The differences to be discovered between them in this respect are much more due to what each of them knew than to what each wanted to say. They are quantitative rather than qualitative. There are hardly any fragments of Mark which Matthew and Luke or one of them has not failed to reproduce and in the majority of cases where they have failed to do so no theological reasons can be discovered for the omission.[2]

We have also to ask ourselves how far a particular fragment which is peculiar to one evangelist expresses his own particular ideas. One concrete example will help us here. In Matthew v. 19 are the words 'Whosoever therefore shall break one of these least commandments, and shall teach men so, he shall be called the least in the kingdom of heaven'. Even if it was quite certain that, as has been sometimes supposed, these words were originally directed against the apostle Paul and that they reflect the sentiments which certain Jewish Christian circles felt towards him, it would not be right for us to attribute to Matthew a legalist antipauline position. Matthew may quite well have reproduced this saying somewhat mechanically without perhaps seeing its antipauline prejudice.[3] In short, there is

[1] This is proved by the way in which ideas have developed concerning what has been called the paulinism of Mark. See *Introd.*, I, pp. 358 ff., and M. Werner, *Der Einflusspaulinischer Theologie im Markusevangelium*, Geissen, 1923. It is true that we can find ideas in Mark's gospel which bear a striking resemblance to Paul's but by the time the gospel was compiled they had passed into the common currency of the church. The idea that Paul exercised a direct influence on the gospel is contradicted by wide differences in terminology.

[2] But there is one exceptional case. It belongs to two primitive stories of healing (vii. 32-37; viii. 22-26) where Jesus does not effect the cure by a word but by gestures which are not effective at once but have to be repeated. It is certain that Matthew and Luke failed to reproduce them because they did not correspond with their idea of the way in which Jesus' healing power worked. But there is such a strong contrast between them and other stories of healing given by Mark that we are led to suppose that he gave them because he found them in his sources, the ideas which originally inspired them being, however, quite foreign to his own.

[3] In the same way it is foolish to attribute to Luke peculiar ideas about poverty and wealth because his gospel contains some pieces which are inspired by what is called an Ebionite tendency. See in particular the form of the beatitudes and

nothing to show that Matthew has adopted a particular position of his own.

On this point we can draw more decisive conclusions from negative observations. Unfortunately it is something quite exceptional for us to be able to make any precise inference. There is one, however, which deserves mention. In the synoptic apocalypse Matthew (xxiv. 20) makes Christ advise his hearers to pray that their flight be not in winter or on a sabbath-day; Mark (xiii. 18) does not mention the winter while Luke mentions neither the winter nor the sabbath, although he (xxiii. 25) has the sentence which comes before it in Mark and Matthew, the one concerning the misfortune of women who will be with child when those days shall come. It is illegitimate to infer that Matthew wrote in an environment which was still loyal to keeping the sabbath, as he may have reproduced somewhat mechanically what he found in his source. On the contrary, if Mark omitted the reference to the sabbath, it proves that its observance did not interest him and Luke's omission of both the sabbath and the winter shows that his interest in the eschatological drama is purely theoretical and is not connected in his mind with any concrete circumstances.

Essentially what helps us to see the character of the religious and theological position of the evangelists is the way in which they use their material. As they had no conscious intention of making their work personal, it also represents the position of the communities in which they lived. The main outlines of Mark's narrative are to be found in Matthew and Luke, although they have become rather disjointed through the insertion of fresh material taken chiefly from the Logia and also in the case of Matthew through his tendency to put together blocks of similar material. But this is due to purely literary causes and is in no way to be accounted for on theological grounds. In these circumstances it is much better to consider the three synoptics together.

We can discover certain differences in the presentation of Jesus due to the fact that the material used in the composition of the gospels corresponds to different stages in the development of

the corresponding curses (vi. 20-26) and also the story of the rich man and Lazarus (xvi. 19-31), i.e. those pieces which seem to make poverty a ground for salvation and wealth a bar to it. There is in effect nothing to show that we are here dealing with pieces created by Luke. They may reflect the conceptions of a particular circle of believers whose tradition was already fixed when he used it, or they may quite well correspond to a particular aspect of the actual teaching of Jesus.

christology. For instance, the story of the baptism even as it is told in Mark shows us an adoptionist christology changing into an ontological one, as soon as we see that what was originally a vision revealing to Jesus his vocation is on the way to becoming his manifestation as Messiah to John Baptist and the people. Jesus' messiahship, which is thus publicly proclaimed, before his ministry has even begun, is described towards the end of the Galilean period in the story of Peter's confession as a disclosure which has just been made to the disciples[1] and as a secret which they are to keep to themselves. A little later on in the story of the transfiguration the messiahship, which Peter had confessed before the Twelve and in their name, is described as a secret entrusted to the three intimate disciples which they are forbidden to divulge until the Son of Man is risen from the dead. None of the evangelists seem to have been troubled by these incoherences. We can therefore conclude that neither they nor the communities to which they belonged and for whom their works were intended had any real interest in the philosophical aspect of christology. It is for that reason also that there is almost no mention in the gospels of anything which might explain the person of Jesus or could be interpreted as an explanation. But Jesus is always shown as a transcendent personality. At the end of each story from the first expulsion of the demon in the synagogue at Capernaum (Mark i. 21-28 and par.) right up to the discovery of the empty tomb (Mark xvi. 1-8) there is always a note giving the impression produced by the words and acts of Jesus. The phrases used express surprise, admiration, and fear. There is no reference to that kind of vague terror and discomfort which men feel when they are faced with facts they cannot explain. They all refer to a feeling purely religious in nature which is felt in face of the manifestation of a transcendent and peculiarly divine power. This feeling was particularly acute in a Jewish environment because the Jewish mind was obsessed with the gulf which separates man from God and with the conviction that it is a terrible thing for sinful man to be found in the presence of God, the holy one.

It must also be noted that Matthew and Luke omit some statements in Mark attributing human emotions to Jesus.[2] This may not be so much a new attitude towards Jesus adopted by Matthew and Luke as Mark's attitude carried to its logical conclusion.

---

[1] This aspect of the incident is plainly underlined by Matthew, but it seems implicitly to have meant the same thing for Mark and Luke.

[2] See *V. de J.*, p. 152 and *Life of Jesus*, pp. 172 f.

THE BIRTH OF CHRISTIANITY

There is no need to insist on the important place given to the moral teaching of Jesus in the gospel together with the conception of Jesus as the pattern and lawgiver. The Sermon on the plain in Luke (vi. 20-49) and more particularly the Sermon on the Mount in Matthew (v-viii) are the charter of a new society. The idea which we have here of Jesus as revealing a new way of life certainly originated in a current of thought which belonged to Palestine, as is proved by the resemblances it bears to the conception of Christianity which we find in the epistle of James and the *Didache*.[1]

But beside this in the gospels, Jesus is the man who came to accomplish the drama of redemption by which the kingdom of God will be realised and salvation assured to those who have believed on him, followed him, and have not been ashamed of him before the world. This shows plainly the influence of Paulinism.

Mark's narrative is divided into two parts which are joined together by the story of Peter's confession (viii. 27-30). As a corollary there follows immediately the first declaration of the necessity of the sufferings, rejection, death and resurrection of the Son of Man (viii. 31-33) and a prediction of sufferings to be endured by the disciples also (viii. 34-ix. 1). The transfiguration then gives these declarations divine confirmation (ix. 2-8). It is of little importance that this grouping of incidents has only the faintest connection with what really happened; what matters is the significance Mark attributes to them. In Mark's narrative the questions put by Jesus, 'Whom do people say . . . whom do you say that I am' have no real context; neither have they any connection with the situation depicted by John (vi. 66 ff.), where Jesus is described after the crisis in Galilee as having been deserted by many of those who had followed him up to then and wishing to know if he could at least count on the little group who were still faithful to him.[2] The gospels show and explain the life of Jesus as a drama which disclosed and accomplished a plan prepared by providence and from it has been deleted almost all remembrance of the actual circumstances which had in fact determined its course and pattern.

Mark gives to the proclamation of Jesus' messiahship the character of the confession of a fundamental and essential belief and the announcement of the sufferings of the Son of Man is the twin pole of this belief and cannot be separated from it. When the evangelist is speaking of the sufferings which will be the lot of those who wish to follow Jesus, he is not so much concerned with the

[1] See pp. 373 ff.   [2] See *V. de J.*, p. 122 and *Life of Jesus*, pp. 378 ff.

circumstances in which these words were spoken as with the idea that it was important to impress them on the minds of his readers. Paul is always returning to the same idea and it forms also the essential theme of the first epistle of Peter, to know that only by suffering and dying with Christ can a man also share in the glory of his life and reign.

While the evangelists affirm in the most categorical way possible that the drama of redemption is necessary they are always vague concerning how it is efficacious and by what process. They use images—especially in the words accompanying the distribution of the bread and the cup in the course of the last supper—which express the ideas of ransom, substitution, and life given for those who are his own. We cannot tell how far formal soteriological doctrines are invoked by them; they only show in every case that the evangelists do not attach much importance to their systematic development.

There is, however, one soteriological idea which seems to have determined the thought of the evangelists, i.e. the idea of a victory gained by Christ over Satan and the demons. It is expressed in the stories of healing which, as we know, occupy such a large place in the gospels. In a world dominated by wicked powers Christians felt that they were protected against them by a power superior to them. While they lived in this evil world they did not belong to it;[1] they were strangers in it; they were not interested in what attracted other men's loyalties.[2]

Early on the story of the temptation (Mark i. 12-15) shows Jesus baffling the snares of Satan and compelling him to withdraw after he has received a check. The discussion following on the accusation brought against Jesus that he was casting out evil spirits in the name of, i.e. by the power of Beelzebub, the prince of demons, is equally typical (Mark iii. 22-30 and par.). In particular, the parable of the strong man (iii. 23-27 and par.) shows that the expulsions of the demons wrought by Jesus were only made possible through a victory gained over Satan. We cannot tell what Jesus considered had gained this victory[3] but putting on one side the fact that the saying was spoken during the ministry of Jesus there is no doubt that it suggested both to the evangelists and their readers the idea to be met with in Paul (1 Cor. ii. 6-8; Col. ii. 15. Cf. Eph. i. 21) that Christ had gained a victory by his cross over all the hostile powers who had revolted against God, a victory the full effects of which

---

[1] Harnack, *Mission*, I, pp. 136 ff.   [2] Harnack, *Mission*, I, pp. 238 ff.

[3] It is not impossible that he may be thinking of the ministry of John-Baptist.

would only be disclosed at the parousia (1 Cor. xv. 25-26). Yet the victory has already been gained, as is shown by the saying of Jesus on the return of the seventy disciples, 'I have seen Satan fall as lightning from heaven' (Luke x. 18).[1]

The miracles of healing are both acts of power and acts of deliverance. In reference to a woman who had had a 'spirit of infirmity' for twelve years and whom Jesus healed on a sabbath-day, Luke (xiii. 16) uses this characteristic expression, 'Ought not this woman, being a daughter of Abraham, whom Satan hath bound, lo, these twelve years?' We are not forcing the meaning of these declarations in the gospels in saying that they are not only an interpretation of events which happened during the ministry of Jesus but that they also express what Christians felt they owed to the protection Christ gave to them.[2]

The importance of the drama of redemption in the eyes of the evangelists can be measured in an almost material fashion by the amount of space which their compositions devote to the story of the passion. It forms a coherent whole from the account of the council of the Jewish authorities when they determine to put Jesus to death (Mark xiv. 1-2) to the discovery of the empty tomb in Mark and the resurrection appearances in Matthew and Luke. Criticism shows the existence of fissures in this block and that it is made up of material of unequal value but from the point of view of the significance of the story for the evangelists this has no importance. They made no attempt at all to elucidate a chain of cause and effect which ended in Calvary. The drama which crowns the life of Jesus is for them the unfolding and realisation of a divine plan prepared beforehand. All the actors in the story of the passion are gathered round the story of the last supper which throws a light on them all and shows what interpretation is to be given. In this way the drama ceases to be something afar off and abstract, because it is past, and becomes something very near and closely mixed up with the life of believers. Perhaps we must go further and say that what touches the reader is not something which was one day in the past enacted at Jerusalem but the results which issued from this drama and of which a believer is conscious every time he receives the bread and wine of the eucharist. For the evangelists salvation is linked to a cultus and the church which celebrates this cultus is the framework in which it is realised.

[1] This saying must be considered a metaphor rather than an allusion to a vision.　　[2] Harnack, *Mission*, I, pp. 115 ff.

5.—THE BOOK OF THE ACTS

After the synoptic gospels the book of the Acts, which is a sequel to Luke, must naturally be considered next. It belongs to the same class of documents as the synoptics, being deuteropauline in the wide sense of the term, but its deuteropaulinism is much more distinct because in it there are commingled two currents of thought, one being that of Jerusalemite Christianity and the other being Paulinism. This is shown very clearly in the parallels the narrative draws between Peter and Paul whose personalities dominate the two parts of the book respectively. The author is most careful to find similar incidents in the lives of each of them. Their similarity cannot be considered accidental.[1] He carefully passes over the collisions and conflicts which took place between them and makes them out always to have been in perfect harmony with each other; under the influence of the theory of the institution of the apostleship which had become current in his own time he gives Peter a certain pre-eminence and so for instance he ascribes to him the distinction of taking the initiative in being the first to preach the gospel to the Gentiles. He also avoids giving Paul the title of apostle which is used of the Twelve without exception.[2]

As against the views of the Tubingen school there is no need to see in the deuteropauline character of the book of Acts a systematic manipulation of the facts undertaken to justify primitive catholicism, which according to the pattern of Hegelian logic should be considered to be the completed synthesis of two forms of Christianity which were originally opposed to each other, Jewish Christianity being the thesis and Gentile Christianity being the antithesis. It should rather be considered to reflect the situation as it existed between 80 and 90, when the conflicts of the past had been forgotten and the past had assumed in men's minds an idealised form which was also a justification of the present. We should therefore be making a mistake if we tried to discover if it was the author's purpose

---

[1] By way of examples I find the following parallels : At Samaria Peter came into conflict with Simon the Magician (viii. 18-25) and at Paphos Paul with the magician, Elymas Bar-Jesus (xiii. 6-12). The sick whom Peter's shadow touched were healed (v. 13); in the same way handkerchiefs or linen which had touched Paul's body healed the sick (xix. 11-12). Prison gates opened miraculously before Peter at Jerusalem (xii. 6-11) and before Paul and Silas at Philippi (xvi. 25-34).

[2] There are, however, two passages (xiv. 4, 14) where Paul and Barnabas are called apostles. This is an inconsistency due to the fact that the compiler has forgotten to correct an expression which existed in his source and did not conform altogether to his own ideas.

in writing the Acts to defend Jewish Christianity or Gentile Christianity or to promote their reconciliation. His thought is only the reflection of that of the church of his time when the two currents from Palestine and Greece had met .and combined. Such of Paul's ideas as still survived were debased commonplaces compared with the original 'as universalism was accepted without question.

Beyond this the compiler of Acts is not a theologian in the real sense of the word. One idea, however, running through the whole of his book he tries to demonstrate, which is that Christianity is not a novelty but a sequel to Judaism because it proclaims that Jesus and his work have realised the promise on which the religion of Israel was founded. What attracts him to this idea is its practical value, since, if it is true, Christianity has a right to the same tolerance from the Empire as is given to Judaism.

The author of Acts is so indifferent to theological consistency that he does not mind placing side by side Peter's sermons, which have been taken from a very early source and express a very rudimentary christology and soteriology, with other sermons, which he has edited or have been edited from a deuteropauline point of view and, as the context serves, are put into the mouth of Peter (x. 35-43; xv. 7-11) or James (xv. 14-21) or Paul (xiii. 16-41). But they all express the same dull, tame ideas. He also had no difficulty in finding a place in his work for a sermon—the one which he attributed to Paul at Athens (xvii. 22-31)—in which is sketched out a theory which shows great originality and is much more Greek than Jewish in tone. It presents the Christian revelation as a divine response to the groping and futile quest of mankind after God, whom they have been unable to find, although he was quite near to them.[1] He was also able to give Stephen's speech (vii. 2-53), although it expresses an argument concerning the relations between Christianity and the Jewish religion which are completely different from his own. Although it is true, as we have seen,[2] that this speech has been mutilated and added to, this does not imply that such mutilations and additions must be attributed to the author of Acts and that they were not already there in the source on which he depended.

[1] Concerning this sermon see Ed. Norden, *Agnostos theos, Untersuchungen zur Formengeschichte religioser Roden*, Leipzig, Berlin, 1913. Harnack (*Ist die Rede des Paulus in Athen ein ursprunglicher Bestandteil der Apostelgeschichte?* Leipzig, 1913) tried to maintain the sermon at Athens to be authentic but all his arguments show is that it was not a later addition to Acts, which is no proof whatever that it was Paul's composition. [2] See pp. 172 f.

This not only shows the vague character of the thought of the compiler of Acts but also inasmuch as the book has been preserved and must therefore have met with some success, reveals the general state of religious thought in the church at the end of the first century.

6.—THE FIRST EPISTLE OF PETER

We must not try to find in the epistle of Peter[1] an exposition of a complete theological system. Its concern is solely practical. It is an exhortation to loyalty addressed to believers who were suffering an active or latent persecution. But it is made up partly of ideas and much more of religious sentiments suited for giving instruction to those in this situation. By reminding them of their faith and especially by evoking the example of Christ, the author tries to comfort his readers and to exhort them to be patient. We must try to disengage the religious conception inspiring this exhortation.[2] It has no personal character; it is rather the reflection of a collective faith than the product of individual reflection or speculation. The terms used by the author derive their inspiration from Pauline phrases but lack the realism which belonged to them when they were attached to a mystic experience. The whole epistle is dominated by the idea of salvation. God is the author of salvation which he has predestined for the elect (i. 3-9).[3] The anthropology of the epistle, although it betrays the influence of Paul, approximates to Greek dualism. The way of salvation is the destruction of the flesh rather than its transformation.[4]

[1] The epistle called Peter I cannot be the work of the apostle whose name it bears. It only seems to have been attributed to him sometime after it was written. Certain contradictions to be found in the document, notably those referring to the attitude of the authorities towards Christians, suggest that it was composed in several stages. Originally it may have been as Bornemann supposes ('Der erste Petrusbrief, eine Taufrede des Silvanus?' Z.N.T.W., 1919-20, XVIII, pp. 143-165) a baptismal exhortation which may be attributed to Silvanus on account of v. 12. Its date would then be about 80. Later on, about 110 perhaps, the exhortation may have been developed and adapted to a situation which had worsened and put under the patronage of Peter.

[2] On this point see the careful exposition which, however, is rather too systematic of Jean Monnier, La première épître de l'Apôtre Pierre, Mâcon, 1900, pp. 277 ff.

[3] The idea of predestination did not originate in a speculation about the freedom and omnipotence of God, but in the conviction that faith does not have a human origin and that salvation is a gift of God. It has also been asked (J. Monnier, p. 284) if there was not also the idea of predestination to damnation. The passage ii. 8 may suggest it. It is a question here of the corner stone against which those stumble who have not surrendered to the word. But there seems to be in this passage a statement of fact rather than the affirmation of a divine decree.

[4] Peter does not seem to agree with Paul in his conception of σῶμα as being purely formal. Flesh and body seem to be almost interchangeable conceptions developing into an ethic but also one of the causes determining this development.

While Paul considers Christ to be only spirit in the full sense of the word when he had become Kyrios, Peter considers that he was pre-existent spirit as he was the Spirit who acted through the prophets (i. 11).

Peter's christology shows no development within the frame of a cosmology as can be found in Paul, John, and the author of the epistle to the Hebrews. It is impossible, as has sometimes been done, to use this fact as an argument in favour of the early age of the epistle; it is explained by the completely practical character of its concern. Otherwise Peter is interested in the redemptive work of Christ rather than in any definition of his person. He speaks of his sufferings and death as a cause of salvation but does not develop any systematic argument on the subject and gives no clear description of the way in which they effect it. He clings to phrases which had already become traditional and express no personal thought. Some of them (i. 19; ii. 24; iii. 18) evoke the idea of sacrifice but they are so lacking in connection and co-ordination that they cannot be considered to be anything more than pure metaphors or expressions of belief of a symbolic and somewhat conventional character.

The epistle of Peter contains a doctrine which elsewhere in the New Testament can only be found in a much less precise form, that of Christ preaching to the dead and the rebellious spirits who wait for their final judgement in prison (iii. 19 f.; iv. 6).[1] It represents various preoccupations denoting a stage in the development of thought sufficiently advanced to need a description of what happened between the death of Christ and his resurrection, a manifestation of the unlimited character of the redemptive power of Christ, and finally an effective answer to the idea that an infinite number of men were condemned to perdition solely because they had not had the opportunity of hearing the gospel of salvation preached to them.

We find in the epistle the Pauline idea of the association of the faithful with the sufferings and resurrection of the Saviour without, however, that strict co-ordination with which Paul connected it to the idea of justification. The epistle uses it especially as a motive for encouragement and as a theme for exhortation.

It has been thought that there can be found in Peter a trinitarian formula.[2] In the opening greeting (i. 2) the foreknowledge of God, sanctification through the Spirit, obedience to Jesus Christ and

---

[1] Concerning this conception see my book, *La foi à la résurrection*, pp. 357 ff.
[2] J. Monnier, p. 25.

purification by his blood are associated together. The formula is only trinitarian in appearance. The reference to the Spirit is only a survival of primitive pneumatism and does not correspond to a concrete and actual experience.

Peter makes faith the centre of religious life but his conception of it is hardly precise. It seems to be as far removed from the mysticism of Paul's conception as from the intellectualist conception attacked by James. To have faith in short is to be a Christian. Faith serves as a foundation for hope.[1] This is explained to a large degree by the critical circumstances which were sweeping across the church and directing its thought to the life beyond. This is also the reason why its eschatological perspective is much sharper than what we find in most of the writings of the same period.[2] There is a strong feeling in it that Christians are strangers and travellers far from their real home (i. 1; ii. 11), but there is no mention of the parousia or the apocalypse drama and all the expressions used can only be given a symbolic interpretation and be understood to point to the achievement of salvation independent of the coming of a new age.

Lastly, we cannot help but be struck by the amount of space taken up in the epistle by exhortations to sanctification. This characteristic conforms to the essentially practical purpose which the epistle was intended to serve. This, however, can be judged not only to be a symptom of the way in which Christianity was developed into an ethic but also one of the causes determining this development.

[1] In this respect his thought resembles that of the epistle to the Hebrews. It cannot, however, be inferred from this that one book has influenced the other. It is rather that similar situations have given to the thought of both authors the common orientation we find they possess.

[2] It would then be illegitimate to judge this to be a sign of archaism.

CHAPTER IV

The Epistle to the Hebrews

WE do not find in the epistle to the Hebrews[1] a complete theology but an interpretation of Christ's death, which, although personal in nature, belongs to a current of Greek Christian thought parallel to Paulinism but independent of it; but it approximates to Paulinism on certain essential points, particularly on its treatment of the death of Christ as capitally important for the accomplishment of salvation.

The author of the epistle presumes that the reader knows and accepts the elements of Christian teaching (vi. 1). His purpose is to give teaching on the death of Christ which can only be assimilated by those who have made some progress, not only in their religious convictions, but also in their intellectual beliefs. He is trying to counteract a certain decadence in thought or at any rate a certain sluggishness and intellectual inertia which was perhaps the characteristic of the Christianity of his time rather than of a particular group for whom his work was intended. He reproaches them that, although they must have become teachers themselves since they first received Christian teaching, they still needed to be taught elementary doctrine, or, using an expression also used by Paul (1 Cor. iii. 1-2),[2] which seems to have come from the vocabulary of gnosticism,[3] that they were still being fed on milk, because they were not yet able to eat solid food (v. 11 f.). We must not, however, take this reproach literally since it is the superior doctrine which he goes on to give. We must therefore suppose that the author had in

---

[1] We know nothing about who the author of the epistle to the Hebrews was or where it was written. It seems to have been written between 89 and 90. See my article, 'Hébreux (Épître aux)' in the *Dictionnaire encyclopédique de la Bible de* A. Westphal, Paris, 1932 ff., I, pp. 508-510, in which the most essential bibliographical references are given. Concerning the thought of the epistle to the Hebrews the most important work, although it is now rather old, is that of E. Menegoz, *La theologie de l'é'pitre aux Hébreux*, Paris, 1894.

[2] It is also to be found in 1 Peter ii. 2.

[3] We find it in Philo, *De agricultura*, 9; *De congressu*, 19; *De migratione Abraham*, 24; *De sobrietate*, 8, *De somniis*, ii. 10; *Quod omnis probus liber*, 160 and in Epictetus, ii. 16, 39; iii. 24, 9.

mind the general situation and not the state of a particular group of readers. The method of argument used by him is that of exegesis. In what the Old Testament says of Melchizedech (Gen. xiv. 18) he finds the prototype of the sacrifice of Christ, and in what the law teaches about the sacrifice which each year the high-priest offered in the holy of holies for the expiation of the people, he finds teaching about the unique sacrifice which Christ has offered with his own blood in the heavenly sanctuary. This doctrine is not opposed to other interpretations of Christ's death. The author's intention seems to have been only to develop with greater clearness ideas which may not have been current among those whom he was addressing but were not entirely new to them.[1]

Like Paul the author of the epistle to the Hebrews is a universalist without any reserve, but he wrote at a time when the position of universalism was so strong that it did not need to be justified and defended.[2] It is plain, however, that his ideas concerning the function and significance of the law did not coincide with those of Paul. Paul considers that the law has its own significance which only held good until Christ. For the epistle to the Hebrews the law had an allegorical significance. It is the representation—he calls it the shadow (x. 1)—of an order of higher realities to which Christ and his sacrifice belong. The question of keeping the law has ceased to be relevant, the only idea which it conjures up is that of the sacrifice of expiation and the law governing the ritual for it.

Eschatological expectation is very attenuated. The phrases referring to it are little more than survivals. One idea, however, is still completely valid for the author, the idea of the judgement, by which at the end of time (vi. 2; ix. 27) every individual will be admitted into the kingdom of heaven or excluded from it. This attenuation in eschatological thought is not only the result of wear and tear; it is

---

[1] Weinel (*Bibl. Th.*, p. 534) thought he could perceive in the epistle to the Hebrews a polemic against a judaising form of gnosticism. To justify this interpretation he emphasises as most important the way in which the epistle insists on the superiority of Christ and his sacrifice but all that the epistle contains on this theme is only of a theoretical character and never does more than provide what is needed as a ground for the allegorical interpretation of the Old Testament in order that it may be used to support a doctrine of the sacrifice of Christ. Furthermore, it is impossible to see how a Jewish doctrine of sacrifice could have sprung up at a time when sacrifices had ceased to be offered. Weinel speaks of a 'romantic enthusiasm' (*romantische Schwarmerei*) for the old religion. Such states of mind do not constitute theological positions which can be discussed by the exegetic method as it is used by the writer of the Epistle to the Hebrews.

[2] This also constitutes an objection to Weinel's theory.

also due to the fact that the dualism of the epistle is very much Greek in its outlook. The heavenly realm, the true home of the faithful, from which they have the feeling that they are far removed as pilgrims and strangers (xi. 13) is not so much a new world which will take the place of the old as a higher realm which exists above the world of earth.[1]

The form in which sin is conceived as that which prevents a man from entering into the celestial realm is entirely negative; it is a stain on human nature rather than a corruption. The sinner needs to be purified rather than transformed and recreated. Cleared of sin by the expiation and purification which the celestial sacrifice of Christ has realised he resumes, it may be said, the path which would have led him from terrestrial to celestial life, if sin had not intervened, i.e. the path of sanctification. The way in which the problem of sanctification is stated in the epistle to the Hebrews is not entirely void of contradiction. It categorically affirms that there can be no second repentance for the man who has been enlightened, i.e. who has received forgiveness for his sins and suffers a relapse. He is definitely shut out from salvation (vi. 4-8; x. 26-31; xii. 16-17).[2] If this is true, the logical consequence should be that if sanctity is not realised, salvation is impossible. But it is clear from the exhortations given by the author to his readers that he does not consider them to be entirely holy; in spite of this he does not despair of their salvation. We can only therefore suppose that certain sins of a particularly grave nature are bars to salvation.[3] Other sins the author of the epistle to the Hebrews does not seem to have considered to be radically incompatible with the Christian life but he does not say how the Christian is to be purified, in what way or on what conditions he can obtain forgiveness. He resigns himself to the persistence of sin in such a way as to reveal a lowering in moral ideals. The completely negative character of his conception of expiation as a purification also shows that he envisages sin as a stain which has come upon a man from without.

[1] Although the writer does not express his thought with very great clearness it seems as if the coexistence of the two worlds is not to be thought of as the result of a fall but as a stage in the work of creation.

[2] See my article, 'La doctrine de l'impossibilité de la seconde conversion dans l'épître aux Hébreux et sa place dans l'évolution du Christianisme', *Annuaire de l'École pratique des Hautes Etudes (Sciences religieuses)*, 1931-32, pp. 3-38.

[3] The first epistle of John in the same way as though it was a current idea makes a distinction between two categories of sins, those involving the loss of salvation, and those not necessarily doing so. By inference from what was the custom of the penitentiary at a later date, it may be conjectured that the sins which could not be forgiven were apostasy, murder, and adultery.

The purification of sin is wrought by the sacrifice of Christ. The epistle's christology shows marked analogies with that of the Fourth Gospel both in its ontological character and also through the way in which both works have been strongly influenced by Philo's doctrine of the logos.[1] But although the epistle strongly emphasises the divine and eternal side of the person of Christ (i. 2, 3) it also insists on his humanity, his sufferings and his temptations (ii. 18; v. 18; ix. 26). They make him one with humanity so that he can become the high-priest representing humanity before God on whose behalf he offers intercession (v. 8; viii. 3).[2]

The author of the epistle to the Hebrews interprets the death of Christ in terms of ritual not like Paul in those of jurisprudence. The redemptive act does not actually take place on the cross, which only prepares the ground for it and creates the conditions; it takes place in the heavenly sanctuary into which Christ has gained entrance to offer there the sacrifice of his own blood (viii. 3; ix. 25 ff.; x. 8 ff.).

The tabernacle set up by Moses in accordance with the pattern which had been shown to him on Sinai and the instructions which he then received (viii. 5), is only the likeness of the heavenly sanctuary in the same way that the levitical priest and the sacrifice which it is his office to offer do not belong to the true priesthood with the sacrifice which is really able to take away sin. The true priest is that referred to by the saying from Psalm cx (verse 4), 'Thou art a priest for ever after the order of Melchisedec' (v. 6; vi. 20). The levitical priesthood is not eternal because the high-priests, being mortal, had to be continually replaced (vii. 23). The sacrifice which they offered was not efficacious because it had to be continually repeated. If such a sacrifice could have taken away sin it would have become unnecessary and would have ceased to be offered (x. 2). Furthermore, what is a further proof of its imperfection, sacrifice had to be offered by the high-priest not only for the sins of the people but also for his own sins (vii. 27 ; ix. 7). The purpose of this criticism of the system of Jewish sacrifice is not to attack its legitimacy but to show its true significance. It is a representation of the one real efficacious sacrifice which must be offered by Christ once and for all in the heavenly sanctuary (ix. 28).

[1] On this point see E. Ménégoz, pp. 197 ff.
[2] Paul also insists on the union of Christ with humanity. But the idea was so commonplace in primitive Christianity that we have no right to use it as a proof of Paul's influence on the thought of the epistle to the Hebrews.

Christ is both the high-priest and the victim of this sacrifice. It cannot be repeated as Christ can only die once. That is why those who relapse into sin after they have profited by the sacrifice cannot obtain pardon again.

The thought of the epistle to the Hebrews is very different from Paul's because it borrows from Judaism all the material for its interpretation of Christ's death and so in certain respects is much closer to Judaism. But it is also much further removed from Judaism, which has ceased to be an ideological system and a religion in respect of which Christianity has to define its position and defend its autonomy.

We can find, however, in Paul's epistles certain ideas which, while they are only presented by him in an incidental manner, show a real affinity with ideas developed in the epistle to the Hebrews. Thus, in the epistle to the Romans Paul says that God has made Christ to be a propitiation by his blood for the forgiveness of sins (iii. 25). The word $\lambda\alpha\sigma\tau\dot{\eta}\rho\iota o\nu$ of which we have numerous examples[1] must be understood in the general sense of the means of expiation although there is no direct reference to be found here to the ritual of the Jewish sacrifice of expiation. But this allusion may have suggested to the author of the epistle to the Hebrews an interpretation which he went on to develop.

[1] See Deissmann, '$\dot{I}\lambda\alpha\sigma\tau\eta\rho\iota o\varsigma$ und $\iota\lambda\alpha\sigma\tau\dot{\eta}\rho\iota o\nu$, Eine lexikalische Studie', *Z.N.T.W.*, 1903, IV, pp. 193-212.

CHAPTER V

The Johannine Theology

THE Fourth Gospel and the two first epistles of John,[1] which throw further light on some points in the teaching of the gospel and make some corrections, express the ideas of a group of Christians, which was at first rather a closed circle, although it was not in any way opposed to the church at large. Later its influence gradually extended over the churches of Asia and through them over the whole of Christendom. But behind the Johannine theology can be discerned an original and creative religious personality.

I.—THE FOURTH GOSPEL

The best way of describing the general characteristics of Johannism especially in its purest form as it is found in the

---

[1] In my *Introd.* I (t. II) I have given the reasons which seem to rule out any possibility of retaining the traditional attribution of the authorship of the Johannine writings to the apostle John, the beloved disciple of Jesus, who is supposed to have lived at Ephesus in the last decade of the first century. The Johannine literature came into existence at this period and in this environment, although it is not impossible that the gospel in its first rough form originated at Antioch. The Gospel passed through several stages before it reached the form in which we know it. Consequently it lost something of its freshness and was gradually adapted to the general mind and needs of the church. As for the epistles the second seems to be older than the first which gives an ample exposition of what is briefly sketched out in the first, while the third contains no doctrine at all. They all came out of the same environment as the gospel but are not written by the man who wrote the gospel in its original form at any rate. They clearly belong to a later date and embody ideas to be found in the gospel which are expressed in more clear-cut and possibly somewhat simpler sentences. This seems to have been done in order that they might be used to support theories and practices which were contrary to the thought of the evangelist. The Apocalypse shows certain affinities with the language and thought of the gospel. There is no doubt that this must be explained as due to the fact that all the Johannine literature has the same geographical origin. But the orientation of the thought of the Apocalypse is quite different from that of the gospel. Some time after the composition of the Johannine literature in order to give proper form to the authority which it enjoyed in fact the tradition grew up that the apostle John was both the author of the gospel and the epistles and also of the Apocalypse and in this way a link was forged connecting them all together.

gospel[1] would be to call it a combination of gnostic philosophy and mysticism. John[2] does not possess in the slightest degree a synthetic and constructive mind. His intellectual make-up is expressed in his style which is characterised by little sentences being placed side by side without any organic connection between them.[3] One sentence often corrects another. It is also characterised by his dialectic, which takes the form of one thesis being opposed in argument to another over and over again. Hence his thought lacks coherence; theories are simply stated and put side by side. They are not so much the elements of a system as the record of experiences, the expression of mystic intuitions. Each affirmation has its own value and stands on its own feet. This is owing to the mystic character of Johannine thought. The mind of the mystic, when he is not also a dialectician like Paul, is completely possessed by each moment in his experience, and each of his intuitions as they come. He finds no need to co-ordinate the diverse elements of his religious life.

John is so strongly persuaded of the truth of what he has grasped and is expressing that it is impossible for him to imagine that other people may not be convinced by the evidence. He only replies to objections by repeating statements over and over again, sometimes reinforcing them by his own certitude. He can only find one explanation why everyone is not convinced like him. It is predestination. The truth has only been revealed to those whom God has given to Christ and whom he has brought to him (vi. 37, 65). Others cannot grasp it.[4]

Johanninism is also a gnostic philosophy. There is no doubt that John wishes to know the way which leads to salvation. He declares to his readers that he has written his book, 'that they might believe that Jesus is the Christ, the Son of God, and that believing they might have life through his name' (xx. 31), but at the same time he wants to prove to them how the revelation which this Jesus has brought reveals the mystery of God, the world, man, and his destiny, as he finds Jesus not only the Messiah promised to Israel but also the Word of God, who became flesh and dwelt among us, whose glory we beheld.

[1] The Gospel in the form in which we have it seems, however, to have been subjected to certain revisions which began to make it better adapted to the needs of the church, i.e. to a larger circle of believers than that for which it was originally intended.

[2] I must remind readers that the name John is only used here in an entirely symbolic and purely conventional manner.

[3] Both in the gospel and the epistles connecting particles are particularly rare. In this respect there is a very sharp contrast between John's style and Paul's.

[4] We meet with this idea in Paul. Cf. 1 Corinthians i. 24; ii. 19 ff.

The two aspects of Johannine thought, mysticism and gnostic philosophy, are closely correlated to each other. John expresses his ideas in the form of speeches put into the mouth of Jesus. The themes around which the speeches revolve are those of the arguments which were taking place between Jews and Christians when the gospel was being compiled. That they are anachronisms is obvious. John is using a literary fiction to give greater authority to what he says. He makes Christ speak because he is convinced that he has received his message from him through the action of his Spirit. In his eyes no distinction can be made between Jesus who lived on earth for a period and Christ who through his Spirit returns to visit his own and lead them into all truth (xvi. 13). The Johannine gnostic philosophy is much more mystical in its outlook than speculative. Ideological elements occupy a very small space in it. John attributes the creation to Christ (i. 3) but he does this because he identifies Christ with the logos. He is only interested in this idea as a theory, a passing notion, which he does not stop to explore. It is particularly noticeable that he does not draw from it, as Paul did, any conclusions concerning the position of Christ in respect to the cosmic powers.[1]

Johanninism stands at the junction of several lines of thought, one of which is Pauline. Also in the Palestinian traditions, which have been used in the narrative parts of the gospel, are to be discerned on the theological level influences coming from apostolic Christianity. There exists also in the gospel an extended form of Judaism in spite of the conflict between Jews and Christians which was acute at the time and in the place where the gospel was written. But on this point the situation is shown to be quite complex; it presents a series of problems settled solutions of which are still far from being found. There is no agreement yet what questions should be asked and what features are significant.

John is not only the heir of biblical Judaism; what has been definitely granted, and is also plain, is that he was also the heir of the Hellenised Judaism of Alexandria, especially of Philo's philosophy and what might be called Philo's gnosticism.

Johannine phrases and terminology offer also striking analogies with those of a form of Greek mysticism which was strongly tainted with Oriental influences. It was synchretistic in character and flourished in certain sects on the periphery of Judaism. The discovery

---

[1] In the same way it must be noted that beyond mentioning the devil whom he thinks is the prince of this world the evangelist only speaks of demons.

and publication of the Odes of Solomon[1] and Lidzbarski's translations of the Mandaean writings which formerly were hardly known and are now rendered accessible by them,[2] have made us acquainted with phrases which offer striking resemblances to those of the Fourth Gospel. The documents were compiled later than the Johannine writings, some of them much later. The Mandaean writings in the form in which we have them do not seem to be earlier than the beginning of the eighth century, but they may contain earlier fragments and the ideas expressed in them especially go much further back than the documents which inform us about them. Some authors, too, among whom Bultmann and Bauer must be given special mention, thought that these documents taken together would enable us to revise our ideas of the way in which Christian thought took shape and especially of the way in which Johannine mysticism originated.[3] This was, however, to draw precipitate and rash conclusions from comparisons which certainly are worthy of consideration. For we cannot completely ignore the environments and periods in which the mysticism of the Odes of Solomon and the doctrine of the Mandaeans appeared and took shape. While we must not rule out systematically and *a priori* the idea that a hypothetical premandaeism may have played some part in the shaping of Johannine thought, we must also recognise that the converse hypothesis may also be true. It may have to be supposed that Johanninism influenced the gnosticism of the Odes of Solomon and the Mandaean or

[1] Rendel-Harris, *The Odes and Psalms of Solomon*, Cambridge, 1909,[2] 1911; Rendel-Harris and Mingana, *The Odes and Psalms of Solomon*, Manchester, 1916-20; Harnack, *Eine Psalmbuch aus dem ersten Jahrhundert*, Leipzig, 1910; Labourt and Battiffel, *Les Odes de Salomon*, Paris, 1910; Gressmann, in Hennecke, *Neutr. Apokr.*, pp. 437-472. It seems actually settled that we must look for the origin of these odes in a gnostic sect of the second century.

[2] Lidzbarski, *Das Johannesbuch der Mandäer*, Giessen, 1905-1915, *Mandäische Liturgien*, Berlin, 1920, *Ginza Der Schatz oder das grosse Buch der Mandäer*, Goettingen, 1925.

[3] Some time before the publication of the Mandaean writings the thesis that Johanninism was to some extent influenced by synchretistic mysticism was maintained by Reitzenstein (*Poimandres*, Leipzig, 1904), Bousset (*Kur. Christ.*, pp. 164 ff.) and Wetter (*Phos. Eine Untersuchung uber hellenistische Frommigkeit*, Uppsal, Leipzig, 1915; *Der Sohn Gottes*, Goettingen, 1916). The critics who have most systematically maintained that Johanninism was to some extent influenced by premandaeism are Bultmann, *Der religionsgeschichtliche Hintergrund des Prologs zum Johannesevangelium, Eucharisterion H. Gunkel dargebracht*, Goettingen, 1923, II, pp. 3-26; 'Die Bedeutung der neuerschlossen mandaischen und manichaischen Quellen fur das Verstandnis des Johannesevangelium', *Z.N.T.W.*, 1925, XXIV, pp. 100-146; 'Untersuchungen zum Johannesevangelium', *Z.N.T.W.*, 1928, XXVII, pp. 113-163, 1930, XXIX, 169-192; *Das Johannesevangelium*, Meyer, II[10], Goettingen, 1937 ff.; W. Bauer, *Das Johannesevangelium*[2], Tubingen, 1925,[2] 1933.

premandaean doctrine and on first sight this hypothesis may be the more probable.

The Mandaean fever which seized a whole school of criticism has very much abated.[1] As far back as 1929,[2] Odeberg confined himself to throwing light on certain Johannine concepts by comparing them with parallel ideas found in the Mandaean documents but in doing so he did not pretend that he could throw any light on the origins of Johannine thought. Later on Lietzmann and Loisy[3] both published vigorous articles on the subject showing that not only the Mandaean writings but also the ideas to be found in them and notably the Mandaean baptismal liturgy, which until then had been thought to be very early and original, showed signs of having been profoundly influenced by Christianity.

The problem of the relations between the Fourth Gospel and synchretistic mysticism, especially in the form in which it is found in the Mandaean writings, has not been disposed of but it must be considered as settled that it has to be framed in a different way and in different terms from those in which it was at first envisaged.[4] As long as the history of the synchretist, mystic, and gnostic sects and their relations with Christianity remain undiscovered, if ever they can be known with any satisfaction, we shall have to confine ourselves to analysing ideas, i.e. to try and throw light on the meaning and character of certain concepts such as life, light, and truth, by comparing the way in which John uses them with the way in which they are used in the writings of the sects. But it is quite plain that John did not create them but marked them with his own imprint. But in the actual state of our knowledge it would not be right for us to make these comparisons to use them to reconstruct the early history of these concepts.

[1] It has not, however, completely disappeared as is shown by Bultmann's commentary on the Fourth Gospel.

[2] H. Odeberg, *The Fourth Gospel interpreted in its relations to the contemporary religions current in Palestine and the Hellenistic world*, Uppsal, 1929. See also Omodeo's book, *La mistica giovannea*, Bari, 1930.

[3] Lietzmann, 'Ein Beitrag zur Mandaerfrage', *S.B.A.*, 1930, pp. 596-608; Loisy, *Le mandeisme et les origines chrétiennes*, Paris, 1934. See also my remarks, J.-B., pp. 113 ff.

[4] E. Percy, *Untersuchungen uber den Ursprung der johanneischen Theologie, zugleich ein Betrag zur Frage nach der Entstehung des Gnostizismus*, Lund, 1939. Percy perceives that the real problem is to understand Johannine thought as a Christian creation. But he observes that this does not rule out the problem of the relations between Johannine thought and synchretistic mysticism. But it plainly becomes a secondary problem. Percy (p. 6) recognises that we shall not be able to use Mandaean texts to explain Christian texts, particularly the Johannine, until we have a knowledge of the history of Mandaeism. It is plain that at the moment interest in the Mandaean texts has considerably dwindled.

Our principal task, as far as the interpretation of Johanninism is concerned, must be to grasp it, both by itself and in its relations with other forms of Christian thought. John's Christianity is completely detached from Judaism but we can see from it that the rupture had only recently taken place and that the Jews were the ones who initiated it (ix. 22). The arguments between Jesus and the Jews, which form a large part of the gospel, echo those in which Jews and Christians were involved at the end of the first century. They express the outlook of people who felt that they had something in common. Jews and Christians are depicted as brethren who are enemies but are still brethren who have not accepted the rupture between them as final. Far from being indifferent to each other they make every effort to promote defections from the other side and to prevent them from occurring from their own.

'Salvation is of the Jews', proclaims the Johannine Christ (iv. 22). Jesus Messiah is he 'of whom Moses in the law and the prophets did write' (i. 45; cf. i. 49; v. 46-47; vi. 14; viii. 56).[1] Although John finds in the Old Testament prefigurations of Jesus and his work,[2] his ground is not that of the religion of Israel. Moses gave the law, but grace and truth come through Jesus Christ (i. 17). The place given in discussion to the argument from scripture shows how much he values the Old Testament.[3] It is also significant that the problem of the law is not raised. Universalism had definitely triumphed.

John admits that in theory there has been a natural revelation of God in creation, the work of the logos, and in the reason which has been given to every man (i. 1-5, 9-10) but as humanity has not accepted this revelation it has become almost of no effect so that God has remained unknown to humanity (i. 18; v. 37 f.; vi. 46; xvii. 25); he is only accessible by revelation. God revealed is unique (v. 44; xvii. 3); he alone possesses life (v. 21, 26; vi. 57); he is spirit (iv. 24) and constantly active (v. 17).

The Johannine conception of the world may be described as an ontological and pessimistic dualism. The world in which man lives differs essentially from that from which Christ comes (vi. 14; x. 36 ff.). The world is sinful but John has a less tragic conception of sin than Paul. Before the time of Christ sin was primarily latent and passive.

---

[1] x. 8 refers not to the prophets of the Old Testament but to claimants to Messiahship.

[2] e.g. the brazen serpent (iii. 14) or the manna (vi. 22).

[3] This perhaps is not altogether explained by the fact that the argument from scripture was particularly appropriate for influencing the Jews.

It is ingratitude for the natural revelation of the logos (i. 1-15). It is not so much guilt as a natural deprivation of life (iii. 16-17, 36; v. 24). Left to itself the world is on its way to condemnation; the wrath of God weighs on it (iii. 17-36; xii. 48). It is darkness and deprived of the divine light (i. 5; iii. 19; xii. 46); it is flesh.[1] But the term flesh is not a synonym for the term sin, because the prologue culminates in the affirmation: 'The word was made flesh' (i. 14). Paul's thought is similar as he conceives the flesh of Christ to be exempt from sin but he reckons that the flesh is the means by which Christ has become united to human sin and taken it upon himself. This is not John's conception who considers that the incarnation in some measure unites Christ to humanity but not to its sin. Unlike the Pauline Christ the Johannine Christ is not juridically united to the sin of humanity.

The Johannine Christ has a triple function: he is creator, revealer, and redeemer. His creative function is affirmed in the prologue in no uncertain terms (i. 3) but after John has once stated it he does not return to it. What makes Christ the revealer is the position he occupies towards God due to the fact that as the logos he is orientated towards God ($\pi\rho\dot{o}s$ $\tau\dot{o}\nu$ $\Theta\epsilon o\nu$)[2] and is God ($\Theta\epsilon\dot{o}s$)[3] (i. 2; cf. vi. 46; viii. 55; xvii. 25, etc.). The content of the revelation is the person of the Son, who is so closely associated with the person of the Father that to know one is to know the other (v. 37; viii. 19; xiv. 9, etc.). In this twofold and unique knowledge exists eternal life (xvii. 3). In spite of appearances to the contrary the Johannine christology is not primarily speculative theory. Christ is described in the gospel only as revealer and redeemer. Into the conception of Christ as revealer enters his humanity as it is through that that God has come down to man.[4]

Certain of the attributes ascribed to Christ belong to an older tradition, such as possession by the Spirit (i. 33; iii. 34) and the power

---

[1] It is flesh $\dot{\epsilon}\nu$ $\dot{a}\rho\chi\hat{\eta}$, i.e. both from the beginning and in principle.

[2] The flesh is denoted by its powerlessness, not by its corruption. It is of no help; what comes from it is destructive of the true life (iii. 6; cf. i. 13). A Greek conception that flesh and spirit are antitheses is joined to the Jewish concept of the fall. That is why flesh seemed not only powerless but also sinful.

[3] This affirmation does not mean that the logos is identical with God because the statement $\pi\rho\dot{o}s$ $\tau o\nu$ $\theta\epsilon\dot{o}\nu$ clearly differentiates it from God.

[4] We may note in this sense his presence at the marriage in Cana (ii. 1 f.) his hunger and fatigue at Jacob's well (iv. 6) his tears at Lazarus' grave (xi. 35), the suppression of the incident of Simon of Cyrene, the absence of any reference to the supernatural birth. Jesus is explicitly described as Joseph's son (i. 45; vi. 42; vii. 27-28). It would almost seem as if John, by emphasising features of this kind as he does, wished to point out that in contemplating the divine aspect of the person of Jesus his humanity must not be forgotten. Cf. Bousset, *Kyrios Christos*, p. 261.

of reading the hearts of men (ii. 24-25). Elsewhere older conceptions are given more precise form. In this way the acts of Jesus are not determined by circumstances or by suggestions which may have been made to him but they are always absolutely spontaneous and free (ii. 4; vii. 1 f.; x. 18). Other conceptions are new altogether as, e.g. those of glory (viii. 59; xii. 41; xvii. 5, etc.),[1] and light (i. 4; iii. 21, 26 f. etc.).[2] The term 'Son'[3] is much more frequently used than in the synoptics or the Pauline epistles while 'Lord' less frequently so. It occurs in xiii. 13 where it means much the same as the Pauline conception, faithful one, or slave of Christ. In Thomas' affirmation (xx. 28) the term 'Lord' is directly connected with the term 'God'. The term 'Son of God' is reserved by the evangelist to describe the relations between Christ and God and must be understood in its fullest sense, as is shown among other passages by x. 30 in which Jesus declares 'I and my Father are one' on which his hearers comment 'Being a man, thou makest thyself God' (x. 33).[4] Although John uses the term Son of God in a strictly ontological sense, he lays great emphasis on the perfect spiritual unity between the Son and the Father, the complete subordination of the Son to the Father's will, and his absolute obedience.[5] While it cannot be contested that there is in the Johannine christology a speculative element, it must also be recognised that it contains a conviction of a religious nature, viz. that in the devotion of the faithful believer God and Christ cannot be separated (i. 18; v. 21-23; x. 38; xii. 44 ff.).[6] There is, however, a certain logical incoherence in his christology, because the unity of the Father and the Son and the love of the Father for the Son are sometimes explained as a result of Christ pre-existing before the creation and therefore not being dependent on what Christ may have done (iii. 34 ff.; v. 20; xvii. 23-24), and sometimes as a result of his work (x. 17).

[1] Wetter, 'Die "Verherrlichung" im Johannesevangelium', *Beitr.*, 1915, II.

[2] Wetter' "Ich bin das Licht der Welt", Eine Studie zur Formelsprache des Johannesevangeliums', *Beitr.*, 1914, I.

[3] Cf. Bousset, *Kyrios Christos*, pp. 156 f. The term 'Son' is used three or four times more frequently in the Fourth Gospel than in the Synoptics or the Pauline epistles.

[4] It is better not to place much reliance on the use of the term 'God' in the prologue. In i. 18 the reading μονογενὴς θεὸς is very doubtful. It is only given by אֵ B.C.*L., 33, syr[pesh, hel.] m. *ethiop*. The other manuscripts have μονογενὴς υἱός.

[5] It is not without interest to note that the epistle to the Hebrews which in a different way from the Fourth Gospel uses the term Son in an ontological sense also emphasises like John the obedience of Christ.

[6] Bousset, *Kyrios Christos*, p. 157.

The idea of a prophet, messenger, and son of the gods, who brings a message from the gods to men occupies considerable space in the religious conceptions of Hellenism. This has been the way in which such personalities have been thought of as Pythagoras, Apollonius of Tyana, and Simon of Dositheus, whom Origen mentions.[1] Are we to think, as Wetter and others[2] do, that we have here one of the sources of the Johannine christology? In every case the Greek conception offers something different from a replica of the Christian idea of Jesus, Son of God. Origen does not accuse these people of being imitators; he only says that Celsus is making a mistake in comparing them to Christ. He emphasises their failures which he sees as a proof of the vanity of their pretensions. The origin of the convictions expressed by the term 'Son of God' is not explained as due to apologetic or polemic but they may well have been shaped and moulded by the Greek concept of the Son of God.

The use of the term Son of Man has shrunk considerably in the Fourth Gospel. Where we do happen to find it it has lost its eschatological content[3] and only retains the idea of the heavenly origin of Christ (i. 51; iii. 13; vi. 27, 53). Elsewhere John represents the return of Christ in heavenly glory as the essential factor in redemption (iii. 14; viii. 28 f.) which is exactly the reverse of the eschatological concept.[4]

John is much more concerned to throw light on the benefits received by the faithful through the work of Christ than to explain the way redemption is wrought. Salvation is shown as the work of Christ (i. 16; vi. 28), and as God's gift of his Son whom he offers to the world (iii. 16-17). Sometimes under the influence of Pauline phrases the work of Christ is summed up in his death (iii. 14; x. 11, 17; xi. 50-52) which is in appearance Satan's triumph but in reality is his defeat (xii. 31; xiv. 26; xvi. 33). John sees in the brazen serpent (iii. 14) a figure of Christ who, raised from earth, draws men to him (cf. viii. 28). The death of Christ has ceased to be described as a

[1] Origen, *Contra Celsum*, vi. 11. Cf. vii. 9.

[2] Wetter, *Der Sohn Gottes, Untersuchung uber den Charakter und die Tendenz des Johannesevangeliums, zugleich ein Betrag zur Kenntniss der Heilandsgestalten der Antike*, Gottingen, 1916. Cf. Reitzentstein, *Poimandres*, pp. 222 f.; Norden, *Agnostos Theos.*, pp. 188 f.

[3] In one passage alone (v. 27) do we find the concept of the Son of Man as judge, which is an element belonging to eschatological conceptions. But as v. 28-29 is a gloss (see p. 391, n. 2, *Introd.* II, pp. 358 f.) the words 'because he is the Son of Man' in v. 27 appear to have been added to knit the verses together.

[4] Wetter, *Verherrlichung*, p. 46.

paradox or a scandal.[1] It is the return of the Lord to heaven, a return which opens access to his own; from this comes the importance of the idea of Christ as the way (xii. 31-32; xiv. 6).

The idea of predestination is found in John in a much sharper form than in Paul; salvation is only possible for 'the children of light' (iii. 19-20). For them has been accomplished a work of protection, purification, and sanctification which began in the historical ministry of Jesus and only then acquiring its full force is continued in the action of the paraclete (xiv. 20-21; xvii. 14-19). The action of Christ is more the action of his person than of his work as is also shown in the idea of Christ as the light of the world (viii. 12), which does not mean only that Christ gives light to men but also that he makes them light by giving to them the essence of the life divine (xii. 35-36).

Elsewhere the true life is described as the knowledge of God and Jesus Christ whom he has sent (xvii. 3). But knowledge here does not denote something purely or even principally intellectual; it is equivalent to communion. The life of the believer seemed to be both a result and an extension of the life of Christ. 'Because I live, ye shall live also', he says (xiv. 19). Some contexts speak of the gift of life as present (iii. 36; v. 25; vi. 47), even as complete (v. 24), others as future (iii. 36; v. 24; xi. 26); in some of them present and future are connected together (iii. 36; xi. 26). We have here realised eschatology in a much sharper form than in Paul. John happens to use the future sometimes not because it is a survival of the eschatological conception but because he is making Jesus speak of the bread of life and of the eucharist, which according to his doctrine[2] could only be given to one after Christ had returned into celestial glory.

As has already been remarked in passing, John has a very sharp conception of predestination. Jesus knew in advance who would believe and he protects them so that none of them should perish (xvii. 12; xviii. 9) but he also knows who will not believe. Those destined to salvation are exposed to the hatred of the world because they are not beings of flesh (xvii. 14-16). God has given them to Christ (vi. 37-39; x. 29; xvii. 2, 6) or rather Christ has chosen them and kept them from the world (xv. 18-19). The fact that these two phrases are logically contrary shows that we are not in the presence of a theory but of a religious experience. According to some texts (i. 13; iii. 6, 21; viii. 47, etc.), faith is a result of the very nature of

[1] Wetter, *Ich bin das Licht der Welt*, pp. 183 f.   [2] See *E.P.*, pp. 368 ff.

those who believe, of the fact that they are 'children of God' or 'children of light'; according to other texts faith is a result of divine action which is exercised on them to draw them to Christ (vi. 37, 44, 45, 46, 65).

The object of faith which is the determining condition of salvation is Christ and his sayings (iii. 18; v. 47; vi. 29; viii. 24, etc.). To believe in Christ is to believe in God who has sent him (xii. 44; xiv. 1); it is to recognise his heavenly person behind his human manifestation. Faith contains an intellectual element, i.e. to know who Jesus is. But it is not only of an intellectual quality; it creates a mystic link between the believer and Christ which makes it the source of life (iii. 36; v. 24; vi. 40, 47, etc.). Faith gives life directly and not as in Paul's thought indirectly through the mediation of justification. It comes into being through the person of Christ, through hearing his words and contemplating his works. Jesus expresses both astonishment and regretful reproach when he says, 'Ye have also seen me and ye believe me not' (vi. 36). The miracles reveal the real person of Jesus; they are 'manifestations of his glory' (ii. 11; x. 37-38; xiv. 12).[1] John uses other terms as well as faith to describe the relationship of the believer to Christ; he speaks of 'coming to Christ' (v. 40; vi. 35; vii. 37), of going in through the door (x. 1 ff.) or by the way which Christ is (xiv. 6), and of receiving him (i. 12; v. 43; xvi. 48). In the last part of the gospel obedience to Christ is emphasised (xiv. 15, 21; xv. 10). The disciples are shown as if, when they were going to be separated from their master, they needed all the more to be loyal to his commandments.

The connection of the faithful to Christ and their union with him not only form the determining condition of salvation but make up salvation itself which is shown by love, the love of the faithful for the Lord and of the Lord for them and the love of the faithful for one another (xii. 26; xiv. 21-23).

This union is also realised through the sacraments.[2] The allusions in chapter vi to the eucharist[3] are sufficiently plain to leave no doubt that the omission of any account of the last supper cannot be due to any opposition to sacramentalism. The explanation for this is to be

[1] The desire to see a miracle in iv. 48 (cf. vi. 36) is described as due to lack of faith because it is taken from the synoptic tradition.

[2] Just as Paul shows no contradiction between faith and sacraments, John shows there to be none between the mysticism of love and the mysticism of the sacraments.

[3] Concerning the eucharistic doctrine of John see my book, *L'eucharistie*, pp. 195-215 and *E.P.*, pp. 368 ff.

found in the idea that sacraments could only become efficacious through Christ's death or rather, one should say, through his glorification.[1] In the incident of the feet-washing (xiii. 4 ff.) the gesture of Jesus is to be taken as symbolic representation of the supper making it to be a complementary purification to baptism effacing the impurities which have been contracted since baptism (xiii. 10).[2] But the discourse on the bread of life in chapter vi shows that the significance of the sacrament of the eucharist is in no way weakened.

The life of believers is characterised by the love which they have for Christ and the love which they have for one another (xiv. 23; xvii. 21-23). The concept of believers being slaves to Christ is deliberately avoided and superseded by that of being his faithful friends (xv. 15).[3] Believers continue to see their master after he has left the world (xiv. 19); they are guarded and protected by him against the hatred of the world (xv. 18-20; xvi. 2; xvii. 11-15). This action of Christ over his own is shown as the promise that their prayers will be answered (xiv. 14).

The doctrine of the spirit,[4] through whom Christ acts on his own after he has left them, is practical in character. No explicit definition of the Spirit is given and such indications as John does give us prevent us from thinking that he had any coherent ideas on the subject.

This is particularly noticeable in respect of the relations between the Spirit and the Father and the Son. The Spirit comes from God but is sent at the request of Christ and his action is that of Christ returning to his own. This doctrine is unfolded only in the farewell discourses because they contain the culmination of Christ's teaching and Christian initiation. The hostility of man can do nothing against the Spirit's action; time and place impose no limitations. It enables the disciples to understand what they were unable to grasp during the ministry of Jesus (xiv. 16-26; xvi. 12-14). The complexity of the Spirit's action is expressed in the term $\pi\alpha\rho\acute{\alpha}\kappa\lambda\eta\tau\eta\varsigma$ which is his designation. This word is translated comforter, counsellor,

---

[1] This is the significance of the incident of the piercing of Christ's side (xix. 34). The water and blood which spring from Jesus' side are symbols of baptism and the eucharist. The way in which the evangelist invokes oracular witness in reference to the incident shows the importance he attributes to it.

[2] The same idea is to be found in the miracle of Cana where the water which is changed into wine is in vessels used for the Jewish rite of purification.

[3] Bousset, *Kyrios Christos*, pp. 77 f.

[4] See my article, 'La notion johannique de l'Esprit', Paris, 1902.

advocate, helper, tutor, supporter. Each of these translations contains an element of truth but none of them by itself expresses all that is contained in the concept of the Paraclete. He comforts the disciples in their grief at their separation from their master (xii. 24; xvi. 20 f.); he instructs because he is the Spirit of truth (xiv. 17, 25, 26; xvi. 13); he gives knowledge of the Father and so gives life (xvii. 26); he reveals the future (xvi. 13); at the death of every believer he receives his soul to unite him to Christ (xiv. 3). On the world his action is entirely negative; he exercises judgement upon it and pronounces condemnation (xvi. 8-11).

Through his conception of the Spirit John spiritualises the eschatological tradition without ever explicitly breaking with it. As Paul had done before him, in a more radical fashion he makes his eschatology realised and present, with the result that there is no place now for an anxious waiting for the return of Christ.[1]

As a result of this, the traditional idea of judgement has no meaning for John. We have seen[2] that this was also true of Paul but, while Paul categorically maintains the conception of a judgement which appears superfluous because before it will have taken place the elect have already been separated from the non-elect through their prior resurrection, John goes farther and changes the position of the judgement by transferring it from the last day to the moment when each is brought face to face with Christ and his sentence. He explicitly denies the conception of an eschatological judgement. 'Verily, verily, I say unto you, He that heareth my word, and believeth on him that sent me, hath everlasting life, and shall not come into condemnation; but is passed from death unto life', says the Johannine Christ (v. 24; cf. iii. 36; viii. 51).

The conception of judgement in its traditional form is even the object of a direct polemic. 'I came not to judge the world', says Christ, 'but to save the world' (xii. 47; cf. iii. 17) and again: 'And this is the condemnation, that light is come into the world, and men loved darkness rather than light because their deeds were evil' (iii. 19). Only in this sense has Christ come into the world for judgement (ix. 39). But in reality man brings this judgement on himself by the attitude he adopts towards the words of Christ. It does not concern only those who come face to face with Christ and his words while they are alive on earth but all mankind, as everyone either in this world or while they are in the realm of the dead will be challenged to accept or refuse his words 'Verily I say unto you', says Christ,

---

[1] The word is not found anywhere else in the epistle. [2] See p. 274.

'The hour is coming and now is,[1] when the dead shall hear the voice of God and they that hear[2] shall live' (v. 24-27).[3]

While John teaches that those who receive the sayings of Christ have already passed from death to life, he also has the conception of the resurrection on the last day and the terms in which it is mentioned prevent us from thinking that it is due to interpolations by an editor who wanted to accommodate the gospel to conceptions which were current in the church at the end of the first century. This affirmation is met with not less than four times in the eucharistic discourse in chapter vi. For example Jesus says, 'And this is the Father's will which hath sent me, that of all which he hath given me, I should lose nothing, but should raise it up again at the last day. And this is the will of him that sent me, that everyone which seeth the Son, and believeth on him, may have everlasting life and I will raise him up at the last day' (vi. 39-40; cf. vi. 44, 54). The conception of the resurrection seems then to have been superimposed upon that of eternal life as an immediate possession. These two ideas are closely associated together in the dialogue between Jesus and Martha before Lazarus' tomb: Jesus says, 'Thy brother shall rise again'. Martha replies, 'I know that he shall rise again in the resurrection at the last day'. Jesus then declares, 'I am the resurrection and the life. He that believeth in me though he were dead, yet shall he live; and whosoever liveth and believeth in me shall never die'[4] (xi. 23-26). Under the combined influence of his religious experience and his Greek spiritualism John was led to the conception of a spiritual life, which is independent of physical life over which death has no power but he does not on that account abandon entirely the Jewish idea of resurrection. We have here

---

[1] This expression means that this moment is near (cf. iv. 23).

[2] The same verb ἀκούειν which is used twice in the passage means (1) understand and (2) listen, accept, receive.

[3] In what follows (v. 28-29) we find an entirely different conception. 'For the hour is coming in the which all that are in the graves shall hear his voice (that of the Son of God) and shall come forth, they that have done good unto the resurrection of life; and they that have done evil unto the resurrection of damnation'. The voice of the Son of God is not here the one which calls to salvation but the one which summons the dead before his tribunal. The contradiction between verses 24-27 and 28-29 is clear and distinct. The latter passage is an interpolation by a later editor who thought he found the idea of judgement in v. 24 f. and gave it precision by the addition of verses 28-29.

[4] These words can also be translated, 'will not die for ever', The translation which I give I think must be preferred because it exhibits with greater clarity the paradoxical nature of this saying of Jesus spoken in front of Lazarus' tomb.

a logical contradiction which is easily explained. We are concerned here with one of those phrases which are more than intellectual in their content and derive much of their significance from the emotional coefficient contained in them. A long tradition which John does not care to cast aside had so closely associated faith and hope in the beyond with the affirmation of the resurrection that it preserved its religious significance even when it no longer satisfied as an adequate conception of the life beyond.

We have to understand the declaration of xii. 48 in the same way, 'He that rejecteth me and receiveth not my words hath one that judgeth him: the word that I have spoken, the same shall judge him in the last day'. In form this contradicts the affirmation that judgement lies in the immediate response to the challenge presented by the sayings of Jesus offering salvation. This contradiction bears a close resemblance to the one where Jesus is made to speak of a resurrection on the last day for a believer who has already passed from death to life.

The fact that Johannine thought is somewhat lacking in coherence is not entirely explained by the survival of certain forms of thought due to what might be called the religious potential with which tradition had charged them. It is also due to the fact that John expressed his ideas in the framework of the gospel story and also as much as anything else to the character of his personality. As the gospel is preceded by a prologue which appears to be systematic in character and could be described as the most philosophic bit of the New Testament we might have expected a different conception. Many critics of the nineteenth century among those belonging to the liberal school, notably H. J. Holtzmann, Jean Reville and Loisy,[1] judged the prologue to contain the programme and key to the whole of Johannine thought. This compelled them to discover a scheme in the gospel in which the various elements are fitted together to develop and illustrate the themes laid down in the prologue. The schemes suggested by them show considerable ingenuity and considered separately they all seem plausible if somewhat forced. But they contradict and refute each other. In addition the underlying thesis behind these

[1] H. J. Holtzmann, 'Der Logos und der eingeborene Gottessohn im vierten Evangelium', *Z.f. wiss Theol.*, XXXVI, 1893, I. pp. 385-407; Reville, *Q.E.*, pp. 110-119; Loisy, *Q.Ev.*, pp. 97-98, 153, 199. Loisy expresses the same idea again in his second edition (Paris, 1921). But here it is offered with less exactness because in the interval Loisy took to the theory that the gospel is a compilation from composite sources.

critical essays meets with this difficulty, that, if the logos conception is the key to the gospel, it is impossible to explain why it is never referred to except in the prologue. Harnack observed this and was led to maintain that the gospel was a uniquely religious mystical work and that the prologue which is different in character ought to be considered as a kind of façade, a sort of *captatio benevolentiae* to charm Greek readers.[1] The arguments used by both parties are too weighty to allow either to be ignored. We must then suppose that the problem has been badly conceived. When we try to follow the movement of thought in the prologue we come to recognise that its dominating interest is not philosophical but religious and practical. It unfolds the successive aspects of the revealing action of the logos, in creation, in the life of the individual illuminated by reason, in the religion of Israel, and last of all in the incarnation, but it emphasises the reception given by men at each stage of the revealing process. The interest of the prologue in the logos is practical and religious like the rest of the gospel. Holtzmann, Jean Reville and Loisy are right to maintain against Harnack that the prologue sums up the message of the gospel but Harnack is right to maintain against Holtzmann and the other liberal critics that the gospel is above everything else a religious book and not a philosophic treatise.

John through the instrumentality of the Judeo-Alexandrine philosophy of Philo[2] was much more widely and profoundly influenced by Greek currents than Paul. But the nature of these currents and the extent of their influence must be defined. They effected the framework of the form of his thought, his general conception of the world, with the opposition between the world below and the world above, and the connection between flesh and spirit. The specifically religious element in the gospel has not been touched by Greek influences. The culmination of the Johannine doctrine of the logos is the conception of incarnation, but his conception is not only strange to Philo; it lies at the antipodes of his thought. To interpret the appearance of Christ in history and his work of

[1] Harnack, 'Uber das Verhaltsniss des Prologs des vierten Evangeliums zum ganzen Werk', *Z.f.TH.u.K.*, 1902, II, pp. 189-231.

[2] On this point see the somewhat ancient but still useful works of Reville (*Le Logos d'après Philon d'Alexandrie*, Geneva, 1877; *La doctrine du Logos dans la Quatrieme Evangile dans les œuvres de Philon*, Paris, 1881). See also Aal, *Der Logos*, Leipzig, Grill, Untersuchungen über die Enstatehung des vierten Evangeliums, Leipzig, Tubingen, 1902-23; J. d'Alma, *Philon et le Quatrième Évangile*, Paris, 1910; Langrange, 'Vers le logos de St. Jean', *R.b.*, 1923, XXXI, pp. 161–184; 321-371.

salvation, John did not borrow doctrine from Philo which he might have transposed but only material. At the centre of Johanninism is a religious experience which is quite foreign to Philo, the conviction of what the believer receives from Christ, who is the only source of true life. The principle on which John organises the elements which he borrows from Philo, i.e. the religious spirit with which he endows them he does not owe to Judeo-Alexandrine philosophy. The same thing can be said of what he may have borrowed from rabbinic Judaism[1] or the books of wisdom.[2]

Allowing for its own distinctive originality Johannine mysticism belongs to the main stream of Greek mysticism. For example the Johannine conception of light seems to have been influenced by the ancient conception of a luminous soul, which was trying to free itself from the matter into which it had fallen to return to its original source.[3] Norden[4] showed that the phrase, 'I am the light' (viii. 12), expresses a current theme of Greek mysticism and is to be found in the *Poimandres*.[5] What the Greek said of his god and the Jew of the Messiah for whom he was waiting John says of the Christ in an exclusive sense. The influence is entirely formal and at bottom more negative than positive.

The Fourth Gospel is primarily a religious book expressing a faith and experience but it is also an apology and a polemic. John feels the church to be threatened and he wants to defend it. Certain passages in the farewell discourses refer to the hatred of the world and to the conviction that the enemies of Christians will think that they are doing service to God by putting them to death (xvi. 2).[6] Against this danger he only advises patience. He is more concerned with dangers which the faith is incurring at the hands of groups from whom the faithful do not always perhaps feel

---

[1] Burney, *The aramaic origin of the fourth gospel*, Oxford, 1922, pp. 34 f., 37 f.

[2] Rendel Harris, *The origin of the prologue of the fourth gospel*, Cambridge, 1917; Grill, *Unters.*, I, pp. 155-176; Holtzmann, *Neutestamentliche Theologie*,[2] II, p. 415. On the possibility that Johannine theology may have been subject to Egyptian influences through the agency of synchretism see A. Moret, 'Le Verbe createur et révélateur en Egypte', *R.h.r.*, 1909, LXIX, pp. 279-298; Reitzenstein, *Zwei religionsgeschichtliche Fragen*, Leipzig, 1901. Cf. *Introd.* II, pp. 518 ff.

[3] Wetter, *Ich bin das Licht*, pp. 177 f.; Reitzenstein, 'Die Gottin Psyche in der hellenisteschen und fruhchristlichen Literatur', *S.H.A.*, 1917, p. 10.

[4] Norden, *Agn. Th.*, pp. 298 f. Cf. Wetter, *Ich bin das Licht*, pp. 179, 197.

[5] Paul seems to be thinking of it in Romans ii. 19-20 and Baldensperger (*Der Prolog des vierten Evangeliums*, Freiburg in Breisgau, Leipzig, Tubingen, 1898, p. 11) maintained that the disciples of John Baptist applied it to their master.

[6] These passages seem to belong to an editorial stratum of a later date. Cf. *Introd.* II, pp. 370 ff.

themselves completely separated by as wide a gulf as he would like and who are trying to attract to themselves members of the church. He seems to have in mind three groups, Judaism, the disciples of John Baptist, and Greek mystic sects. John's apologetic is more positive than negative; he always tends to show that faith in Christ alone is able to satisfy men's needs.

In reply to Judaism John emphasises the doctrine that Jesus was the Messiah, making it his main argument. He uses the argument from prophecy and the predictions of the gospel events given in the Old Testament (xii. 16 f., 38 f.; xv. 25; xix. 24, 29-36). For purposes of apology he puts the prediction of the passion right at the beginning of Jesus' ministry (ii. 19, 22; iii. 14) and makes it a public announcement (vii. 33-36; viii. 28; xii. 33-36). The miracles are less numerous than in the synoptics but they are more astounding in character. Their purpose is to create faith by revealing the true character of the personality of Jesus (i. 48 f.; ii. 11; vi. 14, etc.).

The way in which John repeatedly affirms the heavenly origin of Christ is certainly due to christological speculations but he is also in this way replying to the argument of the Jews, when they said that the Messiah could not have come from Nazareth and that no man knew his origin (vii. 27 f., 41, 52). Weinel[1] is right when he says that John unfolds the complete body of Jewish Messianic doctrine to show that Jesus conformed to all its demands.

The fact that the most important of Jesus' activities are placed in Jerusalem is partly due to the character of the sources used by John but possibly, as Baldensperger maintains,[2] it is also because it forms a refutation to the charge brought by some against Christianity that it rested on a series of historical events which did not take place in full daylight but in a remote province of the empire. (Cf. vii, 4).

It is thought that traces can be found in the Fourth Gospel that rivalry existed between the disciples of Jesus and those of John Baptist.[3] The gospel is devoted to showing the absolute superiority

---

[1] Weinel, *Bibl. Theol.*, p. 220.

[2] Baldensperger, *Urchristliche Apologetik*, Strasburg, 1909, p. 30. Cf. Weinel, *Bibl. Theol.*, p. 532.

[3] On the questions concerning John Baptist and his disciples see my book *J.B.* which gives the bibliographical references. I am actually rather chary in believing in the existence of a group of disciples of John Baptist in the community among whom the Fourth Gospel was written and much more inclined to think that they were Jews who made use of some of Jesus' sayings about John Baptist to put him on a pedestal in order to embarrass the Christians.

of Jesus over John Baptist but this does not prove that there was a rival group attached to the Baptist in the church. The argument may well have been purely ideological and the sole concern of the evanglist may have been to reply to Jews who, although not disciples of John Baptist, magnified him to annoy the Christians. With this reserve Baldensperger[1] was right in emphasising the anti-baptist polemic in John. Before John the synoptics had effaced the originality of John Baptist's preaching; he was reduced by them to the almost schematic part of a precursor. This tendency is much more strongly marked in the Fourth Gospel where he is nothing more than 'a man sent by God to bear witness to the truth' (i. 7) and it is stated that 'he was not that light but was sent to bear witness of that light' (i. 8). This statement is so important in John's eyes that he does not hesitate to break the organic development of the prologue in order to make it. In the same way John Baptist's reply to the Jews who question him begins with a categorical negative, 'I am not the Messiah' (i. 20). This plainly implies the existence of a group of people who, either out of conviction or for polemical purposes, were stating or insinuating that the Messiah was John Baptist and not Jesus. Very characteristic also is the narrative of iii. 22-iv. 3 which culminates in this declaration from John Baptist, 'He must increase, but I must decrease' (iii. 30).

The gospel is also a statement in opposition to Greek mysticism. The frequency with which phrases referring to light and glory are repeated over and over again may be explained, as has been suggested,[2] as due to the part they played in a liturgy which more or less resembled that of the mysteries to which Christianity was opposed. But Wetter[3] carries things too far when he says that in John's eyes the Christian worship realised in full what the liturgies of the mysteries were really trying to attain and that the Johannine Christ is the perfect type of the priest represented in the mystery religions, who brought those who trusted him to light and glory. We are reading too much into the gospel, if we interpret the request of the Greeks who want to see Jesus (xii. 20) as the form of words used by the candidate to demand initiation,[4] or draw a comparison between the sayings on sanctification and the rites of initiation,[5] or claim to recognise in Christ's agony an echo

[1] Baldensperger, *Prol. viert. Ev.*, 1898.
[2] Wetter, *Die Verherrlichung*, p. 78; *Ich bin das Licht*, p. 166.
[3] Wetter, *Die Verherrlichung*, pp. 64, 101.
[4] *Ibid.* p. 57.   [5] *Ibid.* pp. 95 f.

of the sentiments of the initiate at the time of his initiation,[1] or 'in the new commandment' the law imposed on the initiate.[2] To do this would be to explain what it must be confessed is not very clear by a very flimsy hypothesis and far-fetched reconstruction. It is true that John's gospel contains a conception which played a great part in the mysteries, namely that the drama of redemption is repeated in each individual,[3] but this originates from Paul's principle that the faithful believer is associated with the sufferings of Christ. The origin of Paul's principle must be found in the peculiar character of his conversion. We are simplifying over much and, what is more, falsifying things, if we presume that Johanninism contains elements taken from a liturgy of the mystery religions. It remains true, however, as Norden rightly observes,[4] that the Fourth Gospel is not the work of a mystic recluse, who composed it as it were shut up in his own cell but it shows contact with affairs and transports us into the thick of a conflict which Christianity was waging with the various forms of Greek religion for the domination of men's souls.

2.—THE FIRST EPISTLE OF JOHN

The conceptions of the first epistle of John are those of the gospel in an extended form but they differ in several ways. In the epistle they are cheapened and given popular form, as without going farther can be seen from the prologue to the epistle (i. 1-14). It is an imitation of the prologue of the gospel but differs from it in this respect that the two terms ἀρχή and λόγος are used in a different sense. ἀρχή does not mean the eternal origin of things but the beginning of the Christian preaching while the logos of life is the preaching of the gospel and not the eternal word of God. The epistle has the same conception of sin as the gospel but is much more concerned about it. This is due to the fact that its author seems to have been mixed up with the life of the church more directly than the evangelist who seems to have lived in a select group of Christians. The epistle is much more directly polemical in purpose than the gospel and has in mind not rival groups but heresies. Lastly the epistle corrects and adds clarity to certain phrases from the gospel, from which not without some show of logic conclusions seem to have been drawn which were contrary to the thought of the evangelist.

[1] Wetter, *Die Verherrlichung*, pp. 60, 62.
[2] *Ibid.* p. 67.   [3] *Ibid.* p. 51.   [4] Norden, *Agn. Ther.*, p. 299.

The problem of sin in the life of the believer weighs much more heavily on the mind of the author of the epistle than on the evangelist's. He states that Christ expiates sins and frees the faithful from the domination of Satan (ii. 2; iii. 8 f.; iv. 10). Sin thus has a positive meaning and is not merely the equivalent of not having received the word of Christ. It would have been impossible for the author of the epistle to have said with the evangelist that sin would not have existed, if Christ had not come and spoken (John xv. 22).[1] But we find in the epistle some ideas which come from the gospel, and are applied not to man in his natural state but to the Christian. They are stated in much more categorical terms than those used in the gospel: 'Whosoever abideth in him sinneth not. . . . Whosoever is born of God doth not commit sin; for his seed remaineth in him: and he cannot sin because he is born of God' (iii. 6-9; cf. i. 18). But the epistle also speaks of sin in the life of the Christian,[2] a statement which can hardly be reconciled with those which have just been quoted. To recognise the existence of sin in the life of a being who, it has been said, cannot sin, and to entertain the idea of a sin which does not necessarily involve the loss of salvation[3] means that experience has triumphed over theory.

There are two reasons apparently why the epistle differs from the gospel in this way: the writer of the epistle (1) had had a more direct experience of what the life of Christians was in fact, and (2) was replying to an antinomist group who may have been justifying their contentions by certain phrases from the gospel. The epistle has antinomism clearly in mind: 'Whosoever committeth sin transgresseth also the law; for sin is the transgression of the law' (iii. 4). The epistle not only replies on the theological level to a dialectical apology for some moral slackness but makes certain practical suggestions. It evolves the conception that some sins which are termed 'mortal' cut a man off from salvation so definitely that it is futile to pray for those who have committed them. Other sins, although in theory they are incompatible with the Christian life, do not necessarily involve the loss of salvation, because forgiveness for

[1] It is true that we find in John the idea that the Passion is a struggle between Christ and the prince of this world (xii. 31; xiv. 30; xvi. 11, 33). But it is cosmic in character. The end of it is to bring the elect from the world below to the world above by victory over the prince of this world who is keeping the elect down. In the epistle the struggle is ethical. Its purpose is to free men from the domination of sin.

[2] Statements such as i. 9 and ii. 2 prevent us from thinking of sins committed before conversion.

[3] But this would happen if the brethren did not intercede.

them can be obtained through the intercession of the church (v. 16-17). The writer has here surrendered something of the primitive moral ideal which was uncompromising and retreated from his theological position that sin was incompatible with the life of a Christian.

In addition to antinomism the epistles attacks two other heresies both of which are christological in character. One of them is a form of Ebionitism (ii. 18-27) and is described by the author as denying the messiahship of Jesus, which simply means that those whom he has in mind had a different conception of messiahship from his own.[1] The other consists in denying that Jesus had come in the flesh, i.e. a form of docetism (iv. 1-3). We shall return to these heresies later on.[2] At the moment we will only note that the epistle judges their appearance to be the realisations of prophecies which had referred to the coming of antichrist. In this context he corrects or rather adds precision to the teaching of the gospel on the action of the Spirit. Generally speaking, he maintains the same doctrine without alteration (ii. 20-27; iii. 14; iv. 13), but the idea that heretics are antichrists, i.e. that they are inspired by the devil, upsets the balance of the doctrine by making it necessary for discrimination to be made between the Spirit of Christ and that of antichrist. The criterion to be used[3] is as follows: 'Every spirit that confesseth that Jesus is come in the flesh is of God: and every spirit that confesseth not that Jesus Christ is come in the flesh is not of God' (iv. 2). The purpose of the author is to harmonise the teaching about the spirit given in the gospel with the doctrine which had been already fixed and formulated in the church. In this way the function of the spirit has been perceptibly narrowed. This is an example of the way in which religious thought loses spontaneity while it gains stability and is precluded from enterprises which are not without risk.

Taken as a whole Johanninism was strongly influenced by Paulinism but is shown to be less tumultuous and tragic in character. This is because the personality who created it was of a different type from Paul. He had not passed through the same experiences or known a catastrophic conversion. The apparent date of the fourth gospel allows us to suppose that John may have been born and bred in a Christian environment and so found his faith in a perfectly natural way. That is why his Christianity is quietistic in tone and his conception of sin attenuated.

---

[1] Concerning the fact that the Ebionite group left the church see p. 408.
[2] See pp. 407 ff.   [3] Paul gives exactly the same criterion in 1 Cor. xii. 3.

There are other differences between them. John's eschatology is realised and spiritualised in a more coherent fashion than Paul's and there is less apocalyptic. This is due to differences in time and environment. Although John shows himself to have been subject to Palestinian influences, he remains a Greek whose outlook has been only superficially and almost only verbally affected by the Jewish conception of a temporal dualism.

We have seen that the gospel seems to have been composed originally within the confines of a small group and that it was edited at a later date to adapt Johanninism to the general outlook and needs of the church. The epistle seems to have been written for the same purpose.

While we have no information concerning in what environment Johanninism came into existence, we may ask ourselves if we may not imagine it to have been a group of men made perfect, spiritual, or gnostics (wise) in the sense which Paul gives to these words (1 Cor. iii. 1 ff.; cf. viii. 1 ff.). This would explain the freedom with which John treats certain traditional ideas such as that of judgement and also the boldness of some of the phrases used by him which, as the revision to which they were subject in the epistle shows, were not adapted to the needs of the church at large. The Fourth Gospel gives us an insight into an aspect of Christian thought for which there is hardly any other evidence and on the existence of a form of gnosticism which was not a heresy and provides an explanation of certain trays in later doctrinal developments.

3.—THE JOHANNINE APOCALYPSE

The book to the Seven Churches forms an introduction to the Apocalypse (i-iii) and seems to have come from the pen of the same author who wrote the rest of the book but to have been written about ten years earlier. It is taken up with two concerns: one refers to a measure of slackness and indifference in the life of Christians which the author strives to withstand, the other to the danger of Christian thought being involved in a heresy called the heresy of the Nicolaitans.[1] In the background can be discerned the threat of persecution. The Apocalypse itself reveals a different situation. The threats of persecution have either become more definite or have begun to be realised, or perhaps it would be truer to say that the author has come to see that the conflict between the church and the empire

---

[1] Concerning the Nicolaitans see pp. 409 ff.

cannot be resolved by compromise but is taking the form of a fight to the death.[1] This he sees as the last and most dramatic episode in a great struggle which began at the creation between God and the demonic powers. In this way John identifies the cause of Christians with that of God and boldly predicts the triumph of the church in spite of the formidable disproportion in the material forces at its disposal. He tries to encourage the church in face of the critical period which it is on the point of entering by suggesting the final triumph and at the same time he exhorts it to faithfulness. In the face of danger a kind of sacred union is made and doctrinal divergencies pass into the background. Only one thing counts, faithfulness in confessing the faith.

To recall the great apocalyptic struggle would seem to be far removed from the serenity of mystic contemplation to be found in the fourth gospel. If, however, we take the thought out of its context there is a striking affinity between the central idea of the Apocalypse and the way in which the evangelist portrays the passion as a struggle between the prince of this world and Christ who proves to be conquered in spite of appearances to the contrary. The saying of Jesus to his disciples, 'In the world you will have tribulation, but be of good courage, I have overcome the world' (xvi. 33) would seem to be the motto of the Apocalypse. That does not imply that the gospel and the Apocalypse were written by the same author, but shows that the two books may have emanated from the same environment, or at any rate environments sufficiently near to one another to have mutually influenced each other.

It is not just due to chance or solely because they date from almost the same period that the fourth gospel, the Apocalypse, and the epistle to the Hebrews are those books in the New Testament which contain the most advanced christology.[2] The christology of the Apocalypse shows some peculiar trays. The term most often used to designate Christ is 'Lord' which is sometimes given in the stronger form 'King of kings and Lord of lords' (xvii. 14; xix. 16).

---

[1] See pp. 524 ff., 535 ff.

[2] No importance can be attached in this respect to the fact that the celestial warrior's name is 'Word of God' (xix. 13). This is a gloss which was introduced under the influence of the gospel because in verse 16 it is said that his vesture and thigh are inscribed with his name which is 'King of kings and Lord of lords'. This also is an addition made by the compiler to his source. Verse 12 says that on his head he carried a name which no one but he knew. This must mean a name written in characters which no one but he could read. Cf. Lohmeyer, *Die Offenbarung des Johannes*, Tubingen, 1926, p. 155.

In this way the sovereignty of Christ assumes a meaning which restores it to the Jewish tradition. The pre-existence of Christ is clearly stated. Christ is the beginning[1] of God's creation (iii. 15), the first and the last, the alpha and omega (i. 17; ii. 8) but the apocalypticist's prevailing interest lies in what Christ has done, in what he is going to do in a future which he portrays as very near[2] and in the victory which he is going to gain over the demonic powers who are at war with God and are tormenting the faithful. He is qualified to do this through the drama of his death and resurrection. The speculative element in the christology of the Apocalypse answers above everything else to the demand to exalt the Christ.[3] A close connection is made between the drama of Christ's death and resurrection and his part on the last day. Christ is the ἀρνίον[4] who has been sacrificed (v. 6, 12), the first begotten from the dead (i. 5), he who was dead and is alive again and possesses the keys of Hades and Death (i. 18).[5] Because he has conquered, Christ is seated with his Father on his throne (iii. 21). Here there are traces of Pauline influence; it is stronger than Johannine christology.

The soteriology of the Apocalypse has two poles: the forgiveness of sins and the final deliverance. The very nature of the book causes the author to lay special emphasis on the latter element. The forgiveness of sins and their deletion through the blood of Christ are firmly stated (i. 5; v. 9-10; vii. 14-15; xiv. 1, etc.). But how this takes place is not explained. That is perhaps because the author of the Apocalypse has no very deep conviction or conception about sin.[6] He does not seem to have considered it to be much more than a defect inseparable from human nature. He speaks of purification rather than transformation. Life on earth is, at least for Christians,

---

[1] Or perhaps the principle.

[2] Cf. I,3. 7 ; III, 3. 10 ; VI, 9 ff. ; XIV, 7 ; XVII, 14 ; XXII, 7, 10, 12, 20, etc.

[3] The description of Christ given in the opening vision of the book to the Seven Churches contains a number of features which have been borrowed from visions of the prophets where they are described as belonging to God.

[4] The word ἀρνίον is usually but inaccurately translated 'the Lamb'. It is true that the word ἀρνίον is a diminutive of ἀρήν which means ram, but in the first century ἀρήν had fallen into disuse and only ἀρνίον was used. As Spitta showed (*Christus der Lamm*, in *Streitfragen zur Geschichte Jesu*, Gottingen, 1907, pp. 172-224) the image used in the Apocalypse originated from the Jewish tradition (Enoch, Testaments of the xii Patriarchs). It does not suggest the idea of a weak animal who suffers without being able to defend himself but a beast full of strength and fire who goes at the head of the herd to lead and defend it.

[5] i.e. the power over Hades and Death.

[6] This is also a point on which the thought of the Apocalypse resembles that of the Fourth Gospel.

tribulation and suffering rather than a cause of sin. Sin belongs to the past; it has been washed by the blood of Jesus; there is no question of its still existing.

The apocalypticist considers that only one thing is needed for the deliverance which he expects from Christ on the last day, i.e. fidelity in witness. In this respect his thinking follows much more closely the lines of Palestinian Christianity than those of Paul. It would seem that for his ideas he owes most to the Jewish tradition and at the same time he seems to have no interest in the gospel history.

CHAPTER VI

Christianity as an Ethical Religion in the Epistle of James and the Didache

I.—THE EPISTLE OF JAMES

BOTH from the literary and historical point of view and in respect of its place in the development of Christian thought, the epistle of James[1] is an enigma. Some scholars consider it to be the earliest Christian document;[2] others even suppose it to be pre-Christian, a Jewish work which has only been superficially made Christian by the introduction of the name of Jesus Christ[3] in two passages (i. 1; ii. 1). Every possible date has been suggested up to the beginning of the second century.[4] As the epistles of Peter and Clement of

---

[1] The most important work on the epistle of James is by Dibelius, *Der Brief des Jakobus*, Meyer, XV[7], Gottingen, 1921; J.-H. Ropes, *The Epistle of St. James*, Edinburgh, 1916; Windisch, *Die katholischen Briefe*, Tubingen, 1911,[2] 1930, pp. 1-36; Chaine, *L'épître de saint Jacques*, Paris, 1927 ; J. Marty, *L'épître de Jacques*, Paris, 1935, can also be consulted with advantage.

[2] F. H. Kruger, *L'épître de Jacques, le plus ancien document du Nouveau Testament*, *Revue chrétienne*, 1887, pp. 605-618, 685-695.

[3] This hypothesis was put forward simultaneously by L. Massebieau ('L'épître de Jacques est-elle l'œuvre d'un Chrétien?' *R.h.r.*, 1895, XXXII, pp. 249-281) and by F. Spitta ('Der Brief des Jakobus', in *Zur Geschichte und Literatur der Urchristentums*, Gottingen, 1896, II, pp. 1-239). These two scholars arrived at the same conclusion quite independently of each other (cf. *Spitta*, pp. iii and iv). Two Jewish scholars, Joseph Halévy (*Lettre d'un rabbin de Palestine égarée dans l'Évangile* (sic), *Rev. sémitique*, 1914, XXII, pp. 197-201) and Joseph Klausner (*Jesus of Nazareth, his Life, Times and Teaching*, translated by H. Danby, London, New York, 1927, Eng. trans., p. 367) produced similar opinions. Without going further, Arnold Meyer (*Das Ratsel des Jacobusbriefes*, Giessen, 1930) considers the epistle of James to be a Christian adaptation of a Jewish writing. His argument greatly impressed Windisch as can be seen by comparing the two editions of his commentary.

[4] There are not lacking other books in the New Testament about which there are wide differences of views on important questions. What is peculiar to the epistle of James is that the differing views are not due to differing conceptions of the whole course and development of primitive Christianity.

Rome appear to be dependent on the epistle of James[1] and refer to it, it cannot have been composed later than 85-90.[2] On the other hand, the author tells his readers in the passage iv. 7 of the 'worthy name by which ye are called'. This can only refer to the name of Christ invoked at baptism and therefore shows quite plainly that the epistle is a Christian document. This is also clear from the discussion on faith and works (ii. 14-26). James here has in mind, if not Paul's doctrine, at any rate his phraseology about the superiority of justification by faith over the works of the law. But he has misunderstood the doctrine; by works James does not mean, as Paul meant, the observance of the Jewish ritual but charity towards one's neighbour who is in need. Faith for James is wholly an intellectual virtue; it is not a mystic union with Christ but the kind of belief in the existence of God which even demons may have. From this fact two conclusions may be drawn. (1) James had no direct knowledge of the Pauline epistles. Although his whole outlook and temperament differed from Paul's, if he had read the epistle to the Romans or the epistle to the Galatians, he never could have so completely misunderstood Paul's thought as he has done. The misunderstanding could only have arisen, because the problem of the law as it arose when Paul formulated his doctrine of justification by faith no longer existed. James then belongs to the post-pauline period and he must have written the epistle before the epistles of the apostle had been gathered into *a corpus* and had begun to become known in the church at large. It is peculiarly typical that in a book which was claimed to be James', the leader of the Jewish Christian party, there is no trace of particularism or Jewish ritualism.

It is none the less true that the Christianity to be found in the epistle of James differs considerably both from Paul's and from the variety to be discovered in the writings of deutero-paulinism. It is essentially ethical. Mystical and christological elements are hardly present at all, although it must not be said that they are completely absent,[3] since the epistle shows a certain familiarity with the

[1] The epistle describes itself as the work of James without defining to which James it refers; but apart from the brother of Jesus there is no James who played any part in Christianity in the first century and possessed such prestige that there was no need to define who he was.

[2] We cannot agree with Guignebert's opinion (*Le Christ*, p. 43) that the epistle belongs to 'the first third of the second century and to the beginning of it rather than the end'.

[3] It might be asked if the impression produced by the epistle of James was not due to the fact that it is an exhortation pure and simple. But if we examine the underlying themes of this exhortation we shall find that they are purely ethical.

tradition giving the sayings of Jesus.[1] But they were only used for purposes of moral exhortation[2] which in other respects still more closely resembles Jewish moral exhortation.[3] In James' eyes Jesus is hardly anything more than the revealer of true wisdom, the wisdom which comes from on high and differs from that taught by the flesh. He does not give much consideration to the idea of sin; for him it has nothing to do with a corruption of nature. The moral ideal is exalted. The author with vigorous emphasis condemns harshness towards one's neighbour, indifference on the part of the rich towards the poor, servility towards the powerful, the exploitation of the disinherited, and an attachment to the goods of this world. He criticises with force hesitating and divided attitudes and moral inconsistencies. We must also note his exhortations to faithfulness in trial and temptation and the way in which he threatens sinners with the judgement of God (v. 1 ff.). He speaks of this judgement as if it was very near. This, however, does not denote a resurgence of eschatological sentiment. What he says of the imminent judgement of God must be taken as a traditional theme in exhortation. It would perhaps be going too far to say with Lietzmann[4] that there is no trace of any peculiarly Christian sentiments in the epistle of James since the moral strength behind the epistle which give it its value comes from the gospel. But Lietzmann is certainly right when he says that Gentile Christianity in the hands of small men who owed nothing to Paul ended in resembling the kind of Judaism which missionaries preached in the diaspora.

To try and define the position of the epistle of James in the history of Christianity it is important to know where it was written. Unfortunately we have no definite sources of information about this. Nothing can be made of what is said in v. 7 about the early and later rains for which the husbandman waits, because (1) there are many districts to which this could refer, and (2) it may be more or less a traditional theme of exhortation which had come to be used in other districts besides the one where it originated.[5] The fact that

---

[1] Ritschl (*Die Entstehung der altkatholischen Kirche*[2], Bonn, 1857, p. 109) remarks that the epistle of James echoes more closely the sayings of Jesus than any other book in the New Testament. For the study of the recollections of the sayings of Jesus in the epistle see R. Patry, *L'épître de Jacques dans ses rapports avec la prédication de Jésus*, Alencon, 1899; Dibelius, pp. 27 ff.; Marty, pp. 258 ff.

[2] A comparison comes to mind with the way in which in the *Didache* the *Book of the Two Ways* is embellished with quotations from the gospels.

[3] It also contains features resembling Greek exhortations. Dibelius' commentary has made this clear.   [4] Lietzmann, *H.* I, p. 217.   [5] Dibelius, pp. 46, 224.

the epistle of James seems to have been known and valued at Rome from the end of the first century onwards, as is shown by the influence which it had on the first epistle of Peter, the epistle of Clement of Rome and the Shepherd of Hermas, is not sufficient for us to consider it to have originated in Rome.[1] Many scholars such as Jean Reville and Johannes Weiss[2] think that it originated in Palestine or Syria, their only reason probably being that the epistle is attributed to a person who seems never to have left Palestine or at any rate did not live very far away.[3] But this argument carries little weight as Paul's epistles show that James was well known in the churches of the Greek world. The absence of any allusion to a concrete fact or situation which could be defined in more than general terms[4] compels us to share Dibelius'[5] opinion that it is best to give up any idea of determining the geographical origin of the epistle.

To try and discover the context of James' Christianity we must therefore confine ourselves to the internal evidence provided by the epistle itself. The only positive hint given to us here is that James' Christianity owes nothing to Paul. We have to understand it to be an offshoot of Palestinian Christianity but one which has been influenced by Hellenism to this extent, that it has been freed from particularism and Jewish ritualism and has become universalist. We saw[6] that Palestinian Christianity had two centres, one in the past, i.e. the historic Jesus, his ministry and teaching, and the other in the future, what Jesus will do when he comes to accomplish his redemptive work on the last day. But at the moment he has no positive function. The eschatological hope died down and grew feeble with the result that the balance of Palestinian Christianity changed. The importance of Christ's return diminished; it remained only as a theory and all that was left for Christ was his function as a teacher, preacher, and revealer of true wisdom and the sound way of life. That is what we find Christianity to be in the epistle of James.

[1] As is done with some measure of reserve by Bruckner ('Zur Kritik des Jakobusbriefes, *Z.f. wiss. Th.*, 1874, XVII, pp. 530-541); Von Soden (*Hand-Commentar zum Neuen Testament*, III, 2³, Freiburg in Breisgau, Tubingen, 1899, p. 176); Grafe (*Die Stellung und Bedeutung des Jakobusbriefes in der Entwickelung des Urchristentum*, Tubingen, Leipzig, 1904, p. 45); Loisy (*Naiss. du christ.*, p. 31).
[2] Reville, *Oirg. de l'épiscop.*, pp. 229 ff.; Johannes Weiss, *Urchrist.*, p. 578, n. 8.
[3] We cannot count in favour of Palestine the fact that the author addresses himself to the Twelve tribes who are in the dispersion (i. 1), because, even if it is something more than a literary fiction, we must understand the term dispersion in a figurative sense and suppose it to mean believers who are still living far from their celestial country.   [4] Dibelius, p. iii.   [5] Dibelius, p. 46.   [6] See p. 99.

2.—THE DIDACHE

The Didache[1] is a document belonging to about the year 100 and appears to have originated in Syria, or perhaps, but less probably, in Egypt. It is partly a catechism, partly a liturgy, but more than anything else a kind of manual containing directions for those who found themselves with the charge of governing the churches and do not seem always to have had clear ideas on what they ought to do or how they ought to act. The Didache seems to have been written for a group of churches which were situated where Christians and Jews lived in contact with each other; their separation was complete but there were certain links between them. The author seems to have dreaded the influence of Jews upon the church and makes every effort to distinguish the two groups, but he emphasises external differences.[2] The Law has ceased to be a question at issue but the author advises his readers to abstain from foods forbidden by the law without, however, insisting on it.[3]

The churches which he has in mind seem to have lacked organisation. The charismatic ministry had almost completely disappeared.[4] It was only surviving in the form of an itinerant ministry of teachers and prophets who are also called apostles.[5] While in principle the authority of inspired persons and inspiration itself was

[1] The full title of the document is 'Doctrine (it might also be translated "Teaching") of the Lord to the nations through the mediation of the Twelve Apostles'. The term nations must be understood to mean the peoples of the world without any distinction being drawn between Jews and Gentiles as there is no allusion to there being any difference in the church between them. As for the term apostles it only occurs in one passage (xi. 3-4) where it is applied not to the twelve who are never mentioned but to teachers and itinerant prophets. We may therefore suppose that the title was added some time after the work was written.

[2] e.g. he advises his readers not to fast on the same days as the Jews who are called hypocrites (viii. 1) and not to use the same forms of prayers as they do but to recite the Lord's prayer (viii. 2). He also wants services of worship to be held on Sundays (xiv. 1) but he does not give as his reason for this the necessity of distinguishing themselves from Jews.

[3] On the subject of foods he advises his readers to do what they can (vi. 3) which shows that he considers that the prescriptions of the law about prohibitions of foods to be still valid to some extent, but there is a sharp contrast between what he says about these prescriptions and his uncompromising prohibition which follows immediately to consume what is offered to idols.

[4] The passage x. 7, which says that the prophet can celebrate the eucharist as he wishes, i.e. improvise the prayers instead of using the forms prescribed in chapters ix and x shows that for a prophet to preside at the eucharist was an exceptional case.

[5] Adventurers crept in among the itinerants. The Didache advises precautions to be taken against them. See E.P., pp. 508 ff.

not called in question, it was causing a certain amount of uneasiness. The charismatic ministry had so far declined in prestige that most of the churches had ceased to gain anything from it, but no other kind of ministry had yet arisen everywhere to replace it and in those places where it was beginning to become established it did not enjoy unquestioned authority.

Between different parts of the Didache are found very distinct theological differences. The contrast is sharp between chapters i to vi which informs us of the teaching which must be given to candidates for baptism and chapters ix and x which gives the text of prayers to be said at the celebration of the eucharist. Chapters i to vi reproduce with the addition of some sayings from the gospels a little treatise of Jewish morality, the *Book of the two ways*. The prayers in chapters ix and x are informed with a kind of mysticism which is not particularly Johannine in character but sufficiently resembles it to show marked affinities with it. These prayers cannot have been composed among people who were satisfied with a Jewish treatise, the *Book of the two ways*,[1] as an instruction to be given to those who wanted to receive baptism. They were borrowed from another circle of people with whom the churches of the Didache were in contact. We are therefore in the presence of a form of Christianity, in which at least two currents, coming from two distinct types of Christianity, meet without completely inter-penetrating each other. We must try to define the character of each of them.

There are, it is said, at the beginning of the moral catechism, two ways, one of which leads to life, the other to death. It goes on to describe each of the two ways. The instruction is therefore divided into two parts. One is positive and describes what one must do to have life; the other is negative describing what leads to death and must be avoided. We have here at the outset a peculiarly Jewish legalistic conception. What is Christian in it, which is far from negligible, is that the moral ideal put forward for realisation is not made up of commandments from the law but from sayings of Jesus. First is given Jesus' summary of the law which he gave (Mark xii. 28-34; Matt. xxii. 34-40) or approved of (Luke x. 25-28),[2] then the golden rule, 'not to do to others as one would not do to

---

[1] The epistle of Barnabas also reproduces the *Book of the Two Ways*, Book VIII of the *Apostolic Constitutions* (1-21) does the same. Cf. Harnack, *Lehre d. zw. Apost.*, pp. 174-176, 178-186. *G.a.L.*, pp. 86 ff. Its use in the church was not therefore an isolated instance.

[2] Cf. Barnabas, xix. 5.

oneself' (Acts xv. 19, Western text) (i. 2) and next the sayings from the Sermon on the Mount concerning the way in which we must regard our enemies (Matt. v. 39-48; Luke vi. 27-36;[1] i. 3-5a).[2] This is followed by a saying which breathes a very different spirit. It is a warning to those who would ask for alms without really needing them and advice only to give alms with care and knowledge. In reference to this, the following saying is quoted:[3] 'Let thine alms sweat in thine hands until thou knowest to whom thou art giving' (i. 5b). This is followed by a series of prohibitions (murder, adultery, sodomy, debauchery, theft, magic, poisoning, abortion, infanticide, etc.). The faithful man will have to love all men. He will reprove some and pray for them; he will love others more than his own life (ii. 1-7).[4] This is repeated in chapter iii but with this difference, that it does not refer so much to sins themselves as to the sentiments and practices which engender them.[5] The last paragraph of the description of the way of life advises a man to reverence as the Lord himself the masters from whom he has received his teaching,[6] to avoid divisions, to give alms in order to obtain forgiveness of sins, to bring up children in the fear of the Lord, and to be gentle with slaves and servants. On the other hand, slaves are advised to submit to their masters who are for them God's representative (iv. 1-12).[7] In conclusion, a man must keep the commandments of the Lord without adding anything to them or taking away anything and, in order that he may not come to prayer with an evil conscience, he must confess his sins in the congregation of the faithful (iv. 13-14).

The way of death is described more briefly.[8] First, there is a catalogue of vices such as the moralists of the time loved to draw up. Then comes a brief conclusion. A man must see that no-one

---

[1] One detail shows that these sayings of Jesus in their profoundest sense were not always understood. The Didache quotes this saying, 'If any man will take from thee what is thine, refuse it not', but he adds the words, 'For other reasons you may not be able'. The form of the saying given here is not quite the same as in the gospels. Translator's note.—The Greek is literally 'for thou art not even able'. As this does not make sense Kirsopp Lake translates 'not even if thou canst'.

[2] The Didache adds the advice to avoid corporeal and carnal passions (i. 4). This was a current theme of Christian exhortation. Cf. Romans xiii. 14; Ephesians ii. 3; 1 Peter ii. 11.

[3] A saying of Jesus which either had come from an extra-canonical tradition or is quoted from an unknown book.

[4] Cf. Barnabas, xix. 3, 5, 7, 11.   [5] Cf. Barnabas, xix. 2, 4-6.

[6] This is a specifically Jewish sentiment which recalls the way in which the rabbi had to be honoured by their disciples.

[7] Cf. Barnabas, xix. 2, 4, 5, 7-11.   [8] Cf. Barnabas, xix. 12.

makes him deviate from the form of teaching which has just been given for he teaches him without God.[1] The man will be perfect who will bear the whole yoke of the Lord. But in the mind of the author of the Didache this is only an ideal standard of perfection indicating rather than anything else what it is best to try and aim at in life. The man who does not feel he can attain it is only asked to do what he can (vi. 1-2). The facility with which the author limits his ambitions shows that he was living among Christians whose standards were somewhat mediocre. He is far removed from the moral vigour of the epistle of James.

A man is invited in this catechism, which it must not be forgotten was a form of instruction preparatory to baptism, to rely on his own natural strength to resist the passions of the body and flesh and to obey the commandments of the Lord. Sin and the way in which forgiveness can be obtained are hardly mentioned. There are only two short notes about it ; iv. 6 advises a man to give alms in order that he may in this way give a ransom for his sins; iv. 14 speaks of confession of sins before the congregation of the faithful but it is not stated to be a condition to be fulfilled to obtain God's forgiveness; by itself it prevents prayer from being spoilt by an evil conscience, which means that by itself it purifies. Christ and his redemptive work and the grace of God are not even mentioned. In addition there is no thought of sanctification being the work of the Spirit of God or Christ. The catechism is pure and unadulterated moralism and in spite of the few sayings of Jesus to be found in it the atmosphere is purely Jewish.

It might be supposed that the character of the instruction had been determined by the nature of the source used and by the fact that the author had not sufficient mastery of it to impose his own outlook upon it. But when we look at the other parts of the book there is nothing to justify an explanation of this kind. To take an example, in reference to baptism forgiveness of sins (vii) is never mentioned. The instruction however is more concerned with the way in which the rite should be administered than with its significance. If forgiveness of sins had been a central idea in the rite, it would be quite surprising if there were not signs of this in the baptismal formula recommended for use.

---

[1] The Spirit is only mentioned in the catechism in iv. 10 which in referring to the proper attitude of the Christian towards his slave or servant says that God is over masters and slaves; he comes not to call men with respect of persons but those whom the Spirit has prepared.

The instructions concerning Sunday worship in chapter xiv must also be considered as they also are in complete agreement with the opening catechism. Before a man breaks bread to celebrate the eucharist he must confess his sins in order that the sacrifice may be pure and, if anyone has a quarrel with his brother, he must abstain from participating in the rite until a reconciliation has been made. There is no suggestion that forgiveness from God is needed. The only idea is that the faithful believer must purify his heart by confessing his sins and becoming reconciled to his enemies in order that he may be able to give God the worship pleasing to Him.

The eucharistic prayers show quite a different type of Christianity which had penetrated from outside the church where the Didache was composed.[1] They describe Jesus as servant ($\pi\alpha\hat{\imath}\varsigma$) of God (ix. 2, 3; x. 2-3), revealer of life, knowledge (ix. 3), faith and immortality (x. 2). This is the language of the Hellenistic mystery religions; in the conceptions used by them to reveal life and knowledge is also to give and to communicate these things. God is glorified because he has given the faithful through his servant Jesus spiritual food and drink (x. 3) and has caused his name to dwell in their hearts (x. 2). One last thing must be noted in these prayers, i.e. the yearning for the time when the church which is now scattered to the four winds will be gathered and sanctified in the Kingdom of God (ix. 4; x. 5).

The presence in these prayers of the ideas of Christ as revealer of knowledge and immortality shows some affinity with Johannine mysticism but the idea of sin receives much less notice than in John. This may be due to the fact that it was influenced less by Paulinism and more by Greek mysticism. It is quite certain that the author of the Didache cannot have composed these prayers himself; it is none the less plain that he would not have adopted them unless he and those among whom he lived had shown themselves amenable to the ideas and sentiments expressed in them. The fact that these prayers were borrowed shows that these people had been influenced by another type of Christianity which, however, was not sufficiently strong to repress the moralising type. It was imposed upon it but did not harmonise.

It is possible that the mystical ideas which we find in the eucharistic prayers penetrated the group of churches for whom the Didache was written through the agency of itinerant preachers. This would

[1] Concerning the conception of the eucharist behind these prayers, see *E.P.*, pp. 362 f.

explain the mixture of respect and embarrassment which the author shows for inspiration and inspired persons. There are other signs showing that pneumatism was not an indigenous element belonging to these churches but had penetrated them from outside.

The Didache thus affords significant evidence for the work of assimilation and interpenetration which was going on at the end of the first century between the various forms of Christianity. In it two types are placed side by side rather than mingled together. One of them belongs to the same species as that represented by the epistle of James. The other is shown to be a mystical type of Christianity, which had been little influenced by Paulinism but may have been a little more so by Johanninism. It is also conceivable that it was a development resembling Johanninism with perhaps this difference. It should be envisaged as a combination of Greek Christianity with Hellenistic mysticism while Johanninism would be more accurately defined as Greek Christianity expressed in the language of Hellenistic mysticism.

CHAPTER VII

The Pre-Catholicism of Clement of Rome

THE Christianity of Clement of Rome, or, to be more exact, the Roman Christianity, which is reflected in the epistle which Clement[1] wrote about 96 to the church at Corinth in the name of that at Rome[2] shows certain trays which are common to the epistle of James and the Didache. It possesses sufficient originality to make it in some respects a novelty, so that it marks an important stage in the long process of Christianity becoming stabilised and organised. It is legitimate to use the term pre-catholicism because we find in

---

[1] There are very many editions of the epistle of Clement. Among the principal ones may be mentioned J. B. Lightfoot (*The apostolic Fathers*, Part I, London, 1869,[2] 1890), Von Gerhardt and Harnack (*Patrum apostolicorum opera*, 1, 1, Leipzig, 1876). These two editions contain exhaustive commentaries and an introduction by Funk, *Patres apostolici*,[2] Tubingen, 1906. A good English translation is to be found in the Loeb texts (*The Apostolic Fathers*, translated by Kirsopp Lake, London, New York, 1914). R. Knopf's commentary (*Lehre der zwolf Apostel. Zwei Clemensbriefe*, Tubingen, 1930) can also be consulted with profit. These editions and commentaries contain many bibliographical references. Among the most important works we will only mention R. Knopf, *Der erste Clemensbrief*, Leipzig, 1899; Harnack, 'Der erste Clemensbrief, Eine Studie zur Bestimmung des Charakters des aeltesten Heidenchristentums', *S.B.A.*, 1909, pp. 38-6 3; *Einf.*, Tradition makes the end of the reign of Domitian the approximate date of the composition of the epistle. Various hints confirm this date. It is a long time after the Apostolic period. The first bishops and deacons whom they appointed have already had successors (44, 2 f.). The church at Corinth has behind it a long history (47, 6). There are in the church at Rome people who have led an irreproachable life from youth to old age (63, 3). The massacres of 64 seem to belong to such a distant past that none living can remember them (see pp. 96 ff. and *E.P.*). Lastly, at the beginning of the letter Clement alludes to a difficult period through which the church has just passed. This is recognised to be a reference to Domitian's persecution. The epistle seems therefore to have been composed shortly after the accession of Nerva when the persecution came to an end.

[2] The epistle itself does not pretend to have been written by Clement. The author always expresses himself in the first person plural. He is the spokesman of the church of Rome. There is nothing to cause us to question the traditional attribution of the epistle to Clement. Hermas (*Vis.* ii. 4, 3) mentions a Clement as being authorised to regulate the relations between the church of Rome and the

Clement's letter certain features strongly delineated which later belonged to the character of early catholicism, in particular, a close association between a theological conception containing a strong moral element, and a theory, which by linking together true doctrine and the church as a stable organisation presents it as the body within which the life of the Christian may advance on the road to salvation, guided by a ministry exercising its functions because it is a divine institution. From Clement onwards the church is a supernatural organism. For Clement it is the concrete church here and now not, as for Paul, the ideal church of eschatological expectations which is an institution of salvation.

The circumstances which determined the composition of this epistle do not by themselves explain the character of its thought. Its style is so emphatic that we must put on one side the idea that it contains a theory improvised to solve a problem which had just arisen. Circumstances only provided Clement with the occasion for expressing ideas which must have been current for some time in the ruling circles of the church of Rome.[1]

Concerning Clement himself we have hardly any exact information. In spite of real difficulties in the way of chronology he is sometimes identified with Paul's collaborator mentioned in Philippians iv. 3, whom tradition says was pope.[2] It is of little importance as the ideas expressed in the epistle are more than personal.

There had been troubles in the church at Corinth after which the presbyters who were in office were deposed.[3] The church at

communities outside. If we identify the Clement mentioned by Hermas with the author of the epistle we are relieved of any difficulties connected with chronology as the Shepherd of Hermas is more than half a century later than the epistle to the Corinthians. For the history of this question which has been a subject of much discussion see Harnack, *Patr. ap. op.*, III, pp. 26 ff. Harnack, who in 1877 declared himself against the identification, has since (*Einf.*, p. 169) declared himself for it. Lightfoot[1] (I, pp. 359 f.) and Dibelius (*Der Hirt des Hermas*, Tubingen, 1923, pp. 422 f., 453) also admit the identification but think that Hermas named Clement because he wanted to antedate the celestial letter which Clement was charged to communicate to the churches outside in order to increase his prestige. Hemmer (*Peres apost.* II, p. xc) inclines to think that Hermas' Clement is an imaginary person. Lelong (*Les Peres apostoliques* IV, *Le Pasteur d'Hermas*, Paris, 1912, p. xlv) thinks it a synonym for the author of the epistle.

[1] For this theory and the question of knowing how far it is true see *E.P.*, pp. 70 ff.

[2] Concerning his place in the early lists of bishops see Lightfoot, I, 1, pp. 46 ff., 92 f., 144-202; Hemmer, pp. 1 ff.

[3] Clement does not enter into any discussion on the complaints made by the Corinthians against their elders. This is perhaps due to the fact that they did not altogether lack foundation in fact but more especially because, as we shall see elsewhere, Clement is more concerned with a question of principle than of fact.

Rome was forced to restore order in her sister church after she had learnt what had happened—we do not know how—and intervened with her counsels. The epistle is firm in spirit and moderate and prudent in form. Clement has great confidence that the Corinthians will accept the counsels given by him. We do not know what was the outcome. Whatever happened, relations between the churches of Rome and Corinth remained excellent as is proved by the correspondence of Denys of Corinth with Rome.[1]

The letter begins with a short introduction apologising for the church of Rome's delay in intervening. Clement then sketches a picture of the splendid condition up till recently enjoyed by the church of Corinth and the reputation which it had acquired (i-iii). To explain what has just happened and to emphasise its gravity, he shows by a number of examples what ravages quarrelling and jealousy cause (iv-vi).[2] He then makes an appeal to penitence (vii-viii) which is followed by a long exhortation extending to chapter xxxix. This has no direct relevance to the events at Corinth. It gives an idea what form preaching must have taken in the church of Rome at the end of the first century. After the exhortation to penitence there follow notes on obedience, faith, and hospitality (ix-xii), God's blessings and man's attitude towards them (xix. 2-xxii. 8) and lastly the resurrection (xxiii. 1-27; xxvii. 7).[3] A brief bridge-passage

The elders do not hold their powers from the community which is therefore not qualified to withdraw them. Clement seems to minimise the conflict somewhat by speaking of those who had provoked it as a few persons (I, 1) and even of two or three (lxvii, 6). In any case these instigators of trouble must have found a response in the latent sentiments of the majority of the members of the church as they followed them. All sorts of hypotheses have been made. Reville (*Orig. de l'épiscop.*, pp. 403 ff.; *Orig. de l'euch.*, pp. 40 ff.) thought that the conflict originated in the elders claiming to be the only persons who had the right to perform certain ecclesiastical acts, particularly that of presiding at the eucharist. Perhaps in the exact form in which he states his hypothesis there is too much conjecture. But it seems true that the conflict was caused by the increasing amount of authority claimed by the elders. We are belittling the significance of the conflict too much if, as Harnack does (*Einf.* p. 92), we think that only personalities were at stake and there were no questions of principle involved, or as Lietzmann thinks (*H.*, I, p. 206) that it was a case of the younger generation being opposed to the old, the young demanding a new division of powers which were entirely in the hands of the old. W. Bauer (*Rechtgl. u. Ketz*, pp. 99 ff.) thought that the conflict was doctrinal in character. He judges it to have been an extension of the conflict waged by Paul at Corinth against gnostics and libertines. The fact that the instructions in the letter on doctrine are in vague, general terms is not favourable to this hypothesis.

[1] Eusebius, *H.e.*, IV, 23, 9-12.
[2] It is in this context that the apostles, Peter and Paul, are quoted as having been victims of these vices. See *E.P.*, pp. 232 ff.
[3] The resurrection of Jesus is mentioned at the beginning but occupies a smaller place in the chain of reasoning than other arguments of a pseudo-rational

(xxviii) refers to the omniscience and omnipotence of God which has been demonstrated by the resurrection and leads to the idea that, as Christians are the object of God's choice, they must accomplish works of sanctification (xxix-xxx). The concluding part of the exhortation describes the way in which man will be blest (xxxi-xxxvi). To this Clement attaches another exhortation that they should submit themselves to God and subordinate themselves to each other as is required of them in the community (xxxvii-xxxix). The letter then returns to its central theme. Chapters xl-xliv treats of the order of the ministry and its institution by God which the Corinthians have disregarded by deposing their elders. The principles are stated from which spring the instructions given to the Corinthians. Chapters xlv and xlvi form a connecting passage; they deal with people of wealth who have been often persecuted and pursued by wicked men. Then in another connecting passage consisting of chapters xlvii-l Clement recalls the warning which Paul had previously given to the Corinthians when their church had been divided into rival factions. He then passes on to more concrete instructions. Those who initiated the movement must confess their sin and make an act of repentance. The church will compel them to leave Corinth (liii-lv). It will pray that they may submit themselves to the will of God (lvi): then comes an appeal to repentance addressed to the rebels themselves (lvii-lviii). This is crowned by a long prayer (lix-lxi) which must be a liturgical prayer in use in the church at Rome.[1] After a doxology it ends with an intercession for those who suffer, the persecuted, the sick, and the poor, and with a triple prayer for forgiveness of sins, peace, and the general good, and those in authority. The whole prayer is again followed by a prayer of thanksgiving. The epistle concludes with a summary of Clement's previous exhortations (lxii-lxiii) and recommends three trusted men, Clausius Ephebius, Valerius Biton and Fortunatus who are sent to Corinth to bring the letter and to add to it their own exhortations (lxiv). It finishes with a greeting (lxv).

There are, it can be seen, two elements in this letter. There is its essence, i.e. instructions for restoring the situation which has been created at Corinth by the revolt against the elders. There are also hortatory and liturgical elements which provide first-hand information about Roman Christianity at the end of the first century. What is most

character such as the succession of day and night, sowing times, and the history of the phoenix bird.
[1] I shall return to this prayer in *E.P.*, pp. 266 ff.

striking about it is its strong ecclesiastical character. The Christian life is only conceived to be possible within the framework of a supernatural society synonymous with a divine institution in which the laity are strictly subordinated to the clergy. For with the epistle of Clement we meet with a clear-cut cleavage between clergy and laity.

There are few quotations and reminiscences of the gospel tradition in the epistle. The life and teaching of Jesus as well as his redemptive work are only on the fringe of Clement's Christianity. One reminiscence of the parable of the sower (xxiv. 5) and two quotations of sayings of Jesus[1] are practically all that can be discovered. The Old Testament is the principal source of Clement's inspiration and provides him with what he considers to be the most suitable incentives with which to impress his readers.[2]

This pre-catholicism imbued with the Roman legalistic spirit has a very marked moralising character and approximates closely to Judaism. Worship, adoration and prayer are addressed to God, while Christ plays only quite a secondary part. It is true that there is a mention of the wisdom, gentleness and piety 'in Christ' formerly possessed by the Corinthians (ii. 2) but this is hardly anything more than a traditional phrase. The point emphasised most by Clement is that they formerly walked according to God's commandments, submitted themselves to their leaders, gave their young good instruction, and kept their wives in submission (i. 3). Christ is not even mentioned in those passages dealing with forgiveness. 'You stretched your hands to Almighty God, beseeching him to be merciful towards any unwilling sin' (ii. 3).

Chapter vii is rather different. As he states in it that he is coming to 'the glorious and venerable rule of our tradition' (vii. 2) we should expect to find the quintessence of Clement's thought here but what follows, 'Let us see what is good and pleasing and acceptable in the sight of our Maker' (vii. 3), shows that he is thinking of God and not of Christ, and that what he finds in the tradition is a rule of life. Yet he invites his readers to reflect how the blood of Christ[3] is precious in the eyes of God, since it was poured out for

---

[1] In xiii. 2 there is a quotation from Matthew v. 7; in xlviii. 8 from Matthew xxvi combined with Luke i. 1-2.

[2] This suggested to many critics that Clement was of Jewish origin. It is by no means impossible. It remains true, however, that this use of the Old Testament corresponds to the general outlook of the church of Rome.

[3] In xii. 7, Clement even speaks of the blood of Christ which gives a purification to all those who believe and hope in God and in xxi. 6, he speaks of the Lord Jesus Christ whose blood has been given for us.

our salvation and brought the grace of repentance to the whole world (vii. 4). This is an echo of Paul's phrases, without any precise significance. What follows shows that the blood of Christ does not directly give salvation but creates repentance. Clement's thought in general lacks firmness; he goes on in vii. 5-7 to show by examples borrowed from the Old Testament that God in every generation brings to repentance those who come back to him.

Penitence therefore gives salvation. Clement states this even when he is using phrases from Paul. Thus he writes, 'And therefore we who by the will of God have been called in Christ Jesus, are made righteous, not by ourselves, nor by our wisdom nor understanding nor by the deeds which we have wrought in holiness of heart, but through faith' (xxxii. 4). But Clement does not mean what Paul meant, since he adds that God has justified all men from eternity. What part then can the sacrifice of Christ play? Paul would never have written as Clement does, 'Let us then join ourselves[1] to those to whom is given grace from God; let us put on concord in meekness of spirit and continence keeping ourselves far from all gossip and evil speaking, and be justified by deeds, not by words' (xxx. 3).

And this is how Clement, after speaking of the good things enjoyed by the elect, defines what gives salvation: 'But how shall this be? If our understanding be faithfully fixed upon God; if we seek the things which are well-pleasing and acceptable to him; if we fulfil the things which are in harmony with his faultless will, and follow the way of truth, casting away from ourselves all iniquity and wickedness, covetousness, strife, malice and fraud, gossiping and evil speaking, hatred of God, pride and arrogance, vain-glory and inhospitality' (xxxv. 5; cf. ix. 1). Christ has no part in all this. Except for the fact that he would not have mentioned Christ by name at all, a Jewish preacher might have expressed himself in exactly the same terms. If Christ calls to a real repentance he is not the only one to do this, since the instruction which begins in chapter viii and is made up of quotations borrowed from the Old Testament is introduced with the words, 'The ministers of the grace of God (he means the prophets and writers of the Old Testament) spoke through the Holy Spirit concerning repentance'. All the exhortations addressed to the authors of sedition or to those who have allowed themselves to be won over by them are directed to bringing them back not to Christ but to God.[2]

[1] There must be understood 'in order to imitate them'.
[2] e.g. xiv. 1; xix. 2; xxi. 1; xxvii. 1; xxix. 1; xxxiv. 4, 5, 7.

Clement has a clear idea of the part played by Christ in the realisation of salvation, but he uses phrases which he has borrowed from a tradition which means nothing to him except in a superficial kind of way. Thus in chapter xxi he shows what instruction in Christ must be given to children. He speaks of the strength of humility before God, the power of pure love before God, of the effects of the fear God inspires, how God saves those whose conscience is pure, searches our thoughts. He says that his breath is in us and when he will he will take it away (xxi. 8-9). Christ's part is only to instruct: it is God who speaks. Clement wants a man to be firm in faith in Christ, but to define this faith he only quotes from passages in the Psalms (xxii. 1-8).

Chapter xxxvi contains a passage in which Clement seems to be speaking of Christ with a little more warmth of spirit and in a more personal tone but, whatever the fervour shown in the passage, it never goes beyond the idea of Christ as educator and revealer of the way of salvation. 'This is the way in which we found our salvation, Jesus Christ, the high priest of our offerings' (xxxvi. 1-6). Clement owes his inspiration for all this directly to the epistle to the Hebrews (ii. 17, 18; iii. 1; iv. 16). But its influence is purely verbal; Clement never recalls the doctrine of the sacrifice of Christ. Clement quotes the statement of Psalm cx. 1 quoted in Hebrews i. 13, 'Sit thou on my right hand until I make thine enemies a footstool of thy feet', and makes this comment on it, 'Who are then the enemies? Those who are wicked and oppose his will.' Both the author of the epistle to the Hebrews and Paul before him had taken this statement in a metaphysical and cosmological sense but Clement gives it a moral significance. The purpose of Christ's work is no longer to purify men from their sin but only to show them what they must do to be saved. 'Let us serve in our army, brethren, with all earnestness, following his faultless commands' and he supports this exhortation by taking as a pattern the discipline prevailing in the Roman army (xxxvii. 1-2). To obey God's commandments is the only way to obtain forgiveness of sins (l. 5). A function, however, is attributed to Christ, since Clement quoting what Psalm xxxi (1-2) says of the blessedness of those who have obtained forgiveness for their sins, adds, 'This blessing was given to those who have been chosen by God through Jesus Christ' (l. 7). A little earlier he had said, 'All the generations from Adam until this day have passed away: but those who were perfected in love by the grace of God have a place among the pious who shall be made manifest at the visitation of the Kingdom of Christ' (i. 3). It follows from this statement that strictly speaking Christ's intervention is not absolutely necessary for men to be able to come to blessedness. His function does not emerge with any greater clearness in lix. 2 where the faithful are asked to pray that through Jesus Christ, his well-beloved child, God may keep the number of the elect intact.

This presumes that Christ exercises protection over them, but we are not told how he does it, and in what follows it is only God who is mentioned. The church's prayer is addressed to God as the one who helps and brings succour. In a beautiful moving oratorical passage the church supplicates Him for all the unfortunate in order that, the concluding passage says, 'all the nations may know that thou art God alone, and that Jesus Christ is thy child, and that "we are thy people and the sheep of thy pasture"' (lix. 3-4). This shows piety of a Jewish type freed from any kind of particularism. Except in one passage which plainly owes its inspiration to the epistle to the Hebrews Christ is not called Son but only 'child' of God. Clement's thought is more closely related to Palestinian than to Greek Christianity. This is clearly apparent in the long final prayer from which we quote two passages, 'O merciful and compassionate, forgive us our iniquities and unrighteousness, and transgressions and shortcomings. Reckon not every sin of thy servants and handmaids, but cleanse us with the cleansing of thy truth, and guide our steps to walk in holiness of heart to do the things which are good and pleasing before thee, and before our rulers'[1] (lx. 1-2). And this is the way in which it ends, 'we praise thee through Jesus Christ, the high priest and guardian of our souls, through whom be glory and majesty to thee, both now and for all generations and for ever and ever. Amen' (lxi. 3).

At the end of the letter Clement describes what he has written as a statement of 'the things which befit our worship, and are most helpful for a virtuous life (ἐις ἐνάρετον βίόν) to those who wish to guide their steps in piety and righteousness' (lxii. 1).

Up to now we have not given any thought to Clement's ideas concerning the organisation of the church but this must be done not only because the incidents at Corinth gave rise to them but also because in Clement's eyes the organisation of the church played an essential part in bringing mankind salvation. The church as well as being a supernatural society, both in principle and in its ends, is also one in its organisation and its manifestations; in actual fact the

---

[1] These rulers appear to be political authorities. Cf. Knopf, p. 114.

form of worship and priesthood as laid down in the Mosaic legislation are applied to it. Its hierarchical organisation, which subordinates the laity to the clergy, was created by the apostles acting
in accordance with the Lord's instructions. As Clement conceives
the church it loses its eschatological character; it has become an
institution for the education of the faithful. Clement does not go as
far as formulating the catholic principle, 'Outside the church, no
salvation', but his thought looks forward to it. If the first task of
the faithful believer is to submit himself to the elders, how could
he be on the road to salvation when he is in revolt against them or
keeps himself apart from the church which they are directing?

Now that the church is settled on earth the question of its relations with the political authorities assumes a growing importance.
We must not make too much of the fact that, to prove the necessity
of obedience, Clement refers to the firm discipline and organisation
of the Roman army (xxxvii. 2) in such terms as show that he felt
proud to be a Roman. But the prayer for those in authority in
chapter lxi shows it, although it follows the lines of Romans xiii,
1 Peter ii. 13 f. and 1 Timothy iii. 1 f.[1] Clement did not think that
Christianity implied an absolute unconcern with the affairs of the
world. After the persecutions of Nero and Domitian that is all the
more significant.

In varying degrees and not altogether in the same way Clement's
Christianity shows affinities both with Palestinian Christianity and
also principally in the forms derived from Paul and the epistle to
the Hebrews with Greek Christianity.

But it is not a development of either. The connection with
Palestinian Christianity is shown by the use of the term servant
(or child) to designate Jesus, by the importance given to penitence
and lastly by an emphasis on morals to which Palestinian Christianity
leads when it is deprived of eschatological belief.[2]

On these points Clement's thought shows striking affinities with
that of the epistle of James and the first part of the Didache. The
incidence of literary influence alone does not explain them. A parallel
development under the influence of the same causes gave birth to
James' Christianity and to Clement's.

But in addition to the resemblances there are also fairly clear
differences. Although it can be maintained without being ridiculous
that James' epistle may be a Jewish writing and certainly that some

[1] See also for a later period Polycarp, *Phil.* xii. 3; Justin, *Apol.* i. 17, 3;Tertullian,
Apologet. 28, 32, 39.   [2] See pp. 373 ff.

of its sources are Jewish, the same hypothesis cannot be put forward for the epistle of Clement of Rome. Two reasons explain the difference between them which is here revealed. One must be found in the influence of Greek Christianity. This influence we saw was superficial and verbal but none the less it preserved in a latent state, as a static if not a dynamic religion the original elements of the gospel as understood by Paul which could not be derived from Judaism. The other is the fact that Clement's thought is shown to be ecclesiastical in character. It does not belong to an individual but to a religious society which felt that it was distinct from the Jewish community even if it had no clear idea where the distinction lay.

CHAPTER VIII

Heresies

PRIMITIVE Christianity in the first generation held the conviction with singular intensity that unity was an essential mark of the church. The church must be one because Christ, its foundation and centre of its being is one. Paul admits that there may be and even that it is inevitable and perhaps good that there should be differing opinions in the church, αἱρέσεις,[1] but there must not be σχίσματα, deep divisions between members of the body of Christ setting them at variance with each other (1 Cor. xi. 18-19; cf. i. 10; xii. 25; cf. Phil. iii. 15-16).

There was the feeling in the latter half of the first century that this unity, capable of description as it was, did not exist. The Johannine Christ does not pray that his disciples may remain one but that they may be one (xvii. 11). The eucharistic prayers of the Didache show nostalgia for unity rather than the presence of it as a reality (ix. 4; x. 5). The church of the end of the first century shows it to be an ideal when it describes the Christians of apostolic times as being 'of one heart and mind' (Acts iv. 32), as 'continuing stead-fastly in the apostles' doctrine' (ii. 42). It was thought that this blessed unity had been destroyed by disloyalty and ambition, i.e. by men's sinfulness and the malice of Satan. Many passages of the New Testament belonging to relatively late books, such as the Pastoral Epistles (1 Tim. iv. 1; 2 Tim. iii. 1; iv. 3) or the first epistle of John (ii. 18; iv. 1) or even admittedly late works like the epistle of Jude (18) or 2 Peter (ii. 1 ff.; iii. 3) declare that in the last times, which are just the times in which the authors of these books feel that they are living, there will arise false prophets, antichrists, masters

---

[1] The word is used here in quite a different sense from what it acquired afterwards.

of error, creators of schisms and heresies. The appearance of these wicked men was in their eyes a symptom of the coming of evil days, which according to Jewish apocalyptic ideas were before the end came to cause Satan to rage with redoubled force because he would feel that his final defeat was near.[1] What happened only corresponded to these predictions, as they were planned out, in a very remote fashion.

The first generation was unaware of any contradiction between sound doctrine[2] and heresy, not because there existed perfect unity in thought but because the phrases used to express belief still only retained their validity so far as they sprung from inward conviction itself, in other words, so far as they expressed experience. There could thus be a wide diversity in the phrases used without any feeling that the unity of the church was in any way compromised thereby. It was different in the second generation when the relationship between experience and expression was reversed, experience ceased to give birth to doctrinal expression which itself created experience and adhesion to a particular doctrinal truth was held as the condition which must be fulfilled for a man to be able to share in salvation. Doctrine in this way came to exist in its own right as it preceded experience and what differed from it appeared as heresy. The two opposing conceptions of sound doctrine and heresy are closely bound together; one defines the other and neither can exist without the other.

Heresy in principle is any line of thought[3] which differs from the official expression of the church's faith and yet claims to have the right to exist and develop within the community. For the period under consideration this definition must be treated as flexible, as no rigorously phrased confession of faith yet existed.[4] Heresy cannot yet be spoken of as being a way of thought opposed to that of the

[1] The traditions of the Palestinian churches with which we are acquainted through Hegesippus (in Hegesippus, *H.e.* iv. 22, 5) show the same idea in a slightly different form. Until Simeon was elected bishop of Jerusalem in place of James who had died a martyr's death, Hegesippus tells us, the church deserved the epithet 'virgin' because no heresy had yet soiled it. But a certain Thebuthis was disappointed because he did not attain his ambition to become bishop and began to corrupt the church by introducing into it the pernicious ideas of the seven Jewish heresies.

[2] It might be called orthodoxy but the term would be rather an anachronism.

[3] Heresy as a conception must be understood to include the practical devotional, and ethical consequences flowing from this way of thinking.

[4] In Paul's epistles there are passages which seem to reproduce formulae belonging to a confession of faith but they vary in form and have no definitive character.

majority of the members of the church, but only one opposed to the ideas of certain groups perhaps not large in numbers, who exercised or tried to exercise a preponderating influence in the church and whose ideas were ultimately destined to be imposed upon it. This explains why, although the exponents of sound doctrine may pass severe judgement on heretics, they do not go so far as to demand their exclusion from the church; it is not because of their moderation as their words show no discretion in this respect, but because they have the feeling that if they asked for strict measures against the heretics, they would not be granted.[1]

The common name heresy covers a wide range of forms of thought, which have in common this feature only, that they do not agree with those forms which prevail on the church or are tending to do so. Some heresies might be described as intra-christian. Some of these are the persistence in certain congregations of archaic forms of thought which the church as a whole has outgrown. Such is the Ebionite heresy which the first epistle of John opposes and such also in a more general fashion is Jewish Christianity after 70. Others might be considered to be logical developments of accepted principles of the faith which none the less somewhat seriously contradict, if not the faith itself, at least the general conception of the faith. Such was antinomism which was deduced from certain phrases used by Paul but was certainly foreign to his thought. Other heresies which we call extra-christian show a synchretistic character. They are a result of introducing into Christian thought elements which had developed outside Christianity and by being integrated within it were in danger of changing its character.[2]

While the appearance of the idea of sound doctrine called into existence the idea of heresy or at any rate the idea of judging certain ways of thought to be heretical and intolerable, on the other hand, the existence and growth of heresy forces sound doctrine to be defined with growing precision and its field to be so enlarged as to include solutions of problems which it would never have raised,

---

[1] On this point see W. Bauer's book, *Rechtgl. u. Ketz.* Of the facts mentioned by him I quote the following by way of example: In his epistle to the Philippians Polycarp is fighting a docetic form of gnosticism (7, 1) and immediately after in 7, 2 he speaks of the vain thoughts of the majority as he had spoken before of the erring ways of this same majority (2, 1). The majority must have been on the side of the heretics whom he was opposing and Polycarp does not mention the bishop probably because he was with them.

[2] This classification of heresies must naturally be understood *cum grano salis.* One heresy may be complex and in its various aspects might simultaneously belong to two of the groups distinguished by us or even to three.

except for the fact that it could not leave their solution to those whom it considered did not possess the truth.

The history of heresy shows that there was in early Christianity a marked difference between the doctrinal position of the general company of the faithful and that of the leading personalities or groups who took the initiative in the struggle against heresy and heretics. At first they were only concerned to put the faithful on their guard against what appeared to them dangerous propaganda. Only by a slow process in the course of the second century when the organisation of the church had become strong did its leaders pass on to the offensive and exclude heretics from the church.

2.—DID THE APOSTLE PAUL REGARD THE JUDAISING CHRISTIANS AS HERETICS?

Must we consider the first stage of the conflict with heresy to be the struggle which the apostle Paul had to maintain with those who tried to impose circumcision upon the Galatians, or with those who took upon themselves, more or less directly on the strength of Paul's own theological principles to assume on certain questions concerning the Christian life, attitudes of which he could not approve?

The epistle to the Galatians clearly shows that for Paul the idea that circumcision was necessary for Gentiles if they were to partake of salvation was not just a mistaken interpretation of the gospel but its negation. He speaks of another gospel preached to the Galatians, but he at once corrects himself, and denies that there could be any other gospel except his even though an angel from heaven or he himself were to preach it (Gal. i. 6-9). Neither the violent apostrophe at the beginning of the epistle nor the more balanced statement of v. 2-4 suggest any other idea except a pure and simple negation of the gospel. To be circumcised is not to misinterpret the faith, it is to give it up. It is to renounce all the benefits accruing from the redemptive work of Christ.[1]

[1] The adoption of Jewish ritualism is described by Paul as a reversion to subjection to 'the elements of the world' (Gal. iv. 9), i.e. to the elementary powers, to the angels to whom the government of the world has been entrusted and whom Paul, following the astrological theology of the time, seems to have identified with the stars (cf. Col. ii. 8, 20). The idea that the Galatians were making a setback comes as rather a surprise, as before their conversion they were not Jews but pagans. We can explain the expression which, as is sometimes the case with Paul, is a little forced, as meaning that to adopt Jewish ritualism is to return to a religious position which had been left behind, a retrogression compared with the gospel which is just as wicked as a return to paganism would be.

The situation at Corinth was infinitely more complex than the one in Galatia[1] and there were other factors at work beside the intervention of judaisers from without.[2] There was also an internal crisis characterised by a certain moral laxity[3] due to the reappearance of the pagan outlook which conversion had repressed rather than exterminated and reappeared, as soon as the first fervour had abated and the church no longer had the benefit of the apostle's firm direction, as he was now pursuing his missionary work in Asia. Simultaneously with the setback we have just mentioned, we recognise that there existed at the basis of the doctrine of the libertines or gnostics which was summed up in the phrase, 'all is permitted' (i vi. 12; x. 23) on the one hand, a misunderstanding of what Christian liberty was intended to mean as preached by Paul, and on the other hand, quite a different idea from Paul's on the relationship between soul and the body and the soul.[4] Although Paul believed that the body, being destined to resurrection, had to be kept holy because from now onwards it was the abode of the Holy Spirit, the gnostics at Corinth seem to have thought that as the body was doomed to destruction nothing mattered as far as religion or morals were concerned about its life (i vi. 13 ff.).[5] Paul does not seem to have taken this into account. There is no doubt that in respect of sexual life he could only regard their argument as a paradox. The attitude which they adopted on the question of meats offered to idols, i.e. of what is left over from sacrifices made to idols appeared

---

[1] See *Introd.* IV, 2, pp. 107 ff.

[2] They do not seem to have censured Paul's gospel but to have set to work in a more or less underhand manner to undermine Paul's authority. We have seen (pp. 305 ff.) that the difference between the agitators in Galatia and those at Corinth seems to have been one of method rather than of intention.

[3] This is shown by the division of the church into rival factions (I, i. 10-17), an excess of tolerance towards a scandalous sinner (I, v. 1 ff.) the custom of submitting differences between Christians to pagan tribunals (I, vi. 1 ff.), the profanation of the Lord's supper (I, xi. 17 ff.) and disorders at the gatherings for worship I, xiv). Possibly some of these happenings were related to doctrinal errors but Paul seems only to have noticed in the Corinthians inconsistencies with the Christian life.

[4] As a Semite Paul could not believe it possible that a spirit could exist without a body. He therefore envisaged the future life in the guise of the resurrection. In i Cor. xv he assails the denial of the resurrection as if it were a denial of any life beyond the grave. This was certainly not the idea of the Corinthians who, as Greeks, considered that the soul only came to its full growth when it had been freed from the body in which it was imprisoned as in a tomb or prison.

[5] From the same principles the weak seem to have drawn opposite conclusions, saying that as the body was a hindrance to the soul's development its life should be reduced to a minimum. Hence the scruples which some felt concerning marriage.

to him to be justifiable in theory, but he considered that it did not have sufficient regard for brethren who were ill-informed or weak in the faith. He discussed their ideas[1] wholly with practical considerations in mind.

There is not what could be accurately called a conflict between sound doctrine and heresy when Paul in Romans iii. 8 protests against those who had accused him of professing a doctrine which favoured sin because he showed that in the end sin would provide an opportunity for God's glory to be revealed.[2] He is only seeking here to defend his gospel against a misrepresentation. Paul judged the great struggle which he sustained against Jewish Christians[3] to be a conflict not between two conceptions of the gospel, one of which was correct and the other not, but between the gospel and a denial of it. Certain aspects of the crisis at Corinth he saw only as moral failings and deficiencies without suspecting that they could have a dogmatic basis. Yet that does not mean that he was convinced that the unity of the church was as complete as might be desired. It is worth while to stop at this point as Paul's position in this respect is in striking contrast to that which was to become current from the time of the second generation.

The first text to be considered is in the epistle to the Philippians.[4] Paul has just explained the great change his conversion made in his life, the change in values resulting from it and his new position since he was seized by Jesus Christ. Yet he emphasises that he is

[1] I shall return to this question when I am dealing with Christian morality. See *E.P.*, p. 561 ff.

[2] Romans iii. 8 is not an isolated piece of evidence. The whole account of the doctrine of justification emphasises the fact that the sinner who has been justified and freed from the domination of sin is thereby pledged to the service of God and bound to the obligation of sanctification. Paul emphasises this so strongly that he shows himself more concerned to defend himself against an accusation of being antinomian than to prevent a doctrine like this being deduced from his theology. Galatians v. 13 ff. must be understood in the same way and not as if it was directed against persons who were ultra-pauline as Ropes (see p. 314, n. 2.) supposes. In it Paul develops the idea that the liberty to which Christians have been called must not serve as an excuse for the flesh.

[3] Only so far as Jewish Christianity came to attack him on his own ground in the churches themselves which he had founded.

[4] At the beginning of the same epistle in i. 15-18 Paul mentions people who had set about while he was in prison to preach the gospel from impure motives, envy and a desire for strife, in order to give him pain while he was in prison. But he does not stop at that but sees one thing only, that Christ was preached and that gave him joy. Paul may have been mistaken but he saw them only as people who were trying to advertise themselves personally not to preach a different gospel from his own. The epistle to the Philippians seems to me to have been written before the conflict between Paul and the representatives of Jewish Christianity had begun.

under no illusion that he has attained the end or realised complete salvation. Salvation and the end are still in front of him; they are still at least in theory uncertain of attainment. Alluding then to the Philippians' conviction that they are 'perfect',[1] i.e. gnostics, Paul says this: 'Let us therefore as many as be perfect, be thus minded: and if in anything ye be otherwise minded, God shall grant us further revelations. Nevertheless our conduct must be in harmony with what we have attained' (iii. 15-16).[2]

Paul wants here to offer as a standard an attitude of humility, which does not consider salvation to be attained and demands a vigilance which must not relax. So far as the Philippians are really perfect as they boast to be, they will approve of the apostle's attitude and, if they do not judge it correct, they have proved that they have not yet attained full knowledge and still need further revelations. From this it may be concluded that there are at least for the time being differences of degrees in Christian initiation and that, as long as there are, there cannot be complete accord of views among believers.

From a different point of view the same idea receives confirmation from what we find in chapter iii of the first epistle to the Corinthians. Where Paul is giving instruction concerning factions he has the feeling, which he tries to express in the mildest tones possible but it comes out in the conclusion which is severe in tone (iv. 14-21), that the opposition to him at Corinth is personal. In the comparisons made between him and Apollos it was alleged that Paul's teaching lacked prestige through want of eloquence and wisdom. His reply to this charge was twofold. First he declared that the gospel is above all a power and that the preaching of the gospel owed its efficaciousness to this power, i.e. to the power of the Spirit. Persuaded that the gospel is not only power but also wisdom, i.e. divine not human wisdom, he adds that he has not offered it as such because the Corinthians had not so far developed spiritually and intellectually as to be able to grasp the gospel as wisdom. They are still carnal and not spiritual, they are children who can yet only take milk, not adults to whom can be given more solid fare (1 iii. 1 ff.). This distinction and the metaphor of the food suitable for two groups are not peculiar to Paul. We find them in the epistle to the Hebrews

---

[1] The word must be understood to mean not those who had come to perfection in salvation but those who had attained a higher degree of knowledge.
[2] I have translated somewhat freely to make the sense plain. A more literal translation would be almost incomprehensible.

(v. 12 f.) and their origin must be looked for in the mystery religions which knew differences of degree in initiation. It is not consistent with the principle laid down by Paul in Romans viii. 9, that if anyone has not the spirit of the Lord he does not belong to him, since, while he states that from the point of view of initiation the Corinthians are not spiritual, he in no way questions that they belong to Christ and have received his spirit. The distinction between σαρκινόι and πνευματικόι only holds good as far as knowledge is concerned; it had penetrated the framework of Christianity from outside. A man's salvation is not in any way compromised because his knowledge has remained in a rudimentary condition and he is only taking milk.

From the fact that all the members of the church have not arrived at the same degree of knowledge it follows that there cannot be uniformity in Christian thought; but the unity of the faith and of the church are not thereby compromised. But Philippians iii. 15 show that this diversity in degrees of knowledge is only provisional in character; it is destined to decrease as both the wise and the foolish receive new revelations; but this will only disappear altogether in the world beyond, since, as long as the present economy lasts, knowledge will remain partial and confused (1 Cor. xiii. 9, 12). The unity of the church, therefore, cannot be realised in the realm of knowledge, only in that of charity.

When Paul comes to deal with the arguments of the libertines concerning the eating of pollutions of idols, i.e. of meats which had been sacrificed to idols, in theory he has no objection to their views but he does not approve of them because anything which in any way touched on idolatry is repugnant to his instincts in virtue of his Jewish origin. But he does not argue. He confines himself to saying that, as well as knowledge which is likely to inflate a man's pride, room must be allowed for considerations of love and of that charity, which takes into account the interests of one's neighbour, especially if he be weak, and is ready to sacrifice something of one's own liberty rather than to run the risk of goading weak men into actions, which run contrary to their inmost convictions, wound their consciences, and in their own eyes are sins (1 Cor. viii. 7; Rom. xiv. 13 ff.). Paul then conceived that the church's unity was not realised in the sphere of knowledge but of love. This is quite a different conception from that of the second generation, when sound doctrine and heresy began to be in conflict with each other.

3.—THE GNOSTICISM OF COLOSSAE

It is none the less curious to find that in one case at least, at Colossae, Paul had to defend his doctrinal position, not as in Galatia against people who were taking diametrically opposed views, but against people who assented to Paul's principles but under the influence of a Jewish Greek form of gnosticism agreed to the worship of Christ being associated with a worship of angels which took the form of abstinences and ascetic practices, belonging to a system which contained both a cosmology and a soteriology. The Christians of Colossae seem to have been worked upon by a propaganda which had its origin outside the church. While they offered no resistance to its influence, they do not seem to have had any desire or intention of giving up the gospel which had been preached to them. To counter this propaganda, Paul's method was positive rather than negative. He put the Colossians on their guard against the worship of spirits and angels but he insists emphatically on the absolute superiority of Christ, who by his Cross had vanquished all powers and spoilt them. As a result of his superiority what one tries in vain to obtain through the worship of angels is fully realised in the worship of Christ. The whole argument of the epistle is summed up in the phrase, 'that in all things he might have the pre-eminence' (ἵνα γένηται ἐν πᾶσιν αὐτὸς πρωτεύων, i. 18).

As Paul develops this idea he is led on, not exactly to give his thought a new orientation, but to emphasise ideas which in the previous epistles had only been hinted at or implied.[1] His theme is Christ's cosmological function. He does not develop his ideas about this out of any philosophical interest. All his efforts go to prove that the hierarchy of heavenly beings are subordinated to Christ in whom it has pleased God for the fullness of divinity to dwell and by him to reconcile all things to himself, both things on earth and things in heaven (i. 19-20). Paul insists on the supremacy of Christ to prevent anyone seducing the Colossians through specious arguments (ii. 8). As Christ alone can assure salvation it is useless and perhaps dangerous for anyone to try and obtain it by the good will of cosmic powers who are incapable of conferring it.

Paul does not make a direct attack on the theories of the gnosticism of Colossae. He concentrates upon the practical consequences

---

[1] E.g. Colossians i. 15 ff. develops an idea which had been hinted at in passing, that of Christ being the image of God, first-begotten and instrument of creation.

to be drawn from them. He forbids the Colossians to keep any rules of abstinence from certain foods or observances connected with feasts, new moons and Sabbaths (ii. 16-17). The gnosticism there was then judaising in character but not purely Jewish as it does not seem to have been concerned with the question of circumcision. As Paul does not have in mind those who were propagating the gnosticism and does not address them with invective or warnings or appeals, it must be supposed that they did not belong to the church but to a synchretistic group outside it.[1]

The form of gnosticism at Colossae had a speculative character but the text which states what it was (ii. 18) is so obscure that it cannot be interpreted with any certainty.[2] Only the general sense is clear. Paul puts his readers on guard against those (evidently representatives of the gnostic group) who would condemn them by insisting on a false humility ($\tau\alpha\pi\epsilon\iota\nu o\phi\rho o\sigma\acute{u}\nu\eta$).[3] This term is associated with the term 'worship of angels' and may have referred to a man being jusified by this cult, the idea being that God is so exalted and so inaccessible that it would be presumptuous to suppose one could address him directly.[4] Paul uses the term $\acute{\epsilon}\mu\beta\alpha\tau\acute{\epsilon}\upsilon\omega\nu$ (ii. 1) to describe the position of the devotees of this cult. He must have borrowed it from the vocabulary of gnosticism. The verb $\acute{\epsilon}\mu\beta\alpha\tau\acute{\epsilon}\upsilon\epsilon\iota\nu$ is found in three inscriptions connected with the cult of Apollo at Claros;[5] it must have referred to initiation. The Colossian gnostics therefore justified their doctrines by claiming that they had had visions. It must then have meant 'the things which he saw at the time of his initiation'. Paul continues with these words, 'Wherefore if ye be dead with Christ from the rudiments of the world ($\acute{\alpha}\pi\grave{o}\ \tau\hat{\omega}\nu\ \sigma\tau o\iota\chi\epsilon\acute{\iota}\omega\nu\ \tau o\hat{u}\ \kappa\acute{o}\sigma\mu o\upsilon$), why, as though living in the world, are ye subject to ordinances, "Touch not; taste not; handle not", which are all to perish with the using;[6] after the

---

[1] It is difficult to estimate how far this group was composed of Jewish elements. But Dibelius (*An die Kolosser, Epheser, An Philemon²*, Tubingen, 1927, p. 29) seems to be quite off the mark when he supposes that Paul might have made a mistake and taken as Jewish ideas which were not so.

[2] For a detailed interpretation I would refer to Dibelius' commentary (*Kol.,* pp. 25 ff.) the main conclusions of which I accept. It does not seem to me impossible for the text to be corrupt.

[3] The term humility seems to have been borrowed from the vocabulary of gnosticism but it is impossible to determine in what sense it was used.

[4] This interpretation is given by Dibelius (*Kol.,* pp. 25 f.) and had been given before in antiquity by Theodorus (iii. 489).

[5] Dittenberger, *Or. inscr.,* II, 530, 13. Cf. Dibelius, 'Die Isiswehhe des Apuleius', *S.H.A.,* 1917, 4, pp. 30-36.

[6] I do not consider the last remark (v. 23) to belong to gnostic phraseology.

commandments and doctrines of men? Which things indeed have a show of wisdom in will,[1] worship, and humility, and neglecting of the body' (ii. 20-23).

If we are to understand the connection between ascetic practices and the cult of angels, we must begin with what the epistle says of the 'elements', $\sigma\tau\sigma\iota\chi\epsilon\hat{\iota}\alpha$, i.e. of the cosmic powers. Paul writes, 'Beware lest any man spoil you through philosophy and vain deceit, after the tradition of men, after the rudiments of the world, and not after Christ' (ii. 8), and a little further on he offers as the essential reasons for resisting the attractions exercised by these doctrines the fact that the faithful are with Christ, i.e. through their faith in him dead to the elements of the world and therefore have ceased to be dependent on them. It is clear then that in Colossian gnosticism it was supposed that a man's destiny depended on his position in regard to the cosmic powers, which explains why it was thought necessary that he should make them kindly disposed towards him. As these powers were identified with the stars which govern the march of time, we see how this led to observing certain days as feasts and others as unlucky days on which no enterprise was to be taken in hand. As these same powers were connected with certain substances, we can understand also how, in the religious system connected with them, certain foods could be placed under a taboo. Paul shows himself relatively moderate because the Colossians were not thinking of asking for salvation from the cosmic powers but were only trying to assure themselves of their good will or at least of their neutrality for the time being, while their salvation was not yet consummated and they still remained subject to their activity.

The agents of gnosticism at Colossae do not seem to have met with any decisive success up to the time when Paul intervened, as he put them on their guard against gnostic practices but was not asking them to give them up. Later on gnosticism had more influence. The epistle to the Ephesians shows that far from having been eliminated it must have grown. Paul seems to have regarded the tendencies which appeared at Colossae as nothing more than an effort to impose upon believers futile observances which were likely to blind them to the essentials of the faith. The doctrines of the gnostics were further removed perhaps from Paul's thought than he himself recognised. They tended to make salvation a cosmological happening while in Paul's eyes it was

[1] See p. 402, n. 3.

essentially something moral and religious set within a cosmic framework.[1]

Gnosticism at Colossae compelled Paul to sketch out a complete theology explaining Christ's cosmological position and function which influenced doctrinal development by forcing him to produce a general explanation of the world so that the erroneous gnosis of the heretics could be thwarted by the true gnosis.

4.—THE GNOSTICISM WHICH IS ATTACKED IN THE EPISTLE TO THE EPHESIANS

The epistle to the Ephesians[2] seems to have been fighting a more complicated form of gnosticism than that found in the epistle to the Colossians. It is probably the same but in a more advanced stage of development, unless it is supposed that the author of the interpolations in the epistle to the Ephesians was better acquainted with it than Paul. It contains a complete theory on the origin of evil and the means by which it can be conquered. Evil has been caused by the rupture of the unity of the cosmos. Salvation, therefore, will be its restoration. Schlier[3] showed that the idea of 'the Ruler of the power of the air' being the cause of sin (Eph. ii. 2) originated in a theory which made out that demonic powers rule in the air and thwart every communication between the world above and the world below and in this way prevent men from participating in the true life. The restoration of cosmic unity, i.e. 'the gathering of all things in Christ, both things in heaven and things in earth' (i. 10) is only made possible by the victory, which he has gained over the cosmic powers. The epistle to the Ephesians lays greater insistence than the epistle to the Colossians on the superiority of Christ over the whole hierarchy of heavenly beings. The gnosticism which it fights does not seem to have denied redemption through Christ. But possibly it excluded from Christ's domination which he had gained through his passion that part of the heavenly hierarchy

[1] Concerning the above see my article, 'La caractère et le rôle de l'élément cosmologique dans la sotériologie paulinienne', *R.h.p.r.*, 1935, XV, pp. 335-359.

[2] Concerning my hypothesis that the epistle to the Ephesians is made up of a genuine Pauline foundation and later interpolations see my article, 'Esquisse d'une solution nouvelle du problème de l'épitre aux Ephésiens', *R.h.r.*, 1935, CXI, pp. 254-284; 1935, CXII, pp. 73-99. The contents of this article correct the conclusions to be found in the chapter devoted to the epistle to the Ephesians in my *Introd.* IV, 2, pp. 431 ff.

[3] Schlier, *Christus und die Geister im Epheserbrief*, Tubingen, 1930.

which had not revolted against God[1] so that it could be worshipped with Christ at the same time.

The interpolator of the epistle to the Ephesians penetrates more deeply than Paul did into the conception which he is fighting; he uses a cosmological conception of salvation but does not cut out those parts of the epistle which express the authentic pauline conception. He envisages salvation as the restoration of cosmic unity and order but he separates himself from the gnostics by affirming that restoration is the work of Christ alone.

Distrustful as he is of gnosticism, the interpolator does not see it as a false doctrine which contradicts that of the church. He does not say that it is inspired by demons nor does he hurl anathemas or appear to consider a rupture a possibility. He makes no appeal to the adherents of gnosticism and makes no effort to bring them back to the true faith. They must be looked for outside the church, perhaps in a group which was close to the church and seems at any rate to have exercised a certain attraction for its members.

5.—THE HERESIES ATTACKED IN THE PASTORAL EPISTLES

The Pastorals reveal quite a different situation from that to be found in the epistles to the Colossians and to the Ephesians; the opposition between truth and error, between the deposit of sound doctrine which the church has received and human speculations contradicting it is more sharply defined.

For several reasons the heresies which are subject to attack[2] cannot be accurately described. Perhaps the author of the Pastorals did not clearly understand them; he may also have been faced with several groups of heretics and have failed to distinguish them clearly; lastly, he was so persuaded that the church possessed the truth pure and unalloyed that he thought it superfluous to discuss the heresies, thinking it sufficient to meet them with the church's teaching and to put them on their guard against the evil consequences to which the heresies were leading them. At the time of the pastoral epistles heretics were not yet separated from the church and were perhaps wanting to discharge ecclesiastical functions. The care taken by the author to emphasise the doctrinal guarantees which

---

[1] What the epistle calls 'Principalities', 'Dominations', 'Powers', 'Lords'.

[2] There are a large number of works about the heresies in the Pastorals. Bibliographical information on this subject will be found in the principal commentaries.

must be shown by aspirants for these offices is typical in this respect.[1]

The only heretics mentioned by name are Hymenaeus and Alexander[2] in one place (1 Tim. i. 20) and Hymenaeus and Philetus in another (2 Tim. ii. 17).[3] As Hymenaeus is mentioned in both places we have no reason for supposing that there are two distinct groups of heretics mentioned here.[4] When the author predicts that other heresies will come (1 Tim. iv. 1 ff.; iv. 3 ff.) he is developing a commonplace theme which was a result of the fiction attributing to Paul letters written in a situation which only came to exist after his disappearance. He says that heretics who will appear at the end of time will forbid certain foods (1 Tim. iv. 3). This taboo is no different from a statement attributed to contemporary heretics that some things are impure in themselves (Titus i. 15). The defence of marriage (1 Tim. ii. 15) proves that the author knew of people who were already attacking its legitimacy just as heretics must have done later on.

The Paul of the Pastorals, when he delivered Hymenaeus and Alexander over to Satan, does not seem to have formally excommunicated them from the church. If proceedings had been taken in hand to excommunicate them, he would have put his readers on their guard against heretics in different terms from those used in Titus iii. 9-11. But while heretics are allowed to remain in the church, the Pastorals do not consider that they really belong to it. The author makes no attempt to bring them back to sound doctrine. He describes them as deceitful and mercenary men who insinuate themselves into houses to seduce ill-informed persons (Titus i. 11; 1 Tim. vi. 5-10) especially women (1 Tim. iv. 7; cf. ii. 14; 2. iii. 6).[5] Heresy is described as a novelty opposed to the traditional teaching

---

[1] Perhaps it must be added with Jean Reville (*Orig. de l'épisc.*, p. 276) that the absence of any reference to the itinerant ministry shows that it was regarded with a certain amount of mistrust and suggests that as by its very nature it was difficult to control in any way, it was used by propagators of heresy.

[2] There seems no justification for identifying him with Alexander, the coppersmith, who, according to 2 Tim. iv. 14, did Paul much harm.

[3] Phygelus and Hermogenes, according to 2 Tim. i. 15, left Paul, do not seem to have been heretics but collaborators with the apostle who had become discouraged. Cf. p. 541 and *Introd.* IV, 2, p. 316.

[4] Contrary to the opinion of Hesse, *Die Enstehung der neutestamentlichen Hirtenbriefe*, Halle, 1889, p. 270.

[5] For this reason the author fearing that young widows having no employment would become an easy prey to propagators of heresy wishes them to remarry (1 Tim. v. 9-15) in spite of the harsh judgement which he passes on second marriages.

and explained as due to the action of demons (1 Tim. iv. 1) and of the passions (2 Tim. ii. 22). They must have been of quite a judaising character as they are described as 'Jewish myths' (Titus i. 14)[1] and many of their adherents were amongst the circumcised (Titus i. 10).

The author only mentions the speculations of heretics in a disdainful tone. They are myths and genealogies[2] without end (Titus iii. 9) which do not edify but provoke disputes (1 Tim. iii. 9), profane and old wives' fables (1 Tim. iv. 7; cf. 2 iv. 3-4). Possibly the author did not understand clearly the arguments which he was attacking and did not try to fight false theory with true. He restricted himself to advising loyalty to the traditional teaching (1 Tim. i. 4-5; iv. 7; vi. 3 f.; 2 Tim. ii. 14-16, 22, 23; iv. 7; Titus i. 13 f.; iii. 9-11).

Heretical thought seems to have been dualist in character. The heretics thought that those men who were involved too deeply in matter could not be saved. To meet this it is declared that God wills all men to be saved (1 Tim. ii. 4-6). The argument of Hymenaeus and Philetus that the resurrection has already taken place is also a dualist conception.[3] The insistence of the author of the Pastorals on the manhood of Jesus (1 Tim. ii. 5) and on his belonging to the race of David suggests that the heretics associated docetism with their dualism, which is after all quite natural.

In actual fact, dualism ended in ascetic practices which the author of the Pastorals describes as being 'the commandment of men' (Titus i. 14). He is referring to a marriage prohibition[4] and rules of abstinence (1 Tim. iv. 3-5). The reactions of the author of the epistles to this kind of asceticism show that it was an essential element of the heresy.

6.—THE HERESIES ATTACKED IN THE FIRST EPISTLE OF JOHN

The conflict against heretics takes up much space in the first epistle of John.[5] It describes them as anti-christ whose appearing shows that the end of the world is near (1 ii. 18). Three groups are

---

[1] 1 Timothy i. 7, 8 also shows us the judaising character of the heresies.

[2] Most probably genealogies of angels.

[3] This makes us think of John v. 24.

[4] The author contradicts this by a eulogy of marriage and maternity (1 Tim. ii. 9-15).

[5] One of the heretical groups to whom the first epistle of John refers, that of the Docetes, is also referred to in the second epistle, which is chronologically earlier than the first but they are treated in a more summary fashion.

envisaged, none of whom seem to have been the kind of gnostics who are attacked in the epistles to the Colossians and the Ephesians or in the pastoral epistles. Two of them professed a christological heresy, the third was antinomian.

Only one of the groups, the Ebionites, were separated from the church. These heretics, who are dealt with in ii. 18-27, denied that Jesus was the Christ, which must only mean that they did not have the same conception of messiahship as John. Perhaps they were the only group who had remained faithful to the earliest christology of all, the one in Peter's sermons, according to which Jesus, a man sent by God, was by his resurrection exalted to God's right hand as Messiah. John sees in this christology a denial both of the Father and the Son. He is fighting with the heretics for the possession of the truth and faces them with his readers, who have a holy unction (ii. 20-27), i.e. the Spirit who teaches truth.[1]

The Ebionites took the initiative in leaving the church. John considers this normal and declares that, although they once were in the church, they did not really belong to it as otherwise they would not have left it (ii. 19).[2]

Another heresy contrasted with that of the Ebionites is dealt with in chapter iv. It is that of the Docetes, i.e. of those who reduced Christ's humanity to pure appearance. They seem to have justified their contentions by claiming that they were inspired, as John withstands them by the argument that before the teaching of the spirit is accepted one must be sure that it comes from God and not the devil.[3] The criterion laid down by him is a confession that Jesus came in the flesh. The Docetes are the only heretical group with whom the second epistle which is earlier than the first is concerned.[4] Their contention is described as if it were a novelty, as it is said of them that they did not abide in the doctrine (II. 9). The heretic is

---

[1] This is one of the customary arguments of antiheretical polemics. It may also be a recollection of the fact that this christology came into existence in an environment where inspiration was unknown or at any rate was restrained in its activities.

[2] The fact that John finds it necessary to justify the departure of heretics from the church shows that everybody did not share his views.

[3] Paul had previously shown the necessity for checking the course of inspiration and had laid down as the criterion whether the teaching harmonised with the faith of the church (1 Cor. xii. 3).

[4] The attitude of the second epistle towards heresies is much more hostile than that of the first. Not only is heretical doctrine condemned but advice is given to avoid contact with heretics, not to salute them or to accept them in one's house (10-11). The last injunction shows perhaps that the heretics referred to were itinerant preachers.

described as the man who transgresses (προάγων) but it is not said what he transgresses. It may be nothing more than the confessional symbol used by the church showing that the heretics did not mean to leave the church but claimed that they were justifying their ideas by interpretations proving that they were not separating themselves from it.

iii. 7 f. deals with a third heretical group made up of antinomians whose position recalls that of the strong or gnostics of Corinth. John lays down as a principle that sin (ἁμαρτία) and transgression of the law (ἀνομία) are identical.[1] He reminds his readers of the opposition between sin and the Christian life and once more connects sin with the activity of the devil (iii. 8). From this it follows that it is incompatible with the Christian life to reject the law. It is then certain that he has in mind a group of heretics who, inspired by principles of Christian liberty, were maintaining that for the justified Christian the law had ceased to count and therefore the possibility of sin had ceased.[2]

7.—THE FIGHT AGAINST HERESY IN THE BOOK TO THE SEVEN CHURCHES

The fight against heresy is one of the dominating concerns of the author of the Book to the Seven Churches written between 75 and 85 and used by its author ten years later as an introduction to the Apocalypse. The heretics involved are the Nicolaitans.[3] There are also heretics described as followers of the doctrine of Balaam. The prophetess Jezebel of Thyatira seems to have been only a particularly active agent of their doctrine. The Nicolaitans may have possibly derived their name from Nicholas, one of the Seven (Acts vi. 5) who was a proselyte from Antioch. But, as all that we know about him comes from late and confused traditions, we cannot know if there is anything concrete behind this designation, just as we cannot decide if the Nicolaitans of the Apocalypse were the precursors of

---

[1] This means the law in the moral sense not in the ritual sense.

[2] This contention has to be harmonised with that of Hymenaeus and Philotus (2 Tim. ii. 17) who maintained that the resurrection had already happened. John v. 24 perhaps throws light on how they are connected. It says that the man who has received the word of Christ has passed from death to life and will not come under judgement. Does not this mean that he has ceased to be under the law? Although the Fourth Gospel does not incline in any way to antinomianism some of the phrases used by it may well have favoured developments in that direction.

[3] Concerning all these fairly complex questions which the Nicolaitans raise I would refer to my article, 'Les Nicolaites', *R.h.r.*, 1937, CXV, pp. 5-36.

the immoral Nicolaitans of the end of the second century or whether the latter claimed to be derived from them without justification.

What is said about the prophetess, who is given what is certainly the symbolic name of Jezebel, yields us the most concrete details about the Nicolaitan heresy. This woman, whose activities were tolerated by the church at Thyatira, seduced the faithful and taught them *porneusai*[1] and to eat things sacrificed to idols. The Lord had given her time to repent, which shows that the heresy had been in existence for some time previous, but she had not taken the opportunity. Now he will cast her on a bed of sickness; her lovers will be afflicted and he will cause her children to perish (ii. 20-23). On those who have not allowed themselves to be seduced by her preaching, and have not, using the phrase of the group, 'known the depths of· Satan', Christ will not impose any further burden in addition to that which they already have (ii. 24-25). At first sight it looks as if the heresy was antimonian and immoral in character. But if it had been, would not John have held up his moral ideal in face of the corruption of the Nicolaitans? The letters show that the life of the churches in Asia was at a rather low ebb but they do not contain any reproof against moral slackness. Those who had committed adultery with Jezebel are summoned to repent, not for their sin but for their deeds. Furthermore, if we remember that adultery is a traditional metaphor for idolatry and doctrinal infidelity and also that the followers of the prophetess are described sometimes as her lovers and sometimes as her children, we shall be ready to interpret the evidence provided by the Apocalypse about Jezebel symbolically. One difficulty is still left in the fact that the verb *porneusai* is joined to 'to eat things sacrificed to idols' which seems to imply that it must be taken literally. But the word *porneia* when used in Acts can only mean conjugal unions within the degrees of kindred forbidden by the Jewish law.[2] This was a relic of ritual law[3] from which the Nicolaitans wanted to liberate Christians. In opposition to them others wanted to be stricter in observing Jewish ritual law. The author does not approve of this tendency and declares that the burden[4] which the church is bearing will not be made heavier.

---

[1] I am not translating this word for the time being.

[2] See p. 299, n. 4.

[3] This is even less than what the decree of Jerusalem asked of the Gentile converts.

[4] The same word is used in Acts xv. 28 in reference to the commands imposed on the Gentiles. The expression also seems to be referred to in *Did.* vi. 3.

The phrase 'to know the depths of Satan' shows that the Nicolaitan doctrine contained speculative elements. Is this, however, a phrase of the Nicolaitans or is it a caricature of one? Paul speaks in one place (1 Cor. ii. 10) of the Spirit who searches the deep things of God. Might not the Nicolaitans have invoked revelations to justify their ideas and their enemies replied that their revelations had come not from God but from Satan? This is possible but the Nicolaitans may have done what the libertines of Corinth did, i.e. justified their claims to freedom by a theory that, as Satan had been conquered by Christ, he had lost all his power over men.

The Nicolaitan heresy found lodgement in only three of the seven churches to whom John addressed his book. The church at Ephesus, luke-warm as it was, rejected the Nicolaitans for whom it had nothing but detestation (ii. 6) and had shown up false apostles (ii. 2) which is easily recognised as a description of the agents of the Nicolaitan heresy. The church at Pergamum is censured for having received Nicolaitans into its bosom (ii. 15). But Thyatira seems to have been the place where the Nicolaitans prospered most, thanks doubtless to the activities of the prophetess Jezebel. But even there, there was no question of their being cut off from the church; they continued as fellow churchmen with those who did not share their ideas.

John considers the presence of Nicolaitans in the church to be an offence and a danger; he is indignant at the culpable indifference with which they are often tolerated. He thinks that it exposes the churches to Christ's anger. Yet neither the Christians of Pergamum nor of Thyatra are explicitly requested by him to expel the heretics. Asiatic Christians in general did not judge the Nicolaitans with the same severity and were unlikely therefore to have complied with such a request.

The phrase with which each of the seven letters ends, 'He that hath an ear, let him hear what the Spirit saith unto the churches', shows that the Apocalypse was at least intended to be addressed to the whole of Asiatic Christendom. That seems surprising, when we realise that the Nicolaitan heresy which in John's eyes was threatening the whole of Asiatic Christendom receives no mention as existing in four of the seven churches.[1] This raises the question as to

---

[1] Zahn (*Einl.* II, p. 608) thinks that Nicolaitan propaganda was still in its infancy but this explanation does not give satisfaction. What is said of Jezebel suggests an activity which had been in existence for some time previous. Besides, if the propaganda had only just begun, it would have been useful to have given a warning to those churches which it had not yet been able to reach.

by what method the particular seven churches were selected as representing Asiatic Christendom. Ramsay[1] suggested that they were the nerve centres from which information and news was carried. The fresh factions which had sprung up at Ephesus would have been transmitted one by one to each of the others and through them would have penetrated the neighbouring communities. The hypothesis is ingenious, but it does not rest on any positive information and conflicts with the fact, that at the end of the first century the church is still far from being organised on any wider basis than that of the local community. W. Bauer[2] made a much more satisfactory proposal by suggesting that John addressed the seven churches which he thought were most likely to hear him. He wondered if Asiatic Christianity, taken as a body, did not think quite differently from John about the Nicolaitans and whether he was not representing a minority who were trying to destroy their influence. May it not be that he does not use his own name as Paul did but writes in the name of Christ because he wanted to impress his readers? Ignatius, a much later representative of the same type of Christianity as John's, wrote only to three of the churches, who had received letters from John,[3] and to the three who had received the letters containing the most favourable appreciations. This may have been because the churches of Pergamum and Thyatira had persisted in their more tolerant attitude towards the Nicolaitans and their successors had become more tolerant still, with the result that Ignatius did not write to them.

The differences between John and the Nicolaitans seem to have been on questions of practice rather than theology. Could a Christian reject every scrap of Jewish ritual law and consider himself free from certain prohibitions which had formerly been thought necessary to assure that the people of God were separated from idolatrous pagans?

The situation revealed by the Book to the Seven Churches to have existed in Asia between 80 and 90 falls into line with the disputes which occurred between Paul and the Jewish Christians. There are also resemblances to the questions which faced the church at Jerusalem probably as a result of the incident at Antioch and which it tried to resolve by the decree the text of which is given in Acts xv.

[1] Ramsay, *The Letters to the Seven Churches of Asia*[2], London, 1906, pp. 171 ff. Ramsay's interpretation has been accepted by many commentators on the Apocalypse. [2] Bauer, *Rechtgl. u. Ketz.*, pp. 81 ff.

[3] Ephesus, Smyrna, and Philadelphia. In addition Ignatius wrote to the Christians of Magnesia and Tralles. Four churches who received letters from John did not receive one from Ignatius (Pergamum, Thyatira, Sardis, Laodicea).

But the Nicolaitans may have had other reasons for their attitude than those which caused Paul to reject the Jewish ritual law. Rivalry between the two groups of Gentile and Jewish Christians may well have survived, although the issues which had first created it had evaporated and no one would have understood them. In its surviving form it seems to have assumed peculiar characteristics in Asia owing to immigration on a considerable scale from Palestine which took place after 70. The fact that the Nicolaitans in some degree inherited Paul's ideas and were attacked by a man whose name for complex reasons was being received with growing respect throughout Asia, may well partly explain what Karl Holl[1] has called the black ungrateful way in which Asia hardly remembered the apostle Paul.

8.—IGNATIUS OF ANTIOCH AND HERESIES

The conflict between John and the Nicolaitans following the opposition between Paul and the Jewish Christians was itself followed by the conflict waged by Ignatius with heretics. Unfortunately the issues are not revealed with any great clarity. In those parts of Ignatius' letters which are concerned with heresies, warnings, exhortation, and invective take up much more space than arguments, which would enable us to form a fairly accurate idea of what the enemies whom he was fighting thought. It must be added that it is certain that the gulf between the heretics and the general body of the church was not as wide in reality as the bishop of Antioch would have wished.

Ignatius is much more a churchman than a theologian. The heretics annoyed him because they had revolted against an authority of which as bishop he felt himself to be the depositary. Bauer[2] found various bits of evidence showing that, although Ignatius bestowed upon the churches of Asia eulogies which were often dithyrambic in quality, their attitude generally speaking was not what he desired. While he commends the church at Ephesus for having stopped its ears, when someone had come to preach to them a wicked doctrine (ix. 1), he does not consider that they are sufficiently grounded in orthodoxy for it to be superfluous for him to put them on their guard against people, who bear the name of Christians but behave in a manner unworthy of God, who are wild beasts and savage dogs biting treacherously (vii. 1). The Magnesians are

---

[1] K. Holl, *Ges. Aufs.* II, p. 66.
[2] Bauer, *Rechtgl. u. Ketz.*, pp. 71 ff.

similarly exhorted to keep unity in doctrine (vi. 1) and put on their guard against strange doctrines, old fables which are profitless, Judaism (viii. 1), celebrating the Sabbath (ix. 1) and evil leaven (x. 2). Can we believe in the unity of a church, which recognises its bishop in their words but disregard him in all their actions (iv. 1)?[1] At Philadelphia Ignatius had to foil the intrigues of heretics (vii.). At Smyrna there were Docetes whom he treated as wild beasts. Their preaching must have had some influence as he advises people to avoid meeting them (iv. 1). The fact that Ignatius is so concerned that the faithful should have no contact with heretics shows how much he feared their influence. Some of them must have occupied important positions as Ignatius declares that no one must get excited because of the position he occupies (Philad. vi. 1).[2]

Ignatius therefore was next to John the spokesman of a group within the churches of Asia which claimed a monopoly of orthodox Christianity. In some of the churches whom Ignatius addresses, the bishop was the leader of this party but everybody did not follow him and perhaps in some cases in matters of doctrine he influenced only a minority. Ignatius considered the orthodox group to be the only true church; but the vehemence of his invectives shows that the majority of Asiatic Christians did not share his intransigence. But his outlook was destined to triumph in the end and the heretics to be expelled from the church.

In his polemics Ignatius seems to have had two distinct groups

[1] In the same way the epistle to the Trallians which begins with an unqualified eulogy ends with an exhortation to them to preserve the unity of the church (xii. 1). This leads us to think that the unity was compromised. The letter to the Philadelphians opens with a long eulogy of their bishop (i). But the remark that he is able to do more by silence than those who use vain words leaves one to infer that Ignatius regretted that he was not more active in preventing heretics from spreading their ideas. In addition, certain members of the church were not prevented from failing in respect towards Rheus Agathopaus and Philon who followed Ignatius (ii. 2; xi. 1). In the same letter the affirmation that the authors of schism will not inherit the Kingdom (iii. 3), the statement that the eucharist is only valid when the bishop or his deputy presides (iv. 1), suggest something very different from a church closely gathered round its bishop.

[2] This is supported by the fact that the epistle of Polycarp begins with the words 'Polycarp and the elders with him' which makes one think that all the elders did not follow him. Irenaeus reports in the *Letter to Florinus* (in Eusebius, *H.e.* v. 20, 7) that when he heard men confessing heresies he whispered, 'Good God, at what a time has thou caused me to live that I should be obliged to put up with this?' Bauer (*Rechtgl. u. Ketz.*, p. 77) remarks that Polycarp makes no reference to the bishop of Philippi and does not anticipate his intervention on the affair of the elder Valens. He must therefore have felt that he was not in agreement with him.

in mind. In the epistle to the Magnesians he takes to task people who were attached to old fables and were judaising but there is no reference to circumcision or to any other Jewish rites but only to the keeping of the Sabbath (ix. 1). Ignatius emphasises the authority of the prophets who lived according to Jesus Christ and received his grace; this might be considered on a rigorous interpretation to be a polemic against a form of ultra-paulinism which was a forerunner of Marcionism. It rather seems as if Ignatius was taking steps to prevent anyone accusing him of underrating the value of the Old Testament. The epistle to the Philadelphians contains a warning against the preacher of 'Judaism' without any reference to circumcision and the Jewish ritual. Ignatius writes, 'It is better to hear Christianity from the circumcised than Judaism from the uncircumcised. But both of them, unless they speak of Jesus Christ, are to me tombstones and sepulchres of the dead, on whom only the names of men are written' (vi. 1). He can only be referring here to preaching which was taking place within the bosom of the church. It could not therefore have been a form of Hellenistic Judaism which had lost its particularism and ritual but it might have been a Jewish Hellenistic gnosis resembling that at Colossae which had come to penetrate into the church.

This is perhaps the kind of 'Judaism' referred to in an obscure passage dealing with people who say 'if I find it not in the charters in the Gospel I do not believe'.[1] This seems to refer to scriptural proofs which some had claimed for their doctrinal affirmations. Ignatius states that this proof exists, but in face of the persistence with which his adversaries kept on doubting this he interrupts his argument and proclaims that for him, 'the charters are Jesus Christ, the inviolable charter is his cross, and death, and resurrection' (Philad. viii. 2). Those whom Ignatius is here attacking must have been men who were extraordinarily struck by the contrast between the gospel and the Old Testament. Possibly they gave a Jewish interpretation to the Gospel instead of a Christian interpretation to the Old Testament.[2] Such an idea may well have originated in a Gentile Christian environment as a result of the part played in the

---

[1] The Greek, without punctuation, is as ambiguous as the English: 'If I find it not in the charters—in the Gospel I do not believe', or, 'If I find it not in the charters, in the Gospel, I do not believe'. Probably the former should be preferred on the ground that 'the charters' probably means the Old Testament. (Note from the Loeb Trans. Kirsopp Lake.)

[2] For another interpretation of this passage see *J. de N.*, p. 94.

THE BIRTH OF CHRISTIANITY

preaching of the gospel by the argument from scripture. This would also explain the sentence in vi. 1 about the uncircumcised who preach 'Judaism'.

The danger of the church being judaised which seems to have concerned Ignatius so much may have been in reference to activities directed against the church from outside. The Fourth Gospel shows that at the end of the first century there was lively controversy between Jews and Christians. The evangelist is very much concerned to withstand efforts made by the Jews to attract or bring back Christians to the synagogue. The Judaism which Ignatius attacks may well have been in line with this kind of propaganda put out by penetrating judaisers.

In addition to this Ignatius carries on a polemic against a christological heresy which in its characteristic essentials seems to have been docetism. Ignatius speaks of people who claimed to be Christians but acted in a way unworthy of God and then describes Christ as the only medicine which can heal. He analyses his character by a series of antitheses. He is both carnal and spiritual, born and yet not born, God in the flesh, life in death, born of Mary and born of God, suffering and impassible (Eph. vii. 1). The heretics have denied one of these series of attributes ascribed by the traditional doctrine in spite of their logical contradiction. The way in which in many passages Ignatius insists on the reality of the flesh, the human birth, the sufferings, death, and resurrection of Christ shows that it was the human side of his person which the heretics refused to recognise. They must therefore have been Docetes. In the passage of the epistle to the Magnesians (ix. 1) in which Ignatius explains that the first day of the week and not the Sabbath must be observed, he is making a polemic against those who deny the resurrection. It cannot be clearly known if he has in mind Docetes or partisans of 'Judaism'. But they are certainly Docetes whom he describes as atheists because they say that Christ only appeared to suffer (Tral. ix. 1-3, 10).

The Docetes seem to have formed a particularly important group at Smyrna. Ignatius shows himself virulent towards them. He calls them advocates of death and not of truth (v. 1). The epithet 'Clothed with a corpse' suits those who deny that Jesus was 'clothed in the flesh' (v. 2). Ignatius refuses to put their name in writing or even to remember them (v. 3). Such men must not be spoken about, neither in public nor in private (vii. 2). He wants to organise a conspiracy of silence against them.

An indirect polemic against docetism can be discovered in the eulogy made by Ignatius on the faith of those men of Smyrna grouped round Polycarp who are the true church. They are 'nailed to the cross of the Lord Jesus Christ, being fully persuaded that he is in truth of the family of David according to the flesh . . . truly born of a virgin . . . truly nailed to a tree in the flesh . . . who has truly suffered and truly died . . .' (i. 1-ii. 1). The word 'truly' which is repeated each time is underlined by the fact that Ignatius adds 'His sufferings were not merely in appearance, as some say', and he finishes with a point of irony, 'but it is they who are merely in semblance, and even according to their opinions it shall happen to them, and they shall be without bodies and phantasmal'. After this he adds to support the reality of the resurrection of Jesus a story of a resurrection appearance, which, according to St. Jerome, was borrowed from the epistle to the Hebrews[1] and is perhaps merely a rather free reproduction of the scene described in Luke xxiv. 39.[2]

What the Docetes seem to have taken most umbrage at was the reality of the passion. The Greek mind found nothing inconceivable in the idea of a god taking a human form; but the idea of a suffering god who died it found invincibly repugnant. The Docetes of Smyrna may have thought with Corinth[3] that the Christ was united with the man Jesus at the moment of the baptism and that they were separated at the moment of the passion.[4] Or perhaps they accepted the doctrine attributed by Irenaeus to Basilides[5] that Simon of Cyrene was miraculously substituted for Jesus and crucified in his place and with his visage.[6] Yet Ignatius seems to have insisted on the sufferings and death, not because it was only the reality of these facts which the Docetes denied but because they formed the core of the debate.

[1] Jerome, *De viris. inl.* 16; *Comm. in Jerem.*, XVIII, *prol.*

[2] See my book, *La foi à la rés.*, pp. 340 f.

[3] Irenaeus, *Adv. Haer.* i. 26, 1; iii. 11, 1.

[4] Some trace of this idea can be found in the Gospel of Peter (19) which says that Jesus, before he expired, was abandoned by his δύναμις.

[5] Irenaeus, *Adv. Haer.* i. 24, 4. Possibly this was not the doctrine of Basilides himself, but only of his disciples. Cf. De Faye, *Gnostiques et gnosticisme*[2], Paris, 1925, p. 53.

[6] This seems to be the theory envisaged in the *Acta Johannis* (ch. 97). It was preserved among the Manichaeans as is shown from the form of the solemn renunciation which was imposed upon them. See Kessler, *Mani.*, Berlin, 1889, I, p. 404.

9.—THE DIDACHE AND HERESIES[1]

The Didache provides little evidence for the history of the conflict between sound doctrine and heresy. But there are some hints available. They have this peculiar interest, that they reflect instinctive reactions rather than a reasoned attitude and on that account seem to show the common feelings of the church.

The author is strongly attached to the traditional teaching of the church just because it is what the faithful have received. That is sufficient; he feels no need to prove or even merely to affirm that the teaching is true and that what contradicts it is only error or vanity. To give any kind of instruction which differs from that of the church is to teach 'without God' (vi. 1). Those must be accepted who give instruction which conforms to what has been received, and is capable of increasing righteousness and knowledge of the Lord; he who does otherwise must be repressed. When the author is warning Christians to take care not to do anything Jewish (viii. 1, 2; xiv. 1) the danger which he wishes them to avoid seems to be that of a return pure and simple to Judaism rather than a judaising of Christian thought.[2]

10.—THE POLEMIC AGAINST HERESY IN THE EPISTLES OF JUDE AND 2 PETER

It is difficult to decide if there is any relationship between the heresies which are attacked in the Book to the Seven Churches, the pastoral epistles, those attacked by Ignatius, and those dealt with in two documents of a rather later date, the epistle of Jude and the second of Peter.[3] In any case, these two groups are separated

[1] If I had followed chronological order in considering heresy I should have taken the Didache before Ignatius. But as it seems possible that the heresies which Ignatius has in mind are related to those which are attacked in the Pastorals and the Book to the Seven Churches I resolved to this small extent to abandon the chronological order.

[2] The author of the Didache is quite indifferent on the question of observing Jewish food prohibitions; he seems to think it the normal thing to keep to them, but he advises their observance only so far as is possible (vi. 3). But on the question of meats sacrificed to idols he is adamant and absolutely forbids their consumption because he says, 'It is the worship of dead gods' (vi. 2).

[3] The epistle of Jude is repeated almost word for word in the second chapter of the second epistle of Peter with this difference, however, that the epistle of Jude quotes two pseudepigraphical books (the Assumption of Moses in verse 9 and the book of Enoch in verse 14) while the epistle of Peter does not give these quotations. This is an indication—and not the only one—that the epistle of Jude is the earlier

418

by an interval of some importance. Heresies are not discussed in these two epistles. Their readers are only put on their guard against them and they are described in general terms. These two epistles are catholic in the most definite sense of the term; they are addressed to all believers. The authors of these two documents had in mind a concrete situation with a particular time and place but at the same time they felt that the same situation existed all over the church and that doctrine was being threateneed by the same heresies everywhere.

The epistle of Jude which is very short is entirely devoted to a conflict against heresy. It is purely negative in character. A caution is given without any account of sound doctrine and unsupported by any attempt to show the errors of those who were rejecting it. Like the author of the Pastorals and Ignatius Jude thinks it sufficient to denounce the heretics and vituperate against them; he thinks it useless to refute their doctrines.

At the beginning of his letter Jude states that he felt pressed to write to his readers to exhort them to fight for the faith[1] which had been delivered once and for all to the saints (3); the faith has been threatened by certain men who have insinuated themselves into the church and whose appearance was predicted beforehand. They are ungodly men turning the grace of God into lasciviousness and denying our only master and Lord Jesus Christ (4). He is referring therefore to antinomists.[2] To prove how grave their sin is and with what severity God will one day judge them, Jude recalls how the rebels of the Old Testament were treated; the days of the wandering in the desert, the angels who joined the daughters of men,[3] and lastly, the inhabitants of Sodom and Gomorrah. The three cases

book. The epistle of Jude seems to have been composed between 100 and 125 or even a little earlier. The second epistle of Peter can be dated approximately 125-150. It is impossible to make any precise guess where these two documents were composed. They may have originated from the same place. The epistle of Jude is offered as the work of the brother of James, and if this James is, as it seems, the same as James the Just, then it would be the work of the brother of Jesus mentioned in Mark vi. 3 and Matt. xiii. 55. It is difficult to think that the ascription can be anything else but spurious. Harnack (*G.a.L.* II, 1, p. 468) revived a hypothesis of Hugo Grotius and conjectured that the words 'brother of James' were added at a later date. As for the second epistle of Peter it is impossible to suppose that it was composed by the apostle.

[1] This word here as in the postoral epistles means doctrine.

[2] It does not look as if to antinomianism is joined a christological heresy as it is not mentioned again. It would seem more natural to suppose that heretics deny their Lord through antinomianism.

[3] Under the influence of the book of Enoch (x. 4-12; xii. 4 ff.; liv. 3-7) and the book of Jubilees (v. 6) the epistle says that the rebel angels were imprisoned in darkness to wait for the judgement.

quoted have to do with sexual shortcomings and in two of them angels are concerned. We have, therefore, reasons for thinking that the heretics justified moral laxity by some theological speculation which had to do with angels intervening. Possibly their argument was purely theoretical like that of the strong at Corinth. It is also said of them that claiming the authority of visions they pollute the flesh (8). They were therefore libertine gnostics who justified their attitude by visions. Jude accuses them of defying authority, which seems to mean that they rejected the teaching of the church which was covered by the authority of the Lord.[1] They insult august names.[2] This seems to mean some theory about the heavenly beings which was thought insulting to them. Jude may also have thought that the immorality of the heretics offended the angels who were charged to see that the law of God was observed.

In face of their presumption Jude takes his cue from the Assumption of Moses and points to the moderation of the archangel Michael, who contending with the devil for the body of Moses did not dare to accuse him of blasphemy but was content to proclaim to him the judgement of God (9). Returning to the heretics who insult the angels, Jude observes that they speak evil of those things which they do not know as their knowledge is purely of physical things, resembling that of the beasts deprived of reason. For that reason they will perish in the same way as Cain, Balaam, and Korah did (10-11).

The heretics are, what is a more concrete description, a spot, i.e. an offence at the agapes celebrated by the church,[3] at which they feast without shame (12). This desecration of the eucharist resembles that against which Paul had to take action at Corinth. The heretics were not then separated from the church but shared in the common meals which served as a framework for the eucharist properly so called. In the same sentence, however, the words 'feeding themselves' (ἑαυτοὺς ποιμαίνοντες), seem to show that they did not follow bishops and elders of the church, perhaps because they rejected even the conception of an order of clergy. This leads us to

---

[1] The author of the Didache advises his readers to receive the man who teaches true doctrine as the Lord himself and says, 'Where the Lord's nature is spoken of (ἡ κυριότης λαλεῖται) there is he present' (iv. 1). Jude possibly drawing inspiration from this idea only wants to say that the heretics reject sound doctrine.

[2] I.e. the angels who remained faithful to their task.

[3] In place of ἀγάπαις the manuscripts A.C. and some others have ἀπάταις 'by their (A.a.: your) passions, which comes from 2 Peter ii. 13. The manuscripts 6. 424 have εὐωχίαις (banquets).

think that the principle laid down by Ignatius that that eucharist alone is valid over which the bishop or his deputy presides had not yet been carried out (Sm. viii. 1). Verses 12 and 13 give no proper description of the heretics but are full of invective against them comparing them to clouds carried about by the wind containing no rain[1] and to trees, which even at the end of autumn bear no fruit. They are twice dead.[2] Like the waves of the sea they foam out their own shame and show off their immorality without reserve. They are wandering stars[3] for whom is prepared eternal darkness. The severity of this condemnation is defended by a prophecy of Enoch (i. 9; v. 4) who spoke of the Lord coming with ten thousands of his saints to judge sinners (14-15). The invective pursues its course without affording us any hints which would enable us to know what the positive characteristics of the heretics were. It is said that they murmur and are dissatisfied with their lot, which may mean that they consider the world to be evil because it was created by a demiurge or ruled not by God but by elementary Powers. This interpretation would give concrete meaning to the expression 'they insult august names' (8), but as we have such little evidence as to the theoretical nature of the heresy we cannot make any positive decision in this sense. Jude may have wished to say that the heretics were dissatisfied with the way in which things were going in the church and were criticising those who were in charge. Nothing concrete can be inferred from the description of the heretics as allowing themselves to be led away by their passions and having their mouth full of arrogant words with which they pay court to men to serve their own ends (16).

In verses 17-19 Jude returns to the idea that the coming of the heretics has been foretold. He recalls the teaching of the apostles of whom he speaks in a solemn style befitting the past. They said[4] that in the last times there will arise mockers who will be led by their

---

[1] It has been suggested that this metaphor helps us to determine where the epistle originated but in addition to the fact that there are several places where a cloud deceives by evaporating without giving forth rain the metaphor could easily have been used in a different place from that where it originated.

[2] This may mean either that after being saved by justification from the death to which their sins destined them, they became death's victims again through giving up the true doctrine or that after rising again for the judgement they would die the second death.

[3] This refers to the planets which, according to a myth fairly widespread in Judaism, had left the place which had been assigned to them (*Enoch*, xviii. 14 f.; xxi. 3; xc. 24. Theophilus of Antioch, *Ad. Autol.* ii. 15).

[4] See Acts xx. 29 f.; 1 Timothy iv. 1 ff.; 2 Timothy iii. 11 ff.; Mark xiii. 6.

THE BIRTH OF CHRISTIANITY

impious passions, who will set up divisions and will divide men into two classes, psychical or carnal, pneumatic or spiritual, and on the strength of this will claim that they are free from ethical rules. Jude takes up this distinction which he had just described as unlawful and uses an argument *ad hominem* to describe the psychic heretics as men who do not possess the spirit. Jude modified the traditional idea of inspiration in one important respect; he considers all individual inspiration to be vain and deceptive and reckons the collective inspiration possessed by the church alone to be valid. To claim the right to defend one's own personal ideas is to prove that one is only carnal.[1]

The last paragraph before the final doxology (20-23) contains the only positive exhortation to be addressed to the readers. They must build themselves up in their most holy faith, praying in the holy Spirit, keeping themselves in the love of God and looking for the mercy of our Lord Jesus Christ unto eternal life (20-21). What follows is obscure and we gain no light by supposing that the text is corrupt.[2] The readers are exhorted to have pity on heretics and to try to save them by looking on them with pity yet maintaining a certain reserve, 'hating even the garment spoiled by the flesh', i.e. avoiding any compromise with their immorality. The epistle finishes with a beautiful and long doxology (24-25) which seems to reproduce a liturgical formula.

The attempts which have been made to identify the heresies attacked by Jude with one or other of the gnostic systems of the second century may be considered to have proved futile. Their very diversity refutes them. The epistle was written before these systems came into being.

In as much as the references to a christological heresy, an amoral antinomism, and angelogy are almost always connected together, we are led to think that Jude is dealing with only one heretical group. His ideas do not seem to have come from Judaism. The analogy which Jude draws between the heretics whom he is attacking and the rebels of the Old Testament is simply a comparison made for the purpose of proving that God's judgement awaits them.[3] The

---

[1] The second epistle of Peter condemns any personal interpretation of prophecy more explicitly.

[2] Unless the obscurity of the text is explained by the fact that it refers to some phrase known to the readers.

[3] The fact that according to the second epistle of Peter the heretics defended their ideas by means of a particular interpretation of the prophets gives us no right to infer that those whom the epistle of Jude is considering did the same.

heretics justified their ideas by dreams and visions (8). When Jude reproaches them for having only animal and material knowledge (10) he must be giving a caricature of the way in which they justify their ideas. Doubtless they must have boasted that they possessed a supernatural gnosis which gave them the right to judge themselves free from all law. Jude reproaches them for allowing themselves to be guided by their passions and for letting their flesh be soiled (18). When he describes them as psychic who do not possess the Spirit he must be answering their claims and is calling in question their contention that they are inspired.[1]

The heretics without being formally separated from the church formed within its confines an opposition group.[2] They do not seem to have been activated by a positive desire to proselytise. Jude seems to have considered them a danger in themselves, not from the conquests which they were trying to make.

The epistle of Jude appears to have been written at a time when the appearance of heresy, at least in the community to which the author belonged, was still relatively speaking a novelty. The beginning of the epistle shows that its author found it necessary to intervene against heresy with such suddenness that he had to give up the project of a message in more general terms which would have treated of their common salvation (3) and would therefore have had a more positive character. Jude says that the arrival of heretics had been foretold to try and weaken the impression which their appearance had caused among his readers. It is also clear that the conflict with heresy had not been organised. The epistle does not even concentrate the attack on any particular point. Jude says that he is writing to enlist his readers in the fight for the defence of the faith, but he gives them no counsel or any practical suggestion as to what form the fight ought to take. An unexpected situation seems to have caught him somewhat by surprise and not to have given him time to consider how it ought to be faced. He denounces the errors of the heretics, tries to inspire his readers with horror at their ideas and conduct, but does not say how their doctrine can be effectively prevented from spreading.

We must not, however, infer from this that the appearance of the heresy was altogether a novelty. Although the epistle gives us only

[1] Possibly Jude like Peter means by individual inspiration, when he is attacking it, individualistic interpretation of the prophets and writings.

[2] The fact that the epistle never envisages the heretics being brought back proves that the author did not suppose that his letter would be read by them. The same can be said of the second epistle of Peter.

incomplete and insufficient evidence about it, its form is sufficiently clear to show that it had been in existence for some time. The only novelty in the situation may well have been that it had penetrated a community which had not been acquainted with it before.[1]

Jude's judgement on heresy is simple and plain. Those professing it are outside the true faith and destined to ultimate destruction. Only inconsistency prevents him from despairing altogether of their final salvation (22-23).

We cannot describe or place the heresies visualised by Jude with any exactness, as the epistle shows no intention of refuting them and speaks of them only in general terms sufficient for its readers to know the subject and persons to whom it is referring. It would be unwise to take the accusations of immorality literally. It was the fashion in polemics against heretics to make mountains out of molehills. Sometimes they may have been well founded; certainly they were not always so.

The accusations against the heretics can be classified under two or three principal headings, antinomianism, angelology, and perhaps christology, if the expressions, 'to deny the only master and Lord Jesus Christ' (4) and 'to despise dominion' (8), i.e. the teaching coming from Christ, are not just conventional phrases used to describe heresies. The description of Jesus Christ as 'only master' (μόνον δεσπότην) does not allow us to think that it refers to a doctrine which in addition to Christ knew of other masters and other lords and thus would resemble the gnosticism at Colossae. In short, the heart of the heresy is not the worship of angels as at Colossae but blasphemy against them (8, 10). It might be connected with some theory which made the angels responsible for evil and sin. But blasphemy against angels might also be connected with antinomianism on the supposition that to speak evil of them was an offence, in virtue of the fact that the Jewish tradition associated them with the promulgation of the law on Sinai.[2]

The only kind of heresy which is beyond question is antinomianism. The immorality with which the heretics are reproached was

[1] This interpretation is supported by the use of the word παρεισεδύησαν (they slipt in, insinuated themselves). It can mean either that they had recently entered the church or that their representatives had penetrated the churches in a district where they had not been previously represented.

[2] The fact that the heretics seem to have invoked visions to justify their doctrine (8, 19) might lead to the inference that they claimed that the doctrines had been revealed to them by angels who had appeared to them. Jude would have considered that it was an outrage for them to suggest this.

partly a product of their theories. We are in the presence of a form of antinomianism which was sometimes inferred from Pauline phrases, sometimes was proclaimed by Paul's disciples and sometimes by his enemies, who imputed it to him in order to attack and compromise him. It also resembles the kind dealt with in the first epistle of John (iii. 4 ff.). The only question which remains to be discussed is whether Jude is dealing with a theoretical form of antinomianism or a practical form which showed itself in the domain of sexual morality. Jude's thought certainly implies the second interpretation. The term ἀσέλγεια which he uses (4), the reference to the angels who loved the daughters of men, the reference to Sodom and Gomorrah, and the expression 'they soil the flesh' leave no doubt on this point.[1] It is unsatisfactory to interpret adultery and debauchery as merely allegorical terms for infidelity to God and the doctrine of the church, and as implying no particular type of heresy. But apart from the fact that antinomianism is definitely referred to it is impossible to grasp what heresy is being attacked in the epistle of Jude.

The mass of the faithful do not seem to have entertained the same feelings as Jude towards the heretics. Otherwise he would not have thought it necessary to give them the serious warning contained in his epistle.[2] Possibly Jude does not go so far as to demand the expulsion of the heretics from the church which he was in no way assured that he would secure because a good number of the faithful looked on them with indulgent or indifferent eyes.

The second epistle of Peter does not show with any greater clearness than that of Jude for whom it was intended. Before he attacks the heretics Peter reminds his readers of what has been given to them which they must take care is not lost, altered, or in any way compromised. At all times, he whose faith does not bring forth fruit is a blind man who has forgotten that he once was purged

---

[1] Although the evidence is rather indefinite and taken by itself would be insufficient, one might quote the comparison of the heretics to beasts without reason (10) and the statement that they allow themselves to be led away by their passions (16). In addition to this the accusation brought against them that they disgrace agapes by feasting at them without shame (12) cannot be considered proved. It resembles the case of certain Corinthians who became drunk at the celebration of the Lord's supper (1 Cor. xi. 21), a statement which does not seem to have been taken literally (cf. E.P. pp. 343 ff.). It might well be that in Jude's eyes the mere presence of heretics was sufficient to profane the supper.

[2] Jude may have been led to describe the heretics in particularly sombre colours by the desire to make an impression on his readers.

of his sins (i. 9).[1] This introduction shows immediately that, while Jude's only concern was to inspire his readers with a horror of heresy, Peter does not feel that sufficient but considers that the life of faith calls, not for immobility, but for effort.[2] He wants to remind his readers that it is necessary to persevere in the faith because a revelation of the Lord has taught him that the time of his departure is at hand.[3] For the last time he seeks to recall his teaching which did not rest on imaginary fables but has been given by him, because he was the witness of the majesty of Christ at his transfiguration. To the authority of the revelation which he received on the holy mountain is added the sure revelation of prophecy. We must, however, take care that no prophecy of scripture is of any private interpretation (i. 12-21). This is a theory of prophecy to which I shall return when later on I shall be speaking of Paul's epistles. The polemic against heresy begins properly in chapter ii in which are found with very little alteration the substance and phrases of the epistle of Jude. The chapter opens by comparing heretics to the rebels of the Old Testament (ii. 1-3). God did not spare the rebel angels but shut them in dark caves where they await the judgement (ii. 4).[4] He condemned the ancient world at the time of the flood, when he saved only Noah (with seven other persons) as a herald of righteousness (ii. 5).[5] By this God showed that he would not let the righteous die with the sinners, which is also proved by the fact that Lot did not perish with the inhabitants of Sodom and Gomorrah (ii. 6-8). Terrible punishments await those who have gone after the flesh with foul covetousness and have despised the lordship of Christ. He is referring to antinomians who reject the teaching of the Lord as professed by the church. The parallelism with the epistle of Jude is complete but the last stroke made by Jude to describe the heretics, 'they despise the dignities' is amplified in the second epistle of Peter. They are described as reckless without shame who do not tremble before dignities but speak evil of them (ii. 6-10) although the angels

---

[1] A similar idea is expressed in 1 Peter iii. 21 where baptism is described as a pledge to a holy life. See *E.P.*, p. 295 ff.

[2] We have here a fact which tells in favour of the priority of Jude as it is easier to conceive of an amplification of thought than of its contraction.

[3] The way in which he mentions impending departure does not suggest the idea of martyrdom.

[4] This idea is present in the epistle of Jude but in a more developed form and is supported by a quotation from the book of Enoch. The suppression of this quotation makes the sentence somewhat obscure.

[5] This may be due to the influence of 1 Peter iii. 20.

themselves did not dare to bring railing accusations before the Lord[1] (11).

As in Jude, the heretics are described as animals without reason living a completely physical life destined to destruction. There follows a description of their life which is like an indictment. They will receive the just reward for their sin because they please themselves in their pleasures; they are soiled and corrupt, they gorge themselves in their lusts (ἀπάταις).[2] We have here a curious variation from the text of Jude who spoke of the scandal of heretics being present at the agapes celebrated by the church. In the interval between the two epistles the situation appears to have changed. The heretics have ceased to participate in the eucharistic reunions unless their participation did not give Peter so much pain and therefore he altered the words to avoid mentioning it. The parallelism of the two texts leaves no doubt that Peter depends on Jude. Participation in the supper is a subsidiary offence in Peter's eyes as heretics are reproached for feasting, for having their eyes set on an an adulteress, for not ceasing from sin, and for offering a bait to hesitating souls. This last tray shows that the situation had changed in another respect. Jude feared the wicked example of the heretics but does not seem to anticipate any propaganda from them. Heresy therefore had grown strong in the interval and had striven to become master of the situation. After a series of invectives which yield nothing in the way of accurate information (ii. 13-17),[3] it is said that the heretics are destined for darkness because they preach futile sermons, and stirring up the carnal passions, seduce people who are almost become victims of their errors, i.e. converted. Slaves of the flesh, they promise liberty (ii. 17-19). Peter is therefore concerned with heretical propaganda which was getting hold of new converts not without success. The conclusion emphasises the unfortunate condition of those who had once escaped the pollutions

---

[1] This phrase of Peter's is somewhat obscure. A comparison with the parallel text in Jude makes it clear: the obscurity is shown to be due to the suppression by Peter of an implicit reference to the Assumption of Moses because it was not a canonical book.

[2] Instead of ἀπάταις which is the reading of the majority of manuscripts B. and some others have ἀγάπαις which is the original reading in Jude 12. The manuscript 1739 and a few minuscules have ἀγνοίαις (in their ignorance).

[3] In ii. 17, the heretics are compared to dried up springs and clouds evaporated by the storm. The simile of the clouds which evaporate without giving forth rain as used by Jude is therefore divided into two, a proof that Peter did not understand it, doubtless because he lived in a district which was not so wet as where Jude lived. This is another indication that 2 Peter depends on Jude.

of the world through the knowledge of the Lord and Saviour Jesus Christ, and are now allowing themselves to be entangled afresh, and are falling into a worse state than that which they left at the beginning. It would be better for them never to have known the way of righteousness. They are like the dog who turns to his own vomit again and the sow that was washed to her wallowing in the mire (ii. 20-22). This conclusion is an amplification of the 'twice dead' of Jude 12. It also shows itself to have been influenced by the doctrine of the epistle to the Hebrews on the impossibility of the second repentance.

After the author has thus vituperated against the heretics he invites his readers to remain loyal to the true teaching. He reminds them of his first letter which was to awaken in them a clear sense of the truth[1] and he also recollects the words of the prophets and the commandments of the apostles of the Lord and Saviour (iii. 1-2). The first thing to know, says Peter, is that in the last days mockers will appear who will walk after their own lusts and who, this being taken for granted, will defy the righteousness of God. 'And saying, "Where is the promise of his coming?", for since the fathers fell asleep, all things continue as they were from the beginning of the creation' (iii. 4).

The heretics therefore denied the parousia and with it the judgement: they made fun of the teaching of the church on this subject and of the disappointment facts had caused them.[2] This is not an isolated instance. The first epistle of Clement of Rome (xxiii. 3-4) and the second (xi. 2-4) quote a passage from a writing replying to the same criticism of the prediction of the final cataclysm. Did this criticism of eschatological doctrine come from Jews or from Christian heretics? One hesitates to answer as the treatise *Sanhedrin* (99*b*) contains a polemic against this kind of argument. To this criticism Peter replies that the critics have forgotten that God once before destroyed the world by water and now he is going to destroy it by fire and in this way punish the impious (iii. 5-7).

[1] There is no doubt that he is alluding to the first epistle of Peter, although it is not very accurately described. Zahn's theory (*Einl.* II, p. 95) which suggests that it is referring to another letter written by the apostle Peter and addressed to the Jewish Christians of Palestine is only a desperate hypothesis to save at all costs the authenticity of 2 Peter.

[2] Windisch (*Kath. Br.*, p. 191) justly remarks that only after the first generation had disappeared can it be supposed that there could be any real criticism of the belief in the parousia in the form envisaged in 2 Peter. He considers this sufficient evidence in itself to rule out the authenticity of the epistle.

They forget that one day is with the Lord as a thousand years, which means that as man cannot appreciate the length of time, he cannot say that the prophecies have not been fulfilled. He adds that if God appears to have delayed, it is because he is long suffering and is giving sinners time to repent. He ends by stating that the day of the Lord will come like a thief. The whole world will then disappear; the faithful must therefore lead a holy life and be irreproachable in their conduct in order to hasten on the coming of the day of the Lord who will create new heavens and a new earth which will be a habitation of righteousness. While they wait they must live in peace, counting that if the Lord shows patience it is an aid to salvation (iii. 8-15).

This is what the beloved brother Paul has also taught in his letters in which some things are difficult to understand, which men who are unlearned and restless twist into a wrong sense, as they do with the other scriptures to their own destruction (iii. 15b-16).[1] In principle, therefore, Peter recognised the authority of the epistles of Paul just as further back he recognised that of the prophets. But he notices that they contain obscurities. In the same way he had said that prophecy is like a torch giving light in an obscure place (i. 19) which consequently can only give an uncertain light. He is therefore concerned by the use which the heretics made both of Pauline phrases and of certain texts from the prophets. It also showed that it was necessary to put his readers on their guard against what he considered to be a reckless way of using the prophecies and the epistles. He thus protests against a personal interpretation of the epistles in the same way as he had previously protested against a personal interpretation of prophecies (i. 20-21). Only the interpretation given by the church in conformity with its own teaching is valid.

The conclusion of the epistle is simple. The readers duly warned and taught in advance of the appearance of heresy must watch that

---

[1] Zahn (*Einl.* ii. 97 ff.) remarks that Peter is speaking of two things, (*a*) a letter received by his readers from Paul which may be one of those in our possession or may be one which has been lost and (*b*) other letters which must be reckoned to have been already collected into a *corpus*. This seems to be what the text implies, but it leaves a problem which Zahn does not even examine. Do we know if this actually was the situation? If 2 Peter is admitted to be unauthentic, it must be thought that the writer is thinking of Paul's letters generally, having the same idea as expressed in the Muratorian canon (lines 56-59) that what Paul writes to one church is addressed to all. There is no evidence which allows us to think that the author of 2 Peter knew of other letters besides those which figure in the *corpus paulinum*.

they do not allow themselves to be seduced but must grow in grace and in the knowledge of our Lord and Saviour Jesus Christ (iii. 17-18).

The few differences to be found between the epistles of Jude and Peter are not so wide as to contradict each other and may be explained in two different ways which, however, do not conflict. Peter may have attacked heresy with greater precision than Jude did or he may have had to deal with a form of heresy which had developed to a greater extent, was more precise in form and more active than that with which Jude had had to deal.[1] At the time when the epistle of Peter was written the heretics seem to have become more sharply distinct from the church than when the epistle of Jude was written. They also have begun to defend their doctrines by prophecy and by Paul's epistles. Of this there is no trace in the epistle of Jude. The criticism of the church's teaching on the ground that the parousia is delayed is the only factor to be noted in the epistle of Peter which cannot be regarded as entirely inherent in the situation depicted in the epistle of Jude. Both epistles judge heresy in the same way. Both of them consider it to be a danger, both to the church in general and to each individual believer. But Jude thinks it sufficient to put the faithful on their guard and to warn them of the danger, while Peter considers it necessary to reply to the heretics by a discussion of their doctrines and producing at least the outline of a refutation. He also is emphatic that they must remain loyal to the traditional doctrine, the value of which he under-lines by emphasising the authority of the revelations on which the apostolic teaching rests, particularly those received by Peter illus-trating it. It may be also that the differences between the two polemics are due to differences in the temperaments of the two authors.

II.—CONCLUSION

The evidence which I have tried to collect together on the first phase of the conflict between sound doctrine and heresy is too disparate in character and on most points too compressed for one to think of composing the history of heresy in the last quarter of the first century and the first quarter of the second.

It offers a series of contrasts: first of all a contrast between the

---

[1] The fact that the polemic of 2 Peter is more detailed is another sign that Jude was composed earlier.

attitude towards heresy of those who *de facto* or *de jure* were the leaders of the church and that of the mass of the faithful. The former were acutely conscious of the pernicious character of heresies and made great efforts to keep those who were committed to their charge free from their influence. There is also a contrast between the way in which heretics were spoken of and the way in which they were treated. The harshest judgements and most categorical condemnations are pronounced against them; vehement invective is showered upon them; but their most determined enemies fail to demand that they should be expelled from the church. It was certainly not liberalism or a love of toleration which led the champions of sound doctrine to take up this attitude. A certain measure of moderation is imposed upon them by their knowledge that they could not take strong measures because the church in general would not agree if they were suggested or asked for.

With Ignatius new tactics appeared; centres of resistance against heresy were formed around those bishops who were loyal to the traditional doctrine, and in these alone, it was maintained, the true church existed. 'There, where Jesus is', Ignatius writes, 'there is the catholic church', but he adds, 'Wherever the bishop appears, let the congregation be present' (Smyrn. viii. 2), which means that the church exists only so far as it is grouped round its bishop.[1] In this way Ignatius does not demand that heretics should be excluded, which he would not have been granted but tries to concentrate the church into groups which were free from their influence.

The history of heresy shows another contrast. It is shown as the negation of truth; yet it was first attacked in the realm of discipline more than in that of doctrine. Theological argument, properly so called, scarcely played any part before the middle of the second century. Heretics were at first condemned, not on account of their ideas but because their ideas were not within the framework of the traditional formulae. Men were less concerned to show that heretics were thinking evil than—what was plainly much easier—to prove that they were not holding to the traditional formulae.

Although the evidence at our disposal does not allow us to say so with complete certainty, it is neither impossible nor improbable

---

[1] For that reason he adds that neither baptism nor a celebration of the agape is allowed without the bishop. At the beginning of the chapter he commanded them to follow the bishop as Jesus Christ had followed the Father and the presbytery as if it were the apostles.

that the heretics at times showed more originality and vigour in their ideas than the exponents of sound doctrine. And perhaps, paradoxical as it may seem, just for that reason sound doctrine prevailed in the end. It offered ideas, which were collectively expressed in phrases to which assent could be given without there being any necessity for personal reconsideration of their meaning. They thus lent themselves to a mass of opinion being formed which could withstand heresy in its various and diverse forms.

CHAPTER IX

Towards Early Catholicism

ONLY in a very relative sense can it be said that the travails and trials of early Christianity to find intellectual expression gave birth to Johannine theology on the one hand and the precatholicism of Clement of Rome on the other. In spite of this, the end of the first century marked a very important stage in the process of development which ended in the constitution of a stable form of doctrine. Just about the time John and Clement's ideas were taking shape, if we may use the phrase in preference to that of finding expression, those who were coming to exercise powers of direction in the church began to feel with more force than had ever been felt before, that the sound doctrinal tradition must be defended against the pernicious innovations of the heretics. The conflicts with them which assumed a clear-cut form with the Book to the Seven Churches, the Pastoral epistles, the first epistle of John, and later on with the epistles of Ignatius, that of Jude and 2 Peter had several consequences. First of all, it resulted in changing not only the general attitude of Christian thought but the very nature of its function, its purpose no longer being to express the content of the faith but to give such a presentation of the traditional doctrine as would reveal its contents in a form which rendered them accessible and made them most easy to assimilate. At the same time it made the tradition challenge heresy encasing it with the whole armoury of apologetic.

Once the battle was set between sound doctrine and heresy, the Christian thinker of the second century, even when his thought showed more originality, was much less conscious than in the first century of the personal nature of his work, i.e. he believed that he was not presenting his own faith and thought but the faith and thought of the church. In this way doctrine became more and more the expression of an objective truth.

Yet, while on the one hand the conflict with heresy should have, it seems, reduced the part played by the theologian as a personal thinker it tended rather to strengthen it, because, as we have already seen, the conflict was taken in hand by a group of men who were not swayed by the convictions belonging to the mass of the faithful who gave them hardly any support at all. The development of Christian thought thus became the work of a class of theologians who, for all practical purposes, were almost completely identified with the clergy as the epistle of Clement of Rome seems to show.

A comparison between Christian thought about the year 100 and Christian thought at the end of the second century as expressed in the early Catholicism of Tertullian and Irenaeus shows certain differences between them which allow us to see the significance and nature of the work of the second century.

First of all, it is to be noticed that while both Johanninism and the thought of Clement of Rome were only local forms of Christianity, at the end of the second century Christian theology had become catholic in the true sense of the word, i.e. universal. This is the result of a process of concentration, conjunction, unification, and synthesis among the differing types of Christianity, which were commingling and interpenetrating diverse communities. But a new factor came into play in the second century. That was a more explicit and thought-out conviction that sound doctrine was one and homogeneous in contrast to the varying forms of heresy. Very typical in this respect is the attitude of Hegesippus, who took a long voyage towards the middle of the second century to assure himself that the same doctrine was taught in all the churches which he visited and that its immutability was assured from one age to another by a regular succession of bishops.[1] In practice unification was much favoured by the fact that the church of Rome both on account of its importance and activity as well as because it was the church of the capital of the empire attracted to itself Christians from every quarter. In particular, men such as Justin Martyr or Irenaeus, who either were born in Asia or converted there, came to Rome or the West and introduced into Roman theology doctrinal and religious elements from Johanninism, which spiritually enriched Western Christianity and so assimilated it to Eastern Christianity.

In addition an important change took place in the second century in the form in which doctrine was expressed. The formulae grew more explicit and it was equipped with a complete armoury of apologetic. In the interval the dangers from heresy to which traditional doctrine was liable had grown clearer first through the growth

[1] Hegesippus, in Eusebius, *H.e.* iv. 22, 1-2.

of Marcionitism and gnosticism and later through the growth of montanism, all of which endangered both the traditions and outlook of the church. If they had triumphed Christianity would not only have assumed a different form from that which it had had up to then and was destined to keep, but a new religion would have been substituted in place of the old. The principal weapons in the defensive armoury of the traditional doctrine were the strengthening of the ecclesiastical organisation and especially of the authority of bishops, the increasing part played by credal confession, but above all, the formation of the idea of a sacred scripture of the New Covenant and the first efforts at determining its essential context. This took place, not in the period of creative activity but in that of organisation and consolidation. It is not therefore within our province to follow its course but a very brief description of its essential characteristics is not out of place since it sprang from forces which in the first century determined what form Christian doctrine took, while the result of it was to stabilise and consolidate the ensuing doctrines.

PART FIVE

The Reactions Provoked by the Preaching of the Gospel

CHAPTER I

The Problem

As the inheritor of Judaism and like it the beneficiary of the divine promise and covenant, Christianity was from the first opposed to every form of Greco-Roman paganism which, to use the phrase of the epistle to the Ephesians, left men 'strangers from the covenants of promise, having no hope, and without God in the world' (ii. 12). While nascent Christianity was closely bound up with Judaism and had no thought of following Marcion and repudiating its heritage, it was not identical with it. Far from that, from the very beginning it felt very strongly that compared with Judaism it offered something absolutely new, that it was a continuation of Judaism but had passed beyond it by putting reality itself in place of image and prophecy.[1] Christianity did not regard itself as a religion which was hostile to Jews or Gentiles and indifferent to them. On the contrary, it possessed the conviction that it was the religion—and the only religion—which could bring salvation to both of them. For some time at any rate, it cherished the hope that it would see the whole Jewish people as a body accept its message and rally round it. When it had to admit that it had been deceived on this point it could scarcely resign itself to the fact, but tried with the apostle Paul to console itself with the hope that Israel would only remain incredulous for a period or, in accordance with the same apostle's suggestion, made a distinction between the spiritual Israel made up of those who believed in Christ and the empirical Israel consisting of the descendants of Abraham, saying that it was not the latter but the former who were the people of God and seeing in the latter only a synagogue of Satan (Rev. ii. 9).

---

[1] Yet in the Jewish environment of Palestine Christianity retained Jewish forms of worship and social life to such an extent that any sense of originality was almost lost.

2.—THE FEELINGS OF THE CHURCH TOWARDS THE EMPIRE AND THE GENTILE WORLD

The infant church might easily from the start have felt itself separated from the Gentiles by the fact that the whole structure of civil society and the empire was permeated and impregnated with paganism. But this went for nothing and the idea that Gentiles could be summoned to salvation and consequently admitted into the church does not appear to have been called in question.[1] The pagan character of the ancient world failed to create an insuperable barrier between itself and Christianity, partly, perhaps, because the Jewish communities which existed everywhere in the Greco-Roman world as they spread outwards and created more or less merely formal ties between themselves and the world outside, in practice if not in theory, paved the way for the idea of the civil society being divorced from the religious society. At any rate they habituated men to the idea that even within the framework of an idolatrous society it was possible to worship the true God and to gain souls for Him.

But in addition in the eyes of primitive Christianity the pagan society and the Roman empire were part of this present world in which the church was called upon to live and to which consequently it would be best for it to accommodate itself, while at the same time it preserved its own essential spirit and safeguarded its own character until the time came when God would destroy it to establish his kingdom.

Because the Roman empire was therefore a reality which God allowed to exist at least for the time being, the infant church not only showed itself ready to accept Gentiles, who individually were ready to come to it, but desired an understanding and *modus vivendi* with pagan society so far as might be possible while it remained strictly loyal to its own principles. Some significant and essential points must be recalled here.

First must be noted the philo-Roman tendency of the story of the passion, which grows more accentuated as we pass from Mark to John[2] and beyond. The four evangelists depict Pilate resisting

---

[1] The only question which caused conflict between Jewish and Gentile Christians was on what terms Gentiles could be admitted into the church.

[2] On this point see my articles: 'Les Chrétiens et l'Empire romain a l'époque du Nouveau Testament', Paris, 1908; 'Juifs et Romans dans l'histoire de la passion', *R.h.r.*, 1910, LXII, pp. 165-182, 296-322, *Life of Jesus*, pp. 464 ff. The tendency to make the Jews responsible and free the Romans of responsibility is further

as far as he could the pressure which the crowd, instigated by their leaders, were bringing to bear upon him to ratify the condemnation of Jesus pronounced by the Sanhedrin. After he had proclaimed, in the clearest and most explicit terms, Jesus' innocence and tried to save him by giving him the advantage of the favour which it was always customary for him to grant at the feast of the passover, he is represented to have complied in the end only because it was in fact impossible for him to do anything else.[1] This is all the more characteristic because in reality the actual course of events was quite different. Whatever may have been the tricks and manoeuvres to which the Jews resorted in order to compel Pilate to intervene against Jesus, one thing is certain; Jesus was tried under Roman jurisdiction, as is proved by the penalty which was imposed upon him and the fact that he was executed by the procurator's soldiers.[2]

In the gospel tradition, therefore, facts have undergone a very distinct transposition. This was not the result of the accidents and imperfections of human memory. Unconsciously perhaps it reflects certain conceptions and concerns, which we may well hesitate to define. The more responsibility is placed upon one of the groups involved in the trial the lighter becomes that of the other. When we study the tradition do we find that it tends to accentuate the responsibility of the Jews or to diminish that of the Romans? In other words, is the tradition to be described as philo-Roman or anti-Jewish? The answer seems as if it must be both.

But so far as the tradition can be described as philo-Roman another question remains. Was the part played by the Romans in Jesus' trial minimised, as we saw it was, out of sympathy for Pilate and the empire which he represented? It might have been done for quite different reasons. The one whom Christians presented to the world as the Son of God, Lord and Saviour, had been condemned by a Roman magistrate to an infamous punishment. The difficulty created by this fact for the preaching of the gospel among the subjects of the empire must not be underestimated. The scandal could

accentuated in the later tradition. For instance, in the gospel of Peter it is not Pilate but Herod who condemns Jesus and sentences him to death. While Pilate washes his hands neither Herod nor the Jewish leaders follow his example (1-2).

[1] *V. de J.*, pp. 360 ff. and *Life of Jesus*, pp. 466 ff.

[2] The procurator did not, as has sometimes been thought, ratify a sentence which had been passed by the Sanhedrin but could not be executed without the approval of the Roman governor. If this had been done Jesus would have been given a Jewish punishment (strangulation or stoning) and not a Roman punishment. (Cf. *V. de J.*, pp. 392 f. and *Life of Jesus*, pp. 471 f.)

not be suppressed. But in order to water it down the explanation was put out that the magistrate was placed in such a situation that, while he could not refrain from pronouncing a verdict of guilty, nevertheless on several occasions he publicly proclaimed the innocence of the man whom he had vainly tried to defend against his enemies. The idea cannot be altogether ruled out that, out of the growing tendency of the tradition to exculpate the Romans from any responsibility for the death of Jesus, emerged that anti-semitism which after 70 became an explicit and pronounced feature of the church's tradition. Furthermore, we cannot help but think that it was prompted by the desire to lessen one of the difficulties which faced the preaching of the gospel in the Roman world. There seems to have been a close connection between Christian antisemitism and the distinctly loyal attitude towards Rome of the first generation of Hellenistic Christians. There also seems to have been other and more profound reasons for them both.

Jesus himself seems to have taken this attitude as is shown both by his opposition to political Messianism and his reply to the Pharisees when they asked him about the tribute money (Mark xii. 13-17 and par.). The meaning of his reply must not be misunderstood. 'Render to Caesar the things which are Caesar's' must not be separated from 'Render to God the things which are God's'. Caesar and God are not put on the same level. Caesar belongs to a world which is doomed to disappear; God is eternal. Caesar's legitimate authority only holds sway as long as the present world lasts.[1] Significant evidence for the loyal sentiments of the first generation of Christians towards Rome is provided by the teaching given in Romans xiii. 1-17.[2] Paul writes, 'Let every soul be subject

---

[1] H. J. Holtzmann, *Die Neue Testament und der romische Staat*, Strasburg, 1892, pp. 12 f.

[2] Loisy (*Remarques sur la litterature épistolaire du Nouveau Testament*, pp. 30 f.) maintains that these instructions were interpolated later. The two reasons which he gives for this suggestion do not appear convincing. It is true that the instructions are not logically connected with what precedes or with what follows, but it is a peculiar characteristic of the hortatory parts of the New Testament that they are not logically developed out of preceding matter but are simply placed side by side with other matter without any connection. Cf. M. Dibelius, 'Rom und die Christen im ersten Jahrhundert', *S.H.A.*, 1941, 42, 2, pp. 7-8. The other reason given by Loisy is that he reckons the instructions to be an anachronism. But it is just the time when we can think it most likely for them to have been given, i.e. before the conflict between church and empire became acute. Positive proof that the instructions are authentic seems to emerge from considerations which I have to put forward in reference to a passage in the second epistle to the Thessalonians.

to the higher powers. For there is no power but of God:[1] the powers that be are ordained of God. Whosoever therefore resisteth the power, resisteth the ordinance of God: and they that resist shall receive to themselves damnation. For rulers are not a terror to good works but to the evil. Wilt thou then not be afraid of the power? do that which is good, and thou shalt have praise of the same: For he is the minister of God to thee for good. But if thou do that which is evil, be afraid; for he beareth not the sword in vain: for he is the minister of God, a revenger to execute wrath upon him that doeth evil. Wherefore ye must needs be subject not only for wrath[2] but also for conscience sake. For for this cause pay ye tribute also: for they are God's ministers, attending continually upon this very thing. Render therefore to all their dues: tribute to whom tribute is due; custom to whom custom; fear to whom fear; honour to whom honour.'

Among other reasons for advising submission to the established authorities Paul may have been moved by opportunism. To submit is the surest means of living in peace. But this is only a secondary consideration; the underlying reason why the apostle asks for obedience is religious, viz. that the constituted authorities have been set up by God and therefore to oppose them is to act against the will of God.

It may be difficult to suppose that Paul was inspired with such political loyalty, when it is recollected that at the time when he was writing to the Romans he had just experienced particularly, in Macedonia,[3] the suspicion and ill-will with which the Roman authorities looked on the preaching of the gospel. The paradox may be explained by the fact that Paul felt that he was already living in the last days when the elect were doomed to be persecuted.[4]

There is one passage which shows how Paul was able to combine the idea that submission to the authorities is necessary with the idea that both the world which they rule and the authorities themselves are subject to Powers destined to perish because they are in

---

[1] Dibelius (*R.u.d. Chr.*, p. 7) rightly sets aside the hypothesis which he had previously maintained (*Geisterwelt*, p. 2000) that the passage is not referring to political authorities but to transcendent demonic powers. This interpretation has been defended by G. Dehn ('Engel und Obrigkeit', in *Theol. Aufs., f. K. Barth*, Munich, 1936, pp. 90 ff.) and O. Cullmann (*Konigsherrshaft Christi und Kirche im Neuen Testament*, Zollikon, 1941) and has been refuted by G. Kittel (*Christus und Imperator*, Stuttgart, Berlin, 1939, pp. 48-54).

[2] I.e. through fear of punishment.

[3] See pp. 475 ff.   [4] Dibelius, *R.u.d. Chr.*, pp. 10 f.

revolt against God (1 Cor. ii. 8). The passage belongs to the instructions in 2 Thessalonians ii. 1-12 where Paul is trying to calm the feverish impatience of his readers who have been thrown into great agitation by the thought that the parousia is almost imminent. He teaches them that it cannot appear 'except there come a falling away first, and that man of sin be revealed, the son of perdition;[1] who opposeth and exalteth himself above all that is called God, or that is worshipped; so that he be as God sitteth in the temple of God, showing himself as he is God.' Recalling the oral teaching which he had given, Paul adds, 'And now ye know what withholdeth[2] that he might be revealed in his time.[3] For the mystery of iniquity doth already work: only he who now letteth will let,[4] until he be taken out of the way. And then shall that Wicked be revealed, whom the Lord shall consume with the spirit of his mouth, and shall destroy with the brightness of his coming: even him[5] whose coming is after the workings of Satan with all power and signs and lying wonders,[6] and with all deceivableness of unrighteousness in them that perish; because they received not the love of the truth, that they might be saved. And for this cause God shall send them strong delusion, that they should believe a lie that they all might be condemned who believed not the truth, but had pleasure in unrighteousness.'

What is this preventive power which intervenes to prevent a premature manifestation of Antichrist and the resulting destruction of the world before what God considers the appropriate time? Before trying to reply to this question we must first take account of the reason why it was necessary that there should not be a premature manifestation of Antichrist. It is this. God's purpose and end first in creation and then in redemption is to create a people who will render to him the worship due to him. This would not be attained if the present world were destroyed before the Messianic people had been recruited from present humanity and formed of those who receive the call to salvation.

---

[1] This refers to Antichrist although the word is not used by the apostle.

[2] τὸ κατέχον. The term used is a neuter.

[3] I.e. at the time fixed by God in his design.

[4] ὁ κατέχων. The term here used is masculine.

[5] I.e. the parousia of the iniquitous one.

[6] I.e. not by counterfeit miracles which might be clever conjuring tricks but by miracles caused by a transcendent power, i.e. Satan which will be done to persuade men to give their loyalty to lying doctrines which can only bring them to death.

We know from various passages, particularly from the synoptic apocalypse (Mark xiii. 5-8 and par.) that one of the recurring themes referring to the happenings at the end and to the signs heralding the parousia was the idea that the return of the Lord would be preceded by revolts, civil and national wars. Nations will be drawn up against nations, and kingdoms against kingdoms. What compelled nations in the first century to swallow their prejudices and to refrain from going to war with each other was the empire which made itself felt in the whole civilised world. The empire is what Paul has in mind when he speaks of the power which is preventing a premature manifestation of Antichrist.[1] We then understand how he can attribute a providential function to the empire, although it belongs to a world doomed to disappear because it is bound to Satan and is ruled by Rulers who are in revolt against God. Its providential function is only provisional in character. It lies only in the present world, but, as long as it lasts, the empire has a part to play in the accomplishment of God's design and to rebel against it is to rebel against God himself. Paul's loyalty springs neither from resignation nor from opportunism; he is loyal from principle and perfectly sincere in his professions. But his loyalty remains provisional in nature because in his eyes the interests of the empire and its own ends have only passing value. Nothing was more foreign to the apostle's mind than the conception of a Christian empire or an imperial church. Church and empire not only belong to different levels of life; they belong to worlds opposed to each other, the empire belonging to the present world while the church is a reality in the world to come and in the present world a prophetic foretaste of what is to come.

Paul then could have no concern for the empire's maintenance and existence or want to transform it so as to bring it into harmony with the gospel. He could only see it as a missionary field offering nothing except opportunities for winning souls for

[1] This interpretation affords us a complete understanding why Paul alternates between the masculine and the neuter. He uses the neuter when he is thinking of the empire and the masculine when he is thinking of the emperor. Tertullian (*Apologeticum*, 32; *Ad Scapulam*, 2; *De carnis resurrectione*, 24) was the first author to recognise κατέχων to be the Roman empire. Following others Dibelius (*R.u.d. Chr.*, pp. 12 ff.) rules out this interpretation and finds in κατέχων only a rather vague traditional apocalyptic idea. What seemed to him to justify this opinion is the parallel between the idea of κατέχων and that of Antichrist. The parallel is beyond question; but Paul borrowed the idea of the κατέχων from the tradition and had to give it a new interpretation making it signify a distinct object of his thought.

Christ. He asked nothing of the empire except to allow the little Christian communities to grow and live in peace. He was ready to comply with all its demands provided they did not conflict with what belonged only to God.

3.—THE ATTITUDE OF JUDAISM TOWARDS THE CHURCH

During the first period which lasted until 70 the attitude of Judaism towards Christianity was not uniform. It depended whether it was that kind of Christianity which remained within the ecclesiastical and ritual framework of Judaism and continued to observe the law or the other kinds, such as those of Stephen and Paul, which had cut themselves free from Judaism. In respect of the former, Judaism was on the whole extremely tolerant. It considered it to be a somewhat peculiar sect, not exactly resembling the large parties of the Pharisees and the Saducees, but more like the somewhat more eccentric groups such as the Essenes or the disciples of the hermit Banus. Towards the other kinds of Christianity it showed systematic hostility and used all the means at its disposal, both direct and indirect, to exterminate them. After 70 the situation changed. Under the blows of national catastrophe Judaism recoiled upon itself, identified itself with Pharisaism, and became radically hostile to anything which did not conform and rejected alike both the legalistic and antilegalist forms of Christianity. A definite cleavage occurred between Judaism and Christianity but the two opposing groups still remembered their common origin. They did not lose interest in each other but tried to recruit members from one another. They were thus compelled to have men who were expert in this kind of propaganda. The argument which lasted for a long time between Jews and Christians has left echoes, first in the synoptic gospels and in the book of the Acts, and later in a more distinct form in the Fourth Gospel and at a rather later period in Justin Martyr's dialogue with the Jew Tryphon. Force of circumstances confined the conflict between Judaism and Christianity to the realm of ideas, as neither party had any direct means of action at its disposal. Justin expresses the feeling of Christians that they were protected against Jewish hatred by the authority of Rome when he says to Tryphon, 'You have not the power to lay hands upon us, thanks to those who are at present our rulers, but every time you could you have done so'.[1]

[1] Justin, *Dial.*, 16, 14.

The year 70 marks the end of the period after which there could remain no illusion that Christianity could develop and live within the framework of Judaism. But it was a little before this that Paul's trial before a Roman magistrate and the massacres of Christians following the fire at Rome in 64 dispelled any hope that a *modus vivendi* could be attained between the church and the empire.

What caused the hopes entertained by the first generation of Christians to evaporate? What resulted from the fact that the church found itself in opposition both to Judaism and the empire? These are the questions which must now be examined.

The church found that it had to defend itself against two adversaries at the same time, (1) Judaism and (2) Greco-Roman paganism represented by the empire. But this did not mean, as might at first be thought, that it was engaged in two separate conflicts with each of them independently of one another, because Christianity had contacts with both of them. In actual fact, both the hostile parties with whom Christianity came into conflict had much closer relations with each other than might at first sight be supposed. For a long time the Roman authorities and public opinion confused the Christians with the Jews and only considered the differences between them to be divergent interpretations of the law which were only of significance within the Jewish community. This mistake so far as it was one—for after all Christianity is in one sense a form of Judaism—was to the advantage of the Christians, as it enabled them in the first generation, in fact until the fire at Rome in 64, with a few exceptions to enjoy the privileged position of Judaism in the empire as a recognised *religio licita*.[1] The representatives of Judaism did their best to relieve the confusion. They certainly did not do it because they wanted to injure the church; but we must not rule out the idea that they may have wished to free Judaism from developments which they saw were taking hold of the infant church and which they could foresee would lead one day to open conflict with the empire. They considered that it would be best for them to avoid this conflict in advance if they did not wish to suffer from it. Judaism was able to obtain and keep a privileged position in the empire because it was a national religion. The Roman authorities, of course, in the end recognised that Christianity was not a national religion and that, although it had some close affinities with Judaism, it had not the same claims to a privileged position

[1] The term *religio licita* which it is convenient to use has no judicial official character. Tertullian (*Apologeticum*, 21, 1) seems to have been the first to use it.

447

in the empire, but it is an undoubted fact that Jewish manoeuvres hastened the time when the Roman authorities became conscious of this. As we shall see further on, the imperial authority resolved to take action against the church at the instigation of Jews. In this way the Jewish and Roman opposition to the church was closely connected. The Jewish campaign which was undertaken to repudiate any connection with Christianity was what showed that it could have no legal status in the empire, that it was fixed on the margin of society so that it was left without any protection against the ill-will and hostility of public opinion, which hardly had any acquaintance with Christianity and perhaps, because Christians enveloped their meetings for worship with secrecy to prevent their being profaned,[1] was ready to believe the direct calumnies which were spread abroad about them.[2] Thus the opposition of the Jews and the Romans to Christianity was inspired by different motives and used different means of action but it was closely connected. It must therefore be considered as one.

4.—THE POSITION OF CHRISTIANITY IN THE EMPIRE. PUBLIC OPINION

In the title to this part of my work I have avoided using the term 'persecutions' and have used the less accurate term 'reactions provoked by the preaching of the gospel'. The word 'persecutions' in the proper sense of the word refers to official, legal, judicial or administrative measures taken for the purpose of thwarting the development of Christianity and even of destroying it. Most historians of the persecutions take the word in this sense and assume that they began with the systematic measures which were taken against the Christians in 64 after the fire at Rome. For instance, that excellent historian of the early church, Gustav Kruger, writes, 'The history of persecutions begins with those which were taken against the Christians under Nero'.[3] Nero's victims were massacred

---

[1] At least those at which the supper of the Lord was celebrated. We know from 1 Cor. xiv. 23 f. that passers by and curious folk could be present at the Christian assemblies at Corinth. This may have been peculiar to Corinth or perhaps the custom may have been modified.

[2] See Dom Leclercq, art. 'Accusations contre les Chretiens', D.A.C.L., I, cols. 265-307.

[3] G. Kruger, art. 'Imperium romanum', R.G.G. III, col. 201. We have only quoted his judgement as a sample. A whole series of judgements similar to this might be added.

not because they were Christians but because from what was said of them as Christians they were judged to be responsible for the fire at Rome. We cannot find a series of systematic measures undertaken expressly for the purpose of extirpating Christianity until we come to the persecution of Decius (249-251).

If we study what happened under Nero—and the same applies to the whole history of persecutions—we find that measures would certainly have never been taken against the Christians or would have been ineffectual if public opinion had not been sympathetic towards them and had asked for them. It follows therefore, that the judicial and administrative measures which were taken against the Christians must not be studied apart from the reactions of an ideological and religious character which were roused by the preaching of the gospel and the establishment of Christian communities.

5.—THE REACTIONS OF THE CHURCH

The church's reactions towards both Judaism and Greco-Roman paganism assumed two forms. One was altogether instinctive and practical, a matter of feeling: it was expressed by hostility which showed itself whenever there was opportunity. The other was ideological. The doctrinal reaction was a source of interminable controversies which Christianity had to sustain with both Judaism and paganism. It had very diverse aspects. The Jewish and pagan polemics against Christianity were not as independent of each other as might have been supposed. Celsus in his 'True Discourse' borrows some of his arguments against Christianity from a 'Jew'.[1] Porphyry and others also took much of their argument from Jewish polemic.[2]

For the early period we have no direct evidence of the objections which the Jewish polemic directed against Christianity.[3] But some idea of the forms they took and the points on which they concentrated can be gained by considering the replies made to such objections in some of the books of the New Testament such as the Gospels.[4]

[1] This 'Jew' is perhaps the rabbi Trypho with whom Justin Martyr argued.
[2] On all these questions see the excellent book by Fr. de Labriolle, *La réaction paienne*, Paris, 1934.
[3] The earliest exposition of Jewish objections to Christianity in our possession is to be found in the *Dialogue against the Jew Trypho* by Justin Martyr.
[4] As an instance the story of the guard being placed at the sepulchre in Matthew xxvii. 62-66 can be quoted which, as the author shows us without disguise, meets a desire to refute the Jews who explained belief in the resurrection to be due to fraud on the part of the disciples who had taken away the body of Jesus.

The pagan polemic only appeared above ground at a later date. Christians only began to offer a defence of their ideological position to pagan public opinion in the second quarter of the first century.[1] This was because, as can be seen from the first pagan references to Christianity in Suetonius, Pliny the younger and Tacitus,[2] public opinion in the Roman world, so far as it was not totally and clearly ignorant of it or did not fail to confound it with Judaism, profoundly mistook its nature. It considered it to be a poor petty oriental superstition which was not worth arguing with and too insignificant to ask for suppression.[3]

[1] Arguments between Christians and pagans only began with the Apologists. See Aimé Puech, *Les Apologètes grecs*, Paris, 1912.

[2] See my observations, *Life of Jesus*, pp. 94 ff.

[3] It must be noted that about 50 Thallus, a freedman of Tiberius according to a fragment of Julius Africanus which has been preserved by the Byzantine chronicler George the Syncellus (810) (C. Muller, *Fragmenta historicorum graecorum*, Paris, 1841-70, III, pp. 517 f.) maintained that the darkness which according to the gospel tradition accompanied the death of Jesus was due to an eclipse. The statements of the gospel tradition were therefore discussed in Rome at an early date. It is true that the environment was one not unconnected with Judaism. See my article, 'Un nouveau témoinage non-chrétien sur la tradition évangelique d'après M. Eisler', *R.h.r.*, 1928, XCVIII, pp. 1-12. Cf. *V. de J.*, pp. 70 f. and *Life of Jesus*, pp. 91 ff.

CHAPTER II

The Reactions of Palestinian Judaism to the Preaching of the Gospel

I.—THE FEELINGS OF JUDAISM TOWARDS CHRISTIANITY UP TO 70 AND ITS METHODS OF ACTION

IT will be useful to examine two important points before we try to form any idea as to the attitude of Judaism towards the preaching of the gospel and the small groups of Christians which, at a quite early date, came into existence in Jerusalem and Judaea. How did Judaism before 70 regard ideas and beliefs which differed more or less from orthodox sentiment and what methods of action were at the disposal of the Jewish authorities under the rule of the procurators for resisting those who were opposed to the doctrines and spirit of Judaism?

The catastrophe of 70 compelled Judaism to recoil upon itself, become identified with Pharisaism, and to assume a hostile attitude towards any movement which did not conform to Pharisaism now that it had become equivalent to Jewish orthodoxy and in the preceding half century Judaism abounded in contrasts. But such divergences of view and differing attitudes failed to cause real contention, internal conflicts or even any positive discomfort. For instance, to take the temple worship and its sacrificial system we see that the Sadducees regarded it as of primary importance while the Pharisees were lukewarm towards it. The Essenes were still more reserved in their attitude: they did not condemn it in principle as they sent offerings to the temple treasure but they abstained from any participation in the sacrifices. As for John Baptist he does not seem to have attached the least importance to the temple *cultus*. But neither John Baptist nor the Essenes were thought of as heretics who ought to be cut off from the Jewish community. Although Messianic ideas were in the centre of Jewish religious thought in the first century, they were extremely fluctuating in character. The conception of the Son of Man was closely associated with that of the Davidic Messiah and there was no difficulty in holding them both simultaneously. It is not impossible that speculations that a second Adam would come and that the Messiah would be some sort of a man had already begun to be entertained by certain circles in Palestine. To declare oneself Messiah might be inopportune and goad the Roman authorities to intervene with dangerous consequences for the whole nation. But the fact that innumerable pretenders to be Messiah were given a warm welcome proves that it was not a heresy. Rabbi Aqiba, a man who was the very embodiment of the spirit of Judaism, hailed Barkochba as fulfilling the prophecy of Numbers xxiv. 17 'there shall come a star out of Jacob' and acclaimed him as the Messiah.[1]

First-century Judaism expected the coming of the Messiah to be the prelude to 'Israel's deliverance' and yet, when John Baptist appeared and proclaimed the appearance of the Messiah as something to be dreaded, his preaching met with a great response and no one thought of accusing him of heresy. Between Pharisees and Sadducees disputes were keen. They centred round points the importance of which were bound to be misunderstood, such as the existence of angels and spirits and the idea of resurrection but neither of them seems ever to have thought of demanding the expulsion of their opponents from the Jewish religious community. Even to predict the coming of catastrophes which would strike at the nation, Jerusalem, and the temple itself, was not heresy.[2]

But while Judaism previous to 70 still showed itself fairly flexible and tolerant of internal differences on one point it was adamant. That was the absolute value and divine origin of the law. With this went the unique privileges and mission of Israel and its exclusive call to salvation. These were dogmas which were not to be called

---

[1] Schurer, *Gesch.* I, p. 685.

[2] This is proved by the incident reported by Josephus (*G.j.* vi. 5, 3) concerning a certain Jesus, son of Ananias, a peasant of modest means, who six years before the Jewish war broke out, began after the feast of Tabernacles in the temple to prophesy and predict the fall of Jerusalem. The ill-treatment which he received from the mob could not silence him. The Jewish authorities intervened, not because the speeches of Jesus, the son of Ananias, appeared sacrilegious but because they were thought inopportune and likely to disturb public order. Jesus was brought not before the Sanhedrin which only took cognisance of religious charges but before the procurator Albinus who was responsible for the maintenance of peace and order. The procurator had him scourged, but he did not succeed in silencing him. He continued to prophesy right up to the time when during the siege he was killed by a stone from a catapult.

in question. If anyone seemed to cast doubts on one of them he could rest assured that he would find the whole of Judaism like a rock ranged against him.

If we penetrate below the surface, what happened at the trial of Jesus[1] supports this contention. At any rate it is not contradicted. The causes of the drama of the passion are complex and events seem to have followed one another with such rapidity that it is not easy to see exactly what happened. But a critical analysis of the tradition gives us assurance on several points. First of all it is certain that popular feeling was not hostile to Jesus but on the whole rather the reverse. Hostility came to him from a more limited group which consisted of the Jewish authorities. The scribes and Pharisees were annoyed to see a man who did not come from their group, and had not been trained by them and was regarded by them as illiterate, putting himself forward as a teacher of the people and claiming for himself real authority. While we must not generalise and say that all the Pharisees were hostile to Jesus, some of them determined to bring about his death, not so much because they thought that he was a heretic who was misleading the people as a dangerous rival to themselves.

The motives which led the Sanhedrin to declare Jesus worthy of death and then induced Pilate to pronounce sentence of death upon him—he had previously been persuaded to give orders for his arrest—were not necessarily the same. To persuade Pilate to act it was sufficient to make out to him that Jesus was one of those claimants to Messiahship who appeared from time to time and created disturbance in the country. But the fact that Jesus had declared himself to be the Messiah, even if it could be proved, would not have been sufficient to persuade the Sanhedrin to condemn him. Jesus, however, had once said to his disciples, not only that he would come again on the clouds of heaven but also that in three days he would destroy and rebuild the temple, i.e. he would change the whole economy of Israel's religion, its structure and worship. This had been reported to the Sanhedrin and could not be forgiven. It was this saying which persuaded the Sanhedrin to declare him worthy of death.

To understand the attitude of the Jews towards the Christians in Jerusalem and Palestine we have not only to consider the feelings with which the various groups of Christians inspired them; we must also take into account the methods of action open to them in dealing

[1] See *V. de J.*, pp. 360 ff. and *Life of Jesus*, pp. 464 ff.

with them. Both the great Sanhedrin at Jerusalem and the local Sanhedrins preserved their existence and competence under the rule of the procurators but they lost the power of imposing capital punishment unless they had first obtained the permission of the Roman governor. We do not know if their activities were restricted further. But whatever may have been the case, the fear of attracting the attention of the Roman authorities and causing them to intervene must have induced the Jewish authorities to act with a certain measure of reserve and discretion. It is difficult to regard it as nothing more than an accident that on the only two occasions when before 70[1] Judaistic Christianity suffered persecution the Roman government lacked complete control of Palestine. The first was in 44 when James the son of Zebedee and almost certainly his brother John were put to death and Peter was hard pressed and had to hurry away.[2] At that time the rule of the procurators had been replaced by the restoration of the kingdom of Herod the Great in favour of his grandson Agrippa I. The other was in 62 when James the Just, the brother of Jesus, was put to death.[3] At that time the office of procurator was vacant for some months between the death of Festus and the arrival of Albinus and consequently, while Roman administration did not collapse, it must have been slack. Perhaps the fact that the persecutions against the Christians in 44 did not last long, when the rule of the procurators was re-established, is not altogether devoid of significance. In any case, this hypothesis must be considered as we know that Jewish religious practices and services were closely watched. Typical proof of this is shown by the rapidity with which the tribune Lysias intervened at the time of the riot caused by the presence of the apostle Paul in the temple (Acts xxi. 31 f.).

2.—THE DESCRIPTION GIVEN BY THE COMPILER OF ACTS OF THE ATTITUDE OF THE JEWISH AUTHORITIES TOWARDS THE CHURCH AT JERUSALEM
A CRITICISM OF HIS DESCRIPTION

If we are to believe the story in the book of the Acts a conflict or at any rate a skirmish between nascent Christianity and the Jewish authorities took place apparently at a very early stage, some time before the preaching of Stephen, by vehemently criticising the Jewish religion caused Jewish public opinion to be deeply disturbed.

[1] Naturally the persecution against Stephen and the Hellenists must be put on one side and considered apart. [2] See pp. 456 ff. [3] See pp. 123 ff.

The occasion of this incident was the healing of an impotent man by Peter and John who took up his post by the gate of the temple to ask for alms. This was what first called the attention of the Jewish authorities to the disciples of Jesus and their preaching.[1] On their appearance before the Jewish authorities[2] they were not condemned, but forbidden to continue to preach in the name of Jesus (iii. 1-iv. 31).

A little later, a second incident which was more serious took place. The Twelve appeared before the Sanhedrin. The narrative in Acts does not tell us what had happened to lead to this. One of the members of the court, Gamaliel, advised his colleagues to take care what they were doing. Supporting his contention by examples to which we will revert later,[3] he maintained that if the Christian movement did not come from God it would collapse of its own accord, but if it came from God it was futile and dangerous to try and withstand it. They then confined themselves to repeating the prohibition, which had been made previously to the apostles Peter and John, but this time they made it more serious and threatened them in a more explicit manner by beating them (v. 17-42). As before, the apostles took no notice of the prohibition but nothing happened.

From whatever point of view we look at them, both these stories especially the second, are inconsistent. In the first we cannot grasp what legal procedure was being followed. It is quite clear that the author intended to tell of a trial but the nature of the accusation is not revealed and the affair ends with a simple prohibition which cannot be interpreted either as an acquittal or a condemnation. Yet it is difficult to suppose that the story is only fiction, as, if it had been, it would have been more coherent in character. What can be retained, it seems, is the idea that nothing more than an enquiry was made into the preaching of Peter and John to which attention had been drawn by an incident of some kind. The practical conclusion of the enquiry was a purely formal prohibition not to disturb public order. It may well be that the prohibition mentioned is an invention of the compiler of Acts whose *a priori* conception

---

[1] In the actual setting of the story the incident is preceded by the story of the events of Pentecost which it cannot be supposed passed unnoticed, but it is plain that the incident of the impotent man was originally supposed to mark the first public appearance of Christianity.

[2] It cannot be clearly discerned whether the compiler has in mind an appearance before the Sanhedrin or simply an interrogation conducted by the officials responsible for the maintenance of law and order in the temple. [3] See p. 457.

of the feelings entertained by Jews for Christians prevented him from thinking it possible for the apostles to appear before the Jewish authorities and being dismissed with anything less than at the very least an order to keep silent with threats of punishment if they did not obey.

The story of the appearance of the Twelve before the Sanhedrin which is given in Acts v. 17-42 is still more inconsistent. There is no organic link connecting it with what precedes it and with what follows. It is preceded by a note of a general kind (v. 12-16) saying that Christians were all with one accord in Solomon's porch without anyone thinking of troubling them.[1] Signs and wonders were wrought by the hands of the apostles. Peter in particular possessed such power of healing that they brought sick people on pallets so that the shadow of Peter passing by might overshadow them. Bluntly and without any further explanation, verse 17 states that the high-priest Annas[2] and the other priests belonging to the Sadducee party had the apostles arrested and put in prison. No explanation of this measure is offered. It is quite arbitrary without anything in the text to support or lead one to suppose that the people and the authorities differed in their attitude towards the Christians.[3] At the end of the story it is said that the apostles were scourged and then released with a warning to stop speaking in the name of Jesus. They took no notice of this (v. 42) but the authorities do not seem to have been disturbed by their negligence.

As for the story of the appearance before the Sanhedrin, the whole point of it lies in the speech of Gamaliel advising moderation so that they would not be exposed to the danger of fighting against

---

[1] Verse 13 says that 'no man durst join himself to them'. As the following verse says that the number of Christians did not stop growing, it must mean that no one cared to meddle in the Christian circle in order to cause trouble.

[2] On the reading 'Annas the high-priest' in p against the evidence of the other manuscripts and versions see p. 91, n. 3. The mistake as to what the name of the high-priest was is not favourable evidence for the value of the tradition which has been used.

[3] This idea, however, is suggested by the fact that it is related that during the night the apostles were miraculously delivered—this perhaps has come from the story concerning Peter in xii. 4 ff. and that on the following morning when they wanted to bring the apostles before the Sanhedrin they found the prison empty, as the apostles were in the temple teaching undisturbed. They had them brought, but did not use violence in order not to hurt popular feelings. We have here a miraculous incident which has no effect on the march of events. The idea of a preliminary imprisonment is borrowed from the story of the appearance in court of Peter and John (iv. 3). There it is due to the time when the arrest was made. In chapter v there is no such reason for it.

God. Gamaliel's argument is that a movement which was purely human would fail of itself. He quotes two cases of this, the revolt of Theudas and a disturbance created by Judas the Galilean at the time of the taxing. Josephus gives accurate information[1] showing that the revolt of Theudas happened when Fadus was governor. He was the first procurator to be sent out when, after the death of Agrippa I, Judaea became a Roman province again.

It must, therefore, have happened after 44. Quite clearly, however, the compiler of Acts places the appearance of the apostles before the Sanhedrin before this date. We cannot solve the difficulty by supposing that the compiler of Acts has made a mistake and anticipated the appearance of the apostles before the Sanhedrin by ten years or more. Peter had left Jerusalem; so doubtless had the other members of the Twelve, while in any case, the direction of the church was not in their hands but in James'. According to Gamaliel's speech Theudas' insurrection was quickly followed by that of Judas the Galilean, both of which he makes out had only recently taken place. Gamaliel states—and this is supported by Josephus—that the revolution led by Judas the Galilean happened 'at the time of the taxing', i.e. in A.D. 7. Gamaliel's speech therefore contains a series of anachronisms. It says that one event very quickly followed another although in fact there was an interval between them of forty years. They are stated to have happened in the reverse order in which they in fact took place, and finally, Gamaliel is speaking of two events as if they had recently happened, when in fact one of them had taken place about twenty-five years before he is supposed to be speaking and the other must have taken place at least ten years afterwards. Hence Gamaliel's speech is an artificial clumsy literary composition.[2] But it is so essential to the story of the appearance

---

[1] Josephus, *A.j.* xx. 5, 1.

[2] It is difficult to explain the cause of the mistake which we have shown was made in the story in Acts. Josephus, after he has mentioned the insurrection of Theudas and its repression in *A.j.* xx. 5, 1 adds (xx. 5, 2) that Tiberius Alexander, Fadus' successor, put to death the sons of Judas the Galilean who had once tried to stir up the people at the time of the taxing made by Quirinius (Josephus mentions this attempt in book xviii. 1, 1). Some authors (Wendt, *Die Apostelgeschichte*, Meyer, III[3], Goettingen, 1913, p. 43; Schmiedel, art. 'Theudas', *E.B.* IV, cols. 5049 f.; Loisy, *Actes*, p. 288) think that the compiler of Acts had only read Josephus' story in a superficial way or was quoting from it from memory, having no clear recollection of it. This is hardly probable as Josephus' story is clearly told and does not lend itself to misunderstanding. There is no doubt that we must adopt the hypothesis put forward by H. J. Cadbury (*Begin.*, II, p. 356) that Josephus and the compiler of Acts depended on the same source which Josephus understood better and used in a more judicious manner than the author of Acts.

before the Sanhedrin that, if it is eliminated, there is nothing left. We must therefore suppose that the story is a complete fiction and has no historical value.

There is one point, however, in the two stories which needs attention. The first states that only in the course of the interrogation was it learnt that Peter and John 'had been with Jesus' (iv. 13); in the second the high-priest makes his complaint against the apostles with these words, 'Did not we straitly command you that ye should not teach in this name? and, behold, ye have filled Jerusalem with your doctrine, and intend to bring this man's blood upon us' (v. 28). These two passages make us question how far the Jewish authorities were led to take action against Jesus and secure his condemnation from the same motives which later on incited them to take action against his disciples.

They did not on the first occasion question Peter and John because they had been preaching in the name of Jesus but because they wanted to know what they were preaching. The information given them on this point seems to have been reassuring as they were not seriously disturbed and the compiler of Acts in spite of his *a priori* conviction that the representatives of Judaism were systematically hostile, allows it to be seen that Christian preaching was able to progress without being perceptibly impeded. When the Twelve later on appeared before the Sanhedrin, they were not accused of giving the people teaching which was blasphemous or contrary to the doctrines and spirit of Judaism, but of presenting Jesus in a favourable light and so making the people sympathetic to him and running the risk of causing a revolt against the Jewish authorities, who had been responsible for his death, 'of bringing this man's blood upon them', i.e. as it cannot be seen what else this expression could mean, of exposing the leaders of the people to the vengeance of those who had become disciples of Jesus. Here the story in Acts cannot be suspected of minimising the opposition to the preaching of the Twelve. The Jewish authorities were therefore shown to be hostile to their preaching, not because it was thought erroneous or blasphemous, but only because it was thought inopportune and likely to diminish their authority or to create a disturbance hostile to them. It cannot be supposed that this was a conception which originated with the compiler of Acts as he considered that Judaism was hostile in principle to Christianity from the start. Probably then, we have here evidence from a good tradition showing that the Jewish authorities regarded Christian preaching

with some mistrust, not on the grounds that it could not be reconciled with Judaism but on the grounds that it was inopportune and
capable of causing a disturbance and so furnishing the Romans with
a pretext for their intervention which was always dreaded.

Paradoxical as it may seem, the Jewish authorities did not feel
for Jesus' disciples the same hatred which they had shown for him.
They—or at any rate those who formed the circle round the Twelve
—did not adopt the attitude which Jesus had taken up at the end
of his ministry, perhaps because they were too strongly attached to
Judaism to understand it. For by then Jesus had despaired of the
conversion of Israel and so came to think that in place of the Jews
the kingdom of God would be realised among the Gentiles, He had
proclaimed that when he returned as the Son of Man and Messiah
he would destroy and then rebuild the temple, i.e. he would reconstruct the religious economy of Israel.

This is confirmed by the fact that both the Jewish people and
their leaders adopted a very different attitude towards Stephen and
the Hellenists who were the real heirs of the last thoughts of Jesus
from that which they showed towards the Twelve.

We have seen further back[1] how Stephen, inspired by the words
of Jesus about the destruction and reconstruction of the temple,
called the religion of Israel one long act of idolatry. We have now
to gather what we can from the story in Acts what reactions Stephen's
teaching encountered.

Two elements rather artificially joined together can be discerned in
the story devoted to Stephen (vi. 1-viii. 3). There is a narrative and in
the narrative is a speech. That the two were joined together at a later
date may be inferred from the fact that the speech, which is in reality
a missionary sermon and a statement of Stephen's teaching handed
down to us in a mutilated and edited form, is offered as Stephen's
defence in reply to an accusation which had been brought by two
false witnesses. The speech is not a protest against a calumnious accusation but reads as a justification of what Stephen was accused of
having said, viz. that he knew that Jesus on his return would destroy
the temple and change the customs which had been given by Moses.

A rapid analysis of the story shows that it combines two traditions
closely resembling one another but differing on one point which
otherwise is of secondary importance. One of the traditions seems
to have been only a variant of the other. It is related that Stephen,
full of grace and power, did great wonders and miracles among the

[1] See pp. 171 ff.

people and taught in the synagogue of the Libertines and Cyrenians, Alexandrians, and people from Cilicia and Asia with such force that no one could resist the Spirit by whom he spoke. His enemies then stirred up false witnesses against him, who accused him of having uttered blasphemies against Moses and God. They succeeded in stirring up the people, the elders and scribes, i.e. both popular opinion and the authorities. They seized him and dragged him before the Sanhedrin (vi. 8-12). We find here two elements which are placed side by side but are not in perfect harmony with each other. There is the idea of a popular movement and the idea of a regular trial. The fact that there were two sources is supported by what is said in verses 13-14 about false witnesses who appear before the Sanhedrin. They do not play the same part as the false witnesses mentioned in verse 11 who are suborned not to initiate proceedings, but in the course of a trial which has already begun, to give evidence in support of a charge which, if proved, would lead to condemnation to death for blasphemy. They affirm that Stephen does not stop speaking against the Holy Place and the law. They say that they have heard him declare that Jesus of Nazareth would destroy this place, i.e. the temple and would change the customs which had been given by Moses. Stephen was questioned about the accusation by the high-priest; his face then became like that of an angel[1] and then he declaimed the speech which we analysed further back (vi. 15-vii. 53).[2]

Stephen's words put his audience in such a rage that they ground their teeth (vii. 54) and did not allow him to continue his speech. It is clear that the end of the speech was so shortened, or rather mutilated to such an extent, that it became almost unintelligible. The compiler of Acts took refuge in this literary artifice to avoid reporting the conclusion of a speech, which in its outspokenness did not agree with his ideas concerning the relationship between Judaism and Christianity. We are told nothing about the end of the trial or its interruption but pass on at once to the story of the martyrdom. Stephen fell into ecstasy and declared that he saw the heavens opened and the Son of Man on the right hand of God (vii. 55-56).[3] Thereupon, those present threw themselves on Stephen, dragged him out of the city and stoned him. Whether they

---

[1] This means that he is filled with the Holy Spirit.
[2] See pp. 171 ff.
[3] This phrase comes from the declaration of Jesus before the Sanhedrin (Mark xiv. 62 and par.).

were judges or witnesses, accusers, or people who had been following the trial, the text does not tell us. Before he expired Stephen said again, 'Lord, Jesus, receive my spirit', and then, 'Lord, lay not this sin to their charge'.[1] We can see that the end of this story is influenced by two ideas which were current in early Christianity, the effect of which can be easily seen in any of the stories of martyrs. One is that the martyr is not a testimony given by a Christian of his faith but a testimony given by God of Himself through his spirit inspiring him. The other is that the martyr, naturally in varying degrees and with varying shades of exactness, imitated the passion of Christ.[2] The two traditions, one showing Stephen as a victim of popular fury, and the other as a criminal condemned by the Sanhedrin after a more or less regular trial are so closely interwoven in the narrative in Acts that it is impossible to distinguish what comes from one and what comes from the other. It is equally impossible to find out which one reproduces with greater accuracy what actually happened. One consideration inclines us to favour the idea that there was a regular trial, although it is not decisive. It is that, if there had been a popular outbreak, it would have been difficult for the Roman authorities to have shut their eyes and refrained from taking measures to quell it. If the compiler of Acts had known of any action on their part he would not have failed to mention it, as it would have supported his cherished prejudice that it was the Roman government which prevented the hatred of the Jews for the Christians having full play. It is of course true that the author of Acts wrote too long after the event for us to be certain that he knew what were the consequences of the murder of Stephen for the Jews. It is not impossible that the Roman government shut its eyes to a popular agitation which was not in any way directed against it.

According to the compiler of Acts (viii. 1) a general persecution of the church at Jerusalem followed Stephen's martyrdom and all its members were compelled to scatter in Judaea and Samaria with the exception of the apostles. Quite naturally those who belonged to Stephen's group and shared his ideas were alarmed and could only secure safety by leaving the city. In addition they were not kept at Jerusalem out of devotion to the temple and its worship. But the

---

[1] These sayings come from those reported in Luke xxiii. 46 and xxiii. 34. As they are not given by Mark it must be supposed that they are due to literary elaboration.

[2] Not only the writers of the stories of the martyrs were influenced by the stories of the passion. It is certain that in many cases at least the martyrs must have forced themselves to assimilate their demeanour to that of Jesus, the martyr's model.

compiler of Acts failed to understand the real relationship between the Hellenist group directed by the Seven and the Hebraic group directed by the Twelve and misunderstood the character of this persecution. Apart from this, we do not see how in a general persecution the apostles, who should have been the first to be threatened, could have remained in Jerusalem without being disturbed. The narrative also fails to explain how it happened that shortly afterwards the persecution ceased and the Hebraists are rediscovered reunited in Jerusalem (ix. 31).

Saul of Tarsus played an important part in the persecution of Stephen and the Hellenists; all the statements referring to this are so clumsily fitted into the narrative that they look as if they were editorial additions (vii. 58; viii. 1, 3). But the compiler may have introduced Saul into a story in which originally he was not mentioned by name, because he had good reason for doing so and knew either from another source or from a tradition worthy of credence that the future apostle had taken an effective part in these persecutions. The question where Paul persecuted the church is then quite unsettled. That he did so is attested by Paul himself in such terms that it cannot be called in question (Phil. iii. 6; Gal. i. 13; 1 Cor. xv. 9; cf. 1 Tim. i. 13). Unfortunately these allusions make no mention of the circumstances of his part in persecution as his readers were perfectly aware of them.

Some scholars[1] think that the statement of Acts (vii. 58; viii. 1-3; ix. 1-2) that Paul persecuted the Christians at Jerusalem must be considered doubtful. They think the future apostle came into contact with Christianity for the first time in the district of Damascus and there first tried to destroy it. In support of their contention they first of all invoke the fact that the high-priest could not give Paul full powers to act in Damascus and bring back to him the Christians whom he found there. The synagogues at Damascus were not under his jurisdiction. But actually the text does not speak of full powers but only of letters of recommendation; the high-priest, we know, enjoyed a moral authority which would allow him to do

---

[1] Mommsen, 'Die Rechtsverhaltnisse des Apostels Paulus,' *Z.N.T.W.*, 1901, II, p. 80; Loisy, *L'ép, aux Gal.*, p. 69; *Actes*, p. 389; Schwartz, 'Zur. Chron.', *N.G.*, 1907, p. 375; Heitmuller, 'Zum Problem Jesus und Paulus', *Z.N.T.W.*, 1912, XIII, pp. 327 ff.; Wellhausen, *Noton*, *N.G.*, 1907, p. 9; *Krit. An.*, *A.G.*, 1914, p. 55; Preuschen, *D. Apgsch.*, p. 55. To the arguments generally used to deny that Paul persecuted in Jerusalem Guignebert (*Le Christ*, pp. 250 f.) adds a new one. He thinks that if Paul had persecuted the church in Jerusalem, he would have considered it part of his duty to have repaired the evil which he had done. This is a rather bold psychological interpretation.

this.[1] Secondly, they invoke the fact that in Galatians i. 17, where Paul is speaking of the period immediately following his conversion he does not say, 'I did not return to Jerusalem', but 'I did not go up', which shows, they say, that he had not been there before his conversion. But the context does not call for any allusion to where Paul was before he went to Damascus. Throughout the whole of the passage Paul takes his conversion to be the beginning of something absolutely new in his life. He tries to offer a very clear picture of his relations with Jerusalem from the time he became a Christian in order to prove that he did not receive his gospel from the Twelve. From this point of view his previous sojourns in Jerusalem are irrelevant. He has no reason to mention them. They also point out that, when Paul is speaking of the period which, after his visit to Peter, he spent in Syria and Cilicia, he says, 'I was unknown by face unto the churches of Judaea which were in Christ. But they had heard only, that he which persecuted us in times past now preacheth the faith which once he destroyed. And they glorified God in me' (Gal. i. 22-24). How then, it may be asked, if Paul had persecuted the churches in Judaea, could he have been unknown to them? But the terms here used by Paul must not be pressed too hard; otherwise we meet with another contradiction, the Christians of Judaea saying that Paul persecuted them and yet they did not know him.[2]

At the time when these persecutions took place the church was not yet an institution set up in opposition to the synagogue. It was only a small group of brethren who continued to worship as Jews but met at each others' houses. Persecution could only have consisted of measures against individuals who had first of all to be hunted out. In such conditions Christians had every possible reason for avoiding meeting their enemies. The struggle might have gone on without any contact taking place between the persecutor and his victims. The result was the emigration of the Hellenists. Also the church grew so rapidly with the result that at the time of which Galatians i. 22-24 is speaking the churches in Judaea must have been made up for the most part of people who were not members in the days when Paul was persecuting them.

It must be added that apart from Damascus we have no evidence at all for the existence of groups of Christians outside Judaea before Paul's conversion. It is easy to understand why a punitive expedition

[1] Ed. Meyer, *Urspr. u. Anf.* III, p. 163.
[2] Ed. Meyer, *Urspr. u. Anf.* III, p. 162. Wernle, 'Jesus und Paulus, Antithesen zu Boussets Kyrios Christes', *Z.f.Th.u.K.*, 1915, XXV, p. 57.

was taken in hand against the Christians at Damascus if their group, which may have been founded by Hellenists who came from Jerusalem, was the only one existing at that time outside Jerusalem.

The arguments used then to try and prove that it was not at Jerusalem that Paul persecuted the Christians are not convincing. But the book of the Acts does not provide strong enough evidence for it to be considered proved that the churches in Judaea were the victims of Paul's persecution. But, as the theories concerning the existence of Christian groups in the diaspora previous to the dispersion of the Hellenists independent of the church in Jerusalem are purely conjectural in character, the hypothesis that Paul persecuted Christianity in Jerusalem seems the most reasonable.

Acts does not say how the persecution against the Hellenists finished. It only remarks, after the story of Paul's conversion, that the church in Judaea, Galilee, and Samaria enjoyed peace (ix. 31). This would have been somewhat surprising, if the aim of the persecution had not been the Hellenists and had not stopped as soon as they had left Jerusalem. Acts does not say explicitly that persecution broke out again at the time of Paul's first visit as a convert to Jerusalem but hints that he then found that he was in danger and had to leave for Caesarea and from there went to Tarsus (ix. 29-30). The epistle to the Galatians (i. 19) to some extent supports this hint, when it says that on his first visit to Peter, Paul acted with reserve and apart from Peter made no contact with anyone but James. Unfortunately we do not know if his attitude was dictated by hostility from the Jews who had been enraged by his sharp turn-round or by mistrust on the part of the Christians in Jerusalem generated by the way in which he was already preaching the gospel to the Gentiles.

The first epistle to the Thessalonians provides evidence, which unfortunately is rather vague, as it is just a bare allusion to the persecution of the churches of Judaea. Speaking of what the Thessalonians have had to suffer at the hands of their fellow citizens, Paul says to them, 'For ye, brethren, became followers of the churches of God which in Judaea are in Christ Jesus: for ye also have suffered like things of your own countrymen, even as they have of the Jews: who hath killed the Lord Jesus, and their own prophets, and have persecuted us; and they please not God, and are contrary to all men: forbidding us to speak to the Gentiles, that they might be saved, to fill up their sins alway: for the wrath is come upon them to the uttermost' (ii. 14-16).

Although Paul's words seem to mean that the persecutions in

Judaea were taking place when he was writing, they must not be understood exactly in that sense. Paul did not have at Corinth where he was writing to the Thessalonians any sources of information at his disposal as to what was happening in Judaea. He seems to have been alluding to what had taken place at the time of the persecution against the Hellenists, to be generalising from what he found in the diaspora by supposing that the situation was the same in Judaea. Thus his statement cannot outweigh the evidence of Acts that persecution ceased after the dispersion of the Hellenists.[1]

There is no doubt that the peace enjoyed by the church in Jerusalem after the departure of the Hellenists must have begun at the end of 29 or 30 and seems to have lasted until 44. In that year a short but sharp storm disturbed the church. Popular Jewish opinion had been disturbed by the concessions, which the pillars of the church at Jerusalem had just made to Paul and Barnabas, who stood for the idea that the Gentiles could be saved without being bound to observe the Jewish ritual law, although they were trifling and paper concessions at that. By an unfortunate coincidence for the Christians Judaea was not at that time being administered by procurators. The old kingdom of Herod the Great had been restored in favour of his grandson, Herod Agrippa I. Although he was really pagan at heart, perhaps just because of this his political policy at home was to humour in the extreme the religious convictions of his subjects.[2] And so he seized this opportunity for doing so and giving them satisfaction by acting with harsh rigour against those who had out-raged the law by showing themselves conciliatory towards Paul.

The compiler of Acts saw no real connection between the con-ference at Jerusalem and the persecution; but he shows that they both happened at the same time because he brackets the story of the persecution between two fragments, one telling of the departure of Paul and Barnabas from Antioch for Jerusalem (xi. 27-30), and the other of their return to Antioch (xii. 25).[3]

The story of the persecution is briefly told with little detail. We are not told why Herod Agrippa determined to act but it does reveal that the king was not condemning the whole church but

---

[1] It is difficult to share Harnack's opinion (*Mission*, I, p. 47, n. 1) that the saying in Matthew x. 17, 'they will deliver you up to the councils', is sufficient to prove the reality of persecutions in Judaea.

[2] For the way in which Herod Agrippa pretended at Jerusalem to be a zealous Jew, see the evidence of Josephus, *A.j.* xix. 6, 1; 7, 3.

[3] Concerning the confused ideas of the compiler of Acts as to the date and purpose of this visit see p. 294, n. 1.

only some of its leaders. It says, 'Herod stretched forth his hands to vex (κακῶσαι) certain of the church. And he killed James the brother of John with the sword' (xii. 1-2). There are very good reasons for thinking that the earliest text or the text of the source had the words 'James and his brother John'.[1] What is said of James (and John) is not an addition to the expression 'vexing certain members of the church' but is given to illustrate it and supports the hypothesis that the persecution was directed only at some of the most prominent personalities who were thought to be responsible for the concessions which had been made to Paul. Peter just escaped being one of them. Encouraged by the favourable impression the killing of James (and John) had made on the Jews, Herod had Peter arrested but delayed his trial[2] because the feast of the Passover and unleavened bread was at hand. While Peter was in prison the church prayed intently for his release.[3] Acts relates that the night before the day when he was to be tried or executed Peter was miraculously released by an angel of the Lord. After he had rejoined the brethren whom he found gathered together at the house of Mary, John Mark's mother, he left the city for what place the story does not say. He seems to have left it for good (xii. 3-17). It is difficult to disentangle from this story what is to be considered historical. Perhaps Peter was not actually put in prison but was only threatened in such a way that he had to flee secretly and the impression was left that only a miracle could have saved him. Perhaps he really was put in prison and managed to escape through a conspiracy[4] on which silence had to be kept, which helped to create a legend that he was miraculously released.

[1] A fragment published by C. de Boor (*Neue Fragmente des Papias, Hegesippus und Pierius aus der Kirchengeschichte des Philippus Sidetes*, Leipzig, 1888, p. 170) contains the following, 'Papias reports in his second book that John the divine and James, his brother, were killed by the Jews'. Mark x. 35-40 contains a prophecy *ex eventu* of the martyrdom of the two brothers (see on this subject my observations: 'Deux notes d'exégèse, *R.h.r.*, 1941, CXXIII, pp. 27-42). For some other clues which go to strengthen Papias's evidence see *Intr.* II, pp. 92 ff.   It must be added that Eusebius (*H.e.* ii. 9, 1-3) relates that according to the *Hypotyposes* of Clement of Alexandria the man who brought James before the council was so touched when he heard him confess his faith that he declared himself a Christian and was beheaded with the apostles. It is difficult to share Dom Leclercq's opinion (art. 'Jacques le Majeur', *D.A.C.L.*, VII, col. 2092) that there is no good reason for rejecting this evidence but it may have been that the tradition received by Clement showed traces that it was remembered that James did not perish by himself.

[2] Or his execution. The text is not clear.

[3] The fact that he alone was the object of the church's prayers leads us to think that no other Christians were imprisoned.

[4] The suggestion of a conspiracy was put forward by Grundmann, 'Die Apostel zwischen Jerusalem und Antiochia', *Z.N.T.W.*, 1940, XXXIX, p. 129, n. 41.

The persecution of 44 was short. Was this only because Herod died before he got it under way?[1] This seems unlikely as the story in Acts informs us that it had already come to an end when Herod left Jerusalem for Caesarea. Possibly the restoration of the rule of the procurator made it more difficult for the Jews to show their hostility to the Christians or to some of them, although the persecution seems to have ended before the king died. Perhaps Jewish public opinion, which had been for a time disquieted by the conference of Jerusalem, was reassured by the transfer, after Peter's departure, of the leadership of the church of Jerusalem into the hands of James, who was a strict Jewish legalist.

The peace which the church of Jerusalem seems to have enjoyed from 44 onwards was not even disturbed in 58, when Paul was the victim of Jewish hatred and the Sanhedrin made every effort to have him delivered to them in order that they might try him for desecrating the temple. In the eyes of the Jews the Christians in Jerusalem were not associated with him.[2]

The peace was not broken in 62 on the death of James, who, as we saw,[3] was killed by force at the hands of the high-priest Annas, who was jealous of his popularity. As the people who were most strongly attached to the law protested at the action of the high-priest, it is clear that Christians at Jerusalem were considered to be a Jewish sect whom no one thought of expelling from Judaism and that some Christians at any rate enjoyed great popularity in the city.

The fact that the Christians left the city before the war or before the siege cannot be considered a sign that there had been a rupture between the church in Jerusalem and Judaism. It only proves that they were not on the side of the Zealots but that was true of many other people.[4]

After 70 force of circumstances brought about a change in the character of the relationship between Jews and Christians. Judaism became completely hostile even to those forms of Christianity, which it had till then tolerated, but it was left without any means of direct action against the Christians. The era of theological discussion between them began. The Jews indulged in systematic apologetic and polemic both to prevent new conversions and to bring back deserters to the religion of their fathers. In reply, the church was not less thorough in trying to prevent returns to Judaism and to make fresh conversions among the Jews.

[1] See pp. 21 f.   [2] See pp. 126 f.
[3] See pp. 319 f.   [4] See pp. 132 f.

The Reactions of the Jews in the Diaspora and the first interventions of Rome prompted by them

THE Roman authorities did not take action against the disciples of Jesus at Jerusalem. We have seen in the preceding chapter that, on the contrary, the rule of the procurators gave the Christians protection against the measures which the Jews might have tried to take against them. From the Roman point of view, the affair Jesus, if the phrase may be used, seems to have been considered definitely closed by the execution of the sentence pronounced by Pilate. After this in every incident right up to Paul's trial, the Roman authorities in Palestine do not seem to have made any distinction between Jews and Christians.[1] At first the same was true in the diaspora: for a long time Christians were confused with the Jews. But the latter went to work to clear up this confusion with such perseverance that we cannot help but think that they were working according to a set plan. So far as they succeeded they rendered the situation of the Christians in the empire very precarious. As soon as they ceased to enjoy the favoured treatment which had been awarded to Judaism, they found themselves without legal status, on the fringe of society and subject to the penalty of death, because they practised an illicit religion.

Judaism enjoyed an exceptional position in the empire. It had received considerable privileges through a series of public decrees which had been renewed and confirmed by Caesar and Augustus.[2]

---

[1] This fact confirms the conclusions which we reached in the preceding chapter concerning the tranquillity which the Christians appear to have enjoyed in Palestine.

[2] See Schurer, *Gesch.* III, pp. 66 ff.; Juster, *Les Juifs dans l'Empire romain*, I, pp. 213-242.

Jewish communities possessed wide powers of self-government; they had rights of association and could exercise discipline over their members. Jews were exempt from all participation in public worship; they could take oaths without calling upon the gods. Their scruples concerning the sabbath were respected. They were not bound to appear in a law-court on that day and, when distributions to the people were made on a Saturday, they were repeated the next day specially for them. All this was possible because Judaism was considered to be the national religion of a people[1] who had been the friend and ally of the Roman people before they became vassals.

In theory, only Jews by race were allowed to practise their religion. They did not possess the right to evangelise on its behalf but in practice every synagogue was a centre of active propaganda and proselytes or 'God-fearers', who became members of the synagogues, seem generally speaking to have been undisturbed.[2] They must have been too few in numbers for anyone, so far as they were known, to think that they constituted a danger to the safety of society and the maintenance of order in the Roman empire. The groups which they formed lacked sufficient organisation and were too exclusive to make them appear dangerous. These privileges are all the more striking as Roman society had a poor opinion of the Jews and misunderstood them. Even Romans of great distinction[3] accepted the most stupid calumnies against them. But their legal position in the empire was so strong that it remained unshaken during the Jewish war and after the capture of Jerusalem.

2.—THE EFFORTS OF THE JEWS TO COUNTER CHRISTIAN PROPAGANDA, ESPECIALLY PAUL'S MISSIONARY WORK

One of the points which interests us most closely is the right possessed by the Jewish communities to exercise discipline over their own members, even over those who possessed the privileges

---

[1] They were attracted to Judaism but did not make any formal profession of their allegiance.

[2] Sometimes it was different as, for example, under Domitian. See p. 529.

[3] See especially what Tacitus (*Hist.* v. 2 ff.) says of the Jews in reference to whom he uses the words *mos absurdus sordidusque*. Similar expressions had previously been used by Cicero (*barbara superstitio. Pro Flaeco*, 28) and by the Elder Pliny (*gens sontumelia numinum insignis, Hist. nat.*, xiii. 4, 46). On antisemitism in the Greco-Roman world see Schurer, *Gesch.* III, pp. 102 ff.; M. Schuld, *Les préventions de Rome contre la nation juive*, Paris, 1882; Hild, 'Les Juifs devant l'opinion romaine', *R.e.j.*, 1885, II, pp. 176 ff.; C. Thiaucourt, 'Ce que Tacite dit des Juifs au commencement du livre V des Histoires', *R.e.j.* XIX, pp. 57-74; Gaston Boissier, *Tacite sur les Juifs in Mélanges offerts à Mgr de Cabrière*, Paris, 1899, I, pp. 81-96.

of Roman citizenship provided of course they wished to remain Jews. The only penalty they could not inflict was that of death, but the 'leaders of the synagogues' had the right of punishing Jews by beating[1] and of pronouncing sentence of excommunication.[2] It seems to have taken two forms, one light, the other heavy. One (*nidda*) was temporary; the other (*heron*) was permanent. We do not know what use was made of these disciplinary measures in the struggle against Christianity, but plainly they could only be used as long as Christians were content to remain within the synagogue and had not resigned themselves to forming themselves into separate groups. More than anything else they must have been used as a means of preventing Jews from being converted.[3]

But the means used by the Jews to hinder the Christian mission were indirect. They made every effort to persuade the Roman authorities that Christians were not Jews or had ceased to be so and consequently had no right to the privileges of Judaism. They seem also sometimes to have created riots for the purpose of giving the impression that the existence of Christian communities was a perpetual cause of agitation and disorder. According to the early church the Jews organised a proper campaign to fight the preaching of the gospel.[4] Justin Martyr, who mentions several times the way in which Christ and the Christians were cursed in the synagogue,[5] when addressing the Jew Tryphon says as follows, 'When you knew that he (Jesus) was risen from the dead and had ascended into heaven, as the prophets foretold, you not only refused to repent but chose delegates whom you sent into the whole world to say that an impious heresy, that of the Christians, had appeared and to publish calumnies against us which people who do not know us repeat'.[6]

[1] Concerning this punishment which was ordained by Deut. xxv. 3, see Strack-Billerbeck, III, pp. 527-530. The apostle submitted to it five times (2 Cor. xi. 24).

[2] Concerning exclusion from the synagogue see Strack-Billerbeck, IV, pp. 293-333. John (ix. 22) is plainly guilty of an anachronism when he speaks of a decision to exclude from the synagogue anyone who acknowledged Jesus as Messiah. It is quite likely that a principle of this kind was decided upon after 70.

[3] For the same purpose the curses against the *minim* and the *nosrim* were used, i.e. against heretics and Christians. The *Schmone Esre*, a prayer which every Jew had to use three times a day, contained them from the first century onwards. The text and translation will be found in Strack, *Jesus, die Haretiker und die Christen nach der altesten judischen Angaben*, pp. 30 f., 64 ff. Cf. Schurer, *Gesch.* II, pp. 463 ff. [4] Harnack, *Mission*, I, p. 61.

[5] Justin, *Dial.* xvi. 4; xlvii. 5; xciii. 4; xcv. 4; xcvi. 2; cviii. 3; cxvii. 3; cxxxiii. 6; cxxxvii. 2.

[6] Justin, *Dial.* xvii. 1; cf. cviii. 2. The same idea is found later on in Eusebius, *in Jesaj.* 18, 1 and in Macarius of Magnesia, iii. 22, 29.

Justin and his successors constantly express the idea, that always and everywhere, the Jews incited the Gentiles against the Christians and are therefore the real people responsible for the persecutions. *Synagogae Judaeorum fontes persecutionum*, Tertullian says.[1] Justin's remarks about a kind of counter propaganda of a preventive kind undertaken by the Jews doubtless originated in the impression conveyed by the book of Acts and certain passages from Paul's epistles such as 1 Thessalonians ii. 15-16, where the apostle speaks of Jews who 'prevent us from preaching to the Gentiles lest they should be saved'.[2] But if we look at these references closer, they do not tell of counter propaganda organised by Jews. The opposition which faced Paul everywhere he went may perfectly well have been a spontaneous product and the natural reaction of the Jews to the preaching of the gospel, which spread in certain districts from town to town, as is shown particularly in the story of the mission to Macedonia.

It is certainly no accident that in the first incident reported in Acts in the story of Paul's first missionary journey, which is his encounter with the proconsul Sergius Paulus at Paphos, his enemy is portrayed to be the magician and false prophet, the Jew Elymas Bar-Jesus, who tries to dissuade the proconsul from becoming a Christian and is struck by Paul with blindness (Acts xiii. 6-12). The incident is full of obscurities.[3] The compiler thinks that it proves the superiority of the gospel and the futility of all its enemies' efforts to prevent its victory. The attitude of the proconsul who

---

[1] Tertullian, *Scorpiacum*, 10. Cf. Justin, *Dial*. xvi. 4; xcv. 4; cxxii. 2; cxxxiii. 6. *Apol*. I, xxxi. 5. Irenaeus, *Adv. Haer*. iv. 28, 3. Origen, *C. Celsum*, vi. 27.

[2] Possibly also Justin and the Christian writers after him thought that allusions in the epistles to the Galatians and the Corinthians to Jewish Christians who troubled the churches of Galatia and Greece referred to Jewish agents of counter-propaganda.

[3] The story is full of obscurities. Particularly noticeable are those concerning the name of the person. D. and some other texts have *Etoimas* instead of *Elymas*, a name which for some unknown reason the compiler considered to be the equivalent of Bar-Jesus (= son of Jesus) (cf. v. 8). According to a conjecture of Hugo Grotius adopted by Grimme (*Elymas der Astrolog. Orient. Litzg*., 1909, pp. 209-211) the name came from the Arabic and means 'the Magician'. But how would a Jew come to have an Arabic name? Burkitt ('The interpretation of "Bar-Jesus"', *Journ. of theol. St*., 1903, IV, pp. 127-129) saw in Elymas a corruption of ὁ λοιμός (= the pest). Rendel Harris ('A curious Bezan reading vindicated', *Expositor*, 1902, VI, 5, pp. 189-195) and Zahn ('Zur Lebensgeschichte des Apostels Paulus', *N. Kirchl. Z*., 1904, XV, pp. 195-200) adopt the reading *Etoimas* from the manuscript D., and identify the person as the Jewish magician Atomos who arranged Felix's marriage with Drusilla (Josephus, *A.j*. xx. 7, 2). The reading Atomos is given by Niese in his edition of Josephus according to the manuscript of Milan and the *Epitomy*. The other manuscripts have '*Simon*'.

listens impartially both to the missionaries of the gospel and their opponents is offered as a model for imitation. Although the significance which the compiler gives to the incident is clear, it is difficult to extract from it its historical core. As Judaism formally condemned magic, how far could a magician be considered to be an authentic' representative of Judaism? The compiler may have described someone as a Jew who was not one.[1] This is supported by the fact that Paul does not use scripture in his argument against him but confines himself to calling him a son of the devil and a corrupter of the ways of the Lord. In any case the compiler would seem to have given the incident a different significance from what it had in the original source.[2] It exemplifies the compiler's theory that Paul's preaching was subject to constant and systematic opposition at the hands of the Jews. The incident also betrays a certain contradiction with the paragraph preceding it, which says, without mentioning any incident, that Barnabas and Paul crossed the whole of the island of Cyprus from Salais to Paphos preaching in the synagogues.

From Cyprus the missionaries went to Antioch in Pisidia where on the Sabbath day Paul preached in the synagogue (xiii. 16-41). We are not told anything of the effect of the sermon; it is only said that they asked that 'these words might be preached to them the next Sabbath' (xiii. 42). This may well mean that, before the authorities gave Barnabas and Paul permission to speak, they wanted to take precautions and at any rate to gain time. We can find confirmation for this hypothesis in the fact that the sermon cannot possibly be Paul's but is the composition of the compiler of Acts.[3] It is said that on leaving the synagogue many Jews went with Barnabas and Paul and listened to their exhortations. Paul's activity, therefore, at Antioch in Pisidia seems at the beginning to have been confined to the synagogue as it is reported that on the following Sabbath the whole town gathered together to hear the missionaries. On this occasion uproar broke out in the synagogue, marked by violent opposition from the Jews. This supports the hypothesis that on the previous Sabbath nothing happened except that the missionaries and the synagogue authorities made contact with each

[1] This would explain the Arabic name according to the hypothesis of Grotius and Grimme. It may be that Elymas belonged to a gnostic syncretistic group.
[2] This is one reason for thinking that it was not a complete invention.
[3] For the reasons which prevent me from attributing the sermon to Paul see *Introd.* III, pp. 233 ff. The essential point is that in xiii. 31 it is said that only those who went up to Jerusalem with Jesus saw him after his resurrection. This is contrary to Paul's most explicit declarations.

other and that the compiler completely changed the story of what happened by introducing into the scene a sermon of his own composition which did not belong to his source. This time when Paul 'proclaimed the word of God' the Jews in the presence of the crowd, whom we must assume listened with favour to the apostle's preaching, set about to contradict him and blaspheme against his words. It was not just the presence of the crowd and Jewish jealousy at Paul's apparent ascendancy over it which created the opposition now appearing. It was Paul's message. It must have shown itself as soon as they met each other. An inevitable rupture took place. Paul declared that the Word of God must first be addressed to the Jews but, as they rejected it and did not consider themselves worthy of eternal life, he was now going to address himself to the Gentiles (xiii. 44-49).

Paul naturally always began his mission in the synagogue both for doctrinal reasons, because in principle the gospel was intended for the Jews first (Rom. i. 16), and for practical reasons, because the synagogue provided the missionaries with a platform ready to hand. He was also very soon excluded from it, at least where he did not leave it himself.[1] But the story in Acts concerning Antioch in Pisidia seems to have been to some extent written up to meet certain *a priori* ideas. It hides the fact that the Apostle was from the beginning received with suspicion and that he did not wait to be hunted out of the synagogue before addressing himself both to Jews and Gentiles at the same time.

Acts makes out that Jewish opposition at Antioch in Pisidia was not altogether doctrinal and religious but used tricks and manoeuvres to make the position of the Apostle difficult. The Jews made use of their influence with some women of high rank who were proselytes and some persons of importance and created a disturbance against Paul and Barnabas which is described as 'persecution'.[2] Barnabas and Paul were pursued and wiping the dust off their feet went to Iconium. But the narrative goes on to note that their work was not in vain; it says that the disciples[3] were full of joy and the holy Spirit. It is all singularly confused and vague. We cannot tell if the missionaries were driven out or if, in face of growing

---

[1] There are domestic reasons for this. The forms of service in the synagogue, even when the Jews were favourable, could find no place for certain essential elements of Christian worship such as baptism and the celebration of the supper of the Lord.

[2] The Western text contains 'a great tribulation and a persecution'.

[3] It means believers òf Antioch in Pisidia.

opposition which was becoming threatening, they thought it preferable to depart. The words, 'they expelled them out of their country', would make one lean to the former interpretation, while the expression, 'they shook the dust off their feet' would favour the latter. There is, however, another possibility to be thought of: Paul and Barnabas may never have intended to stay long at Antioch in Pisidia but to depart because they were content to establish in the town a small Christian nucleus. The vague way in which their departure is mentioned would harmonise perfectly well with such an interpretation.

Amongst the reasons which lead us to think that the compiler of Acts rewrote the narrative concerning Paul and Barnabas at Antioch in Pisidia as he found it in his source, there must be included the striking parallelism between what happened at Antioch and the subsequent events at Iconium (xiv. 2-7). There also many Greeks are converted. It is not said whether they were proselytes, although Paul is not deemed yet to have spoken outside the synagogue. The Jews who remained hostile stirred up the Greeks. The result was a combined attack on the part of the Jews, the Gentiles, and the Jewish authorities to injure the missionaries, who, foreseeing what was going to happen, took precautions and escaped to the towns of Lycaonia, Lystra, and Derbe, where they preached the gospel. The incoherence of this statement which mentions the towns together and the absence in the story of any concrete facts give the impression that the story has been constructed on the same plan and to illustrate the same ideas as the one concerning Antioch in Pisidia.

At Lystra an impotent man is healed: the story offers disturbing analogies with the one reported in chapter ii. Such enthusiasm was raised that Barnabas and Paul were taken for Zeus and Hermes and had the greatest difficulty in preventing sacrifice being offered to them (xiv. 8-18). Without any transition, the situation changed completely. Jews who had come from Antioch and Iconium stirred up the crowd against Paul who was dragged out of the city, stoned, and left for dead. But he got up again, returned to the town and the next morning left for Derbe. Only one sentence mentions the evangelisation of Derbe (xiv. 1-2), after which it is said that the missionaries returned on their steps, passed back through Lystra, Iconium and Antioch, exhorting the brethren that through much tribulation they must enter the kingdom of God. At the same time they set up elders in each town (xiv. 21-23). No explanation is given as to how the missionaries could, without being disturbed, return through the towns from which a little time before they had been chased out with violence. Although the exhortation about the sufferings awaiting the believers hints at opposition to the gospel, it is not the kind of opposition which it is said the apostles have been facing. This is not just opposition directed at the missionaries but at all those who have been converted as well.

The obscurities, incoherences, and even the contradictions to be found in the narrative of the first missionary journey show that the compiler's source for this part of his narrative was inferior to that which he goes on to use when he is recounting the evangelisation of Macedonia. At the most he seems to have had before him a bare itinerary which he has filled out with literary embellishments, combined perhaps with some incidents borrowed from an oral tradition which was already inaccurate and confused, the whole composition being dominated by his *a priori* conception of Jewish opposition to the preaching of the gospel.

The story of the second missionary journey from Paul's arrival in Macedonia provides us with more solid ground. The compiler of Acts had for this an excellent source. Unfortunately he has not reproduced it as a whole but has made excisions and additions. He did this for two reasons. First of all the aim of the compiler, which was to show the progress of Christianity from Jerusalem to the ends of the world, was not that which the author of the source had in view. A companion of Paul, he was most probably the doctor Luke, who simply wanted to recount the apostle's missionary work. Secondly the compiler of Acts had a subsidiary end in view; he wanted his work to be an apology and to show that Christianity was nothing more than an extension of Judaism and remained loyal to the promises which were the core and foundation of the religion of Israel. Consequently, his argument ran, Christianity had the right to enjoy the privileged position in the empire which had been accorded to Judaism and therefore, if sometimes the Roman authorities denied it this right, they had allowed themselves to be deceived by Jewish intrigue.

The story of Paul's activity at Philippi (xvi. 11-40) shows signs of having been abbreviated. The narrative assumes that Paul preached both to the Jews and Gentiles but it does not say how he came into contact with them. After narrating how Lydia, a seller of purple, a native of Thyatira, received Paul and Silas (xvi. 11-15) it is said that the owners of a slave girl, whom Paul and Silas freed from an evil spirit, which had enabled her to practise the art of divination to the pecuniary advantage of her owners, brought the missionaries before the magistrates with an accusation which had nothing to do with the real reasons for their complaint. They accused them of being Jews who preached a way of life which Romans could not follow. The accusation is supported by the crowd, although it is not previously stated that they had been disturbed by the preaching of the gospel. What took place before the magistrates to whom the case was submitted is not reported. This suggests that the compiler did not wish to dwell on facts which failed to support his own pre-conceptions. All that is said, is that the magistrates had Paul and Silas scourged and put in prison.[1] This shows that they were judged guilty on the charge that they were propagating a *religio illicita*.[2] The author of Acts could not entirely pass over what happened at Philippi and did not wish to do so, but he at least wanted to play them down as much as possible; he does this by making out that the motive which set in train the proceedings in which Paul and Silas were involved was of a trivial nature, nothing more than the annoyance of the owners of the slave girl at their material interests being endangered. But the intervention of the crowd shows quite clearly that the motives behind the opposition were of a different kind, being in fact of a religious order. Nevertheless—and this ought to be underlined—the narrative shows clearly that the initiative in the opposition to Paul came not from the Jews but from the Gentiles.

What happened afterwards at Thessalonica supports this con-clusion. Although the source is not reproduced as a whole here, we can arrive at a fairly clear idea of what it described. After a note of a general kind about some proselytes and some of the better-class women being converted by a preaching in the synagogue (xvii. 1-4) the story relates the circumstances which led to the departure of Paul and Silas. The compiler has let fall what in his source referred

---

[1] I Thess. ii. 2 confirms the fact that Paul was a victim of violence at Philippi.

[2] It is afterwards related that Paul and Silas were miraculously released during the night. This bears a striking analogy to the story of Peter's release in chapter xii. Chapter xii, it is certain, is the earlier composition, as Peter's release is effective, while Paul and Silas the next morning are back in prison. The piece is also shown to be an addition by the fact that, after reporting this, the narrative continues as if nothing had happened, with this addition that, when the magistrates knew that Paul and Silas were Roman citizens, i.e. that they had acted illegally towards them, they asked them to leave the town, although, before they knew this, they had without any ado given them back their liberty.

to Paul's preaching to the Gentiles, as the first epistle to the Thessalonians makes it plain that the church at Thessalonica was principally composed of members of Gentile origin who had had to suffer at the hands of their Gentile fellow-citizens (ii. 14 f.). There is no reason for supposing that Paul is alluding only to things which happened after his departure from Thessalonica. This makes us think that the preaching to the Gentiles had created spontaneous opposition in which Jewish intrigue had no part at all.

The narrative in Acts makes the Jews responsible for Paul's departure from Thessalonica, which would more accurately be called an expulsion. Jealous of his success they stirred up vagabonds who haunt public squares and sent them to attack the house of Jason, who had given Paul hospitality.[1] As they failed to find the missionaries there, they dragged Jason and some of the brethren before the magistrates. The accusation levelled against them because they gave hospitality to Paul and Silas shows no sign of Jewish intervention. It is formulated in these words, 'These that have turned the world upside down are come hither also; whom Jason hath received: and these all do contrary to the decrees of Caesar, saying that there is another king (*basileus*)[2] one Jesus' (xvii. 5-7). There are two charges, (1) that Paul and Silas had transgressed a law of the empire, which can only be the one which forbids the propagation of strange religions which have not been adopted or ratified by the senate.[3] (2) That they had proclaimed Jesus *basileus*, which can only mean one thing, i.e. that they were rebels against the lawful *basileus*, Caesar. They were therefore guilty of both the crime of lese-majesty on account of their religious illicit propaganda and the crime of high treason. All this is conceived from the Roman and not from the Jewish point of view. Plainly, it might be imagined that, in order to obtain the expulsion of the missionaries, which they thought desirable, the Jews might have advanced charges which did not interest them but which they knew were the sort that would make an impression on the Roman authorities. But in actual fact this explanation cannot be retained, as there is no allusion to any conflict between the missionaries and the synagogue, which the compiler would have had no reason to pass over in silence,

---

[1] It is only in the course of the narrative that it is said that Jason was Paul's host. The fact that it is not stated explicitly shows that the source has been abridged.

[2] The term *basileus* means both king and emperor.

[3] Cicero (*De legibus*, ii. 8) mentions this law which was thought to go back to Numa. '*Nemo habesset deos sive novos, sive advenas nisi publice adscitos.*' The punishment for transgression of this law was death.

477

if he had found any mention of it in his source.[1] The author seems then to have created the idea that the movement was created by professional agitators hired by the Jews to hide the fact that the preaching of the gospel at Thessalonica met with spontaneous opposition from Gentile public opinion. This is supported by the fact that the story of what happened at Thessalonica before the magistrates is abridged to such an extent that it has become incomprehensible and incoherent. The magistrates were as much impressed, it seems, by the accusation as by the attitude of the crowd, and after making Jason and those with him pay a deposit, sent them away. In the following night the brethren made Paul and Silas leave for Beroea (xvii. 8-10). The story seeks to give the impression that the initiative to get them away was taken by the brethren to appease their minds. But the caution money demanded by Jason must have guaranteed something, which could only have been the departure of men who had just been brought forward as the enemies of the emperor. Jason as their host was entrusted to see that they departed. Their departure then was not voluntary at all but was the result of a decree of expulsion.[2]

What happened afterwards at Beroea supports this interpretation (xvii. 11-15). Paul there, it is said, met with an experience at the hands of the Jews of a very different kind from that which he met at Philippi and Thessalonica. They received his preaching favourably because they took care to meet his teaching with statements from scripture. It is in such contrast with the *a priori* conceptions of the Jewish attitude towards the preaching of the gospel shown by the compiler of the Acts that this detail must be considered historical. No difficulties, it seems, must have occurred at Beroea, but the Jews of Thessalonica learning how Paul had been received, sent agents to create trouble there and compel Paul to depart. As soon as they learnt of this design the brethren of Beroea compelled Paul to depart for Athens. They made him leave then not just the town but the province even before they had had time to get a clear idea of the success which had attended the machinations of the Jews of Thessalonica.[3] That they should have yielded to threats so

---

[1] It must also be observed that even if the initiative came from the Jews the agitation would have come to nothing if it had not found support in public opinion.

[2] The first epistle to the Thessalonians shows that Paul very much wanted to return to Thessalonica after he had been driven from there but had to give the idea up following the news which Silas and Timothy brought him at Corinth.

[3] It should be remarked that the measure had only Paul in mind. It was possible for Silas to remain in Macedonia. Timothy whom Acts xvii. 15 says remained at

quickly, although nothing had happened at Beroea, means that the danger must have been serious. It must therefore be supposed that it was sufficient for Paul's presence at Beroea to be known to the authorities to make his position dangerous. We may therefore infer that the apostle was not merely pursued from Thessalonica but was expelled from Macedonia with the result that it was illegal for him to be at Beroea. The inaccuracy of the whole story explains itself. The compiler wanted as far as possible to hide the fact that Paul's preaching met with such powerful opposition at the hands of the Gentiles that it succeeded in securing his expulsion from the province.

The first epistle to the Thessalonians contains evidence confirming this. Paul does not confine himself to an allusion in i. 6 to the tribulations which accompanied the church's birth at Thessalonica but in ii. 14 f. draws a parallel between the Thessalonians and the Christians of Judaea by saying that the former had had to endure sufferings at the hands of their fellow-citizens comparable to those which the Christians of Judaea had had to endure at the hands of the Jews. This supports the idea that it was the Gentiles who took the initiative in measures against the Christians. In addition to what we learn from Acts the epistle shows us that sufferings came, not only to the preachers of the gospel, but also to those who had been converted.

Paul came to Corinth after he had passed through Athens and undertook there a new enterprise in evangelisation when he recognised that it was impossible to return to Macedonia as he ardently desired. Affairs turned out very differently from what they had done at Philippi and Thessalonica. In accordance with his customary preconceptions, the compiler of Acts reports a rupture between Paul and the synagogue. On this occasion it seems as if it may have been Paul who took the initiative by going and settling in the house of the proselyte Titus Justus (xviii. 5-7).

What we learn from the book of Acts concerning the evangelisation of Corinth is supplemented by information from the letters to the Corinthians. They show us that public opinion and the Gentile public authorities were not hostile to Paul's preaching and the infant church. But at Corinth an incident took place which, because it betrays both the attitude of the Jews towards Christians and Christianity's position in the empire, is of capital importance. It

Beroea in reality went with Paul to Athens. Afterwards it was possible for him to return to Thessalonica (1 Thess. iii. 2).

refers to a charge which the Jews brought against Paul before
Gallio, the proconsul of Achaia, who declined to accept it. We must
examine the incident closer both because it is important and the
author of Acts recognises it to be so.

I shall not return here to my note about the position of the story
when I was dealing with the chronology of Paul's stay at Corinth
and to my reasons for thinking that it has been displaced.[1] In the
earliest tradition the incident seemed to Paul so threatening that he
thought of leaving Corinth. He only decided to stay after he had
received a reassuring vision.

Let us consider the incident itself. The Jews seized Paul and
brought him before the court of Gallio, proconsul of Achaia; they
declared[2] that Paul preached a way of worshipping God 'contrary
to the law' ($\pi\alpha\rho\alpha$ $\tau\grave{o}\nu$ $\nu\acute{o}\mu o\nu$). These words can be taken in two
different senses, according as to whether it refers to the Roman
law[3] or the Jewish law,[4] and also according as to whether it refers to
the content of the preaching or the forms of worship. In the former
case they meant that Paul violated the Roman law by preaching
a religion which had not been authorised by the senate. In the latter
it would mean that what Paul preached was not Judaism. But in
either case, if the Jewish charge had been accepted, the practical
consequences for Paul would have been the same: he would have
been charged with having devoted himself to the propagation of an
illicit religion and he would have been liable to capital punishment.
The only difference would have been that in the former case the
Jews would have formulated an accusation in their desire to secure
the apostle's condemnation while in the latter case they would only
have made a declaration to show that they had nothing to do with
him. Without doubt, they would have reckoned that the proconsul
would of his own accord take measures against him.[5] Perhaps also
they guessed or foresaw that sooner or later Paul's activities would
lead him into a conflict with the state in which they wished to

[1] See p. 22.
[2] For the time being I am avoiding the question whether this was a formal
accusation or something else.
[3] Such is Zahn's and Preuschen's interpretation among others. Zahn, *Einl.*
I, p. 191; Preuschen, *Apgesch.*, p. 113.
[4] This is the interpretation given by Wendt, *Apgesch.*, p. 269; Johannes Weiss,
Der erste Korintherbrief, Meyer, Goettingen, 1910, V, p. xiii; and Loisy, *Actes*,
p. 700.
[5] Such is, practically speaking, the interpretation given by Lake-Cadbury,
Begin. IV, p. 227. Jacquier (*Actes*, p. 552) inclines in the same direction by saying
that the word 'law' is used purposely in an ambiguous manner.

avoid being implicated; that is why they would have solemnly and officially declared that what Paul preached was contrary to the law of Moses. It is difficult to make a definite pronouncement in favour of either of these interpretations at the price of completely excluding one, although in favour of the latter one it may be urged that it is difficult to suppose that the Jews even out of hatred for Paul would have posed as champions of the rights of the Gentile empire. On the other count, the way the incident developed favours the idea that the Jews meant by the law Jewish law. At any rate Gallio understood them to mean this. Without leaving Paul time to reply to his enemies Gallio declared that if they were complaining of some injustice or an act of violence he would listen to them with patience but if it was only a question of disputes about points of doctrine, names, and the law, these were things which were only of interest to Jews about which a Roman could not judge. Thereupon he left the judgement-seat. Gallio refused to consider the conflict between the Jews and the Christians anything except an internal dispute within Judaism.[1]

The way in which the affair ended justifies the interpretation that the law which the Jews invoked was their own. They did not formulate a direct accusation against Paul in proper form but made a declaration by which they showed that they had nothing to do with Paul. Gallio disregarded the declaration; he refused to make any distinction between Jews and Christians. In his eyes Christians remained Jews.

It is easy to see the importance which the author of Acts attaches to the incident and the way in which it supports the main contention of his apologetic thesis. For him Gallio is the ideal type of the Roman magistrate who judges according to right without allowing himself to be influenced by Jewish intrigues and machinations. He recognised that Christianity must be treated as a *religio licita*. But just because the incident illustrates with such exactness a thesis which the compiler had every interest to prove true, we must ask ourselves if it is altogether historical and, if it was, did it have the precise significance which the author gives to it.

---

[1] The story adds that they set about to beat Sosthenes, the chief of the synagogue, and that Gallio was unconcerned. The text does not show us who beat him, whether it was the Gentiles, whose latent antisemiticism was encouraged by the scornful way in which the procurator had just treated the Jews, or whether it was the Christians or even the Jews who reckoned him to blame for the rebuff they had received and accused him of having pleaded the Jewish case in too mild a fashion. If we identify him with the Sosthenes who is named as the companion author of

Loisy[1] discovered in the story a series of details which appear to him of improbable occurrence. He is astonished for instance by the way in which Gallio understood the respective positions of Paul and his opponents at the first glance without asking for any explanations. It also seems to him no less surprising that Gallio from the beginning assumed an attitude which conforms so precisely to the apologetic thesis of Acts. He also thinks that a Roman proconsul would not have acted with such nonchalance and would not have shown himself so completely indifferent to a charge of an illicit religion being propagated.

The justice of Loisy's[1] observations must be allowed to some extent at least but, all things considered, they are only relevant to the way in which the incident is described and not to the substance of the story. They may lead us to doubt if the Jews involved themselves in regular legal proceedings but they lose their significance, if, as we have seen, it is at least probable that they simply made a declaration to try and show that they had nothing to do with a form of propaganda which might possibly endanger their safety since it was in the synagogue where the affair began.

Gallio showed, by refusing to be involved in an examination of the controversy between the Jews and Paul, that he was not taken in and that he well understood that the Jews had acted out of hostility to Paul, not out of love for Rome. Nevertheless his attention had been drawn to the propagation of Christianity and the Jews may have been afraid that, while he was not concerned as to what impression it made upon them, if he had anything to do with it in the future he would not show any special regard for them. Loisy's observations then have a bearing upon the way in which the incident is told but not upon its substance. It is perfectly natural that the compiler of Acts should have simplified and reshaped this incident to make it more impressive, because it had decisive importance for what he judged was the essential thesis his work was written to prove.

the first epistle to the Corinthians, we may wonder whether he failed to make the Jewish accusation with any great firmness because he was already inclining to Christianity, or if the bad treatment which he received, supposing it to have come from the Jews, did not go some way to detaching him from the synagogue. It is much better to refrain from conjectures of this kind as we have not sufficient details to support them and to confine ourselves to the fact that a story which was a literary fiction would not have contained the ambiguities which mark this incident.

[1] Loisy, *Actes*, pp. 700 ff.

The fact that the chronological position of the incident has been changed also confirms the probability that it has been elaborated in a tendentious manner. The compiler separates the reassuring vision from the incident of the Jews accusing Paul. Originally the vision enabled Paul to avoid what would have been the consequences of their complaint. He also notes that after appearing before Gallio Paul remained some days at Corinth and left it entirely of his own free will. He does this because he wants to give the impression that the incident had no significance except to show that in this particular case the Jews' hatred for Paul was powerless. In reality, the affair was not perhaps of such little consequence to Paul as the compiler wants to try and make out. It may well have been that there were some irregularities. Perhaps Paul did not appear in person before Gallio and the Jews without him called on Gallio and complained. If this was so, Paul would have been aware of it but he would not have known for quite a long time what was going to be the end of it. It may have been then, when things were uncertain, that he thought of leaving Corinth.

The action of the Jews of Corinth then put Paul in a very dangerous position. If they had been successful, he would have been condemned on a charge of having indulged in propagating an illicit religion.[1] He would have broken the *lex majestatis* and have been liable to capital punishment. Even if their action had failed, of which one could not have been sure in advance, his position would have remained none the less anxious. At the very least a grave threat hung over the apostle. He could foresee that his enemies would not count themselves beaten but would try again. Another effort with better preparations might meet with success. In any case, the church could no longer find a temporary home in the synagogue as it had done at first.

The compiler of Acts has then given the incident quite a different colour. He turned what was only a retreat on the part of Paul's enemies and perhaps only a partial and temporary retreat into a positive success for the apostle, while in reality it remained a threat which he had only escaped for the time being.[2] To make this transformation he altered the position of the incident so that it ceases

[1] Even if Paul had been considered to be a Jew, his preaching to the Gentiles might have exposed him to legal proceedings. The privileges granted to Jews allowed them to practise their religion but not to make propaganda in its favour. Cf. Juster, I, pp. 254 ff.

[2] It would be wrong to suppose that Gallio by disallowing the Jewish complaint showed that he was tolerating any agitation or propaganda.

to have any connection with the reassuring vision or with Paul's departure, with the result that it looks like an isolated incident in the story of Paul's activity at Corinth, which in fact it is not.

As in Macedonia so in Corinth Jewish intrigues seem to have been especially directed against Paul alone. The epistles to the Corinthians contain no trace suggesting that possibly the Corinthian community had had to suffer at the hands of the Jews, although right up to the last moment they did not throw over the apostle. At the end of his stay in Greece, in the spring of 58, when he was on the point of embarking for Syria, he had at the last moment to change his itinerary and pass through Macedonia and Asia to avoid travelling with Jews, who had planned to make use of any incident which might arise in the course of the voyage, or, if need be, to create one, in order to kill him. The peculiar hostility with which he was regarded by the Jews, which they did not extend to the other Greek missionaries[1] is explained by the fact that the complete volte-face which took place in his life and the arguments which he used to free Christianity from the Jewish ritual made Paul, in Jewish eyes, a renegade and an apostate.[2] They wanted him personally; it was Paul they were trying to catch. It must not be supposed on that account that they showed real tolerance towards the other Greek missionaries but they were certainly less eager in fighting them, no doubt because unlike Paul they were more ready to compromise.

Chapter iii of the epistle to the Philippians[3] reveals one particular aspect of the Jewish attitude towards the Christian mission. It affords a violent polemic against enemies who must be external enemies as there is nothing said which would be likely to win them over or bring them back. As they are described as 'the false circumcision' in contrast to the Christians who are the true circumcision, i.e. who are the true people of God, they can only be Jews[4] who

---

[1] The fact that Silas could remain in Macedonia and that Timothy could return thither, although Paul was forbidden to enter the province, supports the idea that Jewish opposition was especially directed against Paul himself personally.

[2] The Christians of Jerusalem in the same way thought that Paul was devoting himself to a systematic campaign in the diaspora to persuade Jews to give up the Mosaic customs and to stop circumcising their children (Acts xxi. 20-21). In reality Paul was only opposed to the law being imposed on Gentiles who had been converted, but not in any way to Christians of Jewish origin continuing to observe it.

[3] It is reported to have happened at Philippi but it may perhaps have happened to some extent at Ephesus also, where the letter seems to us to have been written. But it is exceedingly probable that similar happenings took place elsewhere.

[4] See *Introd.* IV, 1, pp. 379 ff.

were trying to bring into the synagogue Gentiles, whom Paul had converted from polytheism in order to bring them to the worship of the one true God. Perhaps the other Greek missionaries were not so violently attacked as Paul, because they resisted attempts like these with less ferocity.

We have no direct information as to what opposition Paul may have encountered at Ephesus whether it was Jewish or Roman. The first epistle to the Corinthians (xv. 22, 32; xvi. 9) shows that his ministry in Asia formed a particularly rich and particularly difficult period of activity because of the difficulties which he met there.[1] Ephesus was a centre where the most diverse philosophic and religious currents met and crossed, and controversy was heated; it is all the more curious that we know very little about the beginning of Christianity there, as later on from the end of the first century it was a metropolis of Christendom. The story of Acts telling of Paul in Asia is full of nothing but anecdotes.[2] Perhaps we are not wrong in thinking that the compiler of Acts wanted to pass over in silence what happened at Ephesus because it was not favourable to his apologetic preconceptions. He then may have proceeded to fill in the resulting gap in his narrative by drawing on chance material. Those who consider that the epistle to the Philippians was written at Ephesus while Paul was in prison there, confirm this hypothesis in a remarkable way. According to Acts a rupture occurred between Paul and the synagogue where Paul had begun by teaching for three months, as had happened elsewhere. Owing to the calumnies of the Jews against his teaching he was compelled to leave them and set himself up in the school of Tyrannus which he rented and where he taught for two years (xix. 8-10). It is not altogether certain if, when he set up in the school of Tyrannus, that meant that he had made a complete break with the Jews.[3]

It naturally follows from the hypothesis which we have adopted concerning the composition of the epistle to the Philippians that it is the only document which gives us direct information on Paul's

---

[1] It must be added that it appears from 2 Corinthians i. 8-11 that Paul found himself in such danger in Asia that he despaired of life.

[2] One of these anecdotes, that concerning the disturbance of the coppersmith Demetrius, seems originally to have had no connection with Christianity. In the source it was an anti-semitic outburst.

[3] The text says in conclusion that thus all the inhabitants of Asia, Jews and Greeks, heard the word of the Lord (xix. 10) but it is not clear if this refers to the teaching given in the school of Tyrannus or to that given previously in the synagogue.

position in Asia. Unfortunately, as it alludes to facts of which its readers were already aware, it is not easy to interpret its evidence in any assured fashion. But some points are exceedingly clear. Paul was in prison. Why he had been arrested and what proceedings were being taken against him may for a time have been shrouded in obscurity but at the time he was writing affairs had become clear; not only within the church but outside it was then known that he was not in prison on account of a crime or an offence of the common law but on account of the preaching of the gospel (i. 12-13). The affair in any case was serious, the apostle had to envisage the possibility of being condemned to be put to death. Yet, in his efforts to forecast and prepare for the future he put on one side this possibility and foresaw a favourable end to his trial not from any impartial appreciation of the facts and of the circumstances but from considerations of his life-purpose; Paul foresaw his liberation because he considered that it would be advantageous to the work of evangelisation. He can have had no doubt on this point; the motive for his arrest and trial must be found in an accusation of propagating an illicit religion, but there is nothing which informs us or hints at or even allows us to suppose that the Jews were in any way responsible for this accusation being brought against the apostle.[1]

Much more delicate is the question of knowing what were the reactions of the church to Paul's arrest and what inferences may be drawn as to the character of the affair. O. Cullmann[2] who, it is true, thinks that the epistle to the Philippians was written from Rome, is struck by the fact that where Clement of Rome is speaking of Peter and Paul concerning the attitude of certain preachers of the gospel towards Paul the terms jealousy, spirit, and strife ($\zeta\hat{\eta}\lambda os$ $\phi\theta\acuteo\nu os$) are used again and again as a kind of leitmotiv. This he thinks authorises him to assume that Paul's imprisonment was the result of intrigues and denunciations from enemies he had in the church, probably Jewish Christians.

Various reasons prevent my sharing this opinion.[3] To begin with, what Clement of Rome writes on the dire effects of jealousy and a quarrelling spirit is purely verbal and covers without hiding his almost

---

[1] The fact that Acts does not mention any hostility shown by the Jews at Ephesus to Paul deserves to be noticed.

[2] O. Cullmann, 'Les causes de la mort de Pierre et de Paul d'après le témoignage de Clément Romain', *R.h.p.r.*, 1930, X, pp. 294-300.

[3] Without mentioning the fact that, if the traditional idea that it was written at Rome is given up, it cannot be defended.

complete ignorance of the history of Peter and Paul, beyond what the author could learn through reading Paul's epistles and the book of Acts. In addition, what is still more decisive, Paul mentions persons who have begun to preach the gospel on account of his imprisonment and his consequent inactivity. Amongst them are some whose motives for doing so were not pure but were moved by jealousy, a love of strife, and the thought of giving pain to the apostle while in prison. Two interpretations may be given of this. It may refer to people who were profiting by the inactivity to which Paul had been reduced and were trying to secure themselves a place in the church and gain influence at his expense. Or it may refer to people who are trying to substitute another doctrine in place of the gospel preached by Paul. The former of the two interpretations is certainly the one to be retained as Paul would have reacted much more violently to the preaching of another gospel.[1] He is not referring to some form of doctrinal opposition which had gone so far that, in order to destroy his influence, it had denounced him before the Roman authorities. He is referring to a situation, which had only shown itself in the church after his arrest, or at any rate which only his arrest had disclosed because it brought to light the jealousies his authority had provoked.

i. 13 ff. shows that a certain interval of time had to elapse for the situation created by Paul's arrest to be cleared up and for it to be recognised that it was only his activity as an apostle which had caused his arrest. But in the interval others, even to the extent of two groups, had resumed the task of preaching, which was continued on sufferance after his arrest, and apparently these preachers did not have cause to suffer. This situation surprises us and we must try to analyse its character. Olaf Linton[2] judiciously describes the problem, when he says that the question to determine is whether Paul's cause is synonymous with that of Christianity or not. They were synonymous in the eyes of those who began to preach in order to console Paul with the knowledge that the gospel continued to be preached in spite of his forced inactivity; they were not so in the eyes of those who were animated by a spirit of rivalry and were trying to create anxiety for

---

[1] All the more because, if Paul had found others preaching a different gospel, he would not have explained it as due only to jealousy or a love of strife. In addition it cannot be supposed that those who began to preach at Ephesus laboured for the benefit of another gospel and that Paul knew nothing about it.

[2] Olaf Linton, *Zur Situation des Philipperbriefs in Arbeiten und Mitteilungen aus dem neutestamentlichen Seminar zu Uppsala, herausgegeben von* A. Fridrichsen, 1936, IV, pp. 9-21.

the apostle in prison. We must consider the problem in a wider context.

It would seem odd that Paul can say, as he does in i. 14, that his chains, i.e. the example of his captivity have given confidence and encouragement to a new group of preachers of the gospel. Is this just one of those exaggerations which Paul often uses or must we give the terms precise significance and understand that, as the obscurities which enshrouded Paul's arrest and the beginning of his trial had evaporated, it was recognised that the circumstances surrounding the affair were seen to be such that it in no way directly threatened other preachers of the gospel? This might have been true if Paul was not imprisoned for preaching the gospel but for the way in which he preached it, or in more concrete terms, for offending the Jews by his preaching and setting them up against him. In other words, it may be that Jewish manoeuvres were the original cause of Paul's arrest at Ephesus so that he was arrested not because he was preaching the gospel but because he was the enemy of the Jews. The manoeuvre which failed before Gallio probably succeeded at Ephesus. The fact that in chapter iii Paul puts his readers on their guard against doctrines and not against the intrigues of enemies, among whom we think Jews must be classed, is not perhaps favourable to this interpretation, but it does not constitute a decisive objection.[1] We must give up hope of being able to dissipate all the obscurities on this point. One thing at any rate is certain: although there was some confusion at the beginning as to the circumstances of the affair and time had to elapse before its real character was realised, it was an affair of extreme gravity. Condemnation to death was possible and it looks as if at one moment the apostle thought it so likely that he could think of himself as already present in the arena where the wild beasts were waiting for him (1 Cor. xv. 32). When he was trying to weigh up the circumstances in which he found himself either then or some other time he 'had the sentence of death in himself', as he says in 2 Corinthians i. 9; when he had been set free he felt that God who raises the dead had snatched him from death (i. 9-10). One detail further must be noted concerning 'the trouble which came upon him in Asia'.[1] Paul does not only say that God had snatched him from death; he adds that he places his hopes in God that he will yet deliver him in the future and, that to gain this deliverance, he is counting on

[1] It may be noted on the contrary that the part played by the Jews of Asia at the time of Paul's arrest in Jerusalem (Acts xxi. 27) which is in other ways obscure to us perhaps reveals the memory of a conflict between Paul and Judaism in Asia.

the prayers of the Corinthians (i. 10-11). It may be inferred from this that the danger to which Paul had been exposed had receded but had not disappeared and at any moment might break out again. This is in complete agreement with the position in which Christianity was placed from the moment it ceased to be identified with Judaism, i.e. a religion deprived of any legal status.

3.—PAUL'S TRIAL

We come now to the last part of Paul's life and the long trial which began the day after his arrest at Jerusalem and was continued at Caesarea and Rome. How it ended we do not know.

When Paul departed for Jerusalem he was well aware of the dangers to which he was exposing himself (Rom. xv. 30 f.). According to the story in Acts his apprehensions only assumed definite form in the course of his journey.[1] He saw James on the day following his arrival, who advised him to take some precautions before he introduced him to the church on account of the thousands of Jews who had been converted, but were full of zeal for the law, to whom he had been made out to be a renegade and an apostate (xxi. 20-22).[2] In accordance with his request Paul agreed to give public proof of his loyalty to Judaism by associating himself with a group of brethren, who were under obligation to discharge a vow but were unable to do so for lack of resources.[3] Some people question the authenticity

[1] The Acts describes Paul's journey to Jerusalem as a progress to punishment or at any rate to imprisonment. At Miletus the apostle summons the elders of the church to him and declares to them that they will not see his face again (xx. 25) and the conclusion repeats and emphasises this detail (xx. 38). At Tyre Paul meets disciples who try to dissuade him from the idea of going to Jerusalem (xxi. 4). At Caesarea the prophet Agabus bound his own hands and feet with Paul's girdle and predicted that the man to whom the girdle belonged would be thus bound at Jerusalem and the brethren, like those at Tyre, tried in vain to dissuade Paul from going to Jerusalem (xxi. 10-14). It is also typical, when we think of the early church's customs relating to hospitality, that, as xxi. 16 shows, they thought it necessary to secure Paul a lodging beforehand in Jerusalem at the house of a certain Mnason, whom from the fact that he was an early disciple and a Cypriot we recognise was a Hellenist. According to the text of ms. D Paul and his friends accepted Mnason's hospitality in a village between Caesarea and Jerusalem, where they passed the night.

[2] The text of Acts shows that James did not judge Paul in this way but it does not make it plain that he did all he could to remove this prejudice against Paul.

[3] To help a poor man to discharge a vow was deemed a meritorious act of charity (Josephus, *A.j.* xix. 6, 1. Cf. Strack-Billerbeck, II, pp. 755 ff.). It has been suggested that the necessary money had been deducted previously from the collection (Johannes Weiss, *Urchrist.*, p. 283). To want to know where the money provided by Paul came from is to try to extract a detail from the documents at our disposal which from their nature they cannot supply.

of this detail. Hausrath[1] thinks it as difficult to suppose that Paul agreed to this as it would be to think of Luther vowing to go a pilgrimage to Notre-Dame of Einsiedeln or of Calvin on his death-bed promising a golden robe to the Mother of God. But Paul never taught that those who were of Jewish blood must cease to keep the law. It is possible, as many scholars do,[2] to regard Paul's associating himself with a vow as historical without being obliged to share Renan's view[3] that, owing to the gravity of the situation, he relaxed his principles or Eduard Meyer's[4] that he possessed such a rich and complex personality that his conduct was not always absolutely consistent and rigid. But the historicity of Paul's associating himself with a vow is very much open to question, because, when he was subsequently accused of profaning the temple, he did not defend himself by saying that he had been there for a ceremony of purification and prove it by calling as witnesses those with whom he had been associated.[5]

Paul's fears that the Jews at Jerusalem would show hostility to him had not long to wait before they were realised. Shortly after his arrival,[6] as soon as he was found in the temple, Jews from Asia incited the crowd by accusing him of having profaned the temple by bringing Greeks into it.[7] According to Acts this accusation in the beginning

---

[1] Hausrath, *Der Apostel Paulus*, Heidelberg, 1872, p. 433. Similar opinions have often been expressed.

[2] Schurer, *Th. Ltzg.*, 1882, col. 348; Wendt, *Apgsch.*, p. 304; Harnack, *Neue Untersuchungen zur Apostelgeschichte und zur Abfassungszeit der synoptishen Evangelien*, Leipzig, 1911, pp. 54 ff.; Johannes Weiss, *Urchrist.*, p. 223.

[3] Renan, *Saint Paul*, pp. 517 f.

[4] Eduard Meyer, *Urspr. u. Anf.* III, pp. 65, 71.

[5] Eduard Meyer (*Urspr. u. Anf.* III, p. 70, n. 3) thought that he found an allusion to the vow in xxiv. 18 where Paul says that they found him purifying himself in the temple. But purifications could be undertaken for other purposes besides the accomplishment of a vow.

[6] Doubtless on the fifteenth day. Cf. *Introd.* IV, 2, p. 367, n. 1.

[7] The Romans gave the Jews the right to punish any non-Jew with death, even if he was a Roman citizen, who entered the temple (Josephus, *G.j.* vi. 2, 4; *A.j.* xv. 11, 15). The court of the temple was surrounded with a railing along the whole length of which was inscribed a notice in Greek and Latin saying that any stranger who crossed the boundary mark was responsible for his own death. One of these inscriptions was discovered in 1871 by Clermont-Canneau ('Une stèle du Temple de Jérusalem', *Rev. archéol.*, 1872, I, pp. 214-234, 290-291, pl. X). The text of it has often been reproduced since (e.g. Dittenberger, O.G.I.S.[2], II, 598). It is preserved in the museum at Constantinople. Another example of the inscription has been found at Jerusalem in the district of the gate of the Brebis (*The Quarterly of the Department of Antiquities in Palestine*, 1936, VI, pp. 1-3). Jewish jurisdiction seems to have been competent to deal with any case where the law was broken but there is no doubt that this did not exclude completely the supervision of the Roman authority. Cf. Schurer, *Gesch.* II, pp. 209 f., 272; Juster, II, pp. 142 f.; Strack-Billerbeck, II, pp. 761 ff.

had been due to a misunderstanding. Paul had been seen in the streets of Jerusalem in the company of an uncircumcised Gentile who was a convert to the gospel, Trophimus from Ephesus, and they thought or perhaps imagined that he had gone into the temple with him. In the ensuing riot Paul would have been killed, if the tribune had not intervened, who with his soldiers left the fortress Antonia from which he watched the temple and arrested him (xxi. 27-34).

The mistake concerning Trophimus which is mentioned in the book of Acts is only a fiction to hide the real character of the affair. If Trophimus took any part at all, why did not the populace direct their fury on to him also? The so-called profanation of the temple by the Greeks with Paul as the accomplice is not mentioned when the tribune sends Paul to the Sanhedrin for investigation (xxii. 30-xxxii.11) nor in the report which he makes to the procurator Felix (xxiii. 26-30). When the orator Tertullus, the spokesman of the Jews, makes his speech before Felix, he says that Paul had tried to profane the temple but he does not say precisely how (xxiv. 6). Paul in his reply ignores the accusation that he had caused Gentiles to enter the temple; he remarks on the failure of the Asiatic Jews to appear who ought to have given evidence against him. What Acts makes out to have been the cause of Paul's arrest plays no part in his trial. There is certainly something wrong here.

Acts xxi. 21 shows that the Jews considered Paul an apostate who was leading a campaign in the diaspora to persuade Jews to give up the customs of Moses and to cease having their children circumcised.[1] The compiler of Acts failed to realise that the presence of Paul himself in the temple seemed to be a profanation; through his apostasy it was thought that he had lost his status as a Jew with the right to cross the line marking off that part of the court accessible to the Gentiles.

The story told in Acts of Paul's trial is stocked with later additions the historicity of which must be accepted with some caution.[2] Almost all of them tend to establish and underline the thesis dear to the author that Christians are still Jews.[3] Generally speaking, he has

[1] According to xxi. 28 the Jews from Asia who had created the incident in the temple described Paul as 'the man that teacheth all men everywhere against the people, and the law, and this place (the temple)'.

[2] Wendland, *Urchr.*, Litf., pp. 323 f.

[3] This is what makes some people think that the book of Acts was composed as a defence for Paul in the course of his Roman trial. It is the old theory of Aberle ('Ueber den Zweck der Apostelgeschichte', *Tub. Quartschr.*, 1855, XXVII, pp. 173-266; 'Ueber die Epochen der neutestamentlichen Geschichtsschreibung', *ibid.*,

made the whole story obscure and on some points almost unintelligible, because he failed to understand that the trial revolved entirely round this question: must Paul, although he had the status of a Roman citizen, be judged by the Sanhedrin on the ground that he had profaned the temple by entering it when he was an apostate or must he be thought to be still a Jew in spite of his attitude in preaching the gospel to the Gentiles?[1]

After the tribune had arrested Paul[2] he proceeded to make investigations on his own responsibility. Using the simple and brutal methods of the Roman police, he had the accused beaten until Paul declared his status as a Roman citizen (xxii. 24-29). By doing this he not only escaped the blows of the whip but placed himself under the protection of Rome (xxii. 24-29).[3] If he had been an alien one of two things might have followed. If he had been thought guilty of sedition on account of the riot which he had occasioned, the Roman authorities represented by the tribune would have been competent to have taken cognisance of it, unless the procurator had intervened personally because he thought the affair ought to be moved to his jurisdiction. If it was thought to be a religious offence, Paul could have been tried by the Sanhedrin subject to the sentence being ratified by the procurator, if it was a sentence of death. As Paul was

1863, XLV, pp. 84-98). A similar theory in a less blatant form was set out more recently by F. J. Jackson and K. Lake in *Begin.* II, pp. 179 ff. A hypothesis of a similar kind was defended by Riddle ('The occasion of Luke Acts', *Journ. of Religion*, 1930, X, pp. 545-563) with this particular suggestion that Luke wrote when the first symptoms of Domitian's persecutions appeared. This is a very bold hypothesis because, as we shall see later (p. 529), Christians found their connection with Judaism more compromising than helpful in Domitian's time.

[1] The fundamental work on Paul's trial is still that of Mommsen, 'Die Rechtsverhaltnisse des Apostels Paulus,' *Z.N.T.W.*, 1901, II, pp. 81-96 (reproduced in *Gesamulte Schriften* III, pp. 431 ff.). See also V. Weber, *Die Glaubwurdigheit der Apostelsgeschichte und ihr Kritiker Th. Mommsen, Katholik*, 1902, pp. 1-11; Holzmeister, 'Der heilige Paulus vor dem Richterstuhle des Festus', *Z. f. kath. Theol.*, 1912, XXXVI, pp. 489-511, 742-783; L. V. Velhoen, 'Het Proces van den Apostel Paulus', *Alphen a.d. Rejn.* 1924; E. Springer, 'Der Prozess des Apostels Paulus', *Preussische Jahrbucher*, 1929, CCXVIII, pp. 182-196; H. J. Cadbury, 'Roman law and the trial of Paul', in *Begin.* V, pp. 297-338.

[2] According to Acts xxi. 35 ff. when Paul was on the steps of the fortress Antonia with the soldiers who had brought him thither, he made a speech to the Jews with the permission of the tribune in which he narrated his conversion. It is inconceivable that this could have happened in the midst of the confusion of which the author speaks.

[3] It is striking that Acts xvi. 22 does not say that Paul declared his Roman citizenship at Philippi to avoid scourging as he did at Jerusalem. The reason certainly is that he did not want to separate himself from his people. The situation had changed at Jerusalem where the rupture had already been consummated and consequently Paul had no need to think of them any longer.

recognised to be a Roman citizen, things took a different course. If the charge of sedition had been retained, only the procurator could have tried the case but there is no reference in the whole story to an accusation of this kind. Paul as a Roman citizen and charged with profaning the temple could only be handed over to the Jewish authorities for trial provided the charge was properly founded. This implies that as the charge of having brought a Gentile into the temple was apparently not maintained and not even ever brought, the whole trial revolved round Paul's apostasy. The question to be resolved was whether Paul's faith as a Christian and his missionary activity among the Gentiles deprived him of his rights as a Jew. The whole trial then is concerned with Paul's religious position. Felix had to decide whether he was an orthodox proper Jew. It is hardly surprising that he shrank from doing it and began to allow the affair to drag on.

Once the tribune discovered that Paul was a Roman citizen he could do nothing but refer the business to the procurator giving him what information he had been able to gather. The compiler of Acts did not understand this, and in order to explain Paul's removal to Caesarea imagined that the tribune had had to take extraordinary precautions to protect his prisoner from an attempt by the Jews to assassinate him (xxiii. 12-38).

Once Paul was snatched from the Jews' hands they demanded that he should be referred to the Sanhedrin. They appeared at the trial as prosecutors, not as witnesses. The compiler of Acts may well have narrated the story of the appearance before the Sanhedrin for investigation (xxii. 30-xxiii. 10)[1] in place of the steps taken by Jewish authorities. The trial began some days after Paul had been brought to Caesarea.[2] The high priest came into court with some other priests and a lawyer Tertullus who put forward the Jewish demand. 'Paul was "a pest",[3] he said, 'and a mover of sedition among all the Jews

---

[1] But Wellhausen (*Krit. An.*, *A.G.*, 1914, p. 47) and others think this appearance historical. The hypothesis is plausible but the story of the incident cannot in any case be held to be accurate. It makes the question one of the hope of the resurrection while the debate revolved round Paul's attitude towards the law.

[2] The tribune certainly had to report to Felix. In spite of Zahn's opinion (*Einl.* II, p. 400) the text given in Acts xxiii. 26-30 is suspect of being an editorial element. Nevertheless it corresponds fairly well to the situation as the tribune declared that he had taken nothing out of Paul's charge sheet and expresses the idea that the complaints of the Jews against Paul were on questions about the interpretation of the law. In any case—and this is an important point—Paul never seems to have been prosecuted officially but only at the request of the Jews.

[3] Wendt (*Apgesch.*, p. 323) and Loisy (*Actes*, p. 852) noted that the term 'pest' (λοιμός) may be an allusion to the Senate's decree concerning the alliance between Rome and Simon Maccabee which enjoined the neighbouring states to deliver up

throughout the world and a ringleader of the sect of the Nazarenes. He has tried to profane the temple and for that reason has been arrested. The Jews would have judged him according to their law, but the tribune Lysias came and took him away from their hands and commanded his accusers to come before the procurator. If the tribune is questioned, he will not fail to confirm that this is so' (xxiv. 1-8).[1]

In his reply Paul declared that he had never caused any trouble at Jerusalem and challenged his enemies to prove the contrary. He then touched on the complaint brought against him by the Jews, that he had disturbed the synagogues of the diaspora. He did not deny that he belonged to what the Jews called 'a heresy'[2] but as far as that was concerned he had only remained faithful to the Jewish hope that there will be a resurrection of the dead, both just and unjust. After being absent for many years he came to Jerusalem to bring alms to his nation.[3] Jews from Asia who had seen him go into the temple for purifications had nothing to accuse him of as they had not appeared before the procurator (xxiv. 10-21). There is no explicit mention of the charge of profaning the temple. The whole purpose of Paul's speech was to prove that he was not an unfaithful Jew.

After the two parties had been heard the procurator adjourned giving judgement, until the tribune Lysias arrived.[4] Paul waited in prison. His imprisonment was to some extent mitigated by the fact that he was allowed to receive ministrations from his friends (xxiv. 22-23). The compiler of Acts fails to give any distinct reasons why the affair was allowed to drag on.[5] Felix was very embarrassed. He

to the high priest the 'pests' who had fled from Judaea to be judged according to the law (1 Macc. v. 21).

[1] The text of the end of Tertullus' harangue is uncertain. I have analysed the received text, although it is only found in ψ E. 69. 114 and some other manuscripts. The evidence of D. fails at this passage. In the majority of the manuscripts it is said that the Jews wished to try Paul but the tribune prevented them and that the procurator was asked to question the tribune to convince himself that the Jewish accusations were well-founded. The short text is given by the great majority of the editors and adopted by many critics (e.g. Wendt. *Apgesch.*, p. 372; Lake-Cadbury, *Begin.* IV, pp. 299 f.). The long text is only given in the two editions of Blass but it is adopted by several critics among others by Loisy (*Actes*, p. 853). In favour of the long text it may be remarked that in xxiv. 22 Felix declares that he will give sentence when the tribune comes. The short text might have had its origin in some lines being missed out.

[2] His arrival is not again referred to.

[3] This is the only allusion in Acts to the affair of the collection. It is in other respects fairly vague.   [4] His coming will not be in contemplation.

[5] In xxiv. 25-26 he gives several reasons which are plainly only conjectures on his part. Felix was impressed by Paul's speech and kept him at his disposal in order that he might have an opportunity of treating with him or he hoped that Paul would give him money to obtain his liberty.

shrank from handing over a Roman citizen to the Jews and at the same time he wanted to satisfy them and possibly thought that their request was not unreasonable, as after all, the Jews might seem better qualified than anyone else to decide if Paul was still a Jew or not.

The apostle's captivity lasted two years[1] when Felix was recalled. Acts says that to please the Jews he left Paul in prison and handed on to his successor the task of making a decision on the affair (xxiv. 27); but the moment he failed to pass judgement he could not do otherwise.

It is not said that Paul's enemies made any move to obtain a decision during the two years he passed in prison at Caesarea. Perhaps they were satisfied with knowing that their enemy had been made powerless and hesitated to try and obtain a decision which might prove unfavourable to them. They did not observe the same reserve towards Festus, either because they hoped that the new procurator would be inclined to conciliate his subjects or because they feared that, if they did not renew their plaint, they would be judged to have abandoned it.

When Festus arrived at Jerusalem they requested him to have Paul transferred to them (xxv. 1-3). The compiler of Acts seems to have misunderstood the purpose of the Jews' request. His explanation is that they intended to assassinate Paul in the course of his journey from Caesarea to Jerusalem.[2] Probably the request was similar to that presented to Felix two years previously asking for Paul to be handed over to the Sanhedrin to be tried by it. Festus rejected this request and summoned those who had formulated it to appear before his court at Caesarea (xxv. 4-5). This did not constitute the final formality of rejection, but a return to regular procedure. The audience to which Festus had summoned the Jews took place the day after his arrival at Caesarea. The account given of it in Acts is brief and vague. This may be because the compiler did not wish to give too accurate an account of a phase of the trial which was more unfavourable to Paul than he liked to recognise.

The Jews brought against Paul many grave accusations, but their nature is not defined. The only thing said, which is hardly more than

---

[1] Concerning an interpretation which would make the two years begin not at the beginning of Paul's imprisonment but at the beginning of Felix's term of office see my 'Essai sur la chronologie paulinienne', *R.h.r.*, 1912, LXV, p. 329.

[2] The same explanation was given for Paul's transfer from Jerusalem to Caesarea.

one of the compiler's tricks of style, is that the Jews were unable to prove their charges and that Paul energetically defended himself saying that he had done nothing against the law of the Jews, the temple, or Caesar (xxv. 6-8). The mention of Caesar deserves attention. Up to then not the slightest allusion in all that had been said of the trial had been made to anything brought against Paul which might be considered a crime or offence from the Roman point of view. Only his position in respect of Judaism had been under consideration. We shall see a little later on that Paul's trial certainly changed in character at Rome or rather to the question of jurisdiction was added a trial of fact. In other words, the question, 'must Paul be handed over to the Sanhedrin on the ground of having profaned the temple?' there came to be added or substituted for it another question, 'Was he guilty of a crime punishable by the Roman law, either of having devoted himself to propagating an illicit religion or of having disturbed public order by occasioning divisions in the synagogues and the resulting agitation?' Must then Paul's declaration that he had committed no crime against Caesar be seen as a proof that early on at Caesarea the Roman plaint was added to the Jewish one or has the compiler anticipated what could only have happened later at Rome? We cannot say with certainty which is right; we must be content with observing that, if the procurator had had the impression that serious charges from the Roman point of view could be brought against Paul, he would not have shown himself disposed to give satisfaction to the Jews' request and allow them the right to try him.

The arguments put forward by Paul's enemies must have given the procurator Festus the impression that they were not entirely without foundation, as he took a decision, which in spite of the way in which it is cloaked in Acts was favourable to them. What it was is not clearly expressed in the narrative either because the compiler did not clearly understand the juridical character of what took place or because he wanted to diminish the significance of Festus' decision or for both reasons. According to his story the procurator had proposed to Paul that he should go up to Jerusalem to be tried there by him (xxv. 9). Simply to change the place of trial did not need the consent of the accused. The legal place for the court was where the procurator happened to be. It must then be understood that Festus' decision against which Paul protested was different in character. Festus gave the Jews what they asked for, i.e. he decided that the accused would be tried at Jerusalem by the Sanhedrin: he only gave the accused this guarantee that the trial would take place in his presence. In other words he would see that it was regular. It could hardly be thought a friendly proposal which Paul could either accept or reject. Paul had just passed two years in prison because he denied the competence of the Sanhedrin in this affair. How could the procurator have imagined that he was now going to accept it of his own free will? Festus' decision did not then have the character the compiler gave to it. It gave the Jews satisfaction while at the same time it tried to give Paul some measure of safety. If it had been an offer which Paul was free to accept or reject, would Paul have had recourse to an appeal to the Emperor in order to avoid trial at Jerusalem,[1] in spite of the risks of such procedure and the inevitable prolongation of his captivity which would be the first thing that would happen? After Festus had taken the advice of his counsel he could only acknowledge that Paul had made use of a right which belonged to him and deliver a certificate of his appeal by deciding that he should be sent to Rome[2] (xxv. 10-12).

It was Festus' decision on the question of competence which determined Paul to appeal to the imperial court. If it had given the same decision as Festus, Paul would have had to be taken back to Jerusalem to be brought before the Sanhedrin which would have had to try him. Paul, however, in any case, was not sent back to Jerusalem. According to Acts xxviii. 21 the Jews apparently did not take their complaint to Rome. But that did not mean that the trial was abandoned.[3] There is no positive evidence that Paul was set free at the end of his term of imprisonment at Rome. That can only be explained by supposing that when the imperial magistrates came to examine Paul's affair they decided that his activities as a preacher came within the scope of the law and that he had caused disturbances in various places.

On his arrival at Rome Paul must have been delivered up to the officer who commanded the *frumentarii* and maintained communications between the supreme authority and the detachments stationed

---

[1] There has been much discussion on the question whether Paul himself made *provocatio*, i.e. a request to be tried by the emperor's court, a right which was given to Roman citizens by the *lex Julia de vi publica et privata* (Paulus, *Sent.*, 5, 26; cf. Mommsen, *Strafrecht*, pp. 66 f., 242; *Staatsrecht*, II, 2, pp. 908 f.) or *Appelatio*, a request to obtain a revision of a judgement. See J. Merkel, *Ueber die Geschichte der classischen Appelatio*, Halle, 1883.

[2] The phrase used in xxv. 10, 'I stand at Caesar's judgement seat, where I ought to be judged', exactly sums up the situation.

[3] In spite of Lake's opinion, 'The end of Paul's trial in Rome', *Teyler's Tijdschr.*, 1912, XLVII, pp. 356-365.

in the provinces.[1] He obtained permission while waiting for his trial to live in a private house rented by him with a soldier in charge of him (xxviii. 16). This lasted for two years (xxviii. 30). The two years forms the end of Acts but we are not told how it ended or for what reasons.[2] This is probably because the trial was about to enter on a more active phase.

As for the result of the trial we are reduced to guessing. The traditional hypothesis, which everyone who considers the pastoral epistles authentic[3] must hold, is that Paul regained his freedom either when the Jews gave up their case or through a favourable decision from the court. A fresh period of activity would then have opened for him.[4] Then he must have been imprisoned afresh and this time condemned to die and he must have died a martyr's death. If the authenticity of the pastoral epistles is given up, all this becomes a castle in the air; most scholars who do not feel bound by the tradition give up altogether the idea of a second captivity.[5]

Some fragments from the pastoral epistles which seem to be from notes written by Paul while he was a prisoner at Caesarea and Rome[6] compensate in a small measure for the absence of any direct evidence. The most detailed of these (2 Tim. i. 16-18), which is especially important because it shows how indifferent the church at Rome was towards the apostle while he was a prisoner, only informs us that at a given moment about the time when the story in Acts ends or a little later Paul must have been transferred to a prison. This authorises

---

[1] Mommsen and Harnack, *Zur Apostelageschichte*, 28, 16, *S.B.A.*, 1895, pp. 491 ff. Paul's transfer to the *stratopedarchus* is mentioned by A.B. and some other manuscripts. It is difficult to decide which text ought to be considered the earliest.

[2] Concerning the hypotheses which have been made to explain the abrupt and plainly unsatisfactory character of the end of Acts see *Introd.* III, pp. 326 ff. The most likely is that the author intended to write a third volume in which he would have told of Paul's trial at Rome and perhaps also of his death and that circumstances prevented him from fulfilling his intentions.

[3] For the reasons why I think they are not authentic see *Introd.* IV, 2, pp. 504 ff.

[4] Some of the scholars who suppose that Paul was liberated think that he returned to the East, which is what the pastoral epistles seem to postulate. Others (e.g. Harnack, *Mission*, II, p. 92, n. 2) suppose that he turned to Spain and took up the project which he entertained at the time he was writing to the Romans. Others (J. Zeiller, 'Les origines chrétiennes en Gaule', *Rev. de l'hist. de l'égl. de France*, 1926, XII, pp. 27 ff. and with more reserve, C. Jullian, *Histoire de Gaule*, Paris, 1914, IV, p. 485) think that on his way to Spain he touched at Marseilles or at Narbonne.

[5] This is the position adopted by most of the scholars of the independent school of thought such as Holtzmann, Julicher, Loisy, Guignebert, Eduard Meyer, and Schwartz.　　　　　　　　　　　　[6] See *Introd.* IV, 2, pp. 530 f.

us to think that his trial must have entered on a more active phase. At this time the apostle was painfully impressed by the despondency which had seized some of his friends and made them resolve to leave Rome and return to Asia. 'This thou knowest, that all they which are in Asia be turned away from me; of whom are Phygellus and Hermogenes.[1] The Lord give mercy unto the house of Onesiphorus;[2] for he oft refreshed me and was not ashamed of my chain; but, when he was in Rome, he sought me out very diligently and found me. The Lord grant unto him that he may find mercy of the Lord in that day.[3] And in how many things he ministered unto me at Ephesus, thou knowest very well' (2 Tim. i. 15-18).

When Onesiphorus arrived at Rome, he must have enquired of the church where he would find Paul. This must have taken place after the two years had elapsed during which Paul lived in a house which he was allowed to rent. After this he must have been moved to a prison. The church at Rome was not disturbed about him and did not try and find out where he was. But it might have done as a stranger from Asia was successful in doing so. This is an additional reason for thinking that the church at Rome had very little sympathy for the apostle Paul. If 2 Timothy iv. 16 belongs to the same letter or to one written at the same time, Paul had the feeling that his end was near.

Another fragment, which we cannot determine whether it was written at Caesarea or Rome,[4] speaks of the apostle making a first appearance in court where no one defended him. 'At my first answer no one stood with me, but all men forsook me: I pray God that it may not be laid to their charge. Notwithstanding the Lord stood with me, and strengthened me: that by me the preaching might be fully known, and that all the Gentiles might hear: and I was delivered out of the mouth of the lion. And the Lord shall deliver me from every evil work, and will preserve me unto his heavenly kingdom' (2 Tim. iv. 16-18). If the passage refers only to Paul's appearance before Felix at Caesarea, no decision followed it, but if the hypothesis is accepted —and in any case it is only a hypothesis—that the text refers to Rome, all that is proved is that Paul's trial did not reach any conclusion beyond the preliminary examination of the accused. It would not be right to infer from the apostle's words that, while no decision had been made, the situation appeared in a favourable light. Paul is

---

[1] Having returned to Asia after they had stayed for a certain time with Paul.
[2] It must be presumed that Onesiphorus had died in the meantime.
[3] I.e. of judgement. [4] See pp. 162 f.

expressing his assurance of deliverance to come but it is a super-natural deliverance. The Kingdom of God is where he will be saved. Hence Paul had appeared in court for the first time; his situation seemed so threatening that he felt that he was facing a lion ready to devour him. For the time being he had escaped the danger; but a verdict of acquittal had not been given. His case was not finished; the danger remained and Paul awaited his true deliverance in another order of things.

Paul's imprisonment lasted until the beginning of the summer of 64 just before the terrible fire at Rome broke out which directly affected the whole position of Christians, perhaps even up to the very time when it occurred. If Paul, as at the least is extremely probable, was still in prison at the time, it is hardly probable[1] that he perished in the fire, as the Pretorian camp was in that part of the city which was untouched; but the wave of hatred which then broke out against the Christians may well have finally submerged him. Perhaps he perished with Nero's victims,[2] perhaps persecution merely hastened the end of his trial or caused his trial which had been half-forgotten to be resumed.[3] There are other possibilities besides these, for no strict proof has ever been brought forward to show that his trial ended with the fire of Rome. Paul may have died a martyr's death without the church at Rome being aware of it or his nearest friends informed of the circumstances.[4] He may have been condemned not to death but to the mines. In his exhausted condition he could not have survived the life of a convict put to forced labour and must have quickly succumbed in some corner unknown to anyone, except those who saw him depart in a convoy of prisoners who were being sent to work in the mines. It would have been easy for them to see that he was going to almost immediate death. A last possibility is open to us, that Paul died before his suit came before the court. As we shall see in the next chapter when repressive measures were taken after the fire of Rome, a clear distinction was made between the Christians and the Jews. The former were accounted responsible for the disaster; the latter were not disturbed in any way. The situation was then very different at that time from what it had been twelve years earlier when Gallio at Corinth firmly declined to consider the conflict between Paul and the synagogue to be anything but a domestic concern of

[1] Contrary to the opinion of Ed. Staffer, 'Le mort de St. Paul', *Revue chrétienne*, 1886, pp. 497-507. [2] Hausrath, *Der Apostel Paulus*, pp. 498 f.
[3] Ed. Meyer, *Urspr. u. Anf.*, III, p. 501.
[4] Guignebert (*Le Christ*, p. 324) thinks this.

Judaism. The reasons for this change are certainly very complex, but two of them seem to be of particular importance.

The first relates to the investigation which must have been made at Rome in conjunction with Paul's trial. After attention had been drawn to the apostle's activities the investigation must have led people to recognise that he had been devoting himself to the propagation of an illicit religion, which to a large extent did not come within the category of the Jewish religion the practice of which was freely permitted, and was therefore plainly illegal. Furthermore, such were its external manifestations that Judaism could not be held responsible for it or to have connections with it.

Perhaps, however, Judaism would not have been so completely and explicitly exonerated, if it had not found at Nero's court in the empress Poppaea and the Jewish actor Alyturus valuable allies in its campaign, in which it had been engaged for a long time both to disengage itself from Christianity and to fight it. It is interesting to note that Josephus was in Rome when Paul was being tried.[1] He must not have remained inactive.[2]

Paul's trial marks the end of that period in the history of the relations between Christianity and the empire, when Christianity was either purely and simply ignored or was thought of only as a variant of Judaism. From the time of Paul's trial and the fire of Rome, although the empire did not sharply define its attitude, it felt that Christianity was not a national religion with which it would be possible to accommodate itself as it had done with Judaism.

[1] Josephus, *Vita*, III.

[2] Renan (*L'Antichrist*, Paris, 1873, p. 491) admits that Jewish denunciations played a part in Paul's trial and the massacres of 64. He relies on the fact that Clement of Rome speaks of jealousy concerning Peter and Paul and the victims of Nero. As Dibelius (*R.u.d. Chr.*, p. 21) rightly remarks, Clement's text is too rhetorical in character for it to be able to provide proof. All the same the fact that a clear distinction was made between Jews and Christians in 64 strongly supports the hypothesis that the Jews intrigued against the Christians. Ph. Fabia (*Le règne et la mort de Poppée. Rev. de philologie*, XXII, 1898, pp. 336-337) thinks that it was Poppaea who, at the instigation of the Jews, suggested to Nero that the Christians should be made responsible for the fire of Rome.

CHAPTER IV

Christianity and the Roman Empire

I.—THE CHANGE IN THE SITUATION IN 64 AND ITS CAUSES

THE year 64 saw the fire of Rome which proved the cause or pretext of the massacres of Christians and on that account proved to be a date of capital importance in the history of the relations between the church and the Roman Empire. It was then that for the first time the Roman authorities made a clear and sharp distinction between Jews and Christians. The latter were judged to be explicitly or implicitly responsible for the fire of Rome and were treated accordingly, while the former were not in any way disturbed.[1] Nero apparently resolved to fight Christianity, because he regarded it, not only as a form of atheism which was incompatible with the very principles on which Roman society was founded, but also as a threat to the Empire which it would be suicide to ignore. Up to then so far as Christianity did not pass unperceived or was not confounded with Judaism it was only regarded as an irritant which might stir up trouble and disturb public order. Sometimes action had been taken against those who were propagating it but usually those who practised the new religion were regarded with indifference.

We saw in the preceding chapter[2] that the investigations which Paul's suit at Rome must have set in motion may have revealed the scope of the propaganda in which the apostle had indulged and could only have undertaken in violation of the law. We have also noted that the Jews may have undertaken certain intrigues. This would explain why the Jewish authorities at Jerusalem did not think it wise to follow up their suit and plaint which they had formulated in

---

[1] Only one late document, which has no value, the apocryphal correspondence of Paul and Seneca (ep. xii of *Seneca to Paul*) contains the suggestion that Nero's measures affected Jews as well as Christians. The distinction between them was so sharp that it is difficult to understand how Pohlmann (art. 'Nero', *R.E.* XIII, p. 720) could think that action was taken against the Christians because they constituted the most active part of Jewry at Rome.　　[2] See pp. 500 f.

Jerusalem and Caesarea. They thought that they would more easily by indirect means attain their purpose, which was to rid themselves of a man who was regarded as a renegade and the strongest enemy that Judaism could have met. We must return to this point. Means of action were not wanting to the Jews at Rome. Some of them occupied important places at Nero's court. Poppaea Sabina,[1] first Nero's mistress and then his wife,[2] seems to have been if not a Jewess at any rate a proselyte. In any case, she was sympathetic to Judaism.[3] Through the mediation of the Jewish actor, Alyturus, whose influence was great, Josephus entered into negotiations with Poppaea in 63, when he was sent to Rome to gain the release of some priests whom Festus had sent under accusation to the imperial court. Thanks to the support he received he succeeded in his mission. He even boasts that he received presents from Poppaea.[4] Corssen[5] perhaps is more precise than the evidence warrants when he supposes that these presents must have been a reward for the service rendered by Josephus in denouncing the Christian peril. There is no positive proof that the Jews intervened in this way.[6] Yet we are right in suspecting that they did so at least

[1] Josephus, *A.j.* xx. 8, 11. *Vita*, 3. Tacitus, *Annales*, xiii. 45-46; xiv. 1, 59-61, 63-65; xv. 23; xvi. 6-7. *Historiae*, i. 22. See Ph. Fabia, 'L'adultère de Neron et de Poppée', *Revue de philologie*, 1896, XX, pp. 12-22; 'Comment Poppée devint imperatrice', *ibid.*, 1897, XXI, pp. 221-239; 'Le règne et la mort de Poppée', *ibid.*, 1898, XXII, pp. 333-345.
[2] Nero seems to have had a real attachment for her and to have been strongly influenced by her, although in the end he killed her by kicking her in the belly when she was pregnant.
[3] Poppaea seems to have been a proselyte or at any rate to have inclined towards Judaism. Josephus (*A.j.* xx. 8, 11) describes her as θεοσεβής an expression which Salomon Reinach (*Oeuvres de Fl. Jos.* IV, p. 282, n. 1) calls 'intentionally ambiguous' and makes him think that Poppaea was at least half a Jewess. In the chapter in which he writes of her Josephus says that thanks to her intervention a Jewish delegation of which he was a member obtained the demands for which it had been sent, among others that Jews should not be compelled to pull down the wall which they had built to prevent anyone from seeing what went on in the temple from the additions which Agrippa had made to his palace. Josephus' Autobiography (3) speaks of the mission to Rome in exactly the same terms as the *Jewish Antiquities*, but both documents agree in saying that Poppaea put her influence at the service of the Jews. Tacitus (*Annales*, xvi. 6), after recounting Poppaea's death, says that her body was not cremated according to the Roman custom, but embalmed 'in accordance with the custom of foreign kings' and was then laid in the mausoleum of Augustus.   [4] Josephus, *Vita*, 3.
[5] Corssen, 'Die Zeugnisse des Tacitus und Pseudo-Josephus uber Christus', *Z.N.T.W.*, 1914, XV, p. 140.
[6] Even if what Clement of Rome (6, 1-2) says of the evil which jealousy brought upon the victims of Nero's persecution was to be considered anything more than a stereotyped phrase, nothing justifies its being referred to Jewish denunciations

secretly. So striking is the distinction which the Roman authority made in 64 between Jews and Christians.

From the very moment when the Jews appear to have denounced the Christians the latter became objects of hatred and a conflict broke out between the Empire and the church which the logic of events rendered inevitable. The national cult lay at the base of the Roman Empire. It was a compulsory act of loyalty to participate in it; to abstain under any pretext whatever was to show oneself a rebel. Towards 180 one of the Scillitan martyrs, Speratus, declared to the proconsul Saturninus who was examining him, 'I do not know the empire of this world. If I buy anything I pay the just price because I know my Lord, the master of the kings of all nations.' Another Donata declared, 'I honour Caesar as Caesar, but only God I fear'.[1] When in 258 Bishop Cyprian appeared before the proconsul, Paternus, he ordered him to recognise the order of the sacred emperor, 'Those who do not accept the Roman religion must take part in the Roman ceremonies'.[2] There is no room here for any consideration whether a religion is true or not or whether the gods ought to be worshipped or not. This is borne out by the epigram of Tiberius, 'The gods must be their own avengers'.[3] The privileged status of Judaism did not contradict this idea as it was only tolerated because it was a national religion. Only this peculiarity was taken into account, that the God of the Jews, like His worshippers, was jealous and could not be assimilated. This explains why Christianity could only enjoy the treatment meted out to Judaism for a time. Although it did so for quite a time, it did not fall into the same category as Judaism because it declined to be a national religion.

At an early date the ancient world became suspicious of

as Dom Leclercq does (art. 'Incendie de Rome', *D.A.C.L.*, VII, col. 491). Meliton of Sardis (quoted by Eusebius, *H.e.* iv. 26, 9) says in his *Apologia* written about 170 that Nero allowed himself to be persuaded by wicked men, but he does not say who these wicked men were. The whole literature of Christian apologetic, which could hardly be suspected of goodwill towards the Jews except for one late text, the *Carmen apologeticum* of Commodian, never mentions Jewish intervention in the events of 64. This text (about 825-860) under the inspiration of *Rev.* xi. 9-13 is in apocalyptic form and introduces the legend of *Nero redivivus* persecuting the Christians at the instigation of the Senate which had been driven to it by the Jews. Harnack (*Analecta zur altesten Geschichte des Christentums in Rom.*, Leipzig, 1905, pp. 7 f.) thought that Commodian was making use of a tradition which said that the Senate, driven by the Jews, had made Nero persecute the Christians. But this construction is very bold and has against it the fact that neither Tacitus nor Suetonius make the Senate have anything to do with the persecutions against the Christians.
[2] *Acta Cypriani*, i.
[1] *Passio SS., Scilitanorum*, 6, 9.
[3] Tacitus, *Annales*, i. 73.

Christianity and accepted with disconcerting facility all kinds of legendary calumnies. The fact that Christians were living in the expectation of a new world, which was not in any way peculiar in the first century of our era, was not sufficient to explain how they came to be suspected of being disinterested in the present world. It imperceptibly led people to think that they were its enemies.[1] In any case, we must take into account the mixed feelings of distrust and misunderstanding with which the Roman mind regarded the Oriental religions and the ease with which it accepted the most childish rumours and ridiculous calumnies about them. The secrecy with which the Christians surrounded their meetings, especially those for the celebration of the Lord's Supper from which the catechumens were excluded, may easily have facilitated the spread of calumnies (magic, infanticide)[2] Θυέστια δεῖπνα Οιδοπεδείοι μίξεις. We do not know whether these calumnies were already prevalent in 64. Tacitus in dealing with the fire of Rome speaks of the abominations which had made the Christians odious, but he may be projecting into his story sentiments which belonged to the time when he was writing. Justin Martyr,[3] the first Christian author to allude to these accusations, says that they were made very early on. They were certainly in circulation at the time when the *Annales* were being written and by 117 when Pliny wrote to Trajan and asked him if he was to punish the Christians for the *nomen*, i.e. merely because they were Christians or for *flagitia cohearentia nomini*, i.e. on account of crimes which in popular estimation were inevitably associated with Christianity but had to be proved by the magistrates actually to have been committed.[4] But it cannot be considered proved that these calumnies had begun to be spread as early as the time of the fire of Rome; on the contrary perhaps it ought to be considered that, if the Christians were accounted responsible for the fire, that very fact may have gone a long way in conditioning men's minds for accepting every kind of calumny against them. They disturbed public opinion which not only supported the authorities in their activities against the Christians but also often brought

[1] As has been suggested by Bouche-Leclercq (*L'intolerance religieuse et la politique*, Paris, 1911, pp. 128 f.) and less emphatically by Loisy (*La Naissance*, p. 235) in reference to the accusation brought against the Christians that they started the fire at Rome to which I shall return later.

[2] Cf. Dom. Leclercq, art. 'Accusations contre les Chrétiens', *D.A.C.L.*, cols. 265-307.

[3] Justin Martyr, *Dial.* 10; *Apol.* i. 26; ii. 12. Cf. Tatian, *Or. ad Graecos.* 42; Minucius Felix, *Octavius*, 9, 5 ff.

[4] Pliny, *Ep.* x. 96, 2. It is plain that neither Pliny nor Trajan really believed the accusations which were brought against the Christians.

pressure to bear on the magistrates and compelled them to take severe measures, when they would have preferred to treat the Christians with scornful indifference.[1]

At the beginning the magistrates before whom Christians were brought may have hesitated as to what procedure to apply to them and, as Pliny's letter shows, may have asked themselves if the *nomen*, i.e. the mere fact of confessing oneself a Christian, was a criminal offence in itself. But doubts did not last and quite early on the legal procedure and the law became fixed. Tertullian[2] defines that for Christians there was *confessio nominis* and not *examinatio criminis*.

2.—THE QUESTION OF THE 'EDICTUM NERONIANUM' AND THE PROCEDURE APPLIED TO CHRISTIANS

It is typical that a man like Pliny, before he was sent to Bythinia, had never been present at a trial of Christians and was not able to start proceedings against them until he had received instructions. But the form of proceedings to be taken against Christians existed at the beginning of the second century although it was not always applied with rigour. How long had it been in existence and what was its character? Opinion is very much divided on these points.[3] The essential point under argument is this. Were Christians prosecuted in virtue of particular laws which had been made to exterminate their faith or in virtue of general laws which were already in existence? If special legislation against them was not passed, did the measures taken against them consist of a judicial enquiry (*judicatio*) or were they measures to enforce public order (*coercitio*)? Those who maintain that there was special legislation think it took the form of an *institutum Neronianum* which would have taken this form: *Non licet esse Christianos*. This may be regarded as the traditional opinion. It seems to have been Tertullian's opinion[4] and has been defended

---

[1] The Acts of the Martyrs is full of traces showing that the magistrates often tried as hard as they could to persuade the Christians to give up what they thought was foolish nonsense. Cf. Eduard Meyer, *Urspr. u. Anf.* III, p. 514. The correspondence between Pliny and Trajan shows that the Roman authorities would often have preferred to have had nothing to do with the problem of the Christians.

[2] Tertullian, *Apologeticum*, ii. 3.

[3] Information concerning the history of the discussion will be found in Klette, *Die Christenkatastrophe unter Nero*, Tubingen, 1907, and Dom Leclercq, art. 'Droit persecuteur', *D.A.C.L.* IV, cols. 1646-1648.

[4] See especially *Ad nationes*, i, 7; *Sub Nerone, damnation invaluit . . . Et tamen permansit, erasis omnibus, hoc solum institutum Neronianum*. But we do not know if the word *institutum* here is to be taken in a legal sense.

particularly by Paul Allard, Callewaert, and Dom Leclercq.[1] Others such as F. C. Baur, Overbeck, Aube, and Mgr. Duchesne, think that there was special legislation, but that it was not devised before Trajan's reign.[2]

Tertullian's evidence, which is freely cited in support of the existence of an *institutum Neronianum*, is very far from being decisive. The *Apologeticum* contains many passages which would have inevitably contained a mention of such an *institutum*, if it had been in existence while actually there is not even the slightest allusion to it.[3] What is more convincing than this negative observation is that if an *institutum Neronianum* had been in existence Pliny's letter to Trajan and the emperor's reply to the legate would have been inconceivable. For this reason some scholars have questioned the authenticity of Pliny's and Trajan's letters on insufficient grounds as we shall see[4] and others think there was no special legislation until Trajan's time.[5]

The only evidence which plainly supports an *institutum Neronianum* is late. Sulpicius Severus[6] gives a summary of Tacitus' account of the fire of Rome and the massacre of the Christians and then says this, 'They thus began to take severe measures against the Christians.

[1] Of the numerous works by Paul Allard a list of which will be found in Dom Leclercq's article, *D.A.C.L.* IV, cols. 1565-1648, I shall only quote the last, *Dix leçons sur le martyre*, Paris, 1907, pp. 85 ff.; Callewart, 'Les premiers Chrétiens furent-ils pursuivis par édits spéciaux ou par mesure de police' *R. d'hist. ecol.*, 1901, II, pp. 771-779; 1902, III, pp. 5-15, 324-348, 604-614; 'Le délit de christianisme dans les premiers siècles', *Rev. des quest. hist.*, 1903, LXXIV, pp. 28-55; 'Les premiers Chrétiens et l'accusation de lèse-majesté', *ibid.*, 1904, LXXVI, pp. 5-28; 'Les persécutions contre les Chrétiens dans la politique religieuse de l'Empire romain', *ibid.*, 1907, LXXXII, pp. 5-19; 'La méthode dans la recherche de la base juridique des premieres persécutions', *Rev. d'hist. ecol.*, 1911, XII, pp. 5-16, 635-651; A. Piganiol (*Histoire de Rom. Clio. Introduction aux études historiques*, 3, Paris, 1939, p. 259) is inclined to think that there was special legislation decreed by Nero to punish the Christians. See also Dom. Leclercq's article mentioned above.

[2] F. C. Baur, *Das Christentum und die christliche Kirche in den ersten drei Jahrhunderten*, Tubingen, 1853[3], 1863, pp. 43 ff.; F. Overbeck, 'Gesetze der romischen Kaisern von Trajan bis Mark Aurel gegen die Christen', *Studien zur Geschichte der alten Kirche*, Schloss Chemnitz, 1875, I, pp. 93 ff.; Duchesne, *H.a.* I, p. 107; Aube, *Histoire des persécutions de l'Église jusqu'à la fin des Antonins*[2], Paris 1875.

[3] See for instance v.3: 'Consult your annals; you will see there that Nero was the first to strike with the sword against our sect which exactly at that time was starting up at Rome. That such a prince should have taken the initiative in condemning us is for us a claim to glory.' [4] See pp. 537 ff.

[5] Special legislation under Trajan would only be conceivable if it was proclaimed after he had had his correspondence with Pliny. The fact that neither Pliny's nor Trajan's letters show that they felt that existing legislation could not cope with the situation makes it very unlikely that this happened.

[6] Sulpicius Severus, *Chronica*, ii. 29.

Laws were then enacted to prohibit the religion. In the language of the published edicts none was allowed to be a Christian.' Paul Orosus[1] is less exact as he only mentions orders given by Nero against the Christians.

The theory most generally accepted by historians is that which Mommsen expounded in an epoch-making work[2] in 1890. He maintained that Christians were prosecuted under existing legislation as disturbers of public order.[3]

In any case, from Trajan's reign onward, all proceedings seem to have been taken in hand as if the law forbade the practice of Christianity but its prohibition, the legality of which no one would have thought of questioning, may well have been merely implied from existing legislation.

The two constant complaints against the Christians were atheism and a hatred of the human race (*odium generis humani*). Perhaps we are at first surprised at the former but on reflection we can understand it. From the point of view of the ancient world it was completely justified. Harnack[4] emphasised that the Greek term ἀθεότης had no Latin equivalent before the time of Ornobus and Lactantius. This is because Roman law was not concerned with ideas and still less with spiritual things, but only with the practical nature of the state religion and public worship. The *crimen laesae majestatis*[5] did not consist of holding disloyal views or ideologies but of refusing to participate in national feasts and ceremonies. To do this was to put oneself beyond the bounds of society. This is why the accusation of hatred of the human race was brought. Atheism and *odium generis humani* contained the necessary elements to make them crimes for which there were the most severe penalties. The populace considered

---

[1] Paul Orosus, *Hist. adv. paganos*, vii. 7.

[2] Mommsen, *Religionsfrevel nach romischen Recht Historische Zeitschrift*, 1890, LXIV, pp. 389-429 (a work which was reproduced in *Gesammelte Schriften*, IV, 1907). Cf. *Rom. Strafrecht*, 1899, pp. 567 ff. About the same time a similar theory was developed by K. J. Neumann in his book *Der romische Staat und die allgemeine Kirche bis auf Diocletian*, I, Leipzig, 1890. Only the first volume appeared.

[3] Suetonius (*Nero*, 16) places what he says about the measures taken against the Christians between two measures taken by the municipal police, (1) prohibiting publicans from selling any cooked foods except vegetables, and (2) regulating the chariot traffic in the streets of Rome.

[4] Harnack, *Der Vorwurf des Atheismus in den ersten drei Jahrhunderten*, Leipzig, 1905, p. 9. Cf. Mommsen, *Strafrecht*, p. 569. Eduard Meyer, *Urspr. u. Anf.* III, p. 518.

[5] Tertullian uses a series of terms equivalent to *crimen laesae majestatis*, e.g. *crimen laesae romanae religionis*, *crimen laesae divinitatis*, *sacrilegium*, *crimen majestatis imperatorum*.

that the atheism of the Christians incensed the gods and ran the risk of bringing down their wrath. Public opinion brought pressure to bear on the magistrates and compelled them to be severe with the Christians.[1]

Tertullian wrote, 'They look on the Christians as the cause of every public disaster and every national misfortune. Has the Tiber overflowed into the City? Has the Nile flooded the countryside? Has the weather remained unchanged? Has there been an earthquake? Have plague and famine appeared? Then the cry goes up, "Christians to the lions".'[2]

Harnack[3] thinks that the statement of the Apologists that the *nomen* was punishable with death can only be retained if it is understood that the *nomen* implied refusal to sacrifice to the gods so that a man who bore the *nomen* placed himself beyond the pale of society and became a *hostis publicus*. There was no need for the *non licet essex Christianos* to be officially proclaimed to make prosecutions of Christians possible. Mommsen[4] described the situation in these words, 'In fact proceedings against Christians were as constant as against brigands but they varied in degree. Sometimes they were conducted with mild indifference, at other times with severity'. Commenting on this Eduard Meyer[5] writes, 'The punishment of Christians was a result of the common conception of the state to which the Christians were irreconcilably opposed. Fresh arrangements were not necessary, but proceedings could be taken whenever a case of Christian profession came to the notice of the authorities.' By their whole attitude Christians attacked in a systematic way what in ancient societies was one of the essential prerogatives of the state, i.e. the right to dictate to all that they must participate in the national religion.

Between Christianity and the Roman Empire conflict was fatal. Two conceptions of religion diametrically opposed and irreconcilable clashed.

When Christians were accused of rebellion what form of proceedings were taken?[6] There might be regular proceedings with a

---

[1] Klette, p. 90.

[2] Tertullian, *Apol.* 40. Cf. *Ad nationes*, i. 9. Possibly as we shall see later, it was because the impiety of the Christians had drawn upon the city the anger of the gods, that they were held responsible for the fire of the city.

[3] Harnack, *Mission*, I, p. 458. [4] Mommsen, *Rom. Gesch.* V, p. 523.

[5] Eduard Meyer, *Urspr. u. Anf.* III, p. 512.

[6] A good article on the question will be found in Angar, *Die Frau im romischen Christen prozesse*, Leipzig, 1905, pp. 59 ff.

prosecution, denunciations, evidence from witnesses, pleadings, etc., but there was also a speedier method at hand which consisted of a police-court trial. The magistrates had both the right of judicial investigation (*judicatio*) and that of immediate punishment (*coercitio*). The line between the two possible procedures was not always very clearly drawn. In the majority of cases the magistrate himself chose which to follow. Mommsen thinks that the procedure of *coercitio* was the one most often followed.[1] Ecclesiastical tradition has certainly exaggerated, especially for the early period, the number of martyrs.[2] Except in 64 at Rome and in 177 at Lyon and Vienne up to a little before the middle of the third century, the number of the victims of persecutions was relatively small. Origen definitely says that the number of the martyrs was not very great and could easily be counted.[3] But the Christians lived in a state of perpetual insecurity. The threat of proceedings was constantly suspended over their heads like a sword of Damocles. The least incident or the vaguest of denunciations could start proceedings and create torments.

3.—THE MASSACRE OF CHRISTIANS AT ROME IN 64

The earliest text referring to the massacres of Christians which followed the fire at Rome in 64 is a passage from Clement of Rome which was written about 96. After enumerating the evils caused by jealousy and quarrelsomeness, Clement writes as follows, 'To these men[4] with their holy lives was gathered a great multitude of the chosen, who were the victims of jealousy and offered among us the fairest example in their endurance under many indignities and tortures. Through jealousy women were persecuted as Danaids and Dircae,[5] suffering terrible and unholy indignities; they steadfastly

[1] Mommsen, *Strafrecht*, p. 410. Angar (*Die Frau*, pp. 65 ff.) adopts Mommsen's conclusion but thinks that summary proceedings were only adopted after they had been regularised through regular trials. But neither the text of Tacitus nor that of Pliny hint at such trials.

[2] Harnack, *Mission*, I, pp. 460 ff.; Bouche-Leclercq, p. 145. Bouche-Leclercq certainly goes too far in his reaction against current ideas. It can scarcely be understood how a historian of his class can write, 'Tradition really only knows of two martyrs, Peter crucified and Paul beheaded' (p. 146). This sentence is quite out of harmony with what one reads on the preceding page.

[3] Origen, *C. Celsum*, iii. 8.

[4] No information of any value about the martyrdoms of Peter and Paul can be drawn from what Clement says about the two apostles.

[5] Lightfoot (I, 2, pp. 32 f.) suggests that the text is corrupt and proposes to correct it into γυναῖκες, νεάνιδες, παιδίσκαι (Women, young girls, slaves). This correction is unnecessary. We know (Martial, *Epigr.* 7, 8, 16, 21; Tertullian, *Apol.*

finished the course of faith, and received a noble reward, weak in the body though they were' (vi. 1-2). There is no doubt that Clement is referring in general terms to the massacres which followed the fire at Rome. There is a very significant coincidence between what he says of Danaids and Dircae and what Tacitus tells us of the theatrical display of the victims.[1] What is still more striking is that Clement speaks of a πλῆθος (a large number). The phrase is too reminiscent of Tacitus' expression *multitudo ingens* for the coincidence to be fortuitous.[2] The number of victims was certainly large but it is impossible to estimate the exact number. Klette[3] thinks that victims were counted in hundreds; this is not impossible, especially if, as seems probable, the games lasted for several days.[4] But the same author and others go too far in thinking that the Roman community was wiped out and that a completely new church was set up afterwards in its place.[5] Clement's explanation

15; cf. Friedlander, *Sittengeschichte Roms, II*[6], pp. 412 ff. Knopf, *Lehre der s. Ap. Z., Clembr.*, pp. 53 f.) that the Romans made free use of condemned persons for theatrical representations in which they were compelled to play the part of some mythological hero who met with a cruel fate and no consideration was given to feminine modesty. It is easy to imagine the representation of the Dircae, women bound naked to the horns of a mad bull. It is more difficult to imagine with any clarity what the representation of the Danaids was like. But that does not authorise us as M. Dibelius thinks (*R.u.d.Chr.*, p. 24) to reckon that Clement is only referring to images when he speaks of Dircae and Danaids. Tacitus also alludes to this kind of treatment being inflicted on Christian men and women. On this the highly coloured and brilliant pages of Renan must be read, *L'Antichrist*, pp. 163-181. The epistle to the Hebrews (x. 32-34) recalling the conflicts of former times refers to outrages and sufferings imposed on Christians and uses the expression θεατριζόμενοι. There is no doubt that we have here an echo of the theatrical spectacle which Nero made of the executions of Christians. Cf. Dibelius, *R.u.d.Chr.*, p. 15, n. 1.

[1] The fact that Clement offers the example of the apostles Peter and Paul and of the victims of Nero as belonging to 'our generation', although they took place thirty years before he wrote, cannot be considered a difficulty. The term 'our generation' is used in reference to examples borrowed from the Old Testament (from Abel to David). Irenaeus (*Haer.* v. 30, 3) writing about 190 says that John had had his revelation a short time before almost in our generation and that the Canon of Muratori, written half a century perhaps after the Shepherd of Hermas, says that this book had been written *nuperimme, temporibus nostris*.

[2] The coincidence is still more striking in as much as any direct contact between the two is out of the question. Clement and Tacitus must have used the same source.

[3] Klette, p. 30.

[4] Klette (p. 125), referring to Friedlander, *Sittengeschichte Roms. II*, p. 272, thinks that the games lasted sixteen days from the 4th to the 19th September.

[5] Klette (pp. 30 f.) is led to this conclusion by the fact that Clement has written πόλυ πλῆθος ἐκλεκτῶν and not πόλυ πλῆθος 'ημέτερων. He presses the sense of the words too far for even if the community had been completely reconstituted after being wiped out in 64 it would have had the feeling that it was connected with what had been destroyed. Does not Clement say somewhere else that the

that jealousy caused the massacres has led many scholars to think that the Christians were denounced by Jews.[1] Others like Bouche-Leclercq[2] think that the Christians were divided between themselves and denounced each other. This is drawing an inference from one word which might be only a simple literary stereotyped phrase belonging to a rhetorical scheme into which the reported facts failed to fit. To find seven recent examples as had to be done to correspond to the seven examples which he had borrowed from the Old Testament, Clement was obliged to have recourse to certain artifices. First, he made a distinction between the 'pillars', i.e. the apostles in general and Peter and Paul, who were the only two apostles of whom he knew anything or thought he knew. Then he separates the immense crowd of victims in 64 and the Danaids and the Dircae, who it is certain in fact were some of the victims in 64, and in order to make up the number seven which he wanted to do, he was further compelled to introduce two pieces to fill up, one on marriages broken by jealousy and another on towns and people whose ruin had been caused by jealousy. Clement does not write one word to show any connection between the massacres to which he alludes and the fire at Rome which he does not mention. That he does not claim to be giving an account of the events of 64 has no significance. Taken altogether his evidence amounts to very little and if we only had his text we should not know to what it refers.

Tacitus' account in book xv of the *Annales* gives a more accurate and detailed account, although it was written fifteen years after the letter of Clement.[3] After telling of the fire which broke out at Rome

martyrs had been a magnificent example 'among us'? Suetonius (*Nero*, 16), it is true, says, '*afflicti suppliciis christiani*', but that only means that those Christians who were caught were sent to be punished and does not imply that measures were taken to prevent any escaping. The idea that the Roman community suffered almost complete extermination has been maintained by H. Dannenbauer ('Die romische Petruslegende', *Hist. Zeitschr.*, 1932, CXLVI, pp. 246 f.). Against it see the observations of Leitzmann ('Petrus romischer Martyrer', *S.B.A.*, 1936, p. 397) and M. Dibelius (*R.u.d.Chr.*, p. 19, n. 2).

[1] See further back, p. 501.

[2] Bouche-Leclercq, pp. 125-138. Cullmann ('Les causes de la mort de Pierre et de Paul d'apres le temoignage de Clement Romain', *R.h.p.r.*, 1930, X, pp. 294-300) maintained the same thesis at least so far as the death of the two apostles is concerned.

[3] The *Annales* were published in 115 or 116 (Goelzer, *Tacite, Annales*, Paris, 1923, s., I, p. vi). Hochart (*Étude au sujet de la persécution des Chrétiens sous Néron*, Paris, 1885) maintained that the chapters in Tacitus referring to the Christians were an interpolation. Later on (*De l'authenticité des Annales et des Histoires de Tacite*, Bordeaux, 1890; *Nouvelles considerations au sujet des Annales et des Histoires de Tacite*, Paris, 1894) he went so far as to maintain that Tacitus' work was a late

on the fourteenth day before the kalends of Sextiles (= 19th July, 64) he writes of its causes with such great reserve that, although he is never explicit, we can guess what his personal opinion was. He gives two accounts which were in circulation and pretends that he does not wish to judge between them. According to one it was an unfortunate accident, according to the other Nero was to blame (*forte an dolo principis incertum*). But from chapter xxxviii to chapter xl the story is told with infinite art to give the reader the impression that Nero was the author of the catastrophe. The fire began in that part of the circus which was situated between the Palatine and Coelian Hills and was fed by the goods piled up in the shops which stood against the circus. Favoured by the wind it spread rapidly into the houses which were closely piled together and separated only by narrow alleys. Tacitus makes out that no one dared to fight the flames because people who said that they had had orders to do so withstood every effort to try and fight the fire. Did they want to take advantage of the opportunity offered by the fire for looting or were they agents of the emperor? Tacitus gives both explanations, but in accordance with his apparently self-imposed rule of hinting at Nero's guilt without explicitly saying so, he does not plump for either hypothesis (xxxviii. 2-8).

Nero was at Antium when news of the fire arrived and did not return to Rome until he learnt that the flames had reached the palace which he had built between the Palatine and the gardens of Maecenas. While Tacitus does not say so explicitly, it is plain from his narrative that Nero took upon himself to direct and press forward the fight with the fire. He offered refuge to the homeless crowds by opening to them the *campus Martis* and the monuments which Agrippa had built and even his gardens. He had huts built and food brought which was sold to the people at cheap prices. Tacitus does not lay stress on these measures but he notes that they did not increase the emperor's popularity because it had been noised abroad that, while Rome burnt, Nero sang on the stage of his private theatre the story of the burning of Troy (xxxix).

At last on the sixth day they were able to hold the fire at the bottom of the Esquiline where demolitions were going on to create an open space. The fire revived again at another point but this second fire caused less damage than the first, because it broke out in a quarter where the houses were not so crowded together as in the other parts.

fiction. These suggestions are so fantastic that criticism has no reason to take them seriously.

But it created worse rumours than the first because it began in the domain of Tigillenus, Nero's favourite, and the emperor was credited with the ambition to found a new Rome.

Of the fourteen districts of Rome, four were undamaged,[1] three were destroyed to the ground,[2] of the seven others there remained nothing but ruins. Although Tacitus may have somewhat exaggerated its extent,[3] it was a frightful catastrophe well likely to create a wave of emotion which might have proved dangerous, if measures had not been taken to calm or divert popular feeling.

Chapter xli is devoted to telling of some of the oldest religious buildings and treasures which were a prey to the flames. Chapters xlii and xliii tell of the measures taken by Nero for the reconstruction of the city and the regulations laid down to prevent a recurrence of such a disaster. Tacitus says, 'In addition to the measures which common sense called for, *piacula* were offered, ceremonies for the purpose of propitiating the anger of the gods'. But all this did nothing to efface the prevailing opinion that the fire had been ordered by the emperor (xliv. 3). In order, if possible, to remove the imputation, he determined to transfer the guilt to others. For this purpose he punished a race of men detested for their evil practices, commonly called Christians (xliv. 4). He must not have found it very difficult to make them accounted responsible for the fire. It is at this point that Tacitus gives a parenthesis explaining the origin of the name *Christian* (xliv. 3).[4] The explanation certainly comes from a different source from that used for the account of the measures taken against those who were supposed to be the incendiaries.[5]

First of all, one group of people were seized who confessed themselves guilty (*primum correpti qui fatebantur*) then on the evidence of these men (*indicio eorum*) a great crowd of persons were convicted not so much of having set the city on fire as of hatred of the human race (xliv. 6). Tacitus with disconcerting brevity reduces into this single sentence all that he tells us of the procedure followed. The rest of the chapter is devoted to an account of the torments inflicted.

---

[1] The XIVth (*Transtiberiana*), Ist (*Porta Capena*), Vth (*Esquilinia*), VIth (*Alta Semita*) (Goelzer, *Tacite, Annales*, III, p. 488, n. 6).

[2] The XIth (*Circus Maximus*), Xth (*Palatium*), and IIIrd (*Isis et Serapia*) (Goelzer, p. 488, n. 6).

[3] As Klette (p. 68) thinks who quotes H. Jordan, *Topographie der Stadt Rom im Altertum*, Berlin, 1878, I, pp. 483-491.

[4] See *J. de N.*, pp. 44 ff. *V. de J.*, pp. 73 ff. and *Life of Jesus*, pp. 94 ff.

[5] Corssen, *Z.N.T.W.*, 1914, XV, p. 135.

There were then two stages to the proceedings. First, an indefinite but certainly small number of Christians were arrested;[1] then on evidence provided by them—we do not know whether it was given voluntarily or under compulsion—mass arrests took place. Tacitus does not tell us if the victims were divided into two groups for torment and punishment, one after the other, as in the case of the arrests and trials. We must therefore suppose as well befits the way in which they were made a public spectacle, that to make the torments appear more impressive, they did not proceed until both groups had been condemned.

Two questions arise. On whose information were the first group arrested? Secondly, in what sense are we to understand the words *indicio eorum?* In answer to the first most scholars, with good reasons apparently, think that the Christians who were first arrested confessed their faith.[2] Some think that they admitted themselves guilty of the charge brought against them, that they started the fire.[3] Others have suggested that the text was made ambiguous on purpose.[4] In this case they argue that Tacitus was trying to insinuate that the Christians were guilty, although he could not say so explicitly because the sources at his disposal were not unanimous on this point. We do not think that this hypothesis can hold because Tacitus thought, or at any rate wanted to suggest to his readers, that Nero was responsible both for the fire and for the Christians being accused so that he would be acquitted of blame and would bring popular resentment on others. But it remains a strange fact that Tacitus does not say of the first group of Christians who were arrested something similar

[1] Perhaps on account of the part they played in the community or for some other reason which made them prominent.

[2] This is particularly the opinion of the majority of the translators of Tacitus, e.g. Goeltzer, *Tacite, Annales*, III, p. 491, and many others, e.g. R. Pohlmann, art., 'Nero', *R.E.*, XIII, p. 720, and M. Dibelius, *R.u.d.Chr.* p. 31.

[3] Such is H. Schiller's opinion, *Ein Problem der Tacituserklarung in Commentationes philologicae in honorem Theodori Mommsenii*, Berlin, 1877, pp. 42-47; Keim, *Rom und das Christentum*, Berlin, 1881, pp. 188-189. Such is especially C. Pascal's, *L'incendio di Romae i primi cristiani*, Milan, 1900 (second edition augmented, Turin, 1900); 'A proposito della persecuzione neroniana di cristiani', *Atene e Roma*, 1900, III, pp. 376-381; *Faith é legende de Roma antica*, 1903, pp. 117-185; Bouche-Leclercq, pp. 125 f. Quite often Bouche-Leclercq's thought is rather ambiguous : on p. 133 he notes that according to Christian eschatology the destruction of the world by fire was to be the work of God, but he attributes to the Christians the idea that once the fire had begun to fight it or to allow anyone to fight it would have been to oppose the will of God. Those who said that they had received orders to prevent anyone trying to fight the fire (*esse sibi auctorem*, xxxviii. 8) must have been Christians who thought that they were assisting the will of God.

[4] Klette, p. 109; Eduard Meyer, *Urspr. u. Anf.* III, p. 507.

to what he says of the second, viz. that if they were not guilty of incendiarism they were at any rate guilty of hatred of the human race. I shall return to this point later.

Do the words *indicio eorum* imply that the first group of Christians arrested allowed themselves to betray their brethren more or less of their own accord?[1] Bouche-Leclercq[2] rightly remarks that the text says nothing like this. It only says that through the instrumentality of the first group arrested they were able to arrest many others. The first Christians to fall into the hands of the police were able to provide much information in spite of themselves.[3] We have no reason to think that information was extracted out of them by torture. Neither Tacitus nor any other author who mentions the events of 64 makes the slightest allusion to this method of obtaining evidence.[4] There is no reason either for thinking that one faction had denounced another as there is no evidence to suggest that the church at Rome was in any way divided for such a hypothesis to be thought possible. It might be possible, as Klette thought,[5] that the first Christians who were arrested were convinced of their own innocence and failed to recognise the gravity of their position. Hence they somewhat rashly replied to questions which were put to them about their religion, its adherents, the places where they met for worship, and the police made use both of information they received in this way and of what could be gathered by investigation about the arrested people, their friends and haunts and perhaps also by searching their homes.[6]

Tacitus does not tell us what procedure was used. His story only gives the impression that it was expeditious and that things rapidly came to a head. There were three courts to which the case could have been submitted. Klette[7] thinks that the praetor's court must be ruled out as its procedure would not have been quick enough. The prefect of the city might have proceeded more expeditiously and the emperor's court still more so. Tacitus' story suggests that the emperor intervened personally and therefore we may suppose that the case was brought before his court acting with summary jurisdiction and almost unlimited power.[8]

---

[1] Cullmann, *R.h.p.r.*, 1930, X, p. 299 admits this.
[2] Bouche-Leclercq, p. 125. The text is interpreted in the same way by M. Dibelius, *R.u.d.Chr.*, pp. 31 f.   [3] Klette, p. 110.
[4] Mommsen, *Rom. Strafrecht*, pp. 406 ff. But Pliny made use of it. See p. 537.
[5] Klette, pp. 122 f.   [6] Bouche-Leclercq, p. 125.   [7] Klette, p. 99.
[8] The command of the pretorian guards was at that time discharged by Faenius Rufus and Ofonius Tigellinus (Tacitus, *Annales*, xiv. 51, 5). The latter was Poppaea's confidential attendant (xiv. 60, 4). This information favours the hypothesis that there was Jewish intervention.

Tacitus' story ends with a brief but impressive description of the victims dressed up in various ways and made part of the games of the circus, a refined form of cruelty. For convenience Nero lent his gardens. Dressed as a coachman, sometimes he mixed with the crowd and sometimes he took an active part in the games. The scene varied. Alternately the victims were dressed up as mythological figures and animals of the chase. Christians who had been covered with animals' skins were devoured by fierce dogs, while others were nailed to crosses and covered over with inflammable matter (*tunica molesta*), and when day declined were used as living torches (xliv. 7-8). Tacitus concluded by saying that, although these men were guilty and deserved hard punishment, one could not help but pity them as they were not sacrificed to the public interest but to gratify the whims of one man (xliv. 9).

From what sources did Tacitus obtain the elements of his story?[1] For the history of Nero's reign he made use of three sources, the elder Pliny, Cluvius Rufus and Fabius Rusticus. Cluvius' work seems to have been his principal source. The three sources differed on the question as to who was responsible for the fire. Pliny the elder made Nero responsible, as he speaks of old trees 'which survived up to the time of the fire by which Nero burnt the City'.[2] Klette[3] thinks that Fabius Rusticus shared this opinion and that for his work he used Suetonius as his source, which would prove as an established and incontrovertible fact that Nero burnt Rome.[4] Like Suetonius Fabius Rusticus was hostile to Nero;[5] but this is not sufficient to prove that he held him responsible for the fire. We do not know what his opinion was. Of Cluvius, Rusticus, and Suetonius, one at least believed in Nero's innocence; for it is a fact that Tacitus found that his sources did not agree and so could not give formal expression to his own conviction but was reduced to letting his readers guess what it was. He considered Christians capable of anything and deserving of the most dire punishments but he did not think them responsible for the fire. In his own mind he thought Nero was the incendiary.

---

[1] On this question see the fundamental work by Ph. Fabia, *Les sources de Tacite dans les Histoires et dans les Annales*, Paris, 1893, spec, pp. 184-191, 376-380, 398-404. Cf. Klette, pp. 80 ff.

[2] Pliny the elder, *Hist. nat.* xvii. 4: *Ad Neronis principia incendia quibus cremavit Urbem.*   [3] Klette, p. 80.

[4] Suetonius, *Nero*, 38: *incendit Urbem.*

[5] This is shown by the fact that Suetonius (*Nero*, 28) following Fabius Rusticus tells of the incest of Nero and Agrippina and makes out that Nero took the initiative in it while Tacitus (*Annales*, xiv. 2) following Cluvius Rufus does not believe that the crime was actually consummated but charges Agrippina with attempting it.

Tacitus is the only writer of all those who refer to the massacres of 64 to connect them with the fire of Rome.[1] Suetonius, who mentions the fire in chapter 38 of the *Life of Nero*, attributes it without any hesitation to the emperor. The executions he mentions in chapter 16 where he deals with various measures taken by the municipal police. Evidently he saw no connection between the two things.[2] Klette[3] tries to belittle the significance of this fact by the observation that Suetonius did not arrange his narrative in chronological order like Tacitus but grouped facts together according to their nature. But he does not just mention the tortures of Christians but explains their cause by the words *genus hominum superstitionis novae ac maleficae* (a group of men devoted to a new and evil superstition). If he had known or thought that this evil superstition had impelled them to set fire to Rome, would he have passed it over in silence? But it remains true that from the fact that Suetonius mentions the massacres of the Christians together with police measures which only concerned Rome he seems to think of them as purely local in nature and to have known nothing of any extension of the persecution outside Rome.[4] This plainly favours the hypothesis that the measures taken against the Christians were connected with something that happened at Rome, which is exactly the way in which Tacitus describes events.

In actual fact it is certainly not right completely to rule out *a priori* the possibility that the Christians caused the fire. Christian eschatology, which, generally speaking, had lost considerable force in the second generation, maintained that the final catastrophe must be the work of God, not of men; there may well have been some fanatics among the Christians at Rome who misunderstood this belief and thought it a work of piety to hasten God's vengeance on a corrupt city which was a seat of idolatry.[5] But in the face of the careful reserve shown by Tacitus and the complete silence observed by

---

[1] Except for some late texts such as Sulpicius Severus, *Chron.* ii. 29 and the correspondence between Paul and Seneca (*Ep.* xii of Seneca) which are dependent on Tacitus.

[2] Dibelius (*R.u.d.Chr.*, p. 34) strongly emphasises the fact that except for some notable exceptions, which are of no value as they come from texts dependent on Tacitus, no author, Roman or Christian, gives any indication of the fire and the massacre of the Christians being connected with each other.

[3] Klette, p. 77.

[4] Pohlmann, art. 'Nero', *R.E.*, XIII, p. 721. It is only at a very late date that we find the notion that Nero's persecution extended to the provinces. It is found in Lactantius, *De morte persec.*, 2, and in Paul Orosus, *Hist.* vii. 7.

[5] Piganiol, *Hist. de Rome*, p. 259.

Suetonius, the accusations brought against the Christians cannot be held to be true. Must we then hold Nero to be responsible for the fire in accordance with Tacitus' insinuations and Suetonius' explicit statement to which Renan[1] agrees? Tacitus' story gives the impression that Nero's purpose in proceeding against the Christians was to impress the masses, because the rumours denigrating him had originated with them. Yet, as Klette[2] rightly observes, the masses were always favourable to Nero;[3] right up to the end he remained popular; they refused to believe in his death and for a long time expected him to return.[4] It must then be supposed that the rumours condemning Nero were given credit in more exalted circles such as those from which those who joined Piso's conspiracy were recruited. One of the conspirators, Subrius Flavus, replied to Nero, when he was asked why he betrayed his oath, 'There was a time when no soldier in your army was more devoted to your service, and that was as long as you deserved the esteem of mankind. I began to hate you when you were guilty of parricide; when you became a coachman, a comedian, and an incendiary.'[5] The theatrical torture of men who were supposed to be guilty could hardly destroy rumours which circulated in circles such as this. What is more serious in the charge against Nero is that he made foolish proposals, which were the product of a diseased imagination and an indecent desire to have himself called a founder of the city. What we know of the psychology of this semi-madman makes it possible that he may have passed from dreams to action. But the positive charges brought against him do not allow his guilt to be taken as proved. Most scholars think that in fact the fire was the result of an accident.[6] Bouche-Leclercq[7] in particular has made out a sound case in Nero's favour. He argues that he would have wanted to allow a definite space for the building of the *Domus aurea* and reconstruction of the poor quarters but, if this was his desire, he bungled things badly as the fire destroyed the Palatine, the wealthy quarters, temples, the imperial palace itself and precious works of art. He only came back from Antium when he knew that

[1] Renan, *L'Antichrist*, pp. 144 ff. This is also Pohlmann's opinion (art. 'Nero', *R.E.* XIII, pp. 718 f.) who, however, thinks that the catastrophe assumed proportions far beyond those envisaged by the emperor.

[2] Klette, pp. 82 f.

[3] Dion Cassius (lxii. 18, 3) says explicitly that the charge of having set fire to Rome did not damage Nero's popularity.

[4] Suetonius, *Nero*, 57; Tacitus, *Hist.* ii. 8.

[5] Tacitus, *Ann.* xv. 67, 3-4. Cf. Dion Cassius, lxii. 24.

[6] E.g. Eduard Meyer, *Urspr. u. Anf.* III, p. 502.

[7] Bouche-Leclercq, pp. 115-122.

his own house was on fire; as Tacitus says he tried to fight the flames but (*tamen*) could not stop them before they had devoured the Palatine. If Nero had felt that he was being suspected, would he have started another fire in the gardens of Tigillinus, whom everyone knew was devoted to him? Would he have taken into his confidence a large number of people by ordering them to fight the measures taken to extinguish it and so have told them of his crime? Suetonius[1] holds out as a proof of his guilt the fact that he had buildings of hewn stone demolished by artillery, but he apparently did not know that one is sometimes compelled to make an empty space in front of a fire in order to fight it. If Nero, in the spirit of a morbid dilettante, had wished to enjoy the theatrical spectacle of the burning of Troy would he not have returned to Rome as soon as the sinister outbreak began? The fact that the evidence differs so widely as to where he sang the fall of Troy[2] suggests that all we have here is a legend which may have sprung from some foolish remark of the imperial actor. Rumour ran round that Nero started the fire; Pliny the elder and Suetonius say so explicitly; Tacitus hints at it; Subrius Flavus, at a time when he had nothing to go on, called Nero the incendiary, but Juvenal, who can find no punishment too hard for a wicked fellow like Nero, fails to mention the fire of Rome among his crimes. Except, as I have already remarked, at a quite late period and in direct dependence on Tacitus and Suetonius,[3] Christian writers who were not tender towards Nero make no allusion to Nero as an incendiary, while they attribute to him the initiative in the persecutions.

Whether it be Nero or the Christians who are accused there is no doubt that we must explain these accusations as due to human nature and its inclination to think that no great misfortune can happen without someone being responsible for it. In actual fact, the fire seems to have been due to accidental reasons. Its catastrophic growth was helped by the wind, the way in which the city was built, and the lack of adequate precautions. Although the fire of 64 was particularly terrible, it was by no means the only one which ravaged Rome.[4]

Must the good faith of those who accused the Christians be called in question? It is by no means certain; Tacitus shows by the way in

[1] Suetonius, *Nero*, 38.
[2] According to Tacitus (*Ann.* xv. 39, 4) in his private theatre, according to Suetonius (*Nero*, xxxviii. 6) on the tower of Maecenas, according to Dion Cassius (lxiii. 16) on the top of his palace.
[3] Sulpicius Severus, *Chron.* ii. 29, copies Tacitus and Paul Orosus (*Hist.* vii. 7) follows Suetonius. [4] Bouche-Leclercq, p. 121.

which he expressed himself that they were thought capable of anything. But there is one great difficulty. Tacitus is the only one to provide evidence of any connection between the measures taken against the Christians and the fire. Might it have been simply a guess on his part which historians who followed him did not mention because they were aware of its absurdity?[1] One thing alone can be inferred with any certainty from Tacitus' evidence, that is that the massacres of Christians took place shortly after the fire. It might simply have been nothing but a coincidence.

This is what Dibelius suggests[2] who thinks that the coincidence was the result of a trick on Nero's part to divert attention from the disagreeable rumours which were floating round about him and give public opinion something else to think about by massacring the Christians.

There is another conjecture possible. Tacitus' explanation of the name Christians comes from a different source than the one giving the story of the fire. It therefore may be supposed that Tacitus abandoned his principal source to give the explanation, which he then introduced by a personal remark of his own to the effect that the measures taken by Nero failed to appease the feelings of the masses. In his source what is said of the measures taken against the Christians may have come immediately after what was said of the *piacula*. This would lead one to think that the massacres of the Christians were originally part of the *piacula*. The catastrophe would have been thought of as a sign of the anger of the gods and efforts had been made to try and appease them by dealing severely with those whose impiety had annoyed them.[3]

Suetonius who wrote a little later than Tacitus adds nothing to what he had said.[4] To explain the measures taken against the Christians he preferred another version which incriminated them on the

---

[1] Klette, pp. 139 ff. [2] Dibelius, *R.u.d.Chr.*, pp. 32 f.

[3] This explanation given by Klette (p. 90) in passing he must apparently have preferred to that which he gives in addition on p. 89 in which he suggests that Nero tried to strike the popular imagination by sensational spectacles to create a diversion and stop them thinking too much about the catastrophe. It might also have been supposed as Ed. Cuq ('De la nature des crimes imputés aux Chrétiens d'après Tacite', *Mél., de l'Éc, franc. de Rome*, 1886, p. 129) that the Christians were not accused of actually starting the fire but of having caused it by magic arts. The idea must be avoided that they drew attention to themselves by refusing to take part in expiatory ceremonies after the fire. Only Roman citizens could participate in these ceremonies and the number of Christians at Rome who possessed the privilege of Roman citizenship could not have been large enough for their abstention to have attracted any attention (Bouche-Leclercq, p. 139).

[4] Suetonius, *Nero*, 16.

charge of their *malefica superstitio*. Are we to understand that this means witchcraft in the precise sense of the term? The text is too brief for us to decide definitely one way or the other. But even if we understood the term to mean witchcraft, Suetonius is not explaining the fire of Rome to have been due to this, as he explicitly makes Nero the cause of it. At the very most—and this is very uncertain—it might be suspected that we have here a very slight trace of a divergent tradition which made the Christians guilty.

The *Ascension of Isaiah* refers to the persecution of Nero in the form of a prophecy: 'Beliar, the great prince, the king of this world, who has ruled over it since it came into existence, will come down from his firmament in the form of a king of iniquity and a murderer of his mother; he will persecute the plantation of the twelve apostles of the Well-Beloved; of the twelve one will be delivered into his hands' (iv. 2-3).

There are two things here: a remembrance of Nero's persecution expressed in terms somewhat vague befitting what is supposed to be a prophecy and an allusion to a particular event, i.e. the martyrdom of one of the Twelve. Does this refer to Peter or to Paul?

Mgr. Tisserant[1] thinks that it can only refer to Peter. Such precision may seem arbitrary. But it is of little importance; what matters is that there is no reference to the fire of Rome.

Melitus of Sardis[2] recalls the persecution but makes no allusion to the fire. As he does so he gives vent to a theory which was destined to become classical: only the bad emperors, Nero and Domitian persecuted the Christians. Later on Tertullian adopted this idea and developed it in great detail.[3]

The idea that persecutions began with Nero and that his successors completely disapproved of the measures taken by him and could not annul them but had to be content merely to be moderate in applying them is an apologetic fiction. Nero's part was not as

---

[1] E. Tisserant, *L'Ascension d'Isaie*, Paris, 1909, pp. 29 f., 117.

[2] A fragment from his *apology* preserved by Eusebius, *H.e.* iv. 26, 9 s.

[3] Klette (p. 20) admits that Tertullian may have had other sources besides those with which we are acquainted. This is a very slender conjecture, as, when Tertullian refers the Romans to their Annals (*Apolog.* i. 3, 4), he imagines that the history of Christianity as he thinks of it must be reflected in the works of the Roman historians. His idea of the past of Christianity is quite fantastic. In spite of the ingenious defence put forward by L. Herrmann (*De Golgotha au Palatin*). Tertullian cannot be taken seriously when he relates that Tiberius, on the strength of reports received from Palestinian Syria, asked the senate to recognise Christ's divinity and on his proposal being refused he threatened the accusers of the Christians with death (*Apolog.* v. 2).

decisive as tradition imagined. What he did was entirely due to circumstances and was determined merely by the fact that it was in his reign that the Roman authorities were compelled to realise that Christians were not to be thought of purely and simply as Jews. Perhaps also the fire of Rome gave the latent hostility of public opinion against the Christians the chance to crystallise and appear in the open. From this time onwards the Christians were regarded as *hostes publici* because of their atheism and their hatred of the human race.

4.—FROM NERO TO DOMITIAN

The events which took place at Rome in 64 had no direct repercussions in the provinces in this sense at least, that they did not set in motion general measures against the Christians; none the less they affected the position of the church in the world. For those who all over the place did not like the Christians could not help but be encouraged to persecute and denounce them when they learnt what had just happened at Rome.

The Synoptic evangelists make Jesus predict to the disciples that they will be brought before magistrates and kings and that they will have to confess their faith before them. He promises them for this the help of the holy Spirit.[1] This is all the more significant as the synoptic gospels very seldom mention inspiration.[2] But while the gospels offer clear evidence as to the hostility of the public authorities to the faith and to consequent sufferings for the faithful, the language used prevents one thinking that they were written at a time of sharp persecutions. They belong to a period following persecutions, when at any time what appeared to be a most insignificant incident might provoke fresh ones. The situation is much too general in character for any close connection to be found between this saying and the events at Rome in 64. It springs from a fact which these events did not create but only revealed, viz. that Christians possessed no legal status in the Empire and could not have one, that they were on the edge of society and at any moment for the most trivial causes or even for no reason at all they might be treated as public enemies.

---

[1] Mark xiii. 9-13 (= Matt. xxiv. 9-14; Luke xxi. 12-19); Matt. x. 19-33 (= Luke xii. 2-12).

[2] Apart from the theological thesis that the holy Spirit will enable the disciples to understand the teaching of their master concerning the necessity of his sufferings and his death the only other mention of inspiration is in reference to the appearance of Christians before magistrates and courts.

It is this situation when, however, it had obviously grown worse which the first epistle of Peter discloses, the first draft of which seems to have been composed between 80 and 90. It is an exhortation addressed there is no doubt to Christians in Asia Minor who were being persecuted for their faith not so much by judicial and administrative measures as by ill-will from their neighbours. The author can still hope that if the Christians continue to behave themselves in a manner beyond reproach they will be protected by the magistrates. 'Submit yourselves to every ordinance of man for the Lord's[1] sake; whether it be to the king as supreme; or unto governors, as unto them that are sent by him for the punishment of evildoers, and for the praise of them that do well. For so is the will of God, that with well doing ye may put to silence the ignorance of foolish men' (ii. 13-17).[2] This passage implies that the Christians were subject to calumnies and accused of all kinds of misdeeds but were not being persecuted directly for their faith. But another passage of the epistle discloses a situation so different that we must assume that the document had been revised in the time of Trajan.

'Beloved, think it not strange concerning the fiery trial which is to try you, as though some strange thing happened unto you: but rejoice, inasmuch as ye are partakers of Christ's sufferings; that, when his glory shall be revealed, ye may be glad also with exceeding great joy. If ye be reproached for the name of Christ, happy are ye; for the spirit of glory and of God resteth upon you: But let none of you suffer as a murderer, or as a thief, or as an evildoer or as a busybody in other men's matters.[3] Yet if any man suffer as a Christian, let him not be ashamed; but let him glorify God on this behalf' (iv. 12-16).

The use of the term 'Christian' here shows that the authorities considered it an offence to be one involving the same penal sanctions as murder or theft. The *nomen* had become a crime. This fragment, according to what seems a very probable hypothesis, is reckoned to be the work of a compiler who turned what was originally a baptismal exhortation by Silvanus into a letter from Peter.[4] It also seems correct to attribute to this reviser the probable if not certain designation of Rome as Babylon (v. 13).[5]

---

[1] I.e. from motives of conscience and not simply from expediency.

[2] By revealing that there were no grounds for the accusations brought against the Christians.

[3] Goguel translates the word αλλοτριοεπίσκοπος by intriguer. We have given the translation of the Authorised Version. See Windisch, *Kath. Br.*, p. 77, concerning its interpretation.

[4] Bornemann's hypothesis. See p. 339, n. 1. [5] See pp. 154 ff.

Another document which, like the first epistle of Peter, belongs to the period separating Nero's persecution from Domitian's is the Book to the Seven Churches which is used as an introduction to the Johannine Apocalypse (i. 4-iii. 22). The date of its initial composition must apparently be dated round about 80-85.[1] When this book was composed the churches did not enjoy assured peace; but their situation does not seem to have been very critical. The first indication of the hostility to which Christians were sometimes exposed is furnished by the way in which in i. 7 the return of the Lord is invoked as a threat to his tormentors. The allusion in ii. 3 to sufferings which the church at Ephesus has endured without giving in is really exact enough but does not enable us to know where these sufferings came from. To the church at Smyrna it is predicted that a persecution is near, which will be instigated by the Jews, and that some members of the church will be thrown into prison. It is not said that any of them will perish: the tribulation will last ten days. The term must certainly

---

[1] The language, vocabulary and style of the Book to the Seven Churches are the same as those of the remainder of the Apocalypse. The affinities in ideas are equally striking. But the book cannot have been written at the same time as the rest of the Apocalypse, i.e. at the end of Domitian's reign. It is an earlier work of the prophet John which he revised to use as an introduction to his new work. The reasons justifying this opinion are (1) the initial salutation (i. 4-6) uses the title of the Apocalypse twice (i. 1-3); (2) in iv. 2 the seer falls into an ecstasy although he never states that the ecstasy mentioned in i. 9 comes to an end; (3) one of the dominating concerns of the Book to the Seven Churches, i.e. the struggle against heresy is not mentioned in the remainder of the Apocalypse; (4) persecution is not unknown in the Book to the Seven Churches, but seems to have been fairly intermittent, while in the rest of the Apocalypse persecution is constant. To fix the date when the Book to the Seven Churches was written we must take into account, the fact that one of the towns to which it is addressed is Laodicea which was destroyed by an earthquake in 61-62 and was soon rebuilt out of its own funds (Tacitus, *Annales*, xv. 27, 1). The letter to the Seven Churches contains no allusion to this event and can therefore only have been written well before 61-62 or appreciably much later, when the impression caused by the catastrophe had had time to grow faint. The *terminus a quo* may therefore be supposed to be the year 75 and the composition of the book may be fixed round about 80-85. We do not think that much can be made of i. 9 where it is said that John was at Patmos for the Word of God and the witness of Jesus. Tradition with most of the interpreters think that he was in exile there and Eduard Meyer (*Urspr. u. Anf.* III, p. 557) declares that he does not understand how any other meaning could be given to the passage. I feel that at the very least Bousset's interpretation (*Die Offenbarung des Johannes*, Meyer, XVI[5] Giessen, 1896, p. 223) cannot be altogether ruled out. He thinks that John was at Patmos in the course of a missionary tour. Bousset rightly observes that the scholars who speak of John being in exile at Patmos appear to have no other source than the Apocalypse itself and that the sentence, 'I fell into ecstasy on the Lord's day' (i. 9) and not 'a day of the Lord' implies that John spent only one Sunday in Patmos, which agrees with the idea that he was on a missionary tour and not in banishment.

be understood symbolically: it proves, however, that the persecution will be short (ii. 9-10).[1] The church at Pergamum has known persecution without denying the name of the Lord even in the days when the faithful martyr Antipas was put to death.[2] At the time when the author was writing, the persecution was over; it could not have been very terrible as only one martyr had perished. The author does not seem to have foreseen that it must return (ii. 12-17). The church at Philadelphia also has known persecution; it continues to be threatened with it; it is praised because it has not denied the name of the Lord (iii. 8) but a promise is also made to it that it will be preserved at the time of the great tribulation, i.e. of the final drama (iii. 10). All this as can be seen is quite vague. Each of the seven letters finishes with a promise made to him who shall overcome. To describe the faithful as soldiers was current metaphor in antiquity.[3] We find it in many passages in the New Testament referring to persecution.[4] But in the Book to the Seven Churches it may have special significance and be an exhortation to faithfulness in witness, faithfulness which, if necessary, must go as far as martyrdom which is described as a victory.

One clear allusion to the hatred of the world, i.e. to the persecutions to which Christians will be exposed, is to be found in the second half of the farewell discourses in the Fourth Gospel.[5] The

---

[1] This information is so precise that we are led to think that it is a prophecy *ex eventu*.

[2] Pergamum (Ramsay, *The Letters to the Seven Churches of Asia and their place on the plan of Apocalypse*[2], London, 1906, pp. 281 ff.) was a religious centre of the first importance, the 'Lourdes' of Asia Minor, Lohmeyer says (*Die Offenbarung des Johannes*, Tubingen, 1926, p. 13), with a gigantic altar of Zeus Soter. A temple of Augustus was built there in 29 (Tacitus, *Annales*, iv. 3). Deissmann (*Licht vom Osten*, p. 210, n. 6) thinks that the phrase 'throne of Satan' refers to this altar. But it seems rather that this expression must be explained by the cult of Aesculapius which played a great part at Pergamum. The serpent was one of the attributes of Aesculapius. In Ramsay (*The Letters*, pp. 285 ff., Figs. 23-25) will be found coins from Pergamum on which a serpent figures. One of them shows Caracalla worshipping the serpent-god of Pergamum. It is not surprising that the Christians identified this serpent with Satan.

[3] Cumont, *Textes et monuments figures relatifs au culte de Mithra*, Brussels, 1896-99, I, p. 317, n. 1; *Les réligions orientales dans le paganisme romain*[4], Paris, 1929, pp. x f., 207 f.; Reitzenstein, *Hellen. Mysterienrel.*, pp. 71 ff.

[4] E.g. 2 Cor. x. 4; Phil. I, 30; Col. ii. 1; iv. 12; 1 Thess. ii. 2; v. 8; Eph. vi. 11 ff.; 1 Tim. iv. 10; vi. 12; 2 Tim. ii. 3; iv. 7; Heb. xii. 1. Cf. Harnack, *Militia Christi, Die christliche Religion und der Soldatenstand in den ersten drei Jahrhunderten*, Tubingen, 1905. This work gives an extract of the Christian texts of the first three centuries containing metaphors borrowed from military life.

[5] Concerning the composition of the Farewell-discourses see *Introd.* II, pp. 366 ff.

first half is directly connected with the story of the last supper (xiii. 1-xiv. 31) while the second (xv. 1-xvii. 26) has no organic connection with what precedes it nor with the story of the arrest which follows. The man who pieced together the gospel thought that the last argument of chapter xiv (25-31) was the end of Jesus' discourse and came immediately before the departure for Gethsemane.[1] There is a striking parallel between xiv. 30-31 and the last words spoken by Jesus before his arrest in Mark (xiv. 42). The words, 'Arise, let us go hence' indicate an end. After saying these words Jesus cannot have added a long discourse, especially such a discourse as is contained in chapters xv to xvii, which, on account of their solemn and grave style, could not have been uttered in the hubbub of departure. The words: 'Peace I leave with you' in verse 27 at once recall to mind the Semitic phrase for goodbye. Finally the sentence in verse 30, 'Hereafter I will not talk much with you', which almost certainly should read, 'I will talk no more',[2] cannot originally have been followed by a complete discourse. As Merx[3] says, for chapters xv to xvii to follow xiv. 31 is impossible, both in logic and aesthetic form. Yet they show with what goes before too many affinities both in thought and language for one to be able to attribute them to another hand. We must therefore suppose that they were added by the evangelist at a later date. These chapters have one idea not to be found in chapters xiii and xiv, i.e. that of the hatred of the world for believers. The evangelist added them to introduce this idea. The situation had therefore changed; persecution had begun or was threatening to begin.

The first half of the farewell-discourse proceeds in an atmosphere entirely devotional; it is entirely concerned with the relations of the disciples to Christ. The world is only mentioned twice in quite a negative fashion (xiv 17, 30). The discourse is addressed to men who have not been pressed in any way or at any rate have not been pressed with any violence. They are indeed living in an environment where the church is not understood but not one where Christians are subject to being harassed and still less to persecutions. In the second half the faithful are advised to live united to Christ, which means that they are to resist the action of the world tending to separate them from him. The world hates them, and will persecute them as it

---

[1] Schwartz, 'Aporien in vierten Evangelium', *N.G.*, 1908, III, p. 184. Spitta, *Das Johannesevangelium als Quelle der Geschichte Jesu*, Giessen, 1910, p. 299.

[2] The reading in the Syriac version and in Chrysostom which is adopted by Blass in his edition of the Fourth Gospel and by Merx, *Die vier kanonischen Evangelien nach ihrem altesten erreichbaren Texte*, ii. 2. *Das Evangelium des Johannes erlautert*, Berlin, 1911, p. 383.   [3] Merx, II, 2, p. 384.

persecuted their master (xv. 18-21; cf. xvi. 1-2). Connected with this idea is found that of the world being condemned by the Paraclete (xvi. 8, 11, 33).

The conflict between the church and the world is therefore open; the era of persecution had begun but the evangelist puts into the mouth of Christ the prediction of the condemnation of the world, i.e. the prophecy of his chastisement and of the vengeance of the faithful. This is exactly the same situation as described in the Johannine Apocalypse but by a man of a very different temperament.

The discourse makes persecution to be the logical result and continuation of the incredulity with which Jesus had been received. It might therefore be supposed that the Jews are to be thought of as the enemies of Christians.[1] But we must not attach too much importance to this suggestion. The fourth evangelist is an idealist who was more interested in observing the facts of history transcendentally as a series of events arranged by God rather in tracing their historical development. He makes no distinction between those who were attacking the faith on the plane of ideas and doctrine and those who were tormenting believers. Assuming the date when his book was compiled we must conclude that the second layer of the Johannine discourses reflects the persecution of Domitian.

5.—THE PERSECUTION OF DOMITIAN

From Nero's time to the end of Domitian's reign Christians never knew peace and security. They were continually exposed to personal vexations rather than to administrative or judicial action of a public nature. But their position grew considerably worse at the end of Domitian's reign, especially at Rome with repercussions, however, in the provinces, particularly in Asia.

Christian tradition[2] made Domitian the second author of persecution after Nero. His actions against the Christians and simultaneously against the Jews can only be understood within the general framework of his policy and administration in religious affairs.[3] Domitian was concerned to defend and restore the national religion, which was threatened by an extension of the Oriental cults which Vespasian and Titus had failed to defeat. He was particularly

---

[1] This opinion seems to be confirmed by xvi. 1-2, 'They will put you out of the synagogues . . . whosoever killeth you will think that he doeth God service'.

[2] Meliton, *Apol.*, in Eusebius, *H.e.* iv. 26; Tertullian, *Apolog.* 5; Lactantius, *De morte pers.* 3; Eusebius, *H.e.* iii. 17-20.

[3] See the classic book by Gsell, *Essai sur le règne de Domitien*, Paris, 1893.

distrustful of Judaism which, since the advent of the Flavians,[1] had made notable progress at Rome. In the sphere of administration Domitian's policy was notable for efforts to detract from the authority of the senate to the benefit of the *princeps* and showed almost open hostility for the ancient aristocracy.[2]

Domitian showed great extravagance by the games which he loved to give, by multiplying the number of distributions of largesse to the populace and by the construction of many and important buildings.[3] He had squandered enormous sums and drained the imperial treasury.[4] Persuaded that the fall of Jerusalem and the dispersion of its inhabitants had definitely reduced Jewish fanaticism to impotence, Vespasian, and following him Titus, had treated the Jews with generosity, only demanding that they should declare their religion and pay to the temple of Jupiter Capitolinus the tax of the didrachma which formerly had been paid by them to the temple treasure at Jerusalem (*fiscus judaicus*).[5] Towards the end of his reign Domitian was moved, both by his policy in religious affairs and by his financial policy, to make the *fiscus judaicus* more rigorous in its application.[6] He wanted to impose it, not only on circumcised Jews, but also on all those who had adopted Jewish ways of living. A thorough campaign was taken in hand in which denunciations played a part to discover who could be compelled to pay the *fiscus judaicus;* Christians were found to be included among them. These measures were originally undertaken to relieve the embarrassment of the treasury. Although Domitian did not favour Judaism very much he does not seem at first to have thought of persecuting it.[7]

We know very little about the history of the Roman church between the massacres of 64 and the epistle of Clement of Rome, i.e. between Nero's reign and the end of Domitian's. In these thirty years the church had repaired its losses and made conquests even in the emperor's private circle.

Among Domitian's victims figure members of his own family, Flavia Domitilla his niece, and also almost certainly her husband, the consul Flavius Clemens, but the evidence concerning them does not altogether agree.

[1] He showed himself relatively favourable to the cult of Isis which had been long established in Rome as though he had no desire to canalise towards himself the religious current which the Oriental religions were attracting. Cf. Gsell, pp. 75 ff.   [2] Gsell, pp. 238 ff.   [3] Gsell, pp. 90-119.
[4] Suetonius, *Domitien*, 12; Martial, *Epigr.* ix. 3; Gsell, pp. 119-127.
[5] Josephus, *G.j.* vii. 6, 6; Dion Cassius, ix. 3; cf. Juster, II, pp. 282-286.
[6] Suetonius, *Domitian*, 12; Martial, *Epigr.* vii. 82.   [7] Gsell, pp. 291 ff.

Eusebius[1] says that the flourishing state of the church led profane historians to speak of the persecutions which it sustained under Domitian. He uses the plural, but this seems to be merely literary in character, as in the *Chronica* he only mentions Bruttius[2] who states that many Christians endured martyrdom under Domitian.[3] This Bruttius is unknown but Suetonius and Dion Cassius seem to have used him as a source; possibly then he related the martyrdom of Flavius Clemens and others in terms which, without saying explicitly that they were Christians, did not exclude the possibility. Eusebius then added precision to what he said because he knew or thought that he knew that Domitian's victims had belonged to the church.

Suetonius[4] reports, 'on a very slight suspicion (*ex tenuissima suspicione*) he put to death almost at the time when he was consul,[5] Flavius Clemens,[6] his first cousin,[7] a man who was despised for his idleness and whose sons while they were still young he had named as his heirs'.

According to Dion Cassius[8] Domitian condemned the consul Flavius Clemens with many others, although he was his cousin and was married to Flavia Domitilla, who was also related to him. Flavius Clemens had been convicted on a charge of atheism. Many others were condemned for that and for being inclined to Jewish customs. Some were punished by death; others had their goods confiscated. As for Domitilla she was exiled to the island of Pandateria. There is no difference apparently to be made between the case of Flavius Clemens and his wife being accused of atheism and that of other persons who were in addition accused of a certain inclination to Jewish customs. To live like a Jew might be ranked as atheism if it resulted in abstention from the national cult. There is no doubt that Flavius Clemens, his wife, and those who were accused with

---

[1] Eusebius, *H.e.* iii. 18, 4.

[2] The Armenian version and George Syncelle give the form Brettius.

[3] Eusebius, *Chronica arm.*, ed. Karst, p. 218. *St. Jerome's version*, ed. Helm, p. 192. Cf. George Syncelle, *Chron.* (ed. de Bonn), p. 650; Georges Hamartolos, III, p. 131. [4] Suetonius, *Domitian*, 15.

[5] I.e. doubtless as soon as he quitted office. F. Clemens, ordinary consul in 95, probably remained in office from 1 January to 30 April (Gsell, p. 303). His punishment must then have taken place in May 95.

[6] The identification of Flavius Clemens with Clement of Rome which sometimes has been suggested cannot be retained.

[7] Titus Flavius Clemens was the son of Titus Flavius Sabinus, Vespasian's brother who was prefect of the City. His wife Flavia Domitilla, Vespasian's granddaughter was the daughter of a sister of Domitian who had the same name.

[8] Dion Cassius, lxvii. 14.

them made no formal profession either of Judaism or of Christianity.[1] Dion mentions only a leaning. In the eyes of the Romans Jews and Christians were the same from this point of view. Dion Cassius' text does not allow us to affirm that Flavius Clemens and those accused with him were Christians or that there were Christians among them; nor does it allow us to deny the fact. It does not therefore provide sufficient evidence for us to dismiss the statements as legendary which say that Flavia Domitilla was a Christian.

Philostratus[2] mentions that Flavius Clemens was put to death without saying why.[3] He adds that Domitian compelled his wife to remarry three or four days after her husband had been punished.[4] This contradicts all the other evidence.

Eusebius says in the *Chronica* following Bruttius that many Christians underwent martyrdom under Domitian; in particular he names Flavia Domitilla who was relegated to the island of Pontia because she had confessed her witness to the Christ. He repeats this in the ecclesiastical history;[5] but here he makes Domitilla Flavius Clemens' niece and does not mention his condemnation or Domitilla's connection with the emperor. He names her place of exile as the island of Pontia and not Pandateria which Suetonius gives. On this last point he is in agreement with St. Jerome[6] who relates that Paula visited the island of Pontia which had been ennobled by the exile of Domitilla and the *cellulae* in which she lived.[7]

---

[1] Harnack (*Einf.*, pp. 50 f.) and Dibelius (*R.u.d.Chr.*, p. 39) without formally saying so incline to think that Flavius Clemens and Domitian's other victims were Christians.   [2] Philostratus, *Life of Apollonius*, viii. 25.

[3] Philostratus says that Domitian gave his own sister in marriage to Flavius Clemens. Zahn (*Der Hirt des Hermas*, Gotha, 1868, p. 45, n. 4) suggests that a confusion exists between Domitian's sister and mother who had the same name. Lightfoot (I, 1, p. 44) assumes the text to be corrupt and proposes to correct ἀδελφὴν into ἐξαδελφὴν or ἀδελφιδῆν.

[4] Some authors (e.g. Renan, *Les Evangeles*, p. 296, n. 5) suggested that Philostratus means that he sent her to rejoin her husband. Erbes ('Das Alter der Graber und Kirchen des Paulus und Petrus in Rom', *Jarhrb.*, *prot. Theol.*, 1878, IV, p. 700 f.); Zahn (*D. Hirt. des Hermas*, p. 45, n. 4); Lipsius (*Chronologie der romischen Bischofe*, Kiel, 1869, p. 156); Lightfoot (I, 1, p. 113) seem to have shown this interpretation to be impossible.

[5] Eusebius, *H.e.* iii. 18, 4.   [6] Jerome, *Ep.* cviii. 7.

[7] Because of the divergence between Suetonius and Eusebius certain scholars (De Rossi, *Bull. d. arch. crist.*, 1865, pp. 17 ff., 1875, pp. 69 ff.; H. Achelis, *Acta SS. Nerei et Achillei*, Leipzig, 1893, p. 50 f.; Dom Leclercq, art. 'Domitien', *D.A.C.L.*, IV, col. 1396, art. 'Domitilla (Flavia)', *ibid.* IV, cols. 1401-1404) suggest that there were two Flavias, one the wife of the consul and the other his niece. It is a very bold combination to suggest. The disparity between Suetonius and Eusebius as to the place of exile may be explained by the fact that the two authors independently of each other had a common source (the work of Bruttius) which

Gsell[1] thinks that Eusebius does not mention Flavius Clemens because he did not show the same sympathy to the Christians as his wife. If he had known of a source which spoke of Flavius Clemens and Flavia Domitilla in terms similar to those used by Dion, he would not have described Flavia Domitilla alone as a Christian. He thinks that she was one because of the church's tradition. If Flavius Clemens had belonged to the church officially he would not have followed a senatorial career. Dom Leclercq[2] makes him out to be a convinced Christian, who would have drawn upon himself the emperor's anger if he had refused to participate in any religious ceremony which was laid upon him by his office. But if he had not retired in face of such a scandal would he have passed for the indolent person of whom Suetonius speaks?[3] Would Dion have been likely merely to say that he had been suspected of atheism? And above all would the church have been able to forget such a magnificent example of resistance to idolatry which a consul had shown while in office? Flavius Clemens may have secretly shared his wife's convictions but, anxious to preserve his reputation and his career and not to stand in the way of the future of his sons whom the emperor had adopted, there is no doubt that he decided not to enter the church officially. This explains why he was not remembered as a martyr.[4] Was Flavius Clemens a man lacking in consistency who had not the courage to bring his conduct into line with his convictions? Possibly; but it is possible also he considered the Roman religion to be only a political system and did not see or did not want to see that the worship of the Christ was incompatible with participation in the national cult which was for him only an act of civil duty. He may then have been a semi-Christian rather than an inconsistent Christian.

Domitilla as a woman was not under the same obligations. She may have pledged herself to the church. An inscription uncovered in 1822[5] proves that she possessed an estate on the Atreatine Way a mile

did not state where Domitilla was exiled. The only real difficulty surviving would be concerning her parentage. A conjecture of Gsell (p. 298) could easily solve it. He suggests that Eusebius' source had been slightly corrupted and that it originally read Φλαυίαν Δομετίλλαν Φλαυίου Κλήμεντος [γύναικα Δομετιανοῦ] ἐξ ἀδελφῆς γεγονυῖαν. The words in brackets would have been omitted by the copyist.

[1] Gsell, p. 299.

[2] Dom Leclercq, art. 'Clemens (Titus Flavius)', D.A.C.L., III, col. 1869.

[3] Nor would Suetonius have spoken of a very slight suspicion.

[4] M. Besnier, Les catacombes de Rome, Paris, 1909, p. 117.

[5] Ser. Cornelio Juliano frat(ri) piissimo et Calvis(i)ae ejus, P. Calvisius Philotes, et sibi, ex indulgentia Flaviae Domitill(ae) in fronte p(edes), XXXV, in agro p(edes) XXX (C.I.L., 16, 246).

and a half from Rome. At this spot is the *caemeterium Domitillae*[1] which was identified by J.-B. de Rossi in 1852. This catacomb is in parts very early, but it is impossible to think that it could have been used for the burial of Christians before 95.[2]

While, in conclusion, the supposition that Flavia Domitilla was a Christian does not meet with objections as decisive as in the case of her husband we cannot be sure of it, as Eusebius does not support it, and for many centuries the church at Rome knew nothing of the martyrdom of the Flavian family.[3]

There may have been Christians among the other victims of Domitian of whom Dion speaks without naming them. Must we reckon Glabrion[4] to have been a Christian whom Domitian had wronged in 91 by having him brought into the arena when he was consul in addition to accusing him of atheism. Yet previously he had invited him to Albano at the feast of the *Juvenalia* and there had compelled him to fight an enormous lion, an ordeal through which the consul came unscathed. Suetonius says[5] that after being exiled he was put to death *quasi molitor novarum rerum*, i.e. on the charge of having fomented a conspiracy. He seems to think that he was sent into exile on another charge.[6] A hypogeum of the cemetery of St. Priscilla which is not earlier than the second century was cleared away in 1884 and was found to contain tombs of several Cecilii.[7] This makes it possible that the consul of 91 was a Christian, but in any case he would not have been any more decided in his profession than Flavius Clemens.[8]

---

[1] Besnier, *Les Catacombes de Rome*, pp. 112 f. Dom Leclercq, art. 'Domitilla (Cimetière de)', *D.A.C.L.*, IV, cols. 1404-1442, which gives an abundant bibliography.

[2] These doubts have been much accentuated by the remarks of P. Styger ('Die romischen Katakomben', *Archaologische Forschungen uber den Ursprung und die Bedeutung der altchristlichen Grabstadten*, Berlin, 1933. Cf. 'Stuhlfauth, Die romischen Katakomben, Bermerkungen zu Paul Styger's romischen Katakombenswerk', *Theol. Blatter*, XIV, 1935, cols. 16-24). H. Achelis (*Acta SS. Ach. et Ner.*, p. 51) remarks that the catacomb bearing Fl. Domitilla's name shows no trace of any veneration of her. Those especially venerated there are Petronilla, Nereus and Achilleus.

[3] H. Achelis, *Acta SS. Ach. et Ner.*, p. 51.   [4] Dion Cassius, lxvii. 14.

[5] Suetonius, *Domitian*, 10.   [6] Gsell, p. 304.

[7] Besnier, *Les Catacombes de Rome*, pp. 107 ff. Gsell, pp. 294 ff.

[8] If it were possible that Glabrion was a Christian, then it would be very probable that Civica Cerealis and Salvidienus Orfitus were also Christians as Suetonius relates that they were condemned at the same time as Glabrion. Gsell (pp. 295 f.) remarks that Philostratus (*Life of Apollonius*, vii. 33; viii. 7) mentions Salvidienus Orfitus' indolence and says that Christians suspected of being indifferent to politics were often reproached with being indolent.

The measures taken by Domitian throw light particularly on his concern to protect Roman society from Jewish and Christian propaganda the extent of which had been revealed by the investigations concerning the *fiscus judaicus*. Possibly, as Bouche-Leclercq suggested,[1] he saw with distress Jews and Christians infiltrating into the upper classes which he considered to be just as serious as the conversions which were taking place in the lower ranks of society with its cosmopolitan population.[2] But perhaps he only wanted to safeguard the traditional character of Roman society which was built up on the state-religion, or perhaps he considered Christianity to be a direct threat to the Empire and regarded mention of Christ as the king to be conspiring against the Empire. We should have to accept this explanation if we could regard as well founded the tradition of Hegesippus preserved by Eusebius[3] which states that heretics[4] denounced Jude's grandchildren as kinsfolk of Christ and belonging to the race of David. Domitian made them appear before him and then recognised that they were inoffensive peasants and released them, at the same time publishing an edict putting an end to the persecution. The traditions of Hegesippus are valuable when they tell us of the nature of Palestinian Christianity, but scarcely deserve any confidence when they narrate positive facts.[5] The measures against the *desposunoi* as the descendants of David are sometimes attributed to Vespasian and sometimes to Domitian.[6] At the same time I cannot agree with Eduard Meyer's[7] opinion that Hegesippus had good sources at his disposal. Gsell[8] with a much saner appreciation of things judges that Hegesippus's story is legendary. In addition Eusebius' version of it gives the impression that he does not want to guarantee its accuracy.

It is difficult to reject altogether the tradition that Domitian did not restrict himself to fighting Christian infiltration into the upper

---

[1] Bouche-Leclercq, pp. 180 f.

[2] Ed. Meyer (*Urspr. u. Anf.*, III, p. 555) reckons that this interpretation is supported by the fact that Domitian did not renew Nero's measures against Christianity but reverted to the policy which had been in existence before Nero when there was no distinction between Judaism and Christianity.

[3] Eusebius, *H.e.* iii. 19-20.

[4] Gsell (p. 314) thinks that it may refer to Jews. Their designation as heretics would be evidence that the tradition had come into existence in a locality where Christianity and Judaism were differentiated from each other with precision.

[5] I showed previously (see pp. 127 ff.) that there is little truth in Hegesippus' story of the death of James.   [6] See pp. 134 ff.

[7] Eduard Meyer, *Urspr. u. Anf.*, III, p. 556.   [8] Gsell, p. 313.

classes of Roman society, but also took in hand measures of a more general nature against Christianity.[1]

The Johannine Apocalypse which was written towards the end of his reign is dominated by the idea of a struggle to the death between Rome and Christianity. Such a book may have been written at a time when the church enjoyed peace but, from the way in which the problem of relations with the Empire is stated in all its rigour, it can only be concluded that the book was written in the middle of massacres of Christians. It is an exhortation to the martyr, but most of the victims mentioned by him belong to the past and among them there certainly figure the Jewish martyrs of the Maccabean period and after. The Apocalypse predicts also a great number of martyrs in the future, but it proves that all that happened up to then were a few persecutions in Asia towards the end of Domitian's reign, which it seems were fairly sporadic. What is more significant is that the author of the Apocalypse with true insight, perceived what nobody else of his generation recognised that the conflict which was breaking out here and there between the Roman world[2] and the church was not due to misunderstandings which might evaporate, but was a clash between two opposing conceptions between which no compromise was possible.

A few persons at court who were perhaps only inclined towards Christianity were certainly not the only victims of persecution at Rome. When Clement of Rome wants to explain why the Roman community was slow at intervening with his message in the affair which had divided the church at Corinth, he speaks of 'misfortunes and tribulations which have unexpectedly in succession fallen on the church' (I, 1). This must refer to persecution.[3] The beautiful prayer ending the epistle contains passages confirming this: 'Save those of us who are in affliction . . . raise the fallen, ransom our prisoners' (lix. 4). It is thought that there may be here an echo of the feelings which persecution had aroused in the minds of people

---

[1] Meliton, *Apol.* (in Eusebius, *H.e.* iv. 26); Tertullian, *Apolog.* 5; Lactantius, *De morte persecut.* 3; Eusebius, *Chronicles, arm.* (ed. Karst), p. 218. Jerome (ed. Helm), p. 192. *H. e., III*, 17.

[2] Dibelius (*R.u.d.Chr.*, pp. 17-18) thinks that the city of Rome was the special object of the Apocalypticist's hatred which he explains as due to his memory of the events of 64. It is a fact that he thought of Nero as an embodiment of the demonic power hostile to God, but to a writer whose immediate concerns were with Asiatic Christianity Rome and Nero could have been only symbols of the Empire.

[3] For an explanation of the summary character of Clement's allusion to the events of 64 and its extreme vagueness see p. 551.

of the lower classes as mentioned in the lines of Juvenal in which he says that the artisans did not begin to fear Domitian until he died.[1] This interpretation is far from being certain.[2]

Finally, it has been thought that an echo of a persecution in Bithynia in Domitian's time can be found in the passage of Pliny's letter to Trajan mentioning people who had been denounced as Christians and, when interrogated, replied that they had been Christians once but had ceased to be so, some of them twenty years ago. The latter might well then have abandoned their faith during Domitian's persecution.[3]

Other texts speak of persecutions but give no details, while the nature of their style fails to inspire confidence. The Acts of the martyrdom of Ignatius speak of 'numerous persecutions under Domitian'.[4] Tradition states that this emperor had the apostle John plunged into a cask of boiling oil from which he came out unhurt, after which he was exiled to Patmos.[5] Paul Orosus says that Domitian ordered a very cruel persecution on all sides.[6] Malalas[7], transposing Flavia Domitilla's exile to the island of Pontia, as Lipsius saw,[8] says that Domitian condemned many Christians and that many of them took refuge in the Pontus. Some of these witnesses are suspect, others are vague, but taken together they show that the church remembered Domitian as a persecuting emperor.

The persecution appears to have been short. According to Tertullian[9] the emperor himself recalled those whom he had banished. Hegesippus[10] says the same thing but Eusebius in reporting his evidence does not seem to have been convinced that it ought to be retained, as he says that on Nerva's accession to the throne the Senate passed a law permitting those who had been banished to return and recover their possessions.[11] According to Dion Cassius[12]

---

[1] Sed periit postquam cerdonibus esse timendus
coeperat . . . iv. 153 f.
[2] Gsell, p. 316, n. 3.
[3] Arnold, 'Studien zur Geschichte der plinianischen Christenverfolgung', *Theol. Stud. u. Skizzen aus Ostpreussen*, 1887, p. 275; Gsell, p. 309; Dom Leclercq, art. 'Domitien', *D.A.C.L.*, IV, col. 1397. Karl Muller ('Kleine Beitrage zur alten Kirchengeschichte, I, Zum Pliniusbrief', *Z.N.T.W.*, 1924, XXIII, pp. 214-215), thinks that it refers to apostates, who had been expelled from the church by disciplinary measures after Domitian's persecution and wanted to atone by confessing their faith but had not the courage to keep it up.   [4] *Mart. Ignatii*, I.
[5] Tertullian, *De praescriptione haereticorum*, 36. Jerome, *De viris inl.* 9, etc.
[6] Paul Orosus, *Hist.* vii. 10.   [7] Malalas, *Chron.* X, p. 262 (edit. of Bonn).
[8] Lipsius, *Chronol. der rom. Bisch.*, p. 157.
[9] Tertullian, *Apolog.* v. 1.   [10] In Eusebius, *H.e.* iii. 22, 5.
[11] Eusebius, *H.e.* iii. 20, 8; St. Jerome (*Ep.* 108, 7) speaks of Domitilla's long exile.   [12] Dion Cassius, lxviii. 1.

one of Nerva's first acts was to forbid men being informed against for the benefit of the *fiscus judaicus* and to decree that the tax should be demanded only from those who declared that they wished to remain loyal to the religion of their fathers. This measure was commemorated by a coin being struck bearing the inscription: *Fisci judaici calumnia sublata*.[1]

6.—THE PERSECUTION UNDER TRAJAN

Domitian's murder, the outcome of measures which had made him detested,[2] brought some relaxation in which the Christians shared, but their position still remained precarious. This is shown by the correspondence between Pliny and Trajan.[3] There has been much argument as to its authenticity. It was called in question in the eighteenth century by Semler and has been attacked by Aube, Desjardins Dupuy, Havet, and Guignebert, some of whom maintain that it was apocryphal, others that it had only been subject to interpolations. On the other hand, its authenticity has been maintained by Renan, Gaston Boissier, Allard, Neumann, Harnack, E. Ch. Babut, and Bouché-Leclercq.[4] Babut in particular has put forward arguments in favour of authenticity which seem to me must carry conviction.

After mentioning that his custom was to refer to the emperor whenever he was in difficulty, Pliny goes into the matter and expresses himself thus,[5] 'Having never been present at any trials of the Christians, I am unacquainted with the method and limits to be observed, either in examining or punishing them. Whether any difference is to be made on account of age, or no distinction allowed between the youngest and the adult; whether repentance admits to pardon, or if a man has been once a Christian it avails him nothing to recant;

---

[1] Eckbel, vi. 404; Cogen, *Nerva*, 54 ff.   [2] Gsell, pp. 317 ff.

[3] Pliny the Younger, *Ep.* x. 97, 98 (96, 97 of the edition Keil).

[4] It is impossible to quote here all the literature on the subject. Guignebert, *Tertullien, Étude sur ses sentiments a l'égard de l'Empire et de la société civile*, Paris, 1901, pp. 75-92, gives an excellent summary of the discussions previous to 1901. Guignebert concludes that neither the authenticity nor the inauthenticity of the letters can be proved and thinks that the text of them contains interpolations. Among more recent works mention must be made of the observations of Bouché-Leclercq (pp. 200 ff.) and particularly of the article by E.-Ch. Barbut, 'Remarques sur les deux lettres de Pline et Trajan relatives aux Chrétiens de Bithynie', *R.h.l.r.*, *N.S.I.*, 1910, pp. 289-307. Elsewhere I have given my assent to the conclusion that the text contains interpolations (*L'eucharistie des origines à Justin Martyr*, Paris, 1910, pp. 259 ff.) Babut's arguments do not convince me that it is altogether authentic.

[5] I have used the Loeb translation by William Melmote, pp. 401-407 [trans.].

whether the mere profession of Christianity, albeit without crimes, or only the crimes associated, therewith are punishable—in all these points I am greatly doubtful.

'In the meantime, the method I have observed towards those who have been denounced to me as Christians is this: I interrogated them whether they were Christians; if they confessed it I repeated the question twice again, adding the threat of the capital punishment; if they still persevered, I ordered them to be executed. For whatever the nature of their creed might be, I could at least feel no doubt that contumacy and inflexible obstinacy deserved chastisement. There were others also possessed with the same infatuation, but being citizens of Rome, I directed them to be carried thither. These accusations spread (as is usually the case) from the mere fact of the matter being investigated and several forms of the mischief came to light. A placard was put up, without any signature, accusing a large number of persons by name. Those who denied they were, or had ever been, Christians, who repeated after me an invocation to gods, and who finally cursed Christ—none of which acts, it is said, those who are really Christians can be forced into performing—these I thought it proper to discharge. Others who were named by that informer at first confessed themselves Christians, and then denied it; true, they had been of that persuasion, but they had quitted it, some three years, others many years, and a few as much as twenty-five years ago. They all worshipped your statue and the images of the gods and curse Christ. They affirmed, however, the whole of their guilt, or their error, was, that they were in the habit of meeting on a fixed day before it was light, when they sang in alternate verses a hymn to Christ, as to a god, and bound themselves by a solemn oath, not to do any wicked deeds, but never to commit any fraud, theft or adultery, never to falsify their word, nor deny a trust when they should be called upon to deliver it up; after which it was their custom to separate, and then re-assemble to partake of food—but food of an ordinary and innocent kind. Even this practice, however, they had abandoned after the publication of my edict, by which, according to your orders, I had forbidden political associations. I judged it so much the more necessary to extract the real truth, with the assistance of torture, from two female slaves, who were styled *deaconesses:* but I could discover nothing more than depraved and excessive superstition.

'I therefore adjourned the proceedings, and betook myself at once to your counsel. For the matter seemed to me well worth referring to you—especially considering the numbers endangered. Persons of all ranks and ages, and of both sexes are, and will be, involved in the prosecution. For this contagious superstition is not confined to the cities only, but has spread through the villages and rural districts; it seems possible, however, to check and cure it. It is certain at least, that the temples, which had been almost deserted, began now to be frequented; and the sacred festivals, after a long intermission, are again revived; while there is a general demand for sacrificial animals, which for some time past have met with but few purchasers. From hence it is easy to imagine what multitudes may be reclaimed from this error, if a door be left open to repentance.'

This is Trajan's reply written with *imperia brevitas:*

'The method you have pursued, my dear Pliny, in sifting the cases of those denounced to you as Christians is extremely proper. It is not possible to lay down any general rule which can be applied as the fixed standard in all cases of this nature. No search should be made for these people; when they are denounced and found guilty they must be punished; with the restriction, however, that when the party denies himself to be a Christian, and shall give proof that he is not (i.e. by adoring our gods) he shall be pardoned on the ground of repentance, even though he may have formerly incurred suspicion. Information without the accuser's name subscribed must not be admitted in evidence against anyone, as it is introducing a very dangerous precedent, and by no means agreeable to the spirit of the age.'

The authenticity of the two texts must be examined each separately. The authenticity of Pliny's letter might be inferred from that of Trajan's but it is possible that Trajan's is an interpolation, Pliny's letter may be authentic while Trajan's is not. It is unfortunate that the only manuscript containing Pliny's correspondence from which it was published in 1502 has disappeared, but too many scholars saw it for the hypothesis that it is a renaissance imitation to be thought possible.[1] If the correspondence was faked it must have been so before the time of Tertullian.[2] Let us note the points of Pliny's letter which have created doubts:

(1) It is surprising that Pliny, who was a man of considerable experience, should not have known how to proceed against Christians, as the term used by him (*soleat*) implies procedure which had been fixed if not by law at any rate by custom.

---

[1] Babut, *R.h.l.r.*, N.S.I. 1910, p. 298, n. 3.
[2] Tertullian analyses it in chapter 2 of the *Apologeticum.*

(2) Pliny asks if he is to punish for confessing the *nomen* or for the crimes which go with the *nomen* (*flagitia cohaerentia nomini*), but in actual fact he had answered this question himself by condemning those who refused to declare themselves Christians, when he had nothing with which to reproach them except their stubbornness.

(3) The idea that those who are really Christians cannot be compelled to sacrifice or to curse Christ would have been expected from the pen of a Christian rather than a pagan.

(4) Evidence from apostates throwing a favourable light on Christianity and Christians seems to be suspicious. It hardly agrees with the fact that when Pliny put two deaconesses under torture he found that Christians accepted innumerable evil superstitions.

(5) The information given by Pliny at the end of his letter on the position of Christianity in Bithynia seem as if it is to be accepted with reserve both as to what it says of the number of the Christians and of the desertion of the temples or of the revival of pagan cults after Pliny had begun to take measures.

These arguments may seem impressive but they are not decisive, Pliny may have not known how to proceed against the Christians because there was no special law determining procedure which was always of a more or less improvised character.

We have to distinguish two different periods in his actions. At first some Christians were accused and brought before him: they do not seem to have been a large number. He did not judge the affair to be very serious and all he did was to make a separate case of some Roman citizens whom he thought he must send to the imperial court. He did not even think that an investigation was necessary into the *flagitia* of which the Christians were accused. It is clear that he did not think it necessary, otherwise he would not have been so ready to release those who repudiated their faith and would not have said that he went on to execute the others only because of their obstinacy. He thought that with leniency for the renegade combined with severity for the obstinate he would stop Christianity growing. Soon denunciations showed him that the evil was more widespread than he had believed. When the extent of the movement was revealed to him he may have hesitated because he shrank from assuming more serious responsibilities than he had at first thought necessary. Possibly as Neumann[1] thought, public opinion tried to bring pressure to bear upon him, or, as Babut suggested,[2] he may not have been in

---

[1] Neumann, *Der romische Staat und die allgemeine Kirche bis auf Diokletian*, p. 20.   [2] Babut, *R.h.l.r.*, N.S.I. 1910, pp. 293 f.

agreement with his assistants. But he persisted in his first attitude and only took the additional precaution of assuring himself of the sincerity of their repudiation of Christianity by asking those who were accused to make a sacrifice before the emperor's statue and curse Christ. As Babut clearly sees,[1] it was simply a test. Pliny does not seem to have demanded sacrifice and a curse from those who persisted in their faith in spite of promises and threats. As far as they were concerned he pursued his investigations. After he had learnt both through the evidence of apostates and the deaconesses who were tortured that there was nothing to support the charge of *flagitia* he suspended the trial and referred the matter to the emperor. If we take into account the essential difference between the two successive phases of the affair the contradictions which it was thought Pliny showed disappear. All that remains is that Pliny showed some hesitation when he saw that the business of the Christians was of greater magnitude than he had at first believed.

The difference in the two descriptions of Christianity given by Pliny, one as he found it after his investigation, and the other as it was described by the apostates, does not amount to a contradiction. Pliny was in no way prepared to understand what the Christians believed, but thought of them as inoffensive people at bottom who had foolish ideas which they held with frightful persistence.

As Guignebert has rightly emphasised,[2] Pliny has exaggerated both the extent of Christianity and the amount of damage it had caused to the pagan cults and the trades depending on them as well as the success of his initial measures. Pliny exaggerated both the damage caused by Christianity and the success of his measures to strengthen his own position and obtain the emperor's approval for a line of conduct, of which his assistants did not entirely approve and with which public opinion was not altogether satisfied. Pliny had decided ideas on the best way of treating the Christians. What he was asking from Trajan under the pretence of asking for instructions was for approval so that he could impose his policy both in the face of public opinion and of his assistants who wanted to see stronger measures applied.

Except for the fact that he orders Pliny not to receive anonymous denunciations Trajan entirely approves of the procedure improvised by his legate. But one slight difficulty arises from the fact that Trajan begins by stating that a general rule covering all cases cannot be laid down and then goes on to approve of the procedure which Pliny had

[1] Babut, *R.h.l.r.*, N.S.I. 1910, 302 f.   Guignebert, *Tertullien*, pp. 86 ff.

outlined to him. If a real contradiction existed here, whether we suppose the letter is a fiction or authentic, it would not be explained one way or the other. But if there was a contradiction Trajan must have had in mind procedure which was applicable to Christians everywhere and always. But the emperor had no such idea. He is replying to a precise question asked by Pliny concerning the fulfilment of his mission to restore law and order in Bithynia. While at the beginning Trajan says that a general rule cannot be laid down, he reserves to himself the right of giving other instructions where the situation demanded it, e.g. if the Christians devoted themselves to indiscreet propaganda or assumed an aggressive attitude towards political and religious institutions. The first sentence does not contradict what follows: it only limits its meaning.

The correspondence between Pliny and Trajan reveals therefore a clearly defined situation. Public opinion in Bithynia had become worked up against the Christians no doubt for various reasons. Possibly commercial interests which were directly involved in the prosperity of the temples had made out that the Christians were responsible for the traditional cults being given up. This may have been due to other reasons besides the progress of the new religion. Public opinion clamoured for sanctions and tried to create them by denunciations. Pliny did not share the crowd's feelings. He did not believe in the existence of *flagitia* nor did Trajan either. He thought that public opinion must be calmed rather than excited. But he did not think that Christianity must be tolerated. He considered the Christians *hostes publici* but *hostes* who were not dangerous and he wanted so far as possible to be able to shut his eyes to them.

What happened in Bithynia certainly happened elsewhere, but apart from Ignatius we have no accurate knowledge about the martyrs of Trajan's time.[1] Eusebius in the *Chronica*[2] dates the martyrdom of Ignatius as in the tenth year of Trajan's reign, i.e. 108, but the story given by him in the ecclesiastical history[3] is introduced by the phrase, 'It is related that'; it shows that he had no reliable source at hand. In reality all he knows of Ignatius' martyrdom is extracted from his letters. Jerome[4] also puts Ignatius' martyrdom in the time of Trajan. This tradition must have been fairly widespread and early in date as Origen[5] possesses it and also makes him

---

[1] A certain number of the Acts of Martyrs are dated in Trajan's reign, but they are of no value.

[2] Eusebius, *Chronica, arm.* (ed. Karst), p. 218. Jerome (ed. Helm), p. 194.

[3] Eusebius, *H.e.* iii. 36, 3.

[4] Jerome, *De viris inl.*, 16.   [5] Origen, *Hom, VI in Lucan* (Lomm. v. 104).

the second bishop of Antioch. It would appear legitimate then to maintain that his martyrdom took place in Trajan's reign and at the latest in 117.[1] As Harnack remarks[2] there is nothing decisive to put against this tradition. The Acts of the martyrdom of Ignatius connect it with an occasion when Trajan was passing through Antioch in preparation for a campaign against the Scythians and Dacians,[3] but Eusebius says nothing like this. Ignatius' martyrdom must have created a great impression, as it inspired Lucian's *de morte Peregrini*.[4]

Eusebius[5] tells also of the martyrdom of Simeon in Trajan's time. He was the son of Cleopas, whom Hegesippus says succeeded James as bishop of Jerusalem. According to Hegesippus, whom Eusebius quotes word for word, Simeon was persecuted both because he was a Christian and also because he was a descendant of David: Hegesippus adds that some of those who had accused him were in their turn denounced as belonging to the race of David and on these grounds were put to death.[6] It would be foolish to pretend that elements of historical information can be extracted from a story which tells of Simeon's death at the age of 120 after he had suffered tortures for several days with such hardihood that the magistrates were amazed.

The actual situation and legal position revealed by the correspondence between Pliny and Trajan explain the martyrdoms which took place under this emperor but there was nothing new or final about it. The correspondence is interesting because it offers a lifelike picture of the real position of Christianity and the dangers to which Christians continued to be exposed. The only novelty in the picture lies in the fact that the Christians were coming to be considered legally *hostes publici*, guilty of atheism and high treason, while the magistrates showed some moderation in applying the law, but their

---

[1] Jean Reville (*Orig. de l'épisc.*, p. 447, n. 1) thinks that Ignatius' condemnation may have had something to do with Trajan's stay at Antioch between the end of 113 and 115 and perhaps also with an earthquake which caused much damage in the city at the end of 115. He thinks that in any case it took place later than the correspondence between Pliny and Trajan because Eusebius mentions this correspondence in chapter 33 of book iii of the ecclesiastical history while Ignatius is not mentioned until chapter 36. He also reckons that after Ignatius' trial Pliny could not have written that he did not know how to proceed against the Christians. The last argument does not seem to me convincing as the persecution at Antioch may perfectly well have been a local happening.

[2] Harnack, *G.A.C.L.* II, 1, p. 406.

[3] *Martyr, Ign.*, 2. It was the custom to send condemned persons to Rome to be exposed there in the amphitheatre, if anything in particular made them worthy of it. [4] Renan, *Les Evangeles*, pp. 493 f.

[5] Eusebius, *H.e.* iii. 11. [6] Eusebius, *H.e.* iii. 32.

moderation did not go so far as to withstand the pressure of public opinion which was constantly hostile to the Christians.

Using the terms employed by Trajan there was nothing yet *in universum* and no *certa forma*, but all the same there was a definite attitude. Christianity was beyond the law and would remain so until the time of Constantine. The extreme consequences which might have followed from this situation were not always drawn. The position of Christians varied much according to time and place. The church was destined to know periods of peace; security it never knew. It was clearly perceived that the church and the Empire were incompatible. They were destined to remain so until the Empire in the time of Constantine became Christian.

CHAPTER V

How Christianity re-acted to Persecution

CHRISTIANS were placed in their relations, both with the Jews and with the Romans, in such a position that they could not think of resorting to force and violence to defend themselves, even if they were to ignore the precepts of the gospel, the principle of non-resistance to the wicked, Jesus' commandment to offer the left cheek when one is struck on the right (Matt. v. 39), the charge to bless those who curse you and to pray for those who despitefully use you and persecute you (Matt. v. 44 ff.; Luke vi. 32 ff.).[1] Even when Christians were at the height of their sufferings and were inspired with the most hostile feelings for their enemies, they did not look to themselves but to God alone to deliver them and avenge their wrongs. Paul concludes his indictment against the Jews who created obstacles to his missionary work by declaring that the wrath of God will await them at the last (I Thess. ii. 16). In the same way in the second epistle to the Thessalonians (i. 5 f.) he calls upon the righteous judgement of God which on the day of Jesus' appearing will bring tribulations on his persecutors. In the epistle to the Philippians (i. 28-30) he says that the patience of the Christians is an evident token of the salvation which awaits them and of the perdition which will come to their enemies. The first epistle of Peter proclaims that the time is come when God is going to judge the world. If it has begun with the elect (a reference to persecutions) what will be the fate of those who have not believed the gospel? (iv. 17-19). In the Apocalypse (vi. 9 ff.) the souls of the martyrs cry for vengeance but it is God alone whom they ask to take vengeance on those who have put them to death.[2] We look in vain in the Apocalypse, which exhorts its readers to resist at any cost, for

---

[1] Exceptional cases can naturally be found, in which Christians had the material sources at hand to be able to reply to their adversaries with violence and succumbed to the temptation to do so. Such may have been the case before the judgement seat of Gallio. See pp. 480 ff.

[2] See also James v. 1 f. although this passage refers rather to the poor who had been exploited and oppressed by the rich.

the least encouragement to profit by any opportunity which might offer for using violence, either against those who said that they were Jews but formed a synagogue of Satan, or against the worshippers of the Beast and his image. The author of the book of Acts saw a divine punishment in the execution after Peter's deliverance of the soldiers who were supposed to guard him and particularly so in the sudden death of Herod Agrippa, which followed closely upon the persecution unleashed by him against the church (xii. 19-23). In the same category of thought must be added the fact that, to judge by the way in which the evangelists make Jesus predict the fall of Jerusalem, they judged the catastrophe of 70 to be God's punishment for the crime which the Jews had committed against the Lord, for refusing to listen to Peter's exhortations to repent, and for treating the disciples as far as possible in the same way as they had treated the master.

The possibility of taking violent action against the Gentiles was much more hopeless. Yet at certain times the spirit of revolt rumbled in the hearts of those who suffered either through measures taken by the authorities or through the ill-will of the Gentiles among whom they lived and on whom they often found themselves economically and socially dependent. Instructions like those in Romans xiii. 1-7, 1 Peter ii. 13-17, and 2 Timothy ii. 1-2 advising submission to the established authorities as a religious duty and not merely as a wise and opportune attitude, try to fight such feelings. The exhortations to patience which are a special characteristic of the first epistle of Peter try to do the same.

Christianity took and advised this attitude, not only because it felt that it was powerless to adopt any other and that any attempt at revolt would only aggravate things, but also because very largely, as Apocalypse shows, it was felt that the most active agents of persecution were not the real people responsible but only the unconscious instruments of the demonic powers who were in conflict with God. Christianity inherited this idea from Jewish apocalyptic and all the more easily could appropriate it, because it provided a powerful source of encouragement to persevere in a situation which, from a material point of view, could only seem desperate if the forces at the disposal of each side were compared.

The violent attacks on Christians both from Jews and Romans created then only the feeblest reactions. The reactions therefore provoked by persecution have to be considered from an entirely different point of view. First we must see if the Christians made any attempts to disarm their adversaries and next to find out if there were no internal reactions, in other words, if the hostility created by Christianity against itself did not exercise some passing or lasting influence on its own structure, its doctrines, and its adherents. But a distinction must be made between the reactions which may have been provoked by what has just been shown to be persecution from Jews and those provoked by persecution from the Romans.

There is one point to be noted first. Christians whether we are considering before 70 Pauline Christianity or after 70 other forms never had the feeling that Jewish hostility might be the result of misunderstanding which could more or less easily be removed. As a result they did not look for common ground in the hope of building a compromise or establishing a *modus vivendi*. Christians developed an apologetic devised to meet Judaism; it began with Paul, is developed in the synoptic gospels, gains emphasis in the Fourth Gospel, is advanced in Justin Martyr's *Dialogue against the Jew Tryphon* and continues throughout the whole history of the early church and even beyond. But it was entirely ideological and doctrinal in character. It was part of a dogmatic controversy, which the Christians maintained before everything else to prevent members of the church deserting their faith or merely being disturbed by Jewish objections to Christian doctrine, and also in addition to make conquests among the Jews.

Theoretically two attitudes were possible. One, which was that adopted by the primitive church and symbolised by the name of Paul but also developed in non-pauline centres of thought, consisted in claiming for Christianity the religious and spiritual heritage of Judaism which it was maintained Judaism had repudiated and denied by refusing to accept Jesus and his message. The other attitude, which was destined to be shown by Marcion in the second third of the second century, consisted of the opposite, i.e. the complete rejection of the Jewish tradition. I cannot discuss it, because it did not appear in the period which I am considering, and more especially because the church rejected Marcionitism without being called upon to struggle in order to destroy it. The idea that the church was the inheritor of Judaism was definitely embedded in Christian dogma.

I have no desire to withdraw what I said further back concerning Paul's conception of the connections between Christianity and Judaism, but only to emphasise the fact that the theory or rather the theories which were developed about them were dictated, not only by a desire to compel the Jews to put an end to their activities against the Christians or to prevent Christians being influenced by Jewish propaganda,[1] but also to justify the new attitude towards Judaism which his conversion had imposed upon him.

It was not until after 70 that the controversy with Judaism really became apologetic in character. Two stages can be discerned. The synoptic gospels, especially Matthew and Mark[2] signal the first; they develop a complete system of Messianic dogma, which is built up as is especially emphasised by Matthew on an argument from prophecy the purpose of which is to show that the gospel story and the doctrine of salvation through the sufferings, death, and resurrection of Christ implied in it realise the Messianic programme of the Old Testament. The second stage we find in the Fourth Gospel which concentrates discussion entirely on the question of christology.

This explains the paradox that the rupture with Judaism which came to a head in 70 did not stop Christianity and its forms of doctrine and worship from being influenced by the traditions of Judaism but on the contrary that influence grew in intensity as is shown particularly by two facts, (1) the description of the eucharist as a sacrifice ($\theta v\sigma\iota\alpha$) which we find in the *Didache* (xiv. 1-2) and became more common and definite as time went on[3] and (2) the idea first projected by Clement of Rome that the Jewish priesthood was the prototype of the Christian clergy (41 ff.).

Christianity could not at first defend itself on the ideological level against its Roman adversaries; there was no occasion for it to do so, because it did not meet with objections to its ideas of a critical kind but with accusations, which did not even admit of argument and sometimes were not expressed in words but only implied in pronouncements of condemnations. As for discussions of a more general nature which might have been instrumental in effecting public opinion, there could be no thought of resorting to them because Christianity, so far as it was not ignored, was too much misunderstood for it to be possible to obtain a hearing from those who would

---

[1] But sometimes Paul seems to have had this kind of concern, notably in Chapter iii of the epistle to the Philippians which is directed against Jews who were trying to attract to themselves Gentiles whom Paul by his preaching had freed from polytheism. But it must be remarked that this chapter takes the form of exhortations and cautions with invective and not of inference and argument.

[2] Luke less so, no doubt because he was writing for Gentile Christian readers.

[3] The basic conception of the epistle to the Hebrews that the great expiatory sacrifice in Jewish worship is the prototype of the sacrifice of Christ paved the way for this idea which was at first just a figure.

have had to be persuaded. The work of apologetic, properly so-called, could only begin about the middle of the second century. It then had two principal ends in view. First, Christians tried to establish their right to exist by a repeated insistence that it was the worst of the emperors such as Nero and Domitian who attacked Christianity, instigated persecutions, and so created a tradition and state of things against which the best of their successors were powerless. They also tried to show that there were no solid grounds for the condemnations which had been pronounced against Christians, for despising them and still less for dismissing their religion out of hand and without examination. Secondly, they tried to prove that between Christianity and what was most valuable and good in Greco-Roman thought there was no fundamental and irreducible contradiction, and furthermore, Christian doctrine was supported by the books of the Old Testament which were much older than the works of the philosophers. It could not therefore be dismissed as a novelty and on that account suspect. These efforts of the Apologists of the second century, of whom Justin is the most eminent and characteristic representative, are organically connected in the closest way possible with the whole movement of Christian thought leading to its Hellenisation. This contributed to the strength and ultimate success of the tendency of Christianity to become a Greco-Roman religion of the West and not a Jewish religion of the East which it originally was. This was the logical conclusion of the movement initiated by Paul and the rupture between Christianity and Judaism which took place in 70.

But this concerns only the period beginning in the middle of the second century and does not apply to the previous one. Up to then it cannot be said that Christian thought possessed any real apologetic orientation or that the work of apologetic had any influence on the structure of Christianity. Nevertheless, from the end of the first century onwards the reaction provoked by persecution was perceptible. As we have seen, Christians when persecuted waited only for their deliverance and revenge from God which they envisaged as the destruction of the present world and the establishment of the kingdom of God. At certain times, notably in the Johannine Apocalypse, persecution produced a resurgence of eschatological sentiment, and in a more general way the feeling regained strength that the faith and the church had their true foundation and purpose, not in the present world but in the world beyond. This balanced the tendency of the church to become rooted in this world devoting itself to its development and organisation. Christians at such times remembered that they were only pilgrims and strangers on earth.[1]

But such feelings were not general. So far as one can judge they seem to have been exceptional. Although the situation at the end of the first century must have made the idea that the gospel might penetrate the world seem utterly chimerical, Christians did not recognise it. They did not resign themselves to living on the edge of society.

It is the merit of an article by Martin Dibelius, which I have already quoted, 'Rome and the Christians in the first century', that it shows up a tendency in early Christianity, which has not always received the importance it deserves. It was one of the factors which went to the formation of Catholicism as a religion the function of which was not only to lead believers to the happiness of heaven but also to organise the life of humanity on earth and to serve as a protection for it.

We have seen[2] how Paul, in spite of the persecution which he had experienced, took up a patriotic attitude towards Rome in the epistle to the Romans and how it was possible for him to do so because he believed that, while the present world had only a temporary life and was near its end, it had a part to play in the divine plan which would be consummated in the coming of the heavenly world. This conception of the temporary function of the present world and consequently of the Roman empire, which in the first century symbolised it, must have been deeply rooted in the Christian conscience for it to have survived the massacres of 64 and the persecution of Domitian even in Rome, although it was the scene of these tragic events.

The first epistle of Timothy (ii. 1-2) remains faithful to the attitude adopted by Paul when it advises prayers, supplications, and intercessions to be made for emperors and all who exercise authority. But there is a slight difference. It justifies this instruction, by an appeal not to principles but to considerations of expediency. If Christians are loyal they will be able to live in peace and quietness. We are breathing here the same atmosphere as in the first epistle of Peter the author of which thinks that Christians by good conduct will close the mouth of their enemies (ii. 13-17).

Intercession for those in authority was not the creation of

---

[1] It is interesting to note that these expressions are only found in the two books of the New Testament belonging to a period of persecution (Heb. xi. 13; I Pet. i. 1; ii. 11).　　　　　　　　　　　　[2] See pp. 442 ff.

Christianity: it had its origins in Judaism.[1] It has an important place in the great liturgical prayer given in the epistle of Clement of Rome, which, as we have seen is a Jewish prayer in a revised form. It reads: 'Grant that we may be obedient to thy almighty and glorious name, and to our rulers and governors upon the earth. Thou, master, hast given the power of sovereignty to them through thy excellent and inexpressible might, that we may know the glory and honour given to them by thee, and be subject to them, in nothing resisting thy will. And to them, Lord, grant health, peace, concord, firmness, that they may administer the government which thou hast given them without offence. For thou, heavenly Master, king of eternity, hast given to the sons of men glory and honour and power over the things which are on the earth; do thou, O Lord, direct their counsels according to that which is "good and pleasing" before thee, that they may administer with piety in peace and gentleness the power given to them by thee, and may find mercy in thine eyes' (lxi. 1-2).

Directly inspired by 1 Timothy ii. 1-2, Polycarp in part of his letter which exists only in the Latin version (xii. 3) advises prayer also (*etiam*) to be made for kings,[2] magistrates, and princes and by the word *atque* connects the prayer with that for persecutors and enemies as commanded in the Sermon on the Mount (Matt. v. 44). This shows a perceptible shift in the motive. The Roman authorities are to be prayed for because they are enemies of the Christians. But we cannot determine how far this change must be put down to the author of the Latin version.

Evidence of prayer for the emperors is given by Tertullian who reports that when feasts are being kept in their honour Christians showed that their enthusiasm surpassed that of pagans by decorating their houses with garlands and torches.[3] This does not prevent him from describing the position of the church in another passage by the phrase, 'Nothing is further from us than the public interest'.[4]

---

[1] It was used in the synagogues of the diaspora. At Jerusalem a sacrifice for the emperor was offered every day. It was a kind of compromise as it served as a proof which the Jews could give of their loyalty in place of emperor worship in which they refused to participate. See on the subject Ps. Aristeus, 45; 1 Macch. vii. 33; Josephus, *A.j.* xii. 10, 5; *G.j.* ii. 10, 4; *Against Apion* ii. 6; Philo, *Leg. ad Cajum*, 157, 317; *Pirke Aboth* iii. 2. Cf. Schurer, *Gesch.* I, pp. 483 f. Juster, *Les Juifs dans l'Empire romain*, I, pp. 346 f. When they stopped offering this sacrifice in the summer of 66 (Josephus, *G.j.* ii. 17, 2-4) it was to use Wellhausen's expression (*Israelitische und judische Geschichte*[2], Berlin, 1897, p. 360) the equivalent to a declaration of war from a theocracy. Cf. Schurer, *Gesch.* I, p. 602.

[2] The word 'king' which translates βασιλεύς is equivalent to emperor.

[3] Tertullian, *De idolatria*, 15; *Ad uxorem*, 2, 6.

[4] *Nec ulla res aliena quam publica. Apologeticum*, 38.

We have no better evidence for the attitude of the early church towards the Roman authorities than the epistle of Clement. I have already observed that when Clement is explaining why the church at Rome was delayed in sending its message to the church at Corinth, he alludes to Domitian's persecutions in the vaguest of terms making them out to be an accident pure and simple. As Dibelius says, 'συμφοραὶ (incidents) and περιπτώσεις (accidents) are very mild terms. We might think that we were listening to a Stoic philosopher, who in spite of himself had plunged back into the corrupting stream of desires and dislikes.'[1] Clement may not have given any details because the Corinthians knew what had happened but this does not explain why he speaks of the persecution with such detachment.

The extremely vague way in which he recollects the persecution of 64 is no less surprising.[2] What is more astonishing still, is that its victims are described as heroes of patience, victorious athletes in a moral conflict within themselves, not witnesses and heroes of the faith.[3] They are victims of envy and jealousy, not soldiers of Christ who fell in the great conflict waging between God and the demonic powers.

Why did Clement make these changes and soften down the burning memories which the persecutions of Nero and Domitian had left in the hearts of the Christians of Rome and ought logically, so it seems, have led them not to enter into conflict with the imperial authorities, as they lacked the material means to do so, but at any rate to take up a passive hostile attitude towards them? Dibelius,[4] I think, has the answer, and therefore I cannot do better than give a summary of his views.

Clement used the memories of the persecution of Nero as a text for a moral exhortation presenting the Christian athlete and reduced the persecution of Domitian to a simple incident because he did not want the church to take a blind alley by assuming a hostile attitude towards the Empire. He wanted to safeguard the loyalty of Christians as it had been expounded by Paul in the epistle to the Romans; he wanted them to continue to use from the bottom of their hearts the prayer for the authorities in their worship. He hoped of course that by such loyalty the church would place itself beyond the reach of

[1] Dibelius, *R.u.d.Chr.*, pp. 18 f.
[2] No reliable evidence concerning Peter's and Paul's martyrdom can be inferred from what Clement says about them.
[3] Dibelius, *R.u.d.Chr.*, pp. 22 ff.   [4] Dibelius, *R.u.d.Chr.*, pp. 24 ff.

fresh persecutions.[1] But his attitude was determined at bottom by a reason of another kind. The earthly powers held their power from the master of the universe (lxi. 1); harmony must exist between the order of the universe and that of the church which is like a microcosm within a macrocosm. Clement finds his ideal of this order and harmony in the organisation of the Roman army (xx. 11; xxxiv. 7; xl. 5; lx. 4; lxi. 1; lxiii. 2; lxv. 1). 'Learn to submit yourselves' (lvii. 2), is the fundamental axiom of Clement's theory and practice. This is the principle which must rule the church's life both internally by obedience to the established elders and externally by submission to the political authorities.

Clement's ideal was not rejected by the age of the Apologists.[2] Only very rarely do they show the feeling that there was a conflict of principle between the church and the Empire, the Christian faith and the world. Generally speaking, if they had felt this, would they have laboured to bring the faith and the spiritual and intellectual traditions of the ancient world into harmony? Would they have tried to explain the persecutions as due to misunderstandings, false accusations and the inability of the authorities to repeal measures which had been adopted by a Nero or a Domitian?

Melito of Sardis in his Apology addressed to Marcus Aurelius, a fragment of which has been preserved for us by Eusebius,[3] proclaims in the most explicit terms the principle of absolute submission by Christians to the imperial decisions, a submission which must go as far as acceptance of death, even if it is the emperor's will. He only asks Marcus Aurelius to sift the evidence for himself and not to permit measures to be taken in his name which he would not approve of if he examined things for himself. His fundamental principle is that the welfare of the Empire and Christianity are one, because they came into existence in the same period and have grown up together. Hippolytus[4] also notes the fact that Jesus was born in the reign of Augustus, but he draws from it the opposite conclusion to that of Melito, considering it to be a proof of the opposition between the church and the Empire.

[1] It must be emphasised that they are not merely Clement's own feelings, as they are clearly expressed in the great liturgical prayer which Clement had borrowed from the liturgy of the church of Rome (lx. 4-lxi. 2).

[2] The *Martyrdom of Polycarp* (x. 2) reports that Polycarp when questioned by the proconsul declared that, although he would not defend himself before anybody else, he would do so before him, because he had been taught by Christians that they must render honour as is meet to powers and authorities established by God.

[3] Eusebius, *H.e.* iv. 26, 5-11.

[4] Hippolytus, *Com. in Danielem*, iv. 9.

Yet, although Christians wanted the church and the Empire to be reconciled they could not but be affected by the way in which they were treated. Two streams flowed together, traces of which can be seen after the persecutions had ended and throughout the church's history. In alternate periods and sometimes even at the same time the church can be seen holding itself aloof from this present world and thinking only of the city of God in the realm beyond and contrariwise compelled to create it here and now by organising society on the principles of the gospel.

APPENDIX

BIBLIOGRAPHY

MODERN WORKS IN ENGLISH

BARNES, W. E. *The Testimony of Josephus to Jesus Christ.* London, 1920.
Beginnings of Christianity, edited by F. J. Foakes Jackson and Kirsopp
Lake, 5 vols., London, 1920-33.
BELL, H. IDRIS. *Jews and Christians in Egypt*, London, 1924.
BEVAN, E. R. *Christianity*, London, 1938.
BRANDON, S. G. F. *The Fall of Jerusalem and the Christian Church*,
S.P.C.K., London, 1951.
Tubingen Vindicated ? art. in *The Hibbert Journal*, vol. xlix, 1950.
CLARKE, W. K. L. *New Testament Problems*, London, 1929.
CREED, J. M. *The Gospel according to St. Luke*, London, 1950.
DAVIES, W. D. *Paul and rabbinic Judaism*, London, 1948.
DODD, C. H. *The Apostolic Preaching and its Developments*, London,
1944.
History and the Gospel, London, 1938.
The Epistle to the Romans, London, 1940 (1932).
The Parables of the Kingdom, London, 1941.
DUNCAN, G. S. *St. Paul's Ephesian Ministry*, London, 1929.
FILSON, FLOYD V. *The New Testament against its environment*, London,
1950.
GOODSPEED, E. J. *New Solutions of New Testament Problems*, Chicago,
1927.
HARRISON, P. N. *The Problem of the Pastoral Epistles*, Oxford, 1921.
HOWARD, W. F. *The Fourth Gospel in Recent Criticism and Interpretation*,
London, 1931.
HUNTER, A. M. *Paul and his Predecessors*, London, 1940.
JALLAND, F. J. *The Origin and Evolution of the Christian Church*, London,
1950.
KELLY, J. N. D. *Early Christian Creeds*, London, 1950.
KNOX, W. L. *St. Paul and the Church of Jerusalem*, Cambridge, 1925.
St. Paul and the Church of the Gentiles, Cambridge, 1939.
Some Hellenistic Elements in Primitive Christianity (Schweich Lectures,
1942), London, 1944.
The Acts of the Apostles, Cambridge, 1948.

LAKE, KIRSOPP. *The Earlier Epistles of St. Paul*, London, 3rd Ed., 1930.
Landmarks in the History of Early Christianity, London, 1920.
Paul, his Heritage and Legacy, London, 1934.
LAKE, K. and S. *An Introduction to the New Testament*, London, 1938.
LIGHTFOOT, R. H. *History and Interpretation in the Gospels*, London, 1935.
Locality and Doctrine in the Gospels, London, 1938.
The Gospel Message of St. Mark, Oxford, 1950.
MITTON, C. H. *The Epistle to the Ephesians*, Oxford, 1951.
MOFFATT, J. *Introduction to the Literature of the New Testament*, Edinburgh, 1933 (3rd Ed. revised, 1918).
The First Epistle of Paul to the Corinthians, London, 1943 (1938).
MOORE, G. F. *Judaism*, 3 vols., Cambridge (Mass.), 1927.
MUNCH, J. Israel and the Gentiles in the New Testament, art. in the *Journal of Theo. Studies*, vol. ii, 1951.
NOCK, A. D. *St. Paul*, London, 1938.
PARKES, J. *The Conflict of the Church and the Synagogue*, London, 1934.
RAWLINSON, A. E. J. *St. Mark*, 5th Ed., London, 1941.
RENDALL, G. H. *The Epistle of St. James and Judaic Christianity*, Cambridge, 1927.
SCHONFIELD, H. J. *History of Jewish Christianity*, London, 1936.
STREETER, B. H. *The Four Gospels*, London, 1924.
The Primitive Church, London, 1929.
TAYLOR, V. *Behind the Third Gospel*, Oxford, 1926.
The Formation of the Gospel Tradition, London, 1945 (1935).
The Gospel according to St. Mark, London, 1952.

Index

ALLARD, Paul, 507, 537
Ambrosiastre, the, 159
Apollonius of Tyana, 355
Aquiba, Rabbi, 452
Ascension of Isaiah, 522
Aube, 507, 537
Aulen, 229

BABUT, 537, 540
Baldensperger, 364, 365
Basilides, 417
Bauer, Walter, 7, 179, 184, 293, 330, 350, 412, 505
Belser, 159
Bengel, 159
Bergson, 11, 65, 75, 81
Boissier, 537, 540
Bouche-Leclerq, 516, 519, 534.
Buissière, Baron de, 76 f.
Bultmann, 350.

CALLEWAERT, 507
Cappel, Jacques, 159
Cappel, Louis, 157
Celsus, 62, 441.
Clement of Alexandria, 112, 128, 130
Clement of Rome, 20, 164, 241, 323, 434, 486, 510 ff., 548, 550, 552.
Clerc, Jean le, 155
Corssen, 503
Cullmann, O., 486
Cyprian, 504

DEISMANN, 155, 198, 507
Denys of Corinth, 309, 385
Dibelius, M., 376, 521, 550
Didache, 267 ff., 277, 334, 377 ff., 548
Dion, Cassius, 6, 21, 530 ff., 536
Duchesne, Mgr., 137 f., 507
Dupuy, Desjardins, 557

EISLER, 128, 130
Elchasai, 144
Epiphanes, 6
Epiphanius, 6, 138, 140 f., 144
Erbes, 25
Eusebius, 6, 23, 24, 125, 128 ff., 138 ff., 155, 157, 159, 530, 531, 533, 534, 536, 542, 543, 553

FRIDRICHSEN, 302

GSELL, 532
Guignebert, 537, 541

HARNACK, 24, 109, 137, 185, 188, 264, 268, 282, 362, 508, 509, 537, 543
Hausrath, 490
Harduin, 157
Havert, 537
Hegesippus, 6, 127, 128, 130, 131, 133, 134, 136, 139, 434, 534, 536, 543
Heitmuller, 174
Hippolytus, 553
Holl, Karl, 413
Holtzmann, 362

IGNATIUS, 1, 140, 146, 147, 188, 322, 413 ff., 421, 431, 536, 543
Irenaeus, 1, 140, 159, 261, 417

JEROME, 6, 37, 43, 137, 140, 144, 157, 531, 542
Josephus, 6, 24, 25, 124, 126 ff., 137, 138, 159, 503
Justin, 1, 139, 140, 470, 505, 547, 549
Juvenal, 520, 536

KLETTE, 511, 516, 517, 519
Knopf, 154

Kruger, Gustav, 448
Kuhl, 154

Leclerq, Dom, 507, 532, 537
Leeuw, Van den, 288
Leitzmann, 127, 316, 351, 375
Linton, Olaf, 487
Lipsius, 184, 536
Lods, Ads., 200
Lohmeyer, 174
Loisy, 3, 351, 362, 481, 482
Lucian, 543
Luther, 83 f.

Malalas, 536
Marcion, 195, 547
Melitus of Sardis, 522, 553
Meyer, Edouard, 113, 125, 127, 137, 145, 490, 509, 534
Mommsen, 536

Neumann, 537, 540
Norden, 208, 363

Odeberg, 351
Origen, 125, 139, 140, 180, 355, 542
Orosus, Paul, 508, 536
Overbeck, 507

Pausanius, 154
Philo, 167, 230, 349, 362
Philostratus, 531
Pliny the Elder, 154, 517, 520
Pliny the Younger, 450, 506, 507, 537 ff.
Polycarp, 551
Polycrates, 266
Porphyry, 449

Ratisbonne, 76, 77, 85
Reinach, Salomon, 155, 156, 362

Renan, 1, 490, 519, 537
Reville, J., 376
Rossi, J. B. de, 533
Rufus, Cluvius, 517
Rusticus, Fabius, 517

Sabatier, Auguste, 13, 227
Schlier, 404
Schurer, 24, 125, 132
Schutz, 174
Schweitzer, Albert, 1
Schwertz, 25, 56, 130
Semler, 537
Severus, Sulpicius, 507
Simon of Dositheus, 355
Soter of Rome, 309
Speratus, 504
Strauss, 1
Suetonius, 6, 158, 450, 517 ff., 532
Sundar, Singh, 76 ff.
Symmachus, 139

Tacitus, 6, 24, 450, 505, 507, 511 ff.
Termier, Pierre, 4
Tertullian, 1; 192, 241, 506, 507, 509, 522, 536, 551
Tisserant, Mgr., 522
Tryphon, 139, 470
Tylor, E. B., 80

Victor of Rome, 261, 266

Weinel, Heinrich, 271
Weiss, Bernard, 153 f.
Weiss, James, 141
Weiss, Johannes, 376
Wendland, 208
Wetter, 355, 365
Willamowitz-Moellendorf, von P, 208

Zahn, 125, 128, 130, 136, 161